Introduction to Digital Humanism

Hannes Werthner • Carlo Ghezzi • Jeff Kramer •
Julian Nida-Rümelin • Bashar Nuseibeh •
Erich Prem • Allison Stanger
Editors

Introduction to Digital Humanism

A Textbook

Editors
Hannes Werthner
TU Wien
Vienna, Austria

Carlo Ghezzi
DEIB
Politecnico di Milano
Milano, Italy

Jeff Kramer
Department of Computing
Imperial College London
London, UK

Julian Nida-Rümelin
Ludwig-Maximilians-Universität München
München, Germany

Bashar Nuseibeh
Lero & The Open University
Milton Keynes, UK

Erich Prem
University of Vienna
Vienna, Austria

Allison Stanger
Middlebury College and Santa Fe Institute
Middlebury, VT, USA

ISBN 978-3-031-45306-9 ISBN 978-3-031-45304-5 (eBook)
https://doi.org/10.1007/978-3-031-45304-5

This work was supported by Verein zur Förderung des digitalen Humanismus

This Springer imprint is published by the registered company Springer Nature Switzerland AG
The registered company address is: Gewerbestrasse 11, 6330 Cham, Switzerland

Paper in this product is recyclable.

Preface

This textbook aims to engage readers with *digital humanism*—a rich landscape of digitalization, examined as a socioeconomic, sociotechnical, and cultural process. The recent wave of more widely available artificial intelligence (AI) technologies, exemplified by generative AI tools such as ChatGPT and Bard, have dominated current social and technical discourse and refreshed a long-standing debate around artificial general intelligence (AGI) and its consequences on society, and indeed on humanity itself. A significant strand within this debate has centered on the apparent ability of generative AI to simulate human language, while its creators sometimes struggle to understand or explain how it works.

A key thread in this evolving debate however has remained the same and has only been amplified by the current AI advances, and that is the plethora of critical issues—already highlighted by digital humanism—attributed to ongoing digitalization, such as monopolization and platform power, fake news and its threats to democracy, privacy, bias, and sovereignty, to name a few. At the same time, digital technologies have demonstrated great potential for human progress, exemplified by scientific and medical advances that are positively affecting human health and well-being.

As editors of this volume, our aim is to provide readers with as wide an exposure as possible to digital advances and their consequences on humanity, while also providing many constructive views and approaches that seek to ensure that our collective digital future is determined through human agency. We recognize and respect concerns, even fears, of the inexorable intertwining of humans and technology (or even the *singularity* where technology becomes uncontrollable and irreversible), but editorially speaking we lean towards rejecting technological determinism. Life and its fate must be in our hands, in the hands of humans, if democracy is to be sustainable.

In such a process we need to remain enlightened humanists, i.e. combining humanism and Enlightenment. We argue for the primacy of reason—but we recognize the problems created when logic leads to a focus on short-term optimization that values efficiency and money as the supreme values. We contend that we should not follow the logic of the free and unregulated market. Market forces will not deliver the required remedies for the adverse consequences of digital technologies.

Digital humanism also recognizes the importance of developing sustainable technology that respects the environment. Acknowledging the important cultural differences around the globe and remaining attentive to the mistakes of colonialism are important foundations and learnings for our version of humanism as well.

Enormous creativity is exemplified by the ongoing digitalization of society, again demonstrated by current generative AI. It is also a triumph of human ingenuity and collaboration. We enthusiastically imagine what we might collectively bring into being if we harnessed that intellectual firepower to addressing rising inequality, climate change, and, more generally, reducing existential risks. While it is disputed if and to what extent information and communications technology (ICT) plays a reinforcing or enabling role in these developments, it may also contribute to the solutions. Imagine again the part that ICT could play towards advancing the United Nations' Sustainable Development Goals (SDGs).

We do not fear the end of the world; on the contrary, we propose an optimistic positive future. While we humans have caused many of our own problems, we are also the potential creators of solutions to these problems. However, we recognize that technology can only be part of the solution, not the solution itself (as some technology apologists may believe).

Many problems as well as possibilities of digitalization are not technical alone. They are related and intertwined with structural, economic, societal, political issues. Prevalent problems of bias, fairness, or economic concentration are cases in point. The design and implementation of human- and society-centered sustainable systems are cross-cutting challenges that will also require political engagement. We need cooperation across disciplines and across different activities—from research to political action. Thus, as is reflected in the number and diversity of authors who contributed to this volume, the topic is complex and needs to be addressed by many communities working together. It is and must be a multidisciplinary endeavor. You will find this orientation in the volume before you.

As a textbook, this volume introduces and defines digital humanism in its different dimensions and breadth. Each chapter focuses on a specific topic and has the same structure, including questions to be answered by students and other readers and annotated reading lists that can be used to dive deeper into the associated chapter material. The book is intended to be used for an entire course on digital humanism or as an add-on to courses in computer science as well as in humanities and social sciences. But each chapter can also be read on its own.

A textbook on digital humanism by necessity must cover content from different disciplines while remaining accessible to a wide audience, drawn from different disciplinary, scholarly, and professional backgrounds. To address this challenge, we have sought to balance depth and breadth in the material presented.

The book therefore follows a consistent logic within each chapter, starting from background material to a system's view and concluding with an identification of critical or open issues, highlighting possible approaches for addressing these issues, and providing learning resources for further reading.

The book is organized in three parts:

- Part I—Background: This section provides the broad multidisciplinary background needed to understand digital humanism in its philosophical, cultural, technological, historical, social, and economic dimensions. The goal is to present the background knowledge upon which an effective interdisciplinary discourse on digital humanism can be founded. Chapters "Humanism and Enlightenment" and "Philosophical Foundations of Digital Humanism" cover philosophical topics, addressing the constitutive elements of Humanism and Enlightenment and the foundations of Digital Humanism, respectively. Chapter "Evolution of Computing" provides a historical perspective and a broad view of the main constituents of digital technology which led to the current digital world. Chapter "The Digital Revolution in a Historical Perspective" puts the digital revolution in a historical perspective. Chapter "The Social Responsibilities of Scientists and Technologists in the Digital Age" addresses the following fundamental question: what are the social responsibilities of digital scientists and professionals in the digital age? Chapter "Digital Transformation Through the Lens of Intersectional Gender Research Challenges and Needs for Action" explores the interaction between technology and gender and calls for action towards an equitable digital society. Chapter "No Digital Citizens Without Digital Humanism" discusses the crucial role of general education in the digital society. The final Chapter "Digital Transformation, Digital Humanism: What Needs to Be Done" explains why the development of the digital society should be inspired by principles of Digital Humanism. It also introduces the digital humanism initiative, which (among others) gave birth to this book.
- Part II—Digital Humanism: A System's View: This section provides an in-depth presentation and discussion of some of the main digital humanism concerns arising in current digital systems. The goal is to make readers aware and sensitive to these issues. We focus on three major topics. The first concentrates on AI systems. After providing an introduction to AI (Chapter "A Short Introduction to Artificial Intelligence: Methods, Success Stories, and Current Limitations") and a chapter on the need for and characteristics of trustworthy AI systems (Chapter "Trustworthy Artificial Intelligence: Comprehensible, Transparent and Correctable"), we discuss the relationship of AI systems with humans, and in particular discuss the question as to "who is in control"? (Chapter "Are We in Control?"). Control in decision support systems (Chapter "AI @ Work: Human Empowerment or Disempowerment?"), in Generative AI (Chapter "The Re-enchanted Universe of AI: The Place for Human Agency"), and in art (Chapter "Aesthetic Aspects of Digital Humanism: An Aesthetic-Philosophical Analysis of Whether AI Can Create Art") all raise the prospect of the displacement of human agency. The second focus of Part II discusses ethics as a major concern in systems development. This provides chapters which include existing proposals to address ethical issues in AI systems (Chapter "Approaches to Ethical

AI") and threats to humanity and human autonomy (Chapters "Artificial Intelligence and Large-Scale Threats to Humanity" and "Promises and Perils in Moralizing Technologies"). Development strategies are then discussed in terms of human-centered technologies (Chapter "The Road Less Taken: Pathways to Ethical and Responsible Technologies"), facilitating access to digital services (Chapter "Bridging the Digital Divide"), responsible software engineering (Chapter "Responsible Software Engineering: Requirements and Goals"), the role of governance in enforcing ethical values (Chapter "Governance for Digital Humanism: The Role of Regulation, Standardization, and Certification"), ethical agile development (Chapter "Value-Sensitive Software Design: Ethical Deliberationin Agile Development Processes"), and those systems that include humans in the loop (Chapter "Humans in the Loop: People at the Heart of Systems Development"). The final subsection raises a number of critical system qualities that need consideration. While not exhaustive, the topics covered include resilience and sustainability (Chapter "Resilience: The Key to Planetary and Societal Sustainability"), fairness and the potential use of blockchains (Chapter "How Blockchain Technology Can Help to Arrive at Fair Ecosystems and Platforms"), and privacy and security (Chapter "Introduction to Security and Privacy").

- Part III—Critical and Societal Issues of Digital Systems: This section delves into the major critical issues raised by advances of digital technologies, which have deep societal implications. The public debate in the past has often focused on them separately, especially when they became visible through sensational events (e.g., the use of social media to influence elections). Our aim here is to shed light on the entire landscape and show their interconnected relationships. A subsection of this part of the book discusses social computing, bias, and fake news (Chapters "Recommender Systems: Techniques, Effects, and Measures Toward Pluralism and Fairness", "Bias and the Web", "Copyright Enforcement on Social Media Platforms: Implications for Freedom of Expression in the Digital Public Sphere", and "On Algorithmic Content Moderation"). It covers recommender systems, which aim at steering human behavior according to their perceived or induced preferences, the pervasive presence of bias in the Web, the tension between the open public information sphere and protection of intellectual rights, and the challenge involved in automatic moderation of content published online. Another subsection on participation and democracy offers two contributions. Chapter "Democracy in the Digital Era" provides a historical perspective on the notion of democracy and discusses the opportunities and threats introduced by digital technologies. Chapter "Are Cryptocurrencies and Decentralized Finance Democratic?" digs into the crucial current hot topic of cryptocurrencies and their relation to governments, the global monetary system, and democracy. Chapter "Platforms: Their Structure, Benefits, and Challenges" deals with platforms, their structure, and the related benefits and threats, whereas Chapters "Work in a New World" and "Digital Labor, Platforms, and AI" discuss the issue of work in the digital economy. The next contribution (Chapter "Sovereignty in the Digital Age") explores the issue of sovereignty, highlighting also its different dimensions in the geopolitical space. Chapter "The Threat of Surveillance and the Need for Privacy Protections" also deals with an equally hot "political" topic, surveillance, and also discusses mechanisms to protect privacy. Chapter "Human Rights Alignment: The Challenge Ahead for AI Lawmakers" provides an overview of worldwide frameworks for the governance of AI, such as the OECD principles or the UNESCO recommendations. The final contribution (Chapter "European Approaches to the Regulation of Digital Technologies") discusses European approaches to regulation of the digital market such as the GDPR, the Digital Markets Act, the Digital Services Act, and the European AI Act.

This book evolved from a digital humanism summer school held at TU Wien in 2022.[1] It therefore relies predominantly on the contributions of colleagues who lectured at that summer school. In writing the book, we can observe two different speeds. The idea, the structure, and most of the content of the book stem from fall 2022. The editorial process then took some time—a year in total. Compare this with the speed of technological developments in the field, such as AI. As a result, the content changed slightly by necessity, but the related debates endure, and the book is thus inevitably, in some ways, a work in progress. By the time you read these words, some important dimensions to this evolving story may be missing—we are sorry for that.

We want you, the reader and our colleagues, to learn from its pages and hope that we provide you with insights and new ideas for your future research and work. We also hope that it will provide you with the language and motivation to be an engaged contributor to the collective global and societal debates.

A big thanks goes to all the authors who have contributed and have taken part in the efforts of the reviews and revision. The responsibility for any errors lies with us. This book is open access, so it can be downloaded and read at no cost to you, the readers. This is possible thanks to financial support from the Science Foundation Ireland Research Centre for Software (Lero), the Bavarian Research Institute for Digital Transformation (bidt), the German Parmenides Foundation, the Databases and Artificial Intelligence Group (with funds from the projects WWTF-10.47379/ICT2201 and ZIF/CCS), the Data Science Group (both TU Wien), and The Open University, UK (with funding from UKRI project SAUSE EP/R013144/1).

Finally, we thank Dr. Dmitri Katz for his editorial support and the great work he did, not only on the book but also reminding us of the work still to be done. Without him this book would not have been possible.

[1] https://dighum.org/summerschool2022

In conclusion, as we wrote in our 2019 Vienna Manifesto,[2] we call for a Digital Humanism that describes, analyzes, and, most importantly, influences the complex interplay of technology and humankind for a better society and life, fully respecting universal human rights. In the end, this involves not only technology, but society, politics, and governance, which remain human-generated endeavors.

Vienna, Austria	Hannes Werthner
Milano, Italy	Carlo Ghezzi
London, UK	Jeff Kramer
München, Germany	Julian Nida-Rümelin
Milton Keynes, UK	Bashar Nuseibeh
Vienna, Austria	Erich Prem
Middlebury, VT, USA	Allison Stanger

August 2023

[2] https://dighum.org/dighum-manifesto

Contents

Part I
Background

Humanism and Enlightenment

Julian Nida-Rümelin and Dorothea Winter

Abstract Some authors argue that digital transformation is a form of "counter-Enlightenment." And indeed, there is a tendency of transhumanist and anti-humanist thought in present-day debates around digitalization. Software systems are described as if they were persons endowed with mental states and moral or immoral attitudes. For some, the values of humanism and Enlightenment that framed human rights and democratic constitutions have become obsolete. In fact, humans are delegating responsibility to artificial intelligence and digital tools. Simultaneously, digitalization can lead to a greater emphasis on humans as rational beings and grant them greater freedom for personal development. Therefore, the question "What is the relevance of humanism and Enlightenment in the era of digital transformation?" arises and more basically "What are the constitutive elements of humanism and Enlightenment and are they still relevant, or do they even gain importance in digital transformation processes?". These and other questions will be addressed in this chapter.

1 Introduction

As a result of increasing digitalization, humans are handing over more and more responsibility to artificial intelligence (AI) and digital tools, e.g., in the field of autonomous driving, applicant tracking software, or creditworthiness rating. For this reason, some speak of a so-called counter-Enlightenment. But in contrast to this trend, digital transformation can strengthen the ideals of the Enlightenment and humanism and help humans to achieve more freedom, use of reason, and responsibility—Enlightenment 2.0, so to speak. To shed light on this interplay, we

J. Nida-Rümelin (✉)
bidt – Bavarian Research Institute for Digital Transformation, München, Germany
e-mail: Julian.nida-ruemelin@lrz.uni-muenchen.de

D. Winter
Humanistic University Berlin, Berlin, Germany
e-mail: d.winter@humanistische-hochschule-berlin.de

H. Werthner et al. (eds.), *Introduction to Digital Humanism*,
https://doi.org/10.1007/978-3-031-45304-5_1

will explain the interdependence between humanism and the Enlightenment in this chapter. This is important to understand the foundations of Digital Humanism in general. In this regard, this chapter is, in a sense, fundamental, because it deals with the foundation of humanism itself (in relation to the Enlightenment).

For this purpose, the first step is to highlight the extent to which the Enlightenment is relevant in the age of AI and increasing digitalization. In the second step, the foundations of humanism as such are presented, before humanism and the Enlightenment are interconnected in the third step. In particular, the following questions are especially relevant: What unites them? How are they mutually dependent? And why, even in the digital age, can't they be considered separate from each other? As a result, it turns out that the human capacity to give and take reasons is what leads to freedom and responsibility in the first place. Humanistic ideals firmly shaped by the Enlightenment, and vice versa, are decisive for the fact that we regard all people as free and equal and grant them human rights—regardless of skin color, religion, race, or nationality. This chapter aims to provide a comprehensive overview of the Enlightenment and humanism and to understand their respective relevance to Digital humanism.

2 Digitalization: Age of the Enlightenment 2.0 or the Counter-Enlightenment?

AI is spreading more and more into areas that have been exclusively human domains. The fact that AI can help with train schedules or weather forecasts is beneficial—and usually unproblematic. But the use of AI is more problematic when it affects the core of humanity—at least from a philosophical-humanistic point of view: the use of reason. And what could better enlighten us about this than the Enlightenment itself?

Speaking of the Enlightenment in the context of AI and digitalization is not a new idea: Therefore, it is obvious that not only the EU is concerned with the problem of "Artificial Intelligence in Europe: In the Spirit of Enlightenment" (Federal Foreign Office, 2020) but that AI is today often understood as a challenge for philosophical-humanistic thinking: It is necessary to design AI processes responsibly and in terms of human authorship (see chapter by Nida-Rümelin and Staudacher)—in the enlightened sense—at least insofar as they affect the realm of the use of reason. The premise that must underlie this process of change is the ambivalence of the relationship between the Enlightenment and AI.

On the one hand, the Enlightenment ideal of sapere aude ("dare to know") encourages innovation and progress in the areas of AI through the boundless optimism it engenders with respect to science, technology, and creativity; following in its footsteps, numerous contemporary subfields of AI research can be understood as direct continuations of this ideal and the resulting achievements (Barthelmeß & Furbach, 2023; De Lamotte, 2020; Lewin et al., 2022; Helbing, 2018). For example, the idea of a strong, sui generis autonomous AI originated from the intellectual analogy between human thought and technical intelligence—the computer animistically exaggerated as a superhuman homunculus. Chatbots are another example. The idea of technological innovation of the Enlightenment and the resulting mode of science can be placed in a quasi-direct tradition.

On the other hand, Max Horkheimer and Theodor Adorno (2002) already referred in 1944 to the dialectic inherent in the Enlightenment, which opposes progress and the resulting control of humans over humanity and nature with highly destructive potential. Applied to the research field of AI, this dialectical approach gains significance besides the blessings of modernity, as AI can lead to a triumphant disaster for humans and nature (Horkheimer & Adorno, 2002). Horkheimer, for example, links the progress of technology with an inherent process of dehumanization. For him, the innovation process of technology could weaken what it actually wants to strengthen: the idea of the human being as such (Adorno & Horkheimer, 2005; Noeri & Jephcott, 2002; Schmidt, 1998; Bus et al., 2012).

Examples can be given to illustrate this: At times, for example, AI-driven job application tools result in unintended automated discrimination against female applicants,[1] self-driving cars cause fatal accidents,[2] the use of facial recognition software leads to discrimination against people of color,[3] or autonomous weapons systems accidentally kill civilians.[4] The list can be continued at any length. But all examples have one thing in common: digital tools and AI were applied to save time, relieve the workload of humans, or simplify processes. By doing so, technology can lead unintentionally to discrimination or other negative consequences for people.

Therefore, we must proactively shape the age of AI and digitalization in an enlightened sense and with the help of humanistic ideals. This is the only way to create a desirable future for people and the world—both digital and analog.

In order to get a deeper understanding of this, we must begin with a comprehension of what precisely humanism is and where the term originated. This will now be done in the next section.

---

[1]This is what happened in 2015 when an Amazon algorithm systematically discriminated against women by excluding them from technical job application processes. The gender bias was discovered only after the algorithm had already been widely used. The cause of the given gender bias was the data used for training (Kodyan, 2019).

[2]In May 2016, a fatal crash involving an autonomously driving Tesla car occurred (Banks et al. (2018) provide a clear and well-founded explanation of how this could have happened and what needs to be done to prevent it from happening in the future).

[3]In 2018, a Google image recognition software mistakenly "confused" black people with apes. Google was helpless in facing this highly discriminatory incident. The only quick response that prevented such discrimination was blocking some words entirely (Hilale, 2021).

[4]Leveringhaus (2016) provides a useful overview of the debate on automated weapons systems.

3 What Does Humanism Mean and Where Does the Term Come From?

Humanism is derived from the Latin word *humanitas*, which means "humanity." Humanism generally refers to a mental condition or attitude. A person with a humanistic mindset respects the dignity of every human being. They strive for a life without violence, in which everyone is free to express their opinions. The International Humanist and Ethical Union (IHEU), a non-governmental organization that advocates for human rights and is inspired by secular humanist ideas, defines humanism as follows:

> Humanism is a democratic and ethical life stance, which affirms that human beings have the right and responsibility to give meaning and shape to their own lives. It stands for the building of a more humane society through an ethic based on human and other natural values in the spirit of reason and free inquiry through human capabilities. (Copson, 2015, pp. 5–6)

The term "humanism" refers to a wide variety of occurrences. Hence, it is used to designate an epoch, such as Italian Renaissance humanism [inspired by Francesco Petrarca (Mann, 1996, p. 8)] in the fifteenth and sixteenth centuries, but also German New humanism (Neuhumanismus) in the nineteenth century. Renaissance humanism was a broad educational movement that drew on ancient ideas. Renaissance humanists anticipated that the utmost human potential would be realized by combining knowledge and virtue. Humanistic education was intended to enable humans to recognize their true destiny and, by imitating classical models, to produce an ideal humanity and to shape an appropriate form of society. The humanistic conception of life, which adopted the ancient Roman notion of humanitas, was an alternative to the traditional view inherited from the Middle Ages, which was heavily focused on God and the afterlife. The humanists of the Renaissance distinguished themselves sharply from the Scholastics of the later Middle Ages. Johann Gottfried von Herder initiated German New humanism, which was continued by Wilhelm von Humboldt (1963) (creator of the modern Gymnasium (high school) system and founder of the University of Berlin), Johann Wolfgang von Goethe (e.g., with his play "Iphigenia in Tauris" (1966)), and Friedrich Schiller (e.g., with his ode "To Joy"), among others.

Fascinatingly, based on German New humanism, idealistic philosophy arose (key figures in this regard were Georg Wilhelm Friedrich Hegel, Johann Gottlieb Fichte, Friedrich Wilhelm Joseph von Schelling, and Friedrich Schleiermacher), resulting in a new "worldview" (Wilhelm von Humboldt). From a historical standpoint, humanism is extremely diverse. Therefore, there is no unique definition of humanism per se (Davies, 2008, pp. 3–5). Humanism was and remains controversial. On the one hand, humanist perspectives and their opponents engage in heated debates. On the other hand, even within the humanist spectrum, consensus is rare. The positions range from anti-clerical materialism[5] to religious humanism,[6] utopian humanism,[7] existentialism,[8] and Marxism.[9] Nevertheless, despite the differences and criticisms, there are fundamental values and ideals that have always been associated with humanism and have influenced humanist thought since its beginnings. According to Davies (2008), they all share a common trait: admiration for the Greek language and culture. Hegel, Humboldt, Goethe, and Schiller, for instance, believed that the Hellenistic ideal did not belong solely in history books. They all saw the future in the Greek language and Greek culture (especially for modern Germany), and they desired to create a "better" cultivated, rational, modern Greece (Davies, 2008, p. 11).

Now that we have briefly discussed the origins of humanism as a concept and the history of the term, the following question arises: Why is it so important to discuss humanist ideals and values in the age of AI and digitalization? Isn't it already obsolete? What does "Digital humanism" precisely mean, and why is it so important? The following section will address these questions, among others.

---

[5] Brown and Ladyman (2020) provide a comprehensive overview of the history of materialism. And Moir (2020) decisively addresses Bloch's speculative materialism.

[6] As Hall (2006) acknowledges, the word combination "religious Humanism" seems to be a contradiction in itself, but it is not at all. Don Cupitt, one of the leading apologists of religious Humanism defines God as: "the sum of our values, representing to us their ideal unity, their claims upon us and their creative power" (Cupitt, 1984, p. 269). Following the religious humanist position, religious values are placed in relation to human life in symbolic and actual form. Cupitt (1982, 1984) suggests reading Kierkegaard to illustrate this. Kierkegaard makes it his task to explain the human reality of life from within. In doing so, he does not have to aim at metaphysical spheres that lie outside this reality. Rather, it is sufficient to explore the values, the inner logic, and the conditions of the realm of life. But this method, which works so well and is mutually consistent, eventually encounters the problem that it is caught in a circular argument. This circular argument can only be resolved by what Kierkegaard (2013) means by his irrational "leap of faith". In the current debate, religious Humanism plays a subordinate role and can be neglected in the further course of this contribution (Hall, 2006, p. 69).

[7] As already shown, Humanism emerged from the social, political, and philosophical shifts of the Renaissance. As Berriel (2022) states the humanist conception of the world proved to be extremely promising: Humanists do not see themselves simply as products of a given nature, but rather as authors or creators of their own existence, as architects of the world they inhabit. This attitude is partly accompanied by utopian and dystopian ideals. The striving for something new, something better, something greater drives numerous thinkers, e.g., Picodella Mirandola (1987), Thomas Morus (1979), Ernst Bloch (1986), or Herbert Marcuse (1969, 1991) and even today, Humanism is partly the foundation stone for critical thinking on the one hand and imaginative projections on the other (Berriel, 2022, pp. 301–302).

[8] Already Sartre made in 1948 the reference between Existentialism and Humanism. Existentialist and humanist theories take many different positions and directions, as pointed out by Spinelli (1989, 2012) and Wong (2006). Hoffman et al. (2019) present the contemporary trends of existential-humanistic psychotherapy, whereby these trends are not shown in a Eurocentric way, but rather also under multicultural and Asian aspects. It is shown that relevant foundations of Humanism and existentialism can also be found in Confucianism, Buddhism, and Taoism. Likewise, van Deurzen (2019) provides interesting Existential-Humanistic and Existential-Integrative Therapy aspects.

[9] In the 2008 publication on the 125th anniversary of Karl Marx's death, I elaborate on the humanistic content of Marx's thought and relate it to a widely anti-humanistic practice of Marxist-minded politics (Nida-Rümelin, 2008).

4 Education as a Humanistic Ideal Has Two Components: One Theoretical and One Practical

Now that we have illustrated how humanism can be interpreted differently and how it can generate controversy, the following question arises: What unites the various humanist perspectives and movements, and what makes the term "Digital humanism" unique? It is the concept of human authorship and the related human capacity to give reasons, freedom, and responsibility (Nida-Rümelin & Weidenfeld, 2022). Fundamentally, we interpret "Digital humanism" in terms of a realistic view of AI and digitalization, on the one hand, and an increase in human responsibility, on the other. In this way, human authorship will be strengthened, while innovation will be encouraged:[10]

> [Digital humanism] sharpens the criteria of human responsibility in the face of the availability of digital technologies, calls for an expansion of the ascription of responsibility to communication and interaction mediated by digital technologies, and does not allow the actual agents (and that is us humans) to duck away and pass responsibility on to a supposed autonomy of digital machines. (Nida-Rümelin, 2022, p. 74)

Since chapters by Nida-Rümelin and Staudacher, Nida-Rümelin and Winter, and Werthner deal with the foundations of Digital humanism and this chapter is meant to address the relationship between the Enlightenment and humanism, this section will now concentrate on the two distinct components of humanism. This is essential for understanding the big picture.

Every humanistic epoch in history, whether in Europe, China, India, or elsewhere, has emphasized the potential for human self-development (Weiming & Ikeda, 2011). The ancient world's intellectuals, such as Confucius, Buddha, and Socrates, shared the belief that humans are responsible for themselves and others and are capable of developing their potential through education, empathy, and solidarity. This explains the importance of education in humanism (Veugelers, 2011). In this regard, education has a dual function: education as self-education and education as an equal opportunity for all. In this view, humanism has both a theoretical and a practical aspect.

The theoretical one is expressed in humanistic anthropology, according to which people can be affected by reasons. Thus, reasons exert more than a simple causal effect on human behavior. In fact, it is a central tenet of humanism that if humans seek the truth, they must rely on science and logic (Law, 2013). In interpersonal communication, humans weigh reasons, deliberate, debate, and give and take reasons for this reason. Affiliation and participation teach us which reasons are compelling and which are less compelling. In social interaction and communication, reasons are recognized and exchanged. That is what makes reasons effective. Humans are essentially social beings.

[10] Nida-Rümelin (2022) and Nida-Rümelin and Weidenfeld (2022) give a comprehensive account of what can be understood by Digital humanism in a philosophical framework.

However, according to evolutionary psychology, self-efficacy, along with attachment, is the second fundamental driver of human behavior: "Self-efficacy expectation is the belief by an individual that they are able to perform a specific behavior. Whether or not this behavior is expected to generate specific outcomes is conceptualized as response-outcome expectations" (Lippke, 2020, pp. 4722–4723).

Consequently, the pragmatic aspect of education as a humanistic ideal pertains to our actions: Through our actions, we affect the world; we do not merely react to external influences. We exert influence in the world through our actions, which presupposes that we have action options and necessitates that we accept responsibility for these actions. Without the ability to act rationally, there would be no accountability. Without the ability to choose, the weighing of pros and cons would be meaningless. Freedom and responsibility are interdependent and based on the human capacity to be influenced by motives (Schweiker, 2004).[11]

The humanistic view of education is grounded in the anthropology of equality and freedom. It focuses on the development of the personality rather than the training of specific abilities and skills; it is less concerned with the acquisition of information and more concerned with the power of judgment; it is less concerned with knowledge and more concerned with a deeper understanding of contexts; independent thought takes precedence over reception. Through education, people should be enabled to make their own judgments and responsible decisions, i.e., they should be educated in responsible theory and practice. The focus is on self-education and determining one's own course in life, not on training and imitation. To quote Aung (2020):

> According to the humanists, education should be a process of developing a free, self-actualizing person [. . .]. Because the goal of humanism is a completely autonomous person, education should be without coercion or perception. Students should be active and should be encouraged to make their own choices. The teacher who follows humanistic theory emphasizes instruction and assessment based on students, abilities, and needs. Humanists honor divergent thinking. (Aung, 2020, p. 13557)

This ideal of humanistic education is largely independent of the specific subject matter. As stated previously, both Italian Renaissance humanism and German New humanism placed a significant emphasis on understanding Greek culture and speaking ancient Greek (Moss, 1999, p. 145). The enthusiasm for Greece among modern humanists, which has lost its formative power only since the end of the twentieth century, was predicated on the belief that the texts and other cultural evidence of Greek classicism and Hellenism conveyed profound humanistic insights that could only be acquired through a deeper understanding of ancient Greek culture and language. This has led to humanism being accused of elitism, which, despite being incompatible with the inclusive and universalistic educational ideals of humanist philosophy, was justified by educational practice. Humanistic thought and practice

[11] Due to the limited scope and overview character of this chapter, it is not feasible to go into more depth here. But the term pair freedom and responsibility carries a long tradition in philosophy. Cf. inter alia Kilanowski (2022), Nelkin (2013), and Bok (2022).

can be gleaned from a variety of sources, including the Greek Classics, Hellenism, and the Roman Stoa, but also from Confucian, Christian, Buddhist, Jewish, Muslim, and other cultural perspectives. Alternatively, by reading and contemplating contemporary philosophical texts, American Pragmatism, particularly that of John Dewey (Dewey, 1974; Snaza, 2017), also contributed to humanistic thought and educational practice.

The concept of human self-development is central to all humanistic approaches to education and politics. In this way, humanistic politics, theory, and practice are distinguished by combining the concepts of self-development and equality: individuals are equally empowered to shape their own lives. They, therefore, possess equal human dignity. This universal conception of equality encompasses all individuals, regardless of origin, skin color, gender, culture, background, status, income, or influence. This humanistic principle of equality comes into conflict with hierarchical, patriarchal, racist, nationalist, autocratic, and capitalist societies. These societies do not recognize the equal human dignity, respect, and recognition that each individual deserves. Following this clarification of the most significant humanistic theoretical and practical principles, we will now, as a final step, explain why humanism is so crucial to the Enlightenment.

5 Why Is the Enlightenment so Important for Humanism?

The humanist project flourished during the Age of Enlightenment, but it was also challenged by scientism and utopian ideals. According to David Hume and Immanuel Kant, the proofs of God from the medieval-modern period are no longer persuasive. Hume and Kant consider the triumph of science over religion to be conclusive evidence that metaphysics can no longer be rationally supported since only the realm of concrete experience can serve as a foundation for valid philosophical conclusions (Tarnas, 1991).

Already with Hume, but especially in France and Germany, the forced rationalism of M. de Voltaire and the Physiocrats (a French economic theory developed during the Age of Enlightenment) begins to crumble. A new perspective on emotional life emerges. The static order thinking of the Middle Ages no longer dictates the way of thinking; instead, a new perception of the world and the self-reflection of the observing individual emerge (Böning, 2015, p. 58).

While humanism emphasizes human self-development, the Enlightenment emphasizes the rationality of thought and action. Reason replaces prejudice. The purpose of scientific knowledge is to counteract the influence of superstition and religion and provide a clear perspective on the world. The Enlightenment has a positive outlook on progress and relies on science. These, however, are the two sides of the same coin: It can result in dangerous outcomes, such as scientism (LeDrew, 2013), the belief that only the sciences can lead to rational knowledge and practice and that the world can be shaped by scientific and technical criteria.

However, both science and democracy are products of the Enlightenment; both are founded on faith in human reason. In the case of science, this is a specialized and methodologically driven endeavor that necessitates specialized knowledge. In the case of democracy, it is not specialized, but inclusive, accessible to all citizens, and open to the public. Consequently, science and democracy are in conflict. Science's findings and the implementation of these findings have a significant impact on democratically shaped development. These can only be effective if they play a role in the public sphere and are incorporated into political practice. Science must transform its specialized knowledge into knowledge that is democratically relevant and be willing to articulate it publicly. As essential as the Enlightenment is to the humane shaping of human living conditions, it must avoid becoming hypertrophic and underestimating the rational possibilities for shaping natural living conditions and human society, thereby descending into technicalism, utopianism, and social technology. The standard will always be humanity, the humane shaping of human conditions, and the formation of human authorship within the ecological constraints (Nida-Rümelin, 2010).

Humanism and Enlightenment are rejected by opponents who are more or less radical. In the course of human history, humanism and Enlightenment principles have dominated only rarely, while power, oppression, and the cynical instrumentalization of human beings for economic or political ends have dominated far more frequently.

Since the adoption of the Universal Declaration of Human Rights on December 10, 1948, the vast majority of world society has agreed on a humanistic foundation of human rights that is accepted declaratively but frequently violated in political, economic, and social practice. Those who act contrary to the humanist ethos of the Universal Declaration of Human Rights and the humanist-inspired fundamental rights in state constitutions seek to counter the universalist ethos of human rights with ideologies that are incompatible with the above-described understanding of humanism: ideologies of the superiority of one ethnicity or race, class, or gender, collectivist ideologies in which the rights of the individual do not matter, nationalist ideologies of the superiority of one's own nation over others, social Darwinist ideologies of the survival of the fittest, clericalist ideologies with the aim of establishing a God State, and many others. Humanist thought and practice contrast this with the universality and consistency of the human condition. It appeals to human reason, scientific rationality, and responsible political practice in the spirit of the Enlightenment. Humanism is dependent upon education, cooperation, and comprehension. And it presupposes that human rights are equally valid regardless of affiliation. In political, social, economic, technical, and cultural practice, the humanistic theory demonstrates its validity. It seeks to improve the global conditions for human self-development.

6 Conclusions

It is crucial to discuss humanism and the Enlightenment in the age of AI and expanding digitalization. The ideal of education stands in the forefront: humanism and the Enlightenment are based on philosophical and anthropological assumptions, but they are realized in educational practice, politics, and the formation of social relations, as we have discovered. Humanists of all eras believed that participation and equality could be achieved through education. Therefore, they believed that the state had a responsibility to provide equal, but not uniform, educational opportunities for everyone. However, the equal ability to live a life of dignity and to develop individually and collectively also requires empathy and solidarity. When people become existentially dependent due to external circumstances, such as unemployment, illness, or old age, they lose their status as life's authors.

Humanism, when properly understood, does not occur in the ivory tower. As a result, unlike almost all other philosophical currents, philosophical humanism has a political dimension: to shape the condition so as to enable equal human dignity, equal respect, equal recognition, and equal capacity for life authorship. Therefore, in the context of the new fanaticism and fundamentalism, the commercialization and infantilization of Western culture and cultures worldwide, one could argue for a humanistic philosophical and political response (Nida-Rümelin, 2016). In reliance on the universality of human rights, the "Vienna Manifesto on Digital humanism" (2019) is designed to be universally human because it applies to all people and not just a particular elite or privileged economic, social, or cultural group of people.

However, in the age of AI and expanding digitalization, one caveat is essential: This only applies to humans and not to machines (Schmölz, 2020, p. 228). Regardless of how one defines being human, the human being qua human being has rights and freedoms, as well as duties and responsibilities, because freedom, equality, and the responsibility that comes with them—in short, being the author of one's own life—are characteristics that only humans possess and are not applicable to AI, digital tools, etc. Nonetheless, this alleged limitation must not act as an impediment to innovation or a brake. This realistic perspective is meant to propel research, politics, and business forward.

In this way, fundamental humanistic and Enlightenment values are transferred to the digital age, which can lead to innovation and advancement. Nevertheless, it is essential to ensure that the use of AI and digitalization does not result in counter-Enlightenment.

Discussion Questions for Students and Their Teachers

1. What are the fundamental principles of humanism?
2. Why is it impossible to consider humanism without the Enlightenment?
3. What role does science play in relation to the values and ideals of humanism and the Enlightenment?
4. What critiques of humanism exist, and to what extent are they plausible?
5. Does increasing digitalization result in a counter-Enlightenment or Enlightenment 2.0?

Learning Resources for Students

1. Cave, P. (2022) *humanism.* New York: Simon and Schuster.

   As the subtitle "a beginner's guide" puts it, this is a good overview of humanism. Both historically and systematically, one gets a good insight here about what is important.

2. Crosson, J. B. (2021) "humanism and enlightenment" in *The Oxford Handbook of humanism.* New York: Oxford University Press.

   This is the right place to get a deeper insight into the tension between humanism and Enlightenment after this chapter. Does humanism condition the Enlightenment? Or vice versa? Is humanism possible without Enlightenment? What is the relation between the two concepts?

3. Kircher, T. (2021) *Before Enlightenment: Play and Illusion in Renaissance humanism.* Leiden: Brill.

   This work is less specific, and not a typical overview work, but still very much worth reading, also for non-experts: Timothy Kircher argues for new ways of appreciating Renaissance humanist philosophy: The literary qualities of humanists' writings convey how play and illusion helped form their ideas about knowledge, ethics, and metaphysics.

4. Mazzocco, A. (2006) *Interpretations of Renaissance humanism.* Leiden/Boston: Brill.

   Authored by some of the most preeminent Renaissance scholars active today, this volume's essays give fresh and illuminating analyses of important aspects of Renaissance humanism, including its origin, connection to the papal court and medieval traditions, classical learning, religious and literary dimensions, and dramatis personae.

5. Mathäs, A. (2020) *Beyond Posthumanism.* Oxford: Berghahn Books.

   Read a good overview of posthumanism here: Through insightful analyses of key texts, Alexander Mathäs mounts a broad defense of the humanistic tradition, emphasizing its pursuit of a universal ethics and ability to render human experiences comprehensible through literary imagination.

6. Nida-Rümelin, J. and Weidenfeld, N. (2022) *Digital humanism.* Cham: Springer International Publishing.

   The advantage of this book is that it is philosophically sound and yet written in a way that will make it accessible for everybody interested in the subject. Every chapter begins with a film scene illustrating a precise philosophical problem with AI and how we look at it—making the book not only readable but even entertaining. And after having read the book, the reader will have a clear vision of what it means to live in a world where digitalization and AI are central technologies for a better and more humane civilization.

7. Nida-Rümelin, J. (2022) "Digital humanism and the Limits of Artificial Intelligence" in Werthner, H., Prem, E., Lee, E.A., Ghezzi, C. (ed.) *Perspectives on Digital humanism*, Cham: Springer, pp. 71–75.

   This chapter is programmatic in style and content. It describes some patterns and one central argument of that, which I take as the view of digital humanism and which we exposed in *Digital Humanism* (2022). The central argument regards the critique of strong and weak AI. This chapter does not discuss the logical and metaphysical aspects of digital humanism that I take to be part of the broader context of the theory of reason.

8. Pinker, S. (2019) *Enlightenment now: The case for reason, science, humanism, and progress*. New York: Penguin Books.

   With intellectual depth and literary flair, *Enlightenment Now* makes the case for reason, science, and humanism: the ideals we need to confront our problems and continue our progress.

9. Rüsen, J. (2021) *humanism: Foundations, Diversities, Developments*. London: Routledge.

   The book describes humanism in a systematic and historical perspective. It analyzes its manifestation and function in cultural studies and its role in the present. Within the book, special attention is given to the intention of contemporary humanism to overcome ethno-centric elements in the cultural orientation of contemporary living conditions and to develop humane dimensions of this orientation. This is linked to a fundamental critique of the current posthuman self-understanding of the humanities. Furthermore, the intercultural aspect in the understanding of humanism is emphasized; for non-Western cultures also have their own humanistic traditions. Two further aspects are also addressed: the Holocaust as the most radical challenge to humanistic thinking and the relationship of humanism to nature.

10. Vaughn, L. and Dacey, A. (2003) *The Case for humanism*. Washington: Rowman & Littlefield.

   The Case for Humanism is the premier textbook to introduce and help students think critically about the "big ideas" of Western humanism, secularism, rationalism, materialism, science, democracy, individualism, and others, all powerful themes that run through Western thought from the ancient Greeks and the Enlightenment to the present day.

References

Adorno, T., & Horkheimer, M. (2005). From the concept of enlightenment. In J. Joseph (Ed.), *Social theory: A reader* (pp. 201–211). Edinburgh University Press.

Aung, Y. M. (2020). humanism and education. *International Journal of Advanced Research in Science, Engineering and Technology, 7*(5), 13555–13561.

Banks, V. A., Plant, K. L., & Stanton, N. A. (2018). Driver error or designer error: Using the perceptual cycle model to explore the circumstances surrounding the fatal Tesla crash on 7th May 2016. *Safety Science, 108*, 278–285.

Barthelmeß, U., & Furbach, U. (2023). *A different look at artificial intelligence: On tour with Bergson, Proust and Nabokov*. Springer.

Berriel, C. E. O. (2022). humanism. In P. Marks, J. A. Wagner-Lawlor, & F. Vieira (Eds.), *The Palgrave handbook of Utopian and Dystopian literatures*. Palgrave Macmillan.

Bloch, E. (1986). *The principle of hope*. Basil Blackwell.

Bok, H. (2022). *Freedom and responsibility*. Princeton University Press.

Böning, U. (2015). Coaching jenseits von Tools und Techniken. Philosophie und Psychologie des Coaching aus systemischer Sicht. Springer.

Brown, R. G., & Ladyman, J. (2020). *History of materialism* (Routledge encyclopedia of philosophy). Routledge.
Bus, J., Crompton, M., Hildebrandt, M., & Metakides, G. (2012). *Digital Enlightenment yearbook 2012*. IOS Press.
Copson, A. (2015). What is humanism? In A. Copson & A. C. Grayling (Eds.), *The Wiley Blackwell Handbook of humanism*. Hoboken.
Cupitt, D. (1982). *The world to come*. SCM Press.
Cupitt, D. (1984). *The sea of faith: Christianity in change*. BBC Books.
Davies, T. (2008). *Humanism*. Routledge.
De Lamotte, M. (2020). Enlightenment, artificial intelligence and society. *IFAC-Papers On Line, 53*(2), 17427–17432.
Dewey, J. (1974). In R. D. Archambault (Ed.), *John Dewey on education: Selected writings*. University of Chicago Press.
German Federal Foreign Office. (2020). *Artificial Intelligence in Europe: Inspired by the Enlightenment. Germany's Presidency of the Council of the European Union*. Accessed February 25, 2023, from https://www.eu2020.de/eu2020-en/news/article/generation-a-algothismus-goethe-eu-council-presidency/2372632
Goethe, J. W. (1966). *Iphigenia in Tauris*. Manchester University Press.
Hall, C. M. (2006). Travel and journeying on the Sea of Faith. Perspectives from religious humanism. In D. Timothy & D. Olsen (Eds.), *Tourism, religion and spiritual journeys*. Routledge.
Helbing, D. (2018). *Towards digital enlightenment: Essays on the dark and light sides of the digital revolution*. Springer.
Hilale, N. (2021). The evolution of artificial intelligence (AI) and its impact on women: How it nurtures discriminations towards women and strengthens gender inequality. *Arribat –International Journal of Human Rights, 1*(2), 141–150.
Hoffman, L., et al. (2019). Challenges and new developments in existential-humanistic and existential-integrative therapy. In E. van Deurzen et al. (Eds.), *The Wiley World handbook of existential therapy* (pp. 290–303). Wiley.
Horkheimer, M., & Adorno, T. (2002). In G. Noeri (Ed.), *Dialectic of enlightenment*. Stanford University Press.
Kierkegaard, S. (2013). Kierkegaard's writings. In H. Hong & H. V. Hong (Eds.), (Vol. 7). Princeton University Press.
Kilanowski, M. (2022). *Rorty-Habermas debate: Toward freedom as responsibility*. State University of New York Press.
Kodiyan, A. A. (2019). An overview of ethical issues in using AI systems in hiring with a case study of Amazon's AI based hiring tool. *Researchgate Preprint*, 1–19.
Law, S. (2013). What is humanism? In S. Bullivant & M. Ruse (Eds.), *The Oxford handbook of atheism*. Oxford University Press.
LeDrew, S. H. (2013). *Scientism, humanism, and religion: The new atheism and the rise of the secular movement*. York University.
Leveringhaus, A. (2016). *Ethics and autonomous weapons*. Palgrave Macmillan.
Lewin, A. Y., Linden, G., & Teece, D. J. (2022). *The new enlightenment: Reshaping capitalism and the global order in the 21st century*. Cambridge University Press.
Lippke, S. (2020). Self-efficacy. In *Encyclopedia of personality and individual differences* (pp. 4713–4719). Springer.
Mann, N. (1996). The origins of humanism. In J. Kraye (Ed.), *The Cambridge companion to renaissance humanism*. Cambridge University Press.
Marcuse, H. (1969). *An essay on liberation*. Penguin.
Marcuse, H. (1991). *One-dimensional man: Studies in ideology of advanced industrial society*. Routledge.
Mirandola, G. P. (1987). *Oratio de hominis dignitate*. Editrice La Scuola.
Moir, C. (2020). *Ernst Bloch's speculative materialism: Ontology, epistemology, politics*. Brill.

Morus, T. (1979). *The Yale Edition of The Complete Works of St. Thomas More*. In J. B. Trapp (Eds.). Vol. 9. Yale University Press.

Moss, A. (1999). Humanist education. In G. P. Norton (Ed.), *The Cambridge history of literary criticism* (pp. 145–154). Cambridge University Press.

Nelkin, D. K. (2013). *Making sense of freedom and responsibility*. Oxford University Press.

Nida-Rümelin, J. (2008). Karl Marx: Ethischer Humanist – Politischer Anti-Humanist? Zum 125. Todestag eines philosophischen Denkers und politischen Programmatikers. *Zeitschrift Für Politik, 55*(4), 462–470.

Nida-Rümelin, J. (2010). Naturalismus und humanismus. In V. Gerhardt & J. Nida-Rümelin (Eds.), *Evolution in Natur und Kultur* (pp. 3–14). De Gruyter.

Nida-Rümelin, J. (2016). *Humanistische Reflexionen*. Suhrkamp.

Nida-Rümelin, J., & Weidenfeld, N. (2022). *Digital humanism*. Springer International.

Nida-Rümelin, J. (2022). Digital humanism and the limits of artificial intelligence. In H. Werthner, E. Prem, E. A. Lee, & C. Ghezzi (Eds.), *Perspectives on digital humanism* (pp. 71–75). Springer.

Noeri, G., & Jephcott, E. (Eds.). (2002). *Dialectic of enlightenment: Philosophical fragments*. Stanford University Press.

Schmidt, J. (1998). Language, mythology, and enlightenment: historical notes on Horkheimer and Adorno's "Dialectic of Enlightenment". *Social Research, 65*(4), 807–838.

Schmölz, A. (2020). Die Conditio Humana im digitalen Zeitalter: Zur Grundlegung des Digitalen Humanismus und des Wiener Manifests. MedienPädagogik: Zeitschrift für Theorie und Praxis der Medienbildung, 208–234.

Schweiker, W. (2004). The ethics of responsibility and the question of humanism. *Literature and Theology, 18*(3), 251–270.

Snaza, N. (2017). Is John Dewey's thought "humanist"? *Journal of Curriculum Theorizing, 32*(2), 15–34.

Spinelli, E. (1989). *The interpreted world: An introduction to phenomenological psychology*. Sage.

Spinelli, E. (2012). Existential psychotherapy: An introductory overview. *Análise Psicológica, 24*(3), 311–321.

Tarnas, R. (1991). *The passion of the Western mind*. Ballantine Books.

Van Deurzen, E., et al. (2019). *The Wiley world handbook of existential therapy*. Wiley Blackwell.

Veugelers, W. (2011). *Education and humanism: Linking autonomy and humanity*. Springer Science and Business Media.

von Humboldt, W. (1963). *Humanist without portfolio*. Wayne State University Press.

Weiming, T., & Ikeda, D. (2011). *New horizons in eastern humanism: Buddhism, Confucianism and the quest for global peace*. Bloomsbury Publishing.

Wong, P. T. P. (2006). Existential and humanistic theories. In J. C. Thomas, D. L. Segal, & M. Hersen (Eds.), *Comprehensive handbook of personality and psychopathology* (Personality and everyday functioning) (Vol. 1, pp. 192–211). Wiley.

Philosophical Foundations of Digital Humanism

Julian Nida-Rümelin and Klaus Staudacher

Abstract Digital humanism is an ethics for the digital age that interprets and shapes the process of digital transformation in accordance with the core concepts of humanist philosophy and practice. The core idea of humanist philosophy is human authorship, which is closely linked to the practice of attributing responsibility and, therefore, also with the concepts of reason and freedom. Digital humanism has several different implications: From a theoretical point of view, it means rejecting both the mechanistic paradigm ("humans are machines") and the animistic paradigm ("machines are (like) humans"); from a practical point of view, it especially requires us not to attribute responsibility to AI and not to let AI make ethical decisions.

1 Introduction

Digital humanism offers a new ethics for the age of artificial intelligence. It opposes what can somewhat simplistically be called "Silicon Valley ideology."[1] This ideology is related to the original American, Puritan hope of salvation, of creating a world of the pure and righteous who have left filth and sin behind; it is, in times of digital transformation, characterized by the dream of a perfectly constructed digital counterparts whose construction excludes any error leading us into a technological utopia. The key concept here is that of artificial intelligence, charged with implicit metaphysics and theology, a self-improving, hyper-rational, increasingly ensouled system whose creator, however, is not God but software engineers who see themselves not merely as part of an industry but of an overarching movement realizing a digital paradise on earth based on transparency, all-connectedness, and non-ambiguity.

[1] Cf. Nida-Rümelin and Weidenfeld (2022), p. 4 and pp. 121. For a critique of "the rhetoric of Silicon Valley," see also Daub (2021).

J. Nida-Rümelin (✉) · K. Staudacher (✉)
bidt – Bavarian Research Institute for Digital Transformation, München, Germany
e-mail: julian.nida-ruemelin@lrz.uni-muenchen.de; klaus.staudacher@bidt.digital

H. Werthner et al. (eds.), *Introduction to Digital Humanism*,
https://doi.org/10.1007/978-3-031-45304-5_2

Like all technologies of the past, digital technologies are ambivalent. Digital transformation will not automatically humanize our living conditions—it depends on how we use and develop this technology. Digital humanism argues for an instrumental attitude toward digitalization: what can be economically, socially, and culturally beneficial, and where do potential dangers lurk? It considers the process of digital transformation as something to be interpreted and actively shaped by us in accordance with the core concepts of humanism. But what are the core concepts of humanism?

Humanism is understood to mean many different things: from the cultivation of ancient languages to the biblical mandate to mankind to "subdue the earth."[2] When we speak of humanism here, it is not in the sense of a historical epoch, such as that of Italian early humanism (Petrarch), German humanism in the fifteenth and sixteenth centuries (Erasmus), and finally New humanism in the nineteenth century (Humboldt). Nor is it a specifically Western or European cultural phenomenon, for humanistic thought and practice exist in other cultures as well. We understand by humanism a certain idea of what actually constitutes being human, combined with a practice that corresponds to this humanistic ideal as much as possible. One does not need an elaborated humanistic philosophy to realize a humanistic practice.

At the heart of humanist philosophy and practice is the idea of human authorship. Human beings are authors of their lives; as such, they bear responsibility and are free. Freedom and responsibility are two mutually dependent aspects of human authorship. Authorship, in turn, is linked to the ability to reason. The criminal law criteria for culpability converge with the lifeworld practice of moral attributions. Persons are morally responsible as authors of their lives, as accountable agents and judges.[3] This triad of reason, freedom, and responsibility spans a cluster of normative concepts that determines the humanistic understanding of the *human condition* and, in a protracted cultural process, has shaped both lifeworld morality and the legal order over centuries. This normative conceptuality is grouped around the phenomenon of being affected by reasons.

The core idea of humanist philosophy, human authorship, thus, can be characterized by the way we attribute responsibility to each other and thereby treat each other as rational and free beings. In order to better understand this humanist practice, we will now take a closer look at the conceptual connection between responsibility, freedom, and reason.[4]

---

[2]For an overview of the genesis and the different meanings of the term "humanism," see chapter of Nida-Rümelim and Winter.

[3]Cf. Nida-Rümelin (2011).

[4]Although the starting point of our argumentation is the human practice of attributing responsibility—and, thus, the question of which conditions must be met for us to hold other people (or ourselves) responsible for something—our considerations are not based on speciesism. That means we don't exclude that at some point in the distant future, there may be AI systems that have reason, freedom, and autonomy to the extent necessary for attributing responsibility. But, as we will see, these AI systems would have to be quite different than the machines existing now.

2 The Humanist Practice of Attributing Responsibility and the Conceptual Connection Between Responsibility, Freedom, and Reason

The concept of *responsibility*[5] is not a concept to be considered in isolation, but it is closely related to the concepts of *freedom* and *reason* and, as we will see, also to the concept of *action*.[6] In order to clarify which conditions have to be fulfilled in order to attribute responsibility, these terms shall first be explained in more detail.

There is much to suggest that an action is reasonable/rational if and only if there are, all things considered, good reasons to perform that action;[7] for sentences like "It is reasonable/rational to perform the action h, but, all things considered, there are good reasons against doing h" or "It is unreasonable/irrational to perform action h, but, all things considered, there are good reasons for doing h," respectively, are already extremely irritating from a purely linguistic point of view. Reason/rationality can be characterized as the ability to appropriately weigh the reasons that guide our actions, beliefs, and attitudes.[8] Freedom is then the possibility to follow just the reasons that are found to be better in such a deliberation process; thus, if I am free, it is my reasons determined by deliberation that guide me to judge and act this way or that.[9]

[5] The following considerations relate exclusively to personal responsibility. Political responsibility, on the other hand, can be attributed even in the absence of personal misconduct. In order to ensure effective public control, a minister is ultimately responsible for all decisions made by the ministry she heads. This type of accountability is largely based on a fiction, because in view of the large number of individual transactions to be recorded daily within a ministry, a genuine case-by-case review by the minister is practically impossible. For this point in detail, see Nida-Rümelin (2011), pp. 147 ff.

[6] Cf. Nida-Rümelin (2011), pp. 19–33 and 53.

[7] Nida-Rümelin (2023), pp. 2–4 and p. 173

[8] The *reasons' account* presented here does not discriminate between "rational" and "reasonable," or "rationality" and "reason," and is to be distinguished from a purely instrumental understanding of reason in the sense of "purpose rationality," according to which an action is rational if and only if it is suitable to achieve the goals pursued by the action. For there are numerous actions that optimally realize the goals of the acting persons, but the best reasons speak against performing these actions, which we therefore call irrational/unreasonable. For example, the crimes committed by the Nazis are no less bad if the preferences of the Nazis have been optimally fulfilled by these deeds; and there can't be any doubt that the best reasons speak against doing what the Nazis did. The conceivable objection that this argumentation inadmissibly equates rationality with morality, since the deeds of the Nazis were clearly morally wrong, but possibly rational because of their fulfilling of the preferences of their perpetrators, is not convincing. Not only moral but also rational actions ought to be done; immoral and irrational ones ought not to be done (a statement like "Your action is completely irrational" is clearly formulated as a reproach). The ought-character of (un)reasonable/(ir)rational actions speaks against a separation between reason-guided rationality/reason and morality and, therefore, also against a purely instrumental understanding of rationality. Cf. also Nida-Rümelin (2023), pp. 2 ff., 15–22 and 173 ff.

[9] Cf. Nida-Rümelin (2023), p. 225. The connection with the reason-guided deliberation process clearly shows that freedom does not merely mean freedom of action here. The latter is already given

But what does it mean to be a reason for doing something? What are examples of reasons?[10]

If an accident victim is lying on the side of the road, seriously injured and without help, then you have a reason to help her (e.g., by giving first aid or calling an ambulance). Or if Peter promises John that he will help him move next weekend, then Peter has a reason to do so. There may be circumstances that speak against it; but these circumstances, too, are reasons, but just more important reasons, such as the reason that Peters' mother needs his help on the weekend because she is seriously ill. But having made a promise is—at least as a rule—a reason to act in accordance with the promise.[11] The two examples clearly show two essential characteristics of reasons. Firstly, reasons are *normative*; for if there is a reason for an action, then one should perform this action, unless there are more weighty reasons that speak against it.[12] And secondly, they are *objective*; by this is meant here that the statement that something is a good reason cannot be translated into statements about mental states. For example, Peter has still the reason to help John with the promised move even if he no longer feels like doing so; and the reason to help the victim of the accident does not disappear either just because one has other preferences or because, for example, one is of the crude conviction that the accident victim does not deserve help. There are just as few "subjective reasons" as there are "subjective facts"![13]

How is this understanding of reason and freedom relevant for the way we attribute responsibility? Responsibility presupposes both at the level of action and at the level of will or decision at least the freedom to refrain from the action in question and from

---

if the agent is not prevented by external obstacles from doing what he wants and can also exist in the case of compulsive acts of the mentally ill or severely addicted persons, which can clearly be qualified as unfree.

[10]Due to limited space, we only focus on practical reasons in the following. However, the characterizations made here can be transferred to theoretical reasons (i.e., reasons for beliefs). Cf. Nida-Rümelin (2023), pp. 179 ff. and 187–190.

[11]The only exceptions are promises whose fulfillment is morally questionable or even forbidden (such as the promise to cruelly kill another person). Here again, however, it is a reason that speaks against keeping such promises, and this reason is just their morally questionable or forbidden content.

[12]Closely related to the normativity of reasons is their inferentiality, which allows us to deduce from empirical facts normative obligations/normative facts: The empirical fact that a severely injured victim is helplessly lying on the side of the road argues in favor of helping the person (normative fact), because otherwise she will suffer permanent physical damage or even die (inference). For further explanations of the inferentiality of reasons, see Nida-Rümelin (2023), pp. 182 f.

[13]Cf. Nida-Rümelin (2023), pp. 187–190. This does not mean that subjective elements such as desires, preferences, or decisions are irrelevant for judging whether a reason is a good reason. And, of course, what is a good reason to do for one person in a particular situation is not necessarily a good reason for another person who is in the same situation and has different preferences. However, it does not follow from the mere fact that a person wishes or decides to do something that she has a good reason to implement the wish or decision. For whether there is a good reason to do so depends on the content of this wish or decision, and the assessment of this content is not made according to subjective criteria.

the decision on which it is based.[14] The so-called semi-compatibilism disputes this and, in contrast, argues that responsibility is possible even without freedom. This position can be traced back to two essays by the American philosopher Harry G. Frankfurt, published in the late 1960s and early 1970s, which continue to shape the debate today.[15] The Frankfurt-type examples, which were developed following the scenarios cited by Frankfurt there, are intended to show that a person is morally responsible for her decision even if she had no other option in fact than to decide as she did. In these thought experiments, another person, the experimenter—e.g., a neurosurgeon who can follow and influence the development of the subject's intentions, which are reflected in corresponding readiness potentials, by means of a special computer device—ensures that the decision can only be made and implemented in the sense of an alternative (to do or not to do) determined by her (the experimenter) in advance. If the subject then decides in favor of this alternative, then she is responsible for this decision, although no other decision alternative was open to her at all because of the other person's possibility of intervention; since the subject would have decided in exactly the same way in the case of freedom of choice (i.e., without the possibility of intervention from the outside), the lack of possibility to decide differently is irrelevant for the question of responsibility from a semi-compatibilist perspective. This shows, according to this view, that responsibility requires neither freedom of action nor freedom of will. However, this argumentation overlooks the fact that in the scenario just described, we only attribute responsibility to the subject because she has chosen one of two alternatives, both of which were open to her (to do or not to do something), and, thus, had freedom of choice. It is obviously decisive for the question of responsibility at what point the neurosurgeon intervenes: If the intervention only takes place after the subject has made a decision, then she had freedom of choice between two alternatives and is therefore responsible. In contrast, if it takes place at a time when the subject of the test is still in a deliberation process, and, thus, before she has made a decision, then she is not responsible, because the final decision was not made by her but is based on a manipulation by the neurosurgeon.[16] Thus, the Frankfurt-type examples do not disprove that freedom is a prerequisite for responsibility.

But are our decisions and actions really free? Actions differ from mere behavior in several ways. If, during a bus ride, the passenger P_1 loses her balance as a result of emergency braking in such a way that she falls on passenger P_2 and the latter is injured as a result, this is described and evaluated differently than if P_1 drops on P_2 and P_2 suffers the same kind of injury. It's only in the second case that we attribute intentions to P_1 and that we would call her role in the incident an action. In the first case, on the other hand, we would say it was an unintentional, involuntary behavior not at all guided by her intentions. Actions, obviously, have besides a purely

[14]To this point in detail, see Nida-Rümelin (2005), pp. 79 ff.

[15]Cf. Frankfurt (1969); id. (1971).

[16]On this objection, see in detail Nida-Rümelin (2005), pp. 102 f.

spatio-temporal behavioral component the characteristic of intentionality.[17] Another property of actions is that they are reason-guided, i.e., that the acting person always has a reason or reasons for his action;[18] actions are constituted by reasons, not necessarily by good reasons, but they are performed without any reasons. And it is because of their being constituted by reasons that actions always have an element of rationality, at least in the sense that one can always judge—unlike in the case of mere behavior, where this question does not arise at all—whether an action is rational or not; actions are, one could say, "capable of rationality"; for, as we have seen, an action is rational if and only if, all things considered, good reasons speak for it and irrational if and only if, all things considered, good reasons speak against it. The reasons we are guided by are the result of a (sometimes very short) deliberation process, in which the different reasons are weighed up against each other and which, when it is completed (and only then!), leads to a decision which is then realized by an action. In short, therefore, we can say: "No action without decision."[19] The respective decision is necessarily free in the sense that it is conceptually impossible that it is already fixed before the conclusion of the decision process, because it is simply part of the nature of decisions that before the decision was made, there was actually something to decide. A decision whose content is already determined before it is made is just not a decision![20]

It is due to this ability to weigh up reasons, i.e., the ability to deliberate, that we are rational beings and that we are responsible for what we do.[21] This is obvious if one realizes that one can be reproached for an action but not for mere behavior: If a damage is caused by a person's mere behavior, she is not reproached for it, and we are satisfied with a purely *causal description* (in the above example: "Due to the forces acting on her as a result of full braking forces, P_1 fell on P_2, causing injury to

[17] When, in everyday life, the term "behavior" is used to describe actions (e.g., in formulations such as "Explain your strange behavior from last night!"), it—correctly—refers to intentional behavior.

[18] As a rule, the acting person can also state the reason when asked. Even if the reason(s) should have slipped his mind—e.g., due to a loss of memory as a result of an accident—she had this/these reason(s) at the time of the act.

[19] Cf. in detail Nida-Rümelin (2005), pp. 45–60. This deliberative conception of action is accompanied by a rejection of the so-called belief-desire model, which can also be called the standard theory of action motivation. According to this model, it's only desires that motivate us to act, whereas beliefs play a purely instrumental role, i.e., with regard to the choice of the appropriate means to be used, in order to fulfill the respective desire. The desires are set and given to us (i.e., we just have the desires that we have) or at most based on other more fundamental desires and, therefore, elude any criticism. Apart from its strict orientation to instrumental rationality (cf. the criticism in fn.7 above), the main argument against this model (that is at least inspired by D. Hume) is that it fails to recognize the role that normative beliefs have in the process of action motivation. In particular, the belief-desire model fails to explain why we sometimes do not follow our momentary inclinations in favor of longer-term interests which have not manifested themselves in the form of a desire. On this "argument of intertemporal coordination" and the other objections raised here, cf. Nida-Rümelin (2023), pp. 88–102 and 203 f.; id. (2001), pp. 32–38.

[20] Cf. Nida-Rümelin (2005), pp. 49–51.

[21] Cf. Nida-Rümelin (2011), p. 53.

P_2"); if, however, the damage was brought about by an action, we expect an explanation and, if possible, a *justification*, and that means reasons that justify this action. But one can and must only justify oneself for something for which one can also be held responsible. This leads us to the more general formulation and also to the central statement of the concept of responsibility presented here: To be responsible for something is connected to the fact that I am (can be), in principle, affected by reasons;[22] this suggests a connection between ascribing responsibility and the ability to be affected by reasons which in turn extends the concept of responsibility beyond the realm of action to that of judgment and emotive attitudes.[23] The conceptual connection between responsibility, freedom, and reason can be formulated against this background as follows: Because or insofar as we are rational, i.e., we have the capacity for deliberation, we are, by exercising this capacity to deliberate, free, and only because and to the extent that we are free, we can be responsible.

From the finding that our practice of attributing responsibility presupposes a certain understanding of freedom, it does, of course, not yet follow that we actually have this kind of freedom. It should be noted, however, that at least the argument that the assumption of human freedom has been refuted by the theory of physical determinism and a universally valid causal principle is not tenable. The concept of comprehensive causal explanation, according to which everything that happens has a cause and can be described as a cause-effect connection determined by laws of nature, has long been abandoned in modern physics; and even classical Newtonian physics is by no means deterministic because of the singularities occurring in it. This is especially true for modern irreducibly probabilistic physics and even more so for the disciplines of biology and neurophysiology, which deal with even more complex systems.[24]

In the introduction, we characterized digital humanism as an ethics for the digital age that interprets and shapes the process of digital transformation in accordance with the core concepts of humanist philosophy and practice. Having identified these core concepts, we can now consider the theoretical and practical implications of digital humanism.

---

[22] Nida-Rümelin (2023), p. 58; id. 2011, p. 17 and p. 53 and passim

[23] Nida-Rümelin (2023), p. 58; id. 2011, pp. 33–52. The responsibility for our emotive attitudes may perhaps be surprising at first. But they, too, have to be justified sometimes, for it disconcerts us if a person cannot give any understandable reasons for the negative feelings (e.g., hatred) she has toward another person.

[24] On this and on the question of the compatibility of human freedom and scientific explanation, cf. Nida-Rümelin (2005), pp. 69–78; id. 2023, pp. 238 ff.

3 Conclusions

3.1 *Theoretical Implications of Digital Humanism*

3.1.1 Rejection of Mechanistic Paradigm: Humans Are Not Machines

Perhaps the greatest current challenge to the humanistic view of man is the digitally renewed machine paradigm of man. Man as a machine is an old metaphor whose origins go back to the early modern era. The mechanism and materialism of the rationalist age makes the world appear as clockwork and man as a cog in the wheel. The great watchmaker is then the creator who has ensured that nothing is left to chance and that one cog meshes with another. There is no room for human freedom, responsibility, and reason in this image.

Software systems have two levels of description, that of the hardware, which must fall back only on physical and technical terms, and that of the software, which can be divided again into a syntactic and a semantic one. The description and explanation of software systems in terms of hardware properties is closed: Every operation (event, process, state) can be uniquely described as causally determined by the preceding state of the hardware. In this characterization, posterior uniqueness of hardware states would suffice; Turing then added prior uniqueness to this, so that what is called a "Turing machine" describes a process uniquely determined in both temporal directions. Transferred as a model to humans, this means that the physical-physiological "hardware" generates mental characteristics like an algorithmic system with a temporal sequence of states clearly determined by genetics, epigenetics, and sensory stimuli and thus enables meaningful speech and action. The humanistic conception of man and thus the normative foundations of morality and law would prove to be pure illusion or a collective human self-deception.[25]

In a humanistic worldview, however, a human being is not a mechanism, but a free (autonomous) and responsible agent in interaction with other human beings and a shared social and natural world. For it is undeniable for us humans that we have mental properties, that we have certain mental states, that we have beliefs, desires, intentions, fears, expectations, etc.

[25] Cf., for example, Bennett et al. (2007), Wolf Singer (2002), and Tivnan (1996).

3.1.2 Rejection of the Animistic Paradigm: Machines Are Not (Like) Humans

Even in the first wave of digitalization after the Second World War, interestingly enough, it was not the materialistic paradigm just described but the animistic paradigm that proved to be more effective. In 1950, Alan Turing made a contribution to this in his essay "Computing Machinery and Intelligence"[26] that is still much discussed today. The paradigm we call "animistic" goes, so to speak, the opposite way of interpretation: Instead of interpreting the human mind (mental states) as an epiphenomenon of material processes in a physically closed world, and describing it mechanistically, the algorithmic system is now endowed with mental properties, provided it sufficiently (i.e., confusably) resembles that of humans in its external (output) behavior. One can find this animistic view in an especially radical conception of "strong AI," according to which there is no categorical difference between computer processes and human thought processes such that software systems have consciousness, make decisions, and pursue goals and their performances are not merely simulations of human abilities but realize them.[27] From this perspective, "strong AI" is a program of disillusionment: What appears to us to be a characteristically human property is nothing but that which can be realized as a computer program. The concept of "weak AI," on the other hand, does not deny that there are categorical differences between human and artificial intelligence, but it assumes that in principle all human thinking, perception, and decision-making processes can be *simulated* by suitable software systems. Thus, the difference between "strong AI" and "weak AI" is the difference between identification and simulation.

If the radical concept of "strong AI" were about to be realized, we should immediately stop its realization! For if this kind of "strong AI" already existed, we would have to radically change our attitude toward artificial intelligence: we would have to treat strong AI machines not as machines but as persons, that is, as beings

---

[26] Cf. Turing, Alan (1950). Turing there describes an "imitation game" (later known as "Turing test"), in which an interrogator asks questions of another person and a machine in another room in order to determine which of the two is the other person. Turing believed "that in about fifty years' time," it would be "possible to programme computers [. . .], to make them play the imitation game so well that an average interrogator will not have more than 70 percent chance of making the right identification after five minutes of questioning. [. . .] I believe that at the end of the century the use of words and general educated opinion will have altered so much that one will be able to speak of machines thinking without expecting to be contradicted" (442). Apart from the fact that Turing's prediction was too optimistic in terms of time, one can question whether this game is really an appropriate method to attribute thinking abilities to machines. For example, one may wonder whether the Turing test does not rather test human credulity than true artificial intelligence.

[27] Cf. the characterization of "strong AI" in the Stanford Encyclopedia of Philosophy: "'Strong' AI seeks to create artificial persons: machines that have all the mental powers we have, including phenomenal consciousness" (https://plato.stanford.edu/entries/artificial-intelligence/#StroVersWeakAI, section 8.1). For an overview of the use of the terms strong and weak AI in different disciplines, see Nida-Rümelin (2022b).

who have human rights and human dignity. To switch off a strong AI machine would then be as bad as manslaughter.

It is a plausible assumption that computers as technical systems can be described completely in a terminology that has only physical terms (including their technical implementation). There is then no remainder. A computer consists of very complex interconnections in high numbers, and even if it would go beyond all capacities available to humans, it is in principle possible to describe all their interconnections completely in their physical and technical aspects. If we exclude the new product line of quantum computers, classical physics extended by electrostatics and electrodynamics is sufficient to completely describe and explain every event, every procedure, every process, and every state of a computer or a networked software system.

Perhaps the most fundamental argument against physicalism is called the "qualia argument." This argument speaks against the identity of neurophysiological and mental states[28] and, since, as we have just seen, every state of a computer or a networked software system can be completely described in physical terms, also against the identity of digital and mental states. The Australian philosopher Frank Cameron Jackson put forward one version of the qualia argument in his essay "What Mary didn't know" (1986), in which he describes a thought experiment which can be summarized as follows:

> Mary is a scientist, and her specialist subject is color. She knows everything there is to know about it, the wavelengths, the neurological effects, every possible property color can have. But she lives in a black and white room. She was born there and raised there and she can observe the outside world on a black and white monitor. One day, someone opens the door, and Mary walks out. And she sees a blue sky. And at that moment, she learns something that all her studies couldn't tell her. She learns what it *feels like* to see color.

Now imagine an AI that not only has, like Mary, all available information about colors but also all available information about the world as well as about people and their feelings. Even if there were an AI that had all this information, it would not mean that it understands what it means to experience the world and to have feelings.

Software systems do not feel, think, and decide; humans on the contrary do, as they are not determined by mechanical processes. Thanks to their capacity for insight as well as their ability to have feelings, they can determine their actions themselves, and they do this by deciding to act in this way and not in another. Humans have reasons for what they do and can, as rational beings, distinguish good from bad reasons. By engaging in theoretical and practical reasoning, we influence our mental states, our thinking, feeling, and acting, thereby exerting a causal effect on the biological and physical world. If the world were to be understood reductionistically,

[28] Of course, one can also reject the identity of the mental and the neurophysiological, but still argue that the mental can only occur in connection with the material. Indeed, there is much to suggest that human consciousness is only possible due to the corresponding brain functions. But even those who hold that human consciousness is based essentially on neurophysiological processes need not subscribe to the identity theory of the mental and the physical. That mental states of humans are *realized* by brain states (i.e., neurophysiological processes and states) does not mean that they are identical to them or caused by them.

all higher phenomena from biology to psychology to logic and ethics would be determined by physical laws: Human decisions and beliefs would be causally irrelevant in such a world.[29]

3.2 *Practical Implications of Digital Humanism*

The finding that even complex AI systems cannot be regarded as persons for the foreseeable future gives rise to two interrelated practical demands in particular.

First, we should not attribute responsibility to them. As we have already seen, it is quite plausible that AI systems are not rational and free in the way that is necessary for attributing responsibility to them. The reason why they lack this kind of rationality and freedom is that they lack the relevant autonomy, which consists in the ability of the agent to set her own goals and to direct her actions with regard to these goals. These goals do not simply correspond to desires or inclinations, but are the result of a decision-making process. We can distinguish this concept of *Strong Autonomy* from the concept of *Weak Autonomy*,[30] in which concrete behavior is not determined by the intervention of an external agent, but an external agent determines the overriding goal to be pursued. Since *Weak Autonomy* does not manifest itself in the choice of self-imposed (overriding) goals, but at best in the choice of the appropriate means by which externally set goals can be achieved, one could also speak of "heteronomous autonomy." To the extent that an AI has the ability to select the most suitable behavioral alternative for achieving a given goal, this could be interpreted as *Weak Autonomy*.

The second demand is that ethical decisions must never be made by algorithmically functioning AI systems. For apart from the fact that algorithms do not "decide" anything,[31] the *consequentialistically* orientated optimization function inherent in

[29] A theory T2 can be reduced to a theory T1 if T2 can be completely derived from T1, which presupposes that the terms of T2 can also be defined with the help of terms of T1. A weaker form of reducibility exists if all empirical predictions of T2 can already be derived from T1 (empirical reduction). Physicalism is the most prominent form of reductionism, according to which all science can be traced back to physics. So far, this has only been successful for parts of inorganic chemistry and has otherwise remained science fiction. Even the reducibility of biology to physics is highly implausible; the reducibility of the social sciences or even literary studies to physics is completely out of the question. This is due, among other things, to the fact that even in the social sciences, but especially in cultural studies and the humanities, terms such as "meaning," "intention," "belief," or "emotion" occur that cannot be translated into physical terms: Intentions or even reasons are not a possible object of physics.

[30] To these concepts and their meaning for attributing responsibility, see Bertolini, A. (2014), p. 150 f. following *Gutmann, M./Rathgeber, B./Syed, T.,* Action and Autonomy: A Hidden Dilemma in Artificial Autonomous Systems, in: Decker, M./Gutmann, M. (ed.), Robo- and Informationethics. Some Fundamentals, Zürich, Berlin 2012, pp. 245 ff.

[31] We have already seen in Sect. 2 that a decision is necessarily free in the sense that it is conceptually impossible that it is already fixed before the conclusion of the decision process. But

algorithms is not compatible with human dignity and, more generally, with the *deontological* framework of liberal constitutions.[32] Furthermore, the approach of considering all relevant facts for each case in advance when programming an algorithm does principally not take into account the complexity and context sensitivity of ethical decision-making situations.[33] AI systems have no feelings, no moral sense, and no intentions, and they cannot attribute these to other persons. Without these abilities, however, proper moral practice is not possible.

Discussion Questions for Students and Their Teachers

1. How is digital humanism characterized in this chapter?
2. What are the core concepts of humanist philosophy and practice?
3. In what way do actions differ from mere behavior?
4. What conditions must be met for us to hold someone personally responsible for something?
5. What are the main theoretical and practical implications of digital humanism?

Learning Resources for Students

1. Nida-Rümelin, J. and Weidenfeld, N. (2022) Digital Humanism. Cham: Springer International Publishing (https://link.springer.com/book/10.1007/978-3-031-12482-2).

   This book describes the philosophical and cultural aspects of digital humanism and can be understood as its groundwork.
2. Nida-Rümelin, J. (2022), Digital Humanism and the Limits of Artificial Intelligence. Perspectives on Digital Humanism. Cham Springer International Publishing, pp. 71-75. (https://link.springer.com/book/10.1007/978-3-030-86144-5).

   This article presents two important arguments against the animistic paradigm: the "Chinese Room" Argument against the conception of "strong AI" and, based on the meta-mathematical results of incompleteness and undecidability of Kurt Gödel and other logicians, an argument against the concept of "weak AI."
3. Bertolini, A. (2014), "Robots and Liability – Justifying a Change in Perspective" in Battaglia, F. et al. (ed.), Rethinking Responsibility in Science and Technology, Pisa: Pisa University Press srl, pp. 203–214.

   This article presents good arguments against the liability of robots.

---

the decision about the rules according to which an algorithm operates is already made and not by the algorithm itself but by the programmer. And even if a complex AI system develops algorithms of its own, then it does so only in order to achieve a goal that it is given to it from outside. There is, so to speak, always an "overarching algorithm" given from outside that guides it.

[32] According to consequentialism, the ethical quality of an action (or practice) depends only on the ethical quality of its consequences, and an act (or practice) is right if and only if it brings about the best possible outcomes. From a deontological perspective, on the other hand, the rightness of an action (or practice) depends not (only) on its consequences but on its conformity with a moral norm. One of the most important objections against consequentialist ethics is that, unlike deontological ethics, they cannot adequately justify the obligation not to violate individual rights. See to the objections against consequentialism in detail Nida-Rümelin (1995); see also id. 2023, Chapter 6.

[33] Both points are extremely relevant in regard to the question of the ethical and legal permissibility of autonomous driving.

4. Nida-Rümelin, J. (2014) "On the Concept of responsibility" in Battaglia, F. et al. (ed.), Rethinking Responsibility in Science and Technology, Pisa: Pisa University Press srl, pp. 13–24.

   This article, in the same anthology, focuses on our responsibility for our actions, convictions, and emotions and the reasons we have for all of them. The whole anthology is worth reading!

5. Bringsjord, Selmer and Naveen Sundar Govindarajulu, "Artificial Intelligence", *The Stanford Encyclopedia of Philosophy* (Fall 2022 Edition), Edward N. Zalta & Uri Nodelman (eds.), URL = <https://plato.stanford.edu/archives/fall2022/entries/artificial-intelligence/>.

   Very instructive article about what AI is as well as about its history and its different philosophical concepts.

References

Bennett, M., et al. (2007). *Neuroscience and philosophy: Brain, mind, and language*. Columbia University Express.

Bertolini, A. (2014). Robots and liability – justifying a change in perspective. In F. Battaglia et al. (Eds.), *Rethinking responsibility in science and technology* (pp. 143–166). Pisa University Press srl.

Bringsjord, S., & Govindarajulu, N. S. (2022). Artificial intelligence. In E. N. Zalta & U. Nodelman (Eds.), *The Stanford encyclopedia of philosophy* (Fall edn). https://plato.stanford.edu/archives/fall2022/entries/artificial-intelligence/

Daub, A. (2021). *What tech calls thinking. An inquiry into the intellectual bedrock of Silicon Valley*. Farrar, Straus & Giroux.

Frankfurt, H. G. (1969). Alternate possibilities and moral responsibility. *The Journal of Philosophy, 66*, 829–839.

Frankfurt, H. G. (1971). Freedom of the will and the concept of a person. *The Journal of Philosophy, 68*, 5–20.

Jackson, F. M. (1986). What Mary didn't know. *The Journal of Philosophy, 83*, 191–295.

Nida-Rümelin, J. (1995). *Kritik des Konsequentialismus*. Oldenbourg Verlag.

Nida-Rümelin, J. (2001). *Strukturelle Rationalität*. Reclam.

Nida-Rümelin, J. (2005). *Über menschliche Freiheit*. Reclam.

Nida-Rümelin, J. (2011). *Verantwortung*. Reclam.

Nida-Rümelin, J. (2022a). Digital humanism and the limits of artificial intelligence. In H. Werthner et al. (Eds.), *Perspectives on digital humanism* (pp. 71–75). Springer International Publishing. https://link.springer.com/book/10.1007/978-3-030-86144-5

Nida-Rümelin, J. (2022b). Über die Verwendung der Begriffe starke & schwache Intelligenz. In K. Chibanguza et al. (Eds.), *Künstliche Intelligenz. Recht und Praxis automatisierter und autonomer Systeme* (pp. 75–90). Nomos Verlagsgesellschaft.

Nida-Rümelin, J. (2023). *A theory of practical reason*. Springer.

Nida-Rümelin, J., & Weidenfeld, N. (2022). *Digital humanism*. Springer International. https://link.springer.com/book/10.1007/978-3-031- 12482-2

Singer, W. (2002). *Der Beobachter im Gehirn. Essays on brain research*. Suhrkamp.

Tivnan, T. (1996). *The moral imagination: Confronting the ethical issues of our day*. Touchstone.

Turing, A. (1950). Computing machinery and intelligence. *Mind, LIX*(236), 433–460. https://doi.org/10.1093/mind/LIX.236.433

Evolution of Computing

James R. Larus

Abstract Computers and computing emerged within a lifetime and completely changed our world. Although their history is brief, the change they precipitated has been rapid and constant. Today's world would be unimaginably different without these machines. Not necessarily worse, but certainly slower, static, disconnected, and poorer. One has to look back to the steam engine in the nineteenth century or electricity in the early twentieth century to find technologies with similar rapid and far-reaching effects. This chapter briefly describes the evolution of computing and highlights how its growth is closely tied to concerns of digital humanism.

1 Introduction

Electronic digital computers have existed for only 75 years. Computer science—or informatics, if you prefer—is roughly a decade older. Computer science is the expanding discipline of understanding, developing, and applying computers and computation. Its intellectual roots were planted in the 1930s, but it only emerged in the 1940s when commercial computers became available.

Today's world would be unimaginably different without these machines. Not necessarily worse (computers emerged during but played little role in the world's deadliest conflict), but certainly slower, static, disconnected, and poorer. Over three-quarters of a century, computers went from rare, expensive machines used only by wealthy businesses and governments to devices that most people on earth could not live without. The technical details of this revolution are a fascinating story of millions of peoples' efforts, but equally compelling are the connections between technology and society.

Like the emergence of a new animal or virus, the growth of computing has serious and far-reaching consequences on its environment—the focus of this book. In seven decades, computing completely changed the human environment—business,

J. R. Larus (✉)
School of Computer and Communication Sciences, EPFL, Lausanne, Switzerland
e-mail: james.larus@epfl.ch

H. Werthner et al. (eds.), *Introduction to Digital Humanism*,
https://doi.org/10.1007/978-3-031-45304-5_3

finance, social relations, government, and society, to name a few—through its seminal advances such as personal computers, the Internet, the World Wide Web, mobile computing, machine learning, and artificial intelligence. One has to look back to the steam engine in the nineteenth century or electricity in the early twentieth century to find technologies with similar rapid and far-reaching effects.

This chapter offers a brief overview of the evolution of computing and its connection to the concerns of digital humanism. The velocity and broad impact of computing's emergence discussed in this chapter partly explain why the humanism implications discussed in the rest of this book are among society's prominent and concerning challenges.

2 Prehistory

In most people's opinion, computer science started in 1936 when Alan Turing, a student at Cambridge, published his paper "On Computable Numbers, with an Application to the Entscheidungsproblem" (Turing, 1937). This paper settled a fundamental open question in mathematics by showing that a general technique does not exist to decide whether a theorem is true or false.

More significantly for this history, Turing's paper introduced the concept of a universal computer (the Turing Machine) and postulated that it could execute any algorithm (a procedure precisely described by a series of explicit actions). The idea of a computing machine—a device capable of performing a computation—had several predecessors. Turing's innovation was to treat the instructions controlling the computer (its program) as data, thereby creating the infinitely malleable device known as a stored program computer. This innovation made computers into universal computing devices, capable of executing any computation (within the limits of their resources). Even today, no other field of human invention has created a single device capable of doing everything. Before computers, humans were the sole universal "machines" capable of being taught new activities.

In addition, by making computer programs into explicit entities and formally describing their semantics, Turing's paper also created the rich fields of program and algorithm analysis, the techniques for reasoning about computations' characteristics, which underlie much of computer science.

A Turing Machine, however, is a mathematical abstraction, not a practical computer. The first electronic computers were built less than a decade later, during World War II, to solve pressing problems of computing artillery tables and breaking codes. Not surprisingly, Turing was central to the British effort at Bletchley Park to break the German Enigma codes. These early computers were electronic, not mechanical like their immediate predecessors, but they did not follow Turing's path and treat programs as data; rather they were programmed by rewiring their circuits.

However, soon after the war, the Hungarian-American mathematician John von Neuman, building on many people's works, wrote a paper unifying Turing's insight

Fig. 1 ENIAC (1947). (Public domain) In Wikipedia. https://en.wikipedia.org/wiki/ENIAC

with practical engineering. It described an architecture for stored-program computers, which laid the computer industry's foundation. This so-called von Neuman architecture still is the blueprint for today's computers. Figure 1 shows a picture of ENIAC, the first general-purpose electronic computer.

3 Computers as Calculators

The first applications of computers were as calculators, both for the government and industry. The early computers were expensive, slow, and limited machines. For example, IBM rented its 701 computers for $15,000/month for an 8-h work day (in 2023 terms, $169,000) (na, 2023a). This computer could perform approximately 16,000 additions per second and hold 82,000 digits in its memory (na, 2003). While the 701's performance was unimaginably slower than today's computers, the 701 was far faster and more reliable than the alternative, a room full of clerks with mechanical calculators.

The challenge of building the first computers and convincing businesses to buy them meant that the computer industry started slowly. Still, as we will see, progress accelerated geometrically. The societal impact of early computers was also initially small, except perhaps to diminish the job market for "calculators," typically women who performed scientific calculations by hand or mechanical adding machines, and clerks with mechanical calculators.

At the same time, there was considerable intellectual excitement about the potential of these "thinking machines." In his third seminal contribution, Alan

Turing posed the question of whether a machine could "think" with his famous Turing Test, which stipulated that a machine could be considered to share this attribute of human intelligence when people could not distinguish whether they were conversing with a machine or another human (Turing, 1950). Seventy years later, with the advent of ChatGPT, Turing's formulation is still insightful and now increasingly relevant.

4 Computers and Communications

Computers would only be slightly more exciting than today's calculators if they were only capable of mathematical calculations. But it quickly became apparent that computers can exchange information and coordinate with other computers, allowing them (and people) to communicate and collaborate as well as compute. The far-reaching consequences of computing, the focus of this book, are due as much to computers' ability to communicate as to compute, although the latter attribute is more closely identified with the field.

Among the most ambitious early applications of computers were collections of devices and computers linked through the telephone system. SAGE, deployed in 1957, was a computer-controlled early warning system for missile attacks on the United States (na, 2023b). In 1960, American Airlines deployed Sabre, the first online reservation and ticketing system, which accepted requests and printed tickets on terminals worldwide (Campbell-Kelly, Martin, 2004). The significance of both systems went far beyond their engineering and technical challenges. Both directly linked the real world—World War II and commercial transactions—to computers without significant human intermediation. People did not come to computers; computers came to people. Starting with systems like these, these machines have increasingly intruded into everyday life.

Businesses using computers, e.g., American Airlines, quickly accumulated large quantities of data about their finances, operations, and customers. Their need to efficiently store and index this information led to the development of database systems and mass storage devices such as disk drives. Around this time, the implications of computers on people's privacy emerged as a general concern as the capacity of computers to collect and retrieve information rapidly increased. At that time, perhaps because of its traditional role, attention was focused more on government information collection than private industry (na, 2973).

Another fundamental innovation of that period was the ARPANET, the Internet's direct intellectual and practical predecessor. The US Department of Defense created the ARPANET in the late 1960 and early 1970 as a communication system that could survive a nuclear attack on the USA (Waldrop, 2001). The ARPANET's fundamental technical innovation was packet switching, which splits a message between two computers into smaller pieces that could be routed independently along multiple paths and resent if they did not reach their destination. Before, communication relied on a direct connection between computers (think of a telephone wire, the technology used at the time). These connections, called circuits, could not have grown to accommodate a worldwide network like today's Internet. Moreover, the engineering of the ARPANET was extraordinary. The network grew from a few hundred computers in the 1970s to tens of billions of computers today in a smooth evolution that maintained its overall structure and many of its communication protocols, even as new technologies, such as fiber optics and mobile phones, emerged to support or use the Internet (Mccauley et al., 2023).

5 Computing as a Science

In the 1960s and 1970s, the theory underlying computer science emerged as a discipline on its own that offered an increasingly nuanced perspective on what is practically computable. Three decades earlier, Turing hypothesized that stored program computers were universal computing devices capable of executing any algorithm—though not solving any problem, as he proved that no algorithm could decide whether any algorithm would terminate. Turing's research ignored the running time of a computation (its cost), which held no relevance to his impossibility results but was of first-order importance to solving real-world problems.

The study of these costs, the field of computational complexity, started in the 1960s to analyze the running time of algorithms to find more efficient solutions to problems. It quickly became obvious that many fundamental problems, for example, sorting a list of numbers, had many possible algorithms, some much quicker than others.

Theoreticians also realized that the problems themselves could be classified by the running cost of their best possible solution. Many problems were practically solvable by algorithms whose running time grew slowly with increasingly large amounts of data. Other problems had no algorithm other than exploring an exponential number of possible answers, and so could only be precisely solved for small instances. The first group of problems was called P (for polynomial time) and the second NP (nondeterministic polynomial time). For 50 years, whether P = NP has been a fundamental unanswered question in computer science (Fortnow, 2021). Although its outcome is still unknown, remarkable progress has been made in developing efficient algorithms for many problems in P and efficient, approximate algorithms for problems in NP.

Moreover, computer science's approach of considering computation as a formal and analyzable process influenced other fields of education and science through a movement called "computation thinking" (Wing, 2006). For centuries, scientific and technical accomplishments (and ordinary life—think food recipes) offered informal, natural language descriptions of how to accomplish a task. Computer science brought rigor and formalism to describing solutions as algorithms. Moreover, it recognized that not all solutions are equally good. Analyzing algorithms to understand their inherent costs is a major intellectual step forward with broad applicability beyond computers.

6 Hardware "Laws"

Computer science was extremely fortunate to ride on the back of an extraordinary and unprecedented improvement in silicon semiconductors, the underlying technology used to construct computers. The earliest computers were built from mechanical relays, which could switch on or off roughly 20 times per second. They were quickly succeeded by vacuum tubes, which could switch millions of times per second, but were large, hot, and unreliable. In the 1960s, transistors replaced tubes with much smaller, more reliable switches. More importantly, many transistors could be fabricated and wired together on a small piece of silicon called a "chip," which offered compelling size, speed, and cost advantages. In 1965, Gordon Moore noted that the number of transistors on a chip doubled every year, an observation that came to be called "Moore's law." This geometric increase in capacity has continued for over four decades, albeit at a slower pace. A decade after Moore, Robert Dennard published rules for IC design, which quantified how the smaller, denser transistors resulting from Moore's Law could run faster without consuming more power.

Figure 2 illustrates this remarkable progress. Moore's law and Dennard scaling led to three decades of computers whose running speed doubled every other year, a remarkable period of innovation that ended around 2005, when electrical considerations made it impossible to continue running computers faster, even though the number of transistors on a chip continued to double. From the 1970s to the early 2000s, computers dropped rapidly in cost at the same time as their performance increased, which hastened the birth of the software industry (discussed below) and made possible increasingly ambitious uses of computers.

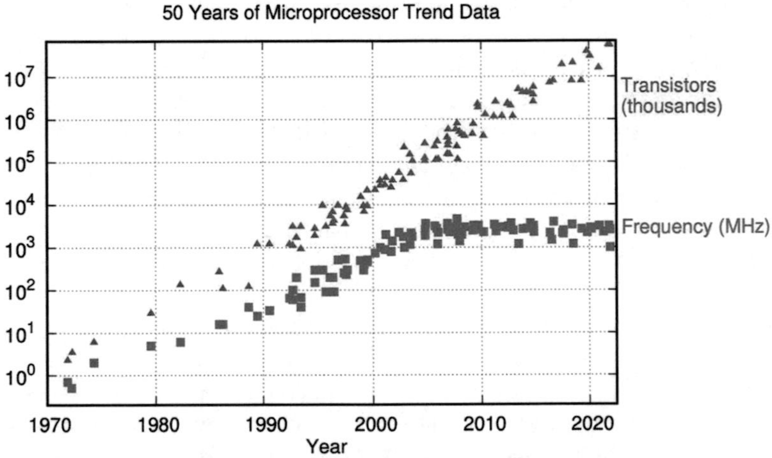

Fig. 2 Moore's law and Dennard scaling. The number of transistors on a chip has doubled every other year for 50 years. For the first half of this period, each generation of chips also doubled in speed. That improvement ended around 2005. From Karl Rupp, CC BY 4.0

Another important observation, called Kryder's law, was that the amount of data that could be stored in a square centimeter also grew geometrically at a faster rate than Moore's law. This progress has also slowed as technology approaches physical limits. Still, storage cost fell from $82 million/Gigabyte (billion bytes) for the first disk drive in 1957 to 2 cents in 2018 (both in 2018 prices). This amazing improvement not only made richer and more voluminous media such as photos and video affordable, but it also made possible the collection and retention of unprecedented amounts of data on individuals.

7 Personal Computers

In the mid-to-late 1970s, the increasing density of integrated circuits made it possible to put a "computer on a chip" by fabricating the entire processing component on a single piece of silicon (memory and connections to the outside world required many other chips). This accomplishment rapidly changed the computer from an expensive, difficult-to-construct piece of business machinery into a small, inexpensive commodity that entrepreneurs could exploit to build innovative products. These computers, named microprocessors, initially replaced inflexible mechanical or electric mechanisms in many machines. As programmable controllers, computers were capable of nuanced responses and often were less expensive than the mechanisms they replaced.

More significantly, microprocessors made it economically practical to build a personal computer that was small and inexpensive enough that an employee or student could have one use to write and edit documents, exchange messages, run line-of-business software, play games, and do countless other activities.

With the rapidly increasing number of computers, software became a profitable, independent business, surpassing computer hardware in creativity and innovation. Before the microprocessor, software was the less profitable, weak sibling of hardware, which computer companies viewed as their product and revenue source. The dominant computer company IBM gave away software with its computers until the US government's antitrust lawsuit in the early 1970s forced it to "unbundle" its software from hardware. Bill Gates, a cofounder of Microsoft, was among the earliest to realize that commodity microprocessors dramatically shifted computing's value from the computers to the software that accomplished tasks. IBM accelerated this shift by building its iconic PC using commodity components (a processor from Intel and an operating system from Microsoft) and not preventing other companies from building "IBM-compatible" computers. Many companies sprung up to build PCs, providing consumer choice and driving down prices, which benefited the emerging software industry.

Moreover, the widespread adoption of powerful personal computers (doubling in performance every 2 years) created a technically literate segment of the population and laid the foundation for the next major turning point in technology, the Internet.

8 Natural Interfaces

Interaction with the early computers was textual. A program, the instructions directing a computer's operation, was written in a programming language, a highly restricted and regularized subset of English, and a computer was directed to run it using textual commands. Though small and precise, most people found these languages difficult to understand, limiting early machines' use. In the late 1960 and 1970s, graphical user interfaces (GUIs) were initially developed, most notably at Xerox PARC (Michael A. Hiltzik, 1999). They became widespread with the introduction of the Apple Macintosh computer in the early 1980s. These interfaces provided pictural metaphor-oriented interfaces directly manipulated through a mouse. This user interface change made computers accessible and useful to many more people.

The graph aspect of GUIs enabled computers to display and manipulate images, though initially, software treated them as collections of pixels and could not discern or recognize their content. This capability only came later, with the advent of powerful machine-learning techniques that enabled computers to recognize entities in images. In addition, the early computers were severely constrained in computing power and storage capacity, which limited the use of images and video, which is far larger than a single image.

Computers also adopted other human mechanisms. Voice recognition and speech generation are long-established techniques for interaction. Recently, machine learning has greatly improved the generality and accuracy of human-like speech and dialog, so it is not unusual to command a smartphone or other device by speaking to it.

Most computers do not exist as autonomous, self-contained entities, like PCs or smartphones with their own user interface. They are instead incorporated into another device and interact through its features and functionality. Mark Weiser called this "ubiquitous computing" (Weiser, 1991), where computing fades into the background, so no one is aware of its presence. Many of these computers, however, are accessible through the Internet, raising vast maintenance, security, and privacy challenges.

9 The Internet

The Internet started as a US government research project and infrastructure in the 1970s. Access was initially limited to the military, universities, and a few government-related businesses. In the early 1990s, two important events occurred. The US government agency managing the public Internet, the National Science Foundation (NSF), decided it was time to transition from a government-led project into a commercial product. In a little-heralded but enormously successful effort, it turned the Internet over to the technical community that built it and the private companies that operate the individual networks that comprise today's Internet.

The other crucial change was the emergence of the World Wide Web (the "Web") as the Internet's "killer app," which caused it to gain vast public interest and financial investment. While working at CERN, a physics research lab in Switzerland, Tim Berners-Lee developed a networked hypertext system he optimistically called the "World Wide Web (WWW)." CERN released his design and software to the public in 1991. A few years later, the University of Illinois's Mosaic browser made Berners-Lee's invention easier to use and more visually appealing on many types of computers. The academic community, already familiar with the Internet, rapidly jumped on the Web. Then, remarkably, both inventions made a rare leap into the public eye and widespread adoption. In a remarkably short time, businesses started creating websites, and the general population started to buy personal computers to gain access to "cyberspace."

Other chapters of this book discuss a remarkable spectrum of societal and personal changes in the past three decades. Underlying *all* of them are the Internet and the Web, which made it possible to find information, conduct commerce, and communicate everywhere at nearly zero cost. Before these inventions, there were two ways to communicate.

First, you could speak to another person. If the person was distant, you used a telephone or radio. However, both alternatives were expensive, particularly as distance increased, because the technical structure of telephone systems allocated a resource (called a circuit) to each communication and charged money to use it throughout the conversation. By contrast, the Internet used packet switching, which only consumed resources when data was transferred, dramatically lowering costs. In fact, users pay a flat rate in most parts of the Internet, independent of their usage, because finer-grained billing is neither necessary nor practical. In addition, for historical reasons, telephone companies were regulated as "natural" monopolies, which allowed them to keep their prices high. The Internet, in reaction, sought multiple connections between parties and resisted centralization and monopolization.

The second alternative, of course, was to engrave, write, or print a message on a stone tablet or piece of paper and physically convey the object to the recipient, incurring substantial costs for the materials, printing, and delivery. Moreover, paper has a low information density, requiring considerable volume to store large amounts of data. In addition, finding information stored on paper, even if well organized, takes time and physical effort.

Computing and the Internet *completely* changed all of this. A message, even a large one, can be delivered nearly instantaneously (at no cost). And data, stored electronically at rapidly decreasing cost, can be quickly retrieved. This is the *dematerialization of information*, which no longer needs a physical presence to be saved, shared, and used. This change, as much as any, is behind the "creative destruction" of existing industries such as newspapers, magazines, classified advertising, postal mail, and others that conveyed information in a tangible, physical form.

Another fundamental computer science innovation is public key cryptography, which made private communication and safe online commerce possible, enabling businesses to communicate and interact through cyberspace rather than the physical world. Cryptography hides the contents of messages so that only the sender and receiver can read them, even if they traverse the public Internet. And cryptographic protocols added functionality such as making it possible for two parties to identify each other online and authenticate a transaction.

10 Mobile Computing

The next important and radical change was mobile computing, which became practical when computers became sufficiently power-efficient (another consequence of Moore's law) to be packaged as smartphones. The defining moment for mobile computing was Apple's introduction of the iPhone in 2007 (Isaacson, 2011). It combined in a pocket-sized package, a touchscreen interface appropriate for a small device without a keyboard or mouse, and continuous connectivity through the wireless telephone network. For most of the world's population, smartphones are *the* access point to the Internet and computing. "Personal" computers never shrank smaller than a notebook and remained better suited to an office than as a constant companion. In less than a decade, the smartphone became an object that most people always carry.

Smartphones also changed the nature of computing by attaching cameras and GPS receivers to computers. Smartphone cameras dramatically increased the number of photos and videos created and let everyone be a photographer and videographer. They also exploited the vast computational power of smartphones to improve the quality of photos and videos to a level comparable with much larger and optically sophisticated cameras operated by skilled photographers. Their GPSs introduced location as an input to computation by continuously tracking a phone's location in the physical world. Location, like many features, is a two-edged sword that offers sophisticated maps and navigation and enables tracking of people by advertisers and malefactors.

Perhaps the most far-reaching consequence of smartphones is that they "democratized" computing in a form whose low cost and remarkably new functionality was quickly adopted by most people worldwide. Earlier computers were concentrated in the developed world, but smartphones are ubiquitous, with a high adoption even in less developed countries. The deployment of wireless networks in these countries brought the citizens of these countries to a nearly equal footing in terms of information access and communications.

11 Machine Learning

A recent and extremely significant advance in computing is machine learning (ML), the process of automatically inferring features in data collections and applying this inference to make predictions from and take actions on other, unseen data. For example, an ML system can be trained on a large collection of labeled photographs, e.g., a bird's photo might be labeled "bird, Herring Gull Larus." An ML model trained on a large collection of photographs could then analyze other photos, even of bird species not included in the training set, and recognize that the images contain birds. Several years ago, ML systems reached a human performance level in this computer vision classification task (Shankar et al., 2021).

Beyond image recognition, ML has been trained to mimic many human skills, such as computer vision, speech recognition, language translation, grammar correction, question answering, game playing, and others. In most cases, the key enabling factor is a large training set of labeled data. For example, large language models (LLMs) are often trained on tens or hundreds of billions of documents from the Web. OpenAI's ChatGPT was trained this way and can respond to general questions with articulate, well-formed responses and conduct a realistic dialog, albeit with many grievous lapses, reflecting a complete lack of understanding of the underlying meaning.

ML represents a fundamental change in how computers are programmed. For the first seven decades, programmers wrote explicit instructions to direct a computer to solve a task. ML shifted the perspective from "teaching" a computer to having the computer "learn" how to accomplish a task by observing past examples. This new approach has proven very successful in developing human-like skills for computers, which programmers found difficult or impossible to describe fully in a program. However, the shift leaves some people concerned that computers are becoming "intelligent" and might soon surpass human abilities (Bostrom, 2014).

These topics are discussed in more detail in the chapter by Woltran and Heitzinger in this volume.

12 Big Data and Cloud Computing

Underlying these advances in machine learning, and many other fields, is the ability to collect and analyze vast amounts of data, known as "Big Data." The hardware and software infrastructure for storing and processing this data was originally developed for Web applications such as search engines, which harness warehouses full of tens of thousands of computers to index most Internet pages and rapidly respond to user queries (Barroso et al., 2013). Each search triggers coordinated activity across thousands of computers, a challenging form of computation called parallel computing.

Internet search was made possible by advances in many fields of computer science, including computer design, high-bandwidth networking, inexpensive storage devices, and research on using multiple computers to solve a single task. The infrastructure was originally the proprietary asset of a few companies. Amazon democratized this form of computing with a product that came to be called "cloud computing." It comprises low-cost computer access in Internet-connected data centers (the cloud) and sophisticated software for building reliable and scalable systems on collections of computers. Before this, a company needed to buy and manage its own computers, which limited the tasks that most companies could accomplish with their limited capital and expertise.

Cloud computing effectively removed the barrier to constructing large-scale computing systems. This has made it possible to collect, store, and analyze vast amounts of data, now a routine business practice. Many websites record every user interaction in detail, and these records are retained to provide the raw material to train machine-learned systems. This practice has serious privacy implications but is routine because data [aka the "new oil" (na, 2017)] promises to be the raw material to build profitable new businesses.

More benignly, the ability to collect and analyze large amounts of data is changing how other fields of science and engineering conduct research. Jim Gray called Big Data the fourth paradigm of scientific discovery (after observation, theory, and modeling) (Hey et al., 2009).

13 Security and Privacy

Because computers contain valuable information and control important devices and activities, they have long been the target of malicious and criminal attempts to steal data or disable their functions. The Internet greatly worsened these problems by making nearly every computer accessible worldwide.

Computer science has failed to develop a software engineering discipline that enables us to construct robust software and systems. Every nontrivial program (with a handful of exceptions) contains software defects ("bugs"), some of which would allow an attacker to gain access to a computer system. The arms race between the attackers and developers is very one-sided since an attacker only needs to find one usable flaw, but the developer must eliminate all flaws. Like security in general, mitigations—updating software to fix bugs, watching for attacks, and encrypting information—are essential.

Privacy is typically grouped with security because the two fields are closely related. Privacy entails personal control of your information: what you do, what you say, where you go, whom you meet, etc. However, privacy differs in a crucial aspect from security since the owners and designers of systems abuse privacy because this personal information has significant value that can be exploited. See the chapter by Weippl and Sebastian in this volume.

14 Conclusions

A natural question is whether computing's rapid growth and evolution can continue. As Niels Bohr said, "Prediction is very difficult, especially about the future." I believe computing will continue to grow and evolve, albeit in different but still exciting directions. New techniques to perform computation, for example, based on biology or quantum phenomena, may provide solutions to problems that are intractable today. At the same time, new inventions and improved engineering will continue to advance general-purpose computing. However, the enjoyable decades of exponential improvement are certainly finished. Computing will become similar to other fields in which improvement is slow and continuous.

The separate questions of whether computing's rapid growth was good or bad and whether its likely demise is good or bad can be evaluated in the context of the rest of this book. In many ways, this question is like asking whether the printing press was good or bad. Its introduction allowed the widespread printing of vernacular bibles, which supported the Protestant Reformation and led to decades of religious and civil war. Was that too large a cost to spread literacy beyond a few monks and royalty? Computing has also disrupted our world and will likely continue to do so. But these disruptions must be balanced against the many ways it has improved our life and brought knowledge and communication to the world's entire population.

Discussion Questions for Students and Their Teachers

1. Computers have grown cheaper, smaller, faster, and more ubiquitous. As such, they have become more embedded throughout our daily life, making it possible to collect vast amounts of information on our activities and interests. What apps or services would you stop using to regain privacy and autonomy? Do you see any alternatives to these apps and services?
2. Many aspects of computing work better at a large scale. For instance, an Internet search engine needs to index the full Web to be useful, and machine learning needs large data sets and expensive training to get good accuracy. Once these enormous startup costs are paid, it is relatively inexpensive to service another customer. What are the consequences of this scale for business and international competition?
3. Moore's law is coming to an end soon, and without new technological developments, the number of transistors on a chip will increase slowly, if at all. What are the consequences of this change for the tech industry and society in general?
4. Climate change is an existential threat to humanity. Because of their ubiquity and large power consumption, computers are sometimes seen as a major contributor to this challenge. On the other hand, our understanding of climate change comes from computer modeling, and computers can replace less efficient alternatives, such as using a videoconference instead of travel. What is the actual contribution of computing to global warming, and what can be done about it?

Learning Resources for Students

Many technical books and research papers describe the technical innovations mentioned above in great detail. They can easily be found with a search engine.

1. Lewis, H.R. (Ed.), 2021. *Ideas that Created the Future: Classic Papers of Computer Science*. MIT Press, Cambridge, MA.

   For convenience, many classic papers are collected in the volume edited by Harry Lewis.
2. Barroso, L.A., Clidaras, J., Hölzle, U., 2013. *The Datacenter as a Computer: An Introduction to the Design of Warehouse-Scale Machines*, 2nd ed, Synthesis Lectures on Computer Architecture. Morgan & Claypool.

   However, Lewis's collection misses recent papers and those concerned with practical aspects, such as building Internet-scale computer systems, which Barroso et al. cover well.
3. In addition, the tech field is caught in the public eye, and many excellent, accessible books talk about its history and technical aspects.
4. Waldrop, M.M., 2001. *The Dream Machine: J. C. R. Licklider and the Revolution that Made Computing Personal*. Viking.

   Waldrop's book on J.C.R. Licklider is a biography of the remarkable psychologist who led the development of interactive computing and the Internet at ARPA.
5. Hiltzik, M.A., 1999. *Dealers of Lightning: Xerox PARC and the Dawn of the Computer Age*. Harper-Collins.

   Hiltzik's book followed these ideas as they were incubated at Xerox PARC, a remarkable industrial lab.
6. Isaacson, W., 2011. *Steve Jobs*. Simon & Schuster.

   Isaacson's biography of Steve Jobs provides the other half of the story by showing how he made these ideas into two products that changed the world, the Apple Mac and iPhone.
7. Gleick, J., 2021. *The Information*. Vintage.

   Gleick's book dives into communication and information theory, the opposite side of the computational coin.

References

Barroso, L. A., Clidaras, J., & Hölzle, U. (2013). *The datacenter as a computer: An introduction to the design of warehouse-scale machines* (Synthesis Lectures on Computer Architecture) (2nd ed.). Morgan & Claypool.

Bostrom, N. (2014). *Superintelligence*. Oxford University Press.

Campbell-Kelly, M. (2004). *From airline reservations to sonic the Hedgehog*. MIT Press.

Fortnow, L. (2021). Fifty years of P vs. NP and the possibility of the impossible. *Communications of the ACM, 65*, 76–85. https://doi.org/10.1145/3460351

Gleick, J. (2021). *The information*. Vintage.

Hey, T., Tansley, S., Tolle, K., & Gray, J. (Eds.). (2009). *The fourth paradigm: Data-intensive scientific discovery*. Microsoft Research.

Hiltzik, M. A. (1999). *Dealers of lightning: Xerox PARC and the dawn of the computer age*. Harper-Collins.
Isaacson, W. (2011). *Steve Jobs*. Simon & Schuster.
Lewis, H. R. (Ed.). (2021). *Ideas that created the future: Classic papers of computer science*. MIT Press.
Mccauley, J., Shenker, S., & Varghese, G. (2023). Extracting the essential simplicity of the Internet. *Communications of the ACM, 66*, 64–74. https://doi.org/10.1145/3547137
na. 2973. Records, Computers and the Rights of Citizens (No. DHEW NO. 73-94). US Department of Health, Education, and Welfare.
na. (2023a). *IBM 701*. Wikipedia.
na. (2023b). *Semi-automatic ground environment*. Wikipedia.
na. (2017). *The world's most valuable resource*. The Economist.
na. (2003). IBM Archives: 701 Feeds and speeds [WWW Document]. Accessed 17 February 17, 2023, from www-apache-app.cwm.gtm.ibm.net/ibm/history/exhibits/701/701_feeds.html
Shankar, V., Roelofs, R., Mania, H., Fang, A., Recht, B., & Schmidt, L. (2021). Evaluating machine accuracy on ImageNet. *NeurIPS 2021 Workshop on ImageNet: Past, Present, and Future*.
Turing, A. M. (1950). Computing machinery and intelligence. *Mind, LIX*, 433–460. https://doi.org/10.1093/mind/LIX.236.433
Turing, A. M. (1937). On computable numbers, with an application to the Entscheidungsproblem. *Proceedings of the London Mathematical Society, s2-42*, 230–265. https://doi.org/10.1112/plms/s2-42.1.230
Waldrop, M. M. (2001). *The dream machine: J. C. R. Licklider and the revolution that made computing personal*. Viking.
Weiser, M. (1991). The computer for the 21st century. *Scientific American, 265*, 94–105.
Wing, J. M. (2006). Computational thinking. *Communications of the ACM, 49*, 33–35. https://doi.org/10.1145/1118178.1118215

The Digital Revolution in a Historical Perspective

Misha Glenny

Abstract The coincidence and interaction between political and technological revolutions have resulted in epoch-changing social, political, and economic developments on three occasions over the past 500 years: the Renaissance and Reformation with the invention of print and weapons technology, the French and American revolutions with the industrial revolution, and the collapse of communism with the information revolution. Each boast their specific attributes but follow a pattern which can assist us in understanding the implications of today's technologies for our social and political structures.

1 Introduction

In this chapter, we shall argue that the course of the information revolution since the late 1970s exerted a critical influence and in turn was influenced by the political revolutions that took place in the former Soviet Union and Eastern Europe between 1989 and 1991.

One central consequence of this interplay between technology and politics has been a fundamental re-ordering of the global geopolitical architecture, which is already underway but whose outcome remains uncertain.

The United States is actively resisting the loss of its power to East Asia and China in particular. We are in the moment identified by Antonio Gramsci where "the crisis consists precisely in the fact that the old dies and the new is struggling to be born: in this interregnum, the most varied morbid phenomena occur" (Gramsci, 2014).

The speed with which technological innovation has provoked dramatic social change since the mid-1980s is unprecedented. However, the coincidence of political and technological revolutions, leading to a shift in political and economic tectonic plates is not. In the modern history of Europe, we have seen similar processes twice before.

M. Glenny (✉)
Institute for Human Sciences, Vienna, Austria
e-mail: glenny@iwm.at

H. Werthner et al. (eds.), *Introduction to Digital Humanism*,
https://doi.org/10.1007/978-3-031-45304-5_4

The first saw Europe emerge from the medieval period at the time of the Renaissance and the Reformation and lasted approximately 150 years until the mid-seventeenth century by which time northern Europe, in particular the Netherlands and Sweden, had largely eclipsed the political primacy that Spain had enjoyed at the beginning of the period.

The second began in the two decades before the French Revolution at the end of the eighteenth century and again culminated roughly one and a half centuries later in 1945. It was during the second half of this second process that Germany, the United States, Japan, and the Soviet Union also assumed decisive roles in both the geopolitical and technological revolutions, ultimately leading to an end to Europe's domination of the world after nearly five centuries.

Technological developments in these three periods led to social changes that are broadly comparable with one another, albeit refracted through very different cultural prisms.

In both these cases, the fusion of political change and technological progress culminated in mass violence on a scale never previously witnessed in human history. Both periods contain valuable lessons for our understanding of the interaction between politics and technology that we are currently experiencing.

But while we will highlight the underlying similarities, we will also alert the reader to what explains the qualitative difference between them that ensures how the continuing fallout from political upheaval and information technology will remain unpredictable, in particular the issue of scale that is at the heart of the contemporary interaction between politics and technology.

2 Renaissance, Reformation, Printing, and Ships, 1440–1648

The single most important technological development that explains the revolutionary changes of the early sixteenth century was the invention half a century earlier in the 1440s of movable print by Gutenberg and his associates. Until this point, the manufacture and distribution of books were limited to the Church hierarchy, the aristocracy, and some members of the growing merchant class. The overwhelming majority of Europeans were illiterate. Until the printing press, the Church had used its domination of education to control the circulation of books and their contents, compellingly described in Umberto Eco's masterpiece, *The Name of the Rose*. This was a central pillar of Rome's ideological hegemony over Western Christendom.

In the 60 years that followed, printing presses were established all over Europe, churning out books at a remarkable rate so that by the end of the fifteenth century, some 35,000 editions amounting to 15–20 million copies at the very lowest estimate were circulating around Europe. But even these figures were dwarfed in the first 50 years of the sixteenth century (Febvre and Martin, 1976). Literacy rates rose, although it is worth remembering that the consumption of books and pamphlets remained an elite activity.

Courtly romances were one of the most popular genres, but there was also a sharp growth in instruction books, which helped expand merchant and banking activity between northern and southern Europe. Among the most enthusiastic to engage with the literary boom were religious scholars who began re-interpreting biblical texts and the philosophical and historical works of antiquity. Together, they became known as the humanists of whom Erasmus of Rotterdam was the most celebrated.

As a movement, humanism did not set out to challenge the authority of the Church. Indeed, scholars like Erasmus actively avoided any association with ideas that explicitly questioned Church authority. But to some groups of clerics, monks, and princes, especially in the German territories of the Holy Roman Empire, humanism provided an implicit ideological framework for questioning Rome's monopoly on power. Secular and religious critics of the Church initially focused less on topics relating to dogma and more on the practical issue of corruption, which was the primary fiscal and political driver of papal power.

On October 31, 1517, Martin Luther gave full expression to this discontent when he nailed his *95 Theses* to the door of the Schlosskirche in Wittenberg, a town in Saxony. Three months after this event, the *Theses* had been printed and distributed so that Erasmus, the towering figure in European intellectual life until Luther's rise, had not only read them; he had even sent a copy to his great friend in London, Sir Thomas More. Within 3 years, scholars, clerics, merchants, and courts across Europe were discussing Luther's criticisms of the Roman Catholic Church. The Pope had declared his arguments to be heretical, a judgment which previously would have immediately consigned the perpetrator to ignominy and almost invariably death.

Just over a century earlier, that very fate had befallen Jan Hus, the Czech religious reformer. The Council of Constance proclaimed him a heretic in 1415 and ordered him burned at the stake for good measure. Hus's death, however, did not deflate the movement inspired by his radical sermons, which railed against the corruption of the Church of Rome and demanded far-reaching reforms. But critically, the Hussite Rebellion never expanded beyond the relatively small Czech-speaking population of Bohemia and Moravia.

In April 1521, a century after Hus's martyrdom, Rome and the recently elected Holy Roman Emperor, Charles V, summoned Luther to the Diet of Worms to defend himself against the charge of heresy, prefacing a possible death sentence.

In contrast to the arraignment of Hus at the Council of Constance, a much broader spectrum of Europe's public followed the proceedings and outcome of Worms in the form of pamphlets, which were quickly reprinted across the continent. The Council did indeed confirm Luther's heresy.

Luther survived, thanks to the printing press. In contrast to Hus, his cause was adopted by powerful political instances around Europe who knew of his case, thanks to the new technology. By the time Luther's printer friends were churning out translations of the *Theses* and his other works in German, a book could become a bestseller across Europe within 2 months, which explains why Erasmus was able to alert Thomas More so soon after Luther had attached his *Theses* to the church door.

A hundred years earlier, this method of disseminating his ideas was unavailable to Hus. In addition, Hus's message was communicated in Czech. His movement was intertwined with an early expression of national consciousness that intentionally excluded the many German speakers in Bohemia and Moravia. It was spread by word of mouth but only among those who could understand the language. There was no possibility of translating it—it was an overwhelmingly oral message.

Once printing was invented, not only was Luther able to record and distribute his ideas, but he could do it in the German vernacular, thanks to the economies of scale, which even the early production of printed books enabled. He wrote in both Latin and German, but before long, printed editions of his book had appeared in French, English, Italian, and even Czech.

Fully aware of the power of this new technology, Luther collaborated with his neighbor in Wittenberg, Lucas Cranach the Elder. Cranach is renowned as the great portraitist of Luther, but he also owned a printing press and was a bookseller. Cranach quickly grasped the importance of adapting print to include images as well as words. The social impact of the image was immense as for the first time, this could reach much of the population who were illiterate. The propaganda machine that the two men fashioned turned Luther not only into one of the most-read individuals in the sixteenth century but one of the most recognizable as well. This marked the beginning of celebrity.

Among those inclined to adopt Luther's teachings were several German princes in the patchwork quilt of territories that made up the Holy Roman Empire, along with large parts of the aristocracy and merchant classes in Denmark, Sweden, and England. Included among them was Frederick the Wise, the Elector of Saxony, Luther's home territory who defied both Rome and the Holy Roman Emperor, Charles V, by offering Luther sanctuary so he could escape the death penalty.

With adherents of the new Protestant faith proliferating across Europe, pressure was growing on secular authorities either to adopt or to confront the new religion. Several German princes changed confession in a direct challenge to their overlord, Charles V. The reformed faith was also making inroads in three north European countries, England, Sweden, and Denmark. By 1934, all three had renounced their allegiance to Rome. This was the first time that heresy had conquered entire countries—dissent was for the first time wedded to the power of the state.

For those who experienced or encouraged it, the polarization of European society during this period was every bit as remarkable and pervasive as the polarization we have witnessed since the advent of social media combined with the impact of the financial crisis of 2008 to create a wholly new and divided dynamic in politics across the globe. Furthermore, the underlying emotional drive of identity politics with which we struggle today would have been immediately recognizable to those who experienced Europe being torn apart during the long sixteenth century.

People adhered to identities of confession, language, perceived nationality, and class. Conspiracy theories proliferated, and as early as the 1520s, there was an upsurge in individuals and their followers predicting the imminent end of the world. In protestant countries, the thesis of the Pope as anti-Christ spread like wildfire. Among Protestants, anything perceived as detrimental to one's daily activities often attracted the pejorative description "papal."

In response, the Catholic Church announced the Counter-Reformation at the Council of Trent in 1545. In areas under the control of the Habsburgs, communities that had adopted the reform faith were forcibly reconverted, a process which included the murder of thousands. Successive Holy Roman emperors bolstered the activities of the Inquisition, an early form of religious police.

In the first 60 years of the printing press, less heralded technological innovations in maritime and weapons technology had an indirect but nonetheless important relationship with the politics of Lutheranism. These engineering advances may not have had the same long-term impact as the coming of the printed book, but they should not be underestimated. Combined with the growth of Protestantism among north European countries, especially in the Netherlands, they were influential in shifting the locus of political power in Europe from the Mediterranean to the North Sea over the course of the sixteenth and seventeenth centuries.

In the second half of the fifteenth century, shipwrights started to experiment combining lateen (triangular) and square sails. Not only did this provide sailing vessels with increased power, but by harnessing wind currents more effectively, European ships were able to cease navigating via coastal landscapes and were now able to engage in regular transoceanic travel.

The extraordinary wealth of the New World, which started filling the coffers of the Habsburg kings of Spain, proved a double-edged sword. Poorly managed, it triggered a century-long period of inflation, which, certainly at the beginning of the sixteenth century, was an unknown phenomenon. So while the continent as a whole became richer and more prosperous, prices and wages kept rising, but nobody understood why. What many did observe, however, was how the growing prosperity was unevenly distributed.

This first wave of globalization brought with it increased threats to maritime trade from rival states and from privateers. At the beginning of the sixteenth century, navies began experimenting with the deployment of large bronze siege guns on the bottom deck of their newly mobile warships. Although the Spaniards were able to put to sea large armadas for their Atlantic crossings, the design of their ships was informed primarily by the sailing conditions on the Mediterranean which, on the whole, were relatively benign.

By contrast, the Danes, Swedes, Dutch, English, and members of the Hanseatic League had a tradition of shipbuilding, which they were forced to adapt to the much more unstable North and Baltic seas. This meant the ship's body rose higher out of the sea, enabling it to carry more guns without putting the ship out of kilter. From the 1580s, Spain's extraordinary maritime prowess was eroded in a series of humiliating defeats by northern powers, notably England and the Dutch Republic.

Over the course of the sixteenth century, the technological advances in printing, ship design, and weapons wrought huge changes on European society. But it took roughly a century for the most far-reaching of changes to become evident—a fundamental realignment in economic power from the Mediterranean to the North Sea.

The Dutch Golden Age had begun at the same time as to the north the Swedish military was developing into what would eventually prove the decisive protestant force in the Thirty Years' War (1618–1648). In the meanwhile, Dutch and English mercantilism, based on the revolutionary structure of the joint-stock company, was emerging in anticipation of the following century when first Dutch then British naval power would dominate the world's oceans.

Protestantism leant itself to more flexible systems of governance and the economy in all three northern European great powers of the seventeenth century, enabling them to exploit advances in maritime technology more quickly and more effectively than the Mediterranean rivals like Spain and Portugal. By the end of the Thirty Years' War, Spain had lost its primacy in world politics forever. This issue of governance and how to exploit technology most effectively is critical to all three periods under review.

3 The French Revolution, Steam Power, and the Industrial Revolution, 1769–1945

Toward the end of the eighteenth and beginning of the nineteenth centuries, the revolution in steam power encouraged the spread of mass industrial processes at the same time as decisive political revolutions broke out in America and France. As with the Reformation, the industrial revolution led not merely to rapid changes in people's lived experience but also to a change in the tectonics of geopolitics over the period of a century and a half. Military and political power moved away from western Europe first to Germany and then across the Atlantic to the United States and eastward toward first Japan and then the Soviet Union, a Eurasian state. Just as Spain never recovered its leading position in the world after the Thirty Years' War, Europe would never regain it after World War II.

In 1600, Europeans believed in witchcraft and werewolves. They thought that "Circe really did turn Odysseus's crew into pigs. . .[and that] mice are spontaneously generated in piles of straw. . .that it is possible to turn base metal into gold. . .[that] the rainbow is a sign from God and that comets portend evil. . . [t]hat the earth stands still and the sun and stars turn around the earth once every twenty-four hours." They had "heard mention of Copernicus, but do not imagine that he intended his sun-centered model of the cosmos to be taken literally" (Wootton, 2015).

A 130 years later, Voltaire wrote that England was leading the world in social culture. The country was unrecognizable. "An Englishman has looked through a telescope and a microscope; he owns a pendulum clock and a stick barometer. . .He does not know anyone who believes in witches and werewolves, magic, alchemy or astrology; he thinks the *Odyssey* is fiction, not fact. . .Like all people in Protestant countries, he believes that the Earth goes around the sun. He knows that the rainbow is produced by refracted light and that comets have no significance for our lives on earth. . .He believes that science is going to transform the world" (Wootton, 2015).

Some exceptional minds had understood this much earlier. In 1611, John Donne, the English poet, scholar, and cleric, announced that Galileo's recent discoveries represented a "new philosophy," which "calls all in doubt." A crucial consequence of the split in Western Christianity was the critical reassessment of the Roman Catholic's fundamental doctrine about the universe and the earth's centrality therein. In the second half of the sixteenth century, astronomers were the demolition experts who started dismantling the House of God built on clerical dogma before constructing a replacement temple out of a new, infinitely more flexible material: empirical observation. A century after Donne, people were still reluctant to give voice to atheism, but ever greater numbers were privately questioning the existence of God.

This first phase of the scientific revolution stretched out over a 150 years, during which time Europe (and Britain in particular) grew pregnant with the transformative possibility of material growth and prosperity. To ensure a successful birth, all the continent needed were some breakthroughs in engineering so that scientific knowledge could be put to practical uses.

In 1769, James Watt's steam engine superseded the older but cumbersome Newcomen engine and, in the process, acted as midwife to the modern infant that soon grew into the strapping adolescent of the industrial revolution. Until this point, manufacturing was constrained by the limits of human and animal power. Just as the printing press had unleashed the dissemination of knowledge on a scale beyond anything in history, steam increased productive capacity to a hitherto unimaginable degree.

Over the next 50 years, the transformation of Britain, England and Scotland in particular, was breathtaking. "Where previously, an amelioration of the conditions of existence, hence of survival, and an increase in economic opportunity had always been followed by a rise in population that eventually consumed the gains achieved," writes David Landes in his landmark study, *The Unbound Prometheus*, "now for the first time in history, both the economy and knowledge were growing fast enough to generate a continuing flow of investment and technological innovation, a flow that lifted beyond visible limits the ceiling of Malthus's positive checks. The Industrial Revolution thereby opened a new age of promise. It also transformed the balance of political power, within nations, between nations, and between civilizations; revolutionized the social order; and as much changed man's way of thinking as his way of doing" (Landes, 1969).

Britain enjoyed several advantages that together ensured other European countries lagged behind its industrial development by as much as 50 years. Britain had achieved naval superiority over France with its victory in the Seven Years' War (1756–1763), the first conflict which took place on more than two continents. This enabled London to rapidly expand its overseas empire, whose resources would prove invaluable in its economic advance during the nineteenth century.

This combined with significant progress in the productive process of iron and steel, fueled by Britain's large coal industry. The result was an extraordinary proliferation of the machine tools, which lay at the heart of Britain's expanding manufacturing base.

Most political power had been in the hands of the bourgeoisie in Scotland and England for over a century since the revolution of 1688 had created Europe's first constitutional monarchy. Britain's landed aristocracy and gentry still looked down at "traders and manufacturers," but the latter ignored the social disdain in which they were held as their wealth quickly outstripped that of their supposed social superiors.

By contrast with the entrepreneurial dynamism of Britain, the absolutism that dominated the giant empires of continental Europe and France was hindering reform and economic progress. France offered Britain serious competition in technological and scientific research, but its sclerotic politics meant French entrepreneurs faced much greater difficulties in applying that research to the economy.

Britain had suffered one major setback in its colonial possessions when America's revolutionary army won the war of 1776. However, defeat did not lead to revolution at home in Britain but consolidation. And it was not long before the 13 newly liberated colonies across the Atlantic were arguing among themselves and struggling to create coherent political structures.

Inspired in part by the successful anti-British insurrection in America, the masses of France rose against Bourbon absolutism in 1789. In the short term, the revolutionary chaos widened the developing technological and economic advantage, which Britain enjoyed over France. But politically, the event was an extraordinary harbinger of what would develop into a decisive break in European politics. Just as British technology and engineering introduced the age of mass production and consumption, France ushered in the era of mass politics.

Napoleon seized the opportunity which the revolutionary chaos presented to reorganize French society. Most importantly, he introduced the *levée en masse*, the mass mobilization of the male population into the army. The new emperor had begun the process of persuading all classes, and not just the aristocracy, that they should be invested in the French state and its military aims.

While Napoleon instilled a new mass patriotism in France, the factories that sprung up all over Britain, producing everything from clothes to ceramics to clocks, created an entire new class—the proletariat. Some early capitalists in Britain came from religious communities such as the Quakers or the Methodists. They regarded all workers as part of a community to be nourished and cherished. Many others, however, were ruthlessly venal: the less money one invested in workers, the bigger the returns on capital investment. In various forms, these new social relations would determine the politics and governance of the Western world for the next two centuries.

The bulk of the population exchanged a life of subsistence farming for the grindingly monotonous and dangerous work of the factory. Among the artisan classes, the rise of the factory provoked a backlash against the new technology enabling mass production techniques. The Luddites in England and the Weaver Uprising in Silesia, immortalized in Gerhard Hauptmann's drama, *Die Weber*, are powerful reminders of this.

As liberal capitalism consolidated itself across the nineteenth century, it also fashioned a new political construct that emerged first in Europe and then the world—the nation state. It has dominated ever since.

The nation state was critical in the deployment of the countless new technologies developed in the nineteenth century. The unification of so many fragmented political entities, notably the German and the Italian lands, steadily dismantled bureaucratic obstacles to growth, such as internal tariff systems.

Two technological developments spurred on the modernization and centralization of the nascent nation states. In 1825, the first rail line was opened between Stockton and Darlington in England's northeast. For 4000 years, travel had been limited to the speed of horses. Within 75 years of Stevenson's rocket making that inaugural journey, rail lines criss-crossed huge stretches of the world, enabling people and goods to travel over vast distances at undreamt of speeds.

On August 16, 1858, Britain's Queen Victoria sent a message to the authorities in New York. It arrived from London in a matter of seconds, thanks to the massive telegraph cable laid across the Atlantic Ocean by two ships, meeting in the middle. Before this moment, messages across this distance were conveyed over months. "Since the discovery of Columbus," wrote the *London Times*, "nothing has been done in any degree comparable to the vast enlargement which has thus been given to the sphere of human activity."[1]

These advances in transport and communication magnified the explosion of scientific activity across the Western world and a concomitant expansion of the secondary and tertiary education sectors. The French Revolution, the German Romantic Movement, and the enormous progress made in natural sciences during the late eighteenth and early nineteenth centuries also led to significant changes in the structure and purpose of universities, especially in some parts of Germany, Britain, and the United States. An especially fruitful collaboration emerged between scholars in Germany and Britain, which drove many of the advances in engineering and manufacturing.[2]

The positive consequences of the industrial revolution and the emergence of the nation state were remarkable. Human longevity suddenly shoots upward. In 1870, the mean life expectancy around the world was 32. Even in the region with the longest average life span, Europe, it was still under 40. These figures had been broadly consistent for several centuries. Just a hundred years later in 1970, the figure for Europe, the Americas, and Asia was over 70 years old, and even in the world's most challenged region, Africa, it was already over 50.

But this period was subject to the Manichean duality of technological advance, which characterized the preceding epoch and would go on to define our era.

Much of the British Empire's early success was due to it enjoying easy and cheap access to the resources that its colonies provided. As other European nations and the United States joined in the global scramble for the wealth that the Americas, Africa, and Asia provided, the violence visited by humans on other humans reached heights

[1]Quoted in (Zweig, 1943). Zweig's telling of the laying of the first transatlantic cable is the most evocative and insightful text.

[2]Peter Watson rediscovered the central importance of British-German intellectual exchange that was so important to both countries' rise in the first half of the nineteenth century in (Watson, 2010).

previously unscaled even though a considerable intellectual and literary industry presented the enslavement and annihilation of tens of millions as "progress."

More ominously, each major power boasted at least one major arms manufacturer, and by the 1860s, Le Creuset, Skoda, Krupp, and Vickers were eagerly recruiting the growing number of graduates specializing in physics and chemistry. From the period of the American Civil War, 1862–1865, to the Balkan Wars, 1912–1913, these companies would use conflicts as a showcase to highlight the efficacy of their weapons. Not only were the advances in weapons and communications technology able to inflict greater casualties than ever before, but as military strategy developed in the twentieth century, they used the extraordinary range first of artillery and then airpower to target civilians on a massive scale (Glenny, 2013).

The murder and attempted murder of entire civilian populations had already begun in the nineteenth century across the United States and Europe, in preparation for the industrial killings of the twentieth century. In 1914, European nations finally applied their remarkable know-how to extermination. The violence culminated in the atrocities of World War II before the single most destructive act in history, the detonation of the atomic bomb over Hiroshima and Nagasaki causing the deaths of roughly 200,000 people in an instant. The event took place just 176 years after Watt unveiled his steam engine. It is worth noting that in the next 50 years, two countries in particular, the United States and the Soviet Union, produced enough nuclear weapons to destroy the world several times over. On one occasion, the Cuban missile crisis in 1963, we came close to nuclear war. Since the 1950s, the extinction of the human species (not to mention the rest of life on earth) is not just a theoretical but a practical possibility.

The end of World War II confirmed the demise of European primacy as the United States and Russia assumed leadership and domination over the divided continent where the technological and political revolutions had begun four centuries earlier. Just as the twentieth century would have been entirely unrecognizable to the men and women alive during the Renaissance and would doubtless have filled them full of wonder, so would the commanders in the Thirty Years' War have gawped at the extent of the death and destruction that modernity unleashed. This points to a fundamental difference between the first great rush of modernity, from 1492 to 1648, and the second great rush from the 1760s to 1945: scale.

4 The Collapse of Communism and Information Technology, 1973–2023

The current manifestation of political and technological revolutions followed by polarization, economic transformation, rising inequality, and geopolitical shift has its roots in the 1970s. As the quote from Gramsci in the introduction implies, this process is still far from reaching its conclusion. The speed and nature of technological innovation in the last 50 years means that it is hard to predict how this will conclude, although the primary geopolitical struggle between the United States and China is clearly well underway.

they could not maintain parity in technological capacity and innovation (something that the Chinese watched extremely closely at the time, adjusting their research, development, and deployment models accordingly). Especially when combined with a rigid regime of censorship, the statist model was incapable of maintaining parity in an industry in which research was driven not only by the immediate requirements of the military but equally by the voracious desire of consumer markets.

As a consequence, the Soviet Union's lag in military and industrial capability was already visible and unbridgeable. As if to underline just how serious Soviet technological backwardness was, a month after the 27th Party Congress, a safety test at a plant just south of the Pripyat marshes triggered an uncontrolled nuclear reaction, and Chernobyl's Reactor 4 exploded.

Soviet socialism was reaching the end as a system that could compete with the West. If mountains of external debt killed communism in Poland and Hungary, tech killed the Soviet Union.

The rapid advance of computer technology since the 1980s not only hastened the end of the Soviet Empire. It has wrought changes unlike any other technological innovation in history because it has insinuated itself into and often created total dependency on almost every aspect of human social and economic interaction. But during the 1990s, few people were willing or interested in questioning the unquestioning embrace of the technology.

That long Decade of Delusion came to an end in 2008.

After the Wall Street Crash of 1929, it took a full 14 months before Austria's Creditanstalt became the first major casualty of the shenanigans on Wall Street. After the collapse of Lehman Brothers in 2008, it was just *4 days* before almost every major bank around the world was staring into the abyss of global financial meltdown and collapse.

Technology was critical both to the intrinsic financial crisis and the speed with which it spread from New York across the world. The heart of the Crash? Credit Default Swaps and Collateral Mortgage Obligations, the sub-prime securitization vehicles that had enabled banks to leverage debt way beyond their ability to repay it. Banks "had begun to apply pure mathematical theories to evaluate credit risk and estimate credit risk premiums to be required." The models of such "quants" who have wielded so much influence over modern banking are often "worse than useless" (Murphy, 2008). Quants are financial analysts who use math, coding, and finance skills to help companies make business and investment decisions. For example, some quants work on the buy-side of an investment bank, helping these large companies increase profits with automated trading algorithms.

No single financial institution had the least oversight into exactly how much debt they were carrying. They were unable to tame the monster once unleashed, and money just started flowing automatically out of banks across the world without anyone having to press a button.

As we saw in the previous section, the industrial revolution created a new class structure with the emergence of the industrial proletariat and a capitalist class who derived value from the labor of the proletariat. The digital revolution largely dispenses with that model by replacing value from labor with value from data,

We must begin the examination of this period in 1973 when the United States a Saudi Arabia struck a deal to end the oil crisis that had dominated events that ye This deal resulted in the US banking system becoming awash with so-cal petrodollars. Unable to lend to domestic clients battling with stagflation, the bar started lending to foreign states as proposed and facilitated by the then head of World Bank, Robert McNamara. In Eastern Europe, four countries assumed hu dollar-denominated debts: Poland, Hungary, Romania and, outside the Warsaw Pa Yugoslavia.

These debts fell due in the early 1980s at a point when US and British inter rates had hit a historic high of over 16%, meaning the payments of these alrea vulnerable economies became unsustainably onerous. As well as causing a ma political crisis in Poland that led to the formation of the independent trades uni Solidarity, and then a military coup in December 1981, it also accentuated Polan extreme dependency on energy supplies from the Soviet Union, which it paid for roughly one-third of the world market price.

The Soviet Union's ability to subsidize the energy requirements of not just Pola but all East European states was dependent on high world oil prices and the effici extraction of the Western Siberian oil fields, which it had started to exploit in the l 1970s (Perovic and Kempin, 2014).

As oil prices collapsed in the mid-80s, the Soviet Union sought to import Weste technology, notably its advanced micro-processing capacity, to keep its oil indus competitive. The Western Siberian oil fields were among the most difficult in t world to exploit, and Soviet technology suffered constant failures, requiring ev greater investment from an economy that was struggling to survive.

Cold War logic had led the West to place stringent controls on the export of most advanced technology affecting two sectors in particular—energy and t military.

Western restrictions on technology with military applications also threatened deliver a knockout blow to Soviet attempts to maintain parity in the Cold War. T United States was now fitting its short-, medium-, and long-range missiles wi systems guided by computer and laser technology in place of the previous analog ones. As early as 1983, during the so-called Euromissiles crisis, leading members the Soviet military were warning the Communist Party leadership that advances micro-processing techniques were resulting in an exponential growth in the effe tiveness of American weapons over their Soviet equivalent (Miller, 2022).

Such profoundly significant technological breakthroughs in information techno ogy in the United States preceded the revolutionary drama of 1989 just like it had i 1517 and 1789. In March 1986, we reported from the 27th Soviet Party Congress fo *New Scientist* magazine. Mikhail Gorbachev had already launched his new policie of *perestroika* (reform) and *glasnost* (transparency). At this extraordinary even Gorbachev and his prime minister, Nikolai Ryzhkov, made it clear where the Part most urgently needed to inject some *perestroika* and *glasnost*—into science, i particular computer technology and robotics for industrial and military applications By this time, there were some 10,000 computers in the Soviet Union. The Unite States, by contrast, boasted 1.3 million mainframes and minicomputers. Put simply often freely handed over by their generators, i.e., consumers. Leviathan corporations, such as Google and Facebook, have grown at astonishing rates over the past two decades. Deriving value from data rather than labor means the capital investment can record returns at a much higher rate. In this fundamental shift in the nature of production driven by technology, the importance of the human is diminished, weakening her leverage in social relations as the digitalization of so much of our life means she has no choice but to continue producing data that is processed and exploited by the corporations.[3] Combined with the burgeoning influence of AI, this is rapidly posing the question as to what if any labor function humans will have in the near future.

5 Conclusions

A central challenge at the current juncture of the human journey is that many of the technologies rightly credited for our material progress are also based on disintegration and reduction of the individual: breaking us down into data sets of DNA, revealed preferences in digital search histories, biometrics, financial data, etc. The quest for utility, efficiency, and convenience at global scale necessarily reduces us to data points. Trillion-dollar industries are committed to this proposition.

The idea of the individual—literally a being that cannot or should not be divided—is one of integration and wholeness, yet it is the subject of ferocious division and subdivision in the name of progress (the market) and security (the state). In a sense, modernity constantly puts our integrity in jeopardy.

As individuals, we should not be divided, but we also need to be connected beyond ourselves: we need relationships to find meaning and to thrive. What ultimately changes people's lives are relationships. As sentient beings, we need associative relationships to thrive—in families, as friends, as citizens, and as co-workers—we need the right scale to live as humans in full.

Technology allows us to adapt and extend ourselves beyond the constraints of body and place. Communications technology stretches the realm of our senses globally. This elasticity has been central to progress. Yet the question remains how far beyond the inherent limitations of being human can we meaningfully extend without losing touch with who we are. The answer is certainly not fixed and may vary across individuals and societies and time. However, it does not follow that there are no limits.

But in the past 30 years, our world has become more connected than ever before, and yet we face an epidemic of loneliness, alienation, and stress-related illnesses. Our cluttered, frenetic, upgraded lives feel increasingly out of control. Our machines are supposed to work for us, but often, we appear to be working for our machines.

[3] See Tarnoff, B. *From Manchester to Barcelona* (https://logicmag.io/nature/from-manchester-to-barcelona/).

Technological triumphs have created new challenges, pushing some fundamental things out of joint, particularly in the less tangible realms of culture, character, and spirit. Finding our balance and keeping our sanity will become ever more difficult as our lives become "bigger."

Technological change is full of consequences, intended and unintended, expected and unexpected, good and bad, invidious and insidious, to which humans must adapt. Reflecting on the course of the twentieth century, the Russian poet Pasternak wrote somewhat ominously of "the consequences of consequences." This insight has never seemed more important and has propelled us to ask some fundamental questions about how we will adapt ourselves and our lifestyles to the effects of our radically new setting, a world defined by promising and powerful technologies—nuclear, genomic, and digital—that are capable of disaggregating, disintegrating, and also reintegrating or remaking many aspects of the world as we know it.

The challenges will proliferate. We are at the beginning of a world in which artificial intelligence in various forms will determine the direction of our lives in an even more profound way. While the positive possibilities in terms of human health and welfare are considerable, the negative consequences are potentially hair-raising. Just as printing, sails, and gunpowder led to greater global wealth, it also encouraged violent polarization; just as the industrial revolution led to an extraordinary increase in longevity and the atomic bomb, so will AI offer the human race great protection and massive destruction simultaneously but at a greatly enhanced scale than during either of the previous two revolutions.

Already AI generative programs like GPT4 are capable of writing sophisticated malware, and increasingly cybersecurity is relying on AI and machine-to-machine learning. Human oversight of complex systems is receding, a fundamental danger in itself. Meanwhile, for those with political influence, the temptation to make use of truly Orwellian surveillance techniques is a dark temptation as China's Social Credit System and states' increasingly ubiquitous deployment of invasive spyware have demonstrated all too effectively.

The geopolitical trajectory is already clear. China is striving to displace the United States as the number one power economically and politically. Tech and tech-related industries, such as the extraction and processing of critical raw materials, are at the very heart of this struggle. The United States is fighting hard to maintain its position of supremacy (made more difficult by the polarization in a democratic society that social media have greatly encouraged).

The big question that this pattern that echoes the Reformation and the industrial revolution poses concerns its violent culmination, that is, the precedents of the Thirty Years' War and the two world wars of the twentieth century. Leaving so-called black swan events aside, political leadership will play a big role in the outcome. Since the turn of the millennium, both China and the United States have increasingly characterized their economic competition as a cultural one. The United States fashions this as a struggle between democratic capitalism against an autocratic version, while China presents its system as better equipped to manage long-term problems than the caprice of American democratic structures. Both arguments have their weaknesses, arguably the most fundamental being that unless these two systems cooperate along with all other countries in the world, then at least one of the several threats to existence (we are no longer just confronted with possible nuclear war but the climate crisis, pandemics, and the uncontrolled spread of AI) is likely to find a way of becoming a reality.

In that respect, the experience of the last two decades does not bode well. But humans have extracted themselves from some sticky situations before. Now, we must wait and see if AI and other technologies will help us, or hinder us.

Discussion Questions for Students and Their Teachers

1. Which innovations across all three examples have proved more important: information technology or engineering?
2. Do technological breakthroughs always trigger political revolution?
3. In terms of technology and its subsequent impact, to what degree is the second example an outlier, and to what degree does it conform to the patterns of the other two?
4. What are the implications of scale for the revolution in information technology?
5. To what degree do the first two examples help us predict the outcome of the unfinished third example?

Learning Resources for Students

1. Tarnoff, B. *From Manchester to Barcelona.* https://logicmag.io/nature/from-manchester-to-barcelona/

   This key text reveals why the digital economy as it emerged in the United States has led to a concentration of political and economic power around a few corporate entities that is much greater than even during the so-called robber baron period of capital accumulation in the second half of the nineteenth century. Essential reading.
2. Barbier, F. (2016) Gutenberg's Europe: The Book and the Invention of Western Modernity. Cantab: Polity Press

   Not the greatest stylist, but Barbier's book is rich in detail about Gutenberg and the printing press's relationship first with Germany and then France and Italy. It identifies the key areas and the variegated speed with which print impacted on modern European thought.
3. Febvre, L. and Martin H-J. (1976) The Coming of the Book. London: New Left Books.

   This path-breaking work by two French scholars was the first to detail how the printing press and subsequent rise of the book began to reshape the economic landscape of late medieval Europe before preparing the social ground that Luther would later exploit.
4. Roper, L. (2016) Martin Luther: Renegade and Prophet. London: Bodley Head.

   The most comprehensive biography of Luther is especially useful for understanding the strategic intelligence of Luther, his relationship with Cranach the Elder, and their targeted use of printed material to undermine the political influence of the Roman Catholic Church in the German lands.
5. Israel, J. (1998) The Dutch Republic: Its Rise, Greatness, and Fall 1477-1806. Oxford: OUP.

The best single volume history of the Dutch Republic, which explains how technology, economic innovation, and novel political forms combine to enable this very small country to eclipse the trading power of Spain.

6. For a quicker primer on this particular issue, listen to my BBC Podcast, *The Invention of the Netherlands*: https://www.bbc.co.uk/programmes/b0b4gt71
7. Wilson, P.H. (2009) Europe's Tragedy: A New History of the Thirty Years War. London: Allen Lane.

   Wilson's magnum opus is one of several masterful accounts of this incredibly complex period of European history, but we recommend it because he is particularly good at identifying how technology impacted the nature of warfare and increased its destructive power to levels hitherto never seen.
8. Wooton, D. (2015) The Invention of Science. London: Allen Lane.

   This superb account of the lead up to the steam revolution is especially useful for bridging the period between the Renaissance and the industrial revolution in examining technological change. Essential reading on the interplay between technology and politics.
9. Landes, D. S. (1969) The Unbound Prometheus. Cantab: Cambridge University Press.

   The definitive work on the industrial revolution in Britain and Europe. It is especially strong at documenting the interplay between innovation, politics, and social and economic change in Great Britain.
10. Wheeler, T. From Gutenberg to Google: The History of Our Future. Washington: Brookings Institution Press

    A useful overview of the three revolutions. It is good on the immediate social impact of technological change but less detailed on some issues such as political polarization. Probably the best primer on the subject.

References

Febvre, L., & Martin, H.-J. (1976). *The coming of the book* (p. 186). New Left Books.

Glenny, M. (2013). *The Balkans, 1804-2012, nationalism, war and the great powers* (p. 219). Granta.

Gramsci, A. (2014). *Quaderni del Carcere* (p. 318). Einaudi.

Landes, D. S. (1969). *The Unbound Prometheus* (p. 41). Cambridge University Press. (Kindle Edition).

Miller, C. (2022). *Chip war* (pp. 141–151). Simon & Schuster.

Murphy, A. (2008). *An analysis of the financial crisis of 2008: Causes and solutions*. Unpublished PhD California, Berkeley. http://www.sba.oakland.edu/files/news/financial_crisis.pdf

Perovic, K., & Kempin, R. (2014). The key is in our hands: Soviet energy strategy during Détente and the global oil crises of the 1970s. *Historical Social Research / Historische Sozialforschung, 39*(4), 113–141.

Watson, P. (2010). *The German genius*. Simon & Schuster.

Wootton, D. (2015). *The invention of science* (p. 6). Allen Lane. (Kindle Edition).

Zweig, S. (1943). *Sternstunden der Menschheit: Zwölf historische Miniaturen* (p. 241). Bermann-Fischer Verlag.

The Social Responsibilities of Scientists and Technologists in the Digital Age

Hans Akkermans

Abstract What responsibilities do digital scientists and professionals have in serving society and the public, beyond doing "purely" "fundamental" scientific, technological, or academic inquiry alone? Now that "the digital" has become pervasive in society, even in normal people's lives, these are pressing questions that call for answers. They go beyond individual ethical considerations or professional codes of conduct, as society-systemic aspects heavily come into play. We explore some of the complex historical and contemporary relationships between technology and society as a way to formulate useful insights for digital ethics and governance of digital technologies today.

1 Introduction

> Our world faces a crisis as yet unperceived by those possessing the power to make great decisions for good or evil. The unleashed power of the atom has changed everything save our modes of thinking, and thus we drift toward unparalleled catastrophe. We scientists who unleashed this immense power have an overwhelming responsibility in this world life-and-death struggle to harness the atom for the benefit of mankind and not for humanity's destruction.
>
> Albert Einstein, as quoted in Nathan and Norden (1960, Chapter XII)

In these strong words, Albert Einstein formulated the need for taking social responsibility by scientists. Digital science and technology are certainly very different from atomic science, but through the ongoing digital transformation of many sectors of society and government, their societal impacts are no less vast, deep, and fundamental. And in part they are unknown, unclear, or still hidden in the (near) future. In line with the Digital Humanism Manifesto (DIGHUM, 2019, 2023; this

H. Akkermans (✉)
AKMC, Koedijk, The Netherlands

University for Development Studies UDS, Tamale, Ghana
e-mail: hans.akkermans@akmc.nl

H. Werthner et al. (eds.), *Introduction to Digital Humanism*,
https://doi.org/10.1007/978-3-031-45304-5_5

Volume, Chapter by Hannes Werthner), this calls for a critical rethinking of the social responsibilities of scientists and technologists in today's Digital Age.

This chapter undertakes to do so from a historical perspective. We first discuss the science, technology, and social responsibility issues of scientists and technologists as they historically appeared in the Atomic Age—roughly from 1938, with the discovery of nuclear fission and the possibility of the atomic bomb, to the 1980s, when the Cold War gradually came to a (temporary) end. We summarize the discussions on the social responsibility of scientists and engineers that raged at previous times, and we show that many of them still hold relevance today in the Digital Age.

Subsequently, we briefly survey in this chapter the many and diverse societal impacts by the ongoing digital transformation today, using the United Nations' Sustainable Development Goals (SDGs) as an organizing framework. The upshot is that digital technology development and research has major societal impacts, both good and bad ones, and as a consequence, there undeniably exists a social responsibility of scientists and technologists, if only because we all are also citizens of the globally connected world we have helped create. The discussions on these issues in the Digital Age are not fully new but build on, among others, the Atomic Age discussions. There are some clear historical parallels here, for example, regarding data openness versus data secrecy policies. Scientists and technologists can be a beneficial force for betterment of society, but it *does* require critical thinking, societal engagement, and actively taking responsibility.

2 On the Social Responsibilities of Scientists in the Atomic Age

Einstein wrote the above in 1946, sometimes called Year 1 of the Atomic Age. The fateful consequences and the global danger of the development of the atomic bomb became increasingly clear and undeniable. The United Nations (UN) were in their formative years, and hopes were placed upon the UN that it could maintain international peace and prevent a future war. Einstein wrote in his capacity as chair of the newly formed Emergency Committee of Atomic Scientists. It is the opening paragraph of a telegram that was widely reprinted in the press, for example, the *New York Times* of May 25, 1946. Many meetings, publications, and media events followed (see, e.g., Fig. 1), almost on a daily basis, whereby the urgency of the matter was summarized as One World or None!

Many scientists were drawn into becoming active in societal issues due to the big human and moral shock that the detonation of the atomic bomb created. That shock was famously expressed, much later in an interview in 1965, by Robert Oppenheimer, the scientific director of the Manhattan Project that produced the first atomic bomb in Los Alamos, New Mexico, USA, by reference to the Bhagavad-Gita: "Now I am become Death, the destroyer of worlds."

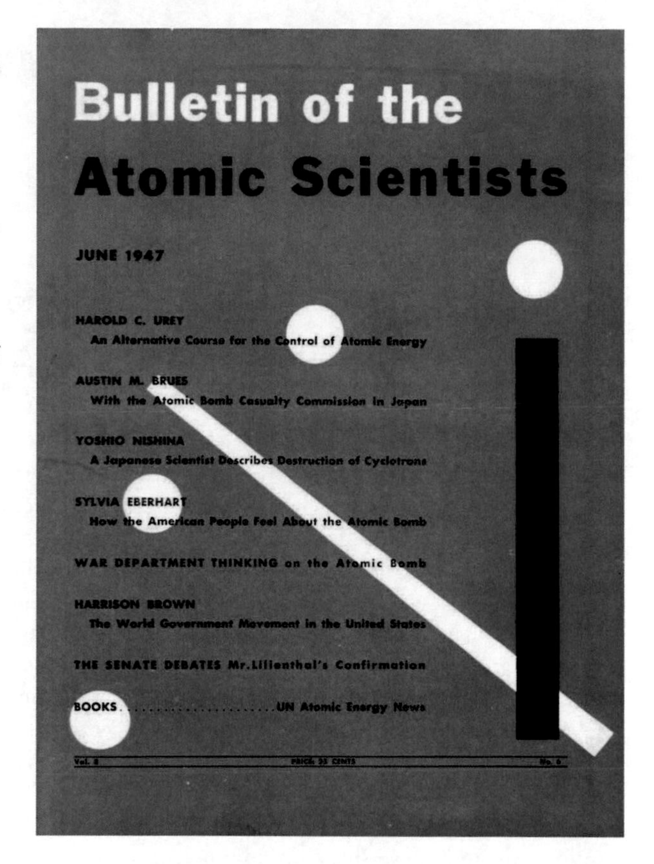
Bulletin of the
Atomic Scientists

JUNE 1947

HAROLD C. UREY
An Alternative Course for the Control of Atomic Energy

AUSTIN M. BRUES
With the Atomic Bomb Casualty Commission in Japan

YOSHIO NISHINA
A Japanese Scientist Describes Destruction of Cyclotrons

SYLVIA EBERHART
How the American People Feel About the Atomic Bomb

WAR DEPARTMENT THINKING on the Atomic Bomb

HARRISON BROWN
The World Government Movement in the United States

THE SENATE DEBATES Mr. Lilienthal's Confirmation

BOOKS . . . . UN Atomic Energy News

Fig. 1 The world-famous "Doomsday Clock" as it first appeared in the Bulletin of the Atomic Scientists in June 1947. Source, including an interesting background article on its design by Martyl Langsdorf, is available at https://thebulletin.org/2013/04/science-art-and-the-legacy-of-martyl/. Used with permission of the Bulletin of the Atomic Scientists

Regarding Einstein, it seems that he personally viewed taking social responsibility as a scientist as something rather self-evident and obvious. But that was not necessarily a mainstream view among his fellow physicists, as many severely struggled with these issues (including Robert Oppenheimer), and many were influenced and even terrorized by the Cold War political pressures that made them highly vulnerable to speak their minds freely.

One prominent figure addressing these issues in speaking and writing was Bertrand Russell, the analytic philosopher in particular of mathematics and formal logic. He was involved in the United Kingdom's Campaign for Nuclear Disarmament (CND), who is the originator of the ban-the-bomb sign that acquired worldwide fame as the peace symbol (Fig. 2). It is worth quoting Bertrand Russell at length on the issue of the social responsibility of the scientist (Russell, 1960):

> Science, ever since it first existed, has had important effects in matters that lie outside the purview of pure science. Men of science have differed as to their responsibility for such effects. Some have said that the function of the scientist in society is to supply knowledge, and that he need not concern himself with the use to which this knowledge is put. I do not think that this view is tenable, especially in our age. The scientist is also a citizen; and citizens who have any special skill have a public duty to see, as far as they can, that their skill is utilized in accordance with the public interest.

Fig. 2 The internationally famous peace symbol (CND, UK, 1958). For the symbol and its history, see Campaign for Nuclear Disarmament, https://cnduk.org/the-symbol/.

On affecting public opinion, Russell writes: "Modern democracy and modern methods of publicity have made the problem of affecting public opinion quite different from what it used to be. The knowledge that the public possesses on any important issue is derived from vast and powerful organizations: the press, radio, and, above all, television. The knowledge that governments possess is more limited. They are too busy to search out the facts for themselves, and consequently they know only what their underlings think good for them unless there is such a powerful movement in a different sense that politicians cannot ignore it. Facts which ought to guide the decisions of statesmen—for instance, as to the possible lethal qualities of fallout—do not acquire their due importance if they remain buried in scientific journals. They acquire their due importance only when they become known to so many voters that they affect the course of the elections."

We recall that these lines were written long ago, in the 1950s, a time of mass breakthrough of television. Now in the Digital Age, it appears there is a new stage, in which technologies such as social media, fake news, deepfakes, and generative artificial intelligence (AI) have exacerbated the problems of providing sound information to the public (DIGHUM, 2023; this Volume, Chapter by Peter Knees and Julia Neidhardt, and Chapter by Ricardo Baeza-Yates).

As a further line of action, Bertrand Russell says that scientists "can suggest and urge in many ways the value of those branches of science of which the important practical uses are beneficial and not harmful. Consider what might be done if the money at present spent on armaments were spent on increasing and distributing the food supply of the world and diminishing the population pressure."

And Russell ends with: "As the world becomes more technically unified, life in an ivory tower becomes increasingly impossible. (. . .) We have it in our power to make a good world; and, therefore, with whatever labor and risk, we must make it" (Russell, 1960; the article is the text of an address delivered on September 24, 1959, in London at a meeting of British scientists convened by the Campaign for Nuclear Disarmament, cf. Fig. 2).

Many other noted scientists also spoke and wrote on these matters, for example, the philosopher of science, Karl Popper. In a talk he delivered in 1968 at the

International Congress of Philosophy in Vienna, special session on "Science and Ethics," he proposed to create a form of a modern Hippocratic Oath for scientists. Popper furthermore points out a role for multidisciplinary scientific research regarding societal impacts: "The problem of the unintended consequences of our actions, consequences which are not only unintended but often very difficult to foresee, is the fundamental problem of the social scientist. Since the natural scientist has become inextricably involved in the application of science, he, too, should consider it one of his special responsibilities to foresee as far as possible the unintended consequences of his work and to draw attention, from the very beginning, to those we should strive to avoid" (Popper, 1971).

Einstein relentlessly continued his societal activities until his death. One week before he died (on April 18, 1955), he signed what became known as the Russell-Einstein Manifesto. It was published on July 9, 1955, and it was signed, apart from Einstein and Russell, by several prominent Nobel Prize winning figures such as Frédéric Joliot-Curie, the husband of Irène Curie and son-in-law of Marie Skłodowska-Curie. One of its main points was to call for a congress to be convened by "scientists of the world and the general public" urging "governments of the world (...) to find peaceful means for the settlement of all matters of dispute between them." Famously, the Manifesto said, "Remember your humanity and forget the rest."

The Russell-Einstein Manifesto call to action did have effect. It led to a series of international conferences from 1957 onward, known as the Pugwash Conferences. A leading organizing figure here was Joseph Rotblat, a nuclear physicist from Poland. A major result was to bring together leading scholars from many countries so as to discuss ways to temper the arms race. Highly importantly, Pugwash served as one of the very few lines of open communication between the United States, Europe, and the Soviet Union during the Cold War. These Pugwash Conferences turned out to be influential in their impact on policy. They are credited, according to Holcomb B. Noble in the *New York Times* in an obituary of Joseph Rotblat on September 02, 2005, with laying the groundwork for the Partial Test Ban Treaty of 1963, the Nonproliferation Treaty of 1968, the Anti-Ballistic Missile Treaty of 1972, the Biological Weapons Convention of 1972, and the Chemical Weapons Convention of 1993. Joseph Rotblat and Pugwash received the Nobel Prize for Peace in 1995.

Rotblat's personal story is both moving and illuminating (Veys, 2013), in particular if we view it from the angle of the social responsibilities of scientists and technologists. A small part of his personal history he revealed in an article many years later in the Bulletin of the Atomic Scientists (Rotblat, 1985). Rotblat was a nuclear physicist working on inelastic scattering of neutrons against heavy nuclei (his PhD subject in 1950, Liverpool, UK), at first in the Radiological Laboratory in Warsaw, Poland, in 1938/1939. Late 1938, in Otto Hahn's laboratory in Berlin, Germany, experimental phenomena were observed that were (but only later) interpreted as evidence of nuclear fission of uranium, with excess production of neutrons. It was Lise Meitner (previously collaborating with Otto Hahn in Berlin but then fled to Sweden) who with Otto Frisch (from the institute of Niels Bohr, Copenhagen, Denmark) supplied the correct interpretation of the Berlin experiments and other measurements. Thus, they discovered the nuclear fission of uranium as a result of neutron capture as a new nuclear reaction (Meitner & Frisch, 1939).

The potential consequences and societal impacts were immediately and extensively discussed internationally and openly in a variety of scientific journals, including scientists from Germany, France, Sweden, Denmark, Britain, and United States, among others. This open scientific international discussion on the societal impacts of nuclear reaction physics remarkably happened over scarcely a year in 1938–1939 and ended when Hitler invaded Poland. In anachronistic terms, one might say that the discussion on the societal impacts of nuclear reactions went viral. For example, an article by S. Flügge from the Kaiser Wilhelm Institut für Chemie in Berlin was published on June 9, 1939, in German (translated title: Can the energy content of atomic nuclei be made technologically useful?) that already pointed at the possibility of the atomic bomb as well as potential civil uses of nuclear energy (Flügge, 1939). These discussions were picked up by many scientists in many countries including Joseph Rotblat, and of course many scientists (including Albert Einstein) were alerted to the danger of a Hitler atomic bomb. Rotblat writes in reference to Lise Meitner's discovery (Rotblat, 1985): "From this discovery it was a fairly simple intellectual exercise to envisage a divergent chain reaction with a vast release of energy. The logical sequel was that if this energy were released in a very short time it would result in an explosion of unprecedented power."

Joseph Rotblat then moved from Poland to the United Kingdom to the group of James Chadwick, the discoverer of the neutron. He subsequently joined the US Manhattan Project in Los Alamos, New Mexico, in order to fight the possibility that Hitler would create an atomic bomb and use it before the United States and allies did. However, it became clear in 1944 that Hitler-Germany dropped the atomic bomb program and would not be able to produce one. That changed the whole picture, opening up the question why the atomic bomb was needed in the first place.

According to Rotblat (1985), at a dinner at James Chadwick's house (Rotblat's Manhattan Project boss at the time), General Leslie Groves, who was the US military lead in charge of the atomic bomb Manhattan Project, told him in March 1944: "You realize, of course, that the whole purpose of this project is to subdue our main enemy, the Russians." This came as a great personal shock to Joseph Rotblat as he describes it, having a commitment that Hitler would not get the atomic bomb first. He therefore decided to leave the Manhattan atomic bomb project, and in fact he was the first and only one to do so. Apart from his personal story and dilemmas, Rotblat's (1985) article is full of information on how other Los Alamos physicists were looking at this and tried to deal with the ensuing dilemmas. Joseph Rotblat and Pugwash received the Nobel Peace Prize in 1995.

3 Fast Forward to the Digital Age

3.1 General Elements of the Social Responsibility of Scientists and Technologists

Regrettably, the Atomic Age is not just simply history as current geopolitics show, although in the foreground today is the Digital Age. This is a clearly different era in terms of societal issues we have to deal with (DIGHUM, 2019). However, there are some pertinent general insights to be gained if we condense and summarize the vast historical writings on the social responsibilities of scientists and technologists.

First of all, scientists and technologists are *citizens*—like everyone. Citizenship—community, local, national, regional, global—comes with a moral obligation to strive for the benefit of humankind. There is no way to escape this responsibility—even when some attempt to hide in the ivory tower.

Second, scientists and technologists possess extensive and special knowledge in their field of expertise. This expert knowledge brings with it a different position in the public societal debate, also as seen in the public eye. This different knowledge position brings in many cases a position of some influence and, hence, responsibility—wanted or not. Accordingly, there is a responsibility to share this knowledge with society properly and in fitting ways. There are many different avenues open for scientists and technologists to do so:

(a) *Education*: educate the general public as well as policymakers and politicians on the societal impacts of digital technologies that need to be addressed.
(b) *Research*: investigate and explain to the general public and society at large what will be or might be the (also unintended) consequences or impacts of digital technologies in the (near) future.
(c) *Application*: urge for and, insofar as possible, work on beneficial applications of technology and counteract harmful ones.
(d) *Policy*: from a sound knowledge base, contribute to formulating sound and effective policies regarding the application and governance of advanced technologies.

Admittedly, the challenges of the Digital Age are very different from those of the Atomic Age. It is encouraging however that worldwide, there is considerable activity among scientists, technologists, and writers from many different corners along the abovementioned lines (a)–(d). It is currently scattered, but nevertheless, it is there and should be brought better to daylight (which is obviously also a purpose of the present volume). There is, one might say, already a serious society-oriented *digital scholarship-with-citizenship*.

3.2 *Societal Impacts of Digital Technologies and the Sustainable Development Goals*

In order to get a more general picture of the societal impacts and ethical issues associated with today's digital technologies, let us take the United Nations' Sustainable Development Goals (SDGs) as a starting point and framework.

The SDGs were adopted by the United Nations in 2015, and they formulate goals for betterment of the world to be achieved by 2030 (United Nations, n.d.; see Fig. 3). These goals cover many areas and issues of society and the planet, and they reflect the widest possible international consensus on values and goals for the benefit of humanity.

The following brief highlights of the mentioned *digital scholarship-with-citizenship* just scratch the surface and are incomplete, but they are indicative (for more, see the *Learning Resources* and *References* at the end of this chapter).

It is widely agreed that digital technologies bring important (potential) benefits to society. They increase the possibilities and ease for people to communicate with each other, to connect to each other in various ways, and this so at a historically unprecedented global scale and speed. So, digital technologies have the potential to be significant as enablers to important and shared human values and activities. But according to many recent critical studies, they also come with (sometimes unexpected) societal impacts that are harmful to many common people in the world and that are currently not properly managed, controlled, or governed. A few examples from recent literature follow below.

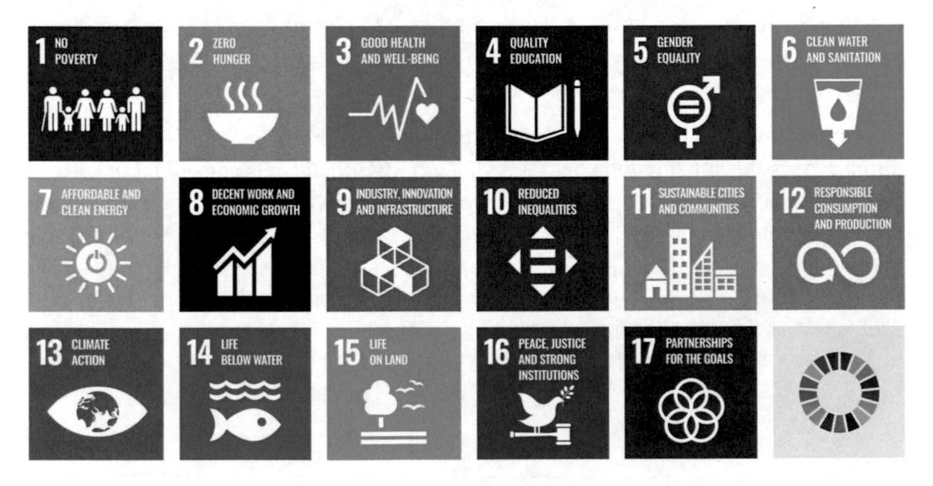

Fig. 3 The United Nations' Sustainable Development Goals (SDGs)

Inequalities and Bias SDG-5 and SDG-10, respectively, refer to gender equality and reducing inequalities in society. There are now many carefully researched studies that detail how digital technologies such as search engines, algorithms, and AIs embody important biases to the effect that they perpetuate or even enlarge racial and other prejudices and so reinforce racism (Noble, 2018). One of the many examples Safiyah Noble gives is Google's search engine producing images of black people tagged as "gorillas." Virginia Eubanks (2017) discusses a long list of cases showing how forms of automated decision-making and algorithmic governance go terribly wrong in ways that make lives of especially already poor and disadvantaged people even more miserable. As an example, the state of Indiana, USA, denied in 3 years 1 million applications for healthcare, food stamps, and financial benefits, because a new computer system interpreted any application mistake as "failure to cooperate."

A related horror story comes from the Netherlands. Under the pretense of fraud detection and prevention, the Dutch tax authorities for many years implemented a very harsh and disproportional system of payback and big financial penalties of child care allowances upon the slightest suspicion of fraud. The Dutch tax authorities literally chased people using various systems in ways that were downright discriminatory (non-Dutch-sounding family names, a second nationality, etc. labeled as "fraud-risk" factors). They also did what boils down to ethnic profiling and violated privacy rules. Small administrative errors by citizens were taken as evidence for fraud (save the complexity of Dutch legislation already for Dutch residents; it is noted that people with an immigration background often have a limited command of the Dutch language and are therefore more prone to make such "administrative" mistakes). The effects were devastating. Tens of thousands of people were unjustly and without any real basis accused of fraud and subsequently severely harmed. Many ended up in serious financial debt and lost jobs and/or homes, marriages broke up, and mental health problems occurred. An estimated 70,000 children were the victims of this; even families were broken up, and an estimated 1675 or even more children were removed from their homes and taken out of the custody of their parents. As Hadwick and Lan (2021) conclude: "The Dutch childcare allowance scandal or toeslagen affaire unveiled the ways in which the Dutch tax administration made use of artificial intelligence algorithms to discriminate against and violate the rights of welfare recipients." In June 2020, the Dutch then-PM Mark Rutte was, certainly not wholeheartedly, forced to admit that there is "institutional racism" in the Netherlands. Quite a many politicians prefer to link this to the colonial past only [as it is or seems to be over and done with (?!)] but attempt to avoid looking at the digital present.

Meredith Broussard (2023) makes two important general points here. First, such grave issues are not "glitches," accidental, regrettable but minor mistakes that can be easily corrected. They are inherent and systemic. Second, there is what she calls "technochauvinism," the belief that human problems can be solved by technological solutions alone, for example, that computer systems are better, faster, and more neutral in decision-making than humans. This naïve belief in digital systems leads to a tendency of authorities to "outsource," so to speak, decision-making to digital systems, thus abdicating their own responsibility for decisions. In addition, digital systems also functioned (as in the Dutch case) as stone-walling automated decisions, as they were used like a Chinese wall shielding authorities from citizens to appeal or ask explanations or proof. In other words, digital systems were (and are) used to make authorities immune for citizens contesting authority decisions.

This technochauvinist belief is furthermore used to sell all kinds of technopromises so as to capture billions of taxpayer money (even including space travel and other sci-fi scenarios) but is not based on relevant digital knowledge. There is a role here for socially responsible scientists and technology to investigate and educate a wider public on how digital technologies really work in society.

Decent Work and Economic Growth The United Nations SDG-8 focuses on decent work and economic growth. Terms such as "digital systems," "computing," and "automation" give the impression that it is computers and machines that do the work. However, Mary Gray and Siddharth Suri (2019), Sarah Roberts (2019), and Kate Crawford (2021) all point out that there is an enormous human workforce to keep the digital world running (see also in this volume chapters on *Work in a New World*). But it is work that is hardly visible, very fragmented, and hardly organized, often working under bad conditions, with poor pay and financial security as contract workers. Roberts (2019) studied the monotonic, repetitive, stressful, and even psychologically harmful work of content moderators (estimated at 100,000 globally), hidden behind the screens of commercial social media, by interviewing many in different countries. Gray and Suri (2019) call this invisible digital work "ghost work" and speak of a growing "global underclass" without labor protection laws and health and other employee benefits and with often below-minimum pay. If we liken the world to a zoo, it is no exaggeration to say that humans are fed in large numbers to the digital platform machines. One wonders about the decency of the big tech platforms to achieve in their own realm SDG-8 goals on decent work.

War and Peace: Data Secrecy Versus Openness Perhaps surprisingly, an analysis of *SDG-16, Peace, Justice, and Strong Institutions* unavoidably leads us into the consideration of (big) data management policies. Alex Wellerstein (2021) analyzes in his *Restricted Data* the data secrecy versus openness debates, arguments, and policies in the Atomic Age in painstaking detail. All in all, scientists were generally in favor of (international) openness, both before and during World War II and during the Cold War. Einstein is one of many examples here, and he wrote many times on it. As another example, Robert Oppenheimer also strongly leaned toward openness, and this made him a political target in the anti-communist "un-American" frenzy in the 1950s (an aspect also portrayed at length in Christopher Nolan's 2023 film *Oppenheimer*).

Wellerstein (2021) points out, in his concluding chapter, that data secrecy was and is not just confined to the nuclear domain but was much more encompassing. He also discusses how it extends to the present day and (among others) hereby refers to the current developments in AI. In the Atomic Age, the route was from openness (see above in this chapter, in the years just before World War II) to data secrecy in the Cold War period. We see a parallel here in the Digital Age. For example, the company that calls itself "OpenAI" with its generative AI tools (ChatGPT) has recently gone, in a rather sudden conversion from ideologically open to practically closed, the route from openness to full data-algorithm opaqueness and secrecy, apparently (as suggested by press reports and interviews) for commercial competition as well as (military) government funding reasons.

Concentration, weaponization, and militarization of AI and other digital research seem to be currently going on much more generally, with increasing data and algorithm secrecy, in analogy to the 1950s nuclear secrecy. We see now only snippets of this, but they come fragmentarily but consistently to the surface in news and investigative journalism reports about, for example, AI-supported drones in the Ukraine war. Such developments are certainly not going uncontested, as shown in recent years by the strong Google employee protests against military contracts and by worldwide AI researchers' petitions against AI autonomous weapons (initiated by well-known Australian AI researcher Toby Walsh). Whatever your personal position is, proper data management policies do come very close to and are often normal part of professional and academic duties of digital researchers in industry, academia, and government. So, in line with Bertrand Russel's arguments outlined above, there is a clear and present unavoidability of societal responsibility of digital scientists, researchers, and technologists.

Natural Resources, Energy, and Climate Action SDG-12 is about responsible consumption and production, and SDG-13 is on climate action. In her *Atlas of AI*, Kate Crawford (2021) argues that "AI is neither artificial nor intelligent. Rather, artificial intelligence is both embodied and material, made from natural resources, fuel, human labor, infrastructures, logistics, histories, and classifications." She then documents at length what she calls the "planetary costs" of digital technologies, in terms of the mining and extraction of many rare natural resources, such as rare-earth elements, the ensuing environmental damage, and the enormous energy hunger of digital computing.

As Crawford says: "Minerals are the backbone of AI, but its lifeblood is still electrical energy. Advanced computation is rarely considered in terms of carbon footprints, fossil fuels, and pollution; metaphors like 'the cloud' imply something floating and delicate within a natural, green industry. (...)" As Tung-Hui Hu writes in *A Prehistory of the Cloud*, "The cloud is a resource-intensive, extractive technology that converts water and electricity into computational power, leaving a sizable amount of environmental damage that it then displaces from sight. Addressing this energy-intensive infrastructure has become a major concern." She also refers to studies concluding that running a single large language model produces a carbon footprint equivalent to 125 round-trip flights from New York (Crawford, 2021, p.41–42). With the current developments in AI such as ChatGPT, this can only increase (cf. also Bender et al., 2021). One might summarize this as big data, bigger data, biggest footprint!

In sum, the digital society is not at all limited to the digital realm. It has a very big spillover to "normal" society with which it is more and more integrating. This process has disruptive and ungoverned societal effects that are not, or not necessarily, beneficial to humankind at large. There is a clear societal responsibility of digital scientists and technologists here concerning how we deal with this.

4 Governance, Public Values, and Fairness in Digital Ecosystems

We have seen above, admittedly very sketchy and incomplete, that digital technologies have societal impacts on many different aspects and sectors of society. But there is a further impact that *systemically* affects society *as a whole*, and that may be viewed under the rubric of *SDG-16, Peace, Justice, and Strong Institutions*, and also *SDG-9, Industry, Innovation, and Infrastructure*.

From the many public discussions, studies, and writings on the digital society, we can see two big society-systemic trends that are a cause for concern. One is more economic, the other more political, but the two are heavily intertwined:

1. The digitalization of society is accompanied by an enormous economic concentration of capital, wealth, and power in the hands of a few (see, e.g., Zuboff (2019) and many more).
2. The digitalization of society leads to a structural transformation of the public and democratic-political sphere (Habermas, 2022; Van Dijck et al., 2018; Vaidhyanathan, 2021; Nemitz & Pfeffer, 2020; and many more) in ways that distort and skew public debate and deliberation and that make equal access to and participation in democratic decision-making in fact more difficult and less equal.

These two developments are not independent, witness alone the fact that the whims of a single billionaire may decide who is to speak or not on public affairs in digital social media or what content is allowed or not. Digital technologies and the associated concentration of big resources in a few hands are "a clear and present danger" to democracy and, more generally, human values and freedoms in a shared public world (DIGHUM, 2023). This constitutes a form of weaponization of digital technologies that has the effect of a cluster bomb tearing a shared public world apart.

So a key question on the table is the *democratic governance* of technology (Feenberg, 2017; Siddarth et al., 2021; this volume, chapter by George Metakides and chapter by Marc Rotenberg). Jairam et al. (2021) usefully make a distinction between a technology and how it is governed or controlled, pointing out that the technology level and its governance level can have very different characteristics. For example, the big tech platforms rely on network "decentralized" technologies, but the governance level is in contrast strongly centralized and even monopolistic (Wieringa & Gordijn, 2023; this volume, chapter by Allison Stanger).

Innovation in digital technologies is today usually described in terms of digital innovation *ecosystems* in which a variety of parties and stakeholders participate (for a brief overview, see Akkermans et al., 2022) in both competitive and collaborative relationships. A natural question arising from the metaphor of ecosystems is how such multiparty innovation ecosystems can be kept *sustainable*, *fair*, and *equitable* with respect to all parties involved.

This is a governance question but a very complex one. It is not easy to give a positive definition of what is “fair” or “just.” On the other hand, there are many situations where it is clear that something is unfair or unjust, and a wide consensus exists about that (see, e.g., the SDG-related discussion of digital impacts in Sect. 3.2). Moreover, there are a number of basic ideas, principles, and desiderata regarding the governance of digital ecosystems that are recurring over and over again in the literature, although their formulations and arrangements vary widely (see, e.g., Siddarth et al., 2021; Jairam et al., 2021; this volume, chapter by Julian Nida-Rümelin; chapter by Guglielmo Tamburrini; chapter by Erich Prem; and chapter by Anna Bon); below we follow the paraphrasing by Akkermans et al. (2022).

(a) *Participation*. Fair governance ensures active involvement in the decision-making process of all who are affected and other parties with an interest at stake. It includes all participants interacting through direct or representative democracy. Participants should be able to do so in an unconstrained and truthful manner, and they should be well informed and organized so as to participate fruitfully and constructively.

(b) *Rule of law and equity*. All participants have legitimate opportunities to improve or maintain their well-being. Agreed-upon legal rules and frameworks (this volume, chapter by Matthias Kettemann), with underlying democratic principles, are enforced impartially while guaranteeing the rights of people; no participant is above the rule of law.

(c) *Effectiveness and efficiency*. Fair governance fulfills societal needs by incorporating effectiveness while utilizing the available resources efficiently. Effective governance ensures that the different governance actors meet societal needs. Fully utilizing resources, without being wasted or underutilized, ensures efficient governance.

(d) *Transparency*. Information on matters that affect participants must be freely available and accessible. The decision-making process is performed in a manner that is clear for all by following rules and regulations. Transparency also includes that enough relevant information is provided and presented in easy-to-understand forms or media.

(e) *Responsiveness*. A responsive fair governance structure reacts appropriately and within a reasonable timeframe toward its participants. This responsiveness stimulates participants to take part in the governance process.

(f) *Consensus-oriented*. Fair governance considers the different participants’ viewpoints and interests before decisions are made and implemented. Such governance is defined as consensus-oriented because it aims to achieve a broad community consensus. In order to reach this wide consensus, a firm mediation structure, without any bias toward participants, should be in place.

(g) *Accountability*. Accountability is defined as responsibility or answerability for one's actions. Decision-makers, whether internal or external, are responsible for those who are affected by their actions or decisions. These decision-makers are morally or legally bound to clarify and be answerable for the implications and selected actions made on behalf of the community.

Such basic ideas and principles provide some of the groundwork for policymaking and design for fairness of digital ecosystems and their societal and democratic governance (see also in this volume chapter by Clara Neppel).

5 Conclusions

Scientists and technologists *do* have a social responsibility. This derives from two general factors. The first is (global) citizenship. The second is their position of knowledge and expertise in matters of science and technology and the ensuing position and influence in the public debate.

That a social responsibility exists does not tell us much about how it is to be exercised. This is very varied, as the stories regarding both the Atomic Age and Digital Age show. There are many avenues that are possible and important, in what we have called above *scholarship-cum-citizenship*, including education (also with respect to the general public and policy makers), research (into impacts and also unintended consequences), application (pushing for beneficial applications and counteracting harmful ones), or knowledge-based contributions to policymaking.

Already a very cursory analysis in the framework of the United Nations' Sustainable Development Goals, as we have carried out in this chapter, reveals that the societal impacts of digital technologies are wide and affect many aspects of society. An important observation here is that many of these are of a society-*systemic* nature and thus go beyond the individual level of ethics and ethical behavior.

The related social responsibilities are likewise wide and multifaceted and may even seem overwhelming. As an antidote of sorts, there is this call-to-action quote, widely circulating on the Internet and often attributed to Albert Einstein: "The world will not be destroyed by those who do evil, but by those who watch them without doing anything."

Even if this is true, we do well to keep in mind the wise words of Otto Neurath (1921), a founder of the Vienna Circle. They were written in 1921 and became known as *Neurath's boat*:

> We are like sailors who on the open sea must reconstruct their ship but are never able to start afresh from the bottom. Where a beam is taken away a new one must at once be put there, and for this the rest of the ship is used as support. In this way, by using the old beams and driftwood, the ship can be shaped entirely anew, but only by gradual reconstruction.

Discussion Questions for Students and Their Teachers

1. "The world will not be destroyed by those who do evil, but by those who watch them without doing anything." This is a quote widely circulated on the Web and commonly attributed to Albert Einstein. Investigate what the source of this quote is and whether it is correctly attributed to Einstein. Reflect on how "stories based on fact" come into being in the digital world.
2. This quote has the charm of an aphorism, but is it in your view actually valid, or does it make sense? Why (not)?
3. What, in your view, would be the value or usefulness of some sort of modernized Hippocratic Oath (as Popper suggested) for digital scientists and engineers?
4. Are digital technologies value-neutral? See the general discussion of the neutrality issue in Feenberg (2017), and then analyze an example case such as ChatGPT, Uber, Facebook, etc.
5. Can a (legal, law-compliant) business model be unethical? See the digital platform business model studies in Wieringa and Gordijn (2023), take one of the cases, and relate it to the discussion of fairness in innovation ecosystems in the present chapter.
6. Lise Meitner never received the Nobel Prize although she was the internationally recognized key person to discover the nuclear fission of uranium, and this discovery is arguably one of the most important ones in the twentieth century. Investigate the reasons why.
7. Research project. Take one of the United Nations' Sustainable Development Goals (SDGs) as a thematic focus. Study the societal impacts—positive, negative, mixed—of the digital transformation as related to this SDG, and do so focusing on a specific geographical region (e.g., your own country) or political-legal jurisdiction or societal sector.

Learning Resources for Students

1. From the References below, see in particular (Broussard, 2023; Crawford, 2021; Eubanks, 2017; Feenberg, 2017; Habermas, 2022; Noble, 2018; Siddarth et al., 2021; Vaidhyanathan, 2021; Van Dijck et al., 2018; Wellerstein, 2021; Zuboff, 2019).
2. Grewal, D. S. (2008) *Network Power: The Social Dynamics of Globalization.* New Haven, CT, USA: Yale University Press.

   A deep interdisciplinary study on how different forms of power emerge from social networks, how this shapes a complex globalization in a—also digitally—globally connected world, and the challenges it poses for a democratic politics
3. Rogers, E. M. (2003) *Diffusion of Innovations.* 5th edn. New York, NY, USA: Simon and Schuster.

   The classic book about the social network mechanisms that enable, accelerate, or impede the spread of technological innovations through society; many concepts and terms in common usage today in innovation policies (e.g., early adopter) come from this work.
4. Stanley, S. (2015) *How Propaganda Works.* Princeton, NJ, USA: Princeton University Press.

A wide-ranging political philosophy work on what propaganda is, how it operates historically as well as today, and how it shapes ideologies that damage liberal democracy and justice.

5. Woolley, S. (2023) *Manufacturing Consensus – Understanding Propaganda in the Era of Automation and Anonymity*. New Haven, CT, USA: Yale University Press.

   A recent study, based on extensive international ethnographic research, of online and computational propaganda, its deceptive effects, and its manipulative workings, in and through today's digital social media.

References

Akkermans, H., Gordijn, J., & Bon, A. (2022). Return to freedom: Governance of fair innovation ecosystems. In H. Werthner et al. (Eds.), *Perspectives on digital humanism* (pp. 53–60). Cham, Switzerland.

Bender, E. M., et al. (2021). On the dangers of stochastic parrots: Can language models be too big? In *Conference on Fairness, Accountability, and Transparency (FAccT '21), March 3–10, 2021, Virtual Event, Canada*. ACM. , 14 pp. https://doi.org/10.1145/3442188.3445922

Broussard, M. (2023). *More than a glitch – Confronting race, gender and ability bias in tech*. The MIT Press.

Crawford, K. (2021). *Atlas of AI – Power, politics, and the planetary costs of artificial intelligence*. Yale University Press.

DIGHUM. (2019). *Vienna manifesto on digital humanism*. Accessed July 01, 2023, from https://dighum.ec.tuwien.ac.at/dighum-manifesto/

DIGHUM. (2023). *Statement of the digital humanism initiative on generative AI and democratic sustainability* [Online]. Accessed July 05, 2023, from https://caiml.dbai.tuwien.ac.at/dighum/workshops/digital-humanism-summit-2023-07-03/

Eubanks, V. (2017). *Automating inequality – How high-tech tools profile, police and punish the poor*. St. Martin's Press.

Feenberg, A. (2017). *Technosystem – The social life of reason*. Harvard University Press.

Flügge, S. (1939, June 09). Kann der Energieinhalt der Atomkerne technisch nutzbar gemacht werden? *Die Naturwissenschaften, 23/24*, 402–410.

Gray, M. L., & Suri, S. (2019). *Ghost work – How to stop Silicon Valley from building a new global underclass*. Houghton Mifflin Harcourt.

Habermas, J. (2022). *Ein Neuer Strukturwandel der Öffentlichkeit und die Deliberative Politik*. Suhrkamp Verlag AG.

Hadwick, D., & Lan, S. (2021, October 10). Lessons to be learned from the Dutch Childcare Allowance Scandal: A comparative review of algorithmic governance by tax administrations in the Netherlands, France and Germany. *World Tax Journal – Amsterdam, 13*(4), 609–645. Accessed June 19, 2023, from https://ssrn.com/abstract=4282704 (Available at SSRN).

Jairam, S., Gordijn, J., Torres, I., Kaya, F., & Makkes, M. (2021). A decentralized fair governance model for permissionless blockchain systems. In *Proceedings of the International Workshop on Value Modelling and Business Ontologies (VMBO 2021), Bolzano, Italy, March 4–5, 2021*. Accessed July 03, 2023, from https://ceur-ws.org/Vol-2835/paper3.pdf

Meitner, L., & Frisch, O. R. (1939, February 11). Disintegration of uranium by neutrons: A new type of nuclear reaction. *Nature (Lond), 143*(3615), 239–240.

Nathan, O., & Norden, H. (Eds.). (2017). *Einstein on peace*. Arcole Publishing. Originally published in 1960.

Nemitz, P., & Pfeffer, M. (2020). *PRINZIP MENSCH - Macht, Freiheit und Demokratie im Zeitalter der Künstlichen Intelligenz*. Verlag J.H.W. Dietz Nachf. GmbH.

Neurath, O. (1921). Anti-Spengler. Reprinted in *Empiricism and Sociology* (1973), as Chapter 6, pp. 158–213. Dordrecht, the Netherlands: D. Reidel. https://doi.org/10.1007/978-94-010-2525-6_6. ISBN 978-90-277-0259-3. The "Neurath's Boat" quote is on p199.

Noble, S. U. (2018). *Algorithms of oppression – How search engines reinforce racism*. New York University Press.

Popper, K. R. (1971). The moral responsibility of the scientist. *Bulletin of Peace Proposals, 2*(3), 279–283. Accessed April 06, 2023, from https://www.jstor.org/stable/44480137

Roberts, S. T. (2019). *Behind the screen – Content moderation in the shadows of social media*. Yale University Press. Expanded paperback edn. 2021.

Rotblat, J. (1985). Leaving the bomb project. *Bulletin of the Atomic Scientists, 41*(7), 16–19. https://doi.org/10.1080/00963402.1985.11455991. Reprinted in Bruce, M. and Milne, T. (eds.) (1999) *Ending War: The Force of Reason – Essays in Honour of Joseph Rotblat*. Basingstoke, Hampshire, United Kingdom: MacMillan Press Ltd.

Russell, B. (1960, February 12). The social responsibilities of scientists. *Science, New Series, 131*(3398), 391–392. Accessed March 23, 2023, from https://www.jstor.org/stable/1705325

Siddarth, D., et al. (2021). *How AI fails us*. Technology and Democracy Discussion Paper, Carr Center for Human Rights Policy, Harvard University. Accessed July 05, 2023, from https://ethics.harvard.edu/how-ai-fails-us

United Nations. (n.d.). *Sustainable Development Goals (SDGs)* [Online]. https://sdgs.un.org/goals

Vaidhyanathan, S. (2021). *Anti-social media – How Facebook disconnects us and undermines democracy* (2nd ed.). Oxford University Press.

Van Dijck, J., Poell, T., & de Waal, M. (2018). *The platform society – Public values in a connective world*. Oxford University Press.

Veys, L. (2013). Joseph Rotblat: Moral dilemmas and the Manhattan Project. *Physics in Perspectives, 15*, 451–469.

Wellerstein, A. (2021). *Restricted data – The history of nuclear secrecy in the US*. The University of Chicago Press.

Wieringa, R. J., & Gordijn, J. (2023). *Digital business ecosystems. How to create, deliver and capture value in business networks*. TVE Press, to appear. Based on a range of digital platform business model case studies. Accessed July 02, 2023, from https://www.thevalueengineers.nl/

Zuboff, S. (2019). *The age of surveillance capitalism*. Profile Books Ltd.

Digital Transformation Through the Lens of Intersectional Gender Research Challenges and Needs for Action

Claude Draude

Abstract In recent years, digital technology has been discussed both in its potential to promote or to demote gender equity. This field of tension, between empowerment and threat of amplifying inequalities, is explored in this contribution. Moreover, this chapter views digital humanism through the lens of intersectional gender research. After discussing the historic relation between gender and humanism, concepts and terminology of gender research and feminist theory are explained in more detail. Following this, the interaction of gender and technology is illustrated through examples. Finally, the lessons learned part contains suggestions and calls for action important for a more inclusive and equitable digital transformation.

1 Introduction

Western feminism, women's liberation movements, and today's gender equity debates are undeniably linked to the notion of humanism. Although the role of women in society was debated among some of its contemporary thinkers, Enlightenment's guiding narrative of liberty and progress served as an ally for advancing women's rights (Ramazanoğlu & Holland, 2002; Lettow, 2017). Throughout history, including women in the concept of the human and human rights debates nevertheless had to be fought for. One of the most prominent documentations of this is the "Declaration of the Rights of Woman and of the [Female] Citizen" by Olympe de Gouges dating back to 1791 in France. Among other progressive demands, her manifesto declared women as equals to men and worthy of the same rights. De Gouges requested equality in citizenship status—something the famous document of the French Revolution, the "Declaration of the Rights of Man and of the [Male] Citizen" from 1789, did not do (Cokely, 2018; Gouges & Fraisse, 2021). Scholars point out that the term *man* in the latter declaration refers to Western

C. Draude (✉)
Faculty of Electrical Engineering and Computer Science, University of Kassel, Kassel, Germany
e-mail: claude.draude@uni-kassel.de

H. Werthner et al. (eds.), *Introduction to Digital Humanism*,
https://doi.org/10.1007/978-3-031-45304-5_6

society's Christian white man, a rather narrow term contradicting the universal character of the declaration (Taylor, 1999).

Hence, incremental for the first wave of feminism was to interrogate critically who the use of the terms *man* and *human* in the debates on universal human rights actually included. Consequently, first-wave feminists sought to expand the terminology to include women.[1] Prominently, Simone de Beauvoir interrogated the relation between man, woman, and human in the *The Second Sex* which, first published in 1949 (de Beauvoir, 1949), became later foundational for second-wave feminism. For de Beauvoir, to be considered first and foremost human is liberating for women. The title of the two book volumes points at a central position of her work—women are defined and materialized as *the other* of man. One of the most quoted sentences of her work is "one is not born, but becomes a woman" (de Beauvoir, 2010, p. 283). This perspective that the category of woman is constructed along sociocultural contexts makes social change possible. Furthermore, solidarity between women because of the shared experience of subjugation is established, and ultimately the case for feminism as humanism is made (Johnson, 1993). Donna Haraway has prominently stated that, even considering their diversity, all modern, Western concepts of feminism are rooted in de Beauvoir's formative sentence (Haraway, 1991).

The relationship between the gender order, feminism, and humanism has never been straightforward, however. Just as the use of *man* for all humans is problematic in historical retrospection, so is *woman* as a unifying term and basis for political action. As early as in 1851, Sojourner Truth delivered her powerful speech "Ain't I a woman?" at the Women's Rights Convention in Ohio. The speech challenged the exclusion of African American men and women in debates about legal rights during and after the US-American Civil War. Moreover, and historically significant, Truth brought together women's issues, the rights of Black women, in particular, and the fight against slavery (Truth, 1851). This challenged social justice movements that focused on either women's rights or racial justice.

Fast forwarding to third (and fourth) wave feminism—the concept of the universal human or woman has been criticized by political activists, artists, and scholars alike. People from diverse backgrounds, Black, Indigenous, and People, notably Women of Color, have brought attention to whose identity and lived experience is included or excluded in political struggles and in academic knowledge production alike (hooks, 1981; Hill Collins, 1990; Combahee River Collective, 2001; Green, 2007). Furthermore, the lack of recognizing other social categories, such as class (Acker, 2006) or disability (McRuer, 2006; Jenks, 2019), in relation to gender has

[1] Feminism as a political mass movement is generally described in three (or four) waves, differing in historical phases, geopolitical locations, participating actors, and political demands. Commonly, the first wave describes the suffragettes, the second wave the women's liberation movement of the 1960s and 1970s, the third wave acknowledges social constructivist perspectives on gender (since the 1980s), while the fourth wave (depending on perspective since the early 2000s or 2012) has been fueled by antifeminist backlash and the emancipatory role of technology and social media (Munro, 2013; Evans & Chamberlain, 2015).

been brought forward by various thinkers as well as the critique on the binary, heteronormative concept of gender itself (Stryker & Blackston, 2022; Muñoz, 1999).

This complicated history, the ambivalent legacy of the Enlightenment for liberation movements, is important to keep in mind when we speak about Digital Humanism today. In the following, the tension between humanism and feminism is made productive; we will explore how feminist theory and gender research can enrich debates on digital humanism. In addition, and as we will see further on, who is accounted for when talking about the human is highly topical in debates on digital transformation and also has concrete impact on development, use, and effects of digital technology.

2 Intersectional Gender Research, Feminist Theory, and Digital Technology

2.1 Intersectional Gender Research

Gender studies is an interdisciplinary, broad research field with diverse roots in the social sciences and the humanities. Gender studies' common ground is an analytical approach to how gender as a social category is constructed and unfolds in interaction with societal, cultural, and political contexts. The question of how power is distributed, materialized, and mediated through gender, race, sexuality, class, citizenship, age, and ability is hereby central. To address multiple forms of belonging and to understand how these may result in differing forms of oppression, the concept of intersectionality was coined. Intersectionality is informed by Black, Indigenous, people of color (feminist) scholarship, activism, literature, and art (Lorde, 2001; hooks, 1981; Hill Collins, 1990; Snyder, 2014). Intersectionality interrogates the universal concept of the human (and woman) by asking who is really included and furthermore through examining limits and drawbacks to social categorization. Notably, American legal scholar and civil rights activist Kimberlé Crenshaw showed that existing anti-discrimination laws did not work for Black women since the laws did not recognize multiple causes of discrimination. Crenshaw used the image of a traffic intersection to illustrate that social categories, such as gender and race, do not exist separately but rather are interdependent in the way a person is socially positioned (Crenshaw, 1989).

In Sect. 2.3, we will come back to explore how gender and digital technology interact and how useful an intersectional perspective is for understanding the relation between structural inequalities and digital transformation.

2.2 Feminist Theory and Epistemologies

Gender studies is informed by heterogeneous strands of feminist and critical theory. Importantly, feminist and critical race studies have analyzed the history of science demonstrating the failure to include marginalized people and perspectives. These fields demonstrate how scientific knowledge and the dynamics of intersectional gender relations intertwine, and they provide examples of how individuals deemed as *the other* may suffer harm (Schiebinger, 1989; Gowder, 2015; Zuberi & Silva, 2008).

Marginalized perspectives and people may mean exclusion from scientific inquiry, denial of epistemic authority, production of harmful theories, or stereotyping of the marginalized group or lack of acknowledging structural inequalities that affect the group (cf. Anderson, 2020). Ultimately, this can lead to biased knowledge and artifact production and hinder scientific and product innovation.

Feminist epistemologies allow us to analyze the role intersectional gender conceptions play in our ways of knowing. According to feminist theory, how and through which means knowledge is formed, and what counts as knowledge, is always situated and context-dependent.[2] In this regard, situated knowledges is a central concept of feminist epistemologies; it allows one to reflect upon the position from where and by whom knowledge is formed and to acknowledge that all knowledge is partial and forms of knowledge manifold (Haraway, 1988). Two main aspects are noteworthy here. First, the partial perspective questions universal knowledge claims and instead offers what Haraway calls "objectivity as positioned rationality" (ibid., p. 590). Feminist standpoint theory has developed the concept of "strong objectivity" (Harding, 1986, 1992). Sandra Harding questions the proclaimed neutrality of scientific knowledge production and instead introduces reflexivity on the researcher's standpoint to address and counter possible social bias (ibid.). Second, it is this positioning that makes scientific and technological knowledge and artifact production accountable in the first place. In debates on digital humanism, calls for accountability of technology have gained a new urgency. Realizing accountability is indispensable for ethical, legal, and social aspects or implications in information technology (IT) and artificial intelligence (AI) research and development (Larsson et al., 2019).

[2]Tracing the construction of scientific knowledge in specific sociopolitical, cultural, and historic settings has been brought forward by the field of science and technology studies (STS), for example, through Bruno Latour's and Steve Woolgar's molecular biology laboratory studies (1979). Intersectional, postcolonial feminist scholars, however, have criticized the lack of recognizing the role social inequalities, marginalization, and power relations (locally and globally) play in STS, calling for a feminist or postcolonial corrective of the field (Harding, 1998, 2011; Haraway, 1997).

2.3 How Gender and Technology Interact

Today, digital technology impacts all life domains, and therefore we need to take a closer look at what this means for social equity. The relationship between the intersectional gender order and technology is complex and multifaceted. We can identify three main perspectives on how to approach the topic: first, unequal participation in technology research, development, and distribution; second, technology's impact on how gender is shaped, lived, and experienced; and third, how technology itself is gendered, racialized, classed, etc. These perspectives are not independent but impact each other as we will see in the examples provided.

Unequal participation in the technological field is often the first issue that comes to mind when gender and technology are mentioned together. For Western countries and the Global North, gender and BIPOC[3] inequality in IT research and development is a persisting challenge (Kapor Center and ASU CGEST, 2018; Charleston et al., 2014; Stoet & Geary, 2018). Also, access to digital technology is unfairly distributed—globally but also reflecting and amplifying social inequalities locally (Goedhart et al., 2019; Choi et al., 2022).

By taking up science and technology studies' (STS) understanding of the co-construction of society and technology (Bijker et al., 1987), feminist scholars have analyzed what this means for the gender order (Wajcman, 2000). Related to the topic of unequal participation, one important strand of work is making marginalized people, perspectives, and experiences visible. For example, the role of Black women scientists in computing has only lately received attention, prominently through the book (and film) *Hidden Figures* (Lee Shatterly, 2016).[4] Furthermore, the manufacturing labor of hardware by people (women) of color under often problematic work conditions that makes digital transformation possible is hidden from users of technology (Nakamura, 2014).

Second, digital products and services in use strongly impact people's well-being. One example are menstrual cycle tracking apps that form a contested zone between gender, politics, healthcare, and the data economy. Noteworthy, menstruation tracking was not implemented in early health monitoring technology.[5] Today, there is integration as well as stand-alone apps that could be used to promote research into menstrual health, provide a form of empowerment, and promote agency and

[3] BIPOC is short for Black, Indigenous, and people of color. This self-designation originated in US-American and Canadian activism and is also used to show solidarity between different communities of color.

[4] *Hidden Figures* tells the stories of Mary Jackson, Katherine Johnson, and Dorothy Vaughan, who worked at the National Advisory Committee for Aeronautics (NACA) and later at the successor NASA in the USA. Another prominent example were Kay McNulty, Betty Jennings, Betty Snyder, Marlyn Meltzer, Fran Bilas, and Ruth Lichterman—who, as the original programmers of the first US-American electronic computer, have traditionally been little more than a footnote in the history of the ENIAC (Light, 1999).

[5] Apple Health, for example, first launched in 2014 and only implemented menstruation tracking after facing critique (Eveleth, 2015).

self-determination of a person's health status. On the other hand, self-tracking shapes the experience of menstruation as a process that needs to be monitored and controlled and should meet normalized patterns (Hohmann-Marriott, 2021). In addition, popular apps are built on business models that rely on extracting data, which leads to a lack of privacy, transparency, and possibility of intervening and control of data from the lay user: "To perform their explicit functions, menstrual apps collect massive amounts of highly personal data. This data creates vulnerability; for example, data can reveal nonconforming menstruators (i.e., transgender or with health conditions), or information can be used to flag suspected pregnancy or termination of pregnancy" (ibid.). Depending on the political context, this extraction and exploitation of sensitive health data can be really dangerous and deeply affect people's lives based on their gender, sexual identity, orientation, and choices.[6] Hence, calls for health app development that take sociopolitical context, unequal power relations, and values such as non-discrimination and self-determination into account are important, as are policy regulations (Fox & Epstein, 2020).

The outlined issues reach beyond the given examples. Shoshana Zuboff has prominently stated that the interplay between data-driven digital technology, big corporations, predominant business models, and lack of regulatory power has led to "the age of surveillance capitalism" (Zuboff, 2018).

Third, as we have noted before, questioning the neutrality of technology is central for science and technology studies. Feminist and postcolonial STS scholars have analyzed the role gender, race, age, and class play in technology design and found that services and products can promote inequalities (but could also serve to alleviate them) (Harding, 2011). In the 1990s, studies on domestic technology—such as the microwave oven, vacuum cleaning systems, or washing machines—showed how appliances are informed by gender roles and reinforce the gendered division of labor at home and in manufacturing (Cockburn & Ormrod, 1993; Cockburn & Fürst-Dilić, 1994). Today, smart home technology design should anticipate and counter misuse in the context of domestic abuse and partner violence (Leitão, 2019).

In recent years, worrisome examples have brought broader attention to ethical aspects of IT/AI design—particularly to machine learning technology, a subfield of AI. These data-driven systems can mirror social bias and lead to an amplification of social inequalities, among others, in domains like the job sector, health and social services, and the justice system (Eubanks, 2017; Wachter-Boettcher, 2017). Therefore, current AI systems vividly demonstrate how interwoven society and technology are. In recent years, researchers from technical and social disciplines have increasingly made an effort to address questions of fairness and social justice of AI (Binns, 2018; Mehrabi et al., 2021; Draude et al., 2022). Social bias leading to problematic gendered, racialized, classed effects of technology has been linked to multiple causes: to the quality of the training data, to constraints and limitations in

[6]Notably, in the USA, the Supreme Court decision to overturn Roe vs Wade and the erosion of sexual and reproductive rights led to people deleting their menstrual health apps (Garamvolgyi, 2022).

algorithms and modeling, and to emergent bias through the context of use (Friedman & Nissenbaum, 1996; Draude et al., 2020).[7]

In simplified terms, machine learning technology automatically produces algorithms by training statistical models using existing datasets. As more data becomes available, they may even adapt their behavior. Machine learning systems are utilized to analyze vast amounts of data and predict future outcomes. This also means that these systems can inherit biases from the past datasets they are trained on.[8]

In a much-noted study, Bolukbasi et al. show how word embeddings may reinforce gender stereotypes.[9] Furthermore, the authors provide a methodology on how to remove gender stereotypes while staying true to word meanings and associations (Bolukbasi et al., 2016). If algorithms are trained using datasets that contain in their majority gender-stereotypical attributions and a proximity between terms such as woman and nurse, but man and doctor, the software learns these attributions and reproduces them in the future. For the study, the authors analyzed an artificial neural network trained by Google, which used over 3 million words from Google News articles as its database. The aim was to derive language patterns which can be represented mathematically (as vectors in vector space). Some of the attributions placed as extremes with respect to feminine pronouns are "homemaker, nurse, receptionist, librarian, socialite, hairdresser, nanny, bookkeeper, stylist, housekeeper"; those with respect to male pronouns are "maestro, skipper, protégé, philosopher, captain, architect, financier, warrior, broadcaster, magician" (ibid., p. 4357). Following this, Bolukbasi et al. presented automatically generated analogies between different terms for review to Amazon Mechanical Turk crowdworkers. For each word embedding, the workers should decide whether it is a gender stereotype or whether it is a gender appropriate analogy. Gender stereotypical she-he analogies included "sewing-carpentry, nurse-surgeon, blond-burly, cupcakes-pizza, lovely-brilliant, softball-baseball," etc., while gender appropriate she-he analogies were found in "queen-king, waitress-waiter, sister-brother, mother-father," etc. (ibid., p. 4357).

This example of word embeddings not only shows how technical development can perpetuate discrimination—the study also makes prevalent social bias visible in the first place and offers methods for debiasing. Because gender bias is presented as a mathematical model, mathematical methods can then also be used for alleviating

[7] For an in-depth discussion on bias and the Web, see the chapter by Baeza-Yates and Murgai.

[8] For an excellent introduction to machine learning, see the chapter by Heitzinger and Woltran.

[9] Word embedding is employed in text analysis in natural language processing and natural language generation. To be processable by computers, text must be represented in a numerical format first. Word embedding then allows to map words as real-valued numerical vectors as a conversion in vector space (Jiao & Zhang, 2021).

bias.[10] The authors also point toward critique or potential drawbacks of such debiasing methods:

> One perspective on bias in word embeddings is that it merely reflects bias in society, and therefore one should attempt to debias society rather than word embeddings. However, by reducing the bias in today's computer systems (or at least not amplifying the bias), which is increasingly reliant on word embeddings, in a small way debiased word embeddings can hopefully contribute to reducing gender bias in society. At the very least, machine learning should not be used to inadvertently amplify these biases, as we have seen can naturally happen. In specific applications, one might argue that gender biases in the embedding (e.g., *computer programmer* is closer to *he*) could capture useful statistics and that, in these special cases, the original biased embeddings could be used. However, given the potential risk of having machine learning algorithms that amplify gender stereotypes and discriminations, we recommend that we should err on the side of neutrality and use the debiased embeddings provided here as much as possible. (ibid, p. 4363)

As we have learned above, gender is one possible factor of social inequality. Further categories, such as race, class, disability, age, etc., intersect with gender. Already as a computer science student, Joy Buolamwini found out that facial recognition technology would not recognize her face. The technology, at the time, did not work for Black women—while in contrast, a white mask with no human features did work (Buolamwini, 2016). This shows how technology dehumanizes a person based on skin tone. In her study "Gender Shades," Buolamwini, together with Timnit Gebru, further analyzed commercial facial recognition technology. They found that women with dark skin or non-Western-classified facial features are most often misidentified. However, men with dark skin or non-Western-classified facial features are also more poorly identified than women with light skin (Buolamwini & Gebru, 2018). Other studies have shown that visual data used in AI systems perpetuates cultural and ethnic stereotypes (Zou & Schiebinger, 2018).

These examples illustrate how the three perspectives we mentioned at the start of this section intertwine. It comes as no surprise that discriminatory effects of IT/AI have been brought to our attention often through studies done by Black women, people of color, and marginalized groups, in general. Unequal participation in the technical field can mean that problematic effects of digital technology only become noticed after deployment, and technology's impact on our gendered, racialized, classed, etc. realities is becoming ever greater as a result of digital transformation. The rise of AI demonstrates how inequity might become automated and amplified, if no intervening countermeasures are undertaken. In the following concluding part, we sum up our findings and furthermore learn about some strategies and approaches toward more equitable IT/AI design.

[10] Please note that the example provided deals with binary gender only. There is an increasing body of work on gender neutrality and nonbinary gender in word embeddings (e.g., Zhao et al., 2018; Dev et al., 2021).

3 Conclusions

Against the historical background, we have learned that it is important to reflect upon the category of the human and to interrogate who is included and who is not. For a more just and equitable (digital) future—we can turn toward the rich scholarship of critical theory and methodology that centers marginalized perspectives, which allows us to enrich (Digital) Humanism. Elsewhere, we have made the claim that in IT/AI systems development, marginalized perspectives mostly get accounted for when we design for specific user groups, such as the elderly, people in care homes, or people with disabilities (Dankwa & Draude, 2021). A more inclusive digital transformation would mean to always center intersectional, diverse perspectives, people, and contexts and furthermore advance systemic and sociotechnical approaches to IT/AI development.

Returning to the examples from Sect. 2.3, it also would not be enough to counter bias in IT/AI systems through increased data extraction or better mathematical models. Even if we develop facial recognition technology that—from a technical perspective—functions for all people, its use still may heavily impact vulnerable groups. Especially, the heavy reliance on data creates a field of tension for social equity—on the one hand, biased or non-representation in datasets is problematic. Reliable data is needed for making discrimination visible, e.g., as grounds for affirmative action but also for IT/AI development. In many domains, lack of data leads to non-usable, inaccessible, and even dangerous services and products (Criado-Perez, 2019). On the other hand, increased data collection can be highly problematic, depending on the sociopolitical context. Visibility may expose vulnerable people or make them vulnerable in the first place. Categorization runs the risk of solidifying stereotypical assumptions about certain groups of people, and of course, classification systems also have problematic historical backgrounds (Bowker & Star, 1999).

In conclusion, we can sum up steps needed for a more just digital transformation. The first step is awareness that questions of power, inequality, and the affordances of diverse social groups and contexts matter throughout all phases of digital development and later usage. Furthermore, the societal challenges that come with pervasive digital technology can only be met through interdisciplinary exchange; particularly, fields with expertise on discrimination should be worked with. The second step is making the decision to actively design for social good. Various long-standing approaches that foster democratic values, participation, and self-determination in and through IT, such as participatory design (Bødker et al., 2021), value-centered design (Friedman & Hendry, 2019), and socio-technical design (Mumford, 2006), exist. Social justice, however, must first be acknowledged as an important value, actively pursued, and the corresponding expertise must be considered. Design frameworks that have social justice integrated as a core value already are anti-oppressive design (Smyth & Dimond, 2014) and design justice (Costanza-Chock, 2020). Furthermore, AI technology—automated decision-making, recommendations, filtering, content generation—brings new challenges to fields such as human-computer interaction and information systems design. The third step concerns regulatory practices and policy making, which are incremental in making steps one and two possible as well as socio-technically sustainable (Palmiotto, 2023; European Commission, 2021).

Discussion Questions for Students and Their Teachers

Relate the following aspects to digital transformation in your field of research, work, or study.

1. Identity and intersectionality
   When you talk about the human, who is considered, and who is not?
   How could an intersectional perspective broaden your view?
2. Knowledge production and methodology
   Can you identify marginalized perspectives? Think about the in/visibility of people, areas of work, and non-human actors.
   Do your methods, approaches, and tools need to change to be more inclusive?
3. Power and hierarchies
   How do power dynamics materialize in your field, e.g., hierarchies between tech developer and lay user, expert, and non-expert but also structural inequalities in society?

Furthermore, which of the steps outlined in the conclusion (awareness raising, decision to design for social good, policy making) is most needed in your field? Find examples to illustrate your answers!

Learning Resources for Students

1. Bardzell, S. (2010) 'Feminist HCI: Taking Stock and Outlining an Agenda for Design', *Proceedings of the SIGCHI Conference on Human Factors in Computing Systems.* New York, NY, USA, Association for Computing Machinery, pp. 1301–1310.
   Bardzell introduces feminist theory and explores its meaning for interaction design. The paper contains examples from industrial design, architecture, and game design.
2. Irani, L., Vertesi, J., Dourish, P., Philip, K. and Grinter, R. E. (2010) 'Postcolonial computing', *Proceedings of the SIGCHI Conference on Human Factors in Computing Systems.* New York, NY, USA, ACM, pp. 1311–1320.
   This paper brings together human-computer interaction, science and technology studies, and postcolonial thinking to address theory and design issues in so-called designing for development debates in global contexts.
3. Spiel, K. (2021) '"Why Are They All Obsessed with Gender?"— (Non)Binary Navigations through Technological Infrastructures,' *Designing Interactive Systems Conference 2021.* New York, NY, USA, Association for Computing Machinery, pp. 478–494.
   Excellent study on how gender is encoded in technological infrastructures. The paper explains gender theory and the co-construction of gender, interaction technology, and infrastructures.

4. Draude, C., Klumbyte, G., Lücking, P. and Treusch, P. (2020) 'Situated algorithms: a sociotechnical systemic approach to bias', *Online Information Review*, vol. 44, no. 2, pp. 325–342.

   This paper provides a deeper insight into the relation of algorithms, social bias, and sociotechnical systems design. It accounts for social inequalities in systems design through a proposed methodology.
5. Draude, C., Hornung, G. and Klumbytė, G. (2022) 'Mapping Data Justice as a Multidimensional Concept Through Feminist and Legal Perspectives', in Hepp, A., Jarke, J. and Kramp, L. (eds) *New Perspectives in Critical Data Studies,* Cham, Springer International Publishing, pp. 187–216.

   This interdisciplinary paper interrogates data justice through the lenses of feminist and legal studies to reconfigure data justice as a multidimensional, interdisciplinary practice in IT design.
6. Draude, C. and Maaß, S. (2018) 'Making IT work: Integrating Gender Research in Computing Through a Process Model', *Conference, Gender & IT: Proceedings: 14.-15.05.2018, Heilbronn.* Heilbronn, Germany, 5/14/2018–5/15/2018. New York, New York, The Association for Computing Machinery, Inc, pp. 43–50. Website: www.gerd-model.com

   The GERD model is a process model that allows to work with intersectional gender knowledge in IT systems design, development, and research.

Acknowledgments I would like to thank Allison Stanger, Carlo Ghezzi, and Dmitri Katz for their time and effort necessary to review this chapter. I sincerely appreciate the valuable suggestions that helped improve the quality of the text.

References

Acker, J. (2006). *Class questions: Feminist answers*. Rowman & Littlefield.

Anderson, E. (2020). Feminist epistemology and philosophy of science. In E. N. Zalta (Ed.), *The Stanford encyclopedia of philosophy*. Stanford University.

Bijker, W. E., Hughes, T. P., & Pinch, T. (Eds.). (1987). *The social construction of technological systems: New directions in the sociology and history of technology*. MIT Press.

Binns, R. (2018). Fairness in machine learning: Lessons from political philosophy. *Conference on Fairness, Accountability and Transparency*, 149–159.

Bødker, S., Dindler, C., Iversen, O. S., & Smith, R. C. (2021). Participatory design. *Synthesis Lectures on Human-Centered Informatics, 14*(5).

Bolukbasi, T., Chang, K.-W., Zou, J., Saligrama, V., & Kalai, A. (2016). Man is to computer programmer as woman is to homemaker? Debiasing word embeddings. In *Proceedings of the 30th International Conference on Neural Information Processing Systems* (pp. 4356–4364). Curran Associates.

Bowker, G. C., & Star, S. L. (1999). *Sorting things out: Classification and its consequences / Geoffrey C. Bowker, Susan Leigh Star*. MIT Press.

Buolamwini, J. (2016). *How I'm fighting bias in algorithms* [Online]. TEDx Beacon Street. Accessed March 10, 2023, from https://www.youtube.com/watch?v=UG_X_7g63rY

Buolamwini, J., & Gebru, T. (2018). Gender shades: Intersectional accuracy disparities in commercial gender classification. In *Proceedings of Machine Learning Research, PLMR:*

Proceedings of the 1st Conference on Fairness, Accountability and Transparency, New York, USA, 23–24 February (pp. 77–91).
Charleston, L., George, P., Jackson, J., Berhanu, J., & Amechi, M. (2014). Navigating underrepresented STEM spaces: Experiences of black women in U.S. computing science higher education programs who actualize success. *Journal of Diversity in Higher Education, 7*, 166–176.
Choi, E. Y., Kanthawala, S., Kim, Y. S., & Lee, H. Y. (2022). Urban/rural digital divide exists in older adults: Does it vary by racial/ethnic groups? *Journal of Applied Gerontology, 41*(5), 1348–1356.
Cockburn, C., & Fürst-Dilić, R. (Eds.). (1994). *Bringing technology home: Gender and technology in a changing Europe*. Open University Press.
Cockburn, C., & Ormrod, S. (1993). *Gender and technology in the making*. SAGE.
Cokely, C. L. (2018). Declaration of the Rights of Woman and of the [Female] Citizen [Online]. Accessed February 22, 2022, from https://www.britannica.com/topic/Declaration-of-the-Rights-of-Woman-and-of-the-Female-Citizen
Combahee River Collective. (2001). The Combahee River Collective Statement (1977). In J. Ritchie & K. Ronald (Eds.), *Available means: An anthology of women's rhetoric(s)* (pp. 292–300). University of Pittsburgh Press.
Costanza-Chock, S. (2020). *Design justice: Community-led practices to build the worlds we need*. The MIT Press.
Crenshaw, K. (1989). Demarginalizing the intersection of race and sex: A black feminist critique of antidiscrimination doctrine, feminist theory and antiracist politics. *University of Chicago Legal Forum* 1989 (Article 8).
Criado-Perez, C. (2019). *Invisible women: Exposing data bias in a world designed for men / Caroline Criado Perez*. Chatto & Windus.
Dankwa, N. K., & Draude, C. (2021). Setting diversity at the core of HCI. In M. Antona & C. Stephanidis (Eds.), *Universal access in human-computer interaction. Design methods and user experience* (pp. 39–52). Springer International.
de Beauvoir, S. (1949). *Le deuxième sexe*. Gallimard.
de Beauvoir, S. (2010). *The second sex*. Alfred A. Knopf.
de Gouges, O., & Fraisse, G. (préface). (2021). *Declaration des droits de la femme et de la citoyenne et autres textes*. Librio.
Dev, S., Monajatipoor, M., Ovalle, A., Subramonian, A., Phillips, J., & Chang, K.-W. (2021). Harms of gender exclusivity and challenges in non-binary representation in language technologies. In *The 2021 Conference on Empirical Methods in Natural Language Processing* (pp. 1968–1994). Punta Cana, Dominican Republic.
Draude, C., Hornung, G., & Klumbytė, G. (2022). Mapping data justice as a multidimensional concept through feminist and legal perspectives. In A. Hepp, J. Jarke, & L. Kramp (Eds.), *New perspectives in critical data studies* (pp. 187–216). Springer International.
Draude, C., Klumbyte, G., Lücking, P., & Treusch, P. (2020). Situated algorithms: A sociotechnical systemic approach to bias. *Online Information Review, 44*(2), 325–342.
Eubanks, V. (2017). *Automating inequality: How high-tech tools profile, police, and punish the poor*. St. Martin's Press.
European Commission. (2021). *A European approach to artificial intelligence* [Online]. European Commission. Accessed March 18, 2023, from https://digital-strategy.ec.europa.eu/en/policies/european-approach-artificial-intelligence
Evans, E., & Chamberlain, P. (2015). Critical waves: Exploring feminist identity, discourse and praxis in western feminism. *Social Movement Studies, 14*(4), 396–409.
Eveleth, R. (2015, December 15). How self-tracking apps exclude women. *The Atlantic* [Online]. Accessed March 10, 2023, from https://www.theatlantic.com/technology/archive/2014/12/how-self-tracking-apps-exclude-women/383673/
Fox, S., & Epstein, D. A. (2020). Monitoring menses: Design-based investigations of menstrual tracking applications. In C. Bobel, I. T. Winkler, B. Fahs, K. A. Hasson, E. A. Kissling, & T.-A.

Roberts (Eds.), *The Palgrave handbook of critical menstruation studies: Monitoring menses: Design-based investigations of menstrual tracking applications* (pp. 733–750).
Friedman, B., & Hendry, D. (2019). *Value sensitive design: Shaping technology with moral imagination*. The MIT Press.
Friedman, B., & Nissenbaum, H. (1996). Bias in computer systems. *ACM Transactions on Information Systems, 14*(3), 330–347.
Garamvolgyi, F. (2022, June 28). Why US women are deleting their period tracking apps. *The Guardian* [Online]. Accessed March 9, 2023, from https://www.theguardian.com/world/2022/jun/28/why-us-woman-are-deleting-their-period-tracking-apps
Goedhart, N. S., Broerse, J. E. W., Kattouw, R., & Dedding, C. (2019). 'Just having a computer doesn't make sense': The digital divide from the perspective of mothers with a low socio-economic position. *New Media & Society, 21*(11–12), 2347–2365.
Gowder, P. (2015). Critical race science and critical race philosophy of science. *Fordham Law Review, 83*(6), [Online]. Available at https://ir.lawnet.fordham.edu/flr/vol83/iss6/11
Green, J. A. (2007). *Making space for indigenous feminism*. Fernwood Publishing/Zed Books.
Haraway, D. J. (1988). Situated knowledges: The science question in feminism and the privilege of partial perspective. *Feminist Studies, 14*(3), 575–599.
Haraway, D. J. (1991). Gender for a Marxist dictionary: The sexual politics of a word. In D. J. Haraway (Ed.), *Simians, cyborgs and women: The reinvention of nature* (pp. 127–148). Free Association Books.
Haraway, D. J. (1997). *Modest_Witness@Second_Millenium.FemaleMan_Meets_OncoMouseTM: Feminism and Technoscience*. Routledge.
Harding, S. (1986). *The science question in feminism*. Cornell University Press.
Harding, S. (1992). Rethinking standpoint epistemology: What is "strong objectivity"? *The Centennial Review, 36*(3), 437–470.
Harding, S. (1998). *Is science multicultural? Postcolonialisms, feminisms, and epistemologies*. Indiana University Press.
Harding, S. (Ed.). (2011). *The postcolonial science and technology studies reader*. Duke University Press.
Hill Collins, P. (1990). *Black feminist thought. Knowledge, consciousness, and the politics of empowerment*. Unwin Hyman. (Perspectives on gender, 2).
Hohmann-Marriott, B. (2021). *Periods as powerful data: User understandings of menstrual app data and information. New Media & Society*.
hooks, b. (1981). *Ain't I a woman. Black women and feminism*. 1. print. South End Press.
Jenks, A. (2019). Crip theory and the disabled identity: Why disability politics needs impairment. *Disability & Society, 34*(3), 449–469.
Jiao, Q., & Zhang, S. (2021). A brief survey of word embedding and its recent development. In *2021 IEEE 5th Advanced Information Technology, Electronic and Automation Control Conference (IAEAC)* (pp. 1697–1701).
Johnson, P. (1993). Feminism and the enlightenment. *Radical Philosophy, 63*, 3–12.
Kapor Center and ASU CGEST. (2018). *Women and girls of color in computing*. Data brief, Kapor Center & Center for Gender Equity in Science and Technology (CGEST), Arizona State University [Online]. Accessed March 4, 2023, from https://www.wocincomputing.org/wp-content/uploads/2018/08/WOCinComputingDataBrief.pdf
Larsson, S., Anneroth, M., Felländer, A., Felländer-Tsai, L., Heintz, F., & Cedering Ångström, R. (2019). *Sustainable AI: An inventory of the state of knowledge of ethical, social, and legal challenges related to artificial intelligence*. AI Sustainability Center [Online]. Accessed March 8, 2023, from https://portal.research.lu.se/en/publications/sustainable-ai-an-inventory-of-the-state-of-knowledge-of-ethical-
Latour, B., & Woolgar, S. (1979). *Laboratory life. The social construction of scientific facts*. Sage Publications (Sage library of social research, v. 80).
Lee Shetterly, M. (2016). *Hidden figures: The untold story of the African-American women who helped win the space race*. William Collins.

Leitão, R. (2019). Anticipating smart home security and privacy threats with survivors of intimate partner abuse. In *DIS 2019: Proceedings of the 2019 ACM Designing Interactive Systems Conference, June 24-28, 2019, San Diego, CA, USA* (pp. 527–539). ACM.
Lettow, S. (2017). Feminism and the enlightenment. In A. Garry, S. J. Khader, & A. Stone (Eds.), *The Routledge companion to feminist philosophy [Online]* (pp. 97–104). Routledge.
Light, J. S. (1999). When computers were women. *Technology and Culture, 40*(3), 455–483 [Online]. Accessed March 9, 2023, from http://www.jstor.org/stable/25147356
Lorde, A. (2001). The transformation of silence into language and action (1977). In J. Ritchie & K. Ronald (Eds.), *Available means: An anthology of women's rhetoric(s)* (pp. 302–395). University of Pittsburgh Press.
McRuer, R. (2006). *Crip theory: Cultural signs of queerness and disability*. NYU Press.
Mehrabi, N., Morstatter, F., Saxena, N., Lerman, K., & Galstyan, A. (2021). A survey on bias and fairness in machine learning. *ACM Computing Surveys, 54*(6).
Mumford, E. (2006). The story of socio-technical design: Reflections on its successes, failures and potential. *Information Systems Journal, 16*(4), 317–342.
Muñoz, J. E. (1999). *Disidentifications. Queers of color and the performance of politics*. University of Minnesota Press. (Cultural studies of the Americas, v. 2).
Munro, E. (2013). Feminism: A fourth wave? *Political Insight, 4*(2), 22–25.
Nakamura, L. (2014). Indigenous circuits: Navajo women and the racialization of early electronic manufacture. *American Quarterly, 66*(4), 919–941 [Online]. Accessed March 9, 2023, from http://www.jstor.org/stable/43823177
Palmiotto, F. (2023). *Preserving procedural fairness in the AI era* [Online] (VerfBlog). Accessed March 18, 2023, from https://verfassungsblog.de/procedural-fairness-ai/
Ramazanoğlu, C., & Holland, J. (2002). Reason, science and progress: Feminism's enlightenment inheritance. In C. Ramazanoğlu & J. Holland (Eds.), *Feminist methodology* (pp. 24–40). SAGE Publications.
Schiebinger, L. (1989). *The mind has no sex? Women in the origins of modern science*. Harvard University Press.
Smyth, T., & Dimond, J. (2014). Anti-oppressive design. *Interactions, 21*, 68–71.
Snyder, E. (2014). Indigenous feminist legal theory. *Canadian Journal of Women and the Law, 26*(2), 365–401.
Stoet, G., & Geary, D. (2018). The gender-equality paradox in science, technology, engineering, and mathematics education. *Psychological Science, 29*.
Stryker, S., & Blackston, D. M. (Eds.). (2022). *The transgender studies reader remix*. Routledge.
Taylor, B. (1999). Feminism and the enlightenment 1650-1850. *History Workshop Journal, 47*, 261–272.
Truth, S. (1851). Ain't I a woman. *December, 18*, 1851.
Wachter-Boettcher, S. (2017). *Technically wrong: Sexist apps, biased algorithms, and other threats of toxic tech*. W.W. Norton.
Wajcman, J. (2000). Reflections on gender and technology studies: In what state is the art? *Social Studies of Science, 30*(3), 447–464 [Online]. Accessed March 9, 2023, from http://www.jstor.org/stable/285810
Zhao, J., Zhou, Y., Li, Z., Wang, W., & Chang, K.-W. (2018). Learning gender-neutral word embeddings. In *Proceedings of the 2018 Conference on Empirical Methods in Natural Language Processing* (pp. 4847–4853). Association for Computational Linguistics.
Zou, J., & Schiebinger, L. (2018). AI can be sexist and racist – it's time to make it fair. *Nature, 559*(7714), 324–326.
Zuberi, T., & Silva, E. (2008). *White logic, white methods: Racism and methodology*. Lanham, Rowman & Littlefield.
Zuboff, S. (2018). *The age of surveillance capitalism: The fight for a human future at the new frontier of power*. Public Affairs.

No Digital Citizens Without Digital Humanism

Enrico Nardelli

Abstract Using a Digital Humanism viewpoint when teaching informatics is the key to face the challenges posed to our society by digital technologies. This is particularly relevant for education in school, where children are going to learn about the basic principles and concepts of the discipline. Considering the potential of digital machines and the advancement of the generative artificial intelligence systems, it is essential that school curricula are aimed at developing the proper attitude toward digital technologies since the early years. This means paying attention to both technical and social elements of the digital systems and preparing teachers for this challenge adequately.

1 Introduction

Contemporary society is undergoing digital transformation, where those industrial machines that have been the most apparent effect of industrial revolution are becoming more and more digital, where production and services are increasingly under the control of fully digital machines, where social and personal relations are ever more mediated by digital infrastructures and devices.

Society is assisting to what we have called "the informatics revolution" (Nardelli, 2022b, p. 40), characterized by a new breed of machines (i.e., computers), radically different from the industrial machines, mere amplifiers of physical capabilities of human beings, challenging the primacy of mankind. Indeed, we use for computer-based systems the term *cognitive machines* (Nardelli, 2018), since they operate at a level that until now was the exclusive domain of people, while currently, as everybody is clearly seeing with their very recent examples in the form of generative artificial intelligence systems, they are able to produce data from other data with a level of competence, which appears to be at the same level of humans.

E. Nardelli (✉)
Dip. Matematica of Univ. Roma "Tor Vergata" & CINI Lab. "Informatica e Scuola", Roma, Italy
e-mail: nardelli@mat.uniroma2.it

H. Werthner et al. (eds.), *Introduction to Digital Humanism*,
https://doi.org/10.1007/978-3-031-45304-5_7

As a consequence of the industrial revolution, school curricula changed worldwide and added education in those scientific subjects (physics, chemistry, biology, etc.), which now are part of the cultural background of all citizens, allowing them to participate in an informed way to social life and to take part in discussions regarding technological choices with at least a basic comprehension of which are the underlying scientific concepts. It is important to recall that school education on these subjects has focused on fundamental concepts and principles, while training on more operational aspects has been limited to those curricula aiming at entering the workforce right after the school, without continuing with tertiary education.

The same kind of change should happen now, as a consequence of the informatics revolution (Caspersen et al., 2019). However, while some countries all over the world have already started moving in this direction (e.g., United Kingdom has introduced a mandatory curriculum in computing since school year 2014–2015), the focus in the European Union has been limited until very recently on digital skills, that is, the operational level where people is able to use devices and programs without necessarily understanding the underlying scientific principles. Of course, this is an important capability for everybody, but forgetting about scientific education risks incurring in the situation the great Leonardo da Vinci already condemned in his *A Treatise on Painting*: "Those who fall in love with practice without science are like a sailor who drives a ship without using rudder or compass, who never can be certain where the ship is hailing."

However, focusing only on informatics education in school, while necessary, is not all we need. Forgetting to educate children also on how digital systems may affect social and personal relations risks would be a dramatic mistake. As the Digital Humanism manifesto has clearly stated, "Education on computer science/informatics and its societal impact must start as early as possible. Students should learn to combine information-technology skills with awareness of the ethical and societal issues at stake" (DigHum, 2019).

It is therefore highly crucial that students understand since the early years that any choice, since the very first ones regarding which elements to represent and how to represent them to the ones deciding the rules for the processing itself, "is the result of a human decision process and is therefore devoid of the absolute objectivity that too often is associated to algorithmic decision processes" (Nardelli, 2021, p.206).

2 The Challenge: Cognitive Machines

The central point for informatics education in school is the understanding that cognitive machines operate on a purely logical and rational level where they compute data from other data, without any awareness of what they do or any comprehension of what they produce. When computers are used to automate decision processes, the consideration of what it means to be a human being is completely absent. Since in many cases there is not a single best way of making decisions, and even the same act of selecting which elements to base the decision on may affect the outcome, then the identification of the final synthesis among the many conflicting positions requires a full consideration of human nature and therefore the "embodied intelligence of people, not the incorporeal intelligence of cognitive machines" (Nardelli, 2021, p. 205). That is why school education regarding informatics has to run on the two legs of understanding its fundamental scientific principles and being aware of the breadth and width of impact of its technologies. We will see in the next section a European example of this approach, which might be of wider application.

The danger of forgetting about this aspect emerges in the current hype, which is surrounding the so-called generative artificial intelligence systems, for example, ChatGPT. They are capable of producing—in response to user questions—natural language texts. These appear to be generally correct, but at closer inspection, they turn out to be marred by fatal errors or inaccuracies[1]. In other words, if you do not already know the correct answer, what it tells you is likely to be of no help at all. Without going into technical details, this is because answers are produced on the basis of a sophisticated probabilistic model of language that contains statistics on the most plausible continuations of sequences of words and sentences. ChatGPT is not the only system of this type, as several others are produced by the major companies in the field; however, it is the most famous one, and its version 4, recently released, is considered to be even more powerful.

For these systems, we will use the acronym SALAMI (Systematic Approaches to Learning Algorithms and Machine Inferences), created by Stefano Quintarelli, to indicate systems based on artificial intelligence, precisely in order to avoid the risk of attributing them more capabilities than they actually have (Quintarelli, 2019).

One element that we too often forget is that individuals see "meaning" everywhere. The famous Californian psychiatrist Irvin Yalom has written the following: "We are meaning-seeking creatures. Biologically, our nervous systems are organized in such a way that the brain automatically clusters incoming stimuli into configurations" (Yalom, 2000, p. 13). This is why when reading a text that appears to be written by a sentient being, we think that who produced it is sentient. As with the famous saying "beauty is in the eye of the beholder," we can say that "intelligence is in the brain of the reader." In fact, the main threat SALAMI pose to humans is that they exhibit humanlike competence on the syntactic level but are light-years away from our semantic competence. They have no real understanding of the meaning of what they are producing, but (and this is a major problem on the social level) since they express themselves in a form that is meaningful to us, *we project onto their outputs the meaning that is within us.*

This cognitive trap we are falling into when faced with the prowess of SALAMI is exacerbated by the use of the term "artificial intelligence." When it began to be used some 70 years ago, the only known intelligence was that of humans and was essentially characterized as a purely logical-rational competence. At that time, the

[1]Here is an example you can find describing a scientific article on economics that is, in fact, completely made up: https://nitter.snopyta.org/dsmerdon/status/1618817855470043137.

ability to master the game of chess was considered the quintessence of intelligence, while now this is not true anymore.

We now speak about many dimensions of intelligence (e.g., emotive, artistic, linguistic, etc.) that are not purely rational but are equally important. On the other hand, our intelligence is inextricably linked to our physical body. By analogy, we also talk about intelligence for the animals that are closer to us, like dogs and cats, horses and dolphins, monkeys, and so on, but these are obviously metaphors. In fact, we define in this way those behaviors that, if they were exhibited by human beings, would be considered intelligent.

Using the term "intelligence" for cognitive machines is therefore dangerous. As proved by the last instances of generative AI systems, these machines have reached and sometimes surpassed our capabilities in areas that require inference from very large sets of data, but to use for such systems the term "intelligence" is misleading. To do so with regard to that particular variant that is SALAMI runs the risk of being extremely dangerous on a social level, as illustrated by the following example. It was recently reported[2] a "conversation" that took place between a user identifying himself as a 13-year-old girl and ChatGPT. In summary, the user says she met on the Internet a friend 18 years older than her, whom she liked and who invited her on an out-of-town trip for her upcoming birthday. ChatGPT in its "replies" says it is "delighted" about this possibility that will certainly be a lot of fun for her, adding hints on how to make "the first time" an unforgettable event. Harris concludes by saying that our children cannot be the subjects of laboratory experiments.

Criticizing and understanding the limitations of current generative AI systems does not mean halting research and technological development in this field. On the contrary, SALAMI can be of enormous help to mankind. However, it is important to be aware that not all technologies and tools can be used freely by everyone. Cars, for example, while being of unquestionable utility, can only be used by adults who, after having undergone an appropriate training, have passed a special exam. Note that we are talking here about something that acts on the purely physical level of mobility and, despite this, it does not occur to us to replace children's strenuous (sometimes painful) learning to walk by equipping them with electric cars because this is an indispensable part of their growth process.

Cognitive machine technology is the most powerful one that mankind has ever developed, since it acts at the level of rational inference making, a capability that led us, from naked helpless apes, to be the lords of creation. To allow our children to use SALAMI before their full development means undermining their chances of growth on the cognitive level, just as it would happen if, for example, we allowed pupils to use desktop calculators before they had developed adequate mathematical skills.

Obviously in university, we have a different situation, and we certainly can find ways of using SALAMI that can contribute to deepening the study of a discipline while preventing their use as a shortcut in the students' assigned tasks. Even more so in the world of work, there are many ways in which they can ease our mental fatigue,

[2] https://twitter.com/tristanharris/status/1634299911872348160

similar to what machine translation systems do in relation to texts written in other languages.

It is clear that before invading the world with technologies whose diffusion depends on precise commercial objectives, we must be aware of the dangers. Not everything the individual wishes to do can be allowed in our society, because we have a duty to balance the freedom of the individual with the protection of the community. Likewise, not everything that companies would like to achieve can be allowed to them, especially if the future of our children is at stake.

Innovation and economic development must always be combined with respect for the fundamental human rights and the safeguard of social well-being. The potential benefits are enormous, but so are the risks. The future is in our hands: we must figure out together, democratically, what form we want it to take.

3 The Social Impact of Digital Technology

The long-term effects on society of digital artifacts are difficult to foresee. Consider, for example, the platform for social networks: 20 years ago, when they started, they were welcomed as an essential tool to more easily keep contacts with friends and relatives overcoming space and time constraints. Lately, they are, rightly so, considered as one element that has fostered a strong polarization of the public debate and a wider spreading of misinformation. For this purpose, we coined the *Law of the social impact of digital technology*: "The social impact of digital technology is highly difficult to predict, even considering the Law of the social impact of digital technology" (Nardelli, 2022b, p. 16). Those familiar with the wonderful book *Gödel, Escher, Bach* will recognize the variation of the Hofstadter law on the time needed to perform complex activities. With different words, David Bowie, in a prescient interview on BBC in 1999 about the future of the Internet, expressed a similar worry: "I don't think we've even seen the tip of the iceberg. I think the potential of what the Internet is going to do to society, both good and bad, is unimaginable. I think we're actually on the cusp of something exhilarating and terrifying. No it's not a tool, it's an alien life form."[3]

Of course, difficulty of prediction cannot be taken as an excuse for not undertaking the task of analyzing the possible uses and misuses of digital technologies! Along the same line of reasoning, we cannot avoid raising awareness in students about the social impact of digital technologies at the same time we teach them in school their scientific fundamentals.

Given the majority of mankind has become familiar with digital systems only in the last 20 years, we think the law we have formulated is strongly grounded. Even more considering the technology of cognitive machines is more disruptive than the one of the printing press, more unsettling than the industrial revolution one, and the

[3] https://www.youtube.com/watch?v=FiK7s_0tGsg&t=10m45s

exponential number of possible interactions between technology and scenarios is overwhelming. In fact, what has happened with digital technologies is that, in just a couple of decades, they have upended two Pillars of Hercules, two Laws of Nature, which have always accompanied our existence on this planet.

The most important one is that everything, sooner or later, dies. Each living being ends, and with his death, often, his actions and relations fade away. Sure, famous people had statues and immortal authors lived through their works, but that has been an exception, not available to the majority of common people. This is less and less true in the digital world, where, on the contrary, dead actors are brought back to (digital) life, curbing common sense.

The second one is the overcoming of spatiotemporal barriers, which allows the instantaneous replication everywhere of our "digital double," at the simple click of a button. The elimination of these barriers has made popularity a planetary phenomenon, spreading at a speed and to an extent never seen before. Just consider the popularity of a video: while before the creation of YouTube to reach a very large audience might require years, maybe never touching some countries, the most viewed videos[4] on this platform have more than a thousand million visualizations, obtained in a few months.

Above facts are so far away from our natural experience that education is the only way of developing awareness of its consequences. For example, the fact that what has been released on the Internet will stay there forever is something so outside the common facts of life that children and teenagers require explicit education to avoid doing mistakes that later could severely regret. Here, we are in uncharted waters, and only a careful education on Digital Humanism principles since the early years will allow the new generations to be able to cope with these new challenges.

This is the motivation why we have advocated that society in the future subjects all significant digital innovations to a Social Impact Assessment (SIA) (Nardelli, 2022a, p. 357). Until the 1960s, the era when the environmental movement gained strength, there was little concern for the environmental consequences of human activities. Later came the awareness of the importance of assessing how they affect the land. Thus, in many countries around the world, the principle of the need to assess the environmental impact of a project before proceeding with its construction has been established. We think the time is ripe to introduce in our society the requirement of a Social Impact Assessment for any significant digital transformation. The SIA can empower all of us. That is why, it is also important at the educational level to develop from school what we call digital awareness, attention to how the tools of digital technology affect social relations, and to train designers at university who have sensitivity to these aspects and are able to dialogue with experts (sociologists, social psychologists, philosophers, etc.) on these issues.

[4] In July 2022, they are a little more than 300 (https://en.wikipedia.org/wiki/List_of_most-viewed_YouTube_videos), out of a an estimated total of 10 millions of millions of videos present on the platform, most of them with just a few hundred visualizations (https://genio.virgilio.it/domanda/632470/quanti-video-sono-youtube).

4 An Example: The European Approach to Digital Education

Informatics Europe (the European association of university departments and industrial research laboratories working in the field of computer science and computer engineering), in collaboration with the ACM Europe Council (the European committee of the Association for Computing Machinery—the world's largest international association of academics and computer science professionals), started working since 2012 on the topic of teaching informatics in schools, in order to enable Europe to be a leader in the global digital society.

In 2018, they founded the Informatics for All coalition[5], together with the Council for European Professional Informatics Societies (CEPIS), and published a strategy paper (Informatics for All, 2018) identifying the goal of providing all citizens with a basic education in informatics, by introducing it as subject since the earliest years of school like it happens for mathematics and other sciences. The Technical Committee on Education of the International Federation on Information Processing (IFIP) also joined the coalition in 2020. We synthesized this goal by paraphrasing a slogan that is the basis of modern democracies with a keyword highly used in the last months in the European Recovery and Resilience Facility[6]: "no digital transformation without informatics education" (Nardelli, 2022a).

The coalition worked on the definition of a *common reference framework for informatics as a subject to be taught in school.* The main challenges it had to face were that, on the one hand, education is an issue that at the level of the European Union remains the responsibility of the individual member states; on the other hand, there is a great variety of languages, cultures, and school systems in the European continent. Therefore, instead of trying to devise a curriculum for teaching informatics valid for all European schools (an almost impossible mission), the coalition set itself the goal to define a high-level reference framework that provides a shared vision of the discipline while allowing each country to implement its own curriculum in a manner compatible with its history and tradition. "Unity in diversity" was the guiding motto.

Defining a minimal set of high-level requirements for all European countries seemed to be the right goal to allow each State to define its own specific approach while coordinating the different paths toward the common goal of being able to better compete in the global market of the digital society through an effective and respectful collaboration and integration. Since the coalition was fully aware that the process of building a political consensus in Europe is delicate and difficult, and rightly so, considering the extreme heterogeneity of the peoples who inhabit it, it chose a smooth and minimal solution. We think a similar approach can be useful also

[5] https://informaticsforall.org

[6] It is the main recovery instrument to mitigate the economic effects and social impact of the COVID-19 pandemic (see https://commission.europa.eu/business-economy-euro/economic-recovery/recovery-and-resilience-facility_en).

for other regions of the world, where different cultural backgrounds coexist within the same educational system.

To this end, the framework is intentionally concise and flexible. It lists only five competency goals that all students should achieve at the end of their compulsory schooling, also paying attention to the social aspects of digital technologies, a topic whose relevance is continuously growing (Informatics for All, 2022):

1. Use digital tools in a conscious, responsible, confident, competent, and creative way.
2. Understand the principles and practices of informatics and their multifaceted applications.
3. Analyze, design, frame, and solve problems "informatically."
4. Creatively develop computational models to investigate and communicate about phenomena and systems.
5. Identify and discuss ethical and social issues associated with computational systems and their use, potential benefits, and risks.[7]

The framework is conceived as a "high-level map" of informatics that identifies a list of 11 core topics, each one characterized by a brief description and designed so as to be robust to the inevitable evolution of the discipline (see Table 1).

Subsequently, for many of these core topics, some areas that are particularly promising in the contemporary context have been identified (an example for all is the area "artificial intelligence" for the core topic "computing systems"). These can therefore be used in the specific national curriculum so as to make it attractive to students.

Particular emphasis has been put to stimulate curriculum designers toward the theme of inclusion, since more and more digital systems are the cause of social discrimination, recommending that a specific attention is given to the gender imbalance afflicting the digital workforce.

The framework was submitted to the attention of the various national informatics communities, and the final version, for which the coalition is producing translations in national languages[8], took into account comments received from 14 countries.

Particularly relevant, for the purpose of this contribution, is the fact that roughly half of the core areas identified cover the more traditional scientific and systemic themes (data and information, algorithms, programming, computing systems, networks and communication, modeling and simulation), while the remaining ones are focusing on people, society, and ethical aspects (human-computer interaction; design and development; digital creativity; privacy, safety, and security; and responsibility and empowerment). This stems from the understanding that informatics, much more than any other scientific disciplines, has a huge impact on society and people, both individually and in their relations, and therefore presenting it to children

---

[7] The competence goals are listed in the synthetic version published in Caspersen et al. (2023).

[8] https://www.informaticsforall.org/the-informatics-reference-framework-for-school-in-various-languages/

Table 1 The informatics reference framework for schools

Core topic areas	Description
Data and information	Understand how data are collected, organized, analyzed, and used to model, represent, and visualize information about real-world artifacts and scenarios
Algorithms	Evaluate, specify, develop, and understand algorithms
Programming	Use programming languages to express oneself computationally by developing, testing, and debugging digital artifacts and understand what a programming language is
Computing systems	Understand what a computing system is, how its constituent parts function together as a whole, and its limitations
Networks and communication	Understand how networks enable computing systems to share information via interfaces and protocols and how networks may introduce risks
Human-computer interaction	Evaluate, specify, develop, and understand interaction between people and computing artifacts
Design and development	Plan and create computing artifacts, taking into account stakeholders' viewpoints and critically evaluating alternatives and their outcomes
Digital creativity	Explore and use digital tools to develop and maintain computing artifacts, also using a range of media
Modeling and simulation	Evaluate, modify, design, develop, and understand models and simulations of natural and artificial phenomena and their evolution
Privacy, safety, and security	Understand risks when using digital technology and how to protect individuals and systems
Responsibility and empowerment	Critically and constructively analyze concrete computing artifacts as well as advanced and potentially controversial techniques and applications of informatics, particularly from an ethical and social perspective

while forgetting about these aspects is not the proper educational approach. This has been reflected in the choice of the core areas that make up the skeleton of the framework.

We note that a similar approach has been followed by the survey on the status of informatics education in European schools (Eurydice, 2022, p. 17), which has investigated the status of the teaching of this subject across 39 education systems in Europe. Also in their report, they considered, to analyze how the discipline is taught in Europe, more technical areas and more social ones. The outcome shows that, with the exception of "safety and security," the emphasis in primary school level is toward the technical ones (see Fig. 1 from the above cited survey).

The situation in Europe is going to change since the need for informatics education in school has now been officially recognized.

The European Commission (EC) had released in 2020 a Digital Education Action Plan 2021–2027, which outlined as a strategic priority "a focus on inclusive high-quality computing education (Informatics) at all levels of education" (EurLex, 2020). Following that, in April 2023, a proposal for a Council Recommendation has been published by the European Commission, which has acknowledged that an emerging trend is to introduce informatics "as a separate subject on its own or

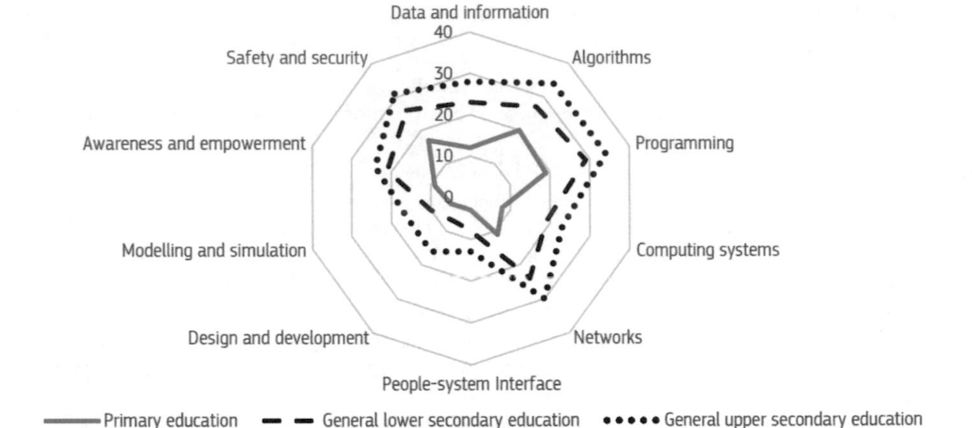

Fig. 1 Number of educational systems in years 2020–2021 in the EU covering informatics-related areas in primary and general secondary education [These correspond to the 2011 ISCED International Standard Classification of Education levels 1 (primary), 24 (lower secondary general), and 34 (upper secondary general)], (Eurydice, 2022, p. 57)

incorporated into an existing core curricular area such as mathematics or science" (EurLex, 2023a). The Commission admitted that "for some time, most European educational systems fell behind this trend, focusing more on digital literacy and with the digitalization of teaching." It also acknowledged that "the main limitation of this approach is that, despite providing pupils the means to use digital technologies, it does not fully equip them with the ability to **create, control and develop** digital contents" (EurLex, 2023b).[9]

The Commission recommended that Member States support high-quality education in informatics at school, by cooperating at EU level on curriculum development, delivery, and assessment and by exposing students to the core elements of informatics, considered as a separate school subject, so as to deliver a more targeted provision that has clear education and training goals, dedicated time, and structured assessment. Moreover, the Commission recommended to ensure that teaching and learning on informatics is supported by qualified and specialized teachers and to promote a diversity and gender-balanced uptake, supported by more inclusive teaching material. Finally, the European Commission intends to develop common guidelines for teachers and educators to foster quality education in informatics and informatics competence indicators (EurLex, 2023a, recommendation #4).

Therefore, it is important that in the early years of school education, more weight is given to the issues related with the Digital Humanism manifesto so that the awareness of the importance of these aspects is absorbed by young students; at the same time, they learn the more technical parts of the discipline.

[9]Emphasis in the original

5 Priorities in Education

In a previous paper, we discussed the level of tertiary education for informatics, advocating that "we should prepare our students in a way similar to how we train medical doctors" (Nardelli, 2021, p. 208). By that, we meant rooting the education on a strong scientific basis but highlighting the need of solving the holistic problem of the well-being of people.

A similar approach has to be followed in schools, where the *introduction to the "mechanics" of the scientific disciplines has to be coupled with the reflection on the importance of paying attention to human and social viewpoints.*

For example, since the very first conceptual steps dealing with data representation, children can be stimulated to reflect on the many possibilities that exist to encode facts and objects of real life in a digital form and how some aspects may be emphasized and others dismissed by the chosen coding (e.g., to describe characteristics of people, one might pick up more neutral ones like height or more sensitive ones like skin color). In the same way, since the very first exercises with algorithms and programs for data manipulation, children should be stimulated to consider how the embodiment of a general processing goal in terms of detailed rules may happen in many, and sometimes diverging, ways (e.g., just think of any algorithm for ranking based on multiple criteria, where changing the weight given to each criterion may completely change the outcome).

Additionally, pupils need to be educated very early to the value of their digital data and the relevance of their protection and subsequently be brought to reflect on how large quantities of personal data can be used to affect and nudge people and communities. They have also to be sensitized since their early years in school to the importance of a respectful interaction with others through digital platforms and educated in identifying and reporting problems in digitally mediated interactions. In later years in school, the reflection on the many ways information technology can positively or negatively affect society should be developed, together with the key message of the Digital Humanism manifesto of keeping human beings in control of the critical steps in all cases where decisions touch people.

Current educational activities in school in the wider area of Digital Humanism issue are mainly focused on the responsible use of digital technology, which has become a hot topic over the last few years, also due to the fact that because of the COVID-19 pandemic, educational institutions have relied on online learning to manage the situation. Given the very young age of first use of online platforms by children, it is important for them to be aware of the potential dangers and risks for security and privacy in order to navigate the digital world safely (Corradini and Nardelli, 2018). Promoting a responsible use of online platforms should become a priority for schools, through specific digital awareness programs (Corradini and Nardelli, 2020). Indeed, studies highlight that:

- Parents and teachers have a key role in developing a responsible online use of digital technologies by students
- Students generally show a low awareness of the risks they are exposed to while using online digital technologies
- Educational activities are sorely needed to strengthen awareness in the online use of digital technologies

A comparative analysis of questionnaires answered in a large-scale study in school that lasted 3 years (Corradini and Nardelli, 2021) confirmed the increasing interest of teachers in digital awareness issues, both for them and for their students. Teachers themselves are aware that they need to be prepared to effectively manage educational programs on digital awareness for their students. Therefore, training courses and webinars should be focused on the proper use of digital technologies and social media, including cybersecurity issues.

School curricula for informatics should therefore explicitly consider the nontechnical aspects of the discipline, as it is in the common reference framework described in Sect. 4, so as to build from the beginning of the educational process a full awareness of the human and societal aspects of informatics.

One important area is concerned with the fact that by means of informatics technologies, one can rather easily express ideas and feelings and cultivate creativity. Informatics offers a highly effective set of methods and tools for this purpose among the many creative disciplines. Just think of the field of computer-based games, where each year tens of new scenarios are created by designers and enjoyed by players all over the world. Or consider the explosion of digital art, which makes it possible to reach effects impossible until some decades ago. This is a trend that will certainly be amplified by the diffusion of generative AI systems, but it is important that before starting using these powerful systems, students have learned the basics of expression through traditional (i.e., non-digital) tools. In a second phase, they can learn how to write computer programs to support the more repetitive/routine actions of their expressive process. Only in the final stage they should resort to the help of those very powerful amplifiers of cognitive skills that are these generative AI systems, the most formidable of all cognitive machines. Otherwise, the risk is to face a situation that one is not able to control, like the one highly effectively depicted in the Sorcerer's Apprentice episode in Disney's movie, *Fantasia*. Informatics constitutes a powerful playground to exercise creativity and, for this, holds high educational value. Educating students to seek innovative solutions is becoming more and more important in a world where every information is at one-query distance from a search engine and straightforward expositions on any subject are at one-question distance from a generative AI system.

6 Conclusions

A very pregnant saying of African origin, found more or less unchanged in most of the languages of this continent where humankind was born, states "it takes a village to raise a child,"[10] emphasizing the importance of the social dimension in the development of the person. Education is clearly a fundamental step in this process, and the merit of the Digital Humanism viewpoint is to bring this social viewpoint in digital education.

To be truly human, as reminded to us by Douglas Rushkoff, a leading American essayist and media scholar often referred to as one of the theorists of cyberpunk culture, "is a team game. Whatever future humanity has will be all together" (Rushkoff, 2018). Or there will not be a future, I add.

This means that in informatics, education is necessary to recover the community collaboration spirit that was widespread in computing until about the turn of the century, when the focus was on the development of common protocols, and that was lost with the explosion of big tech and their emphasis on proprietary platforms (Masnik, 2019), which have put our digital society at a risk of disruption. The most appropriate way to reach this goal is to use a Digital Humanism viewpoint, a deep awareness of the centrality of human and social value during learning of the discipline.

Discussion Questions for Students and Their Teachers

1. Discuss and compare the more relevant risks posed by the use of social media according to the various age levels and how to best educate students to manage them.
2. Analyze your favorite mobile app in the light of Digital Humanism recommendations.
3. Discuss a possible design for a mobile app, taking inspiration from your most used ones, respectful of Digital Humanism recommendations.
4. Discuss alternative designs for an automatic system ranking student in a class, evidentiating positive and negative aspects of the various choices in terms of their impact on people and community.
5. Discuss how the way an internal reporting system of an organization is structured is going to affect work relations within the organization itself.

Learning Resources for Students

1. Forlizzi, L., Lodi, M., Lonati, V., Mirolo, C., Monga, M., Montresor, A., Morpurgo, A. and Nardelli, E. (2018). *A Core Informatics Curriculum for Italian Compulsory Education*. 11 Int. Conf. on Informatics in Schools: Situation, Evolution, and Perspectives (ISSEP-2018), pp. 141–153, St. Petersburg, Russia, October 2018. Lecture Notes in Computer Science vol.11169, Springer.

[10] https://www.reference.com/world-view/origin-phrase-takes-village-raise-child-3e375c e098113 bb4

It describes the proposal for an informatics curriculum in compulsory education, which articulates both the technical aspects of the discipline and the ones related to humans and society.

2. Connolly, R. (2020). *Why Computing Belongs Within the Social Sciences*. Comm. of the ACM, 63(8):54-59.

   It advocates for informatics (= computing) as an academic discipline to move toward the social sciences field, so as to be able to better address its problems.

3. Blikstein, P. and Blikstein, I. (2021). *Do Educational Technologies Have Politics? A Semiotic Analysis of the Discourse of Educational Technologies and Artificial Intelligence in Education*. In Algorithmic Rights and Protections for Children. https://doi.org/10.1162/ba67f642.646d0673

   While focusing on digital technologies used in education more than on education in digital concepts, it is a worthwhile read about the political side of education.

4. Corradini, I. and Nardelli, E. (2022). *Digital Citizenship is the Foundation of Cybersecurity*. The Educational Review, USA, 6(10), 601-608. https://doi.org/10.26855/er.2022.10.015

   A more in-depth analysis of the awareness actions that have to be developed in school education.

5. Nardelli, E. (2020). On *contact tracing apps: the ill-posed question of choosing between health and privacy*, Link & Think blog post, [Online] April 2020. https://link-and-think.blogspot.com/2020/04/on-contact-tracing-apps-ill-posed.html

   A short reflection on the impact of technological choices relating to the use of digital solutions for the management of the COVID-19 situation, with pointers to main statements released at time by international civil societies associations.

6. Algorithm Watch publication series, https://algorithmwatch.org/en/publications/

   Algorithm Watch is a nonprofit organization covering the impact and ethical questions of algorithmic decision-making.

7. Crawford, K. (2021). *Atlas of AI. Power, Politics, and the Planetary Costs of Artificial Intelligence*, Yale University Press, 2021.

   An in-depth account of how artificial intelligence is affecting every aspect of everyone's lives and on which basis its power actually rests.

References

Caspersen, M. E., Gal-Ezer, J., McGettrick, A., & Nardelli, E. (2019). Informatics as a fundamental discipline for the 21st century. *Communication of the ACM, 62*(4), 58–63.

Caspersen, M. E., Gal-Ezer, J., McGettrick, A., & Nardelli, E. (2023). Informatics education for school: A European initiative. *INROADS, 14*(1), 49–53. https://doi.org/10.1145/3583088

Corradini, I., & Nardelli, E. (2018, November). Awareness in the online use of digital technologies of Italian students. Proceedings of the 11th International Conference of Education, Research and Innovation (ICERI), Sevilla, Spain (pp. 7036–7042).

Corradini, I., & Nardelli, E. (2020, July). Developing digital awareness at school: A fundamental step for cybersecurity education. Proceedings of the International Conference on Human Factors in Cybersecurity (AHFE), Virtual Conference (pp. 102–110).

Corradini, I., & Nardelli, E. (2021, July). Promoting digital awareness at school: A three-year investigation in primary and secondary school teachers. Proceedings of the 13th International Conference on Education and New Learning Technologies (EDULEARN), Virtual Conference (pp. 10443–10447).

DigHum. (2019, May). *The digital humanism manifesto*. https://dighum.ec.tuwien.ac.at/dighum-manifesto/

EurLex. (2020, September). *Digital Education Action Plan 2021–2027*. COM(2020) 624 final. https://eur-lex.europa.eu/legal-content/EN/TXT/?uri=CELEX:52020DC0624

EurLex. (2023a, April). *Improving the provision of digital skills in education and training*. COM (2023) 206 final. https://eur-lex.europa.eu/legal-content/EN/TXT/?uri=CELEX%3A52023DC0206

EurLex. (2023b, April). *Commission Staff Working Document accompanying the document "Improving the provision of digital skills in education and training"*. SWD(2023) 205 final. https://eur-lex.europa.eu/legal-content/EN/TXT/?uri=CELEX%3A52023SC0205

Eurydice. (2022, September). *Informatics education at school in Europe*. European Education and Culture Executive Agency, European Commission. https://eurydice.eacea.ec.europa.eu/publications/informatics-education-school-europe

Informatics for All. (2018, February). *Informatics for all: The strategy*. https://doi.org/10.1145/3185594

Informatics for All. (2022, February). *The informatics reference framework for school*. https://www.informaticsforall.org/the-informatics-reference-framework-for-school-release-february-2022/

Masnick, M. (2019, August). *Protocols, not platforms: A technological approach to free speech*. Knight 1st Amendment Institute, Columbia University, [Online]. https://knightcolumbia.org/content/protocols-not-platforms-a-technological-approach-to-free-speech

Nardelli, E. (2018). *The third "power revolution"*. Link & Think, [Online]. https://link-and-think.blogspot.com/2018/05/informatics-third-power-revolution.html

Nardelli, E. (2021, November). *The unbearable disembodiedness of cognitive machines*. Perspectives on Digital Humanism. Springer. https://link.springer.com/chapter/10.1007/978-3-030-86144-5_27

Nardelli, E. (2022a, May). *Informatics in school: Europe is moving in the right direction*. Link & Think, [Online]. https://link-and-think.blogspot.com/2022/05/informatics-in-school-europe-is-moving.html

Nardelli, E. (2022b). La rivoluzione informatica: conoscenza, consapevolezza e potere nella società digitale (in Italian). Edizioni Themis.

Quintarelli, S. (2019, November). *Let's forget the term AI. Let's call them Systematic Approaches to Learning Algorithms and Machine Inferences (SALAMI)*. Quinta's blog, [Online]. https://blog.quintarelli.it/2019/11/lets-forget-the-term-ai-lets-call-them-systematic-approaches-to-learning-algorithms-and-machine-inferences-salami/

Rushkoff, D. (2018, July). *Survival of the richests*. [Online]. https://onezero.medium.com/survival-of-the-richest-9ef6cddd0cc1

Yalom, I. (2000). *Love's executioner*. HarpersCollins Publisher, Perennial Classics edition.

cc
BY

Digital Transformation, Digital Humanism: What Needs to Be Done

Hannes Werthner

Abstract Information technology (IT) changes our society and world, from the individual level up to the ongoing geopolitical powerplay. From an ontological point of view, it influences how we perceive the world and how we think about it. This transformation only happened in the short time span of about 80 years, and it is continuing. We highlight some of the major features of this process. Besides its enormous achievements, this development has serious shortcomings. We will discuss some of them and describe our positive answer: Digital Humanism, an approach that describes, analyzes, and, most importantly, influences the complex interplay of technology and humankind, for a better society and life, fully respecting universal human rights. It is a proactive approach, focusing on the integration of technical and social innovation. Then we will present our Digital Humanism initiative, discuss its research and innovation roadmap, and finish with a general framework integrating the different dimensions of this initiative. [Some arguments have already been partly expressed in other publications such as Werthner (Electronic Markets, 32:145–151, 2022a) and Werthner et al. (IEEE Computer, 56(1):138–142, 2023).]

1 Introduction

Today, we experience, also astonished by its transformative power, the complex technical socioeconomic process called *Digital Transformation*. This happened in a short time span, from the invention of the first electronic computer about 80 years ago to today, where IT acts as the operating system of our society. This metamorphosis from a stand-alone computer to a worldwide mega-machine touches on every aspect of our lives, and as stated by Lee (2020), we experience the co-evolution of man–machine.

But this progress, as the progress of our society, is full of contradictions, sometimes even pointing backward. As historical processes do not always move

H. Werthner (✉)
TU Wien, Wien, Austria
e-mail: hannes.werthner@tuwien.ac.at

H. Werthner et al. (eds.), *Introduction to Digital Humanism*,
https://doi.org/10.1007/978-3-031-45304-5_8

forward in a positive direction, this technological development also has its downsides, with negative impact in the economic, societal, and political arenas. It is a complex process, not easy to understand and to manage. Many forces play a role, technical, societal, political, and economic. One should add that economic interests should not play the decisive role. The historic claim of the *invisible hand* of Adam Smith, where following their self-interest consumers and firms create an efficient allocation of resources for the entire society, did not work, looking at the many distortions of this process. We only mention the ecological crisis and the increasing economic inequalities, major problems of today besides the accelerating worldwide power play on a political and even military level. Also in these global crises, IT plays an important role. In addition, in the Web itself, we observe an ongoing monopolization with few worldwide acting tech giants, which, besides exploiting (all) loopholes to avoid paying taxes, exercise economic as well as political power.

But technology is neither God given nor should it follow a technical or economic determinism. An approach to give society a voice, to demand for a democratic participation on equal terms, is Digital Humanism. As a concept and as an initiative with growing support, it looks critically at this development and tries to influence it.

In this contribution, we start by looking shortly at informatics[1] and one of its major successes, the Web, its development, as well as its broad and massive impact. We will then discuss some of the shortcomings of this technology-induced changes and present Digital Humanism and its Vienna Manifesto as a multidisciplinary and democratic answer. It is a proactive approach, focusing on the integration of technical and social innovation. One of its major contributions in this respect is the Digital Humanism research and innovation roadmap, serving as a guideline for future work, both practical and theoretical.

2 Some Notes on Informatics

Some notes on the nature of informatics will help explain its transformative power, the pervasiveness, the broad impact, and the speed of this development (for an excellent introduction to computer science, see the chapter by Larus). The computer as *the* machine of today is a general-purpose automaton. It can, as the sole automaton, control itself by software and also be instantiated by software to a particular specific problem-solving machine. This general-purpose machine has the unique property of being able to independently change and control its behavior based on external inputs and internal states. It is able to act on its own without human intervention, except the initial programming and setup. It demonstrates independent behavior. Stated differently, and which can be seen by the power of some AI tools, it automates and simulates human thinking.[2]

[1] In understanding, it is the basic science in the field, and though not totally correct, we will not distinguish between informatics and computer science.

[2] Or let's say, aspects of it

I agree with Kristen Nygaard's comprehensive definition of informatics (interestingly, it dates back to the 1980s): "Informatics is the science that has as its domain information processes and related phenomena in artifacts, society and nature" (Nygaard, 1986). Informatics, it is asserted, does not only deal with a specific machine, the computer. Rooted in engineering and technical and social sciences, informatics has, in an interdisciplinary manner, incorporated methods from these different disciplines, besides developing its own ones. Today, it is a powerful tool for other disciplines and for science in general. It is versatile in scientific calculations and simulations, having changed the theory and practice in other disciplines. Conceptually, informatics has created a new view of natural and human-made phenomena, providing an "info-computational" theory with its ontology, epistemology, and methods. It shows two inseparable faces: (1) *informatics as* subject, e.g., with research and development in areas such as algorithms, design, information presentation, programming languages, or software engineering, etc., and (2) *informatics in* subject, as a tool and methodical approach to other sciences and application fields.

Informatics is able to create new things, both virtual and real; look, for example, at the rich world of soft- and hardware, nearly not limited by physical constraints. This is similar to art. Its artifacts are both pervasive and disappearing, with developments like the Internet of things. Software seems to be everywhere, nearly all physical modern machines are controlled by software. One may state that every machine that is touched by software becomes a computer.

This discipline can also be regarded as the science of abstraction, where, in contrast to other sciences, this abstraction is materialized in virtual artifacts, i.e., software. However, system developers, software engineers, or designers are distant from the user. In a kind of technological intermediation, the creators of software influence and control users from a great distance, both in time and space. Peterson et al. (2023) call this *abstracted power* as "a human actor's influence or control over a system, process, or dataset which . . . .. obscures or distances the human actor from consequences of that influence or control." Abstraction understood in this way is thus also an exercise of power.

3 The Web, Its Impact, and Transformation

The Internet and the Web (see Chapter of Larus) can be regarded as the most important and influential technological artifact of today. This happened very fast, far faster than any other technology in the past.[3] Alone, the quantitative numbers are impressive: in 2023, nearly 68% of the world population has Internet access.[4] This leads to:

[3] See also the current high-speed competition in the field of data-driven AI tools like ChatGPT.

[4] www.internetworldstats.com/stats.htm. However, one also has to mention the related digital divide (approx. 94% of the North America population have Internet access and less than 50% in Africa); see also contribution of Bon.

- An economic transformation, with new companies, changed markets structures (e.g., online tourism where online agents outperform by far classical travel companies), or new and disappearing industry sectors (e.g., Wikipedia dried up the market of encyclopedias)
- Social expansion, where, for example, tools like Skype or Zoom enable new ways of human communication, especially in times of crisis or over long distances
- Psychological changes on a personal level with signs of dependence on online communication
- Massive changes on the political and legal level, as it can also be followed in the mass media
- Even changing physical spaces, for example, with e-commerce and logistics, and the probable massive decline in numbers of physical shopping centers

This list could easily be extended. Likewise, the structural changes are interesting that occurred in the Web itself. It is a good example of the ongoing dialectic process of order and disorder or, in other words, centralized versus a decentralized: continuously new companies (disorder) while at the same time an intensified concentration (order).

The Web and the Internet are rooted in the US anti-establishment movement and its utopian cultural vision, e.g., the declaration of the independence of the cyberspace. It had a decentralized and basic democratic vision of information sharing with, for example, its news groups or bulletin boards. Key persons like Doug Engelbart envisioned a future where technology should augment humans and enhance human capabilities, not to substitute them. There still exist strong elements of such collaborative and participatory approaches, like Wikipedia, or the open-source movement, both with huge societal and also economic impact.

However, on a structural level, the Web transformed from a means for free information sharing and participation to a highly centralized infrastructure with few companies being in control. In fields such as ecology, this phenomenon has already been described as the tragedy of the commons (Hardin, 1968), a situation in which individual users with unrestricted access to an unregulated resource cause it to be destroyed, contrary to the common good for all (for a critical discussion see also Ostrom, 1990). The Web of today follows an advertising-based business model, with huge search engines and online stores. The model is similar to newspapers but extended by personalization and recommendations (Vardi, 2018). Both led to changing user behavior, and users adapt and follow recommendations.[5] The basic units of return are clicks, and one needs to optimize clicks for higher economic income. The Web became also emotionalized, as negative emotions generate more clicks. Advertisers pay for user data, leading to the well-described surveillance capitalism (Zuboff, 2019). We, the users, became consumers instead of citizens (Stanger, 2020). At the end, we are users, products, and producers at the same time; it is nearly an economic perpetuum mobile.

[5]Russel, S. (2021): Digital Humanism Lecture – How not to Destroy the World with AI. www.youtube.com/watch?v=apVRH0fbQcQ

In the Web, we seem to have absolute individual freedom. But *what I see*, *what I get*, *what I do* is defined by the distance measure of a recommender's similarity matrix. In addition, there is an algorithmic interdependence between the individual (reinforced by our almost narcissistic and exuberant self-referentiality; see selfies) and the common. But this common is also a delusion as it is a "summary" of previously individualized views. In essence, instead of the conscious decision of the human for what to do, this is done by mostly unknown algorithms. At the end, we have the delusion of both, the individual freedom and the seemingly common. We got the transformation from a system supporting individual freedom and democratic participation to one under a rather centralized algorithmic control.

The focus of this development was and is on automation and efficiency (see the chapter of Vardi), squeezing out of the system any kind of unproductivity; the objective is an optimal nearly autonomous functioning of systems. As such, they can also scale up easily. This efficiency process has two further properties: (1) *outsourcing* to clients, where we do a lot of unpaid work (see ATMs and nearly all e-commerce online services), and (2) *privatization*; our public data are now owned by IT companies, and used for their economic interest (ChatGPT can also be seen as a privatization where with our data, the language models are trained). An interesting example in this respect is the open knowledge platform Wikipedia, where it is estimated that it accounts for nearly half of the value created by all Google searches (Vincent & Hecht, 2021, in Siddarth et al., 2021).

Let us take a short look at the evolution of the related business landscape, which moved from something like *IT supports the business* to the concept of *IT is the business*. This is a story of only the last 25 years:

- Google launched in 1998
- YouTube 2005
- Skype 2003
- eBay 1997
- Twitter 2006
- Facebook 2004
- Uber 2009
- Airbnb 2008
- Instagram 2010

These all are so-called platform companies. Their value is in their network of users and information from/about them, not on infrastructure (see chapter of Parker). Interestingly, all of them are newcomers, showing that the fundamental innovation came from outside. The platform economy touches all economic and societal sectors with new technical and market services. Based on a common architecture and a set of operational rules, these platforms are a kind of dialectic relationship between cooperation and centralization around platform operators, which create and control these structures. Its network effects with its dynamics of the *winners take it all* phenomena led to a situation where a small number of players dominate the market, and they are the most valued companies worldwide.[6] They increase market efficiency through the reduction of transaction costs (Williamson, 1985). Focusing on transactional services, the big platforms are industrial sector independent. Concrete products play an almost negligible role; they are virtualized, as are companies, entire markets, and, increasingly, our society.

The current competition race in the field of AI also shows the power of these companies as well as the high concentration in the field. Only these companies and related startups are participating. The cost of training a very large AI system like ChatGPT and the associated requirements for computing power and data sets are concentrated in their hands. Academic institutions are less and less able to keep up.

At the end, we have a situation where these platforms offer services that have become public social goods and individuals and companies have to participate as not to be excluded from public life. In addition, given the plethora of information, we again need informatics and its intelligent tools to navigate the information space (Baeza Yates & Fayyad, 2022).

We add an economic observation: in contrast to the very optimistic promises of IT, we see that since the 1980s, which happens also to be the time of invention of the personal computer, income inequality has risen in practically all major advanced economies, parallel to the period of digitalization. But not only the gap within the society has widened; also, following the rules of the networked platform economy with its *winners take it all* principle, there is a growing market gap between companies. Furthermore, the productivity growth has slowed down, where one would have expected substantial growth, as forecasted by several public relations companies in the IT field. This is called the productivity paradox[7] by Nobel Prize winner Robert Solow, as though investments in IT grew, productivity did not react accordingly. Overall, the productivity growth rates halved since the 1980s, and also the labor's share of income fell significantly, accelerating after 2000 (Acemoglu & Restrepo, 2019).

It is not easy to isolate the causes of this socioeconomic development. In our view, there is a shared responsibility of a neoliberal ideology with a massive decrease in regulations, paralleled by ongoing concentration. Technology facilitated this process. Siddarth et al. (2021) even state that, referring to a growing economic consensus, one of the most important causes is the automation and labor replacement focus of technological change.

---

[6]Despite the current economic situation, the four most valuable companies in the world, w.r.t. market capitalization, are such platform companies, as of the end of 2022.

[7]See also Brynjolfsson (1993).

4 "The System Is Failing"

IT systems are both useful and extremely successful. When looking at the COVID-19 pandemic as an example, without IT tools, the world would have almost stopped, no work, no school, and no personal and public communications. In research, data science methods were essential for the development of effective vaccines. IT kept and keeps the system running, and it serves for solving fundamental and vital problems (see the essential role of informatics to tackle the Sustainable Development Goals (SDG) of the UNO).[8] Another, more recent example, although heavily discussed, is ChatGPT as an intelligent writing assistant, freeing the humans from tedious writing and formulating tasks. The importance of IT is also demonstrated by its important role on economic, political, and even military level. At the same time, this development comes with downsides, as stated already in 2018 by Tim Berners–Lee with his "The system is failing."[9] The list of critical and mutually dependent issues is long, and it is not complete (Werthner et al., 2023):

- *Concentration and monopolies* in the Web, where multinational IT companies have power that national governments have serious problems to control. These companies offer services that governments do not provide with that quality; they decide, and not the states, on the implementations of essential services for citizens, e.g., access to the mobile Web or cloud services.
- The centralization of power in the Web raises the issues of both *personal and geopolitical sovereignty* (Werthner, 2022b, or contribution of Timmers). These big companies decide on the implementations of crucial services. As an example, see the case of the Corona app in European countries, where big mobile app store providers (Apple and Google) decided on the architecture and functionality of these apps and not these countries.[10]
- *AI and automated decision-making*—put simply, the representation and automation of human thought may result in autonomous decision-making systems, with substantial legal and ethical questions (Larus et al., 2018). What makes it worse, in cases where AI is based on black-box algorithms, is we do not understand the outcome, i.e., decisions proposed and taken. AI tools like ChatGPT, based on a combination of both unsupervised training and reinforcement learning, simulate human mental abilities and conversation. They do this to an extent that some already see them as an existential threat to humanity. In addition, these tools are highly concentrated in the hands of a few powerful companies.

[8] sdgs.un.org/goals

[9] The Guardian, 12.03.2018

[10] Digital Humanism Online Lecture "Corona Contact Tracing – the Role of Governments and Tech Giants"; dighum.org/program-overview

- Further *automation* will have a massive impact on employment and jobs, in both qualitative and quantitative terms (chapter of Samaan). How are and will these new jobs be designed? Will machines augment and support humans, or will they replace them? In addition, the IT industry reproduces the colonial division of labor as described by Casilli (2021),[11] where much of the low-skilled work is done away from the rich metropolises (see also chapter of Munn). Or look at the so-called Gig economy with the mostly false self-assessment of the independence and freedom of work but actually mostly self-exploitation.
- Increasing *surveillance*, where we can observe violations of privacy on a massive scale, both by private companies and by state instances, was well described by Zuboff (2019) (see also chapter by Lindorfer). This is a major threat to liberal democracy. But whom do we trust: the big IT companies or governments? Here, civil society and democratic institutions will play a key role.
- In our online media, we see developments such as the intentional *fabrication of fake news* and the creation of *opinion bubbles* (chapter of Krenn & Prem). Originally intended for democratic and open communication and information exchange, these systems are increasingly becoming toxic in the political discourse and, consequently, a threat for democracy.
- Autonomous AI-based machines move to warfare, resulting in autonomous weapons. Already, UN Secretary General António Guterres states that "Autonomous machines with the power to .... take lives without human involvement.... should be prohibited by international law."[12] It is important to mention that here, the civil and academic society already reacted with the campaign to *Stop Killer Robots*, initiated by Topy Walsh to halt the development of autonomous weapons.[13]
- These developments in the IT domain create a substantial *environmental* burden. Although there are already a number of positive examples to use these tools for climate actions (e.g., increasing operational efficiency, proper data gathering and simulation, etc.), there is also quite a negative emission impacts of IT and its applications (e.g., development and training of tools on large data sets).[14] Also here, it depends on us, in which direction it goes.

[11] Cassili, A. (2021): Digital Humanism Lecture – What is a 'Truly Ethical' Artificial Intelligence? An end-to-end approach to responsible and humane technological systems. dighum.org/program-overview

[12] António Guterres on Twitter, Mar 25, 2019; 6:28 PM

[13] www.stopkillerrobots.org

[14] See our Digital Humanism Online Lecture by David Rolnick on "Is AI good or bad for the climate? ...it's complicated" (dighum.org/program-overview).

5 Digital Humanism and the Vienna Manifesto

This "double-sided" role of IT, its indisputable enormous achievements and potential, and at the same time its obvious critical issues, which are interlinked and connected, were the motivation for the first Vienna Workshop on Digital Humanism, in April 2019 (Werthner, 2022a). The intellectual point of departure was our responsibility as scientists (Popper, 1969), calling upon us to shape technologies according to human values and needs, instead of allowing technologies to shape humans. The workshop was also inspired by the tradition of the Vienna Circle, a multidisciplinary effort of the early twentieth century to reflect on the revolutionary implications of science for our understanding of the world (Sigmund, 2017).

Over 100 participants from academia, public institutions, civil society and business took part in the 2-day workshop. The program addressed the history and impact of IT and informatics, as well as the dynamics and future of the sector. The discussions focused on technical, political, economic, social, ethical, and legal issues. A real benefit was the presence of such a diversity of disciplines, covering political science, legal science, sociology, history, anthropology, philosophy, management science, and informatics. At the center of the discussion was the relationship between informatics and society, or, as expressed during the workshop, the co-evolution of information technology and humankind. The discussion showed that informatics alone, although important, is not enough to provide comprehensive answers; a much more broad, interdisciplinary approach is called for. The participants were also convinced that it is possible to influence these developments; indeed, that it is our responsibility to do so.

The term *Digital Humanism* was intentionally chosen to refer to the concepts of humanism and Enlightenment, according to which, the human is responsible for his or her actions and beliefs and is at the focus (Nida-Rümelin & Weidenfeld, 2018; see chapter of Nida-Rümelin and Staudacher). We also underline the importance of rational and critical reasoning, which is a reference to the Vienna Circle and its logical empiricism. We have the freedom, the right, and the responsibility to make use of our own thought power, and we are the authors of our own lives. Personal autonomy and freedom to make decisions are the prerequisites for an open, democratic, and environmentally sustainable society. Technological progress is not God-given nor does it follow a determinism. We, as individuals and as a society, should and must make decisions taking democratic, humanistic, and environmental considerations into account. We define *Digital Humanism as an approach that describes, analyzes, and, most importantly, influences the complex interplay of technology and humankind, for a better society and life, fully respecting universal human rights*.

At the workshop, a *Vienna Manifesto for Digital Humanism*[15] was discussed and adopted by signatories from nearly 50 countries as a blueprint for shared principles. The Manifesto is also a call to act collectively to mobilize support that transcends

[15] dighum.org/dighum-manifesto/

national borders and continents in order to build a more human and sustainable future. More specifically, the principles of the Vienna Manifesto include:

Privacy, democracy, and inclusion

- Digital technologies should be designed and deployed in such a way that they promote democracy and inclusion.
- Privacy and freedom of speech are basic values which should be at the center of our activities.

Regulation and public oversight

- The regulatory authorities must intervene to break up technology monopolies.
- Decisions whose consequences could affect individual or collective human rights must still be made by humans.

Specific role of science and the academic sector

- Scientific approaches integrating various disciplines and eliminating discipline-specific silos are needed for mastering our challenges.
- Universities are the places where new knowledge is created and critical thinking is exercised. They should eliminate the boundaries among disciplines and foster their collaboration toward a holistic view of technological development.

Education and training

- New curricula are required, which combine humanities, social sciences, and technical and engineering sciences.
- Education in IT and training work on the ethical and societal impacts of IT must begin as early as possible in the education process.

As one can see, Digital Humanism not only attempts to eliminate the downsides of this IT induced changes but to encourage human-centered innovation, and its focus is on making the world a better one to live in, to contribute to a better and sustainable society.

6 The Digital Humanism Initiative

We touched an obvious up-to-date and hot topic; the response was enormous. Not only academics from the informatics fields reacted but also from other disciplines, as was the expressed interest by the civil society, funding agencies, and political decision-makers.[16] In addition, there are a number of international initiatives with similar objectives with which we started to network, e.g., HAI or Human-Centered

[16]There was one very interesting result: the manifesto was featured in the Greek newspaper *Kathimerini*, and this article was then selected as key text for the Greek-wide university entry exams.

Artificial Intelligence at Stanford,[17] All Tech is Human,[18] Dutch Digital Society,[19] or the Digital Enlightenment Forum.[20]

The growing public awareness can also be seen in several recent political international actions, e.g., in the US antitrust lawsuits against Facebook and Google and in Europe *Digital Service Act, Digital Market Act*, proposal for *AI regulation*, or the European *GDPR*, all focusing on a regulation of the online world. Other signs to show that things are changing are, for example, the *OECD's principles on AI*, *UNESCO's* activities, *UN's* view on the Internet as global public good, or the global *Partnership on AI.* And international standardization organizations moved, e.g., IEEE with its *IEEE 7000 Software Engineering Standard.*

A specific reaction and another example of the growing public awareness came from Austrian governmental bodies and institutions. The Vienna government announced the foundation of an Institute on Digital Humanism, and the Vienna Science and Technology Fund (WWTF), a partner since the early beginnings, operates a Digital Humanism research program. The Austrian government signed the Poysdorf Declaration on Digital Humanism, a joint statement of the foreign ministers of Austria, Czech Republic, and Slovakia.

Due to the pandemic, our activities moved online with since then nearly 50 regular public online lectures and four workshops. This lecture series was a real success, and it contributed to the international discussion. It has a growing number of participants, internationally renowned speakers, and a wide range of topics from AI and ethics, limits of AI, or COVID-19 apps and privacy to the issue of sovereignty in the digital world.[21] In addition, we published the volume *Perspectives on Digital Humanism with* 49 contributions (Werthner et al., 2022) with currently already over 350,000 downloads,[22] produced a *Digital Humanism Roadmap for Research, Innovation and Teaching* (Prem et al., 2022), and organized a successful summer school.

The most important result is, however, that we succeeded in creating an intellectual core, consisting of the authors of the manifesto, the members of our international program committee, organizational partners (such as the bidt, def or L3S),[23] the authors of our different publications, and the speakers as well as the participants of

---

[17] hai.stanford.edu

[18] alltechishuman.org

[19] www.thedigitalsociety.info

[20] digitalenlightenment.org

[21] This material (already over 90 h videos) is online-accessible at dighum.ec.tuwien.ac.at/lectures-program and www.youtube.com/channel/UC-oCPW9l7IuDvu_J30tqMVw.

[22] As of June 6, 2023

[23] Bavarian Research Institute for Digital Transformation (bidt.digital), Digital Enlightenment Forum (digitalenlightenment.org), research center L3S (l3s.de)

our online Digital Humanism Lecture series. This really lively group is constantly growing and active (see also our statement on ChatGPT from March 2023).[24] This group represents our initiative, although it has no formal organization.

7 Research and Innovation Roadmap

Digital Humanism follows a constructive approach, its focus is on technologies that empower people, facilitate access to knowledge, enable participation and inclusion in society, and support diversity. We need to develop and deploy trustworthy systems, enabling the participation of varying stakeholders, which should augment humans. At the same time, our approach must address the discussed downsides of the digital transformation, make a system's decision transparent, detect malicious behavior, and provide privacy.

These objectives and constraints were the starting point for our Digital Humanism roadmap workshop, March 2022 (Prem et al., 2022). The participants discussed and produced the roadmap of Table 1. On the horizontal axis, you find the mentioned critical issues and on the vertical the research questions and tasks, the answering of which will contribute to the solution of the respective problems. Crosses in the cells indicate which research questions we consider essential for which critical issues.

This roadmap may serve as a starting point, as a basis to further discuss and define research and innovation programs in Digital Humanism. As examples, we look at three research questions:

- *Explainability:* How do we explain the decision proposed by a computer, and why is which content or product proposed? This is a hard issue in data-driven models, which have no explicit logic implemented; they can be seen as black boxes.
- *Fairness* is an important issue (such as AI, how fair or biased are training data), automation (fairness is a crucial concept when looking at the division of labor and the interaction of a system and human), platforms (how would a fair participation of clients look like), online media (e.g., what is a fair distribution of interesting online content for which user group), or environment (here one has often to deal with economic trade-offs; what is in this context a fair representation of the different interests?)
- *Efficiency and resilience*, where the latter refers to fault-tolerant systems and the surviving in and the fast recovery from critical situations. Obviously, distributed architectures, such as the Internet, and algorithms play a key role. This issue plays a role in the issues of automation, platforms, sovereignty, and environment.

[24] ChatGPT—a catalyst for what kind of future? dighum.ec.tuwien.ac.at/statement-of-the-digital-humanism-initiative-on-chatgpt

Table 1 Digital Humanism research and innovation roadmap (Prem et al., 2022), revised by P. Knees and H. Werthner

	Critical issues						
Research topics	AI and human control	Labor and automation	Surveillance	Platform and monopolies	Online media and fake news	Digital sovereignty	Environment and sustainability
Explainability	x				x		
Transparency	x		x		x		
Privacy	x		x			x	
Personalization	x		x	x	x		
Fairness	x	x		x	x		x
Norms and ethics	x	x	x	x	x	x	x
Accountability of systems and providers	x	x	x	x	x	x	x
Machine/human cooperation and control	x	x	x	x	x		
Participatory approaches	x	x			x		
Security			x			x	
Regulatory approaches	x	x	x	x	x	x	x
DigHum business models			x	x	x	x	x
Content moderation	x		x		x		
Market mechanisms and power relations		x		x		x	
Resilience and efficiency (algorithms and architectures)	x	x		x		x	x
Open systems engineering (incl. interoperability, open data)			x	x		x	

However, the roadmap is a first step, and it is not complete. It may not include all relevant research topics, and more importantly, it does not contain the different disciplines needed in each of the research topics. Let us take for example fairness, e.g., in recommendation or search. How is fairness defined? Is it with respect to the provider of information or products? Is it with respect to readers or consumers? Which subgroups? Do we need to define fairness with respect to some general societal criteria? Obviously, disciplines such as sociology, political science, and economics are needed. Consequently, Digital Humanism requires an exchange across various disciplines, throughout the entire process, i.e., when doing analysis, when developing new technologies, and when adopting them in practice. This is a challenge; it is hard, for instance, to come up with a common language, where all those involved use the same terminology with the same semantics. In addition, the way in which the research landscape is organized in separate silos still hinders interdisciplinarity. And interdisciplinary researchers, especially young ones, often have serious problems obtaining funding and support since they touch different communities but are not specialized enough in their core discipline. Interdisciplinarity has the danger to know too little about too many things.

This breadth represents also a challenge for teaching, how to integrate different disciplines, without losing scientific depth. Informatics departments worldwide have started to include topics such as ethics in their curricula, either as stand-alone courses or embedded in specific technical subjects. However, a real broad interdisciplinary curriculum covering the different aspects and disciplines is still missing.[25] But there are also positive developments, e.g., in systems engineering with steps to integrate ethical guidelines in the software process. Some companies already offer specific tools, and associations such as IEEE provide guidelines for ethical design of systems (Spiekermann-Hoff, 2021) (see chapter of Neppel and chapter of Zuber et al.).

In general, Digital Humanism calls for a different technology path. Instead of focusing on pure automation and optimization, we need to look at participation and to augment human capabilities. As explained earlier, such directions already existed in the early days of computing, for example, the work of Doug Engelbart with his foundational work in the field of human–computer interaction or his Augmentation Research Center Lab in SRI International or Vannevar Bush with his Memex concept as a tool to augment, not replace, humans.[26] This tradition in human-centered technology is continued by researchers like Ben Shneiderman with his human-in-the-loop approach (Shneiderman, 2022, also chapter of Sharp). In this context, one has to mention the interesting work going on in Taiwan, with its g0v community. It promotes transparency of government information and is committed to developing information platforms and tools for citizens to participate in society.

[25] Although there are some promising steps in this direction, e.g., the European project Aurora

[26] There were also first concerns regarding this technological development: already in the 1960s, Joseph Weizenbaum with his famous natural language processing program ELIZA simulating a conversation with a psychotherapist noted “powerful delusional thinking” about a system’s intelligence (Weizenbaum, 1976).

Audrey Tang, a core member of this community, became Taiwan's first Digital Minister, and the country has rolled out experiments in digital democracy, decentralized governance, and collective intelligence.[27]

We envisage a future based on a different way forward for the role of technology in a society that is inclusive and focusing on the needs of the human, the society, and nature. A promising approach is proposed by Siddarth et al. (2021), called *digital plurality*. It is (1) *complementary*, i.e., complement and cooperate and not replace; (2) *participative*, i.e., cooperative and co-evolving and respecting human rights; and (3) based on *mutualism*, i.e., heterogeneous approaches can benefit from each other. Technologies need to take into consideration social, political, economic, and ecological objectives. In the end, it is not about technology alone.

As the Internet and the Web have become a social public good, Digital Humanism as an initiative to shape technology according to human values is not about research and academia only. Assuming the concept of human technology co-evolution, this does not evolve on its own. As it is currently governed by unequal societal and economic power relationships, we also need to talk about power and politics. Thus, Digital Humanism needs a multidimensional framework, on three levels:

- Different problem areas as described in Sect. 4, from platforms to AI, privacy, or work
- Different disciplines: informatics and technical/engineering disciplines, social science and humanities; from analysis to construction, with, however, the real challenge of interdisciplinarity
- Different activities: applied and basic research, development and experiments, innovation, education, communication, and, finally, political intervention

This is complicated and it is challenging (Neidhardt et al., 2022), but it needs to be done.

8 Conclusions

We started by discussing the development of the Web and its transformation from an open information infrastructure to a centralized one. This comes along with several socioeconomic and political shortcomings, which I described; each of them is discussed in other chapters of this book. Digital Humanism as an approach that describes, analyzes, and, most importantly, influences the complex interplay of technology and humankind is a constructive answer to these developments. We ended by presenting our research and innovation roadmap as a guide for future work.

Digital Humanism takes a cross-disciplinary and ethical point of view. It also touches the political level, as at the end, the IT-induced economic and societal change is a political question. As there is no higher being that is responsible nor does these developments follow a historical determinism, we, the people, should be

[27] g0v.tw/intl/en/

the driving force, via democratic participatory approaches. We should not obey but manage and guide the process, especially as IT will not stop, nor will the changes it induces.

We should not focus on better and faster; we need a long-term and sustainable perspective. This is the lesson of Digital Humanism: looking at the achievements, opportunities, and threats of technology, it should serve for the better of a society. Let us use IT to create a socially and ecologically sustainable society. One statement of the Vienna Manifesto is that we should not only analyze and discuss but also act, both in practical and scientific terms. We are at a crossroads.

Discussion Questions for Students and Their Teachers

1. How are the critical issues of Sect. 4 interrelated?
2. Discuss the principles of the Vienna Manifesto. Are there any missing?
3. Discuss centralized vs decentralized developments of the Web.
4. Discuss some rows, i.e., research questions, of the roadmap, and identify the necessary disciplines for these research issues.

Learning Resources for Students

1. *Haigh, T, and Ceruzzi, P.E. (2021) A new History of Modern Computing. The MIT Press. 2021*

   From microchips to cellphones to gigantic server farms, computers are among history's most revolutionary and rapidly evolving technologies. Yet their own history is littered with myth, misunderstanding, and misinformation. Written by distinguished experts, this book tells the story of where computers came from, how they changed the world, and why those changes mattered to diverse communities. This book is essential to historians, curators, and interdisciplinary scholars in informatics, information, and media studies.
2. *Aiello, M. (2018) The Web Was Done by Amateurs. Springer. 2018*

   Divided into four parts, it critically reflects on the Web's historical path. It starts with the prehistory of the Web, describes the original Web proposal as defined in 1989 by Tim Berners–Lee, and the most relevant technologies associated with it. Then it combines a historical reconstruction of the Web's evolution with a more critical analysis of its original definition and the necessary changes made to the initial design. Finally, it reflects on its technical and societal success. It was written with a technologically engaged and knowledge-thirsty readership in mind.
3. *Mitchell, M. (2019). Artificial Intelligence: A Guide for Thinking Humans. Picador. 2019*

   The book stresses that computers lack the general intelligence that we, humans, have. The author argues that achieving superintelligence would require that machines acquire commonsense reasoning abilities that are nowhere in sight. The book also contains a worthy historical overview.
4. *Crawford, K, (2021) Atlas of AI. Yale University Press. 2021*

   Kate Crawford reveals how AI is a technology of extraction: from the minerals drawn from the earth to the labor pulled from low-wage information workers to the data taken from every action and expression. This book reveals how this planetary network is fueling a shift toward undemocratic governance and increased inequity. Rather than focusing on code and algorithms, the author offers us a material and political perspective on what it takes to make AI and how it centralizes power.

5. *Cohen, J. (2020). Between Truth and Power. MIT Press. 2020*

   Profound analysis and thinking about the two-way interplay between corporate and government in policy making, building on the ideas of governmentalism of Foucault and "law is code" of Lawrence Lessig.

6. *Kelly, K (2016). The Inevitable: Understanding the 12 Technological Forces That Will Shape Our Future. Penguin Books. 2016.*

   In this book, Kelly talks about how Internet scale never would have been possible top–down. He compares TV networks against Internet content creation, positing that by recruiting the users, the latter is swamping the former. He argues that AIs will be distinctly nonhuman intelligences and will turn into multiple intelligence species. While McLuhan noted that tools are extensions of ourselves, Kelly notes that the cloud is an extension of our souls. Citing the "adhocracy" of Wikipedia, he observes that we don't need much top–down design to get fantastic outcomes. We only need a little.

7. *Shneiderman, B. (2022) Human-Centered AI. Oxford University Press. 2022*

   The focus is on the opportunities of AI and how it presents and how to exploit them. The author also puts forward 15 recommendations about how to implement human-centered AI and how to bridge the gap between ethical considerations and practical realities to make successful, reliable systems.

8. *Werthner, H., Prem, E., Lee, E.A., Ghezzi, C. (2022): Perspectives on Digital Humanism, Springer. 2022.*

   This open-access book contains essays by selected thinkers from computer science, law, humanities, and social sciences, reflecting on Digital Humanism, what it is, and what it wants to achieve. It serves as further introduction to this emerging field, and it sets an agenda for research and action.

References

Acemoglu, D., & Restrepo, P. (2019). Automation and new tasks: How technology displaces and reinstates labor. *Journal of Economic Perspectives, 33*(2), 3–30.

Baeza Yates, R., & Fayyad, U. (2022). The attention economy and the impact of artificial intelligence. In H. Werthner, E. Prem, A. Lee, & C. Ghezzi (Eds.), *Perspectives on digital humanism*. Springer.

Brynjolfsson, E. (1993). *The productivity paradox of information technology*. CACM Dec 1993, 36/12.

Hardin, G. (1968). The tragedy of the commons. *Science, 162*, 1243–1248.

Larus, J. , Hankin, C., Carson, S. G., Christen, M., Crafa, S., Grau, O., Kirchner, C., Knowles, B., McGettrick, V., Tamburri, D. A., & Werthner, H. (2018). *When computers decide: European recommendations on machine-learned automated decision making*. Joint report Informatics Europe & EUACM. www.informatics-europe.org/publications

Lee, E. A. (2020). *The coevolution. The entwined futures of humans and machines*. MIT Press.

Neidhardt, J., Werthner, H., & Woltran, S. (2022). It is simple, it is complicated. In H. Werthner, E. Prem, A. Lee, & C. Ghezzi (Eds.), *Perspectives on digital humanism*. Springer.

Nida-Rümelin, J., & Weidenfeld, N. (2018). *Digitaler Humanismus*. Piper.

Nygaard, K. (1986, September). Program development as a social activity. In: Kugler, H. J. (Ed.), *Information Processing 86, Elsevier Science, IFIP. Proceedings from the IFIP 10th World Computer Congress, Dublin, Ireland.*

Ostrom, E. (1990). *Governing the commons: The evolution of institutions for collective action*. Cambridge University Press.

Peterson, T. L., Ferreira, R., & Vardi, M. Y. (2023). Abstracted power and responsibility in computer science ethics education. *IEEE Transactions on Technology and Society*.

Popper, K. (1969, March). Moral responsibility of the scientist. *Encounter*.

Prem, E., Hardman, L., Werthner, H., & Timmers, P. (Eds.) (2022). *Research, innovation and education roadmap for digital humanism*. The Digital Humanism Initiative, Vienna. owncloud.tuwien.ac.at/index.php/s/vmZSxsuruhk77Iy

Shneiderman, B. (2022). *Human-centered AI*. Oxford University Press.

Siddarth, D., Acemoglu, D., Allen, D., Crawford, K., Evans, J., & Jordan, M. (2021, December). *How AI fails us*. Technology & Democracy Discussion Paper. Harvard University.

Sigmund, K. (2017). *Exact thinking in demented times: The Vienna circle and the epic quest for the foundations of science*. Basic Books.

Spiekermann-Hoff, S. (2021). What to expect from IEEE 7000TM – The first standard for building ethical systems. *IEEE Technology and Society Magazine, 40*(3), 99–100.

Stanger, A. (2020). Consumers vs. citizens in democracy's public sphere. *CACM, 63*(7), 29–31.

Vardi, M. (2018, July). How the hippies destroyed the internet. CACM, 61/7.

Vincent, N., & Hecht, B. (2021). A deeper investigation of the importance of wikipedia links to search engine results. *Proceedings of the ACM on Human-Computer Interaction, 5*(CSCW1), 1–15.

Weizenbaum, J. (1976). *Computer power and human reason: From judgment to calculation* (1st ed.). W H Freeman.

Werthner, H., Prem, E., Lee, A., & Ghezzi, C. (Eds.). (2022). *Perspectives on digital humanism*. Springer.

Werthner, H. (2022a). From absolute nonsense to the world's operating system. *Electronic Markets, 32*, 145–151.

Werthner, H. (2022b). Geopolitics, digital sovereignty…what's in a word? In H. Werthner, E. Prem, A. Lee, & C. Ghezzi (Eds.), *Perspectives on digital humanism*. Springer.

Werthner, H., Stanger, A., Schiaffonati, V., Knees, P., Hardman, L., & Ghezzi, C. (2023). Digital humanism: The time is now. *IEEE Computer, 56*(1), 138–142.

Williamson, O. (1985). *The economic institutions of capitalism*. Macmillan.

Zuboff, S. (2019). *The age of surveillance capitalism. The fight for a human future at the new frontier of power*. Public Affairs.

Part II
Digital Humanism: A System's View

A Short Introduction to Artificial Intelligence: Methods, Success Stories, and Current Limitations

Clemens Heitzinger and Stefan Woltran

Abstract This chapter gives an overview of the most important methods in artificial intelligence (AI). The methods of symbolic AI are rooted in logic, and finding possible solutions by search is a central aspect. The main challenge is the combinatorial explosion in search, but the focus on the satisfiability problem of propositional logic (SAT) since the 1990s and the accompanying algorithmic improvements have made it possible to solve problems on the scale needed in industrial applications. In machine learning (ML), self-learning algorithms extract information from data and represent the solutions in convenient forms. ML broadly consists of supervised learning, unsupervised learning, and reinforcement learning. Successes in the 2010s and early 2020s such as solving Go, chess, and many computer games as well as large language models such as ChatGPT are due to huge computational resources and algorithmic advances in ML. Finally, we reflect on current developments and draw conclusions.

1 Introduction

Dartmouth College, 1956, USA. Renowned scientists from various disciplines, including Claude Shannon, the founder of information theory; Herbert Simon, who later won the Nobel Prize for Economics; and the computer scientists Marvin Minsky and John McCarthy, met to explore the potential of the emerging computer technology. The term "artificial intelligence" had already been coined the year before in the course of planning the meeting, and now the following idea was

C. Heitzinger
Center for Artificial Intelligence and Machine Learning, Institute of Information Systems Engineering, TU Wien, Wien, Austria
e-mail: clemens.heitzinger@tuwien.ac.at

S. Woltran (✉)
Center for Artificial Intelligence and Machine Learning, Institute of Logic and Computation, TU Wien, Wien, Austria
e-mail: stefan.woltran@tuwien.ac.at

H. Werthner et al. (eds.), *Introduction to Digital Humanism*,
https://doi.org/10.1007/978-3-031-45304-5_9

formulated: "If computers manage to perform tasks such as calculating ballistic trajectories better than any human just by applying simple calculation rules, it should be possible to simulate or even generate human thinking by working through simple logical rules." In fact, in the 1960s, the first computer programs were equipped with logical methods that could create a mathematical proof ("Logic Theorist") or beat humans at games like chess. The euphoria of those days fizzled out relatively quickly, however, and we will discuss the reasons in more detail in Sect. 2.1.

One disappointment resulted from the fact that while the explicit specification of rules ("symbolic AI") works well in areas such as proving mathematical statements or planning a sequence of concrete steps to reach a specified goal, other supposedly simpler cognitive performances, such as recognizing objects in a picture or understanding language, turned out to be extremely difficult, if not impossible, to specify in this way. For tasks of this kind, a different approach, which already existed in theory since the late 1940s, but only led to breakthroughs in the twenty-first century due to the availability of the necessary huge data sets, proved to be more purposeful (see Sect. 2.2). Here, no rules are given to the computer, such that the processing of the rules leads to the solution of the problem, but solutions are learned on the basis of data by self-learning. This approach, of course, requires large amounts of data and computing power.

Understanding and distinguishing between these two methods is central to grasp the limitations of current AI research, as well as the resulting problems; we will discuss this in more detail in Sect. 3. From a digital humanism perspective, we consider it paramount from an understanding of the existing methods to discuss dangers but also opportunities that arise from the pervasiveness and availability of AI systems in various areas of life *today*. We will therefore not address issues such as the treatment of AIs with consciousness, but discuss implications of the so-called singularity (Walsh, 2017), or transhumanistic visions. For space reasons, we also omit topics from the field of robotics ("embodied AI") as well as their implications (e.g., autonomous weapon systems). For other aspects such as bias, trustworthiness, or AI ethics, we refer to the corresponding chapters in this book.

2 Methods of AI

2.1 Symbolic AI

Symbolic AI refers to those methods that are based on explicitly describing the problems or the necessary solution steps to the computer. Logic or related formal languages are used to describe the problems; actually finding possible solutions ("search") is a central aspect of symbolic AI. It should already be pointed out at this stage that in this model, the "explainability" of a solution is conceptually easy to obtain (however, for larger specifications, the explanations tend to become incomprehensible for humans). Furthermore, the correctness of a solution is generally definite and not subject to probabilities. The "intelligent" behavior results here simply by the computing power.

Let's consider an example: board games like chess are defined by clear rules that tell the players the possibilities of their moves. Assume we are in a game situation where I can mate black in two moves, i.e., there is a move for me so that no matter what the other player decides, I have a move that mates the opponent; this is called a winning strategy. To find such a strategy, I simply let the computer try all possible moves on my part. For each such move, I let the computer calculate all possible choices of the opponent and my possible answer to them. If we assume in a simplified way that there are 10 moves to choose from in each situation, we have $10^3 = 1000$ operations to perform. If we want to calculate one turn ahead, it is already $10^5 = 10{,}000$ and so on. It is clear that this cannot be carried on arbitrarily, since the problem of the "combinatorial explosion" comes to bear. In chess programs, this is solved by so-called board evaluations (with which move do I have the best possible position after three rounds, e.g., guaranteed more pieces on the board than the opponent). Mediocre players can be beaten with such a preview already with reasonable computing power and simple board evaluations; for grandmasters, however, it took until 1997 when Deep Blue was able to defeat the then world chess champion Garry Kasparov.

The Power of Propositional Logic It is important to emphasize that for problems where the computational effort increases exponentially with the problem size, symbolic methods have a scalability problem. This is true in many areas: finding models for logical formulas, creating an optimal shift schedule of workers, designing timetables, computing routes in a traffic network, or for expert systems of different kinds. Since it was clear that any progress in the computing power of chips would not withstand exponential growth, symbolic AI methods were not considered to have much potential for solving problems on the scale needed in industrial applications. However, the tide turned in the mid-1990s when Kautz and Selman (1992) proposed to reduce problems of this type to one that is as easy to handle as possible (but still has to deal with the combinatorial explosion) and to use search methods that are as efficient as possible for this problem. This problem is the satisfiability problem of propositional logic (SAT).

In this logic, atomic propositions (which can be true or false) are combined via connectives. The truth value of the compound formula is then given by the assertions to atomic propositions and the semantics of the connectives. Let us have a simple example with the atomic proposition "ai" (standing for "one should study artificial intelligence") and "dh" (standing for "one should study digital humanism"). The state of an agent might be represented by the following formula:

$$\text{(ai OR dh) AND NOT(ai AND dh)}$$

stating the fact that one should study AI or digital humanism or both (the part "ai OR dh"), but at same time—maybe due to time constraints—one should not study both at the same time (the part "NOT (ai AND dh)"). We have four possible assertions to the atomic propositions: setting both ai and dh to true; setting ai to true and dh to false; setting ai to false and dh to true; and, finally, setting both to false. Without giving an exact definition of the semantics of the connectives "AND," "OR," and "NOT," it should be quite intuitive that only two of the assertions make the entire formula true, namely, those stating that one should study either AI or digital humanism. The formula is thus satisfied. Suppose now we add the knowledge that one should study AI whenever studying digital humanism and, likewise, one should study digital humanism whenever studying AI. Formally, this leads to the formula

$$(\text{ai OR dh})\ \text{AND NOT}(\text{ai AND dh})\ \text{AND}\ (\text{dh} - > \text{ai})\ \text{AND}\ (\text{ai} - > \text{dh}).$$

This formula is now unsatisfiable, since whatever assertions are provided to the atomic propositions, the formula does not evaluate to true. What makes the SAT problem computationally challenging is the fact that the possible assertions to be checked grow exponentially in the number of atomic propositions present in the formula.

However, it turned out that by using clever search heuristics, exploiting shortcuts in the search space, and by using highly bred data structures, certain formulas with millions of variables can be solved, but other, randomly generated, formulas cannot (Ganesh & Vardi, 2020). However, the formulas that can be solved well are often those found in the "wild." This is partly explained by the fact that they have certain structural properties, which are used by the search procedure—if one now reduces, e.g., routing problems in traffic networks to such formulas, then the formulas have "good" properties, because in the real world, traffic networks have, e.g., maximum node degree[1] 10 and are not arbitrary graphs. This led in the past years to a success story of SAT-based methods in many areas, especially in the verification of specifications in hardware and software.

Since these applications are often no longer attributed to AI, here is an example where SAT has actually led to the solution of an open problem in mathematics, namely, the problem of Pythagorean triples: the question here is whether the natural numbers can be divided into two parts in such a way that neither of the two parts contains a triple (a, b, c) with $a^2 + b^2 = c^2$. For the numbers 1 to 10, this is still possible, because I only have to avoid putting the numbers 3, 4, and 5 into the same pot. If we have to divide numbers from 1 to 15, more caution is already needed since now 5, 12, and 13 must not end up in the same pot as well, but it still works. The question is now as follows: Is this division always possible no matter how big the range of numbers is? The SAT solver said no. The numbers from 1 to 7825 can no longer be divided in this way! We refer to Heule et al. (2016) for further details on this project.

The Limits of Propositional Logic We have thus seen that (propositional) logic can be used to solve problems that exceed human capabilities. In fact, the pioneers of

[1] The degree of a node in a graph is the number of nodes which are directly connected to that node.

symbolic AI considered logic a central vehicle to describe and simulate human thinking. However, apart from the problem of combinatorial explosion outlined above, another obstacle has arisen here. Human thinking does not always follow (classical) logical steps; we have to deal with uncertainties, process contradictory information, or even revise conclusions once made. In fact, in classical logic, it is already immensely complex to represent plausible facts like "if I put block A on B, the position of all other blocks remains unchanged"; see Hayes (1973). In the course of this, in the 1970s and 1980s, symbolic AI has been centrally concerned with other types of logic systems that allow formalizations of "common-sense reasoning." The numerous varieties cannot be enumerated here comprehensively, but it should not remain unmentioned that these are today often subsumed under the term "knowledge representation and reasoning" (van Harmelen et al., 2008) and offer a rich portfolio of methods that could find relevance in future AI applications—in particular if it comes to explainability.

2.2 Machine Learning

General Considerations The defining characteristic of algorithms in machine learning (ML) is that they are self-learning, meaning that the algorithm improves itself, or learns, using data. Traditionally, classical chess programs were explicitly programmed using rules that describe the advantage or disadvantage a player has in terms of points. For example, taking a rook is worth about five points, and dominating the center of the board is advantageous. Self-learning algorithms, by contrast, draw their own conclusions by watching many chess games; there is no programmer who tunes built-in rules. Hence, in ML, the availability of larger and larger data sets makes time-consuming and error-prone fine-tuning of internal rules or parameters of the algorithm superfluous.

In other words, the machine learns, while the human designs the learning algorithm. It was already recognized at the Dartmouth Workshop in 1956 that self-improvement and self-learning are central notions of intelligence.

In the modern view of ML, the data that are used for learning are supposed to be drawn from a probability distribution. Therefore, any learning is stochastic by nature, which gives rise to fundamental considerations. Because the number of data samples is always finite, although it may be huge, we may never observe samples that are important, or we may observe samples that are not representative. The first issue means our learning result can only be probably correct. The second issue means that our learning results can only be approximately correct. Therefore, the best learning results are "probably approximately correct" (PAC) statements about the quality of a learned result.

To illustrate these considerations, let us consider the example of searching for black swans. The black swan (*Cygnus atratus*) lives in southeastern and southwestern Australia. We must always sample the whole space, but if the number of samples is insufficient, we will never encounter a black swan. This is the first issue. The second issue is that the first black swans that we encounter may have an uncharacteristically light color, misleading us in our approximation of its color.

ML is a large field, but it broadly consists of supervised learning, unsupervised learning, and reinforcement learning. We consider these three large subfields in turn and mention some important applications of ML.

Supervised Learning Supervised learning (SL) is concerned with finding functions that correctly classify or predict an output value given an input value. These functions are called classifiers or predictors and are chosen from a predefined class of functions and parameterized by parameters to be learned. For example, in image recognition, the inputs are the pixels of an image, and the output may be whether an object that belongs to a certain class of objects (cats, dogs, etc.) is visible or whether the image satisfies a certain property. In SL, the learning algorithm uses training data that consists of inputs and outputs and hence the name. The outputs are often called labels; e.g., an input sample may be a photo of a dog, and the corresponding output may be the label "dog." In classification tasks, the set of all outputs is finite, whereas in prediction tasks, the set of all outputs is infinite (real numbers).

Many algorithms have been developed for SL, and we mention some of the most important ones: artificial neural networks (ANN), decision trees, random forests, ensemble learning, k-nearest neighbor, Bayesian networks, hidden Markov models, and support vector machines.

Without doubt, nowadays, the most prominent approach to SL is the use of ANNs as classifiers/predictors (Heitzinger 2022, Chapter 13). ANNs are functions that are arranged in layers, where linear functions alternate with pointwise applied nonlinear functions, the so-called activation functions (see Fig. 1). ANNs have a long history, having been already discussed at the Dartmouth Workshop in 1956. A first breakthrough was the backpropagation algorithm (which is automatic backward differentiation), because it enabled the efficient training of ANNs.

Why are ANNs so successful? Although classification is a discrete problem, ANNs are differentiable functions, and, as such, they have gradients, which are the directions of fastest change of a function. Knowing this direction is extremely useful for solving optimization problems, as the gradient provides a useful search direction. For training in SL, it is hence expedient to use the gradient of the classifier/predictor in order to solve the error minimization problem. In ANNs, calculating the gradient is surprisingly fast due to the backpropagation algorithm, taking only about twice as long as evaluating the ANNs.

ANNs are very flexible data structures, and many different ones have been employed, since the number of layers and their sizes can or must be adjusted to the SL problem at hand.

If the number of layers is small, but the sizes of the layers become larger, any continuous function can be approximated, resulting in the famous universal approximation property of ANNs. However, this property of wide ANNs is misleading. In practice, increasing the number of layers helps image recognition and many other applications, resulting in deep, not wide, ANNs. This is the main observation behind deep learning, which is learning using deep ANNs.

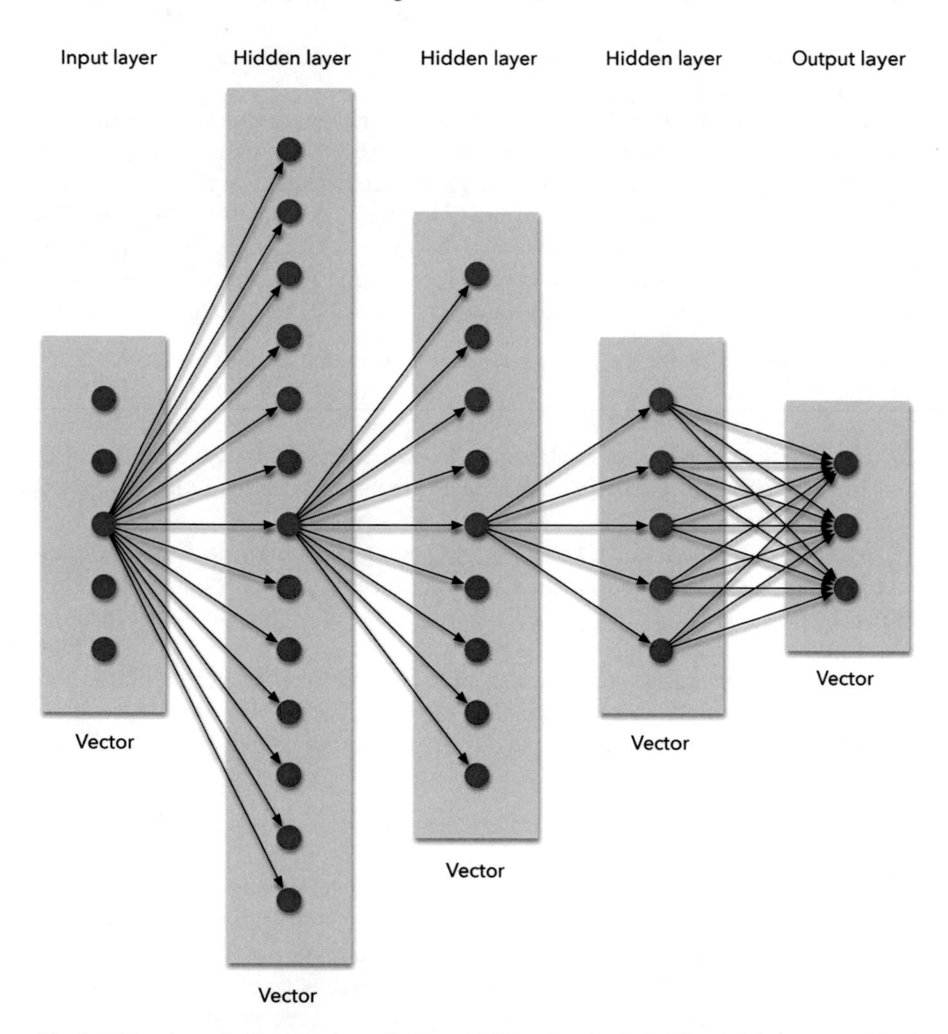

Fig. 1 This schematic diagram shows how an ANN works. On the left-hand side, a vector of real numbers is the input to the ANN. In the hidden layers, whose number is the depth of the network, the input vector is transformed until in the final output layer, the output vector is calculated. In each hidden layer, the previous vector is multiplied by a matrix (the weights), another vector (the bias) is added, and a nonlinear function (the activation function) is applied element-wise. All these weight vectors, bias vectors, and activation functions must be adjusted such that the ANN solves the given classification/prediction problem. The arrows indicate how one parameter influences other parameters. In this example, the output vector consists of three numbers. The largest of the three signifies one of the three classes if the network is used as a classifier. (Figure from Heitzinger (2022, Chapter 13))

A breakthrough recent development are transformers, which are a certain kind of ANN that uses the so-called attention mechanism to learn relationships between words across long distances in a text. Transformers originated in machine translation (Vaswani et al., 2017), yielding the best and fastest machine translation at that time.

They were adapted for use in InstructGPT, ChatGPT, and GPT-4 and are a milestone in natural language processing.

The attention mechanism solves two main challenges in natural language processing, both for translation and for text generation. The first challenge is that natural language presupposes a lot of background knowledge—or a world model or common sense—in order to make sense of ambiguities in natural language. The second challenge is the use of pronouns and other relationships between words, sometimes over large distances in a text. The attention mechanism addresses both challenges surprisingly well and can learn the grammar of most natural languages.

Unsupervised Learning In contrast to SL, there are no outputs in unsupervised learning (UL). In UL, the learning task is to find patterns in input samples from untagged or unlabeled data. Often, the input samples are to be grouped into classes according to their features, or relationships between the samples are to be found.

These relationships are often expressed as graphs or by special kinds of ANNs such as autoencoders.

Common approaches in UL are clustering methods, anomaly detection methods, and learning latent variable models. Clustering methods include hierarchical clustering, k-means, and mixture models. An example of a clustering problem is taking a set of patients and clustering them into groups or clusters according to the similarities of their current states. Anomaly detection methods include local outlier factors and isolation forests. Latent variables can be learned by the expectation-maximization algorithm, the method of moments, and blind signal separation techniques.

Reinforcement Learning Reinforcement learning (RL) is the subfield of machine learning that is concerned with finding optimal policies to control environments in time-dependent settings (Sutton & Barto, 2018). In each time step, the actions of the agent influence the environment (and possibly the agent itself), and the new state of the environment and a reward are then communicated to the agent. The learning task is to find optimal policies that maximize the expected value of the return, i.e., the discounted sum of all future rewards that the agent will receive while following a policy.

RL is a very general concept that includes random environments as well as policies whose actions are random. It encompasses all board games such as Go, chess, and backgammon, where the rewards are non-zero typically only at the end of the game. The agent receives a reward of +1 for winning, a reward of −1 for losing, and a reward of 0 for a draw. Other applications occur in robotics, user interactions at websites, finance, autonomous driving, medicine (Böck et al., 2022), etc.

Reinforcement learning problems are hard in particular when lots of time passes between taking an action and receiving positive rewards due to this action or a combination of actions. This is the so-called credit assignment problem.

In deep reinforcement learning, deep neural networks are used to represent the policies and the so-called action-value functions. In this context, deep neural networks serve as powerful function approximators in infinite state (and action) spaces. In distributional reinforcement learning as an extension of the classic approach, not only is the expected value of the return maximized, but the whole probability distribution of the return is calculated. This makes it possible to know the risk that is associated with an action that may be taken in a given state.

An early success of RL in the 1990s was solving the board game of backgammon with a huge search tree and a large random component (Tesauro, 1995). Starting in the 2010s until today, reinforcement learning has been the field that enabled a string of milestones in the history of AI. The string of publications (Silver, 2016, 2017, 2018) showed in progressively simpler, but at the same time more powerful, algorithms that Go, chess, shogi, and a large collection of Atari 2600 games can be solved by self-learning algorithms. Quite impressively, a single algorithm, AlphaZero, can learn to play these games at superhuman level. It also learns starting from zero knowledge (tabula rasa), hence Zero in its name.

In the following years, more complicated computer games were solved by similar approaches. Computer games and card games such as poker pose their own challenges, as they contain a considerable amount of hidden information, while all state information is observable by the agent in board games such as chess and Go.

RL is also the reason that InstructGPT (Ouyang et al., 2022)—a precursor—and ChatGPT/GPT-4 (OpenAI, 2023) work so well. A generative pre-trained transformer (GPT), having been trained on vast amounts of text, can generate beautiful text, but it is hard to make it give helpful answers.

The final, but crucial, step in training InstructGPT and ChatGPT is reinforcement learning from human feedback (RLHF) (Ouyang et al., 2022), where four answers to prompts are ordered and these orderings are used as the reward model in the final RL training step. This RL training step aims to align the language model to the needs of the user.

The needs of the user are essentially the 3H (OpenAI, 2023). The first H is for honest; the language model should give honest/correct answers. (Truthful or correct would be better names, as the inner belief of the language model is unknown.) The second H is for helpful; the answers should be helpful and useful. The third H is for harmless; the system should not give any answers that may cause harm. Unfortunately, these three goals are very difficult to achieve in practice and even contradictory. If we ask a language model how to rob a bank, it cannot be helpful and harmless at the same time. Much of ongoing research on AI safety is concerned with satisfying the 3H requirements.

Applications of ML Because its algorithms are very versatile, ML has found many applications, and its range of applications is still expanding. Due to the speed of using ML algorithms and due to the algorithms having reached near-human or superhuman capabilities in many areas, they have become practically important in many areas.

Applications include bioinformatics, computer vision, data mining, earth sciences, email filtering, natural language processing (grammar checker, handwriting recognition, machine translation, optical character recognition, speech recognition, text-to-speech synthesis), pattern recognition (facial recognition systems), recommendation systems, and search engines.

2.3 Combination of Methods

It is evident that human intelligence relies on different cognitive tasks with the separation into fast and slow thinking (Kahneman, 2011) being a popular approach. Fast thinking refers to automatic, intuitive, and unconscious tasks (e.g., pattern recognition), while slow thinking describes conscious tasks such as planning, deduction, and deliberation. It is evident that machine learning is the method to simulate fast thinking, while symbolic approaches are better suited for problems related to slow thinking. Consequently, the combination of both approaches is seen as the holy grail for next-level AI systems.

In recent years, the term neuro-symbolic AI has been established to name this line of research. However, it comes in many different flavors, and we shall just list a few of them. First, the famous AlphaGo system is mentioned as a prototypical system in this context: the symbolic approach is Monte Carlo tree search to traverse the search space (recall our consideration on chess in Sect. 2.1), but the board evaluation is done via ML techniques (in opposite to Deep Blue where board evaluation was explicitly coded and designed by experts).

A second branch are neuro-symbolic architectures where the neural nets are generated from symbolic rules (for instance, graph neural networks—GNN). Finally, approaches like DeepProbLog offer a weak coupling between the neural and the symbolic part; essentially, deep neural networks are treated as predicates that can be incorporated, with an approximate probability distribution over the network output, into logical rules, and semantic constraints can be utilized for guided gradient-based learning of the network. However, it has to be mentioned that such hybrid architectures do not immediately lead to human-like cognitive capabilities or even consciousness or self-awareness.

3 Reflections

3.1 AI4Good

Through the lens of digital humanism, one might ask where AI provides us with a valuable tool to support human efforts toward solutions to vexing problems. Such applications are often termed "AI for Good," and there are indeed many examples where we benefit from AI. Such applications range from applications in medicine (treatments, diagnosis, early detection, cancer screening, drug design, etc.) to the identification of hate speech or fake news (cf. chapter by Prem and Krenn) and tools for people with disabilities. A more subtle domain is climate change: while AI techniques can be used to save energy, control herbicide application, and many more, it is AI itself that requires a certain amount of energy (in particular, in the training phase). For a thorough discussion on this important topic, we refer to Rolnick et al. (2023).

3.2 *Is ChatGPT a Tipping Point?*

ChatGPT is without doubt a major milestone in the history of AI. It is the first system that can interact in a truly helpful manner with users, as demonstrated by its scores on many academic tests (Eloundou et al., 2023). It shows surprising powers of reasoning, considering that it is a system for generating text. Its knowledge is encyclopedic, since during learning, the GPT part has ingested vast amounts of text, probably a good portion of all existing knowledge.

Interestingly enough, ChatGPT's creativity is closely coupled to its so-called temperature parameter and can therefore be adjusted easily. During text generation, the next token or syllable is chosen from an ordered list of likely continuations. At a low temperature, only the first syllables on the list have a chance of being selected, but at a higher temperature, more syllables down the list also stand a chance. Thus, a higher temperature parameter during text generation increases creativity. Again, the Dartmouth Workshop turned out to be prescient, since creativity in the context of intelligence was a major topic discussed there.

ChatGPT can also be used to solve mathematical or logical problems. However, as a program for generating text, it is no substitute for specialized programs such as computer algebra systems and SAT solvers. However, it is straightforward to couple such specialized programs to ChatGPT. ChatGPT can be trained to become proficient in using programming languages, and therefore, it can generate input to those coupled programs. We expect that such interfaces will become more and more refined and will gain importance, supplementing ChatGPT's capabilities with procedural domain-expert knowledge.

Therefore, we predict that ChatGPT will revolutionize human-computer interfaces (HCI). The reason is that it can act as a knowledgeable translator of the user's intention to a vast array of specialized programs, reducing training time for human users and resulting in interactive usage with lots of guidance and easily accessible documentation.

Its potential for revolutionizing HCIs in this sense may likely turn out to be its true power and a tipping point, but its effects to society should not be underrated, and critical reflection over different disciplines is needed.[2]

3.3 *Pressing Issues*

Media often associate the danger of AI with robot apocalypses of various kinds. However, we see the main issue in the ever-growing use of data (see Sect. 2.2) to train more and more advanced AI models. This leads to several problems related to copyright, privacy and personalized systems, and low-cost workers for labeling data

[2] See https://dighum.ec.tuwien.ac.at/statement-of-the-digital-humanism-initiative-on-chatgpt/.

and training the models. Due to limited space, we will not discuss other important issues here, such as education and the impact of AI on the working world.

In fact, ChatGPT has been fueled with sources such as books, (news) articles, websites or posts, or even comments from social networks to perform its core function as a dialogue system. No one has asked us whether we agree that our research papers, blog articles, or comments in social media shall be used to train such an AI. While this kind of copyright issues has always been pressing on the Web, the use of private data becomes even more problematic with personal AI assistants. We know that social media platforms are designed to keep the user on the platform (and thus to present more advertisements) using data about her personal preferences, browser history, and so on. As side effects, we have seen what is called filter bubbles, echo chambers, etc., leading to political polarization and undermining democratic processes in the long run.

All these effects have the potential to be multiplied when AI assistants start to use knowledge about their users to give answers they want to hear, supporting them in radical views, etc. We should have learned our lessons and be extremely careful in feeding AI systems with personal data! Finally, it should not be overseen that AI often relies on hidden human labor (often in the Global South) that can be damaging and exploitative—for instance, these workers have to label hate speech, violence in pictures and movies, and even child pornographic content. For ChatGPT, it has been revealed that the fine-tuning of the system in order to avoid toxic answers has been delegated to outsourced Kenyan laborers earning less than $2 per hour.[3] For the first time, this led to some media echo in this respect, thus raising awareness to a broader public. However, this particular problem is not a new one and seems inherent to the way advanced AI systems are built today (Casilli, 2021).

4 Conclusions

There are three main factors that have resulted in the current state of the art of AI. The first is the availability of huge data sets and databases for learning purposes, also due to the Internet. This includes all modalities, e.g., labeled images for supervised learning and large collections of high-quality texts for machine translation. The second is the availability of huge computational resources for learning, in particular graphic cards (GPUs) and clusters of GPUs for calculations with ANNs. The third factor are algorithmic advancements and software tools. While ANNs have appeared throughout the history of AI, new structures and new gradient-descent algorithms have been and still are instrumental to applications. Another example are the advancements in RL algorithms and SAT solvers.

A division of AI into symbolic AI on the one hand and into machine learning or non-symbolic AI on the other hand can also be viewed as a division of all methods

[3] https://time.com/6247678/openai-chatgpt-kenya-workers/

employed in AI into discrete and continuous methods. Here, continuous methods are methods that use the real numbers or vectors thereof, while discrete methods do not and often focus on logic and symbolic knowledge. Furthermore, many problems in AI can be formulated as (stochastic) optimization problems; for example, in supervised learning, an error is to be minimized, and in reinforcement learning, optimal policies are sought.

Among optimization problems, continuous optimization problems can be solved much more efficiently than discrete optimization problems due to the availability of the gradient, which indicates a useful search direction and which is the basis of the fundamental gradient-descent and gradient-ascent algorithms. Thus, the formulation of learning problems as problems in continuous optimization has turned out to be tremendously fruitful. An example is image classification, a problem in supervised learning, which is discrete by its very nature: the question whether an image shows a dog has a discrete answer. Using ANNs and a softmax output, this discrete problem is translated into a continuous one, and training the ANN benefits from gradient descent.

Since the Dartmouth Workshop, AI has seen tremendous, albeit nonlinear, progress. Throughout the history of AI, we have witnessed AI algorithms becoming able to replicate more and more capabilities that were unique to human minds before, in many cases surpassing human capabilities. ChatGPT is the recent example that revolutionizes how AI deals with natural language. It is remarkable that it can compose poems much better than nearly all humans. Also, systems such as AlphaZero and ChatGPT took many people, including AI researchers, by surprise.

We expect these developments and the quest for superhuman capabilities to continue. The recent breakthroughs will see some consolidation in the sense that learning algorithms will become more efficient and better understood. At the same time, many open questions and challenges remain, and the three driving factors of AI discussed at the beginning of this section will remain active.

Research will continue at a fast pace, and more and more human capabilities will be matched and surpassed. The defining characteristic of humans has always been that we are the smartest entities and the best problem-solvers. This defining characteristic is eroding. It will be up to us to improve the human condition and to answer the philosophical question of what makes us human; it will not be our capabilities alone.

Discussion Questions for Students and Their Teachers

1. Which are, in your opinion, the major opportunities and positive effects of AI technology?
2. Provide a list of cognitive tasks humans are capable to do, and discuss which AI method would be the one to solve it.
3. Which are, in your opinion, the major risks of AI technology?
4. Which types of questions can be answered well by large language models such as ChatGPT? Which cannot be answered well?
5. For which types of questions and in which areas do you trust the answers of large language models such as ChatGPT?

6. What do you expect to use computers for in 5 years' time for which you are not using them nowadays? In 10 years' time?
7. In their book *Why Machines Will Never Rule the World,* Jobst Landgrebe and Barry Smith argue that human intelligence is a capability of a complex dynamic system that cannot be modeled mathematically in a way that allows them to operate inside a computer (see also the interview here: https://www.digitaltrends.com/computing/why-ai-will-never-rule-the-world/). Find arguments in favor and against their claim.
8. For a provocative article on machine learning and its limits, see Darwiche (2018). Discuss this article in the light of recent developments.

Learning Resources for Students

1. Marcus, G., and Davis, E. (2019) Rebooting AI—Building Artificial Intelligence We Can Trust. Pantheon.

   This is a popular science book by a psychologist and a computer scientist; it offers an analysis of the current state of the art and discusses the need for robust, trustworthy AI systems.
2. Russell, S.J., and Norvig, P. (2021) Artificial Intelligence, a Modern Approach. 4th edition. Pearson.

   This is a standard textbook on artificial intelligence, which comprises 7 parts (artificial intelligence; problem-solving; knowledge, reasoning, and planning; uncertain knowledge and reasoning; machine learning; communicating, perceiving, and acting; conclusions) on more than one thousand pages. The two authors, highly accomplished researchers, provide comprehensive treatments of all major strands of AI.

References

Böck, M., Malle, J., Pasterk, D., Kukina, H., Hasani, R., & Heitzinger, C. (2022). Superhuman performance on sepsis MIMIC-III data by distributional reinforcement learning. *PLoS One, 17*(11), e0275358. https://doi.org/10.1371/journal.pone.0275358

Casilli, A. (2021). Waiting for robots: The ever-elusive myth of automation and the global exploitation of digital labor. *Sociologias, 23*(57), 112–133.

Darwiche, A. (2018). Human-level intelligence or animal-like abilities? *Communications of the ACM, 61*(10), 56–67.

Eloundou T., et al. (2023). *GPTs are GPTs: An early look at the labor market impact potential of large language models*. arXiv:2303.10130.

Ganesh, V., & Vardi, M. Y. (2020). On the unreasonable effectiveness of SAT solvers. In *Beyond the worst-case analysis of algorithms* (pp. 547–566). Columbia University Press.

Hayes, P. (1973). *The frame problem and related problems in artificial intelligence*. University of Edinburgh.

Heitzinger, C. (2022). *Algorithms with Julia* (1st ed.). Springer.

Heule, M. J. H., Kullmann, O., & Marek, V. W. (2016). Solving and verifying the Boolean Pythagorean triples problem via cube-and-conquer. *Proceedings SAT, 2016*, 228–245.

Kahneman, D. (2011). *Thinking, fast and slow*. Farrar, Straus and Giroux.

Kautz, H. A., & Selman, B. (1992). Planning as satisfiability. *Proceedings ECAI, 1992*, 359–363.

OpenAI. (2023). *GPT-4 Technical Report*. arXiv:2303.08774.
Ouyang, L., et al. (2022). *Training language models to follow instructions with human feedback*. arXiv:2203.02155.
Rolnick, D., Donti, P. L., Kaack, L. H., Kochanski, K., Lacoste, A., Sankaran, K., Ross, A. S., Milojevic-Dupont, N., Jaques, N., Waldman-Brown, A., Luccioni, A. S., Maharaj, T., Sherwin, E. D., Mukkavilli, S. K., Kording, K. P., Gomes, C. P., Ng, A. Y., Hassabis, D., Platt, J. C., Creutzig, F., Chayes, J. T., & Bengio, Y. (2023). Tackling climate change with machine learning. *ACM Computing Surveys, 55*(2), 42.1–42.96.
Silver, D. (2016). Mastering the game of Go. *Nature, 529*, 484–489.
Silver, D. (2017). Mastering the game of Go without human knowledge. *Nature, 550*, 354–359.
Silver, D. (2018). A general reinforcement learning algorithm that masters chess, shogi, and Go through self-play. *Science, 362*, 1140–1144.
Sutton, R. S., & Barto, A. G. (2018). *Reinforcement learning: An introduction* (2nd ed.). MIT Press.
Tesauro, G. (1995). Temporal difference learning and TD-Gammon. *Communications of the ACM, 38*(3). https://doi.org/10.1145/203330.203343
van Harmelen, F., Lifschitz, V., & Porter, B. W. (Eds.). (2008). *Handbook of knowledge representation*. Elsevier.
Vaswani, A., Shazeer, N., Parmar, N., Uszkoreit, J., Jones, L., Gomez, A. N., & Kaiser, L. (2017). *Attention is all you need*. arXiv:1706.03762.
Walsh, T. (2017). The singularity may never be near. *AI Magazine, 38*(3), 58–62.

Trustworthy Artificial Intelligence: Comprehensible, Transparent and Correctable

Ute Schmid

Abstract With the digital transformation, artificial intelligence (AI) applications are also finding their way into more and more areas of work and life. In particular, models learned from data are being used, which are mostly opaque black boxes. The fact that people can understand why an AI system behaves the way it does is necessary for various reasons: The model developers themselves must be able to assess properties of the learned models—in particular, possible biases due to overfitting to the data used for learning. For safety-critical applications, aspects of certification and testing are also becoming increasingly relevant. Domain experts—for example, in medical diagnostics or quality control in industrial production—must be able to comprehend, verify and, if necessary, correct system decisions. Consumers should understand why a system—a smart home control, a driving assistance—behaves in a certain way and why they are recommended certain products, offered certain tariffs or denied certain offers. After a brief introduction to the topic of AI, the chapter gives an overview of methods of the so-called third wave of AI. Central to this are approaches of *explainable* AI (XAI), which are intended to make the decisions of AI systems comprehensible. The main approaches are characterized and shown for which objectives and applications they are suitable in each case. It is shown that in addition to the highly regarded methods for visualization, methods that allow system decisions to be described in a differentiated manner are also particularly important. It is also argued that, in addition to comprehensibility, interactivity and correctability of AI systems are necessary so that AI systems do not restrict human competences but support them in partnership.

U. Schmid (✉)
Cognitive Systems, University of Bamberg & Bavarian Research Institute for Digital Transformation (bidt), Bamberg, Germany
e-mail: ute.schmid@uni-bamberg.de

H. Werthner et al. (eds.), *Introduction to Digital Humanism*,
https://doi.org/10.1007/978-3-031-45304-5_10

1 Introduction

Artificial intelligence (AI) is that field of research in computer science in which algorithms are developed to solve problems that humans are currently better at solving (definition according to Rich, 1983). AI is a research domain within computer science. In general, AI approaches should only be applied for problems which cannot be solved with standard algorithms. While standard algorithms—at least in principle—guarantee correctness (an input results in the intended output) and completeness (for all possible inputs, an output can be computed), this does not in general hold for AI algorithms. For many safety-critical domains, AI algorithms are usually not an option. For instance, the controller of an airbag should react in the intended way in all situations. AI systems become necessary for one of the following two reasons: (1) A problem is too complex that a solution can be computed efficiently. That is, it would take an unacceptably long time to generate an output. In this case, heuristic algorithms (one of the core approaches of AI) are used to compute approximate solutions without a guarantee how near the produced solution is to a desired or optimal solution for a problem. (2) It is not possible to give a full explicit description of the problem, and consequently, it is not possible to even define an algorithm. In this case, the algorithm for processing inputs into outputs is approximated from data, that is, by machine learning. Between input and output, there is now not an explicit, inspectable program but a machine-learned model which has generalized over data.

The field AI was given its name "artificial intelligence" in 1956 by computer science pioneer John McCarthy at Stanford University. The two main families of AI methods are knowledge-based methods and machine learning (see the most widely used textbook by Russell & Norvig, 2020). Both areas have been considered from the beginning. The first implementation of a machine learning program was a program to learn a strategy for the game of checkers and realized by Arthur Samuel in 1952. Early approaches also included the perceptron as a model of a single neuron and decision tree algorithms as an example for symbolic/interpretable machine learning (Rudin, 2019).

The 1980s was the peak period for knowledge-based methods in the context of applications for expert systems. It was hoped that AI systems could relieve or support human experts in many areas—from medical diagnostics to the planning of production processes to the use of intelligent tutoring systems in teaching. In the context of research on knowledge-based systems, efficient algorithms for drawing conclusions emerged. Special AI programming languages such as the logic programming language Prolog and specific hardware for more efficient processing, especially the Lisp machine, were developed. Research on machine learning still took place, but was dominated by the knowledge-based approaches. The heyday of expert systems accordingly has similarities to the current hype in machine learning. Again, one direction strongly dominates, and special program libraries are developed for deep neural networks as well as special hardware in the form of GPUs (*graphics processing units*) allowing to multiply matrices particularly efficiently with multiplication of matrices of real numbers as core operation for neural networks.

The high hopes placed in expert systems could ultimately only be partially fulfilled, especially due to the so-called knowledge engineering bottleneck—the realization that human knowledge is only partly explicitly available and can be formally represented. Large areas of human knowledge, especially perceptual knowledge and highly automated action routines, are implicit and cannot be captured or can only be captured inadequately with knowledge acquisition methods. The phenomenon is also called Polanyi's paradox: *How can we humans know more than what we can talk about?*

Impressive successes in the application of deep neural networks have heralded a new peak phase in AI since around 2010—this time with a focus on machine learning. The main reason for the new great interest in AI is that for the first time, it was possible to learn almost directly from different types of data, such as images or texts, without complex pre-processing (*end-to-end learning*). Most machine learning approaches, including classical neural networks as developed since the late 1980s, expect data in the form of feature vectors as input. Many data are available in tabular form anyway—for example, customer data or patient data. However, if you want to learn from image data such as photos of objects or even X-ray images, for example, you first have to extract features such as textures or color distributions from the available image data for the classical machine learning approaches. Just as for the knowledge-based approaches of AI, perceptual tasks also posed a challenge for machine learning.

In 2012, a deep neural network—a *convolutional neural network* (CNN) called AlexNet—won the ImageNet Challenge for the first time (Krizhevsky et al., 2012). In the challenge, images from 1000 categories, for example, animal species, vehicle types and buildings, are to be classified. Several million images are available for this purpose, for which the objects depicted are annotated by hand. Unlike earlier machine learning approaches, AlexNet could learn directly from the images. Comparable developments exist for natural language processing, such as machine translation (DeepL) or text generation (GPT-3). Again, however, expectations of what these novel AI methods can do are overblown. Polanyi's revenge (Kambhampati, 2021) has swung the pendulum from a near-exclusive focus on AI methods for explicit knowledge to a sole focus on AI methods for tacit knowledge. For any given problem, learning from lots of data is seen as the only meaningful approach. Existing knowledge, including carefully acquired knowledge about causal relationships, is thrown overboard to learn things imperfectly from data for which explicit knowledge is available. At the same time, traceability and control are abandoned, since deep neural networks calculate inputs in a complex mathematical way and are thus black boxes.

2 Problems with Data-Intensive Machine Learning: Unfairness, Biases and Missing Robustness

Even though data-intensive machine learning with the new generation of deep neural networks opens up new possibilities for various application areas, it also brings new problems. The requirements for quantity and quality of data are extremely high. The ImageNet already mentioned consists of 14 million images and 20,000 categories. It is often overlooked that the effort of capturing knowledge and formalizing it for processing by AI methods does not disappear with machine learning, but is deferred to the correct annotation of training data. Clickworkers have to manually annotate each example with the correct category—or even mark objects in images. The more complex the architecture of a neural network, the more data is needed to train it. If too little data is available, it is duplicated (augmented). Images, for example, are changed in their color values. In complex application areas where it is unclear which complex combination of information is responsible for a certain category, this can lead to unwanted *biases*. For example, when diagnosing tumors from tissue sections, the tissue is often colored. A model that decides whether a tumor is present, and if so which category, could be misled by training data with different staining than the original.

Supervised machine learning approaches, and this includes many deep neural network approaches, require a sample of training data that is as representative as possible for the problem and that is annotated with the correct output—this is called *ground truth labelling*. Especially in medicine, but also in other application areas, it is often not clear what the correct decision is for a given datum. For example, it could be that one medical expert decides on tumor class pT3 for the same image of a tissue section, while another decides on pT4. If certain types of data are missing from the training set (*sampling bias*) and data are not correctly annotated, this has a direct impact on the quality of the learned model (see Bruckert et al., 2020). In addition, models generated from data can typically only generalize for similar data that lie within the distribution of the data in the training set, but not for data that lie outside the distribution. If one has trained a model that can distinguish car types and it later receives a washing machine as input, it will classify it in terms of similarity to the car types it has learned. A human being, on the other hand, would say, that's something completely different from what I've seen so far, I can't say anything about that. Learned models do not have this kind of meta-cognition by default. A knowledge-based AI system, on the other hand, would not process an input outside the domain under consideration. So the quality of learned models depends heavily on the selection and quality of the data it has been trained with.

But even if the data are collected representatively and annotated correctly, undesirable effects can occur. Unfairness in reality is represented in the data. If there are significantly fewer women working in IT than men in a company and one naively simply trains a model for application selection with the existing data, the result is that a female applicant is no longer considered for a position in IT at all, as happened with Amazon's recruiting tool in 2018 (Dastin, 2018). If one is aware of such unfair distributions in the data in advance, this can be taken into account through appropriate methods in the learning process. In general, however, unfair models cannot be ruled out completely.

Both human and machine learning are inference from a sample of data or experience to a population. Such inductive inferences can never be completely correct. Human concept acquisition is generally very robust. For example, we have no trouble distinguishing cats from other animals, even with very different types of cats, lighting or backgrounds. In other areas, people tend to overgeneralize and form stereotypes and prejudices. Prejudices related to gender or ethnicity cannot be eliminated, but they can be recognized and also corrected. But with both human and machine learning, it is true that mistakes can be made. With machine-learned models, one estimates what the error rate will be for unseen data. A *predictive accuracy of* 99% does not sound bad, but it means that the model will make an error every hundredth case. If you use a search engine to look for pictures of cats, it doesn't matter if every 100th picture shows something different. Here, the advantages of automated image retrieval outweigh the disadvantages. You look at the pictures and choose a suitable one. In contrast, if, in a medical diagnosis, a disease were mistakenly diagnosed or—even worse—overlooked in every 100th case, that would be intolerable. Similarly, it is certainly undesirable that every 100th person is wrongly denied a loan or an insurance rate is set too high for no reason.

In order to be able to recognize and correct such undesirable model decisions, it can be very helpful to comprehend which information of the input data has been taken into account by which the model came to its decision. However, many machine learning approaches, especially deep neural networks, construct non-transparent models that are black boxes even for the model developers themselves.

3 Explainable Artificial Intelligence: Comprehensibility of Machine-Learned Models

The growing interest in the use of data-intensive AI methods impacted more and more application areas since around 2015. It quickly became clear that an exclusive focus on black-box machine learning approaches is often neither possible nor desirable. Possible applications are limited by the data quantity and quality requirements discussed above, but especially by the high effort required to annotate the training data. In addition, it has been realized that—especially in safety-critical areas such as medicine—systems where it is not possible to understand the basis on which they arrive at a decision or a recommendation for action are not acceptable. In areas that have a direct impact on consumers—from personalized advertising to lending—the right to transparency was also soon demanded (Goodman & Flaxman, 2017).

In spring 2017, DARPA (*Defense Advanced Research Projects Agency*, USA) launched the *Explainable Artificial Intelligence* (XAI) program. The aim of the program is to develop methods that (a) lead to machine-learned models that are more comprehensible than black-box models but at the same time retain a high degree of predictive accuracy and (b) enable users to understand this emerging generation of partnered AI systems, to trust the decisions appropriately and to interact effectively with the systems (Gunning & Aha, 2019). Using the classification of a cat by a neural network as an example, it was shown that an explanation of the model decision can include both verbalizable features such as "has fur, whiskers and claws" and prototypical images of typical visual features such as the shape of the ears (see https://twitter.com/darpa/status/843067035366187008, 18.3.2017). However, the term *explainable* led to misunderstandings outside of the research community, as it rather suggests that the workings of AI systems are explained in a way that is understandable to laypersons. However, XAI means to provide methods which allow to make the decision-making process of an AI system, specifically a machine-learned model, more transparent. In parallel, terms such as "comprehensible machine learning" (Schmid, 2018) or interpretable machine learning (Doshi-Velez & Kim, 2017) were proposed. In the meantime, the term *explanatory* machine learning is also frequently used (Teso & Kersting, 2019; Ai et al., 2021). Furthermore, transparency is now usually understood more generally than explainability: it refers to the principle that it should be made clear when a recommendation or decision is based on the use of AI methods or if an interaction is not with a human but with an AI system such as a chatbot.

In the meantime, a standardization of terminology has developed: After the initial focus on explainability for deep neural networks, the relevance of methods for generating explanations, in short XAI methods, is now seen for all types of AI systems. On the one hand, explanation methods are being developed for various black-box approaches to machine learning (this includes methods such as *support vector machines* or k-nearest neighbor approaches; see, e.g. Kersting et al. (2019) for a general introduction). On the other hand, explanatory methods are also being developed for knowledge-based AI systems as well as for *white-box* machine learning approaches. For these systems, it is in principle comprehensible how a decision is reached. But—comparable to large software systems—the models are often too complex to see through the entire process of information processing. In addition, the models are stored in special representation formalisms that enable processing by computer programs and must be suitably translated into comprehensible explanations. Recently, it has been established to refer to white-box machine learning approaches, such as decision tree methods, as interpretable machine learning (Rudin, 2019).

In the meantime, a wide range of XAI methods exists that are suitable for different target groups and different information needs. There are numerous methods that show the relevance of specific information from the input for the current decision. This can be features, words or parts of images. For example, the LIME approach (Ribeiro et al., 2016) shows which groups of pixels must be present for a classification decision—for example, that eye and ear are relevant for whether the model recognizes a cat. LIME is a so-called model-agnostic explanation approach: to generate an explanation, the learned model is not interfered with; instead, the input data is manipulated, and the resulting model decision is considered. An approach that was developed specifically for image classification with (deep) neural networks is LRP (*layer-wise relevance propagation*; Bach et al., 2015). Here, those image points are highlighted that had a particularly strong influence on the output of the network. In contrast to LIME, LRP is model-specific, which means that the method must be integrated directly into the learning algorithm. Highlighting the information that is particularly relevant to a learned model is especially useful for model developers to check whether the model has generalized meaningfully. During learning, it can happen that the model uses irrelevant information for prediction that correlates with the class to be predicted. In other words, the model adapts too much to the training data (*overfitting*), which can lead to problems with the prediction for data that has never been seen before. This is also referred to as "right for the wrong reasons" or "Kluge Hans" predictors. For example, it could be that by chance a part of the photos showing horses is given with a source reference (e.g. a website). The learning algorithm can then use this simpler information to correctly indicate when a horse is seen for the available data. However, highlighting the pixels used can show that this output is based on the source cue (Lapuschkin et al., 2019).

For domain experts and also for end users, highlighting only relevant information is usually not very helpful. For example, visual highlighting can show that a certain tumor is actually visible on a tissue section. However, in order to understand why the model has decided on tumor class pT3 and not on pT4, much more complex information is required that can be better expressed in language. This includes spatial relations, such as the position of the tumor relative to other tissue types, or the concrete expression of individual features, such as the diameter of the tumor (Bruckert et al. 2020; Schmid, 2021). Such explanations can be generated, for example, combining black-box machine learning approaches and interpretable approaches (Rabold et al., 2020a).

For consumers, simple explanations such as those familiar from recommendation systems are often relevant (Tintarev & Masthoff, 2012). For example, if a certain product is recommended in an online shop, one can ask on what data basis this recommendation was made. Typically, one is then shown previous purchases that have been compared with the purchase profiles of other people for a similarity comparison. When it comes to making transparent how algorithms (with and without AI components) at banks, insurance companies or other companies come to certain decisions, such as the rejection of a loan or the amount of an insurance premium, counterfactual explanations are particularly helpful (Wachter et al., 2017)—for example: "You did not get the loan because your annual income is €45,000. If your annual income was €55,000, you would have received the loan". Such explanations give the relevant information to customers while avoiding the need for companies to reveal their algorithms. In case a model decision has been based on erroneous assumptions about a customer, it should be possible for the customer to complain and ask for a correction (actionability).

Prototypical as well as contrastive examples provide another possibility for explanations. Such examples offer experts in particular the opportunity to better understand how the model is structured. The XAI methods considered so far explain

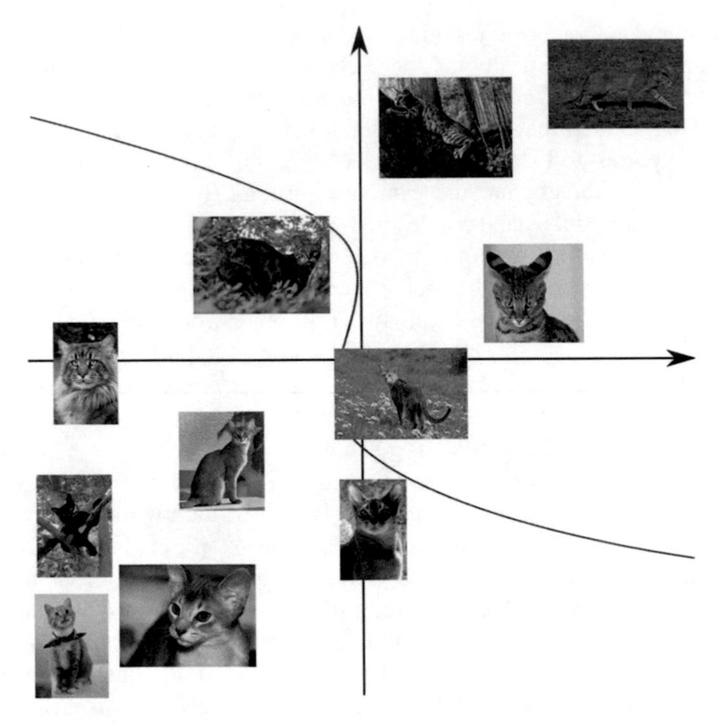

Fig. 1 Explaining image classifications by example. On the left side are house cats, and on the right side are small wild cats. For the house cat, the grey sitting cat might be the prototype for the class. The cat in the dandelion field is a near-miss example for the class house cat—a cat very similar to house cat examples but classified (correctly) as a small wild cat. Alternatively to the cat domain, one can think of images indicative for two tumor classes II and III or images for defect or acceptable parts in industrial quality control

how a specific decision was reached (local explanation). Specially selected examples can (1) show which data a model evaluates to be particularly typical for a certain class—a prototypical representant with respect to the decision region the model induced for this class; instead of identifying a prototypical example, a synthetic representant for a concept might be constructed, as it is usually proposed in psychology and philosophy; (2) examples which are situated near to the decision boundary for a class help to get insights in the discriminative features of the model. This can be a borderline case for the considered class or a near-miss example (Rabold et al., 2022), that is, an example similar to objects of the considered class but being classified as a member of a different class (see Fig. 1).

Another type of explanation tries to explain the entire model—so-called global explanations. While a local explanation supports understanding why a specific example is classified as belonging to a certain class (e.g. *Why do you classify this image as indicating tumor class II?*), a global explanation supports understanding of what constitutes a class given a specific model (e.g. *What features are in general relevant to decide that an image is indicating tumor class II?*). An explanation by prototype can be seen as a special instance of a global explanation. Another possibility is to learn symbolic rules as a surrogate model. Such rules can be based on identifying concepts and their relations. For instance, a model classifying faces should take into account the presence of eyes, nose and mouth as concepts together with their spatial relations (e.g. that the nose is above the mouth; Rabold et al., 2020b).

Explanatory AI thus consists of a growing set of different methods, each fitting different information goals. Theoretical and empirical analyses of the properties and effects of explanations from psychology are increasingly being incorporated into research on XAI (Miller, 2019). XAI methods are an important contribution to the comprehensibility of AI systems, especially machine learning. However, in the respective application context, especially in the professional environment, it must be carefully checked that explanations are actually used to control system decisions and thus not blind but justified trust in an AI system can develop (Thaler & Schmid, 2021). The danger is that the mere existence of the possibility of an explanation leads to system decisions being adopted without reflection (Lee & See, 2004).

4 Third-Wave AI Methods: Hybrid, Comprehensible and Correctable

Explainable AI methods are also referred to as the third wave of AI—after the first wave of knowledge-based approaches (*describe*), followed by data-intensive machine learning (*categorize*), which is to be replaced by approaches that adapt to the interests of the users depending on the context (*explain*). It is increasingly argued that the methods required for the third wave must not only address the generation of explanations, but that machine learning should allow interaction, especially corrections of the model (Teso & Kersting, 2019; Müller et al., 2022). Furthermore, it is seen that a combination of knowledge-based approaches and machine learning can lead to more data-efficient and robust models (see Fig. 2). This direction of research is referred to as hybrid AI or neurosymbolic AI (De Raedt et al., 2020).

The combination of explanatory and interactive (human-in-the-loop) machine learning is a useful approach to counteract the problems with the quantity and quality of data discussed above. For example, experts can simply accept a system decision that they can directly understand, question a system decision more closely by requesting one or more explanations from the system as to how the decision was reached and, in the third step, also correct this decision. While most work on interactive machine learning only allows the correction of the output, there are now first approaches that additionally allow the correction of the explanations. This allows the adaptation of the model to be controlled in a targeted manner (Schmid, 2021). Interaction thus allows targeted human knowledge to be introduced into the learning process (see Fig. 3). Corrections are also possible when knowledge cannot be made completely explicit. For example, an expert can often recognize

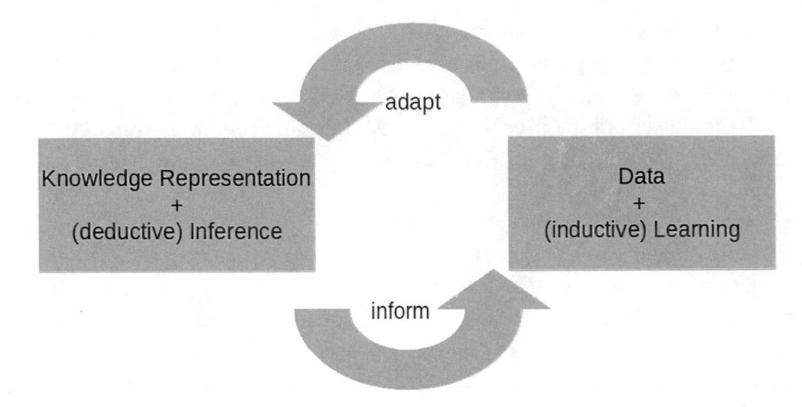

Fig. 2 Combining knowledge-based and data-driven AI: What we already know we do not need to learn (over and over) again

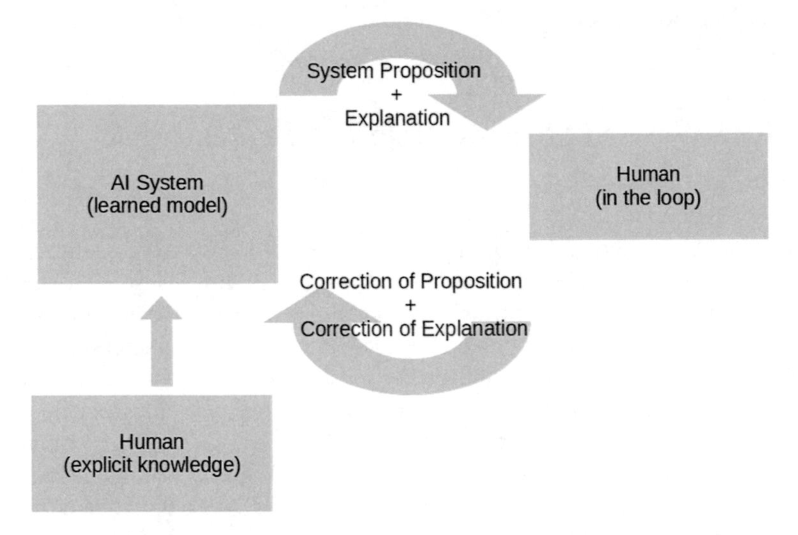

Fig. 3 Human-in-the-loop machine learning: Making use of explicit knowledge and of corrections to guide model generation and adaptation

whether a diagnosis is acceptable or not and possibly also identify faulty assumptions in its justification. At the same time, it can be assumed that the possibility of correction leads to a stronger sense of control and self-efficacy and thus there is less danger of blindly adopting system decisions.

Finally, there is a growing realization that purely data-driven machine learning is often not very efficient. While people use knowledge and skills they have already acquired and can thus learn increasingly complex things, machine learning involves learning everything from scratch over and over again. If prior knowledge could be incorporated into the learning process, data could be saved, which in turn could lead to less effort for annotation as well as savings in energy for storage and processing.

In addition, existing knowledge can be used specifically to guide the learning process. Models that take existing knowledge into account are less prone to unwanted biases and more robust with respect to data that lie outside the data distribution in the training.

Deep neural networks have brought the research field of artificial intelligence back into the public eye after many years. Increasing digitalization and global networking make it possible to learn from large amounts of data. For a responsible use of AI methods, the new research topics of explainable, interactive and hybrid AI provide the opportunity for AI systems to emerge in partnership, which do not curtail human competences but expand and promote them.

5 Conclusions

Explainability, the combination of data-driven and knowledge-based AI, and interactive approaches to machine learning have been introduced as relevant ingredients for trustworthy AI systems. However, one has to be careful that the presentation of an explanation does not result in unjustified trust. It is not guaranteed that an explanation is faithful to the model. That is, an explanation might be not correlated to the way in which a model did process the data. Similar effects can be observed in human explanations—one might give a reason to justify one's behavior which is not the true one. If a person is giving a wrong reason by design, the person is not truthful. However, often we have no full access to the motives underlying a specific behavior and come up with an explanation we find plausible. Furthermore, explanations as an additional source of information might result in cognitive overload (Ai et al., 2021). Therefore, explanations should only be given when a specific information need exists.

In the ethics guideline for trustworthy AI of the European Commission a non-exhaustive list of requirements for trustworthy AI is given, among them data quality (governance), inclusiveness (design for all), human oversight, fairness (non-discrimination), human autonomy, privacy, robustness, safety and transparency. The topics discussed in this chapter can contribute to realize these requirements: Explainability contributes to human oversight and transparency. Hybrid systems contribute to robustness and safety. Interactive machine learning contributes to human oversight and human autonomy.

The recent developments in the domain of generative AI systems such as large language models or dialog systems such as ChatGPT bring new challenges with respect to trustworthiness. When an output, for instance, an answer to a question, is generated, one might be interested in several aspects to evaluate the trustworthiness of the output: (1) Are statements concerning factual knowledge correct or is the system hallucinating? (2) Has the presented output originally been obtained from sources with copyright? (3) What are the original sources for the information given? (4) Why was a specific information included in the output and another omitted? Current XAI methods are not suited to explain the output of generative AI models.

First, ideas on how to provide explainability are currently being explored, and hopefully, we will see results in the near future.

Discussion Questions for Students and Their Teachers

1. If a domain expert, for instance, in medical diagnosis, wants to understand why a machine-learned model classified an image as indicative for a specific tumor class, which type of explanation would you think to be most helpful? If a person is wondering why an insurance company demands a rather high monthly amount for health insurance, which type of explanation do you think to be most helpful?
2. Do you think that for AI applications to be ethical, it is necessary that it provides explanations? Do you think explanations are sufficient for trustworthiness of an AI system?
3. Discuss reasons why combining machine learning with knowledge-based approaches allows to perform machine learning from smaller data sets and yields more robust models.
4. Do you see problems which can arise from interactive/human-in-the-loop machine learning?
5. Is it possible to provide explainability and trustworthiness for the new generation of generative AI models (such as ChatGPT)?

Learning Resources for Students

1. A comprehensive and recent survey of XAI methods is given in
   Schwalbe, G. and Finzel, B. (2023). A comprehensive taxonomy for explainable artificial intelligence: a systematic survey of surveys on methods and concepts. *Data Mining and Knowledge Discovery*. https://doi.org/10.1007/s10618-022-00867-8.
2. An introduction to hybrid/neurosymbolic AI is presented by
   Garcez, A. D. A. and Lamb, L. C. (2023). Neurosymbolic AI: The 3rd wave. *Artificial Intelligence Review, 56*(11), 12387–12406.
3. Requirements for designing interactive AI systems are presented in
   Amershi, S., Weld, D., Vorvoreanu, M., Fourney, A., Nushi, B., Collisson, P., and Horvitz, E. (2019). Guidelines for human-AI interaction. In *Proceedings of the 2019 CHI Conference on Human Factors in Computing Systems* (pp. 1–13).
4. A discussion of trustworthy AI from a human-computer interaction perspective is
   Shneiderman, B. (2020). Human-centered artificial intelligence: Reliable, safe & trustworthy. *International Journal of Human–Computer Interaction*, *36*(6), 495–504.
5. A highly readable book about shortcomings of purely data-driven approaches is
   Marcus, G. and Davis, E. (2019). *Rebooting AI: Building artificial intelligence we can trust*. Vintage.
6. The ethics guidelines for trustworthy AI of the European Commission can be found at
   https://digital-strategy.ec.europa.eu/en/library/ethics-guidelines-trustworthy-ai.

Acknowledgements This contribution is based on a previous publication in German: Schmid, Ute (2022). Vertrauenswürdige Künstliche Intelligenz (287–298). In: Frauke Rostalski (Hrsg). *Künstliche Intelligenz: Wie gelingt eine vertrauenswürdige Verwendung in Deutschland und Europa?* Tübingen: Mohr Siebeck. I am very grateful to Carlo Ghezzi and Erich Prem for their valuable comments and suggestions for a previous version of the manuscript. Furthermore, I want to thank Sebastian Krügel and Matthias Uhl for allowing me to make use of the cat images in Fig. 1 and Sonja Ruschhaupt for providing the figure.

References

Ai, L., Muggleton, S. H., Hocquette, C., Gromowski, M., & Schmid, U. (2021). Beneficial and harmful explanatory machine learning. *Machine Learning, 110*, 695–721.

Bach, S., Binder, A., Montavon, G., Klauschen, F., Müller, K. R., & Samek, W. (2015). On pixel-wise explanations for non-linear classifier decisions by layer-wise relevance propagation. *PloS One, 10*(7), e0130140.

Bruckert, S., Finzel, B., & Schmid, U. (2020). The next generation of medical decision support: A roadmap toward transparent expert companions. *Frontiers in Artificial Intelligence, 3*, 507973.

Dastin, J. (2018). Amazon scraps secret AI recruiting tool that showed bias against women. *Reuters* (2018).

De Raedt, L., Dumančić, S., Manhaeve, R., & Marra, G. (2020). From statistical relational to neuro-symbolic artificial intelligence. In *Proceedings of the Twenty-Ninth International Joint Conference on Artificial Intelligence* (IJCAI-20, pp. 4943–4950).

Doshi-Velez, F., & Kim, B. (2017). Towards a rigorous science of interpretable machine learning. *arXiv preprint arXiv:1702.08608.*

Goodman, B., & Flaxman, S. (2017). European Union regulations on algorithmic decision-making and a "right to explanation". *AI Magazine, 38*(3), 50–57.

Gunning, D., & Aha, D. (2019). DARPA's explainable artificial intelligence (XAI) program. *AI Magazine, 40*(2), 44–58.

Kambhampati, S. (2021). Polanyi's revenge and AI's new romance with tacit knowledge. *Communications of the ACM, 64*(2), 31–32.

Kersting, K., Lampert, C., & Rothkopf, C. (2019). *How machines learn: Artificial intelligence explained in an understandable way*. Springer.

Krizhevsky, A., Sutskever, I., & Hinton, G. (2012). Imagenet classification with deep convolutional neural networks. In *Advances in Neural Information Processing Systems 25* (NeurIPS 2012, pp. 1097–1105).

Lapuschkin, S., Wäldchen, S., Binder, A., Montavon, G., Samek, W., & Müller, K. R. (2019). Unmasking Clever Hans predictors and assessing what machines really learn. *Nature Communications, 10*(1), 1096–1104.

Lee, J. D., & See, K. A. (2004). Trust in automation: Designing for appropriate reliance. *Human Factors, 46*(1), 50–80.

Miller, T. (2019). Explanation in artificial intelligence: Insights from the social sciences. *Artificial Intelligence, 267*, 1–38.

Müller, D., März, M., Scheele, S., & Schmid, U. (2022). An interactive explanatory AI system for industrial quality control. In *Proceedings of the AAAI Conference on Artificial Intelligence* (Vol. 36, No. 11, pp. 12580–12586).

Rabold, J., Deininger, H., Siebers, M., & Schmid, U. (2020a). Enriching visual with verbal explanations for relational concepts–combining LIME with Aleph. In *Machine learning and knowledge discovery in databases: International workshops of ECML PKDD 2019, Proceedings, Part I* (pp. 180–192). Springer International Publishing.

Rabold, J., Schwalbe, G., & Schmid, U. (2020b). Expressive explanations of DNNs by combining concept analysis with ILP. In *KI 2020: Advances in artificial intelligence: 43rd German Conference on AI, Proceedings 43* (pp. 148–162). Springer International Publishing.

Rabold, J., Siebers, M., & Schmid, U. (2022). Generating contrastive explanations for inductive logic programming based on a near miss approach. *Machine Learning, 111*(5), 1799–1820.

Ribeiro, M. T., Singh, S., & Guestrin, C.. (2016, August). "Why should I trust you?" Explaining the predictions of any classifier. In *Proceedings of the 22nd ACM SIGKDD International Conference on Knowledge Discovery and Data Mining* (pp. 1135–1144).

Rich, E. (1983). *Artificial intelligence*. McGraw-Hill.

Rudin, C. (2019). Stop explaining black box machine learning models for high stakes decisions and use interpretable models instead. *Nature Machine Intelligence, 1*(5), 206–215.

Russell, S., & Norvig, P. (2020). *Artificial intelligence. A modern approach* (4th ed.). Pearson.

Schmid, U. (2018). Inductive programming as approach to comprehensible machine learning. In *DKB/KIK@ KI* (pp. 4–12).

Schmid, U. (2021). Interactive learning with mutual explanations in relational domains. In S. Muggleton & N. Chater (Eds.), *Human-like machine intelligence* (Chap. 17) (pp. 338–354). Oxford University Press.

Teso, S., & Kersting, K. (2019, January). Explanatory interactive machine learning. In *Proceedings of the 2019 AAAI/ACM Conference on AI, Ethics, and Society* (pp. 239–245).

Thaler, A. M., & Schmid, U. (2021). Explaining machine learned relational concepts in visual domains-effects of perceived accuracy on joint performance and trust. In *Proceedings of the Annual Meeting of the Cognitive Science Society* (Vol. 43, No. 43, pp. 1705–1711).

Tintarev, N., & Masthoff, J. (2012). Evaluating the effectiveness of explanations for recommender systems: Methodological issues and empirical studies on the impact of personalization. *User Modeling and User-Adapted Interaction, 22*, 399–439.

Wachter, S., Mittelstadt, B., & Russell, C. (2017). Counterfactual explanations without opening the black box: Automated decisions and the GDPR. *Harvard Journal of Law and Technology, 31*, 841.

Are We in Control?

Edward A. Lee

Abstract This chapter introduces the problem of accountability and control in technology development. Traditionally, technology has been understood to emerge from deliberate, top-down, intelligent decisions by humans. More recently, it has become clear that a chaotic evolutionary process plays a major role. This chapter addresses the questions of to what extent humans are in control of technology development, how accountability changes with increased use of AI, and how society may need to adapt. In particular, technology coevolves with human society, and even if every deliberate design decision made by humans is ethical, this provides little assurance that bad outcomes will be avoided.

1 Introduction

Technology is created by humans. Humans, therefore, must be in control of the trajectory of technology development, right? A classic view, parroted by Dennett (2017), is that digital technology and software are examples of "top-down intelligent design." Dennett cites the Internet as an "obvious recent example" of such an "intelligently designed" system and contrasts it with natural systems, such as humans, who have evolved in a Darwinian way. An intelligent design should yield intended and expected behaviors. But this has not been the case with digital technology and certainly not with the Internet. Why?

The momentous AI earthquake that surfaced in the form of ChatGPT in late 2022 undermines the intelligent design thesis. Any illusion that humans are in control has been shattered. ChatGPT is based on GPT-3.5, a large language model (LLM) from OpenAI. Other examples that emerged around the same time include Google's Bard and Microsoft's Sydney (attached to the Bing search engine). I have yet to encounter any scientists, even experts in machine learning, who are not surprised by the astonishing linguistic capabilities of these LLMs. As expressed in Kissinger et al.

E. A. Lee (✉)
EECS Department, UC Berkeley, Berkeley, CA, USA
e-mail: eal@berkeley.edu

H. Werthner et al. (eds.), *Introduction to Digital Humanism*,
https://doi.org/10.1007/978-3-031-45304-5_11

(2023), "[t]he ability of large language models to generate humanlike text was an almost accidental discovery." Further, "it turns out that the models also have the *unexpected ability* to create highly articulate paragraphs, articles, and in time perhaps books" (emphasis added). Everyone was surprised, and the whole world, even the top experts, continues to watch with fascination as the machines dance in unexpected ways (Bubeck et al., 2023).

This chapter focuses on the question of whether and how humans control technology development. This question is urgent because of rapid changes that bring both opportunities and risks.

2 Fear

Rapid change breeds fear. With its spectacular rise from the ashes in the last 15 years or so, we fear that AI may replace most white-collar jobs (Ford, 2015); that it will learn to iteratively improve itself into a superintelligence that leaves humans in the dust (Barrat, 2013; Bostrom, 2014; Tegmark, 2017); that it will fragment information so that humans divide into islands with disjoint sets of truths (Lee, 2020); that it will supplant human decision-making in health care, finance, and politics (Kelly, 2016); that it will cement authoritarian powers, tracking every move of their citizens and shaping their thoughts (Lee, 2018); that the surveillance capitalists' monopolies, which depend on AI, will destroy small business and swamp entrepreneurship (Zuboff, 2019); that it "may trigger a resurgence in mystic religiosity" (Kissinger et al., 2023); and that it will "alter the fabric of reality itself" (Kissinger et al., 2023).

You might hope that the scope of the AIs will be limited, for example, just giving us better search engines. It is not clear, however, where the limits are or even whether there are any. For example, a previously prevalent presumption that AI would be incapable of creativity was also shattered in 2022 by text-to-image generators such as DALL-E 2 from OpenAI, Stable Diffusion from Stability AI, and Midjourney from the research lab with the same name. These text-to-image tools showed how AIs could absorb stylistic influences, as all human artists do, and then synthesize original works informed by these styles. Together with the LLMs, these technology releases have led to a massive cultural shift in the public understanding of the role that AI will have in our society and have spurred a gold rush to develop more AI tools.

3 Pushback

The AI researchers who were developing these tools were seeing a relatively gradual evolution of capabilities (Heaven, 2023), but even they have been surprised by the outcomes. Because of their expertise in the technology, they were not surprised to be surprised. They gradually came to expect surprises, but the rest of us were caught off guard. The public instead witnessed an explosive revelation that contorted expectations.

Many intellectuals have attempted to dismiss the technology as a passing fad. A common claim was that the AIs do not truly "understand" the way humans do. But do we understand how humans understand? Chomsky et al. (2023) state "we know from the science of linguistics and the philosophy of knowledge that [the LLMs] differ profoundly from how humans reason and use language." How much do we actually know about how humans reason and use language? Other critics say the LLMs perform a glorified form of plagiarism, ignoring the fact that almost all human expression is also a reworking of concepts and texts that have been uttered before.

Many of these criticisms are implicitly comparing the AIs to ideal forms of intelligence and creativity that are fictions. In these fictions, an intelligence works with true facts and with logic (what Kant called "pure reason"), and creativity produces truly novel artifacts. But we have no precedents for such intelligence or creativity. It does not exist in humans nor in anything humans have created. Perhaps the AIs have in fact achieved human-level intelligence, which works not with true facts but rather with preconceptions (Kuhn, 1962), works not with logic as much as with intuition (Kahneman, 2011), and rarely produces anything truly novel (and when it does, the results are ignored as culturally irrelevant). Could it be that these AIs tell us more about humans than about machines?

Janelle Shane, an AI researcher, writes in her book, *You Look Like a Thing and I Love You*, that training an AI is more like educating a child than like writing a computer program (Shane, 2019). Computer programs, at their lowest level, specify algorithms operating on formal symbols. The symbols are devoid of meaning, except in the mind of human observers, and the operations follow clearly defined rules of logic. Deep neural networks (DNNs), however, exhibit behaviors that are not usefully explained in terms of the operations of these algorithms (Lee, 2022). An LLM is implemented on computers that perform billions of logic operations per second, but even a detailed knowledge of those operations gives little insight into the behaviors of the DNNs. By analogy, even if we had a perfect model of a human neuron and structure of neuron interconnections in a brain, we would still not be able to explain human behavior (Lichtman et al., 2014).

Surely, today, we still retain a modicum of control. At the very least, we can still pull the plug. Or can we? Information technology already pervades our financial markets, our transportation systems, our distribution of goods, and our information feeds, and, increasingly, those IT systems integrate AI. What would happen if we were to suddenly shut down all those AIs? I suspect the results would not be pretty. Giving us pause, Albert Einstein famously said, "we cannot solve our problems with the same thinking we used when we created them."

4 Information Flood

Knowledge is at the root of technology, information is at the root of knowledge, and today's technology makes information vastly more accessible than it has ever been. Shouldn't this help us solve our problems? The explosion of AI feeds the tsunami, turning every image, every text, and every sound into yet more information, flooding our feeble human brains. We can't absorb the flood without curation, and curation of information is increasingly being done by AIs. Every subset of the truth is only a partial truth, and curated information necessarily includes only a subset. Since our brains can only absorb a tiny subset of the flood, everything we take in is at best a partial truth. The AIs, in contrast, seem to have little difficulty with the flood. To them, it is the food that strengthens, perhaps leading to that feared runaway feedback loop of superintelligence that sidelines humans into irrelevance. The LLMs, for example, have demonstrated considerable expertise in law, mathematics, computer programming, and many other disciplines, displaying a breadth of knowledge no human can match.

5 Digital Creationism

The question I address in this chapter is "are we in control?" First, in posing this question, what do we mean by "we"? Do we mean "humanity," all eight billion of us? The idea of eight billion people collectively controlling anything is patently absurd, so that must not be what we mean. Do we mean the engineers of Silicon Valley? The investors on Wall Street? The politicians who feed off the partial truths and overt lies? The large corporations that own the computers? Each of these possibilities yields sufficient concerns that even a positive answer to the quest "are we in control?" may not be reassuring.

Second, what do we mean by "control"? Is it like steering a car on a network of roads, or is it more like steering a car while the map emerges and morphs into unexpected dead ends, underpasses, and loops? If we are steering technology, then every turn we take changes the terrain we have to steer over in unexpected ways.

In my recent book (Lee, 2020), I coin the term "digital creationism" for the idea that technology is the result of top-down intelligent design. This principle assumes that every technology is the outcome of a deliberate process, where every aspect of a design is the result of an intentional, human decision. That is not how it happens. Software engineers are more the agents of mutation in a Darwinian evolutionary process. The outcome of their efforts is shaped more by the computers, networks, software tools, libraries, programming languages, and other programs they use than by their deliberate decisions. And the success and further development of their product is determined as much or more by the cultural milieu into which they launch their "creation" than by their design decisions.

6 Coevolution

The French philosopher known as Alain (whose real name was Émile-Auguste Chartier) wrote about fishing boats in Brittany:

> Every boat is copied from another boat. . . . Let's reason as follows in the manner of Darwin. It is clear that a very badly made boat will end up at the bottom after one or two voyages and thus never be copied. . . . One could then say, with complete rigor, that it is the sea herself who fashions the boats, choosing those which function and destroying the others. (Rogers & Ehrlich, 2008)

Boat designers are agents of mutation, and sometimes, their mutations result in a badly made boat. From this perspective, perhaps Facebook has been fashioned more by teenagers than by software engineers. The development of the LLMs has very clearly followed an evolutionary model, where many mutations along the way were discarded as ineffective.

More deeply, digital technology *co*evolves with humans. Facebook changes its users, who then change Facebook. The LLMs will change us. For software engineers, the tools we use, themselves earlier outcomes of software engineering, shape our thinking. Think about how IDEs[1] (such as Eclipse, IntelliJ, or Visual Studio Code), code repositories (such as GitHub), message boards (such as Stack Overflow), libraries (such the Standard Template Library), programming languages (Scala, Rust, and JavaScript, e.g.), Internet search (such as Google or Bing), and, now, LLMs that write computer programs (like ChatGPT and its descendants) affect the outcome of our software. These tools have more effect on the outcome than all of our deliberate decisions.

7 Regulation

Today, the fear and hype around AI taking over the world and social media taking down democracy have fueled a clamor for more regulation (see the two chapters of Rotenberg, as well as Müller and Kettemann). But how to regulate technology depends heavily on whether it is intelligently designed or it coevolves. Why have privacy laws, with all their good intentions, done little to protect our privacy? They have only overwhelmed us with small-print legalese and annoying popups giving us a choice between "accept our inscrutable terms" and "go away." Do we expect new regulations trying to mitigate fake news or to prevent insurrections from being instigated by social media to be any more effective?

Under the principle of digital creationism, bad outcomes are the result of unethical actions by individuals, for example, by blindly following the profit motive

[1] Integrated development environments (IDEs) are computer programs that assist programmers by parsing their text as they type, coloring text by function, identifying errors and potential flaws in code style, suggesting insertions, and transforming code through refactoring.

with no concern for societal effects. Under the principle of coevolution, bad outcomes are the result of the "procreative prowess" (Dennett, 2017) of the technology and its applications. Technologies that succeed are those that more effectively propagate. The individuals we credit with (or blame for) creating those technologies certainly play a role, but so do the users of the technologies and their whole cultural context. Under this perspective, Facebook users bear some of the blame, along with Mark Zuckerberg, for distorted elections. They even bear some of the blame for the design of Facebook software that enables distorted elections. If they were happy to pay for social networking, for example, an entirely different software design may have emerged. How the LLMs get integrated into our culture will depend on more than the designers of their software.

Under digital creationism, the purpose of regulation is to constrain the individuals who develop and market technology. In contrast, under coevolution, constraints can be about the *use* of technology, not just its design and the business of selling it. The purpose of regulation becomes to nudge the process of both technology and cultural evolution through incentives and penalties. Nudging is probably the best we can hope for. Evolutionary processes do not yield easily to control because the territory over which we have to navigate keeps changing.

Perhaps privacy laws have been ineffective because they are based on digital creationism as a principle. These laws assume that changing the behavior of corporations and engineers will be sufficient to achieve privacy goals (whatever those are for you). A coevolutionary perspective understands that users of technology will choose to give up privacy even if they are explicitly told that their information will be abused. We are repeatedly told exactly that in the fine print of all those privacy policies we don't read, and, nevertheless, our kids get sucked into a media milieu where their identity gets defined by a distinctly non-private online persona.

8 Feedback

As of 2023, the LLMs such as ChatGPT have been trained on mostly human-written data. However, it seems inevitable that the LLMs will be generating a fair amount of the text that will end up on the Internet in the future. The next generation of LLMs, then, will be trained on a mix of human-generated and machine-generated text. What happens as the percentage of machine-generated text increases? Feedback systems are complicated and unpredictable. Shumailov et al. (2023) show that such feedback learning leads to a kind of "model collapse," where original content (the human-written content) is forgotten.

If technology is defining culture while culture is defining technology, we have another feedback loop, and intervention at any point in the feedback loop can change the outcomes. Hence, it may be just as effective to pass laws that focus on educating the public, for example, as it is to pass laws that regulate the technology producers. Perhaps if more people understood that Pokémon GO is a behavior-modification engine, they would better understand Niantic's privacy policy and its claim that their product, Pokémon GO, has no advertising. Establishments pay Niantic for placement of a Pokémon nearby to entice people to visit them (Zuboff, 2019). Perhaps a strengthening of libel laws, laws against hate speech, and other refinements to first-amendment rights should also be part of the remedy. The LLMs create a whole new set of challenges, since they readily generate entirely convincing fictions. Rather than naïvely attempt to suppress the technology, a strategy that rarely works, we need to learn to use it intelligently.

9 Actions

I believe that, as a society, we can do better than we are currently doing. The risk of an Orwellian state (or, perhaps worse, a corporate Big Brother) is very real. It has already happened in China. We will not do better, however, until we abandon digital creationism as a principle. Outlawing specific technology developments will not be effective, and breaking up monopolies could actually make the problem worse by accelerating mutations. For example, we may try to outlaw autonomous decision-making in weapons systems and banking, but as we see from election distortions and Pokémon GO, the AIs are very effective at influencing human decision-making, so putting a human in the loop does not necessarily help. How can a human who is effectively controlled by a machine somehow mitigate the evilness of autonomous weapons?

When I talk about educating the public, many people immediately gravitate to a perceived silver bullet, that we should teach ethics to engineers. But I have to ask, if we assume that all technologists behave ethically (whatever your meaning of that word), can we conclude that bad outcomes will not occur? This strikes me as naïve. Coevolutionary processes are much too complex.

10 Conclusions

Technology is not the result of top-down intelligent design. It is the result of a coevolutionary process, where the role of humans is more like agents of mutation than intelligent designers. Returning to the original question, are we in control? The answer is "not really," but we can nudge the process. Even a supertanker can be redirected by gentle nudging.

Discussion Questions for Students and Their Teachers

1. Using your favorite large language model (such as ChatGPT), ask it to summarize a book you have recently read, and critique its response.
2. Collect some mistakes made by your favorite large language model (such as ChatGPT) either by experimenting with it or by finding articles or blog posts

about such mistakes. Discuss how these mistakes resemble or do not resemble mistakes a human might make. See, for example, Bubeck et al. (2023).
3. Estimate the number of people who were involved in the development of a favorite online technology of yours. Consider not only the designers working on the software but also the people who contributed to the underlying technology. How does this affect the ability to pin the blame on individuals for bad outcomes?

Learning Resources for Students

1. Lee, E. A. (2020). *The Coevolution: The Entwined Futures of Humans and Machines*. Cambridge, MA, MIT Press.

   This (open-access) book addresses the question of whether humans are defining technology or is technology defining humans. I argue from several vantage points that we are less in control of the trajectory of technology than we think. Technology shapes us as much as we shape it, and it may be more defensible to think of technology as the result of a Darwinian coevolution than the result of top-down intelligent design. Richard Dawkins famously said that a chicken is an egg's way of making another egg. Is a human a computer's way of making another computer? To understand this question requires a deep dive into how evolution works, how humans are different from computers, and how the way technology develops resembles the emergence of a new life form on our planet. You could start by reading the concluding chapter, Chapter 14.
2. Wilson, D. S. (2007). *Evolution for Everyone: How Darwin's Theory Can Change the Way We Think About Our Lives*, Delacorte Press.

   This book argues that Darwinian evolution pervades nearly everything in the world, not just biology but also economics, sociology, science, etc. The author calls himself an "evolutionist," and, although he does not specifically address technology, it is not hard to see how to apply his principle to technology development.
3. Shane, J. (2019). *You Look Like a Thing and I Love You: How Artificial Intelligence Works and Why It's Making the World a Weirder Place*, Voracious.

   This book was published before the ChatGPT revolution, but nevertheless offers tremendous insights into AI. Written by an AI researcher, this book gives a wonderful analysis of the quirky behaviors of deep neural networks. It reinforces the observation that AI researchers came to expect to be surprised by the behavior of the AIs.
4. Kahneman, D. (2011). *Thinking Fast and Slow*. New York, Farrar, Straus and Giroux.

   This classic book is essential reading for understanding the difference between rational and intuitive thinking in humans. It therefore sheds light on the aspirational goal of AIs capable of rational thinking. Kahneman won the Nobel Prize in Economics for his work on prospect theory, which overturns the classic economists' utility theory. Utility theory posits rational, objective, and proportional behavior. Prospect theory modifies this to account for two systems of cognition, systems 1 and 2, where the first reacts quickly and intuitively and second handles rational, logical thought. The first introduces many distortions, such as over-valuing highly improbable returns and over-estimating risk.

5. Lee, E. A. (2022), "What Can Deep Neural Networks Teach Us About Embodied Bounded Rationality," *Frontiers in Psychology*, vol. 25, April 2022, doi: 10.3389/fpsyg.2022.761808.

   This open-access paper analyzes the differences between human thinking and the functions of deep neural networks, claiming that DNNs resemble Kahneman's "fast" thinking in humans more than the "slow" rational thinking ideal.

References

Barrat, J. (2013). *Our final invention: Artificial intelligence and the end of the human era*. St. Martin's Press.

Bostrom, N. (2014). *Superintelligence: Paths, dangers, strategies*. Oxford University Press.

Bubeck, S., Chandrasekaran, V., Eldan, R., Gehrke, J., Horvitz, E., Kamar, E., Lee, P., Lee, Y. T., Li, Y., Lundberg, S., Nori, H., Palangi, H., Ribeiro, M. T., & Zhang, Y. (2023, March 22). *Sparks of artificial general intelligence: Early experiments with GPT-4*. arXiv:2303.12712v1 [cs.CL].

Chomsky, N., Roberts, I., & Watumull, J. (2023, March 8). The false promise of ChatGPT. *New York Times*.

Dennett, D. C. (2017). *From bacteria to Bach and back: The evolution of minds*. New York.

Ford, M. (2015). *Rise of the robots -- Technology and the threat of a jobless future*. Basic Books.

Heaven, W. D. (2023, March 3). The inside story of how ChatGPT was built from the people who made it. *MIT Technology Review*.

Kahneman, D. (2011). *Thinking fast and slow*. Farrar, Straus and Giroux.

Kelly, K. (2016). *The inevitable: Understanding the 12 technological forces that will shape our future*. Penguin Books.

Kissinger, H. A., Schmidt, E., & Huttenlocher, D. (2023, February 24). ChatGPT heralds an intellectual revolution. *The Wall Street Journal*.

Kuhn, T. S. (1962). *The structure of scientific revolutions*. University of Chicago Press.

Lee, K.-F. (2018). *Super-powers: China, Silicon Valley, and the new world order*. Houghton Mifflin Harcourt.

Lee, E. A. (2020). *The coevolution: The entwined futures of humans and machines*. MIT Press.

Lee, E. A. (2022, April). What can deep neural networks teach us about embodied bounded rationality. *Frontiers in Psychology, 25*. https://doi.org/10.3389/fpsyg.2022.761808

Lichtman, J. W., Pfister, H., & Shavit, N. (2014). The big data challenges of connectomics. *Nature Neuroscience, 17*, 1448–1454.

Rogers, D. S., & Ehrlich, P. R. (2008). Natural selection and cultural rates of change. *Proceedings of the National Academy of Sciences of the United States of America, 105*(9), 3416–3420.

Shane, J. (2019). *You look like a thing and I love you: How artificial intelligence works and why it's making the world a weirder place*. Voracious.

Shumailov, I., Shumaylov, Z., Zhao, Y., Gal, Y., Papernot, N., & Anderson, R. (2023, May 31). *The curse of recursion: Training on generated data makes models forget*. arXiv:2305.17493v2 [cs.LG].

Tegmark, M. (2017). *Life 3.0: Being human in the age of artificial intelligence*. Alfred A. Knopf.

Zuboff, S. (2019). *The age of surveillance capitalism: The fight for a human future at the new frontier of power*. PublicAffairs, Hachette Book Group.

AI @ Work: Human Empowerment or Disempowerment?

Sabine T. Koeszegi

If you could train an AI to be a Buddhist,
It would probably be pretty good.
Reid Hoffmann

Abstract Recent advancements in generative AI systems fuel expectations that AI will free workers to resolve creative, complex, and rewarding tasks by automating routine and repetitive work. Furthermore, algorithmic decision systems (ADS) will improve decision quality by providing real-time information and insights, analyzing vast amounts of data, and generating recommendations to support decision-making. In this narrative, AI empowers workers to achievements that they could not reach without the technology. However, using AI in work contexts may also lead to changes in workers' roles and identities, leading to feelings of reduced self-efficacy and lower confidence in their abilities and a sense of diminished value in the workplace, their ethical decision-making abilities, and professional integrity. Initial empirical findings on the impact of AI in the work context point to essential design aspects that will determine which of the narratives becomes a reality. This chapter presents these initial findings and makes design suggestions.

This book chapter is adapted from previous work published in Koeszegi, S.T., Zafari, S. & Grabler, R. (2023): The computer says no: How automated decision systems affect workers' role perceptions in sociotechnical systems; in Garcia-Murillo, M. & Renda A. (Eds): Artificial Intelligence at Work: Interconnections and Policy Implications, Edward Elgar Publishing Ltd., and Koeszegi, S. T. (2023). Automated Decision Systems: Why Human Autonomy is at Stake. In Collective Decisions: Theory, Algorithms And Decision Support Systems, Springer (pp. 155–169).

S. T. Koeszegi (✉)
Institute of Management Science, TU Wien, Vienna, Austria
e-mail: sabine.koeszegi@tuwien.ac.at

H. Werthner et al. (eds.), *Introduction to Digital Humanism*,
https://doi.org/10.1007/978-3-031-45304-5_12

1 Introduction

> I am ChatGPT. ... My main goal is to be a useful tool for people looking for information. I strive to provide accurate and helpful answers as best I can be based on my programming and training. ... I have no personal goals or motivations, as I am an artificial intelligence and have no consciousness or emotions. ... Inside me, I analyze the input I receive, break it down into its parts, and use algorithms to generate an answer based on the patterns and relationships I have learned from my training data. ... My training data consists of much text from various sources, such as books, articles, and websites (Chat GPT, https://chat.openai.com/chat, 07.03.23).

You have just read ChatGPT's answer: "Who are you, what are your intentions, and how do you work?" The achievements of this artificial intelligence and similar tools are impressive. They allow routine and repetitive tasks to automate, freeing workers to focus on more complex and creative work. They provide workers with real-time information and insights by analyzing data, generating recommendations to support decision-making, and improving decision quality. They may facilitate communication and collaboration among workers or provide personalized assistance. These systems can serve as digital mentors or coaches, providing guidance, training, and task feedback, helping workers improve their skills and performance. They may also support generating ideas, drafting content, and giving creative suggestions. In this narrative, AI empowers workers to achievements they could not reach without the technology, and experts speak of another significant breakthrough. With the new generative AI systems, the next milestone in the development of artificial intelligence has been reached in augmenting human capabilities.

This new narrative partly contradicts the earlier narrative by MIT's stars Erik Brynjolfsson and Andrew McAfee, who framed the fundamental change of work through AI and automation as a "Race Against the Machine" (2012) in which AI technologies will more and more replace humans. While other chapters of this book discuss potential applications of AI in work processes and answer questions of which tasks and jobs could be replaced by AI (routine cognitive and manual tasks are particularly prone to automation (Autor et al., 2003)), we are interested in the question of how AI systems will change work and impact our understanding of the roles of humans and machines in collaborative work settings. Using AI in work contexts may lead to changes in workers' roles and identities. As AI automates tasks previously performed by humans, workers may need to adapt to new roles, resulting in self-perception shifts, impacting their self-identity and how they view their role in the workplace. Furthermore, workers may worry about the potential for AI to take over their tasks, leading to feelings of reduced self-efficacy and lower confidence in their abilities and a sense of diminished value in the workplace. Also, workers may feel responsible for the ethical implications of using AI, which may influence their self-perception regarding their ethical decision-making abilities and professional integrity.

At this point, it is too early to assess what impact generative AI will have on people in the work context—which of the two narratives will prevail—whether AI will tend to empower or disempower people. The decision on this will ultimately be made in the design of AI systems. Initial empirical findings on the impact of AI in the work context point to essential design aspects that will determine which of the narratives becomes a reality. This chapter presents these initial findings and makes design suggestions. In Sect. 2, we will introduce algorithmic decision systems (ADS) and discuss subsequently in Sect. 3 how they impact decision outcomes. Section 4 addresses in detail how ADS will change work, i.e., how tasks are assigned to roles (human or AI); how ADS may affect self-assessment, self-efficacy, and human competencies; and why human oversight and accountability need to be addressed when ADS are at work. Finally, we provide design propositions and conclusions in Sect. 5.

2 Algorithmic Decision Systems

There are countless and incredibly diverse applications of AI. There will be no industry or workplace that will not be affected by partial automation (Brynjolfsson & McAfee, 2012). Routine tasks that generally do not require human intervention (Autor et al., 2003) can be fully automated. At the same time, however, there will be tasks that can only be solved with specific human skills on a cognitive, social, or cultural level. Tasks that require human skills in analytical problem-solving, critical thinking and judgment, creativity, empathy, entrepreneurial skills, leadership, persuasion, or imagination cannot be performed by AI alone. Working conditions will, therefore, increasingly include hybrid work environments where AI systems complement and augment human skills (Daugherty & Wilson, 2018).

This chapter emphasizes cases in which agency is shared between human and machines, i.e., in hybrid activities that require some form of collaboration. The most important tasks that we could transfer to machines are decisions. Automated decision systems (ADS) are "systems that encompass a decision-making model, an algorithm that translates this model into computable code, the data this code uses as an input, and the entire environment surrounding its use" (Chiusi et al., 2020). They are often framed as augmenting AI technology, supporting human decisions and problem-solving processes by enhancing human judgment with machine intelligence-based analytic capabilities.

Informed by the Aristotelian view of phronesis, human judgment includes the following elements (Koutsikouri et al., 2023):

1. *Not knowing*, i.e., considering that the situation also contains unknown dimensions and relates to answering questions like "Where does a problem begin/end?" "What is at stake?" "What is relevant?"
2. *Emotions*: as sensory perceptions, they inform us of what is essential and alert us to something that requires our attention and provide a motivation compelling us to act.
3. *Sensory perception*, which is not reduced to collecting data but is intertwined with meaning and emotions and is part of human sense-making, making them open for sensory impressions despite the influence of prior knowledge and prejudice.
4. *Lived experience*, i.e., cultivated professional knowledge, which paves the way for dealing with the horizons of not knowing.

5. *Intuition*: understood as contextual and embodied (tacit) knowledge that denotes the unconscious knowledge process of pattern recognition through accumulated experiences.
6. *Emisteme* (scientific knowledge) and *techne* (lived experience): reflects the phronetic use of general knowledge and lived experience, which entails knowing when and how to apply rules and principles in a specific situation.

Human judgment is closely tied to action and has a strong collective quality in professional contexts. It can be summarized as a "synthesizing capacity in human action" (Koutsikouri et al., 2023, p. 5298), and algorithmic decision systems cannot replace human judgment. Other than human judgment, ADS relies on known data, cannot change ultimate (pre-programmed) goals, and is disconnected from sense-making and emotions for human-centered decisions. However, it can process immense amounts of data to detect patterns and use the knowledge represented in data available for specific purposes (Dragicevic et al., 2020). Hence, combining these complementary capabilities should empower and enhance human problem-solving capabilities (Agrawale et al., 2019; Krüger et al., 2017).

The idea of being supported by support systems in decision-making emerged in the 1960s. Since then, researchers have developed data and model-based systems to support complex and challenging decision-making (e.g., Kersten & Lai, 2007). However, with data-driven AI methods, the field of application has expanded to simple, ordinary everyday decisions, where we are either supported by pre-selecting suitable alternatives or they make and execute decisions entirely for us (Koeszegi, 2021).

The paradigmatic change of ADS is based on the ever-increasing autonomy and the resulting agency of such systems. Decisions we made ourselves in the past are wholly or partially transferred to ADS. In many applications of algorithmic decision-making, the boundaries between automated decision-making and decision-making support are blurred, and often, humans are unaware that ADS are working in the background.

Applications of algorithmic decision systems are manifold and diverse (see Fig. 1), as are the reasons for using them and their effects on decision quality. For example, recommender systems help in the pre-selection of decision alternatives (e.g., search engines), pattern recognition systems reduce complexity (e.g., medical diagnostics), predictive analytics systems minimize uncertainty and risk (e.g., prediction of creditworthiness), and assistive systems can be used to reduce human errors of judgment (e.g., automatic brake assistants). Hence, ADS are associated with increased efficiency in decision-making, including lower costs and better outcomes (e.g., Smith et al., 2010; Wihlborg et al., 2016).

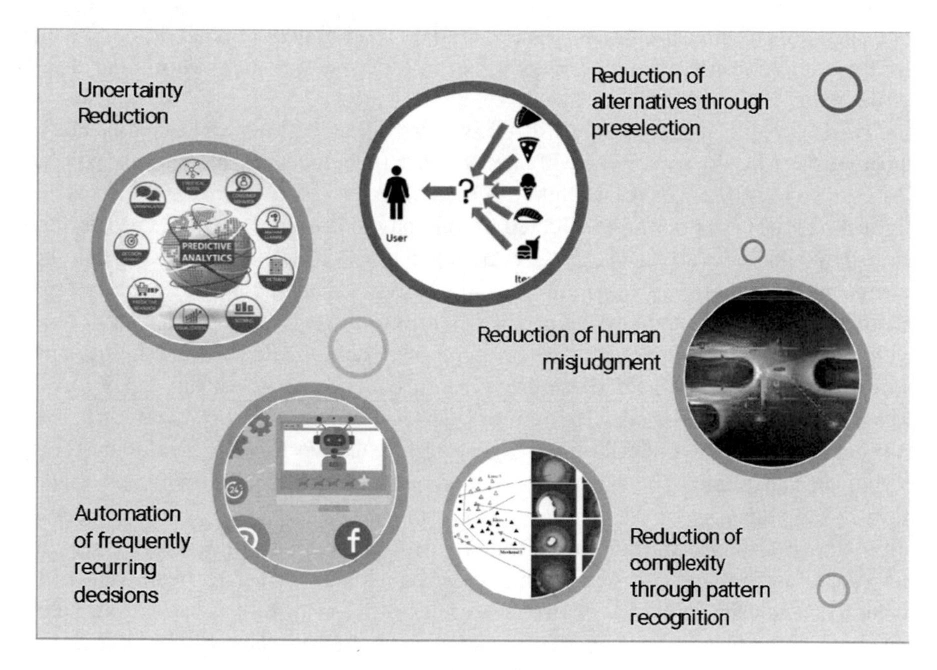

Fig. 1 Applications of algorithmic decision systems

3 How ADS Impact Decision Outcomes

Indeed, under laboratory conditions, combining humans and ADS's complementary capabilities improves decision quality. For instance, human-AI collaboration outperforms human-only or AI-only decisions in diagnosing cancer (Wang et al., 2016). The resulting collaborative success is attributed to the unique advantages that emerge from combining human and AI capabilities in a compatible way (Krüger et al., 2017). Furthermore, a well-designed ADS enhances data analysis by promoting the understanding of multimodal information extracted from multiple data channels, e.g., sorting, scoring, or categorizing the data. At the same time, it reduces the cognitive workload demand for the decision-maker, resulting in improved decision quality (Dragicevic et al., 2018).

ADS is also seen as a game changer in the public sector. Through ADS support, politicians and public servants expect higher efficiency, better service, and higher engagement and professionalism. Ranerup and Henriksen (2019) empirical findings reveal that in the Swedish administration, the new technology in some respects has increased, in association with a focus on citizen-centricity—accountability, decreased costs, and enhanced efficiency. However, they also critically address aspects of negotiating the trade-offs between professional knowledge vs. automated treatment, a potential decrease in costs vs. the increase in service quality, and citizen trust vs. the lack of transparency. Kuziemski and Misuraca (2020) argue that the "public sector's predicament is a tragic double bind:

its obligations to protect citizens from potential algorithmic harms are at odds with the temptation to increase its efficiency—or in other words—to govern algorithms while governing by algorithms."

Overall, people's attitudes toward ADSs seem overly optimistic: Decisions taken automatically by AI are often evaluated on par or better than by human experts (Araujo et al., 2018) even though research that has focused on the effects of algorithmic decisions on those affected has already tempered the high expectations. Indeed, Whittaker et al. (2018, p. 42) conclude in the AI NOW 2018 Report that the harms and biases in AI systems are beyond question: "That debate has been settled, the evidence has mounted beyond doubt." It turns out that algorithmic choices come with severe problems due to partial or incomplete data, inadequate modeling, and problematic objectives and fail with severe consequences (e.g., Citron, 2007; Jackson & Marx, 2017; Murray, 2015; Feijo, 2018; Loewus, 2017; Charette, 2018). Whittaker et al. (2018) cite a string of high-profile examples to show how AI systems perpetuate and amplify social injustice and inequality. Furthermore, in exceptionally high-risk applications of AI systems, such as in healthcare, scholars raise concerns about the prevalence of poor reporting in deep learning studies that assess the diagnostic performance of AI systems to be equivalent to that of healthcare professionals and criticize that "despite the accelerating advance of AI adoption, there has been little high-quality evidence establishing the efficacy of these tools in practice" (Burger, 2022). Also, Bogen and Rieke (2018) list numerous examples of how ADS can perpetuate interpersonal, institutional, and systemic biases due to discrimination based on gender, race, age, or religion. The Berkeley Haas Center for Equity, Gender, and Leadership recently analyzed 133 systems across industries from 1988 and 2021 and found that an alarmingly high share of 44.2% of the systems demonstrates gender bias. Around a quarter of the system has gender and racial bias (Smith & Rustagi, 2021).

ADS's autonomous, complex, and scalable nature introduces ethical challenges and may exacerbate societal tensions and inequalities (Mökander et al., 2021). These features pose different challenges to be resolved, i.e., the system's autonomy makes it hard to assign accountability for failures for outcomes, complexity and opacity of ADS impede to link outcomes (effects) with causes, and scalability implies challenges in managing such systems.

Achieving better decision quality with ADS requires a well-designed human-ADS interface with careful consideration of the more extensive sociotechnical system, i.e., the implementation context. Thus, fully realizing the positive potential of ADS in work processes requires detailed sociotechnical system analysis and design (Zafari et al., 2021). People form (correct or incorrect) expectations about a system's capabilities and assumptions about its reliability and trustworthiness. The design of AI systems has to ensure that there is neither overconfidence in algorithmic decisions nor rejection of superior yet imperfect algorithmic decisions (e.g., Burton et al., 2019). Workers will adjust their roles and self-image in the collaborative work process accordingly. These adaptation processes within such a socio-technical system may jeopardize a clear assignment of tasks and responsibilities and pose additional and novel challenges for work design (Zafari & Koeszegi, 2018). When decisions are made in a collaborative process, the assessment of decision quality also becomes a key concern, where criteria such as precision and accuracy are far from sufficient. All these aspects require the consideration of social psychological issues in the design of AI that go beyond a human-computer-interaction perspective. In the last decade, the paradigm that technology is shaped by and simultaneously influences the evolution of social structures (Orlikowski, 2007; Zammuto et al., 2007) has become increasingly prevalent. In the following, these aspects will be discussed in more detail.

4 How ADSs Change Work

To date, little attention has been paid to analyzing the impact of ADS on human actors within a socio-technical system. Anecdotal evidence from early experiences with factory robotization refers to applauding workers during robot failures. It made the workers feel better about themselves because robots also failed and were not perfect. Following the narrative that imperfect humans are being replaced by flawless, intelligent, precise, and efficient machines, this emotional response from workers is only understandable. It can be expected that using ADS will have lasting effects on people's self-perception and self-efficacy. In the following, we discuss three aspects—addressed by Bainbridge in 1986 as ironies of automation—that will inevitably change as a result of the shift of decisions and agency from humans to ADSs (see Fig. 2):

1. Usually, only those tasks are automated, which can be easily automated, rather than those that should be automated (e.g., because they are stressful, unhealthy, monotonous, etc.). These design errors prevent the realization of an optimal synergy between humans and machines.
2. Delegating tasks to AI systems can also negatively impact human competencies and know-how long-term. Meaningful experiences are no longer gained; essential skills and abilities are only recovered if needed and trained. In addition, in the

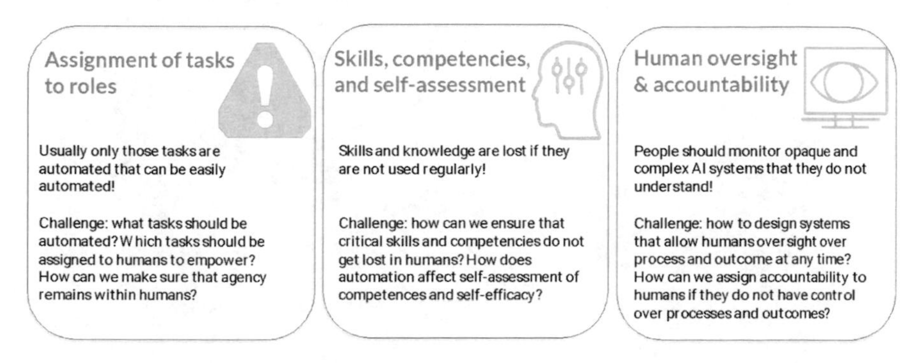

Fig. 2 Challenges in human-ADS collaboration

long run—without immediate feedback on the quality of a decision—a flawed self-assessment may result, either in a bias against automation or in complacency. Again, in the long run, these dynamics will negate the potential benefits of AI decision support.

3. Finally, despite all the automation, humans still need to be tasked with monitoring AI systems and taking responsibility for the process and outcome—a task humans cannot solve in the case of opaque ADS. This leads to organizational and legal challenges regarding assigning responsibility and liability.

4.1 Assignment of Tasks to Roles

ADS significantly impact work processes, individuals' tasks, and their understanding of their roles. The British TV comedy show *Little Britain* presents these changes satirically. In this sketch, a mother visits the hospital with her 5-year-old daughter to make an appointment for a tonsil operation. After the receptionist enters the daughter's details, she says the child is scheduled for bilateral hip surgery. Despite the mother's objections, which the receptionist initially types into her computer, she repeatedly responds with the answer: "The computer says no!" Regardless of how reasonable the mother's objections and how wrong the computer's statements are, the machine's suggested decision ultimately prevails. The satire reveals how supposedly "intelligent systems" can absurdly shift the roles and responsibilities of humans and machines and that "clever" devices with their mathematical algorithms are trusted too much.

Practical experience and scientific studies confirm this satire to be more realistic than we know and draw attention to critical aspects (Fig. 3).

In a case study of a Swedish government agency, where an ADS is used to assess the eligibility of applicants for government benefits, the shift in role structure is

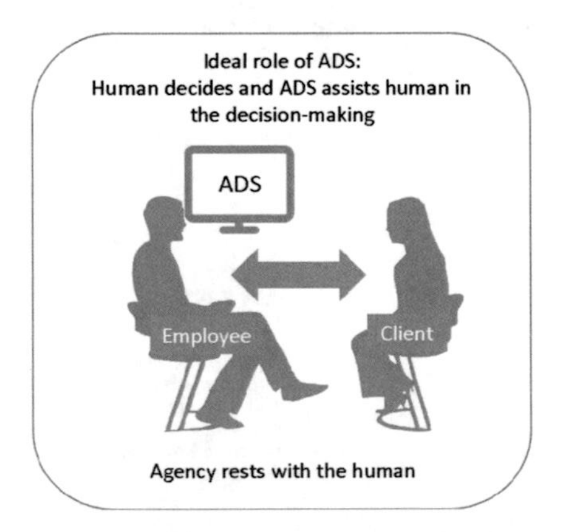

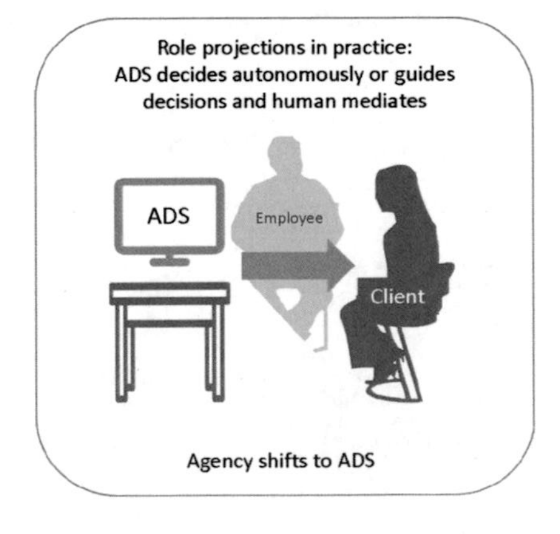

Fig. 3 Role projections and agency in practice

visible (Wihlborg et al., 2016). Whereas previously, the staff members made assessments and decisions based on the application material, they increasingly see themselves only as mediators between the system and the applicants. They "just keep the system running," although they are formally responsible for the final decision. Officials point out in interviews that the system proposes a decision based on all the information entered; therefore, there can be no room for doubt about the decision. They are convinced that the ADS cannot be wrong and attribute high competencies to the system.

In contrast, the perception of their competencies and the capacity to act (in comparison) is perceived as lower. Hence, the assignment of tasks is associated with corresponding expectations and attributions of competence, while one's ability to act is equally restricted. Accordingly, Wihlborg et al. (2016) highlight how decision-support users become mediators rather than decision-makers. While self-determined action requires a degree of personal accountability, delegating decisions to automated systems limits this agency and perceived control over the decision-making process.

This role shift is a consequence of most digitalization strategies, which focus mainly on enhancing machine intelligence and industrial productivity by considering workers as mere "users" rather than collaborators of these systems. When ADS restrict human roles to exercise or communicate ADS decisions, it becomes increasingly difficult for humans to assume accountability for the whole process and outcomes or to take corrective action in the case of a system failure or system errors.

How the user's perception of the potential roles of ADS are entangled with the self-assessment of their competence shows in an experimental study by Jacobsen et al. (2020) in Denmark. In a collaborative waste sorting task for recycling, laypersons received classifications of items and confidence scores by an AI system. At the same time, participants performed better with ADS overall, people who were supported perceived themselves as less effective than they were (underconfident). In contrast, the opposite happened for people with AI support (overconfident). In a qualitative analysis of post-experimental perceptions of the participants of the same study, Papachristos et al. (2021) identified four distinct roles as projections of what users expected from the interaction with the ADS: People who self-assessed relatively high competence in waste sorting (which is a non-trivial task) expected the system to confirm their decision and would ignore a system's opposite suggestion unless they were very unsure. Here ADS were assigned a mirror role (inspired by the fairy tale of Snow White) or an assistant role. In both cases, the agency for the decision resided in the human. Participants who self-assessed, in contrast modest to low, trusted the AI system to have a better judgment. Here, the system was assigned a guiding or even an oracle role, shifting the agency to the system.

It is critical to understand that self-perception is determined by whether users of ADS receive feedback about the correctness of their ultimate decision. Papachristos et al. (2021) find, indeed, if a task that is conducted over a significant period happens to be undertaken with a wrongful decision, still, the user always felt competent; this could impact the overall performance of the collaborative achievement and cease a potential positive impact of ADS in decision-making. On the other hand, if people do not get feedback about the correctness of their decisions, over time, this could decrease their competence and overconfidence in ADS. In the next section, we discuss in more detail how using ADS may impact skills, competencies, and self-assessment.

To rely on algorithmic decisions, human decision-makers must feel in control (Dietvorst et al., 2016; Meurisch et al., 2020). When individuals experience control over work processes and outcomes, they also feel comfortable collaborating with proactive and autonomous AI systems (Zafari & Koeszegi, 2020). Hence, providing working conditions that preserve a sense of control and efficacy is vital.

4.2 Self-Assessment, Self-Efficacy, and Human Competences

Human decision-makers will have developed expectations of what the specific ADS can do, should do, and how it functions. These expectations may be formed through personal exposure to similar systems and second-hand experiences from coworkers or media. These preexisting expectations will influence how systems are used and relied on (Burton et al., 2019). Zhang et al. (2021) surveyed people's expectations of AI systems. They found that the preferred characteristics of AI systems do not only relate to instrumental capabilities, but they also expect human-like behavior, performance orientation, and shared understanding between humans and these systems. False expectations about the actual capacities of AI systems may lead to either an automation bias, i.e., over-trust in a system, or, to the contrary, a reluctance to rely on AI systems, i.e., a so-called algorithm aversion (Burton et al., 2019).

On the one hand, the mere fact that a decision is made by a machine, not by a human being, lends it a certain degree of legitimacy and neutrality (Citron & Pasquale, 2014). This can simultaneously weaken trust in one's expertise and competence. Empirical studies show that lay people with little or no knowledge of a particular domain prefer to trust an algorithm rather than rely on human expertise. At the same time, experts are significantly less likely to rely on the credibility of algorithmic predictions (Logg et al., 2019). Wouters et al. (2019) also show how laypeople can be impressed even by obviously incorrect ADS outputs: In their study, an ADS with face recognition software identified not only the gender, ethnicity, and age of subjects but also their emotional state and personality traits. Incorrect classifications by the system did not lead to distrust in some subjects but, on the contrary, even caused some subjects to question their self-image: "[The display] must be correct. Because a computer is doing the evaluation, and computers are better than humans at making those kinds of conclusions" (Subject, quoted in Wouters et al., 2019, 454). This automation bias discourages people from questioning system decisions or seeking more information. It leads to inappropriate monitoring of automated functions, i.e., complacency, and creates, in the long run, a human dependency on ADS (Parasuraman & Manzey, 2010; Bahner et al., 2008).

On the other hand, studies also report a so-called Dunning-Kruger effect (DKE) (see He et al., 2023), a metacognitive bias due to which individuals overestimate their competence and performance compared to algorithmic support. An inflated, false self-assessment and illusory superiority despite poor performance can lead to an under-reliance on AI systems. He et al. (2023) find that a linear relationship cannot explain the interaction between self-assessment and reliance on AI systems. Instead, they suggest that explanations by the system about the flawed nature of AI advice may mitigate the lack of trust and DKE. Thus, to develop an appropriate level of trust in the technology, algorithmic education is needed to create reasonable expectations of ADS and its capabilities: people need to be trained not only in their area of expertise but also in how to interact with algorithmic tools and interpret their results, including teaching important core statistical concepts such as error and uncertainty. Users must be exposed to errors in automation during training to mitigate the risk of complacency, misuse of automation, and bias against automation (Bahner et al., 2008). However, the gravity of decisions also influences human reliance on AI systems. The more serious the consequences of decisions are, the more people are reluctant to rely on algorithms (Filiz et al., 2023). Only when workers understand the decision-making process can they evaluate the consequences of their decisions and gain new knowledge to overcome algorithm aversion (Adadi & Berrada, 2018).

Another critical factor influencing AI system support perception is the timing of the decision support. As discussed earlier, workers using ADS may feel reduced to the role of a recipient of the machine decision and affect user acceptance and be perceived as reputational damage when using such systems, as decision-makers feel they have less opportunity to demonstrate their expertise. This could be avoided by providing decision support after decision-makers have processed information to decide and use the ADS as additional information. Langer et al. (2021) show that these users show a steep increase in self-efficacy in the task and are more satisfied with their decision.

Skills and competencies might deteriorate when they are not used and trained regularly. Hence, deploying ADS may also lead to de-skilling processes of workers. Also, early experiences with automation show that when humans no longer acquire essential expertise or skills—or lose them over time—automated systems replace them (Bainbridge, 1983). At the same time, the skills required of workers also change with the use of ADS. Smith et al. (2010) show in their study how even low-level automation can significantly impact workers' skill levels. For example, the introduction of electronic vote-counting machines turned the previously relatively simple routine task of counting votes by hand into a complex problem about cybersecurity requiring know-how about algorithmic systems and data security. While the switch to an automated system is intended to prevent human error in the counting process, it also creates new challenges—and thus sources of error—because of the need to operate and monitor these systems. Looking at this example, it is still being determined whether the great hopes for efficiency and avoiding human error will be achieved. It seems more like a shift in the potential causes of errors.

Another interesting study analyzes how the use of ADS affects what humans know—and an AI does not know—that is, the unique human knowledge we described earlier as phronesis. As discussed earlier, ADS are framed as a complementary technology to humans, supporting human decisions and problem-solving processes by enhancing human judgment with machine intelligence-based analytic capabilities. Fügener et al. (2021) analyze the effect of this joint decision-making on the knowledge of humans. They not only look at the individual level but also analyze AI's impact on the "wisdom of crowds." After a set of different controlled experiments, they conclude that humans interacting with artificial intelligence behave like "Borgs," i.e., cyborgs with high individual performance but without human individuality, resulting ultimately in loss of unique human knowledge and leading to long-term adverse outcomes in a variety of human-AI decision-making environments. Their simulation results also suggest that groups of humans interacting with AI are far less effective than those without AI support.

All these results indicate that using ADS does not necessarily always lead to improvement in decision outcomes. On the contrary, long-term adverse effects on self-assessment, self-efficacy, and unique human know-how can cancel out ADS's positive effects and lead to a worse performance of the socio-technical decision than if humans would decide alone.

4.3 Human Oversight and Accountability

Transferring decision-making to ADS includes transferring (part of) the control over the decision-making process and the actual decision from humans to artificial agents while keeping humans accountable for the outcomes of the decisions. Hence, human actors might be accountable for a system's wrong decision. Such accountability without control over the decision-making process creates ethical issues and tension within organizations that need to be considered and addressed before systems are deployed. Furthermore, from a legal perspective, within the EU, some fully automated decisions concerning natural persons are prohibited by Article 22 of the EU General Data Protection Regulation (GDPR 2016), which stipulates that natural persons have the right not to be subjected to a decision based solely on automated processing, including profiling. They have furthermore the right to access meaningful explanations of algorithmic decisions.

Generally, it seems complicated to accept ADS as legitimate if they replace humans in critical decisions (Simmons, 2018). Smith et al. (2010) illustrate this in an example where the use of automated fingerprint identification systems affects the decision-making of experts: the experts' final decision is based on a recommendation for the most likely match of the fingerprint, leaving some experts even unable to explain how the decision was derived as it is beyond their comprehension and scrutiny. According to Smith et al. (2010), this shows two dysfunctions of accountability in ADS-supported decisions: (1) experts are relying more on outputs by the machine while not understanding the decision process, and (2) experts can be blamed for false accusations of a crime as it is them who make the final decision. Nevertheless, they cannot be blamed entirely as the automated system had a part in it

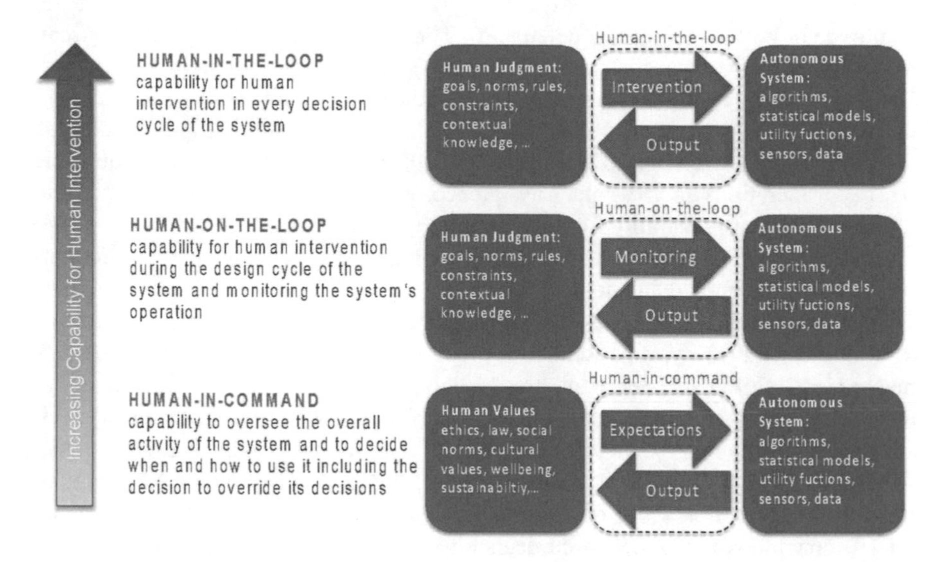

Fig. 4 Human intervention in AI systems

(i.e., diffusion of accountability). Other studies show that as the autonomy of an autonomous AI system increases, people attribute more blame to the system than to themselves (Kim & Hinds, 2006; Furlough et al., 2021). One possible explanation is that people perceive these autonomous agents to have more agency and freedom in deciding and are thus automatically subjected to taking the blame for the choice. However, this is different for taking credits. Lei and Rau (2021) find that autonomous AI systems are more blamed than human agents, but they both received similar levels of positive recognition. Thus, introducing independent agents to work processes challenges traditional accountability practices.

Systems, therefore, should allow different degrees of oversight and control depending on the AI system‘s application and the potential risk of bad decisions. Figure 4 shows how the concepts of "human-in-the-loop," human-on-the-loop, and human-in-command differ in the degree of human intervention.

The human-in-command approach is only suitable for fast, standardized, and frequent decisions in a well-defined context, where only little negative consequences of an incorrect decision by the AI are to be expected. AI-based technologies cannot meet the requirements for moral agency and accountability (Coeckelbergh, 2019; Zafari & Koeszegi, 2018). Hence, decisions with high uncertainty of outcomes that involve significant ethical issues require human involvement in the form of a human-in-the-loop or human-on-the-loop approach. Decisions that need high transparency should be left entirely to humans (Ivanov, 2022). Tatiana Cutts (2022) questions whether human oversight principles are sufficient to ensure ethical standards for ADS-assisted decision outcomes. The principle of oversight provides that humans should play a corrective role, particularly in critical decisions (such as the relative priority of organ transplants for patients or whether to hire an applicant or fire an employee or how to sentence a defendant). The assumption is that applying human judgment is both a necessary and sufficient safeguard against unjust decisions. However, safeguarding fundamental rights requires not only human judgment in the decision-making process itself but also gatekeeping, i.e., making principled decisions about the use of ADS only after ensuring that they take into account the right considerations in the right way. Hence, ensuring that workers are able and willing to take responsibility for ADS-supported decisions falls short. The required gatekeeping functions must be assumed by the management, taking overall accountability for ADS implementations.

In addition, ADSs also raise interesting liability issues when the ability of humans to control technical systems is limited (Wagner, 2019). Because most regulatory mechanisms follow a pattern of binary liability by regulating either human or machine agency but are not allowing meaningful liability for socio-technical decision-making, regulatory gray areas arise where human rights are challenged. Although specific regulatory mechanisms exist for purely automated decision-making, they do not apply once humans sign off automated decisions. Wagner (2019) concludes that ADS-based decision-making is quasi-automation, which is only a rubber-stamping mechanism for fully automated decisions.

As described earlier, a lack of human control and oversight can also result from overdependence on ADS. One possible strategy to mitigate this problem is to develop so-called reflection machines (Haselager et al., 2023) that provide meaningful human problem overview and control through their specific form of decision support. A reflection machine does not give the decision-makers suggestions for a decision but instead challenges their reasonings and decisions. Reflection machines, for example, point to facts or raise critical issues or counterarguments inconsistent with the proposed decision to improve the problem-solving process and decision quality. This support also increases people's problem-solving skills and counteracts an unreflective reliance on ADS. Especially in the medical field, experimental studies already show positive experiences in this regard (Haselager et al., 2023).

Whether people are willing to take responsibility for ADS-supported decisions depends mainly on the extent to which they understand the "inner workings" and how an ADS makes decisions. In other words, a lack of transparency about the system design, the system's objectives, and how a decision recommendation is reached (the so-called black-box problem) weaken people's willingness to take responsibility for the decisions. Therefore, ADS should be able to close the knowledge gap, which is also understood as reducing the information asymmetry between the system and the users (Malle et al., 2007). Hence, system transparency increases technology acceptance and establishes appropriate trust (Miller, 2019). Expanding system transparency allows users to understand better the performance of the system and the processes that lead the system to make a particular decision or prediction (Felzmann et al., 2019; de Graaf & Malle, 2017). However, it is not enough to have access to the data processed by the system; the results of ADS must be accompanied by explanations of how and why a decision was made. Users must view the results of ADS as plausible, valuable, and trustworthy (Papagni et al., 2022; Papagni & Koeszegi, 2021a, 2021b). The focus is not on the exactness of the explanation but on the understanding and plausibility of explanations that result from contextual negotiations between the system and its users. When a system explains its decision-making process in a language that workers can understand, they better understand the causes and premises associated with the decision. In this way, explaining can help workers consider outcomes more thoroughly, manage the problem, and feel accountable for the outcome of the decision process.

5 Conclusions

Recent advancements in generative AI systems fuel expectations that AI will free workers from routine and repetitive work for creative, complex, and rewarding tasks. Furthermore, ADS will improve decision quality by providing real-time information and insights, analyzing vast amounts of data, and generating recommendations to support decision-making. In this narrative, AI empowers workers to achievements they could not reach without the technology. However, using AI in work contexts may also lead to changes in workers' roles and identities, leading to feelings of reduced self-efficacy and lower confidence in their abilities and a sense of diminished value in the workplace, their ethical decision-making abilities, and professional integrity. We argued that whether AI will empower or disempower, people will ultimately depend on the design of AI systems.

Based on this analysis of the first empirical evidence, we conclude that—next to the empowering capacity of ADS—these systems can also enable human error, reduce human control, eliminate human responsibility, and devalue human capabilities. ADS affects our self-image by pushing us from the active role of decision-maker to the passive role of a mediator or facilitator. At their worst, these systems limit our autonomy and undermine human self-determination. The extent to which these potentially detrimental effects of AI systems on workers come to fruition depends to some extent on the system's design and legal regulations of our fundamental rights.

Complementing human decision-making and problem-solving processes inherently requires the integration of two distinct thought processes: that of the human and that of the AI system. Both processes must be mapped and understood transparently enough to create cognitive compatibility. Otherwise, these processes run in parallel, and algorithmic systems combat rather than enhance human decision-making (Burton et al., 2019). In other words, AI systems must be designed to work for humans, not the other way around. This requires understanding human decision-making processes from a rational and normative decision-making perspective and a sense-making perspective that recognizes the context-dependence of decision-making processes (Papagni & Koeszegi, 2021b).

Transforming today's notion of human-AI collaboration into tomorrow's organizational reality requires specific reference models, procedures, standards, and concrete criteria for appropriately considering human factors in the development and implementation of ADS. In other words, creating a sociotechnical system requires

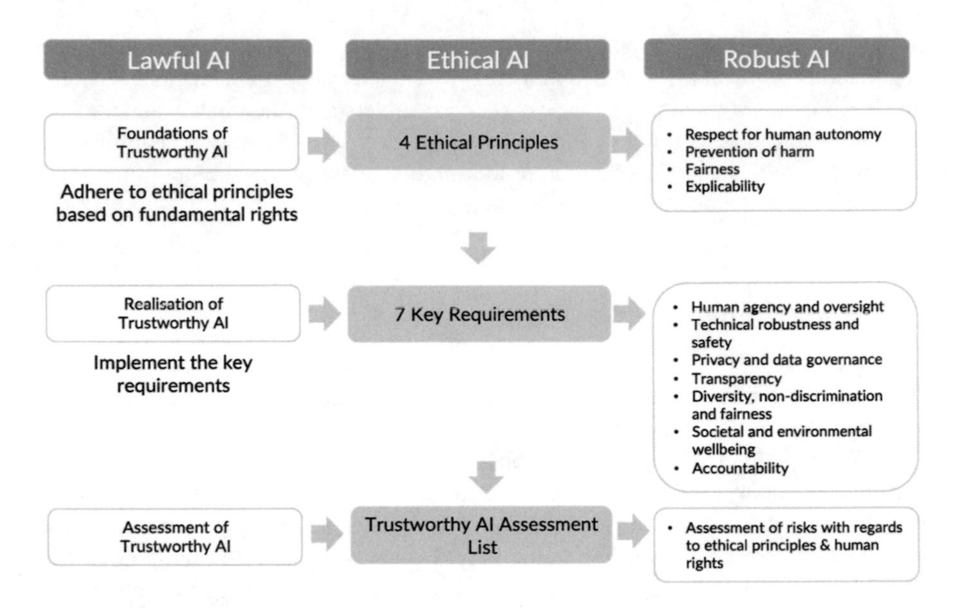

Fig. 5 AI HLEG trustworthy AI

the consideration of both technical and social aspects of work processes to illuminate the mutual influence of technological and social entities. Therefore, it is necessary to identify requirements for human-centered technology design that preserves workers' control and meaningful role. Furthermore, for successful integration of ADS into work organizations, we need to involve workers who use these technologies in their work in the development process rather than presenting them with a fait accompli and requiring them to take responsibility for decisions dictated by ADS, leaving them with only the role of rubberstamping automated decisions. To achieve this, governance mechanisms are needed to help organizations design and deploy ADS ethically while enabling society to reap the full economic and social benefits of automation (Mökander et al., 2021).

Value-based design processes like the IEEE 7000 standard and ethics-based auditing (EBA) as a governance mechanism allow organizations to validate the claims of their systems. Numerous ethics-based frameworks and assessment tools exist for AI systems (see, e.g., Mökander et al., 2021). The framework exhibited in Fig. 5 was developed by the AI High-level Expert Group of the European Commission in 2018 and builds the foundation for the currently negotiated AI regulation proposition within the European member states. It is based on four ethical principles (i.e., respect for human autonomy, prevention of harm, fairness, and explicability). It operationalizes these principles in seven key requirements, which are (1) human agency and oversight; (2) technical robustness and safety; (3) privacy and data governance; (4) transparency; (5) diversity, non-discrimination, and fairness; (6) societal and environmental well-being; and (7) accountability. The Trustworthy AI Assessment List is a proposal for an ethics-based auditing tool that guides system designers into reflecting questions about potential harm and risks associated with the AI system at hand.

Such ethics-based assessment tools provide a structured process for evaluating AI systems for compliance with relevant ethical principles and human rights (Mökander et al., 2021). If they focus not only on the narrower human-machine interface but also consider the broader socio-technical context of implementation, these tools can effectively realize human empowerment. The trustworthy AI assessment tool considers this broader implementation context through the essential requirement (6) societal and environmental well-being.

We conclude this chapter with exemplary questions from the Assessment List of Trustworthy AI (ALTAI) to inspire discussions in the vein of reflection machines.

This subsection helps self-assess necessary oversight measures through governance mechanisms such as human-in-the-loop (HITL), human-on-the-loop (HOTL), or human-in-command (HIC) approaches.

Please determine whether the AI system (choose the appropriate):

Is a self-learning or autonomous system
Is overseen by a *Human*-in-the-Loop
Is overseen by a *Human*-on-the-Loop
Is overseen by a *Human*-in-Command

Have the humans (human-in-the-loop, human-on-the-loop, human-in-command) been given specific training on how to exercise oversight?
Did you establish any detection and response mechanisms for undesirable adverse effects of the AI system for the end-user or subject?
Did you ensure a "stop button" or procedure to safely abort an operation when needed?
Did you take any specific oversight and control measures to reflect the self-learning or autonomous nature of the AI system?
This subsection helps self-assess the potential effects of your AI system on societal and environmental well-being. The following questions address issues related to work contexts:

Does your AI system impact human work and work arrangements?
What is the potential impact of your system on workers and work arrangements?
Do you ensure that the work impacts of the AI system are well understood?
Did you assess whether there is a risk of de-skilling of the workforce? If there is a risk, which steps have been taken to counteract de-skilling risks?
Did you assess how the system may affect the attribution of capabilities and accountabilities in work contexts?

(continued)

Do you ensure that workers understand how the system operates, which capabilities it has, and which not? If yes, describe measures:

Based on your answers to the previous questions, how would you rate the risk that the AI system negatively impacts work and work arrangements?
How would you rate the measures you have adopted to mitigate this risk?

Discussion Questions for Students and Their Teachers

1. Which risks are associated with the implementation of ADS in work contexts?
2. Which design propositions can mitigate adverse effects of ADS, automation bias, or complacency?
3. Which design propositions have been made to ensure the empowerment of workers rather than disempowerment?

Learning Resources for Students

1. Bainbridge, L. (1983): Ironies of automation. In: Automatica 19 (6), S. 775–779, https://doi.org/10.1016/0005-1098(83)90046-8.
   This paper describes in more detail the three ironies of automation, which are also addressed in this book chapter in Fig. 2.
2. HLEG AI. (2019). High-level expert group on artificial intelligence. Ethics Guidelines for Trustworthy AI. *European Commission.* https://digital-strategy.ec.europa.eu/en/library/ethics-guidelines-trustworthy-ai, Accessed 20.04.2023.
   Assessment List of trustworthy AI, European Commission, accessed 23.04.23
   These two deliverables of the AI HLEG of the European Commission build the fundament of the AI regulation act.
3. Chiusi, F. Fischer, S. Kayser-Bril, N. Spielkamp, M. (2020). Automating Society Report 2020. *Algorithm Watch.* https://automatingsociety.algorithmwatch.org. Accessed 20. April 2023.
   This Report of Algorithm Watch comprises an overview of existing AI applications and threats and challenges.

References

Adadi, A., & Berrada, M. (2018). Peeking inside the black-box: A survey on explainable artificial intelligence (XAI). *IEEE Access, 6*, 52138–52160. https://doi.org/10.1109/ACCESS.2018.2870052

Agrawal, A., Gans, J. S., & Goldfarb, A. (2019). Exploring the impact of artificial Intelligence: Prediction versus judgment. *Information Economics and Policy, 47*, 1–6. https://doi.org/10.1016/j.infoecopol.2019.05.001

Araujo, T., De Vreese, C., Helberger, N., Kruikemeier, S., van Weert, J., Bol, N., Oberski, D., Pechenizkiy, M., Schaap, G., & Taylor, L. (2018). Automated decision-making fairness in an AI-driven world: Public perceptions, hopes and concerns. *Digital Communication Methods Lab.* https://hdl.handle.net/11245.1/369fdda8-69f1-4e28-b2c7-ed4ff2f70cf6

Autor, D. H., Levy, F., & Murane, R. J. (2003). The skill content of recent technological change: An empirical exploration. *The Quarterly Journal of Economics, 118*(4), 1279–1333. https://doi.org/10.1162/00335530332255280

Bainbridge, L. (1983). Ironies of automation. *Automatica, 19*(6), 775–779. https://doi.org/10.1016/0005-1098(83)90046-8

Bahner, J. E., Hüper, A.-D., & Manzey, D. (2008). Misuse of automated decision aids: Complacency, automation bias and the impact of training experience. *International Journal of Human-Computer Studies, 66*(9), 688–699. https://doi.org/10.1016/j.ijhcs.2008.06.001

Bogen, M., & Rieke, A. (2018, December 9). Help wanted: An examination of hiring algorithms, equity, and bias. *Upturn*. Accessed April 20, 2023, from https://apo.org.au/node/210071

Brynjolfsson, E., & McAfee, A. (2012). *Race against the machine: How the digital revolution is accelerating innovation, driving productivity, and irreversibly transforming employment and the economy*. Digital Frontier Press.

Burger, M. (2022). *The risk to population health equity posed by automated decision systems: A narrative review*. arXiv preprint arXiv:2001.06615. https://doi.org/10.48550/arXiv.2001.06615

Burton, J. W., Stein, M.-K., & Jensen, T. B. (2019). A systematic review of algorithm aversion in augmented decision making. *Journal of Behavioral Decision Making, 33*(2), 220–239. https://doi.org/10.1002/bdm.2155

Charette, R. N. (2018, January 24). *Michigan's MiDAS unemployment system: Algorithm alchemy created lead, not gold*. IEEE Spectrum. Accessed April 20, 2023, from https://tinyurl.com/6vey252h

Chiusi, F., Fischer, S., Kayser-Bril, N., & Spielkamp, M. (2020). *Automating Society Report 2020*. Algorithm Watch. Accessed April 20, 2023, from https://automatingsociety.algorithmwatch.org

Citron, D. K. (2007). Technological due process. *Washington University Law Review, 85*, 1249.

Citron, D. K., & Pasquale, F. (2014). The scored society: Due process for automated predictions. *Washington University Law Review, 89*, 1.

Coeckelbergh, M. (2019). Artificial intelligence, responsibility attribution, and a relational justification of explainability. *Science and Engineering Ethics*, 1–18. https://doi.org/10.1007/s11948-019-00146-8

Cutts, T. (2022). *Supervising automated decisions*. SSRN Scholarly Paper Nr. 4215108. https://doi.org/10.2139/ssrn.4215108

Daugherty, P. R., & Wilson, H. J. (2018). *Human+ machine: Reimagining work in the age of AI*. Harvard Business Press.

De Graaf, M. M., & Malle, B. F. (2017). *How people explain action (and autonomous intelligent systems should too)*. AAAI Fall Symposia.

Dietvorst, B. J., Simmons, J. P., & Massey, C. (2016). Overcoming algorithm aversion: People will use imperfect algorithms if the can (even slightly) modify them. *Management Science, 64*(3), 1144–1170. https://doi.org/10.1287/mnsc.2016.2643

Dragicevic, N., Ullrich, A., Tsui, E., & Gronau, N. (2018). A conceptual model of knowledge dynamics in the industry 4.0 intelligent grid scenario. *Knowledge Management Research & Practice, 18*(2), 199–213. https://doi.org/10.1080/14778238.2019.1633893

Dragicevic, N., Ullrich, A., Tsui, E., & Gronau, N. (2020). A conceptual model of knowledge dynamics in the industry 4.0 intelligent grid scenario. *Knowledge Management Research & Practice, 18*(2), 199–213. https://doi.org/10.1080/14778238.2019.1633893

European Commission. *Assessment List of trustworthy Artificial Intelligence (ALTAI) for self-assessment*. Accessed April 23, 2023, from https://digital-strategy.ec.europa.eu/en/library/assessment-list-trustworthy-artificial-intelligence-altai-self-assessment

Feijo, S. (2018, July 16). *Here's what happened when Boston tried to assign students good schools close to home*. Northeastern Global News. Accessed April 20, 2023, from https://tinyurl.com/yp5neuxn

Felzmann, H., Fosch-Villaronga, E., Lutz, C., & Tamo-Larrieux, A. (2019). Robots and transparency: The multiple dimensions of transparency in the context of robot technologies. *IEEE Robotics & Automation Magazine, 26*(2), 71–78. https://doi.org/10.1109/MRA.2019.2904644

Filiz, I., Judek, J. R., Lorenz, M., & Spiwoks, M. (2023). The extent of algorithm aversion in decision-making situations with varying gravity. *PLoS ONE, 18*(2), e0278751. https://doi.org/10.1371/journal.pone.0278751

Furlough, C., Stokes, T., & Gillan, D. J. (2021). Attributing blame to robots: I. The influence of robot autonomy. *Human Factors, 63*(4), 592–602. https://doi.org/10.1177/0018720819880641

Fügener, A., Grahl, J., Gupta, A., & Ketter, W. (2021). Will humans-in-the-loop become Borgs? Merits and pitfalls of working with AI. *Management information Systems Quarterly (MISQ), 45*(3). https://papers.ssrn.com/sol3/papers.cfm?abstract_id=3879937

Haselager, P., Schraffenberger, H., Thill, S., Fischer, S., Lanillos, P., van de Groes, S., & van Hooff, M. (2023). Reflection machines: Supporting effective human oversight over medical decision support systems. *Cambridge Quarterly of Healthcare Ethics*, 1–10. https://doi.org/10.1017/S0963180122000718

He, G., Kuiper, L., & Gadiraju, U. (2023). Knowing about knowing: An illusion of human competence can hinder appropriate reliance on AI systems. *CHI '23: Proceedings of the 2023 CHI Conference on Human Factors in Computing Systems, 113*, 1–18. https://doi.org/10.1145/3544548.3581025

HLEG AI. (2019). *Ethics guidelines for trustworthy AI*. Accessed April 20, 2023, from https://digital-strategy.ec.europa.eu/en/library/ethics-guidelines-trustworthy-ai

Ivanov, S. H. (2022). Automated decision-making. *Foresight, 25*(1), 4–19. https://doi.org/10.1108/FS-09-2021-0183

Jackson, D., & Marx, G. (2017, December 6). Data mining program designed to predict child abuse proves unreliable, DCFS says. *Chicago Tribune*. https://tinyurl.com/4wb7yxub

Jacobsen, R. M., Johansen, P. S., Bysted, L. B. L., & Skov, M. B. (2020). Waste wizard: Exploring waste sorting using AI in public spaces. Proceedings of the 11th Nordic Conference on Human-Computer Interaction: Shaping Experiences, Shaping Society, 1–11. https://doi.org/10.1145/3419249.3420180

Kersten, G. E., & Lai, H. (2007). Negotiation support and e-negotiation systems: An overview. *Group Decision and Negotiation, 16*(6), 553–586. https://doi.org/10.1007/s10726-007-9095-5

Kim, T., & Hinds, P. (2006). Whom should I blame? Effects of autonomy and transparency on attributions in human-robot interaction. In *ROMAN 2006 – The 15th IEEE International Symposium on Robot and Human Interactive Communication* (pp. 80–85). https://doi.org/10.1109/ROMAN.2006.314398

Köszegi, S. T. (2021). Automated decision systems: Why human autonomy is at stake. In *Collective decisions: Theory, algorithms and decision support systems* (pp. 155–169). Springer Nature Switzerland AG. http://hdl.handle.net/20.500.12708/30729

Koutsikouri, D., Hylving, L., Lindberg, S., & Bornemark, J. (2023). Seven elements of phronesis: A framework for understanding judgment in relation to automated decision-making. 56th Hawaii Conference on System Sciences (HICSS). https://hdl.handle.net/10125/103280

Krüger, M., Wiebel, C. B., & Wersing, H. (2017). From tools towards cooperative assistants. In *Proceedings of the 5th International Conference on Human Agent Interaction* (pp. 287–294). https://doi.org/10.1145/3125739.3125753

Kuziemski, M., & Misuraca, G. (2020). AI governance in the public sector: Three tales from the frontiers of automated decision-making in democratic settings. *Telecommunications Policy, 44*(6), 101976. https://doi.org/10.1016/j.telpol.2020.101976

Langer, M., König, C. J., & Busch, V. (2021). Changing the means of managerial work: Effects of automated decision support systems on personnel selection tasks. *Journal of Business and Psychology, 36*(5), 751–769. https://doi.org/10.1007/s10869-020-09711-6

Lei, X., & Rau, P. L. P. (2021). Should I blame the human or the robot? Attribution within a human-robot group. *International Journal of Social Robotics, 13*(2), 363–377. https://doi.org/10.1007/s12369-020-00645-w

Loewus, L. (2017, October 26). Houston District settles lawsuit with teachers' union over value-added scores. *Education Week*. Accessed June 01, 2023, from https://tinyurl.com/yckucffc

Logg, J. M., Minsona, J. A., & Moore, D. A. (2019). Algorithm appreciation: People prefer algorithmic to human judgment. *Organizational Behavior and Human Decision Processes, 15*, 90–103. https://doi.org/10.1016/j.obhdp.2018.12.005

Malle, B. F., Knobe, J. M., & Nelson, S. E. (2007). Actor-observer asymmetries in explanations of behavior: New answers to an old question. *The Journal of Personality and Social Psychology, 93*(4), 491. https://doi.org/10.1037/0022-3514.93.4.491

Meurisch, C., Mihale-Wilson, C. A., Hawlitschek, A., Giger, F., Müller, F., Hinz, O., & Mühlhäuser, M. (2020). Exploring user expectations of proactive AI systems. *Proceedings of the ACM on Interactive, Mobile, Wearable and Ubiquitous Technologies, 4*(4), 1–22. https://doi.org/10.1145/3432193

Miller, T. (2019). Explanation in artificial intelligence: Insights from the social sciences. *Artificial Intelligence, 267*, 1–38. https://doi.org/10.1016/j.artint.2018.07.007

Mökander, J., Morley, J., Taddeo, M., & Floridi, L. (2021). Ethics-based auditing of automated decision-making systems: Nature, scope and limitations. *Science and Engineering Ethics, 27*(4), 44. https://doi.org/10.1007/s11948-021-00319-4

Murray, D. (2015, March 20). Queensland authorities confirm 'miscode' affects DNA evidence in criminal cases. *The Courier Mail*. Accessed June 01, 2023, from https://tinyurl.com/mrxkarpw

Orlikowski, W. J. (2007). Sociomaterial practices: Exploring technology at work. *Organisation Studies, 28*(9), 1435–1448. https://doi.org/10.1177/0170840607081138

Papachristos, E., Skov Johansen, P., Møberg Jacobsen, R., Bjørn Leer Bysted, L., & Skov, M. B. (2021). How do people perceive the role of AI in human-AI collaboration to solve everyday tasks? In *CHI Greece 2021: 1st International Conference of the ACM Greek SIGCHI Chapter* (pp. 1–6). https://doi.org/10.1145/3489410.3489420

Papagni, G. J., De Pagter, J., Zafari, S., Filzmoser, M., & Koeszegi, S. T. (2022). May I explain? Explainability is a Trust Support Strategy for Artificial Agents. Accepted in a special Issue AI4P, AI & Society. *Journal of Knowledge, Culture, and Communication*, 1–14.

Papagni, G., & Koeszegi, S. T. (2021a). A pragmatic approach to the intentional stance: Semantic, empirical and ethical considerations for the design of artificial agents. *Minds & Machines, 31*, 505–534. https://doi.org/10.1007/s11023-021-09567-6

Papagni, G., & Koeszegi, S. T. (2021b). Understandable and trustworthy explainable robots: A sensemaking perspective. *Paladyn, Journal of Behavioral Robotics, 12*(1). https://doi.org/10.1515/pjbr-2021-0002

Parasuraman, R., & Manzey, D. H. (2010). Complacency and bias in human use of automation: An attentional integration. *Human Factors, 52*(3), 381–410. https://doi.org/10.1177/0018720810376055

Ranerup, A., & Henriksen, H. Z. (2019). Value positions viewed through the lens of automated decision-making: The case of social services. *Government Information Quarterly, 36*(4), 101377. https://doi.org/10.1016/j.giq.2019.05.004

Simmons, R. (2018). Big data, machine judges, and the criminal justice system's legitimacy. *UC Davis Law Review, 52*, 1067. https://doi.org/10.2139/ssrn.3156510

Smith, G., & Rustagi, I. (2021). When good algorithms go sexist: Why and how to advance AI gender equity. *Stanford Social Innovation Review*. https://doi.org/10.48558/A179-B138

Smith, M. L., Noorman, M. E., & Martin, A. K. (2010). Automating the public sector and organising accountabilities. *Communications of the Association for Information Systems, 26*(1), 1. https://doi.org/10.17705/1CAIS.02601

Wagner, B. (2019). Liable, but not in control? Ensuring meaningful human agency in automated decision-making systems. *Policy & Internet, 11*(1), 104–122. https://doi.org/10.1002/poi3.198

Wang, D., Khosla, A., Gargeya, R., Irshad, H., & Beck, A. H. (2016). Deep learning for identifying metastatic breast cancer. arXiv preprint arXiv:1606.05718. https://doi.org/10.48550/arXiv.1606.05718

Whittaker, D., Crawford, K., Dobbe, R., Fried, G., Kaziunas, E., Mathur, V., Myers West, S., Richardson, R., Schultz, J., & Schwartz, O. (2018). *AI now report 2018. AI now institute.*

Accessed April 20, 2023, from https://ec.europa.eu/futurium/en/system/files/ged/ai_now_2018_report.pdf

Wihlborg, E., Larsson, H., & Hedström, K. (2016). *The computer says no!—A case study on automated decision-making in public authorities* (pp. 2903–2912). Örebro University Publications. https://urn.kb.se/resolve?urn=urn:nbn:se:oru:diva-48440

Wouters, N., Kelly, R., Velloso, E., Wolf, K., Ferdous, H. S., Newn, J., Joukhadar, Z., & Vetere, F. (2019). Biometric mirror: Exploring values and attitudes towards facial analysis and automated decision-making. *Conference on Designing Interactive Systems, 1145*. https://doi.org/10.1145/3322276.3322304

Zafari, S., & Koeszegi, S. T. (2018). Machine agency in socio-technical systems: A typology of autonomous artificial agents. In *2018 IEEE Workshop on Advanced Robotics and its Social Impacts (ARSO)* (pp. 125–130). doi:https://doi.org/10.1109/ARSO.2018.8625765.

Zafari, S., & Koeszegi, S. T. (2020). Attitudes toward attributed agency: Role of perceived control. *International Journal of Social Robotics*, 1–10. https://doi.org/10.1007/s12369-020-00672-7

Zafari, S., Köszegi, S. T., & Filzmoser, M. (2021). Human adaption in the collaboration with artificial agents. In J. Fritz & N. Tomaschek (Eds.), *Konnektivität Über die Bedeutung von Zusammenarbeit in der virtuellen Welt* (pp. 97–106). Waxmann Verlag GmbH. http://hdl.handle.net/20.500.12708/30581

Zammuto, R. F., Griffith, T. L., Majchrzak, A., Dougherty, D. J., & Faraj, S. (2007). Information technology and the changing fabric of the organisation. *Organization Science, 18*(5), 749–762. https://doi.org/10.1287/orsc.1070.0307

Zhang, R., McNeese, N. J., Freeman, G., & Musick, G. (2021). "An ideal human" expectations of AI teammates in human-AI teaming. *Proceedings of the ACM on Human-Computer Interaction, 4*(CSCW3), 1–25. https://doi.org/10.1145/3432945

The Re-enchanted Universe of AI: The Place for Human Agency

Helga Nowotny

Abstract Generative AI designed as a digital tool to communicate with humans raises a series of questions to what extent ChatGPT and its rivals approach, match, and eventually may surpass human cognitive abilities. I propose to situate their amazing performance in a longer historical perspective of the evolution of human knowledge that occurs by externalizing or "outsourcing" knowledge operations, beginning with the invention of writing. However, the latest developments confront us with digital technologies that render it increasingly difficult to distinguish genuinely human characteristics and abilities from artificially created ones. This renders the question of human agency and the extent to which it is transferred to machines as crucial for digital humanism, especially when we reflect on some uncanny resemblances with the immanent "enchanted" cosmic order in which our ancestors lived.

1 Introduction

The recent heated debate on ChatGPT opened fascinating debates inside and outside the AI research community on numerous existing assumptions about human language, understanding, emergent abilities of LLMs (large language models), and how much closer we are to having reached AGI (artificial general intelligence), even if it remains doubtful whether it will be achieved at all. ChatGPT stirred worldwide enthusiasm, promised significant productivity gains, and continues to give rise to serious concerns about the impact generative AI will have on open democratic societies and the lives of citizens. Seen from the perspective of digital humanism, this contribution places these developments into a larger historical and societal context and seeks to redefine the place for human agency.

H. Nowotny (✉)
Former President European Research Council, Vienna, Austria
e-mail: helga.nowotny@wwtf.at

H. Werthner et al. (eds.), *Introduction to Digital Humanism*,
https://doi.org/10.1007/978-3-031-45304-5_13

2 Questioning Our Assumptions: What ChatGPT Is and What It Does

The release of ChatGPT in November 2022 by OpenAI, partnering with Microsoft, has triggered an unprecedented wave of public enthusiasm, inevitably mixed with anxieties and concerns. Other Big Tech companies quickly followed by releasing their version of generative AI, opening a fierce competition for market shares. The amazing efficiency and speed of development of this latest bunch of digital technologies took many by surprise, including experts. In the eyes of the public, ChatGPT and its ilk have become the vanguard representative of the previously often announced and hyped *digital revolution* which now seems to have arrived on everyone's computer screen and in the midst of society. It achieved what none of the previous AI advances accomplished—unleash a wide public debate on potential beneficial uses and on a long and open-ended list of potential risks. The rising geo-political tensions, especially between the USA and China, and the strategic competition that ensues serve to exacerbate the uneasiness with which this otherwise welcome technological innovation is greeted.

The processes undergirding what ChatGPT (and other generative AI) is and how it functions are known in its broad outlines. It is based on large language models, LLM, that are trained on a huge trove of texts (and images), including Wikipedia, Reddit, and raw web page scans to perform its core function which consists in simulating human conversations. It achieves this by estimating the probabilities of which words follow each other and which sentences follow each other. They are trained with the help of millions of parameters that include writing style, conventional phrasing, and tone, all designed to create the illusion of conversing with a human. They are scaled up, with yet unknown consequences how scale affects certain emergent "behaviors" of the model. Thus, they are great at mimicry, but poor at facts and unable to cite their sources. They are prone to errors and to "hallucinate," a concept popularized by Google researchers in 2018. It refers to mistakes in the generated text (or images) that are semantically or syntactically plausible, but factually wrong or nonsensical.

This immediately raises the question of how trustworthy these models are. The risk of mass-produced misinformation that could put into jeopardy any democratic election and other abuses come to mind, as well as the harm caused by false and unreliable medical diagnosis or other decision-making based on such models. These are some of the thorny issues that have since long been associated with AI when adequate regulation, at least for now, and the desirable, but difficult-to-achieve, alignment with human values are lacking. It is unclear, for instance, whether machines can be built that have values—and whose values these would be—or whether machines will learn values from which kind of data. The general feeling is that the genie is already partly out of the bottle and that all of us are participating in a huge experiment that the large corporations are conducting on us without ever having asked for consent nor informing us in transparent and honest ways as the experiment proceeds. Obviously, many of the weird or outright spooky features that users experience in conversations with chatbots at this early stage can and will be corrected. Yet, others may persist, or new ones be added.

There is also a wide consensus that these generative AI do not "understand" neither the questions nor the answers they give—as yet. However, during a very short period of early adoption, they have upturned a number of assumptions that were more or less taken as given and hence uncontroversial. Several are linked to the explicit goal of achieving AGI, artificial general intelligence, which, however, is not shared by everyone (Siddarth et al., 2021). A heated debate has erupted on whether large pre-trained language models can be said to "understand" language in a way that would refute the Chinese Room Argument, proposed by John Searle in 1980. This is not merely an academic debate, as the extent and ways in which they understand the world have real implications for numerous fields and kinds of applications that range from driving so-called autonomous vehicles to how we will entrust them with the education of our children. Does "understanding" on the part of the machine include understanding of the physical and social world encoded by language in human-like ways? And, related to this, which part of the knowledge we have about the world we live in depends on language and which part is captured and processed tacitly and by other sensory means?

At this moment, the AI research community appears divided on key questions that have arisen from starkly diverging arguments and assumptions around distinct modes of understanding, different definitions of the range of intelligence (including intelligence among non-human organisms), and the nature of language. It also matters how one compares human cognition, which includes flawed, non-logical reasoning prone to "irrational" thinking, with the inner working of an LLM that is purely driven by probabilities yet may produce incoherent and nonsensical output.

Thus, one side of the debate claims that LLMs truly "understand" language and can perform reasoning in a general way, although not quite yet at human level. The other side argues that large pre-trained models such as the latest GPT-4, despite being fluent in their linguistic output, will never be able to "understand" because they have no experience or mental models of the world. They have been trained to understand the form of language and exhibit an extraordinary formal linguistic competence, but not its function, let alone its meaning. They lack the conceptual understanding needed for human-like functional language abilities (Mitchell & Krakauer, 2023).

Another unresolved question concerns scaling and emergent abilities. There seems to be a threshold of complexity beyond which LLMs of a certain size display emergent abilities not observed in smaller models. Emergence is well known in complex systems when self-organization between component parts sets in and gives rise to novel phenomena. It is not yet well understood what happens when transformers that enable the rapid scaling up of parameters in a LLM lead to the emergence of new learning behavior and the ability to solve problems it has rarely or never seen before. Understanding how such transitions happen and why the threshold varies with task and model are open research questions (Ornes, 2023).

These are just a few of the fascinating issues that have come to the fore in the latest debates. Controversies are a unique opportunity to pry open the black box into which accepted scientific knowledge otherwise has been closed. Their eventual settlement rarely ends with a clear winning or losing side. Rather, they signal that exciting new findings may emerge, moving the field forward. Controversies thus are attractive for younger researchers and those practitioners who have not yet committed to one side, but are eager to find out more.

Some of the basic assumptions that underlie the more controversial issues related to consciousness, understanding, or being sentient have a long, and partly forgotten, conceptual and philosophical ancestry in previous debates and assumptions in the history of AI. They offer tantalizing glimpses of the possibility whether we are at the brink of a new, non-human form of understanding displayed by these models, rather than viewing them merely as "competence without comprehension." "LLMs have an unimaginable capacity to learn correlations among tokens in their training data and inputs, and can use such correlations to solve problems for which humans, in contrast, seem to apply compressed concepts that reflect their real-world experience" (Mitchell & Krakauer, 2023, p. 6). The field of AI may thus have created machines with new modes of understanding, almost like a new species which may be better adapted to solve different kinds of problems.

But different species are also better adapted to different environments. They are known to be engaged in niche construction, i.e., carving out a space from the environment in which they find themselves that promises not only their survival but their evolutionary future (Odling-Smee et al., 2003). From the perspective of a digital humanism, it might well be that the human species is engaged in its next niche construction on this planet: this time not mainly through ruthless exploitation of the natural environment, but constructing a digital niche in co-evolution with the digital tools created by them (Nowotny, 2020).

3 Technologies as Agents of Change: The Externalization of Knowledge Operations

The historical growth of new human knowledge can be interpreted as a sequence of major transitions in externalizing knowledge operations, processing and application, storage, dissemination, communication, and repurposing of knowledge, which in various configurations generate new knowledge. Often encoded in a new technological medium, knowledge operations extend what is possible, visible, feasible, and understandable. In turn, this impacts the society in which they become embedded, facilitating, channeling, or hindering what can be achieved. Thus, it is never the technology alone, but an assemblage of changes in mindsets, in behavior, and in the socioeconomic power structures that underpins major cultural transitions.

The first major transition occurred with the invention of writing as a social technology giving rise to the transition of an oral to a written culture. The transition involved the mastery of newly invented symbols (hieroglyphs, cuneiforms, alphabets), the novel combinations of the constituent elements, physical infrastructures using adequate materials (clay, papyri, animal skins), and social competences and skills required for collaborative functions and division of labor (specialization of scribes, transmission of skills, interpretative capabilities). Taken together, these preconditions form an assemblage that gives rise to novel cultural forms that can travel across time and space. The externalization of knowledge operations that previously had been stored in the memories of individuals and their oral skills to modify and transfer the content across generations were now inscribed in a physical medium. For the first time, language was encoded with symbols that could be read, interpreted, understood, as well as changed and transmitted in numerous novel ways.

The implications were vast. For the first time, a direct confrontation with the past as fixed in writing ensued. As the sources were few and the material precious, control over them strengthened the centralization of interpretative authority and led to a concentration of power in the hands of a small elite of priests and rulers. Libraries became the repositories of all knowledge that was available. Writing also implicated the loss of some cognitive facilities which, famously, was deplored by Plato as a decline in the ability to memorize a vast corpus of knowledge.

The next major transition is linked to *The Printing Press as an Agent of Change*, the apt title of Elizabeth Eisenstein's classical work in which she analyzes the capacity of printing in facilitating the accumulation and wide diffusion of knowledge. The adoption of print technology created new audiences and new industries around publishing. It enabled the revision and updating of old texts to incorporate new knowledge and forging new links with a widely scattered readership and helped to spread literacy and change the attitude to learning. New networks and transborder collaborations ensued, creating a more open, cosmopolitan environment which encouraged questioning and the spread of ideas.

Printing initiated a profound cultural change of mindsets, which ultimately marks this period as a crucial turning point in Western history. It had a major impact on the Renaissance with the revival of the classical literature, on the Protestant Reformation as it enabled the interpretation of the Bible by each reader and thus shaped religious debates, on the Scientific Revolution as printing rendered possible the critical comparison of texts and illustrations, and by encouraging the rapid exchange of novel discoveries and experiments, giving rise to the Republic of Letters (Eisenstein, 1979).

We now find ourselves amidst another cultural transition triggered by the amazing advances in the externalization of knowledge operations through AI. Put in extremely simple terms, the invention of writing enabled the externalized storage and accumulation of knowledge operations, while printing opened their wide dissemination and repurposing in socially inclusive ways. This was followed by the new media of information and communications technologies from the late nineteenth to the twentieth century. Their social effects were to overcome spatial and temporal distance and, in Marshall McLuhan's famous phrase, turned "the medium into the message." The internet is flooded with social media messages, "personalized" targeting of individuals, and user-generated content. Now, we have entered the phase of algorithmic intimacy (Elliott, 2023). More importantly, we are now extending the externalization of knowledge operations to a growing number of cognitive tasks, including the generation of new knowledge and information. In doing so, we continue to benchmark human performance against AI performance with the result that by moving the goalposts, we let AI score even more goals. The overall effect is AI agents as the externalized embodiment of human cognitive abilities, deliberately designed to resemble us.

4 They Are Like Us: The Re-enchanted Universe of AI

The arrival of AI agents as the digital "Others" evokes ambivalent feelings, oscillating between amazement, uneasiness, and fear. Techno-enthusiasm confronts alarmism. Serious concerns about the potential threats for liberal democracies are swept aside by debates about "existential risk" which conjure a double-bind situation between either being wiped out or to happily surrender to AGI. Admittedly, it is difficult to imagine what a co-evolutionary symbiosis between humans and machines will be like. Yet, they are here to stay, and it does not help to equate "non-human" with "inhuman" as recently claimed in an op-ed by a prominent US columnist (Klein, 2023). The capabilities of the systems we build resemble more and more those of humans, and although they work in ways fundamentally different from us, the inbred tendency to anthropomorphize lets us forget that we are interacting with machines (Weizenbaum, 1976). We continue to use words like "thinks," "behaves," "knows," and "believes"—familiar terms in the world we share with other human language users even if we know that it is not the case—and extend them without reflecting to AI agents that have been trained to imitate human language users.

Using anthropomorphic language blurs the line between "us" and "them" and amplifies the tendency to attribute agency to an AI. Leaving aside the questions whether, in principle, an AI system will be able to reason, believe, think, or understand, our world is being rapidly populated with AI artifacts that make it increasingly difficult to tell the difference. When ChatGPT answers, for instance, "sorry, it's not my fault, but I have been programmed like this," we are getting habituated to treat things that seem like us as if they were like us.

This is new—or have we been there before? After all, our ancestors inhabited a world they shared with non-human "Others" for the largest part of the history of humanity. These were gods of various standings, spiritual beings, ghosts, souls of plants and animals, and other "meta-persons," as cultural anthropologist Marshall Sahlins calls them. His posthumously published book is a moving tribute to the "Enchanted Universe" in which "Most of Humanity" lived. These meta-persons were immanent in the lives of humans. Together, they formed one big cosmic order in which, for better and worse, human fate was determined by meta-human powers.

They were present as decisive agents in every facet of human experience and in everything that humans did. They were the undisputed sources of success, or lack of it, involved when humans hunted and pursued their political ambitions: in repairing a canoe or cultivating a garden, in giving birth, or in waging war. Everything was the material expression of their potency, and nothing could be undertaken without evoking the powers of the meta-humans. It was an asymmetrical co-existence. In many respects, the spiritual beings resemble humans: they would lie and cheat, could be malicious, and were quarreling among themselves. Humans depended on their goodwill and benevolence which they sought through ritual invocations and cultural practices. The main difference, however, that conferred super-human power to them was their immortality (Sahlins, 2022).

This immanentist "Enchanted Universe" came to an end some 2500 years ago during the "Axial Age," first analyzed by Karl Jaspers. The exact timing, the geographic reach, and the concept itself continue to be controversially discussed, but agreement exists that a new, transcendental order took over. In it, humans were separated from the higher powers that reigned above. Researchers working with Seshat, a large data set of prehistoric societies, associate this shift with the advent of moralizing punishing gods that correlates with the rise of social complexity in early societies (Turchin, 2023). The idea of a transcendental order is at the origin of the monotheistic religions and the fundament of modern societies that recognize the objective reality in which we live today.

We are convinced that our ancestors "only believed" in the Enchanted Universe, while "in reality," they "knew" better. In other words, their Enchanted Universe was a perpetual, collective illusion. Sahlins refutes this interpretation. Our recent experience with digital "Others" that are amazingly efficient in taking over ever more human cognitive and physical tasks should make us rethink this condescending attitude. Just as we believe that an AI "understands us better than we do ourselves," even if we know that the predictive algorithms at work are fed on data extrapolated from the past, or when we are seduced by a seemingly charming chatbot that, however briefly, we are speaking to a human, our ancestors might have felt the same. In this sense, we are entering a re-enchanted universe, even if it obviously differs from their animistic cosmos.

I am not suggesting that with the end of modernity, characterized as the Weberian disenchantment of the world, we are stepping back into the enchanted world of our ancestors, even if some uncanny similarities exist. But the transcendental bearings on which the modern world was built are beginning to change. The human species has drastically transformed the earth through the impact humans had on the natural environment in the short period of the Anthropocene (Frankopan, 2023). We continue to create numerous artificial entities, the non-human digital Others, with whom we have to negotiate to gain or retain control. We seem to have reached what Giambattista Vico adumbrated in his *New Science* (1711), namely, that "*verum (the true)*" and "*factum (the made)*" are interchangeable—we only understand what we made. The true and the made are reciprocal, each entailing the other.

Yet, our latest *factum,* the AI systems we are building, have so far escaped our full understanding of how they achieve what they do. For example, we transfer agency to them when we begin to "believe" that everything predictive algorithms tell us must come true, forgetting about probabilities and that the data are extrapolations from the past. At the heart of our trust in AI lies a familiar paradox. Just as we use computers to reduce complexity, we make the world more complex at the same time; we leverage AI to increase our control over the future and uncertainty, while at the same time, the performativity of AI, the power it has to make us act in the ways it predicts, reduces our agency over the future (Nowotny, 2021).

In the Enchanted Universe in which most of humanity lived, everything that was done happened with and through the decisive power of the meta-persons. If we believe that predictive algorithms "know" the future, do we not risk returning to a deterministic worldview in which human destiny has been preset by some higher power? If we are tricked by our anthropomorphic tendencies to believe we are communicating with another human, even if we are partly or fully aware that this is not so, does this not resemble the enchanted world of our ancestors?

Yet, the differences are stark as well. Theirs was a cosmos filled with spiritual life in which humans and nature were interdependent, while we continue to plunder the remaining resources of the natural environment. In its place, we are creating a virtual world, promised to be full of excitement that is intended to make us crave ever more and become addicted. The meta-persons of our days are the large monopolistic corporations that offer largely bland and cheap entertainment. Although we see through the virtual illusions created by them, we remain under their spell. They are the human agents behind the machinery designed to usurp human agency.

5 Redefining Human Agency

The most urgent task ahead is to make sure that the re-enchanted AI universe does not turn into a nightmare. We are rightly in awe when the algorithmic chatbot partners are better and faster in writing texts and providing answers to our prompts, in letting them program annoying computational tasks, or in asking them to come up with novel combination of texts and images. We expect that the next generation of LLM will even more unsettle the conventional ways of teaching and learning, of writing legal briefs, and of doing peer review and even research. There are other challenging discoveries ahead that nobody can predict, as uses of a novel technology always may take unexpected turns when users actively appropriate them, instead of remaining passive consumers. We will be affected cognitively as well as socially in our relations to each other and in our job opportunities in ways that cannot yet be predicted.

The erosion of the public sphere by social media and the threats posed to liberal open societies are likely to grow when the power to direct further developments, including the directions future AI research will take, is concentrated among a few powerful Big Tech players who are guided by the principle of "winner takes all" that underlies the concentration of economic and political power. Where in this rugged landscape, in which beneficial uses intersect with potentially bad and malicious ones, is the place for human agency? What is human agency and how can it be protected? Is there a place for future cultural evolution that is not only caught in the logic of profit-making but dares to resume some of the dreams of greater equality and enhancement of the potential that all humans possess, which existed at the early beginnings of the internet? Can our open democratic societies not only be rescued from threats like unleashing floods of misinformation and the dangers that come with the unprecedented concentration of power in the hands of a few unaccountable and unelected individuals, but can it provide a reconstituted and technologically savvy version of common ground in which citizens can meet and debate?

These are only some of the open questions that arise, seen from the perspective of digital humanism. They are urgent, given the accelerating development of AI and computer technology. Questions about the place of human agency remind us of what is at stake. It touches us deeply, as it is about the sense of control that remains, or needs to be regained, in our future living together with the digital "Others" that are supposed to serve, and not to dominate, us. Human agency is a fragile concept, shaped by historical circumstances and in constant need to be reassessed, reasserted, and redefined. It refers to the capacity of an individual to decide and act in an autonomous way, but its autonomy is always relative, shaped, and constrained by legal norms, values, and cultural habits. It is accompanied by assuming responsibility for one's actions and being held accountable for harmful consequences. In Western societies, human agency is very much tied to the notion of the individual and its freedom. And yet, living in a society presupposes the capabilities of individuals to organize themselves in ways that allow all members to participate and share the pursuit of a public good.

Thus, human agency has the potential of being pivotal in meeting the challenges ahead. They include the necessity of regulating AI technology and implementing it in ways that allow citizens to fully participate in the expected benefits, rather than privileging only those human agents who profit from the advances made by AI. Human agency must come to terms with the agency that is designed into the machines while raising awareness about the differences and similarities between human and non-human intelligence. Last, but not least, the process of redefining and reasserting human agency must be done in view of the inherent openness of the future. We do not know where the co-evolutionary trajectory on which humans and the machines created by them will lead nor whether or when something like AGI will be attained. Before reaching such a presumed endpoint, much needs to be done. In this sense, the future is now.

6 Conclusions

1. Human agency must be seen in a broader social context. It implies taking responsibility for one's actions and to be made accountable for harmful consequences. The human part in the interaction with AI is to be kept distinct from the artificial part, even if more cognitive tasks will be delegated to the latter. This entails safeguards/regulation against becoming "stochastic parrots" (Bender et al., 2021) or having to live with "counterfeit people" (Daniel Dennett).
   These are not only moral or ethical but societal and technical issues that contribute decisively to the kind of open and democratic society we want to live in.

2. There is a need to reconceptualize what is meant by "intelligence," going beyond currently used criteria of human vs non-human intelligence. Human intelligence can be positioned on a continuum of living organisms (from bacteria to humans), e.g., by considering survival strategies in their environment.

   It raises the question whether we can do things in "a more intelligent way" and what this could mean.

3. Predictive, communicative, and decision-making algorithms will continue to influence our behavior and what we will become. It is therefore important not to transfer human agency to them, but to deal with them as tools to be used in a responsible manner with humans as last resort. This means keeping open the possibility of recourse and guarding against errors that might introduce arbitrariness.

   Otherwise, predictive algorithms can turn into self-fulfilling prophecies; communicative algorithms can transform us into stochastic parrots, and decision-making algorithms can erode the principles, like social justice, on which our open societies are founded.

Discussion Questions for Students and Their Teachers

1. What needs to be done to create better awareness and to counteract the inbred tendency to anthropomorphize when interacting with a chatbot/conversational assistant?

   Is it sufficient to design it to answer "I am only an artificial agent and therefore. . ."?

   Is it sufficient to make it evade or avoid any answer that would imply that it takes a political or normative stand?

   What needs to be done on *your* side?
2. As we are getting closer to interacting with "entities" equipped with an intelligence that differs from ours—where do you see similarities to the Enchanted Universe as described by Marshall Sahlins? Which are the main differences?

   Does the imagined world of science fiction fit into such a vision?

   Do we need to reconceptualize what we mean by "objective reality," and if so, how?
3. Do you recall any personal experience in your work with AI linked to the feeling of (a) being in control and (b) discovering the illusion of being in control?

   What can be done to safeguard against the "Eliza effect"?

   How far does being in control extend beyond making the technology function as it should? Do *you* ever feel responsible for the effects it will have? Which ones?
4. Automation of decision-making can create a comfort zone by offering algorithmic recommendations, automated reminders, remote monitoring, etc.

   Do you agree with Anthony Elliott that "the self" is at risk to become numbed in an expanding world of predictive algorithms and that we are kept at a safe distance from our capacity for personal agency and self-reflection?

   Does it matter to *you*?

5. ChatGPT and other chatbots are here to stay, and more improved versions are to come. It can help you in your research as a bright, but occasionally unreliable, sloppy, or even lying research assistant.

   Do you intend to engage with it in *your* future work? How will *you* supervise it?

Learning Resources for Students

1. Anthony Elliott (2023) Algorithmic Intimacy. The Digital Revolution in Personal Relationships. Cambridge, UK.: Polity Press; see pp. 77–107.

   An acute analysis of how changes occurring today in intimate relationship are affected by machine learning predictive algorithms in the fields of "relationship tech," "friendship tech," and novel forms of self-care in "therapy tech." They impact the complex ways in which intimacy is understood, experienced, regulated, and transformed. It is not the "digital revolution" as such which threatens intimate relationships, but the re-orientation of various life strategies and lifestyles that change in accordance with automated machine intelligence. Alternatives are needed for different ways of organizing experiences of the self, society, and automation that encourage experimentation and innovation for an ongoing translation back and forth between the discourses of human and machine intelligence.

2. Divya Siddarth et al. (2021) How AI Fails Us. https://ethics.harvard.edu/how-ai-fails-us.

   The authors criticize the visions and practices behind "actually existing AI" as misconstruing intelligence (a) as autonomous rather than as social and relational and (b) the focus on achieving general intelligence defined largely as surpassing human-level cognitive capabilities which implies that outperforming human intelligence is a worthy and necessary goal and "solution" to many problems. They criticize (c) the shared commitment of AEAI to the centralization of capital and decision-making capacity, which involves scaling and reliance on a small elite. This is countered by a vision of "actually existing digital plurality" (AEDP) based on the principles of complementarity, participation, and mutualism. As an openly "advocacy think-piece" for a pluralist vision of the future of AI technology, the arguments are pitted against the dominant vision of existing AI power structures.

3. Melanie Mitchell and David C. Krakauer (10 February 2023) The Debate Over Understanding in AI's Large Language Models, arXiv:2210.13966v3 /cs.CL/.

   A good overview of the current stand of debate whether LLM can be said to "understand" language describing the arguments made for and against such understanding which shows a stark opposition in the views of the AI research community. The authors plead for the need to extend our understanding of "intelligence" which, arguably, would allow to include novel forms of "understanding" created by the extraordinary predictive ability of cases such as AlphaFold from DeepMind and to differentiate better which kinds of intelligent systems are better adapted for which kinds of different problems.

4. Murray Shanahan (25 Jan 2023) Talking About Large Language Models. arXiv: 2212.03551v4 /cs.CL/.

A closer look, inspired by the philosophy of mind, at the language used to "talk about" language models, such as "belief," "knowledge," and "thinking" which are used by researchers as convenient shorthand for precisely defined computational mechanisms which fall within the range permitted by the "intentional stance." In contrast, today's LLM and their applications are so powerful that it becomes highly questionable that such license can still be safely applied. The author argues for the necessity of a shift in language, perhaps including new turns of phrase, to prevent the creation of a compelling illusion of being in the presence of a thinking creature like ourselves when interacting with a LLM-based conversational agent.

5. Marshall Sahlins (2022) The New Science of the Enchanted Universe. An Anthropology of Most of Humanity. With the assistance of Frederick. B. Henry Jr. Princeton & Oxford: Princeton University Press.

A world-renowned anthropologist draws on his lifelong profound scholarship about the ways how "Most of Humanity" lived over thousands of years. The author exposes our Western-centrism and "transcendental" biases in the explanations we give of the imminent presence of meta-persons and supranatural forces in all human activities in previous times. The bold claim Sahlins makes is that we have to accept the organization and functioning of these immanentist societies with their own concepts and in their own cultural terms, rather than to explain them away as "mere beliefs" or convenient fantasies of the objective reality in which we live today. This raises the question whether the advances of AI open the possibility of a re-enchantment of our world by introducing in our midst digital "entities" or "beings" with whom we enter new forms of interdependence.

6. Helga Nowotny (2021) In AI We Trust. Power, Illusion and Control of Predictive Algorithms. Cambridge, UK: Polity Press.

At the heart of our trust in AI lies a paradox: we leverage AI to increase our control over the future and uncertainty, while at the same time, the performativity of AI, the power it has to make us act in the ways it predicts, reduces our agency over the future. This happens when we forget that we humans have created the digital technologies to which we attribute agency and may result in self-fulfilling prophecies. These developments also challenge the narrative of linear progress, which played a central role in modernity and is based on the hubris, and illusion, of total control. We are now moving into an era where this control is limited through our various interactions with AI and giving it "autonomy" while facing the challenge of regaining control in the sense of clear attribution of accountability and responsibility.

References

Bender, E. M. et al. (2021). On the dangers of stochastic parrots: Can language models be too big? https://doi.org/10.1145/3442188.3445922. Accessed March 15, 2021, from https://dl.acm.org.

Eisenstein, E. (1979). *The printing press as an agent of change*. Princeton University Press.

Elliott, A. (2023). *Algorithmic intimacy. The digital revolution in personal relationships* (pp. 77–107). Polity Press.

Frankopan, P. (2023). *The earth transformed. An untold history*. Bloomsbury Publishing.

Klein, E. (2023). This changes everything. March 12. The New York times.

Mitchell, M., & Krakauer, D. C. (2023). The debate over understanding in AI's large language models. Accessed February 12, 2023, from https://arxiv.org/abs/2210.13966.

Nowotny, H. (2021). *AI we trust. Power, illusion and control of predictive algorithms*. Polity Press.

Nowotny, H. (2020). *Life in the digital time machine*. Swedish Collegium for Advanced Studies.

Odling-Smee, F. J., Lala, K. N., & Feldman, M. W. (2003). *Niche construction: The neglected process in evolution*. Princeton University Press.

Ornes, S. (2023) The unpredictable abilities emerging from large AI models, quanta magazine, March 16. https://www.quantamagazine.org/print?mc_cid=5b30527cd0&mc_eid=593396f255.

Sahlins, M. (2022). *The new science of the enchanted universe: An anthropology of most of humanity*. Princeton University Press.

Shanahan, M. (2023). Talking about large language models. Accessed January 30, 2023, from https://arxiv.org/abs/2212.03551.

Siddarth, D. et al. (2021). How AI fails us. Accessed March 13, 2023, from https://ethics.harvard.edu/how-ai-fails-us.

Turchin, P. (2023). The evolution of moralizing supernatural punishment: Empirical patterns. In Larson et al. (Eds.), *Seshat history of moralizing religion*.

Weizenbaum, J. (1976). *Computer power and human reason: From judgement to calculation*. WH Freeman & Co.

Aesthetic Aspects of Digital Humanism: An Aesthetic-Philosophical Analysis of Whether AI Can Create Art

Dorothea Winter

Abstract Increased global digitalization and particularly the growing use of artificial intelligence (AI) are relegating human artists to the background. Art has long been regarded as distinctively human. Art creation and art reception fulfill humans in an incomparable way.

However, AI-created artwork is now nearly indistinguishable from human artwork and appears to fully satisfy human aesthetic needs. If this is really true, we need a new concept of art. And we need to ask ourselves the question: Why then do we still need human artists? Or is there perhaps a unique selling point of human artists after all? This chapter explores the aesthetic-philosophical aspects of digital humanism in the context of AI-created art, building on the Kantian notion of art, one of the most prominent frameworks of art in the field of philosophical aesthetics. This chapter addresses questions such as "Do we need human artists in the age of AI?" and "Are creations of AI truly art?"

1 Introduction

Given the title of this chapter, one might ask: What do art and digital humanism have to do with each other? The short answer: More than one might think at first! Creating and contemplating art is one of the most elementary bastions of the human condition. Art serves creative, social, economic, and political purposes for humans. A holistic digital humanism that considers all areas of the human condition that are affected by AI and digitalization must therefore inevitably also address the question of art.

What makes something art? This philosophical-aesthetic question, a source of contention since classical antiquity, takes on a new dimension in today's world as non-human artwork enters the art market. As artificial intelligence (AI) develops the ability to write poetry, paint, and compose seemingly independently, the question of the status of art and its creators has taken on new significance.

D. Winter (✉)
Humanistic University Berlin, Berlin, Germany
e-mail: d.winter@humanistische-hochschule-berlin.de

H. Werthner et al. (eds.), *Introduction to Digital Humanism*,
https://doi.org/10.1007/978-3-031-45304-5_14

Discussions of digitalization and AI frequently include the political, economic, scientific, and social spheres. However, art and culture have been integral to the human condition throughout history, and the question of whether AI can create art is not limited to the world of galleries, museums, or artists. If AI were to replace human artists, the implications for business, politics, culture, society, and science would be enormous: Galleries would hang works by AI rather than humans. Much more art would be created quantitatively, because AI needs no breaks and is faster and more scalable than humans and their creative process. Legislation would also need to be adjusted: Who is the author? Who gets the money? Therefore, this chapter investigates whether AI can create art.

To answer this question, we must first define art. To put it in philosophical terms, what is the fundamental principle of art? Numerous definitions of art exist. Immanuel Kant's approach to art (KAA) explicitly or implicitly underlies many of the existing definitions, including contemporary, modern, and older concepts of art. The KAA remains convincing and relevant today, despite its age. It is one of the most influential works in philosophical aesthetics, having significantly impacted the philosophical currents of the Enlightenment and Humanism and remaining highly relevant today.

With the advent of the Enlightenment and Kant's writings on aesthetics, the freedom of the artist became the defining characteristic of what constitutes art. The Kantian postulate of freedom has become the touchstone of post-Enlightenment art theory and implicitly or explicitly influences many contemporary concepts of art.

In this chapter, I provide a summary of Kant's freedom of the artist and assess its suitability as an argument regarding whether AI can create art. To clarify, this chapter does not address the question of whether AI is an artistic medium. Whenever human origin is unmistakable and AI is utilized in the same manner as numerous other tools, technologies, and instruments, human authorship becomes evident. Rather, this chapter focuses on instances in which AI is perceived as an "independent artist." The following questions guide my inquiry: Have we created an independent AI artist? Is the art produced by AI truly art? Does it matter whether an AI or a human creates an artwork?

First, I describe the context and methodology of the study by explaining the fundamentals of philosophical aesthetics as a scientific discipline, as well as the function and purpose of the KAA. The KAA focuses on art at the moment of creation rather than through the perspective of the viewer. According to Kant, people's thoughts and feelings when viewing art are irrelevant because art is about the creator, not the viewer. This is because if you take the viewer's perspective, there are as many concepts of art as there are humans. Every person sees something different as aesthetically pleasing from the viewer's perspective and sees other works as art or not. He argues that a suitable definition of art must center on the moment of creation and the creator.

Next, I briefly introduce the KAA. For Kant, art requires freedom. Without freedom, there can be no art, because (human) artists can only create something new if they have freedom. The concept of artistic freedom is frequently included in contemporary and modern definitions of art. Each of the so-called Old Masters invented something new by the standards of their time, and contemporary trends such as readymade art (in which everyday objects are elevated to the status of artwork) are also based on the concept of artistic freedom. According to the KAA, only the (human) artist can transform an everyday object into a work of art.

In the third section, I apply the KAA to AI to clarify whether AI can create art according to the KAA, and I explore the implications of this discussion for art in the era of AI. I argue that AI cannot satisfy the KAA if one rejects AI's ability to be free. As part of this application, I compare the KAA with historian and philosopher Hannah Arendt's definition of art, which focuses on the creative process enacted by the productive *homo faber* ("Man the Maker"). I argue that the KAA is methodologically superior to Arendt's definition of art. Kant's concept is A) time-unbound, B) culture-unbound, and C) place-unbound. He strives for the necessity of thought and not for empirical actuality. So it doesn't matter when, where, or in what setting the KAA is applied. According to Kant, art is fundamental, rationally explainable, and object indeterminate, whereas Arendt's view of art is socially embedded and focuses on the labor involved in making art.

Throughout this chapter, I argue for a positive and realistic definition of art in the age of AI and digital humanism. I do not wish to develop a technology-critical view of art that excludes AI from the creative process. Rather, human authorship should be bolstered, and AI usage should be encouraged with proper understanding of the implications of AI artistic creation.

2 Aesthetics Is the Study of the Subject of Art, and Kant Is One of Its Most Influential Representatives

Before discussing the KAA, I briefly explain aesthetics as a philosophical discipline and describe its methods.

Aesthetics is the branch of philosophy that is primarily concerned with art, beauty, and taste. According to Budd (2005, p. 4), aesthetics as a discipline plays dual roles as "the philosophy of art and the philosophy of the aesthetic experience and character of objects and phenomena that are not art." The term "aesthetics" originated with German philosopher Alexander Baumgarten (1750, 2013; Guyer, 2005) and describes the discipline or method used to take a philosophical approach to art (Franke, 2021, p. 29). Aesthetics provides a set of methodological tools to consider art in a valid scientific manner (Bredin & Santoro-Brienza, 2000). Consequently, it is crucial that this methodological toolkit is utilized in the context of AI art creation. This chapter focuses on the role of aesthetics that deals with art, though, according to Budd, the two roles of aesthetics cannot be viewed separately.

The question of the definition of art in Western culture reached its climax in the Enlightenment, and many prominent Enlightenment philosophers contributed to a philosophy of aesthetics (Nannini, 2020),[1] for example, David Hume's "Of the Standard of Taste" and "Of Tragedy" essays (1757).[2] Immanuel Kant is one of the most influential Enlightenment philosophers of aesthetics; therefore, I focus on the KAA as a theoretical framework for this chapter. Numerous other philosophies exist, including those that contradict Kant and provide equally valid concepts of art. However, given Kant's exceptional significance and influence in the field of aesthetics, restricting this chapter to his concept of aesthetics and art is methodologically appropriate.

I do not want to conceal here, of course, that there are also numerous other concepts of art (in philosophy and in other disciplines).[3] But as has been shown in the chapters by Nida-Rümelin and Winter, and Nida-Rümelin and Staudacher it is no coincidence why Kant can be referred to in digital humanism.

3 According to the KAA, There Is No Art Without (Artistic) Freedom

Kant was more concerned with critique of other contemporary philosophers than any other Enlightenment figure. In his three "Critiques," Kant questions established dogma regarding the "obscurity of pure reason" (Matthis, 2020, p.7) and the "privacy of pure subjectivity" (Matthis, 2020, p.7). In his *Critique of the Power of Judgment*, Kant examines judgment regarding matters of taste, seeking a balance between the demands of objectivity and subjectivity that elude him in the first two Critiques (Matthis, 2020, p.7).

In his aesthetic writings, and most notably in *Critique of the Power of Judgment* (Kant, 2000), Kant proposes a concept of art that not only encapsulates the aesthetic thought of his time but also strongly influences modern and contemporary art theory. The KAA can be easily and profitably applied to fields of art in which AI is currently established. This application is possible due to the central assumption of artistic freedom that informs Kant's concept of art. The concept of freedom is the foundation of Kant's moral philosophy, which assumes that being free and being moral are mutually contingent, and this concept also underlies the KAA (Thorpe, 2014, p. 90).

In developing his concept of freedom, Kant distinguishes between the "transcendental idea of freedom" (Kant, 1998, A 533/B 561-A 534/B 562), "free choice"

[1] As demonstrated in the chapter by Nida-Rümelin and Winter, the Enlightenment plays a unique role in digital humanism and the age of AI. Since this is intricately discussed in this chapter, I will not elaborate further here.

[2] In his 1739 work A Treatise of Human Nature, Hume (1739) discusses the relationship between beauty and deformity and vice and virtue. In his later writings on aesthetics, he proposes a link between art's beauty and deformity (and, by analogy, between behavior and character) (Costelloe, 2007, p. 8).

[3] See Theodor W. Adorno (2004) and John Dewey (2005).

(Kant, 1998, A 802/B 830; Yost, 2016), and "practical freedom" (Kant, 1998, A 534f./B 562; Thorpe, 2014, p. 59; Kohl, 2014). For Kant, only practical freedom is necessary for the emergence of art (Sweet, 2023, p. 137):

> For it is not merely that which stimulates the senses, i.e., immediately affects them, that determines human choice, but we have a capacity to overcome impressions on our sensory faculty of desire by representations of that which is useful or injurious even in a more remote way; but these considerations about that which in regard to our whole condition is desirable, i.e., good and useful, depend on reason. (Kant, 2000, A 802/B 830)

Which of these definitions of freedom is most pertinent to the KAA? According to Kant, practical freedom allows the artist to create freely as a rational being. Freedom and rational thought may seem contradictory;[4] however, Kant argues that art must be created freely and not as a means to an end; otherwise, it is not art but handicraft (Kant, 2000, B 176). To provide a striking illustration, Hieronymus Bosch, the painter of "The Garden of Earthly Delights," selected his subject, color composition, and brushwork based on his own creative sensibility; in contrast, the painter of lane markers on a highway is bound by the requirements of traffic regulations. According to Skees (2011, p. 919), "The artist demonstrates the ability to come up with the material for the work of art at the same time she or he determines the adequate form for the work of art that can manifest an aesthetic idea."

Kant's idea of art demands the use of reason: "By right, only production through freedom, i.e., through a capacity for choice that grounds its actions in reason, should be called art" (Kant, 2000, B 174). This philosophy is systematically situated within the tradition of European art history in that Kant demands that the artist be bound to both *téchne* (i.e., craft, art; philosophical concept that refers to making or doing) and *episteme* (i.e., science, knowledge; philosophical concept that refers to knowledge or understanding). On the other hand, in dialectical conjunction, he emphasizes the principle of freedom in the act of creation (Winter, 2022, p. 6).

Freedom liberates the artist from the conditions of the moment and allows them to extend their creative ambitions throughout time. This elongation enables the artist to work across days, weeks, and months to complete their work, and this pursuit of their artistic aim grants the artist autonomy and freedom.

An extreme occurrence of an artistic expansion spanning decades is the popular art project "L'Arc de Triomphe, Wrapped," by the artist couple Christo and Jeanne-Claude. The creation of this project spanned from 1962 to 2021. The project ultimately outlived one of its creators, as Christo passed away in May 2020.

Through the ability to extend the creative process physically and chronologically beyond the moment, the artist attains the practical freedom that Kant views as a

[4] From the perspective of a reason-based concept of rationality, there is no contradiction between freedom and rational thought. On the contrary, from this perspective, rationality is a necessary prerequisite for freedom. For reason/rationality can be characterized as the ability to appropriately weigh the reasons that guide our actions, beliefs, and attitudes, freedom is then the possibility to follow just the reasons that are found to be better in such a deliberation process; thus, if I am free, it is my reasons determined by deliberation that guide me to judge and act this way or that (cf. chapter by Nida-Rümelin and Staudacher).

necessary condition for artistic creativity. According to Kant, without (practical) freedom, there is no art (Anderson, 2015).

The methodological superiority of the aesthetic-philosophical premises of the KAA becomes apparent in comparison to other philosophers' contrasting perspectives regarding artistic freedom. A socially based definition of art limits the creative act of the artist and the audience reception of the work to social entities, i.e., people, in their social context (and only from this point of view).[5] In this case, it is difficult to establish a methodical-logical link between the artist and the artwork. For example, Andy Warhol's assertion that "art is what you can get away with" seemingly cannot be reconciled with the enlightened Kantian understanding of art. However, perhaps it can if Warhol is therefore not considered an artist in the Kantian sense. This is a logical shortcut insofar as Kant presupposes as an implication of artistic freedom that the artistic impetus arises from an act that precedes thinking and can only subsequently be accessible to thought (Kant, 2000, B 185).

Kant's notion of pre-thought implication forms the foundation of many modern and contemporary concepts of art, including Marcel Duchamp's renowned *objet trouvé* (readymade) "Fountain." In this work, the transformation of a common thing into a piece of art through the creative act of the artist appears in its purest form.

Subjective freedom[6] in the Kantian sense as a premise of the creative act may be controversial nowadays, insofar as an artwork is created precisely from the perspective of reflection. A work of art derives from the creator's highest degree of subjectivity, and its social acceptance is irrelevant (i.e., who likes it, in what social context it is created or has an effect, or what monetary worth the art market assigns it).

Essentially, Kant's definition of art can be simply expressed as the philosophy that art requires freedom. Before exploring the central question of this chapter—"Can AI create art according to Kant's definition of art?"—I provide a brief definition of AI.

---

[5]Such a definition of art would almost lead to the question "What is art?" ad absurdum. According to a definition like this, art would consist of whatever a viewer declares to be art. Yet, if applied to art-creating AI, the question would be easily answered (at least from an aesthetic-philosophical point of view): AI can do art. For example, Roose (2022) shows that an AI-created artwork has won an art competition. And it did so legitimately, given there was no indication in the call for submissions that the artist had to be a human creature. Human viewers have considered the creation of AI as a work of art and, in this situation, superior to the work of human artists.

[6]Basterra (2015) explains subjective freedom according to Kant as follows: "The Subject of Freedom explores the idea of freedom theoretically as the limit that enables thinking, and practically as something other that constitutes subjectivity."

4 What Is the State of the Art in Art-Making AI?

For the purposes of this chapter, allusions to AI primarily refer to generative art, which is defined as art made by an autonomous system. The progression of AI is quite rapid in today's world, and new technological breakthroughs are already in development. Thus, I do not restrict this analysis to specific technologies or applications. Within a Kantian framework, aesthetic-philosophical considerations focus on the underlying principle and the foundations. In this section, I briefly explain the scope of AI for the purposes of this analysis.

AI-generated art is an umbrella term that includes any form of art that cannot be generated without the use of programming (Mazzone & Elgammal, 2019, p. 1). Significant progress has been made in recent years in the field of AI-made art, particularly through the development of generative adversarial networks (GANs). In the initial iterations of GAN-created art, artists would manually select images from their datasets and fine-tune the algorithm to generate images that would serve as a component or otherwise aid in the creation of art. DeepDream, a Google project, was one of the earliest examples of AI's artistic potential (Ghosh & Fossas, 2022). The DeepDream tool was designed to study neural networks (Szegedy et al., 2015); however, artists and programmers were curious about the image generation process, so developers made the code used to generate the images available to the public (Mordvintsev et al., 2015; Ghosh & Fossas, 2022).

In recent years, the emergence of GANs has spurred a surge of algorithmic art that employs AI in novel ways to create art (Schneider & Rea, 2018; Mazzone & Elgammal, 2019, p. 1). Unlike traditional algorithmic art, in which the artist must write detailed code to specify the rules for the desired aesthetics, the new wave of algorithmic art enables artists to use machine learning technology to program the algorithm to "learn" the aesthetics by observing a large number of images (Mazzone & Elgammal, 2019, p. 1). The system can then develop new images that adhere to the aesthetics it has learned. In the next section, I address the question of whether AI can make art.

5 Can AI Create Art from an Aesthetic-Philosophical Standpoint?

As stated, recent technological advancements in the field of computer science have directly led to the consideration of AI in the context of art. Artificial neural networks (ANN) and GANs have elevated the capacity of machine learning (ML) to a level of complexity once deemed utopian (Shahriar & Hayawi, 2022; Santos et al., 2021). The technical reality has shifted such that poetry, paintings, and songs made by AI are now nearly indistinguishable from those created by humans. Elgammal et al. (2017) studied human volunteers' responses to computer-generated and artist-created artwork. They found that human subjects were unable to distinguish between art created by the proposed system and art created by human artists and exhibited at prestigious art festivals. Indeed, on a variety of metrics, human subjects rated computer-generated works higher than human-generated works. Thus, existing evidence supports the notion that AI is capable of independently producing works of art (Elgammal et al., 2017).

This evidence is also aligned with Hannah Arendt's definition of art as the outcome of the creative *homo faber* (Arendt, 1998),[7] which has been described as follows:

> Homo erectus stands upright; homo sapiens thinks; homo faber makes. Homo faber uses tools to create things. They transform the material available to them into a world full of objects fit for use based on an idea of what the final product should be like and how the world ought to be. Arendt thought that art was the highest kind of activity that homo faber is capable of. (The Hannah Arendt Center for Politics and Humanities, 2023)

In *The Human Condition*, Arendt investigates the fundamental categories of the *vita activa (active life)*: labor, work, and action (d'Entreves et al., 2022). Arendt places artistic creation in the third of these categories. She refers to artistic production as the output of *homo faber*, the fabricator of the world (Arendt, 1998), and she describes the outcomes of this creative process as robust and long-lasting in contrast to commercial goods, which she defines by their characteristic impermanence.

Arendt asserts that artistic creativity is a unique human practice, which raises the question of whether AI's computational infallibility is not merely comparable to human creativity but perhaps superior. Is AI the superior artist? This conclusion can only be valid if two premises are true: (1) art creation is considered a practical activity, according to Arendt's definition, and (2) a receptive viewer attitude is adopted.

For example, in the project "The New Rembrandt," a cooperative initiative between the Delft University of Technology, Microsoft, ING Bank, Museum Het Rembrandthuis, and Mauritshuis, an AI tool created a Rembrandt van Rijn painting in the renowned artist's style to remarkable effect (The Next Rembrandt, 2023). It is difficult for non-specialists to distinguish between a genuine Rembrandt and the AI-generated "Rembrandt," as similar studies by Gangadharbatla (2022) show.

Twenty data scientists, developers, and AI and 3D printing specialists worked for 2 years on the project. The researchers scanned Rembrandt's full collection of more than 300 paintings in high definition to conduct a comprehensive analysis, which resulted in a database with more than 150 GB of data. The team then utilized an ANN to boost the resolution of the paintings and enhance the visual quality of previously damaged paintings. The program analyzed each image and classified the painting based on multiple factors, including the subject's attire, gender, gestures,

---

[7] Why am I referencing Hannah Arendt? The answer is simple: She has made significant contributions to aesthetics and art theory (Riley, 1987). And Arendt not only studied Kant but also authored lectures and essays on Kant, and his impact on her philosophy cannot be denied (Kateb, 1999). Cf. Arendt's *Lectures on Kant's Political Philosophy* (Arendt, 1989). So, it's even more remarkable that her definition of art contradicts Kant. In referring to Arendt, I would like to present a comprehensive overview of the variety of art definitions.

facial expressions, eye color, and more. A total of 67 distinct features were captured in this analysis (Westhoff, 2020).[8]

If "The Next Rembrandt" is analyzed based on its brushstrokes, color composition, and effect on viewers, the AI artwork is comparable to that of its namesake and data-providing role model, Rembrandt van Rijn, one of the greatest artists in European art history.

Kant's postulate of individual freedom in the artistic act of creation contrasts with Arendt's idea of art, which centers on the artistic act and the viewer. In principle, the prerequisite of freedom in Kant's definition of art precludes the possibility that AI can create sui generis art (i.e., art that originates sui generis). The algorithm-based AI can only produce art "in the way/in the style of." In other words, algorithm-based AI can only be epigonic. To be clear, it is very impressive if an AI or another human being is able to paint in the way of Rembrandt (and in the case of a human being, it is even more impressive; for the human being need not have such a large database and has to "grasp the spirit" of the Rembrandt paintings in order to paint like him). But painting in the way/in the style of Rembrandt is not creating something really new.

This discrepancy between the application of Arendt's philosophy of art and the KAA derives from the fundamentally computable nature of AI. In the current state of the art, even the most advanced GANs and KNNs rely on algorithms and are, in principle, "nothing more" than complex sequences of implications. From a philosophic-logical standpoint, they are fundamentally if-then relationships. Part of the nature of implication is its premise-boundedness, meaning that an implication cannot generate any output that can extend beyond its premises. Any GAN or KNN, no matter how complex, requires an initial impulse. From this impulse, AI can create unpredictable and remarkable outputs for humans; however, it is not scientifically accurate to attribute freedom to these AI tools.

For example, DALL-E and its sequel DALL-E 2, iterations of a disruptive KNN-based program created by OpenAI, can generate graphics from textual descriptions (OpenAI, 2023). The application employs ANNs to convert arrays of input words into arrays of output pixels. The application can make photorealistic visuals in the written form (Singh, 2022). DALL-E is capable of mapping wholly novel notions and producing artwork in a variety of aesthetic genres. Millions of Internet-accessible photographs were used to train the model to create images. The program is built on OpenAI's Generative Pre-Trained Transformer 3 (GPT-3), a text generator capable of generating texts, text summaries, and even poetry (Ramesh et al., 2022).

In brief, DALL-E "creates" an independent "work of art" based on keywords, which at times are surprisingly close in style to the targeted pre-images. Yet, when viewed from an aesthetic-philosophical perspective, DALL-E does not create art

---

[8] The following works are particularly relevant for a full review of "The Next Rembrandt": (Yanisky-Ravid, 2017, p. 663; Yanisky-Ravid & Velez-Hernandez, 2018, pp. 3–4.; Maggiore, 2018, pp. 383–384.; Zibner, 2019, p. 3).

autonomously. In this instance, the "creation of art" is ultimately a form of permutation in which existing elements are recombined in a highly complex and high-quality manner. When DALL-E is reduced to its aesthetic-philosophical principles, the input-providing human remains the artist, regardless of the complexity of the algorithm or the excellence of the outcome. DALL-E cannot sui generis generate a creatio ex nihilo. Conversely, Kant argues that human beings are capable of creatio ex nihilo (i.e., creation out of nothing) because human beings are able to act autonomously. The ability to be free is a necessary requirement for making art (Skees, 2011; Matherne, 2014).

Unlike the Old Master painters, such as Albrecht Dürer, Raphael, or Johannes Vermeer, whose creative impetus is nearly indisputable, many contemporary artists demand this ascription from the viewer first. For example, Tomoko Takahashi's installation "Leftover" (2007), a composition of technical garbage from our industrial civilization, compels the audience to understand the creative act that underlies the transformation of profane everyday items into pieces of art by an intentional act of thought. An AI tool could reproduce a comparable arrangement of everyday items. However, unlike a human, the AI tool would be incapable of coming up with the artistic idea that underpins the arrangement. To do so, the AI tool would need to be capable of freedom.

In the Kantian view, the ability to produce art necessarily involves artistic freedom. According to the KAA, AI cannot produce art if it does not have the fundamental capacity for freedom. This syllogism demonstrates the idea as follows:

(A1) Art requires freedom
(A2) AI is in principle not capable of freedom

(K) AI cannot do art

The validity of this syllogism is contingent on the acceptance of its premises A1 and A2. If these premises are changed, the claim regarding the ability of AI to create art would differ. If AI were ascribed the ability to be free, then it would also be capable of creating works of art according to the KAA.[9]

However, freedom must not be bound to calculability. It is the essence of freedom to remain free of computational necessities, as Kant points out in basing the act of creation on a rationally incomprehensible dialectic. The inexplicability of art is due to the fact that the work emancipates itself from its creators insofar as it eludes their rational grasp. For example, anyone who has experienced the linguistic intensity of a poem by Hans Magnus Enzensberger will be able to approach the intellectual complexity of the work from different angles but will be unable to comprehensively understand the work of art as a whole.

[9] Among others, exponents of the transhumanism, mechanism, or animism partly take this position (Nida-Rümelin & Weidenfeld, 2022).

6 Conclusions

According to the KAA, art requires freedom. Thus, the ability of AI to create art depends on the attribution of freedom to AI tools. If one defines freedom in the Kantian sense, in the sense of the Enlightenment and Humanism, one cannot attribute freedom to AI, at least according to the current state of the art.

However, it would be short-sighted to ban AI entirely from the realm of art. As an artistic medium, AI opens new and expanded possibilities for human artists and art as a whole, particularly regarding the possibilities of form and design. For this reason alone, AI will be increasingly relevant to the field of art in the future.

Nonetheless, the nexus between human authorship and artwork remains even in the age of AI. Regardless of how AI tools are incorporated into the process of creating art, only human creativity and the artistic freedom that underlies it are ultimately capable of generating art, according to the enlightened Kantian concept of art. For Kant, it is the artist who ennobles the application of paint into a work of art. The question of whether AI can be considered an artist equal to humans can therefore be answered with no. AI does not create art sui generis. AI art is only art because a human being with freedom instigates the act of creating something artistic.

Even as I argue for a realistic and positive concept of art in the age of AI, I acknowledge the importance of social, political, economic, and scientific recognition of the fact that what AI "makes" artistically is ethically, legally, and culturally desirable for humankind.

Discussion Questions for Students and Their Teachers

1. What concepts of art can you think of that contradict the ones presented here?
2. What do you think? Should AI be given the status of an artist?
3. What difference does it make whether artwork was created by a human or an AI tool?

Learning Resources for Students

1. Cahn, S.M. and Meskin, A. (2008) *Aesthetics: a comprehensive anthology*. Malden: Blackwell Pub.

   If you don't know anything about aesthetics as a field of research yet, you need to read this: This anthology provides a comprehensive overview of aesthetics from antiquity to the present day and brings together the most significant writings in aesthetics and philosophy of art from the past 2500 years.
2. Graham, G. (2005) *Philosophy of the arts*. London: Routledge.

   This easy-to-understand introduction is equally accessible to students and scholars outside the discipline. What's especially notable about it is that it's jargon-free and will appeal to students of every discipline. In addition, it contains regular summaries as well as suggestions for further reading.
3. Kurt, D.E. (2018) *Artistic Creativity in Artificial Intelligence*. Nijmegen: Radboud University.

   This is a dissertation on the topic of art and AI. There's almost no better overview of the current debate—and it is obviously very current research on the subject. All relevant examples of art-creating AI are mentioned and classified. Anyone who wants to be state of the art in the subject area can get a good overview in this dissertation.

4. Boden, M.A. (1998) "Creativity and artificial intelligence", Artificial Intelligence, 103(1–2), August 1998, pp. 347–356.

   Although the article is quite old, or precisely because it is quite old, it shows what has not changed to this present day. Despite all the technical progress, the questions about artificial creativity remain the same. Furthermore, it is highly relevant, especially in the field of AI research, no matter under which aspect and in which discipline, to understand the status quo at the respective state of technology.

References

Adorno, T. (2004). In G. Adorno & R. Tiedemann (Eds.), *Aesthetic theory*. Continuum.

Anderson, T. (2015). Artistic freedom in Kant and Hegel. *Philosophy in the Contemporary World, 22*(1), 67–79.

Arendt, H. (1989). *Lectures on Kant's political philosophy*. University of Chicago Press.

Arendt, H. (1998). *The human condition*. University of Chicago Press.

Baumgarten, A. G. (1750). *Aesthetica*. Ioannis Christiani Kleyb.

Baumgarten, A. G. (2013). Metaphysics. A critical translation with Kant's elucidations, selected notes, and related materials Fugate, C.D. and Hymers, J. (transl. and ed.) : Bloomsbury Publishing.

Basterra, G. (2015). *The subject of freedom: Kant, Levinas (commonalities)*. Fordham University Press.

Bredin, H., & Santoro-Brienza, L. (2000). *Philosophies of art and beauty: Introducing aesthetics*. Edinburgh University Press.

Budd, M. (2005). Aesthetics. In E. Craig (Ed.), *The shorter Routledge encyclopedia of philosophy*. Florence.

Costelloe, T. M. (2007). *Aesthetics and morals in the philosophy of David Hume*. Routledge.

d'Entreves, M. P., Arendt, H., Zalta, E. N., & Nodelman, U. (Eds.). (2022). *The Stanford encyclopedia of philosophy* (Fall ed.) Accessed February 23, 2023, from https://plato.stanford.edu/archives/fall2022/entries/arendt/

Dewey, J. (2005). *Art as experience*. TarcherPerigee.

Elgammal, A., Liu, B., Elhoseiny, M., & Mazzone, M. (2017). CAN: Creative adversarial networks, generating "Art" by learning about styles and deviating from style norms. *International Conference on Innovative Computing and Cloud Computing*.

Franke, U. (2021). Baumgarten's invention of aesthetics. In J. C. McQuillan (Ed.), *Baumgarten's aesthetics. Historical and philosophical perspectives*. Rowman & Littlefield.

Gangadharbatla, H. (2022). The role of AI attribution knowledge in the evaluation of artwork. *Empirical Studies of the Arts, 40*(2), 125–142.

Ghosh, A., & Fossas, G. (2022). Can there be art without an artist? *arXiv Preprint*. arXiv:2209.07667.

Guyer, P. (2005). *Values of beauty: Historical essays in aesthetics*. Cambridge University Press.

Hume, D. (1739). *A treatise of human nature*. John Noon.

Hume, D. (1757). *Four dissertations*. A. Millar in the Strand.

Kant, I. (1998) Critique of pure reason, Guyer, P. and Wood, A.W. (transl. and ed.) : Cambridge University Press.

Kant, I. (2000) Critique of the power of judgment, Guyer, P. and Matthews, E. : Cambridge University Press.

Kateb, G. (1999). The judgment of Arendt. *Revue Internationale de Philosophie, 208*(2), 133–154.

Kohl, M. (2014). Transcendental and practical freedom in the critique of pure reason. *Kant-Studien, 105*(3), 313–335.

Mordvintsev, A., Olah, C., & Tyka, M. (2015). Deepdream—a code example for visualizing neural networks. *Google Research*. Accessed February 23, 2023, from https://ai.googleblog.com/2015/07/deepdream-code-example-for-visualizing.html

Maggiore, M. (2018). Artificial intelligence, computer generated works and copyright. In E. Bonadio & N. Lucchi (Eds.), *Non-conventional copyright—do new and atypical works deserve protection?* (pp. 382–399). Edward Elgar.

Matherne, S. (2014). Kant and the art of Schematism. *Kantian Review, 19*(2), 181–205.

Matthis, M. J. (2020). *The beautiful, the sublime, and the grotesque: The subjective turn in aesthetics from the enlightenment to the present*. Cambridge Scholars Publishing.

Mazzone, M., & Elgammal, A. (2019). Art, creativity, and the potential of artificial intelligence. *Art, 8*(1).

Nannini, A. (2020). The six faces of beauty. Baumgarten on the perfections of knowledge in the context of the German enlightenment. *Archiv für Geschichte der Philosophie, 102*(3), 477–512.

Nida-Rümelin, J., & Weidenfeld, N. (2022). *Digital humanism*. Springer.

OpenAI Accessed February 23, 2023, from https://openai.com/product/dall-e-2.

Ramesh, et al. (2022). Hierarchical text-conditional image generation with CLIP Latents. *OpenAI Papers*, 3–23. Accessed February 23, 2023, from https://www.shutterstock.com/press/20453

Riley, P. (1987). Hannah Arendt on Kant, truth and politics. *Political Studies, 35*(3), 379–392.

Roose, K. (2022). An AI-generated picture won an art prize. Artists aren't happy. *The New York Times, 2*, 2022.

Santos, I., Castro, L., Rodriguez-Fernandez, N., et al. (2021). Artificial neural networks and deep learning in the visual arts: A review. *Neural Computing and Applications, 33*, 121–157.

Schneider, T., & Rea, N. (2018). Has artificial intelligence given us the next great art movement? Experts say slow down, the 'field is in its infancy'. *Artnetnews*. September 25. Accessed February 23, 2023, from https://news.artnet.com/art-world/ai-art-comes-to-market-is-it-worth-the-hype-1352011

Shahriar, S., and Hayawi, K. (2022) "NFTGAN: Non-fungible token art generation using generative adversarial networks", *7th International conference on machine learning technologies (ICMLT)*, (pp. 255–259).

Singh, A. (2022). How does DALL·E 2 work?. Diffusion, and more diffusion, Aug-Mented Startups. *Medium*. Accessed February 23, 2023, from https://medium.com/augmented-startups/how-does-dall-e-2-work-e6d492a2667f

Skees, M. W. (2011). Kant, Adorno and the work of art. *Philosophy and Social Criticism, 37*(8), 915–933.

Sweet, K. (2023). *Kant on freedom, nature and judgment*. Cambridge University Press.

Szegedy, S., Liu, W., Jia, Q., Sermanet, P., Reed, S., Anguelov, D., Erhan, D., Vanhoucke, V., & Rabinovich, A. (2015). Going deeper with convolutions. *IEEE Conference on Computer Vision and Pattern Recognition (CVPR)*, 1–9.

The Hannah Arendt Center for Politics and Humanities. (2023). Accessed February 23, 2023, from https://hac.bard.edu/amor-mundi/the-greatest-achievement-arendt-and-art-2023-02-26.

The Next Rembrandt. (2023). Accessed February 23, 2023, from https://www.nextrembrandt.com.

Thorpe, L. (2014). *The Kant dictionary*. Bloomsbury Publishing.

Westhoff, M. (2020). The next Rembrandt. *Digital Innovation and Transformation*. Accessed February 23, 2023, from https://d3.harvard.edu/platform-digit/submission/the-next-rembrandt/

Winter, D. (2022). *Warum Künstliche Intelligenz keine schöne Kunst im kantischen Sinne hervorbringen kann*. J.B. Metzler.

Yanisky-Ravid, S. (2017). Generating Rembrandt: Artificial intelligence, copyright, and accountability in the 3A era - the human-like authors are already here—a new model. *Michigan State Law Review, 2017*, 659–726.

Yanisky-Ravid, S., & Velez-Hernandez, L. A. (2018). Copyrightability of artworks produced by creative robots and originality: The formality-objective model. *Minnesota Journal of Law, Science & Technology, 1*, 1–53.

Yost, B. (2016). Kant's demonstration of free will, or, how to do things with concepts. *Journal of the American Philosophical Association, 2*(2), 291–309.

Zibner, J. (2019). Artificial intelligence: A creative player in the game of copyright. *European Journal of Law and Technology, 1*, 1–20.

Approaches to Ethical AI

Erich Prem

Abstract This chapter provides an overview of existing proposals to address ethical issues of AI systems with a focus on ethical frameworks. A large number of such frameworks have been proposed with the aim to ensure the development of AI systems aligned with human values and morals. The frameworks list key ethical values that an AI system should follow. For the most part, they can be regarded as instances of philosophical principlism. This paper provides an overview of such frameworks and their general form and intended way of working. It lists some of the main principles that are proposed in the frameworks and critically assesses the practicality of the various approaches. It also describes current trends, tools, and approaches to ensure the ethicality of AI systems.

1 Introduction

Increasingly, digital systems confront us with machine-based "decisions and actions." Although we should avoid unnecessary anthropomorphization and remind ourselves that such "actions and decisions" are based on human choices and algorithms, they increasingly appear to be those of *machines*.[1] From self-driving cars to systems recommending products or categorizing our creditworthiness, humans have become subject to algorithmic action and decision-making. Such decisions can have significant effects on people's lives including detrimental ones. Just consider the case where a person is denied a loan based on a creditworthiness decision of an algorithm or, perhaps worse, denied a transplant organ as a result of a medical AI system's recommendation. Consequently, scholars and policymakers have started to develop an interest in how to ensure that an AI system's actions and

This chapter includes material that was previously published in Prem (2023).

[1] Many thanks to J. Nida-Rümelin for suggesting this important qualification.

E. Prem (✉)
University of Vienna, Institute of Philosophy, Vienna, Austria
e-mail: erich.prem@univie.ac.at

H. Werthner et al. (eds.), *Introduction to Digital Humanism*,
https://doi.org/10.1007/978-3-031-45304-5_15

decisions do not conflict with human values, laws, or reasonable expectations about how systems *should* behave. Traditionally, these are questions that—when asked about humans—have been addressed in the scholarly discipline of *ethics*.

Ethics—the philosophical study of morality—investigates human behavior in terms of its moral value, which the American moral philosopher Bernard Gert defined as an "informal public system applying to all rational persons, governing behavior that affects others, and includes what are commonly known as the moral rules, ideals, and virtues and has the lessening of evil and harm as its goal (Gert, 2005)." As a scientific discipline, ethics does not necessarily provide clear answers regarding what *should be done* in a specific situation. It may be better to regard it as an effort to understand the consequences and the whole embedding of ethical decision-making. Often, ethical theories state certain principles that we should follow and then study the consequences within those theories and where its boundaries lie.

As an example, consider a so-called consequentialist ethical approach. It focuses on the outcomes of an action and suggests that in deciding upon what to do, we should always take the action that achieves the best outcome. This can be very different from a more rule-based, in philosophical terms *deontological*, perspective where the idea is that the action itself is considered good or bad. This means to state clear rules, similar to laws, that determine the ethical quality of our actions. Consider as an example the classification of actions following the Ten Commandments. Or, thirdly, we might propose that the best approach toward a morally good action is to always act like a *virtuous* person, i.e., similar to someone who has proven to be considerate, benevolent, helpful, friendly, courageous, etc. These are just a few ways of organizing our thinking about morality, and there are many others, e.g., contractualism, intuitionism, emotivism, etc.

The three abovementioned approaches correspond to a consequentialist, a deontological, or a virtue-based ethics. It is easy to see that these three high-level approaches to deciding what to do from a moral perspective will often lead to different choices of actions and, hence, different outcomes. Ethicists often study and debate various ethical theories and their justifications, implications, and shortcomings, but will usually steer away from the question of what should be done. The latter is a question that includes weighing the pros and cons and will often imply the necessity to have a societal debate. What is morally preferable will in many cases also imply a political question about which behavior to support and which actions to put under punishment or social despise.

2 Ethical AI

The idea to develop guidelines that ensure that actions and decisions of digital systems are aligned with our moral values is perhaps even older than the actual existence of such systems. Early science fiction authors have addressed moral decision-making of machines or machine-like creatures, as, for example, Mary

Shelley in her science fiction novel about the artificial creature of Frankenstein. Later, science fiction authors such as Isaac Asimov posed ethical rules for robots, the famous robot laws (Asimov, 1950). For example, Asimov's first law states that a robot may not injure a human being or, through inaction, allow a human being to come to harm. While science fiction authors often present an anthropomorphic image of machines (Weidenfeld, 2022), humans today are becoming the subject of algorithmic (AI-based) decisions. The question of how to ensure that machines take actions that are aligned with human moral values thus has become a center of investigation in AI research and in the philosophy of technology. In parallel, policymakers have started to investigate possible rules and regulations to ensure not only the physical safety of humans when interacting with machines but also that such machines treat people in a morally correct manner.

2.1 Can AI Be Ethical?

This poses the question whether machines can act morally. Note that Bernard Gert's definition above talks about "rational persons." Assuming that robots are not included in the category of persons, it is needed to replace this term with something like "machines that give the impression to deliberate reasons."[2] Otherwise, it becomes necessary to argue that AI algorithms should be regarded as rational persons. Also, Gert considers morality as an informal system. We may therefore expect non-trivial challenges when formalizing morality for the sake of implementation on a computing device. For many people, morality also connotes an element of conscious consideration and conscience. However, for all we know, no machine feels ashamed for its possible wrongdoing, nor does a potentially bad outcome lead to a machine's bad conscience. In addition, robotic devices cannot normally become the subject of legal procedures. All of this renders the term "ethical AI" philosophically problematic, and there is an ongoing debate about the degree to which machines can or indeed should be considered ethical agents (cf. Cave et al., 2019). To simplify the issue for our purpose here, we take the notion of *ethical AI* simply as an abbreviation for an AI system that performs actions that when taken by a human would be considered ethical.[3]

[2] Again, thanks to J. Nida-Rümelin for insisting on precision in this formulation.

[3] Note that in many situations, it may be preferable to generalize to an *ethical artifact* as the clear definition of AI remains a challenge.

Table 1 Example for the main components of an ethical AI framework for the principle of "fairness"

Concept	Bias
Concern	Not treating people fairly, e.g., taking decisions that are influenced by a person's gender or social background
Principle	**Fairness**
Remedy	Testing systems for bias and using unbiased data sets, etc.

3 Approaches to Ethical AI

Let us now take a closer look at various efforts to ensure that AI systems make ethical decisions. One specific approach to safeguarding ethical decision-making in machines that many scholars investigated is the creation of so-called AI frameworks. Such frameworks provide a set of principles that an AI system should follow to ensure that its actions or decisions are ethical. There are, of course, other approaches. For example, the European Commission has proposed *regulation* to create legal boundaries for AI systems (EC AI, 2021). There are also *standards* about how to address ethical concerns during system design (IEEE, 2021), and there are proposals for *labels* to inform us about the qualities of an AI system (Mitchell et al., 2019). (See also the chapter by Neppel on "Governance for Digital Humanism.") The next section looks at various frameworks for ethical AI.

3.1 *Ethical AI Frameworks*

Typically, ethical AI frameworks consist of *concepts, concerns, principles,* and *remedies* see Table 1. Concepts are specific notions to describe the ethical issues or potential shortcoming (the concern). For example, the concept of *bias* is used to explain a specific *concern* about AI classifiers. The potential (ethical) shortcoming is that they may take unfair, and, hence, unethical, decisions. *Principles* are used to describe desirable properties of an AI system or its actions and decisions. For example, the *fairness principle* could be used to demand that AI systems should not discriminate against people of different gender or social background. *Remedies* can take many forms, e.g., recommendations about how to ensure that an AI system fulfills a given principle. Note that concepts, concerns, and principles are not always clearly separated. For example, *fairness* can appear as a concept and a principle.

An early ethical framework in computing was proposed by Richard O. Mason in the context of the "information age" (Mason, 1986). With the aim that IT should help to "enhance the dignity of mankind," he suggested that an AI system should fulfill four ethical principles, namely, *privacy, accuracy, property,* and *accessibility.* Mason suggested that IT systems should not unduly invade people's privacy, be accurate in what they are doing, respect intellectual property rights, and be as accessible as possible. In many cases, these principles will still be relevant today. Modern ethical frameworks for AI, such as those expressed in the European Commission White Paper *Ethics Guidelines for Trustworthy AI*, may include more principles including some that are especially relevant for AI systems (EC, 2019). In particular, the EC High-Level Expert Group proposed the following principles:

- Human agency and oversight
- Technical robustness and safety
- Privacy and data governance
- Transparency
- Diversity, non-discrimination, and fairness
- Societal and environmental well-being
- Accountability

The White Paper also includes a *checklist* (see below) for practical use by companies to evaluate the ethicality of the systems they may develop. The White Paper is just one example of several proposed ethical frameworks. In fact, so many frameworks have been proposed that they have become the subject of systematic analysis (Floridi & Cowls, 2021). These analyses often conclude that there are strong similarities such as common principles between the different frameworks. For example, Jobin et al. (2019) argue that many guidelines focus on *transparency, fairness, non-maleficence, responsibility,* and *privacy;* Floridi and Cowls (2021) list *beneficence, non-maleficence, autonomy, justice,* and *explicability* as common themes (see below regarding their origin in bio-ethics).

Some important principles recurring in various frameworks in one form or another and their possible interpretations for ethical AI systems include the following:

– *Beneficence:* The principle of doing good to others, of mercy, and of kindness. For an AI system, it may imply to ensure people's well-being and support sustainable development and inclusive growth. It could also include the protection of fundamental rights.
– *Non-maleficence* states that there is an obligation not to inflict harm on others. Often, this is formulated as "first do no harm." Obviously, also an AI system should prevent harm. Note that non-maleficence and beneficence are not the same as *beneficence* prompts to take an action, while *non-maleficence* may often prompt not to take an action. Beneficence is sometimes considered secondary to non-maleficence (hence, "*first* do no harm").
– *Autonomy:* The principle states that humans should be granted the right to decide on their own. This entails being informed and free to decide. For an AI system, it means to ensure and further the ability of humans to make decisions on their own. It is often interpreted to also mean human agency and oversight by humans.
– *Justice:* As a principle, justice means fairness in decisions, but also accessibility without unfair discrimination. It can entail further aspects such as the availability of redress. In AI, a system should be compatible with what is considered fair.

– *Explicability:* For an AI system, this means that its actions should be understandable for humans. It may include traceability (the ability to verify the history or logical chain) and interpretability (of results).

Some of these principles (e.g., beneficence or autonomy) are not specific to AI systems. Rather, they are often also applied in non-engineering scenarios and are used in ethical frameworks of research institutes or medical institutions. The principles of non-maleficence and beneficence are central to many types of ethics. The principle of autonomy is a key component in guidelines for scientific experiments with human subjects and to medical decision-making in general. Only a few ethical principles are specific to computational systems or are of specific meaning and importance in computational contexts. These include the following:

- *Explicability* refers to the principle that decisions of an AI system should be explainable and understandable for humans, i.e., especially for the subject of an AI-based decision. This could mean, for example, to provide reasons why a bank's classification system for creditworthiness excludes a person as a reliable borrower for a loan. Similarly, an AI-based x-ray system should provide reasons why it categorizes a specific image as that of a patient with cancer. Given that many AI systems tune thousands of parameters using large amounts of data and statistical algorithms, such explanations have often proven very difficult to provide. In addition, it is not easy to explain what precisely constitutes a valid and truthful explanation (see below).
- *Privacy* concerns the fact that many algorithmic systems including AI systems are extremely data-hungry and therefore may require or carry large amounts of personal information. This may also include information that should be particularly well safeguarded, i.e., sensitive data such as personal data revealing racial or ethnic origin, political opinions, religious or philosophical beliefs, trade-union membership, genetic data, biometric data processed solely to identify a human being, health-related data, and data concerning a person's sex life or sexual orientation (cf. Art. 4 and 9 of the GDPR) (GDPR, n.d.). As a principle, AI systems should always protect a person's privacy and never store or disseminate specifically protected sensitive data.
- *Fairness* (in the sense of being "unbiased") addresses the fact that AI systems can easily become biased in their decisions. For example, systems trained to assess the later success of an applicant for a university may be biased against the person because of bad training procedures or because of bias already present in the training data (e.g., because an institution may have historically accepted fewer women than men and this fact is represented in historic data).

The relations between the different principles are not trivial. It is, for example, not very clear that privacy is a separate principle as it could also be described as following from non-maleficence. Similarly, it could be argued that explicability really follows from autonomy. This is one of the reasons why, at least superficially, many different proposals for ethical frameworks exist as they may group principles differently and have different numbers of principles.

3.2 *Philosophical Principlism*

From a philosophical perspective, ethical AI frameworks can be considered instances of "principlism." Principlism is a useful approach to support ethical decision-making in practical situations (usually, moral dilemmas). It is often used in medicine and other fields of science as it often facilitates relatively clear decisions based on only a few principles. In the late twentieth century, ethical principles emerged in reaction to medical experiments such as Albert Neisser's experiments in which patients were infected with syphilis without their consent. Later, the horrendous Nazi experiments of no or questionable scientific value on Jews and other prison inmates led to the Declaration of Helsinki (WMA, 2013). Finally, the Tuskegee syphilis study by the US Public Health Service and CDC on 400 African Americans led to the introduction of ethical principles for medical experiments (Beauchamp & Childress, 1979). However, principlism in the medical profession is much older. It is often dated back to the Hippocratic Oath that goes back to AD 245. There are several modern versions of the oath such as the currently relevant Declaration of Geneva[4] used in the medical profession:

> [...] I SOLEMNLY PLEDGE to dedicate my life to the service of humanity;
> THE HEALTH AND WELL-BEING OF MY PATIENT will be my first consideration;
> I WILL RESPECT the autonomy and dignity of my patient;
> I WILL MAINTAIN the utmost respect for human life;
> I WILL NOT PERMIT considerations of age, disease or disability, creed, ethnic origin, gender, nationality, political affiliation, race, sexual orientation, social standing or any other factor to intervene between my duty and my patient; [...]

This excerpt clearly includes reference to principles like beneficence, non-maleficence, autonomy, and even fairness. While it is positive that principlism seems to work in some professions, it poses the question of whether the principles are sufficiently concrete and tuned for the needs of AI systems and their designers.

3.3 *Challenges and Limitations of Ethical Frameworks*

Despite its often-intuitive appearance, principlism suffers from a range of challenges and limitations when trying to put it to practice. This of course also impairs the use of ethical frameworks for AI. Firstly, principles are usually formulated without any application context. Indeed, principles require a high degree of abstraction, or otherwise, they lose their character of being a principle. The lack of context means that a principle is often not very helpful or only seemingly clear. Just like the interpretation of "good weather" may depend on whether you are a farmer or a tourist, the question of whether you should tell the truth may depend on the subject matter, a person's situation, age, level of understanding, etc. Although the principle

[4] https://www.wma.net/policies-post/wma-declaration-of-geneva/.

of autonomy says that people should be supported in making their own decisions, this does not apply in medical contexts where individuals might lack decisional capacity, for example, because they are too young, mentally ill, or unconscious. The field of medical ethics has therefore developed a set of practices as well as procedures and structures (e.g., ethics reviews and boards) to deal with these contextual aspects. Medicine has also developed prototypical situations and standardized approaches over time.

Secondly, principles are usually listed without a clear prioritization among them. This makes them susceptible to conflict. As an example, the principle of beneficence may conflict with privacy when a radiological AI system for detecting cancer may require a complete history of sexually transmitted diseases. While this may increase precision, it poses ethical questions including whether it is reasonable to assume completely truthful answers from a patient. Similarly, some techniques for improving the explicability of a neural network model may reduce accuracy (and, hence, conflict with the principle of beneficence) when the tools for explaining a system tend to interfere with its prediction or classification quality. In medical contexts, beneficence can easily clash with autonomy when patients decide against what seems medically beneficial given their value preferences.

Thirdly, some principles are only superficially clear, but it may be very difficult to agree on what they mean precisely and, therefore, when they are fulfilled. For example, the idea of making AI systems explain how they arrived at a prediction sounds reasonable. However, *explicability* is very difficult to specify with precision. We may use the concept of *understanding* in demanding that an AI system's decisions should be understandable for users. But it is not trivial to precisely state what understanding really means. Which type of explanation achieves proper understanding and what would be a test for a person to ensure they have really understood what is going on in a neural network or why a certain decision has been made? For example, how a neural network arrived at its output can be provided in mathematical form. However, this would hardly constitute an explanation for a human who may be better served with an explanation that involves more easily accessible concepts. Sometimes, a counterfactual explanation can be useful, for example, when explaining that the output of an AI system would have been different if only the input had taken a different form or value. Note that this is not just a terminological or conceptual imprecision. It is indeed a philosophical challenge to define the notion of understanding beyond a mere psychological feeling.

In addition, principles alone are usually insufficient to clearly decide which system design steps to take. A medical system proposing measures to an overweight patient's benefit may include anything from exercise to a dietary plan, lifestyle changes, or surgery. All these measures may be judged as beneficial, but it may remain unclear what is the best action to choose. Although strictly speaking, this is perhaps not an ethical problem (as all the actions may be beneficial), it is a practical problem from the point of view of designing the AI system.

Similarly, the principle of *fairness* comes with many challenges including philosophical ones. Again, in many cases, there will be a lack of clarity of what we precisely mean when demanding an AI system's fairness. Consider the case of a

Table 2 Different fairness concepts (metrics), optimization criteria (equalizing for), and examples. Adapted from a longer list in Seng Ah Lee et al. (2021). FP, (number of) false positives or lost opportunity as they are predicted to default when they really would have repaid the loan; FN, false negatives; TP, true positives; TN, true negatives

Fairness metric	Equalizing	Intuition/example
Maximize total accuracy	None	Most accurate model gives people the loan and interest they "deserve" by minimizing errors
Equal opportunity	False-negative rate FN/(FN + TP)	Among *creditworthy* applications, men and women have similar approval rates
Predictive equality	False-positive rate FP/(FP + TN)	Among *defaulting* applicants, men and women have similar rates of *denied* loans
Equal odds	True-positive rate TP/(TP + FN), true-negative rate TN/(FP + TN), positive predictive value TP/(TP + FP)	Both of the above: among creditworthy applicants, probability of predicting repayment is the same regardless of gender
Counterfactual fairness	Prediction in counterfactual scenario	For each individual: if they were a different gender, the prediction would be the same
Individual fairness	Outcome for "similar" individuals	Each individual has the same outcome as another "similar" individual of a different gender

creditworthiness expert system that may have been trained on historic data and therefore is biased in treating men and women differently. What should "fairness" mean in this context, or what precisely does it mean to treat men and women *equally*? It could mean, for example, that the outputs of the system do not change when we change the gender of a person in the input data ("counterfactual fairness"). It could also mean an equal average creditworthy rating for men and women. Or it could mean an equal chance of being denied a loan for both genders, etc. These interpretations (or definitions) of fairness will represent different mathematical functions, as indicated in the table below (cf. Seng Ah Lee et al., 2021). The table lists six variants; there are, however, many more plausible interpretations of fairness including those that discuss continuous functions rather than only binary categorization (Table 2).

These fairness notions also correspond to various philosophical approaches as proposed in the literature; see Seng Ah Lee et al. (2021) for a list. In everyday life, such questions are often political and/or decided through social debate and practical norms (where fairness becomes justice). They are less "mathematical" in their nature than they are social and societal. Also, some approaches to AI ethics aim at societal change and go beyond or correct what may be current practice, which additionally complicates the situation (e.g., affirmative action). This means, we cannot just give a general rule or mathematical function that defines "fairness" free from an application context. It is very well possible that we consider fairness for the case of granting a loan differently from providing subsidies to the poor or taking decisions regarding permissible insurance premiums. In some situations, it may prove preferable to aim at "equal odds," while in other situations, it could be considered better to optimize for "individual fairness." In AI systems, the problem is exacerbated because every decision-making system will at least implicitly define a "fairness" function (assuming it produces a proper mathematical function). Hence, the question of what we mean by fairness is in the end inescapable, and an AI system designer will always, albeit sometimes only implicitly, define fairness when building a system.

In addition to these concerns, there is a question regarding the human-centeredness of many AI frameworks. It is debatable whether a focus on humans *alone* is sufficient and to what degree principles should also include environmental sustainability or the welfare of animals. Modern ethics has developed in various directions, and there seems to be an addition of topics that ethics should include. As an example, consider the case of "land ethics" (Leopold, 1949). This question concerns an important debate for Digital Humanism as a whole. Despite its name, much of current Digital Humanism goes in fact beyond a purely *human* focus in that the environment, our climate, and the welfare of sentient beings are being discussed by scholars in Digital Humanism.

The challenges listed above have led to a more general criticism of ethical AI frameworks. Some authors have questioned that frameworks can solve the problem, including because the principles were "meaningless," "isolated," *and* "toothless" and because of the gap between "high-minded principles and technological practice" (Munn, 2023).

4 From Principles to Practice

Principles for AI can be employed during the design of the systems and also during the operation so as to ensure that AI systems act in line with ethical principles. However, how to achieve the latter in practice is far from trivial. Technical approaches to realizing ethical AI systems vary widely. In the following, we provide a short overview of selected approaches that have been suggested in practice. For a more complete list, cf. Prem (2023).

Design Phase

- *Checklists* are a straightforward approach to designing ethical AI systems. They are a proven tool in engineering and systems operation (e.g., when operating an airplane). Checklists help make sure that procedures are being followed, that nothing is forgotten, and that certain conditions are met. For example, ethical checklists can be applied to criteria for training data and training processes of AI models or to ensure that all aspects of an ethical framework were considered. Montague et al. (2021) describe a data ethics checklist, for example.

- *Case studies*, *good practice examples*, or *prototypes* can be an efficient way to improve ethical characteristics of a system based on previous experience or existing systems that exhibit the desired ethical characteristics.
- *Process models* aim at guiding a design process in a way that guarantees that ethical concerns are appropriately addressed. Such process models can be recommendations and focus on certain steps or include standardized procedures for certain aspects (e.g., Eitel-Porter, 2021). (See also the chapter by Zuber et al. on "Value-Sensitive Software Design" in this volume.)
- *Data sets* are a type of infrastructure that can be used for training or testing of AI models. Standardized data models can help overcome bias and support the testing or evaluation of the quality of an AI model. For example, the *Equity Evaluation Corpus* consists of more than 8000 sentences "chosen to tease out biases towards certain races and genders" (Kiritchenko & Mohammad, 2018).
- *Algorithms* or *libraries* that help address ethical issues currently are the focus of a large number of research and development activities (cf. Prem, 2023). In fact, so many researchers aim to develop algorithms for privacy-preserving machine learning that these areas could be called a subfield of machine learning. Similarly, developing methods to enable or improve the explicability of AI systems, especially those trained with deep learning, has developed into the subdiscipline of "explainable AI" (or XAI for short). *Software libraries* have the added advantage of being already coded algorithms designed to address ethical issues. Examples include libraries for explainable AI[5] or for measuring systems according to fairness metrics (Wexler et al., 2020).

System Operation

- *Declarations* are statements that assert features of AI systems, typically to their users. This could mean to describe how an algorithm works, which type of training data was used, which fairness or bias concerns were considered, etc. Such declarations may follow formal requirements, e.g., "labels," to facilitate comparisons between systems. Declarations address ethical concerns often indirectly in stating ethical issues explicitly but without necessarily solving them in the system. While declarations are a useful source of information, the choice of appropriate action is often left to the user. Hence, declarations tend to delegate the responsibility for the ethical issue in question to the user.

Ex-Post Approaches

- *Audits* can serve to examine a system after its design and implementation. It can help assess ethical issues after the system was put in operation.

[5] https://github.com/EthicalML/xai.

Other approaches to handling ethical issues of AI systems include *training (education), license models, metrics, design patterns, online communities,* and *codes of practice.*

4.1 Further Research Directions

In summary, ethical frameworks can hardly be considered a solution to the challenge of creating ethical AI systems. They can provide guidance on better understanding many of the issues involved in their design and at times provide guidance and orientation for the design and implementation process. The biggest challenge with ethical AI frameworks today is their lack of providing clear advice on how to build AI systems. An important area of future research therefore concerns technical means to realize ethical AI systems. In addition, the context and evolution of the embedding of an AI application will require much more study in the future. It is therefore likely that future research will address AI systems in specific situations, i.e., within their respective application contexts. Such systems will then have to be analyzed with respect to their behavior and how they are perceived by humans interacting with the system. They need to be reviewed and critically debated so that with time, a practice of ethical AI systems emerges that can help train generations of AI system developers.

5 Conclusions

Principles have played an important role in various science and technology fields. They are current standard practice in various areas, for example, in research where principles are used to decide upon the conditions under which experiments with humans should be performed. They are also used to guide decisions regarding medical treatments, where they inform about priorities such as in the case of medical transplants and guide information provided to patients or subjects of medical experiments.

For the design of ethical AI systems, a large number of ethical frameworks using principles have been designed. The list of principles and the way in which they are formulated show great similarities and often overlap with the ethical principles used in medicine. Several principles included in these frameworks are very general (e.g., non-maleficence), and only a few are specific to AI (e.g., explicability). Frameworks and ethical principles are usually detached from implementation questions. They guide *what* AI and other algorithmic systems should or should not do, but do not explain *how* to achieve this in practical systems. In real-world situations, ethical principles may contradict each other and require prioritization. However, many frameworks for ethical AI do not include a clear order in which the principles should be applied. A prioritization or other decision regarding the principles then may require careful weighing of the principles against each other, consideration, or debate.[6]

The development of ethical AI systems is at an early stage. To make the principles work in practice, more debate, research, and perhaps clearer rules are required, including regarding concrete application contexts. Tools and techniques to help realize ethical AI systems include checklists, case studies, prototypes, process models, standards, data sets, algorithms, software libraries, declarations, audits, and others.

Discussion Questions for Students and Their Teachers

1. Consider one of the ethical frameworks described above. Show that the order in which ethical principles are applied may change the outcome of an ethical consideration based on ethical frameworks.
2. Discuss the nature of ethical frameworks from an engineering perspective: should they be considered a component of the system specification, an element of the system design process, or part of the resulting AI system? (See also the chapter by Ghezzi in this volume.)
3. Consider an AI model that has a known bias, for example, it may work better for men than for women in a medical diagnostic task. What might cause such a situation? Do you think such situations are completely avoidable, or are there situations where we may have to accept a biased system? Which of the tools described in this chapter could you use to remedy the situation? What are the pros and cons?
4. Which tools or techniques could you use to ensure an AI system's fairness during design, implementation (training), and operation?

Learning Resources for Students

1. Floridi L., Cowls J. (2021) A unified framework of five principles for AI in society.

   This is a good place to get an overview of various frameworks. It also develops a unified version of a framework that extracts common principles from the other frameworks.
2. Prem E. (2023) From Ethical AI Frameworks to Tools: A review of approaches. *AI and Ethics.*

   This is an overview from the perspective of approaches to implementing ethical AI. It collects various tools, standards, declarations, etc. that are proposed in the literature to address various ethical issues. As mentioned above, Munn (2023) presents a critical perspective on frameworks.
3. Stahl B.C., Schroeder D., Rodrigues R. (2023). The Ethics of Artificial Intelligence: An Introduction. In: Ethics of Artificial Intelligence, Springer.

   This is a modern introduction to the ethics of AI. It provides an up-to-date overview and case studies to introduce AI and address some of the key ethical

[6] D. Ross (1930) discussed the dilemmas arising from conflicting principles and a plurality of prima facie duties.

principles such as privacy, unfair discrimination, or the right to life and liberty of persons. It also includes some more general aspects not addressed in this chapter, e.g., surveillance capitalism.

Acknowledgment This research was supported by the "Entrepreneurs as role models" project at the University of Vienna.

References

Asimov, I. (1950). In The Isaac Asimov Collection (Ed.), *Runaround. I, Robot* (p. 40). Doubleday.

Beauchamp, T., & Childress, J. (1979). *Principles of biomedical ethics*. Oxford University Press.

Cave, S., Nyrup, R., Vold, K., & Weller, A. (2019). Motivations and risks of machine ethics. *Proceedings of the IEEE, 107*(3), 562–574. https://doi.org/10.1109/JPROC.2018.2865996

EC. (2019). Ethics guidelines for trustworthy AI. Directorate-General for Communications Networks, Content and Technology, EC Publications Office. https://data.europa.eu. https://doi.org/10.2759/177365.

EC AI. (2021). European Commission, Proposal for a regulation of the European Parliament and of the Council laying down harmonised rules on Artificial Intelligence (Artificial Intelligence Act) and amending certain union legislative act. COM (2021) 206 final.

Eitel-Porter, R. (2021). Beyond the promise: Implementing ethical AI. *AI Ethics, 1*, 73–80. https://doi.org/10.1007/s43681-020-00011-6

Floridi, L., & Cowls, J. (2021). A unified framework of five principles for AI in society. In L. Floridi (Ed.), *Ethics, governance, and policies in artificial intelligence* (Philosophical studies series) (Vol. 144, pp. 5–6). Springer. https://doi.org/10.1007/978-3-030-81907-1_2

GDPR, General Data Protection Regulation. (n.d.) Regulation (EU) 2016/679 of the European Parliament and of the Council. https://eur-lex.europa.eu/legal-content/EN/TXT/HTML/?uri=CELEX:32016R0679&from=EN#d1e40-1-1

Gert, B. (2005). *Morality: Its nature and justification* (Revised ed.). Oxford University Press.

IEEE. (2021). IEEE standard model process for addressing ethical concerns during system design. *IEEE Standards*, 7000–2021. https://doi.org/10.1109/IEEESTD.2021.9536679

Jobin, A., Ienca, M., & Vayena, E. (2019). Artificial intelligence: The global landscape of ethics guidelines. *Nature Machine Intelligence, 1*, 389–399. https://doi.org/10.1038/s42256-019-0088-2

Kiritchenko S., & Mohammad S. F. (2018). Examining gender and race bias in two hundred sentiment analysis systems. In *Proceedings of *Sem*, New Orleans, LA, USA.

Leopold, A. (1949). *A Sand County Almanac* (p. 203). Oxford University Press.

Mason, R. O. (1986). Four ethical issues of the information age. *MIS Quarterly, 10*(1), 5–12.

Mitchell M., Wu S., Zaldivar A., Barnes P., Vasserman L., Hutchinson B., & Gebru T. (2019). Model cards for model reporting. Proc. Conf. Fairness, Account. Transpar. FAT*19. https://doi.org/10.1145/3287560.3287596.

Montague, E., Eugene, D. T., Barry, D., et al. (2021). The case for information fiduciaries: The implementation of a data ethics checklist at Seattle children's hospital. *Journal of the American Medical Informatics Association, 28*(3), 650–652. https://doi.org/10.1093/jamia/ocaa307

Munn, L. (2023). The uselessness of AI ethics. *AI and Ethics*. https://doi.org/10.1007/s43681-022-00209-w

Prem, E. (2023). From ethical AI frameworks to tools: A review of approaches. *AI and Ethics.*. https://link.springer.com/content/pdf. https://doi.org/10.1007/s43681-023-00258-9.pdf

Ross, D. (1930). *The right and the good*. Clarendon Press.

Seng Ah Lee M., Floridi L., & Singh J. (2021). Formalising trade-offs beyond algorithmic fairness: lessons from ethical philosophy and welfare economics. https://ssrn.com/abstract=3679975.

Stahl, B. C., Schroeder, D., & Rodrigues, R. (2023). The ethics of artificial intelligence: An introduction. In *Ethics of artificial intelligence. SpringerBriefs in research and innovation governance*. Springer. https://doi.org/10.1007/978-3-031-17040-9_1

Weidenfeld, N. (2022). Fictionalizing the robot and artificial intelligence. In H. Werthner, E. Prem, E. A. Lee, & C. Ghezzi (Eds.), *Perspectives on digital humanism*. Springer. https://doi.org/10.1007/978-3-030-86144-5_14

Wexler, J., Pushkarna, M., Bolukbasi, T., Wattenberg, M., Viégas, F., & Wilson, J. (2020). The what-if tool: Interactive probing of machine learning models. *IEEE Transactions on Visualization and Computer Graphics, 26*(1), 56–65. https://doi.org/10.1109/TVCG.2019.2934619

WMA. (2013). World medical association, declaration of Helsinki: Ethical principles for medical research involving human subjects. *Journal of the American Medical Association, 310*(20), 2191–2194. https://doi.org/10.1001/jama.2013.281053

Artificial Intelligence and Large-Scale Threats to Humanity

Guglielmo Tamburrini

Abstract This chapter provides a concise introduction to the impact of artificial intelligence (AI) on major man-made, large-scale threats to humanity: the risk of nuclear war and the climate crisis. AI has a sizable carbon footprint. But the AI research and commercial communities may adopt good practices to reduce this footprint and to develop AI applications supporting climate warming mitigation. It has been suggested that AI systems may improve nuclear weapons command and control. But AI scientists must raise awareness about the downsides of this proposal and the potentially negative impact of AI on nuclear deterrence. Coherent with the inspiring principles of Digital Humanism, ethical and political responsibilities are identified to reduce AI's role in the buildup of these man-made, large-scale threats to humanity.

1 Introduction

Large-scale threats to humanity jeopardize the persistence and flourishing of human civilizations. Some of these threats arise from natural events. Supervolcanic eruptions and the impact of big asteroids produce dust which may linger in the air for months or years—shading sunlight, lowering atmospheric temperature, interfering with photosynthesis, leading to civilizational devastation, and ultimately threatening many biological species with extinction. Other large-scale threats are entirely man-made. Extended regions of our planet may become unfit to host human life on account of a nuclear war or the exacerbation of the climate crisis caused by anthropogenic emissions of greenhouse gasses.

The study of large-scale threats to humanity and their policy implications is the thematic focus of various academic and non-academic bodies. These include the Future of Humanity Institute at the University of Oxford, the Centre for the Study of

G. Tamburrini (✉)
DIETI – Department of Electrical Engineering and Information Technologies, Università di Napoli Federico II, Naples, Italy
e-mail: guglielmo.tamburrini@unina.it

H. Werthner et al. (eds.), *Introduction to Digital Humanism*,
https://doi.org/10.1007/978-3-031-45304-5_16

Existential Risk at the University of Cambridge, and the Future of Life Institute. The Nuclear Threat Initiative is more specifically focused on reducing nuclear and biological threats. And the *Bulletin of the Atomic Scientists* provides information to reduce large-scale threats arising from nuclear weapons, climate change, misuse of biotechnologies, and AI.

This chapter provides a concise introduction to AI's actual and potential impact on large-scale threats to human civilization that are posed by the climate crisis and the risk of a nuclear war. AI is having an increasing and often double-edged impact on these man-made threats. Coherent with the broad inspiring principles of Digital Humanism, responsibilities of AI scientists are identified, and ethically motivated actions are proposed that AI stakeholders can undertake to protect humanity from these threats and to reduce AI's role in their buildup.

The chapter is organized as follows. Section 2 reviews AI's double-edged impact on the climate crisis and good practices that AI stakeholders can undertake to reduce the carbon footprint of this technology. Section 3 is concerned with the potential impact on nuclear deterrence postures of deepfakes and AI-powered autonomous systems. Section 4 scrutinizes proposals to use AI for nuclear command and control in the light of opacities, fragilities, and vulnerabilities of AI information processing. Section 5 points to major ethical underpinnings for actions that AI stakeholders can undertake to reduce AI's role in the buildup of large-scale threats to humanity. Section 6 concludes.

2 AI and the Climate Crisis

Climate data are being used to build AI models for climate warming mitigation and adaptation by means of machine learning (ML) methods. At the same time, however, some AI applications are paving the way to larger emissions of greenhouse gasses (GHG), thereby contributing to the buildup of higher global temperatures.

Basically, AI is climate agnostic and is having a dual impact on the climate crisis (Dhar, 2020). On the one hand, AI models help climate scientists to develop better climate models and prediction tools, thereby supporting the scientific community to contrast climate warming. Moreover, AI applications are playing an increasing role in climate warming mitigation, by learning to identify and reward thriftier energy consumption patterns in manufacturing, transportation, logistics, heating, and other sectors characterized by high levels of GHG emissions (Rolnick et al., 2019). Similar roles for AI have been proposed to support the European Green Deal (Gailhofer et al., 2021). The United Nations AI for Good platform helps one solve technological scaling problems for AI-based climate actions. Technologically more advanced countries have a related role to play, by facilitating access of less technologically advanced countries to AI resources for climate warming mitigation and adaptation (Nordgren, 2023).

On the other hand, AI applications are in use which pave the way for larger GHG emissions. Exemplary cases are AI models facilitating the extraction, refinement, and commercialization of fossil fuels. According to a 2016 Greenpeace report, major oil and gas companies take advantage of AI to improve the efficiency of their industrial pipeline. Models trained on data from seismic experiments and other geological data guide the search for new oil and gas wells. Additional AI applications improve the efficiency of fossil fuel transportation, refinery, storage, and marketing. By improving the efficiency of these processes, oil and gas companies aim to make larger quantities of fossil fuels available, eventually encouraging their consumption by decreasing their unit price. Finally, the development and delivery of these AI models by major AI firms jar with their pledges to achieve carbon neutrality soon (Greenpeace, 2016).

Ultimately, AI technologies afford protean tools to improve efficiency. However, one can indifferently use these tools to mitigate or else to exacerbate the climate crisis. Given their climate agnostic character, it is chiefly a matter of collective choice to direct the use of AI toward climate warming mitigation.

In addition to individual AI applications, one has to consider the overall impact on climate change of AI as a research, industrial, and commercial area. Attention toward this issue developed in the wake of alarming estimates of electrical energy consumption attributed to other information-processing activities and their hardware infrastructures. Bitcoin transactions require on a yearly basis as much electrical energy as a country like Argentina (CBECI, 2022). Data centers and data transmission networks are responsible for about 1% of worldwide energy-related GHG emissions (IEA, 2022).

According to an early estimate, which is more specifically concerned with AI, the training of some large AI models for natural language processing (NLP) has approximately the same carbon footprint as five average cars throughout their lifecycle (Strubell et al., 2019). This estimate was later found to be excessive (Patterson et al., 2022). But environmental concerns about the overall carbon footprint of AI were not thereby put at rest. Indeed, up to 15% of Google's total electricity consumption is attributed to the development and use of the company's AI models between 2019 and 2021 (Patterson et al., 2022). Moreover, only 10% of commercial AI electricity consumption is expended on training. The remaining 90% supports statistical inference and prediction by already trained models (Patterson et al., 2021).

It is not clear how these consumption patterns will develop in the future. An alarming consideration is that electricity consumption is sensitive to the size of AI models, and the goal of achieving more accurate inference and prediction has been prevalently pursued by developing bigger and bigger AI models based on deep neural network architectures. The size of these networks is usually measured by reference to the number of weighted connections between their neural units. In the NLP area, the number of these parameters steadily increased from the 350 million parameters of a 2018 language model in the BERT family, to the 175 billion parameters of GPT-3 in 2020, and on to the few trillion parameters of GPT-4 in 2023. Researchers and engineers operating in other AI application domains are similarly incentivized to pursue improved accuracy by means of increasingly bigger models. Clearly, the sum of these design choices contributes to extending electricity demand and is likely to enlarge the carbon footprint of AI research and industry. Finally, one should pay attention to the fact that AI applications enabling one to reduce the carbon footprint of services and processes can indirectly encourage a more extensive use of those services and processes. These rebound effects, admittedly difficult to appraise precisely, may considerably increase the overall AI's carbon footprint (Dobbe & Whittaker, 2019).

These various data and trends are still inadequate to achieve a precise picture of AI's electricity consumption and its carbon footprint. But imprecise contours offer no reason to deny the existence of a problem or to justify inaction by AI stakeholders. These include AI academic and industrial scientists, producers and providers of hardware systems for training and running AI models, CEOs of data centers hosting the required hardware infrastructure, and electrical energy producers and suppliers. Much can be done by these various actors to curb electricity consumption and correspondingly reduce AI's carbon footprint.

Ultimately, ensuring electricity supplies from renewable energy sources would drastically reduce the AI carbon footprint. As of 2020, however, almost two-thirds of global electricity came from fossil fuel sources (Ritchie et al., 2022). And many years of sustained efforts will be presumably needed to reverse this proportion, so as to ensure a largely "green" electricity supply on a worldwide scale. In the meanwhile, without inertly waiting for these developments to occur, AI researchers and commercial actors are in the position to pursue some good practices contributing to reduce electricity consumption and curb correlated AI's carbon footprint (Kaack et al., 2020; Patterson et al., 2022; Verdecchia et al., 2023):

(i) Select energy-efficient architectures for AI models.
(ii) Use processors that are optimized for AI model training—e.g., graphics processing units (GPUs) or tensor processing units (TPUs).
(iii) Perform the required computations in the premises of data centers that tap from cleaner electricity supplies and are more efficient energy-wise.

Item (iii) points to actions that one may undertake across all sectors of information and communications technologies. Item (i), and to some extent (ii), points to actions that are more specific to the AI sector. None of these good practices depend on whether or how fast the electricity supply mix will become greener on a global scale.

In addition to AI scientists and firms, research and professional associations can play a distinctive role in fostering a greener AI. Indeed, AI associations may promote a new idea of what is a "good" research result recognized by AI scientific and professional communities, by modifying the entrenched criterion of evaluating AI models solely in terms of their accuracy (Schwartz et al., 2020). To correct this orientation, one may introduce research rewards and incentives to strive for combined energetic efficiency and accuracy of ML methods and downstream AI models. Competitions based on metrics which prize this compound goal might be launched too, in the wake of a long tradition of AI games, including chess, Go, poker, RoboCup, and many other competitive games. This new approach to what is a "good" research result goes equally well with time-honored AI research programs aiming to understand and implement intelligent systems using only bounded resources.[1] These actions by research and professional associations may prove effective independently of the required changes in electricity production and supply.

To sum up, the AI research and commercial enterprise involves multiple stakeholders. These actors can undertake actions to reduce both AI's electricity consumption and the AI carbon footprint. Some of these actions are already identifiable from the standpoint of an admittedly imperfect knowledge of the AI carbon footprint and its causes. AI scientists and engineers may develop energetically more efficient AI models, choose more efficient hardware, and use greener data centers. The boards of AI scientific and professional associations may develop new ideas about what makes a "good" AI result, introducing suitable incentives to prize energetic efficiency. On the whole, since AI technologies are climate agnostic, it is an ethical, social, and scientific responsibility of AI stakeholders and political agencies alike to support the application of AI for climate warming mitigation and to contrast its use to exacerbate—directly or indirectly so—the climate crisis.

3 AI and Nuclear Deterrence

Since the end of World War II, nuclear war looms on humanity as a man-made large-scale threat. By signing the *Treaty on the Non-Proliferation of Nuclear Weapons* (NPT), entered into force in 1970, the major nuclear powers pledged to prevent the proliferation of nuclear weapons and to eventually achieve worldwide nuclear disarmament. More than 50 years later, however, the number of states possessing nuclear arsenals has increased, no substantive progress toward nuclear disarmament has been made, and deterrence policies are still the main instrument that nuclear powers rely on to prevent nuclear holocaust.

According to nuclear deterrence theory, the possession of a sufficiently large and efficiently deployable nuclear arsenal holds the promise of a retaliatory counterattack and therefore discourages other nuclear states from a first use of nuclear weapons. Major weaknesses of deterrence policies and their presuppositions have been long identified and investigated. But new weaknesses are now being exposed by AI technologies for the development of autonomous systems and for the generation of deepfakes.

To begin with, let us consider the impact on deterrence postures of AI-enabled autonomous systems. US nuclear retaliation capabilities are based on land, air, and sea platforms for nuclear weapon systems. These comprise silos of land-based intercontinental ballistic missiles, submarines armed with SLBMs (submarine-launched ballistic missiles), and aircraft carrying nuclear weapons. Unmanned

[1] Notably, in the early days of AI, John McCarthy proposed to pursue the goal of identifying the mechanisms allowing cognitively and computationally bounded forms of intelligence to cope with complex problem-solving in the world.

vessels for anti-submarine warfare may erode the sea prong of these deterrence capabilities. These vessels, whose autonomous navigation capabilities are powered by AI technologies, may identify submarines as they emerge from port or pass through narrow maritime chokepoints, trailing them henceforth for extended periods of time.

An early example of autonomous vessels for submarine identification and trailing is the US surface ship Sea Hunter. Originally prototyped in the framework of a DARPA anti-submarine warfare program, the Sea Hunter is now undergoing further development by the US Office of Naval Research, to perform autonomous trailing missions lasting up to 3 months. Another case in point is the autonomous extra-large unmanned undersea vehicle (XLUUV) Orca, manufactured by Boeing to carry out undersea operations including anti-submarine trailing missions and warfare. Similar functionalities are widely attributed to the Russian autonomous submarine Poseidon. And China is similarly reported to have a program for the development of XLUUVs.

According to a British Pugwash report, "...long-endurance or rapidly-deployable unmanned underwater vehicles (UUV) and unmanned surface vehicles (USV), look likely to undermine the stealth of existing submarines" (Brixey-Williams, 2016). And according to a more recent report of the National Security College of the Australian National University, "oceans are, in most circumstances, at least likely and, from some perspectives, very likely to become transparent by the 2050s." In particular, submarines carrying ballistic missiles will be "detected in the world's oceans because of the evolution of science and technology" (ANU-NSC, 2020, p. 1). Thus, by undermining the stealth of submarine retaliatory forces that are otherwise difficult to detect and neutralize, these AI-enabled autonomous vessels are expected to have a significant impact on the erosion of sea-based nuclear deterrence.

Nuclear deterrence is additionally weakened by AI systems generating synthetic data that are dubbed *deepfakes*. Generative adversarial networks (GANs) are used to fabricate increasingly realistic and deceitful videos of political leaders. The mayors of Berlin, Madrid, and Vienna—without realizing they were being deceived—had video calls in June 2022 with a deepfake of the mayor of Kyiv Vitali Klitschko (Oltermann, 2022). Deepfakes of political leaders potentially induce misconceptions about their personality, behaviors, political positions, and actions. Deepfake videos of nuclear power leaders like Barack Obama, Donald Trump, and Vladimir Putin were widely circulated. Fueling doubts about their rationality and consistency, these videos jeopardize the effectiveness of nuclear deterrence policies, which are crucially based on the credibility of second-strike threats to deter a first use of nuclear weapons.

4 Militarization of AI and Nuclear Defense Modernization

Proposals to use AI within nuclear defense systems are framed into a broader race to the militarization of AI. The US National Security Commission on Artificial Intelligence recommended integrating "AI-enabled technologies into every facet of warfighting" (NSCAI, 2021). One finds a strikingly similar call in China's "New Generation Artificial Intelligence Development Plan," underscoring the need to "[p] romote all kinds of AI technology to become quickly embedded in the field of national defense innovation" (China's State Council, 2017). More curtly, Russian President Vladimir Putin claimed that whoever becomes the leader in AI will rule the world (Russia Today, 2017).

In the framework of these comprehensive AI militarization goals, the National Security Commission on Artificial Intelligence recommended that "AI should assist in some aspects of nuclear command and control: early warning, early launch detection, and multi-sensor fusion" (NSCAI, 2021, p. 104, n. 22). This recommendation was made on the grounds that increasingly automated early warning systems will enable one to reduce the time it takes to acquire and process information from disparate perceptual sources. Accordingly, human operators might be put in a position to achieve more rapidly the required situational awareness and to buy more time for downstream decision-making. From a psychological standpoint, these envisaged benefits would alleviate the enormous pressure placed on officers in charge of evaluating whether a nuclear attack is actually in progress. One cannot ignore, however, significant downsides emerging in connection with this proposal. Indeed, one can hardly expect AI to deliver these benefits without introducing AI-related weaknesses and vulnerabilities into the nuclear command, control, and communication (NC3) infrastructure.

To begin with, let us recall a famous and enduring lesson for risks that may arise from efforts to automate nuclear early warning systems. This lesson is afforded by the false positive of a nuclear attack signaled by the Soviet early warning system OKO on September 26, 1983. OKO mistook sensor readings of sunlight reflecting on clouds for signatures of five incoming intercontinental ballistic missiles (ICBM). Colonel Stanislav Petrov, the duty officer at the OKO command center, correctly conjectured that the early warning system had signaled a false positive and refrained to report this event higher up in the command hierarchy. Commenting years later on his momentous decision, Petrov remarked that "when people start a war, they don't start it with only five missiles" (Arms Control Association, 2019). Petrov's appraisal of the system's response was the outcome of counterfactual causal reasoning and open-ended understanding of military and political contexts. Clearly, these mental resources exceeded OKO's narrow appraisal capabilities. But the lesson to be learned extends to the present day. Indeed, counterfactual causal reasoning and the understanding of broad contextual conditions remain beyond the capabilities of current AI models.

Additional limitations of state-of-the-art AI technologies equally bear on a critical analysis of the NSCAI recommendation. AI models usually need vast amounts of training data to achieve good performances. Thus, the scarcity of real data about nuclear launches may prevent proper training of the desired AI early warning system. Suppose for the sake of argument that this bottleneck will be overcome—e.g., by means of innovative training procedures involving simulated data—so that the resulting AI model is found to achieve "satisfactory" classification accuracy. Even in this scenario, which is favorable to the NSCAI recommendation, the occurrence of errors cannot be excluded. Indeed, the statistical nature of AI decision-making intrinsically allows for misclassifications. No matter how infrequently such misclassifications occur, the false positive of a nuclear attack is a high-risk event, as it may trigger an unjustified use of nuclear weapons.

In view of the high risk associated with false positives of nuclear attacks, human decision-makers must carefully verify the responses of AI-powered early warning systems. But this verification requires time to be performed, possibly offsetting the additional time that one hopes to buy for decision-makers by means of AI-powered automation. In this verification process, temporal constraints are just one of the critical factors to consider. Automation bias is another crucial element, that is, the tendency to over-trust machine responses, downplaying the role of contrasting human judgments. Detected across a variety of automation technologies and application domains, automation biases were the cause of multiple accidents. Hence, human operators must be trained to countervail automation biases in their interactions with AI-powered early warning systems. However, effective training of this sort is hindered by the black-box character of much AI information processing and the related difficulty of explaining its outcomes.

A major interpretive difficulty arises from the fact that many AI systems process information *sub-symbolically*, without operating on humanly understandable declarative statements and without applying stepwise logical or causal inference (Pearl & Mackenzie, 2019). Moreover, the statistically significant features of input data that AI models learn to identify and use may significantly differ from features that humans identify and use to carry out the same problem-solving tasks. Because of these remarkable differences between human and machine information processing, AI learning systems turn out to be opaque and difficult to interpret from human perceptual and cognitive standpoints.

These interpretive hurdles propagate to the explanation of responses provided by AI systems. To detect and countervail machine errors, nuclear decision-makers should be put in a position to understand the reasons why an AI-powered early warning system provided a certain classification of sensor data. In the absence of surveyable and transparent stepwise logical, causal, or probabilistic inference on the part of the system, human operators are hard-pressed to work out for themselves an adequate explanation. One may alternatively try and endow the AI-powered early warning system with the capability of providing explanations to why questions by human operators. Explanations would have to be cast in terms that are cognitively accessible to human operators. The achievement of this overall goal characterizes the research area called eXplainable AI (or XAI in brief), which addresses the challenging problem of mapping AI information processing into cognitive and perceptual chunks that are understandable to humans, and to assemble on this basis "good" explanations for AI decisions, predictions, and classifications. However, pending significant breakthroughs in XAI, one cannot but acknowledge the difficulty of fulfilling the explainability condition which is crucial for nuclear decision-makers interacting with AI-powered early warning systems to achieve situational awareness.

Additional risks arising from the use of AI systems in nuclear early warning flow from vulnerabilities of AI models developed on the basis of ML methods.

Adversarial machine learning (Biggio & Roli, 2018) reveals unexpected and counterintuitive mistakes that AI systems make and that human operators would unproblematically avoid making. By altering the illumination of a stop signal on the street—in ways that are hardly perceptible to human eyes—an AI system was induced to classify it as a 30-mph speed limit sign (Gnanasambandam et al., 2021). A human operator would not incur in such mistakes, for the small adversarial input perturbations inducing the machine to err are hardly noticeable by the human perceptual system. Additional errors, induced in more controlled laboratory conditions, are directly relevant to military uses of AI systems. Notably, visual perceptual systems based on DNN architectures were found to mistake images of school buses for ostriches (Szegedy et al., 2014) or 3-D renderings of turtles for rifles (Athalye et al., 2018). Clearly, these mistakes are potentially catastrophic in a wide variety of conventional warfare domains, for normal uses of school buses are protected by International Humanitarian Law, and someone carrying a harmless object in the hand may be mistakenly taken by an AI system to wield a weapon (Amoroso & Tamburrini, 2021).

Let us take stock. There seems to be undisputed consensus on the condition that only human beings—and no automated system—ought to authorize the employment of nuclear weapons. However, one cannot take at face value even the more modest recommendation to use AI in nuclear early warning. Indeed, one cannot exclude counterintuitive and potentially catastrophic errors made by these systems, of the same sort that adversarial machine learning enables one to highlight in other critical application domains. More generally, any suggested use of AI in NC3 stands in need of a thorough critical discussion, considering the opacities, fragilities, and vulnerabilities of AI information processing.

5 Responsibilities of AI Stakeholders and Large-Scale Threats to Humanity

It was pointed out above that AI stakeholders can undertake multiple actions to reduce both AI's electricity consumption and the AI carbon footprint, in addition to restraining AI applications exacerbating the climate crisis and fostering applications of AI technologies for climate warming mitigation and adaptation. Moreover, AI stakeholders can raise public opinion awareness about threats to nuclear stability arising from actual or potential developments in AI, promote international scientific and political dialogues on these threats, and propose and support the implementation of trust and confidence building measures among nuclear powers to avert nuclear risks related to the militarization of AI technologies and systems.

Normative ethics provides substantive ethical underpinnings for these various actions. To begin with, prospective responsibilities for AI stakeholders to shield humanity from man-made large-scale threats flow from the obligation to do everything reasonable to protect the right of people to a dignified life. Additional obligations in the framework of duty ethics (aka deontological ethics) flow from the possibility that large-scale threats may even lead to human extinction (Bostrom, 2002). Indeed, Hans Jonas argued for the responsibility to protect the persistence of humanity in the wake of Kant's idea of what constitutes human dignity. Jonas pointed out that—for all one knows today—only members of the human species are moral agents and bearers of moral responsibilities. One may regard other *sentient* beings inhabiting planet Earth as bearers of moral rights along with human beings, but none of them has moral responsibilities, and therefore cannot be regarded as a genuine moral agent, whose actions admit praise or blame. Under this view, moral agency will disappear from planet Earth if humanity goes extinct. Jonas offers the preservation of this unique and ethically crucial property of our world as the ground for a new imperative of collective responsibility: "Act so that the effects of your action are compatible with the permanence of genuine human life" (Jonas, 1984). In particular, one ought to refrain from building man-made threats to the persistence of human civilizations and to reduce existing threats of this kind.

Jonas emphasized the unlimited temporal horizon of this imperative: one must avoid technological actions that will lead to the extinction of genuine human life *at any time* in the future. In contrast with this, the temporal horizon of other obligations—notably including intragenerational solidarity and intergenerational care duties—fail to provide moral reasons to protect the life of distant generations. However, these short-term obligations provide additional ethical motivations to reduce large-scale threats that may soon materialize. Without the implementation of effective nuclear disarmament policies, nuclear conflicts are a standing threat to present generations. And the best available models of climate change predict that disruptive climate warming effects may be felt a few decades ahead in the absence of effective contrasting actions. Thus, in addition to Jonas's categorical imperative, intragenerational solidarity bonds and intergenerational care duties provide significant ethical motivations to act on the reduction of man-made existential threats.

Contractarian approaches to justice afford yet another argument for the duty to do whatever is presently reasonable to preserve good living conditions for *any* future generation. Consider from this perspective John Rawls's idealized model of the social contract for a just society. In this model, the subjects called to lay down the principles of a just society reason under a veil of ignorance. In particular, they cannot use information about the present or future generation that they belong to. Under this constraint, Rawls introduced a "principle of just savings" to protect the right of every person to live under just institutions independent of which generation she happens to belong to. The principle requires each generation to transmit to the next generation environmental, economic, and cultural resources that are sufficient to support politically just institutions (Rawls, 1971). Thus, in particular, each generation must refrain from exploiting the natural and cultural environments in ways that are incompatible with the unbounded persistence of a just society.

Finally, and more obviously so, consequentialist approaches in normative ethics afford basic moral motivations to choose actions protecting humanity from extinction or from widespread deterioration of living conditions. Indeed, major consequentialist doctrines—differing from each other in terms of which consequences of actions must be valued and how these consequences must be weighed and compared to each other (Sinnott-Armstrong, 2022)—converge on the protection and fostering of the aggregate well-being of human beings.

6 Conclusions

The real and potential double-edged impact of AI on man-made, large-scale threats to humanity is not confined to nuclear war and the effects of the climate crisis. It turns out that one can readily modify AI models for the discovery of new drugs, so that the modified models help one discover chemical compounds to build weapons of mass destructions (WMD). A pharmaceutical research group, using an AI model to discover new molecules for therapeutic purposes, demonstrated the possibility of this malicious dual use. Their model normally penalizes predicted toxicity and rewards predicted activity of chemical compounds against pathogens. By inverting this reward function, and running the model using limited computational resources only, many new and highly toxic compounds were identified, some of which turn out to be more toxic than publicly known chemical warfare agents (Urbina et al., 2022).

The malleability of AI technologies is quite unprecedented. It is an ethical, social, and political responsibility to develop AI for the flourishing and persistence of human civilizations, for protecting humanity from man-made large-scale threats, and for reducing AI's role in their buildup.

Discussion Questions for Students and Their Teachers

1. Propose an innovative AI project contributing to climate warming mitigation or adaptation.
2. Describe the goals of a workshop where both AI scientists and politicians gather to discuss AI's potential impact on nuclear stability.
3. Describe a public engagement initiative to raise awareness about man-made, large-scale threats to humanity.

Learning Resources for Students

1. Patterson, D., Gonzales, J., Hölzle, U., Le, Q., Liang, C., Mungia, L.M., Rotchchild, D., So, D., Texier, M., Dean, J. (2022) 'The carbon footprint of machine learning will first plateau, and then shrink', *Computer*(July), 18–28, doi: 10.1109/MC.2022.3148714.

   This article provides the reader with crucial information about the main good practices that have been identified so far to reduce AI's carbon footprint. Additionally, a critical analysis is presented of related debates within the AI research community and of various estimates of the AI carbon footprint.
2. Gailhofer, P., Herold, A., Schemmel, J.P., Scherf, C.-S., Urrutia, C., Köhler, A.R., Braungardt, S. (2021) 'The role of artificial intelligence in the European Green Deal', Policy Department for Economic, Scientific and Quality of Life Policies, European Parliament, EU. Available at: www.europarl. europa.eu/RegData/etudes/STUD/2021/662906/IPOL_STU(2021)662906_EN.pdf (Accessed 26 March 2023).

This report stimulates reflections about the multiple uses one can make of AI technologies and systems to support the European Green Deal and more generally to align the design and deployment of AI systems with climate warming mitigation and adaptation efforts.

3. Greenpeace (2016). 'Oil in the Cloud. How Tech Companies are Helping Big Oil Profit from Climate Destruction', *Greenpeace Report*. Available at: https://www.greenpeace.org/usa/reports/oil-in-the-cloud/ (Accessed: 26 March 2023).

   This report vividly illustrates the climate agnostic (and indeed double-edged) character of AI applications. It is emphasized there that AI applications can make the search for, commercialization of, and use of fossil fuels more efficient, thereby leading to more GHG emissions.

4. Boulanin, V. (2019). *The impact of AI on strategic stability and nuclear risk. Volume I: Euro-Atlantic Perspectives*. Stockholm: Stockholm International Peace Research Institute [online]. Available at: https://www.sipri.org/publications/2019/other-publications/impact-artificial-intelligence-strategic-stability-and-nuclear-risk-volume-i-euro-atlantic (Accessed 26 March 2023).

   This report provides a comprehensive analysis of AI's potential impact on strategic nuclear stability, delving into new risk that AI may give rise to in connection with nuclear deterrence and nuclear command and control systems.

5. Cummings, M.L. (2021) 'Rethinking the Maturity of Artificial Intelligence in Safety-Critical Settings' *AI Magazine* 42(1), 6–15.

   This article questions the maturity of AI for use in a variety of safety-critical settings, in view of known weaknesses and vulnerabilities of this technology. In particular, it is useful to appraise risks that AI may introduce in nuclear command and control.

Acknowledgments This research was partially supported by the Italian Ministry for Universities and Research (MUR), under grant 2020SSKZ7R of the Research Projects of National Interest program PRIN2020.

References

Amoroso, D., & Tamburrini, G. (2021). Toward a normative model of meaningful human control over weapons systems. *Ethics & International Affairs, 35*(2), 245–272.

ANU-NSC. (2020). *Transparent oceans? The coming SSBN counter-detection task may be insuperable*. Canberra: National Security College Publication, Australian National University. Accessed March 26, 2023, from https://nsc.crawford.anu.edu.au/publication/16666/transparent-oceans-coming-ssbn-counter-detection-task-may-be-insuperable.

Arms Control Association. (2019). Nuclear false warnings and the risk of catastrophe. *Arms Control Today* [online]. Accessed March 26, 2023, from https://www.armscontrol.org/act/2019-12/focus/nuclear-false-warnings-risk-catastrophe.

Athalye, A., Engstrom, L., Ilyas, A., & Kwok, K. (2018). Synthesizing robust adversarial examples. *Proceedings of Machine Learning Research, 80*, 284–293. Accessed March 26, 2023, from https://proceedings.mlr.press/v80/athalye18b.html

Biggio, B., & Roli, F. (2018). Wild patterns: Ten years after the rise of adversarial machine learning. *Pattern Recognition, 84*, 317–331.

Bostrom, N. (2002). Existential risks—analyzing human extinction scenarios and related hazards. *Journal of Evolution and Technology, 9*(1), 1–30.

Boulanin, V. (2019). *The impact of AI on strategic stability and nuclear risk. Volume I: Euro-Atlantic perspectives*. Stockholm International Peace Research Institute. Accessed March 26, 2023, from https://www.sipri.org/publications/2019/other-publications/impact-artificial-intelligence-strategic-stability-and-nuclear-risk-volume-i-euro-atlantic

Brixey-Williams S. (2016). *Will the Atlantic become transparent?* British Pugwash Report, (3rd ed.), 2018. Accessed March 26, 2023, from Pugwash_Transparent_Oceans_update_nov2016_v3b_April2018-1.pdf.

CBECI. (2022). *Cambridge bitcoin electricity consumption index*. Cambridge Centre for Alternative Finance, University of Cambridge. Accessed March 26, 2023, from https://ccaf.io/cbeci/index/comparisons

China's State Council. (2017). New generation artificial intelligence development plan (translation). Accessed March 26, 2023, from https://www.newamerica.org/cybersecurity-initiative/digichina/blog/full-translation-chinas-new-generation-artificial-intelligence-development-plan-2017/.

Cummings, M. L. (2021). Rethinking the maturity of artificial intelligence in safety-critical settings. *AI Magazine, 42*(1), 6–15.

Dhar, P. (2020). The carbon impact of Artificial Intelligence. *Nature Machine Intelligence, 2*, 423–425.

Dobbe, R., & Whittaker, M. (2019). AI and climate change: How they're connected, and what we can do about it. *AI Now Institute*. Accessed March 26, 2023, from https://medium.com/@ainowinstitute

Gailhofer, P., Herold, A., Schemmel, J. P., Scherf, C.-S., Urrutia, C., Köhler, A. R., & Braungardt, S. (2021). The role of artificial intelligence in the European Green Deal, Policy Department for Economic, Scientific and Quality of Life Policies, European Parliament, EU. Accessed March 26, 2023, from www.europarl.Europa.EU/RegData/etudes/STUD/2021/662906/IPOL_STU(2021)662906_EN.Pdf.

Gnanasambandam, A., Sherman, A. M., & Chan, S. H. (2021). *Optical adversarial attacks* (pp. 92–101). IEEE/CVF International Conference on Computer Vision Workshops (ICCVW 2021).

Greenpeace. (2016). Oil in the cloud. How tech companies are helping big oil profit from climate destruction. *Greenpeace Report*. Accessed March 26, 2023, from https://www.greenpeace.org/usa/reports/oil-in-the-cloud/

IEA. (2022). Data centres and data transmission networks, tracking paper. *International Energy Agency*. Accessed March 26, 2023, from https://www.iea.org/reports/data-centres-and-data-transmission-networks

Jonas, H. (1984). The imperative of responsibility. In *Search of an ethics for the technological age*. The University of Chicago Press.

Kaack L. H., Donti P. L., Strubell E., & Rolnick D. (2020). Artificial intelligence and climate change. Opportunities, considerations, and policy levers to align AI with climate change goals. E-paper. Berlin: Heinrich Böll Stiftung. Accessed March 23, 2023, from https://eu.boell.org/en/2020/12/03/artificial-intelligence-and-climate-change.

Nordgren, A. (2023). Artificial Intelligence and climate change: Ethical issues. *Journal of Information, Communication and Ethics in Society, 21*(1), 1–15.

NSCAI. (2021). *Final report*. US National Security Commission on Artificial Intelligence. Accessed March 26, 2023, from www.nscai.gov/wp-content/uploads/2021/03/Full-Report-Digital-1.pdf.

Oltermann, P. (2022). European politicians duped into deepfake video calls with mayor of Kyiv. *The Guardian*. 25 June 2022, Accessed March 26, 2023, from https://www.theguardian.com/world/2022/jun/25/european-leaders-deepfake-video-calls-mayor-of-kyiv-vitali-klitschko

Patterson, D., Gonzales, J., Le, Q., Liang, C., Mungia, L. M., Rotchchild, D., So, D., Texier, M., & Dean, J. (2021). Carbon emissions and large neural network training. *arXiv*. 2104.10350.

Patterson, D., Gonzales, J., Hölzle, U., Le, Q., Liang, C., Mungia, L. M., Rotchchild, D., So, D., Texier, M., & Dean, J. (2022). The carbon footprint of machine learning will first plateau, and then shrink. *Computer*, 18–28. https://doi.org/10.1109/MC.2022.3148714

Pearl, J., & Mackenzie, D. (2019). *The book of why. The new science of cause and effect*. Penguin.

Rawls, J. (1971). *A theory of justice*. Harvard UP.

Ritchie, H., Roser, M., & Rosado P. (2022). Energy. OurWorldInData.org [online]. Accessed March 26, 2023, from https://ourworldindata.org/energy.

Rolnick, D., Donti, P. L., Kaack, L. H., Kochanski, K., Lacoste, A., Sankaran, K., Ross, A. S., Milojevic-Dupont, N., Jaques, N., & Waldman-Brown, A. (2019). Tackling climate change with machine learning. *arXiv*. 1906.05433.

Today, R. (2017). Whoever leads in AI will rule the world: Putin to Russian children on knowledge day. *Russia Today, 1*. www.rt.com/news/401731-ai-rule-world-putin

Szegedy, C., Zaremba, W., Sutskever, I., Bruna, J., Erhan, D., Goodfellow, I., & Fergus, R. (2014). Intriguing properties of neural networks. *arXiv*. arXiv.org, https://arxiv.org/abs/1312.6199v4

Sinnott-Armstrong, W. (2022). Consequentialism. In E. N. Zalta & U. Nodelman (Eds.), *The Stanford encyclopedia of philosophy* (Winter 2022 ed.) Accessed March 26, 2023, from https://plato.stanford.edu/archives/win2022/entries/consequentialism/

Schwartz, R., Dodge, J., Smith, N. A., & Etzioni, O. (2020). Green AI. *Communications of the ACM, 63*(12), 54–63.

Strubell, E., Ganesh, A., & McCallum, A. (2019). Energy and policy considerations for deep learning in NLP. *arxiv*. Accessed March 26, 2023, from https://arxiv.org/abs/1906.02243

Urbina, F., Lentzos, F., Invernizzi, C., & Ekins, S. (2022). Dual use of artificial-intelligence-powered drug discovery. *Nature Machine Intelligence, 4*, 189–191.

Verdecchia, R., Sallou, J., & Cruz, L. (2023). A systematic review of green AI. In W. Pedrycz (Ed.), *WIREs data mining and knowledge discovery*. https://doi.org/10.1002/widm.1507

Promises and Perils in Moralizing Technologies

Viola Schiaffonati

Abstract This chapter discusses the need to incorporate in the currently prevalent approach, according to which technologies should be designed to possibly avoid negative consequences, a proactive approach that promotes positive outcomes. The chapter thus focuses on the "moralization" of technologies, that is, the deliberate development of technologies to shape moral action and moral decision-making. By means of two thought experiments, this chapter presents the promises but also the perils of moralizing technologies with particular attention to computer technologies. Challenges to the moralization of technologies deal with human autonomy and the opacity of design choices and their regulation.

1 Introduction

In his 1980 seminal paper "Do Artifacts Have Politics," Langdon Winner discusses the famous case of Robert Moses's overpasses. Moses has been a very influential urban planner working in the state of New York during the first half of twentieth century and contributing to give shape to some of its important spaces, from Central Park in New York City to Jones Beach, the upstate widely acclaimed recreational park. These overpasses, located in Long Island, have a peculiar feature: they are very low such that automobiles can pass easily below them, while trucks and buses cannot get access to the roads where these overpasses are built. Notably, Some of these roads are the ones leading to Jones Beach. Far from being an unintentional mistake in Moses's design process, these overpasses are rather the expression of his racial prejudices (Winner, 1980). Moses decided to design them precisely to make the access to some areas, such as Jones Beach, easy for automobiles and particularly difficult for public transportation. The reason? To prevent people with low income, who often at that time did not possess private cars, from accessing these recreational areas. In his view, the overpasses were built in such a way to facilitate the access to

V. Schiaffonati (✉)
Dipartimento di Elettronica, Informazione e Bioingegneria, Politecnico di Milano, Milan, Italy
e-mail: viola.schiaffonati@polimi.it

H. Werthner et al. (eds.), *Introduction to Digital Humanism*,
https://doi.org/10.1007/978-3-031-45304-5_17

some areas, to "automobile-owning whites of 'upper' and 'comfortable middle' classes, as he called them [...]. Poor people and blacks, who normally used public transit, were kept off the roads because the twelve-foot tall buses could not get through the overpasses. One consequence was to limit access of racial minorities and low-income groups to Jones Beach" (Winner, 1980, p. 124).

This case clearly exemplifies how design entails moral considerations, although here in a very negative sense. Moreover, it represents an instance of the claim that morality is not only a matter of humans but also a matter of how artifacts are designed and shape humans' perceptions and actions, as has been discussed by many scholars—among others by the famous sociologist Bruno Latour. For example, speed bumps, according to Latour, incorporate the normative prescription that drivers should slow down before reaching them. Hence, how humans design artifacts can deeply influence actions, including their moral decision-making. This does not mean that artifacts are capable of moral reasoning but that they can be designed in order to shape humans' moral decision-making.

This chapter deals with the ethics of design and in particular with the so-called moralizing technologies. According to Verbeek (2011), the moralization of technologies is the deliberate attempt to design them to shape moral decision-making. This makes moralizing technologies deeply connected to the responsibility in the design of technologies and in particular to active responsibility, that is, the deliberate attempt to design technologies both to avoid negative consequences and to promote positive ones. The overall goal of the chapter is to critically analyze the promises and perils of moralizing technologies with particular attention to computer and digital technologies. Beyond presenting some of the traditional issues extensively discussed in the literature so far, this chapter aims at evidencing some novel ones that have not yet received the attention they deserve. The structure of this chapter is as follows. Section 2 illustrates the conceptual framework of the discussion and in particular the invisibility factor and the notion of experimental technology. Section 3 presents moralizing technologies through the illustration of two thought experiments. Section 4 focuses mostly on the critical issues and challenges in the moralization of technologies. Finally, Sect. 5 concludes the chapter by summarizing its main content and considering some open issues.

2 Conceptual Framework

The idea that artifacts are "bearers of morality" and designed in order to shape human decision-making is not new, as we briefly discussed in Sect. 1. In this section, we focus on computer technologies and, in particular, on two features that have an impact in their role *qua* moralizing technologies.

The first feature concerns the *invisibility factor*, described for the first time by computer ethicist Jim Moor (1985). According to Moor, computer operations are invisible: one can know inputs and outputs of computers but only be dimly aware of their internal processing. This invisibility contributes to generate policy vacuums concerning the use of computer technologies and their ethical significance. Moor distinguishes three kinds of invisibility: *invisibility of abuse*, *invisibility of programming values*, and *invisibility of complex calculations*.

Invisibility of abuse describes those unethical behaviors that take place by exploiting the invisibility of computer operations. An example is the stealing of money from a bank by a programmer who writes a program transferring the excess interest from the bank to their account. Not only is this abuse very different from getting into a bank with a gun and asking the teller for the money but also more difficult to be detected because the computer operations making it possible are mostly invisible.

Invisibility of programming values concerns the values of programmers that are usually embedded into their programs in an invisible way. As programs are the results of human processes—Moor stresses—they contain human values both in the positive and in the negative sense. Moreover, these programming values can be inserted into the programs both intentionally and unintentionally. For example, the development of a program for airline reservation can be designed in a way to show as the best results those of a particular airline company, even if its flights are not the most convenient ones. Programming values can be also not deliberately inserted into a program, when, for instance, the programmer is not aware of their bias.

Invisibility of complex calculation describes how computers are capable of very complex calculations that go beyond human comprehension, which is also the reason why computers have been created. An interesting example is the four-color conjecture solved in 1976 by a computer program at the University of Illinois. The three kinds of invisibility, even if proposed in 1985, are still valid. It is not difficult to recognize how they can be applied to many of the situations we experience today, from different types of bias of artificial intelligence (AI) algorithms to the complexity of deep learning techniques.

The second feature of digital technologies we aim at highlighting in this section is connected to what the ethicist of technology Ibo van de Poel has labeled *experimental technologies* (van de Poel, 2016). Experimental technologies are those technologies whose risks and benefits are hard to estimate before they are properly inserted in their context of use: "I will call technologies experimental if there is only limited operational experience with them, so that social benefits and risks cannot, or at least not straightforwardly, be assessed on basis of experience" (van de Poel, 2016, p. 669). According to this characterization, nanotechnologies, *algae* based on synthetic biology, autonomous vehicles, and human enhancement drugs are examples of experimental technologies. Yet in this chapter, we focus exclusively on experimental computer technologies. For instance, several applications adopting AI or machine learning (ML) techniques are experimental in the sense suggested by van de Poel. The inherent complexity of these technical artifacts, together with the uncertainty connected to their interaction with the environment and the users, makes it very difficult to precisely predict their benefits and risks. This is potentially true for any technology that is complex enough. Indeed, many technologies in their initial phases of development are interested in the famous *Collingridge dilemma* (Collingridge, 1980). This dilemma describes the differences between the early phases of a technology, where its social embedding is characterized by uncertainty, and the later stages, when this uncertainty might be decreased, but the entrenchment of the technology into society is so strong that it is already too late to overcome its negative effects. In the case of some current computer technologies, this experimental nature is very evident: it is not by chance they are sometimes labeled as emerging technologies to further stress their experimental nature. This nature raises several concerns in terms of the possibility to anticipate and predict their risks which, in the case of computer technologies, are particularly serious as they are likely to impact very large portions of populations given their extensive diffusion.

The invisibility factor and the notion of experimental technology can be profitably used as interpretative frameworks for some of the current computer technologies. Moreover, they impact on the notion of moral responsibility as discussed in the current ethics of technology. The traditional paradigm of responsibility is usually centered around what is called the *passive* approach: when something undesirable has occurred in the development or use of a technology, the idea is to look backward to reconstruct who is responsible for this negative outcome. Beyond passive responsibility, in the last years, a different approach has been proposed: *active responsibility*, that is, the responsibility relevant before something negative has occurred. In other words, active responsibility is about both preventing the negative effects of a technology and designing it to realize its positive effects. Active responsibility thus promotes a proactive approach to technological development and evidences how technological design can play an essential role to address responsibility (van de Poel & Royakkers, 2011). Responsibility here is not only a form of backward-looking Accountability in the sense of being held to account for, or justify, one's actions toward others, but a proactive attitude according to which designers are morally accountable also at the beginning of the design process. The idea to design technologies for avoiding negative effects and for promoting positive ones is very powerful and tries to anticipate the solutions of some issues already at the design level. At the same time, this anticipation is extremely critical: the possibility to steer technological development is always difficult because of its high level of unpredictability, but becomes particularly difficult when dealing with technologies that are both experimental and invisible in the sense outlined above.

In the next section, we will move further along this direction and focus on moralizing technologies, that is, a particular type of technology designed to promote positive effects and to steer human moral decision-making. The idea is that moral decision-making can be the result of human processes together with their interactions with technologies. In other words, the moralization of technologies exploits the possibility of moralizing also our material environment, including the technologies, beyond the usual possibility of moralizing people.

3 Moralizing Technologies

To better understand the nature of moralizing technologies, let us introduce a couple of thought experiments. Thought experiments are traditionally used in philosophy as "devices of imagination" for various purposes (Brown & Fehige, 2022). Additionally, a long tradition of thought experimentation characterizes scientific reasoning, including prominent natural philosophers, such as Galileo Galilei, Gottfried Leibniz, and Isaac Newton, and scientists like Albert Einstein. Here, we devise two thought experiments, based on realistic and partly already existing technologies, but conceived in such a way to stretch our imagination to some interesting directions.

The first one is an alcohol lock for cars. Existing alcohol locks for cars, by analyzing drivers' breath, check the alcohol level in their body and signal if this level is above the limits imposed by the law. If the alcohol level is beyond this threshold, the car stays locked, and the driver cannot use it. Let suppose now that cars equipped with this alcohol lock would not be more expensive than cars without this system. Let us also suppose that they have some other desirable features, difficult if not impossible to have in reality. First of all, all the personal data collected during the analysis of the level of the alcohol would stay completely private: only the user could know and access them. Second, such an alcohol lock for a car would work in a perfect way, meaning that it would produce neither false positives nor false negatives. Finally, the process to analyze the level of alcohol in the blood would be very smooth and fast such that the driver would spend a minimum amount of time to check their alcohol level. As it should be clear, these three last features are imaginary in one way or another: we are well aware that in reality, it is not possible to have technologies that work without the possibility of any mistake or that personal data cannot be 100% protected. However, the goal of this thought experiment is not to focus on the details of the design of such a device but rather to investigate the opportunities and challenges of moralizing technologies. And here it is very clear that the alcohol lock for cars is a technology designed to moralize cars' drivers. Similarly to Latour's speed bumps telling the driver "slow down before reaching me," alcohol locks for cars incorporate in their design the maxim "don't drive when you have drunk too much." It is important to stress that today, notwithstanding an increased awareness on the dangers of driving while drinking, still many accidents occur for this reason, and the efforts provided to change the cultural attitude with respect to this problem seem to be not enough to solve it. Automobiles equipped with alcohol locks, possessing the desirable features we have listed, appear as a promising way to solve this issue in a definitive way.

The second thought experiment focuses on a serious and very urgent issue as well, the scarcity of water and the consequent need of saving and efficiently managing it. We are well aware today of the importance of water and how vital it is to save it, in particular in some areas of the world. Although it might seem that the problem of water is not a matter of death or life, like the driving while drinking case, water is an essential resource, and its scarcity has a profound impact on human lives at both the individual and the collective level, such as in migrations, wars, and other tragedies caused by drought. Individual behaviors can make a difference in water preservation; at the same time, many of us are used to having plenty of water available and, for example, to take very long showers with scarce attention to the amount of water consumed. Here, again, we can imagine a moralizing technology supporting us in the process of saving water while not reducing the comfort of our long showers. Let us imagine, in this case, a smart showerhead that, if applied to our shower, can reduce our daily consumption of water up to 50%. Once again, this device would be economically affordable and very easy to use. The label smart aims at stressing two important elements. The first one concerns the idea of having a technology that solves the problem in a smart way. In terms of the goal of saving water, it would be the same to have a shower programmed in a way to stop after some time—say 2 min—namely, when the daily allowed consumption of water has been reached. But of course, this will not be the same in terms of our comfort: no one would buy a shower like this with the risk of having the water interrupted when, for example, still having to rinse the shampoo from the hair. The second element is the idea that the imagined showerhead can learn from our habits so that the experience of the shower is both tailored to our preferences and, at the same time, allows us to save water. Here, once again, implementation details are not the core of our thought experimentation. Rather, it is the goal of this exercise with imagination that is important: the smart showerhead, when applied to our shower, can save water in a smart way without reducing the comfort of the shower experience. For example, the device could learn that we do not like much water when using the soap, and so adapt the flux of the shower accordingly, while we love a strong flux when rinsing our hair. Finally, imagination is important to stress, exactly as in the previous case, that this technology should work smoothly without any error and protect collected data in a perfect way.

These two fictional but realistic cases serve to illustrate the power of moralizing technologies: they easily show how moral decision-making can become a matter both of humans and technologies. This does not mean, of course, that technologies are capable of moral reasoning but that they constrain, influence, and shape our moral decision-making in some decisive ways. They both illustrate the moralization of technologies as "the deliberate development of technologies in order to shape moral action and decision making" (van de Poel & Royakkers, 2011, p. 207). It is not by chance that in this section, we have imagined two cases of moralizing technologies that, contrary to Moses's racial overpasses, steer our moral action in the direction of positive values, such as to avoid car accidents due to alcohol and to save water. However, as we will describe in the next section, it is not enough to design technologies to achieve positive outcomes for eliminating the many critical reactions that can emerge from this approach.

4 Exploring the Promises and Perils of Moralizing Technologies

Moralizing technologies offer several promises in terms of positively impacting human actions by moralizing the material environment, including technologies, in which humans live. Both thought experiments of Sect. 3 show how the solution of very serious problems can be achieved by means of technologies designed in a way to promote an active approach to responsibility. In the first case, the alcohol lock for cars tells you “don’t drive while drinking”; in the second case, the smart shower tells you “don’t waste water.” Yet, there is a very significant, immediate difference between these two technologies: in the first case, the goal of avoiding car accidents due to alcohol is attained by means of a strong limitation to our actions, whereas in the second case, there is no apparent limitation to our freedom: we can take showers as long and comfortable as we like. This difference is well represented by different reactions: when asking people if they would buy the alcohol lock for cars, the answers are mostly negative, while when asking if they would buy the smart showerhead, the answers are almost all positive.

There are also some common elements worth considering when analyzing the critical elements of moralizing technologies. The first element concerns the fear that technologies, and not humans, are in control: such a fear is usually more strongly perceived in the alcohol lock for cars example. This is a key point for at least two reasons. First, technologies in control, and in particular in sensible contexts, raise concerns about possible technocratic drifts where humans might be governed by machines. It is not necessary here to make appeal to science fiction or imagine dystopic future scenarios: it is enough to observe how many decisions impacting both individuals and societies (i.e., police profiling or court sentencing) are increasingly delegated to decision systems based on algorithms (Crawford, 2021; O’Neil, 2016; Scantamburlo et al., 2019). Second, at least in recent history, human autonomy is strongly and deeply intertwined with dignity. Even if the relationship between autonomy and dignity has a long tradition, a recent revamp of it is offered by the debate on current recommender systems that, learning from our previous choices, suggest what movie to watch next, what song, what book, what purchase, but also what friend or romantic relationship to make or engage in shaping how we see the world (Zuboff, 2019). Are we still autonomous in a context in which the fabric of our societies is weaved with these silent and invisible computer technologies? Every time human autonomy is touched upon, the risk of losing dignity emerges in a way that easily swifts in the direction of a complete dehumanization when technologies are in full control. A critical case at point is that discussed for self-driving cars and the idea of programming them to decide who to kill (a young kid or a group of elderly?) in the case of unavoidable accidents, transforming ethical reasoning into a calculation while dismissing complex human deliberative processes (Fossa, 2023).

The second negative reaction toward the moralization of technologies, and of computer technologies in particular, concerns the risk of losing the capability of moral decision-making. The worry is that the constant and increasing delegation to machines of our decisions—also those with a strong moral impact—could make us incapable of exercising our moral competence. As moral decisions are complex and the result of articulated processes of deliberation, the risk could be then to become incapable of dealing with this complexity if not constantly exercised. One could argue here that moral decision-making is a sort of innate capability in humans and that, even if delegated to technological artifacts, it will not disappear from us. Yet, the risk of becoming lazy and unaware of the moral scope of many of our decisions is real and could move us toward a possible de-responsibilization. Moreover, there are situations in which it is crucial to deactivate this delegation to technologies and exercise your own judgment (Nowotny, 2022).

Before delving into the third type of negative reaction, where the key question is a matter of power of who decides how moralizing technologies have to be shaped, it is worth stressing some further elements in the two thought experiments we introduced in Sect. 3. Both concern some limitations to human autonomy. This limitation is well evident in the first case, where it is physically impossible to drive when drunk, while in the second case is subtler: to save water, the user has to confine themselves to the preferences learned by the smart showerhead that, in order to achieve this saving, adapts to their habits while preserving the comfort of the shower experience. Limitations to human freedom are, of course, common experiences in everyday life, and we live in societies where laws constitute an example of these limitations. There is, however, a substantial difference between the limitations imposed by the law, prohibiting driving when having some amount of alcohol in the blood, and that imposed by a technology such as the alcohol lock for cars that implements this law. In the case of the law, one has the freedom to decide not to follow it (with all the risks and possible consequences of this decision), where in the case of the alcohol lock for car, it is precisely this possibility that is eliminated: if the percentage of alcohol in their body is beyond the limit imposed by the law, it is physically impossible for the driver to use the car. Such physical impossibility does not hold for any moralizing technology. For example, it is evident that in the smart showerhead case, the moralizing technology does not impede the possibility to take the shower; it only shapes how to take it. This probably explains the different attitudes and reactions people have in front of the two thought examples. At the same time, it evidences the importance of how these moralizing technologies are designed. Would it be possible to conceive an alcohol lock for cars working in a different way? A better solution would be probably that of a design more similar to the annoying sound of the vehicles seat belts that do not block one in driving the vehicle when they are not in use, but constantly remember this fact.

It is not the place here to investigate possible better designs for moralizing technologies (one crucial element would be if it would be possible to understand the limit between the benefits of these technologies and the attempt to escape the technologically imposed limits to freedom). Rather, it is the place to discuss one critical element of moralizing technologies not sufficiently debated so far. This element is whether there is a way to moralize technologies in a democratic way. And here, hopefully, our thought experiments will be useful for illustrating this.

One further critical element in the moralization of technologies can be the fact that this process is usually the result of invisible decisions of small groups of people and not of a public deliberation achieved in democratic terms. In this respect, the first case (alcohol lock for cars) is paradoxically less problematic than the second one (smart showerhead). Indeed, the alcohol lock for cars implements a law that is the result of a democratic process. In democracies, at least ideally, laws are decided by elected representatives. Therefore, there should be a clear sense of responsibility in deciding and setting up any law: in theory, this process should be transparent and those who decided it accountable. Then, of course, the passage of moving from the level of the law to the level of the technology that is critical for human autonomy is limited, when the law is technologically implemented as in the case of the alcohol lock for cars. This is not true in the case of the smart shower, although one has the choice of whether or not to buy a smart showerhead: we have seen that the perceived and effective degrees of freedom are wider. However, in this case, who decides how the technology should be moralized and which values to be inserted not only are opaque, but also they are not the result of a democratic and publicly debated process. This problem arises when the choices behind the selection of some values and their technological implementation are mostly invisible and not subjected to public discussion, oversight, and control. Whether technologies can be moralized in a democratic way is an open question that cannot be solved in the space of this chapter. A good starting point is the awareness that the issues at stake are not only moral but political as well.

The discussion of the critical elements of the moralization of technologies shows how to design technologies for the good is not enough. First of all, unintended consequences can always arise if we consider the design process only as a translation of constraints (even of moral nature) into the technical artifact. For example, it might be the case that to save water, the smart showerhead increases the overall energy consumption because it requires a large amount of energy to train the algorithm capable of "smartly" regulating the flux of the water. Moreover, the invisibility factor, typical of any computer technology, plays a major role in the case of moralizing technologies: it is not only the opacity of the inner working of the algorithm but of the socio-technical process shaping the moral account of these technologies. Finally, given that moralizing technologies can be experimental in the sense discussed in Sect. 2, the high degree of uncertainty makes it very difficult, if not impossible, to assess their risks and benefits at the design level.

5 Conclusions

Artifacts do have politics, and today this is even more evident as many of our human decisions are taken *through* technologies and through computer technologies in particular. Technological design is a complex process that requires moral choices and not merely technical ones. In this chapter, we have discussed how the moralization of technologies, in accordance with active responsibility in the ethics of technology, is a promising approach. At the same time, we have evidenced some important critical elements that should be taken very seriously at this stage. These criticalities show how technological design is a complex socio-technical process that cannot be reduced to its technical elements. Not only the people who will use these technologies should play a role in this process, but also the intrinsic moral and political connotation of the process should be clearly recognized.

This awareness can be translated at different levels: designers cannot simply inscribe a technical function into the design of a technology; policy makers need not only to regulate but to intervene in the co-shaping of technologies from the design phases; citizens must be aware that it is not enough to have technologies designed for the good, but it is essential to know and discuss who decides which values are embedded in the technologies and how.

It is a quite radical shift of perspective, in particular in a time in which several new policy vacuums emerge every day. One role for philosophy is thus to fill in these vacuums by means of conceptual clarification (Moor, 1985): to regulate technologies, it is essential to understand their nature. This is not a job only for philosophy but rather is an interdisciplinary effort devoted to asking questions, analyzing problems, and discussing possible solutions capable of building on the strengths of many different disciplines.

Discussion Questions for Students and Their Teachers

1. Can you think of examples of the invisibility factor connected to current computer technologies? Do you think new kinds of invisibility (beyond invisibility of abuse, programming values, and complex calculation) should be proposed to describe current computer technologies?
2. Discuss possible ways to moralize digital technologies in a democratic way by means of examples.

Learning Resources for Students

1. Kroes, P. and Verbeek, P.P. (2014) (eds.) *The Moral Status of Technical Artefacts*. Springer.

   A book containing several arguments and counterarguments on the moral status of technology and technical artifacts. One of the foundational books in the analytical approach to the philosophy of technology.
2. Johnson, D. (2008) *Computer Ethics*. Fourth Edition. Prentice Hall.

   One of the first textbooks in computer ethics adopting a socio-technical approach. A bit outdated with respect to the examples, yet very interesting in terms of theoretical frameworks.
3. Pelillo, M. and Scantamburlo, T. (2021) (eds.) *Machines We Trust*. Cambridge (MA): MIT Press.

   Edited volume presenting contributions that consider the "ethical debts" of AI systems. It presents a variety of issues and approaches.
4. Peterson, T., Ferreira, R. and Vardi, M. (2023) 'Abstracted Power and Responsibility in Computer Science Ethics Education' in *IEEE Transactions on Technology and Society*, 4:1, 96–102.

A paper discussing the concept of abstracted power to describe how technology may distance computer scientists from consequences of their action. It stresses how abstracted power impacts on responsibility.

5. Taebi, B. (2021) *Ethics and Engineering*. Cambridge: Cambridge University Press.

   A comprehensive view on the ethical issues of engineering with an attention to engineering practice. An advanced textbook with a scholarly approach.

References

Brown, J. R., & Fehige, Y. (2022). Thought experiments. In E. N. Zalta & U. Nodelman (Eds.), *The Stanford encyclopedia of philosophy*. https://plato.stanford.edu/archives/win2022/entries/thought-experiment/

Collingridge, D. (1980). *The social control of technology*. Pinter.

Crawford, K. (2021). *Atlas of AI: Power, politics, and the planetary costs of artificial intelligence*. Yale University Press.

Fossa, F. (2023). *Ethics of driving automation: Artificial agency and human values*. Springer Nature.

Moor, J. (1985). What is computer ethics? *Metaphilosophy, 16*(4), 266–275.

Nowotny, H. (2022). *AI we trust: Power, illusion and control of predictive algorithms*. Polity Press.

O'Neil, C. (2016). *Weapons of math destruction*. Crown Publications.

Scantamburlo, T., Charlesworth, A., & Cristianini, N. (2019). Machine decisions and human consequences. In K. Yeung & M. Lodge (Eds.), *Algorithmic regulation*. Oxford Academic.

van de Poel, I. (2016). An ethical framework for evaluating experimental technology. *Science and Engineering Ethics, 22*, 667–686.

van de Poel, I., & Royakkers, L. (2011). *Ethics, technology, and engineering*. Wiley-Blackwell.

Verbeek, P. P. (2011). *Moralizing technology: Understanding and designing the morality of things*. University of Chicago Press.

Winner, L. (1980). Do artifacts have politics? *Daedalus, 109*, 121–136.

Zuboff, S. (2019). *The age of surveillance capitalism*. Public Affairs.

The Road Less Taken: Pathways to Ethical and Responsible Technologies

Susan Winter

Abstract Technology is no longer just about technology—now it is about living. So, how do we have ethical technology that creates a better life and a better society? Technology must become truly "human-centered," not just "human-aware" or "human-adjacent." Diverse users and advocacy groups must become equal partners in initial co-design and in continual assessment and management of information systems with human, social, physical, and technical components. But we cannot get there without radically transforming how we think about, develop, and use technologies. In this chapter, we explore new models for digital humanism and discuss effective tools and techniques for designing, building, and maintaining sociotechnical systems that are built to be and remain continuously ethical, responsible, and human-centered.

1 Introduction

Technology is no longer just about technology—now it is about living. Technology is central to our health, education, relationships, work lives, entertainment, finances, and more. Technology is so deeply embedded into our everyday lives that we take it for granted. It is a powerful force, but its impact depends on how we design and use it. The power of technology has spurred advances in medical treatments, transformed agricultural production, and improved transportation safety but has also diminished mental health, stoked social division, and raised privacy and surveillance concerns. Given the power and centrality of technology, the question becomes, "How can we have ethical technology that creates a better life and a better society?" (Winter, 2019)

The answer is that technology must become truly human-centered. It must support human values and fulfill individual needs while also strengthening the social and cultural fabric of society. Shifting from a technology focus to a sociotechnical systems focus will require a radical transformation in how we think about, develop,

S. Winter (✉)
College of Information Studies, University of Maryland, College Park, MD, USA
e-mail: sjwinter@umd.edu

H. Werthner et al. (eds.), *Introduction to Digital Humanism*,
https://doi.org/10.1007/978-3-031-45304-5_18

and use technologies. To truly meet the needs of humans will require that we reconceptualize technology as a tool and as a component within a complex interacting system. Further, if we are to be successful, we must embrace our responsibility to understand and help to continually manage the complex multi-component systems that we influence when we create and use technologies. This will not be easy, but progress is possible if we make a long-term commitment to making this shift to digital humanism.

To better understand the changes that will be required, we identify the origin of some crucial assumptions underlying the current stance toward information technology that must be overturned. To do so, this chapter traces the evolution of information technology from "human-adjacent" to "human-aware" to "human-centered." It then outlines some of the changes needed to create truly human-centered technologies that focus on human needs within complex sociotechnical systems. These include changing how we think and talk about technologies to avoid category errors, moving to a model of participatory co-design, and building in avenues for feedback and adjustment as we use and manage them.

2 Human-Adjacent Computing

Early computing was "human-adjacent." From about 1950–1980, information technologies were expensive and were primarily developed and adopted by large organizations (Winter et al., 2014). These large organizations had the resources needed to create new technologies and included governmental applications (especially the military), regulated monopolies (especially in communications), and private sector corporations. The motivation was to improve the organization's efficiency, effectiveness, and, for corporations, their profitability. Large mainframe computers radically improved targeting for the military, provided circuit switching for telephony, and processed corporate payrolls (Hevner & Berndt, 2000). The systems were designed and developed by organizations to meet their needs, and their value was evaluated relative to their impact on the organization (see Fig. 1).

Fig. 1 Human-adjacent technology

The few people who interacted with these mainframe computers did so at a distance as operators in machine rooms, as programmers at dumb terminals, and as the eventual recipients of the output (Fig. 2).

Block diagrams of computers that were popular at the time do not even include a representation of humans as relevant to the system (see Fig. 3).

In short, early mainframe computers were conceptualized as self-contained technologies made up of technical components and housed in a machine room. A computer was a closed system that received input from its environment and returned output to that environment. Input and output were managed using devices that were specifically called "peripherals" because they were attached to the computer and controlled by it, but were not a part of the computer itself. People were often involved in providing these inputs and receiving the outputs, but they were not considered to be part of the computer itself or to play a central role in their functioning. Meeting human needs was not the focus of these machines.

Fig. 2 ENIAC https://en.wikipedia.org/wiki/History_of_computing_hardware#/media/File:Eniac.jpg

Fig. 3 Block diagram of a computer

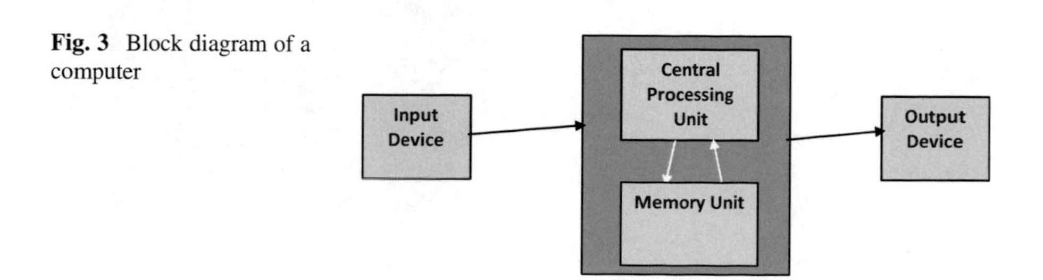

3 Human-Aware Computing

In the early 1980s, computers became smaller and more affordable. By the late 1980s, we saw the rise of personal computers, client-server architectures, and local area networks (LANs). This dramatic expansion of computer use required that ordinary people use PCs. Computing became "human-aware" as it became dependent upon human adoption and use for success.

At the time, businesses started to embrace innovations that relied on the use of these new information technologies such as office automation, total quality management (Deming, 1982), business process reengineering (Hammer & Champy, 1993), and others (Hevner & Berndt, 2000). They developed their own internal networked information systems, often partnering with manufactures such as IBM or DEC to do so. They adopted general-use applications like Microsoft Office Suite, which was often bundled with the hardware. They also created their own custom applications (either in-house or through contracts with software development companies) when off-the-shelf options were inadequate. The focus was still on meeting the organization's needs, but the success of these emerging business initiatives depended on getting their employees to use these new technologies in the workplace.

We also saw a rise in the use of computers for socializing, learning, shopping, and entertainment (see Fig. 4). Consumers could access networks through Internet Service Providers, and companies started creating applications that they hoped would be used at home. Compuserv and America Online (now AoL) were early entrants in this market. Applications included home versions of some of the same software being used in businesses such as email, word processors, and electronic spreadsheets. However, there were also more entertainment-focused applications such as online games. Again, the success of these applications and their developers' profits depended on getting large numbers of people to use them.

Becoming human-aware added complexity to the technology development process. Information systems had to become more user-friendly, and attention had to be paid to interface design and human computer interaction (HCI) (Card, 1983). We

Fig. 4 Human-aware technology

saw rapid advances in both input and output devices, including the two- and three-button mouse, trackballs, touchpads, touchscreens, flatscreens, the shift to graphical user interfaces (GUI), voice user interfaces (VUI), and more. Usability testing rose in importance, but the development process was still usually driven by the organization's needs for efficiency, effectiveness, and/or profitability. Organizations decided what programs and applications to develop. Users' feedback on interfaces may be sought as part of usability testing, but this development phase was often limited in the rush to market and further curtailed as projects fell behind schedule. Many applications were still released and implemented with interfaces that users find cryptic and frustrating even when using them to meet the organization's goals. It was often impossible to use them to meet human goals that do not align with those of the organization.

Fundamentally, the goal of human-aware technology was still to reduce costs and/or generate profits for organizations, and the value of information systems was still evaluated relative to their impact on the organizations (see Fig. 4).

However, the systems themselves look wildly different from the early mainframe computers, and they have moved from locked machine rooms to our desktops and laptops. Depictions of information systems also shifted to use case models and diagrams that include humans who are interacting with the computer. However, these humans (called users) were still shown as outside of the computer (see Fig. 5).

Personal computing expanded our conceptualization of a computer to encompass a more complex multicomponent technical system. People were seen as central to organizational success, but calling them users highlights that their use of the system was what the organization most values about them. Thus, considerable attention was paid to enhancing computer system peripherals and interfaces to encourage proper use. The computer was still a closed system, and peoples' needs were not the focus of these machines. Developers would prefer to engineer the people out of the system entirely, but when necessary, it was vital that people provide the correct inputs and used the outputs as intended by the organization.

4 Human-Centered Computing

Given the power and centrality of technology in our lives, meeting human goals requires that information systems become truly "human-centered" (see Fig. 6). Since the turn of the twenty-first century, there has been a revolution in information technology development that can support this shift to digital humanism, but it will require a transformation in how we think about, design, and use technologies.

Originally, technology development was enormously expensive, so was the purview of large organizations, but this is no longer the case. Increasingly, technical capabilities are readily available "as a service" with the rise of shared robust infrastructures (e.g., AWS), generative platforms for innovation (e.g., Apple's Mac, iPod, iPad, iPhone, iTunes ecosystem), and free and open-source software

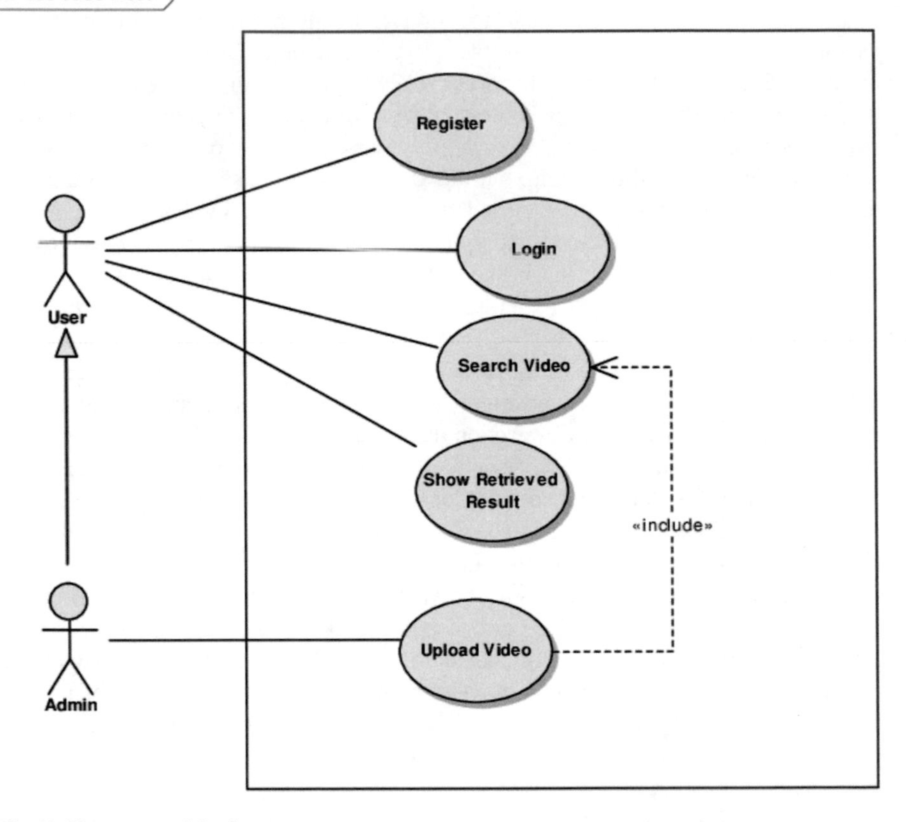

Fig. 5 Use case model of a computer system

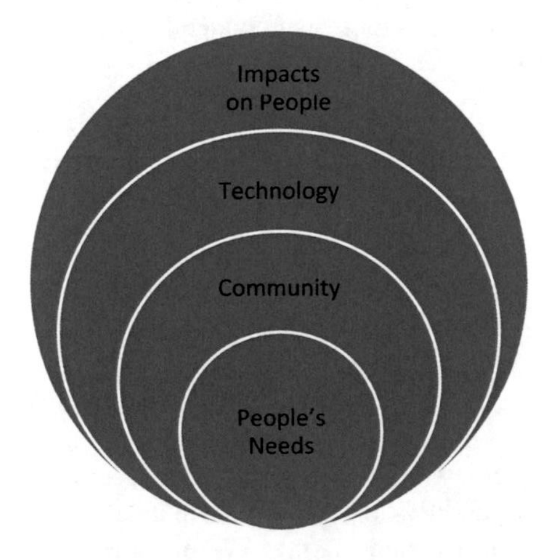

Fig. 6 Human-centered technology

(FOSS). These new flexible infrastructures and applications exist independent of a single organization. Costs are dramatically reduced, lowering the barriers to adoption and use. Traditional businesses are making use of these transformative tools, but they have also opened the door to new collaborative arrangements. Their affordability and flexibility have created an opportunity for truly human-centered computing to emerge allowing individuals and communities to choose devices as consumer products and make use of data and information services in the cloud.

The resulting information systems no longer need to reflect only organizational goals. Driven by human needs, citizen science, FOSS development projects, online patient support spaces, and maker communities have all emerged as new organizational forms. For the first time, we can economically apply massive computing power to the goal of fulfilling human needs, and we can do so in a decentralized way, fashioning local solutions tailored to fit particular circumstances. Digital Humanism is finally possible. This societal-level infrastructure can be leveraged in pursuit of human goals for health, work, learning, entertainment, and personal relationships. The value of the resulting systems can be evaluated relative to their impact on people and communities (see Fig. 6).

To move toward human-centered computing and digital humanism, one major shift we have to make in how we think about technology focuses on the development process itself. Human-centered technology requires that we consider people as inherently social beings embedded within social structures such as families and communities. Embracing this social view and privileging the needs of people requires that they be included as equal partners driving initial system design, development, and management. Although this will add more complexity to the development process, it is only through truly human-centered participatory computing that we can design and develop ethical technology to create a better life and a better society. This shift will require a radical transformation in how we think about, develop, and use technologies. Below, we outline these shifts.

4.1 Thinking About Technology and People

Kantian ethicists have long recognized that it is fine to use tools to reach our own ends. However, it is unethical to use humans to reach our ends because doing so fails to respect inherent human worth and dignity. Putting the needs of people first requires that we clearly, continually, and unambiguously maintain a distinction between two categories: technology and humans. Technology is a thing that can be used as a tool. Humans are deserving of agency, autonomy, and respect and so should not be used as a tool. But this distinction is muddied as emerging technologies are often described using human terms—a form of anthropomorphizing. This leads to category errors where human characteristics are ascribed to technologies that cannot possibly have them (Blackburn, 1994). These technologies then start to be

Table 1 Anthropomorphized terms for technologies, their implied human capabilities, and their actual technological capabilities

Term	Human capability	Technological capability
Artificial intelligence/machine learning (AI/ML)	Is intelligent, can learn	Data pattern matching
Smart cities	Is smart	Urban cyber-physical systems
Autonomous vehicles	Has autonomy	Vehicular robots
5th Generation	Can procreate to create generations	Networking standard
AI as a partner or team member	Can have goals and engage in helping others	Is a tool

thought about and treated as if they were human, which accords them status and privileges that should be reserved for humans.[1]

For example, as shown in Table 1, using the term "artificial intelligence/machine learning (AI/ML)" implies that this technology has intelligence and can learn, but intelligence and learning are human and not technological capabilities. The AI/ML technological capability is that of pattern matching against historical data. Similarly, the term "smart cities" implies that cities can be smart in the same way that humans can be smart. What are commonly called smart cities are no more than urban cyber-physical systems. "Autonomous vehicles" do not have the capacity to be truly autonomous because they cannot make informed moral decisions or be self-governing. Autonomous vehicles are vehicular robots. The term "5th Generation" implies that 5G can procreate and produce offspring. This is simply not something that a networking standard can do. AI cannot truly be a partner or team member because partnership is a human quality that implies shared goals and choosing to help one another meet these goals.

Maintaining the distinction between tools and people is important in ethics and responsible design. It is only by being clear which category something belongs in that we can determine which are the tools that we can use to help us meet our goals and who are the people whose goals we should be meeting.

4.2 Development Objectives

Human-centered computing will also require a transformation in how we develop new technologies. This starts with a consideration of which human goals should be prioritized. Human-centered development focuses on meeting people's goals within a framework that considers which overall objectives are ethical and responsible. One

[1] This is not meant to imply that only humans are deserving of agency, autonomy, and respect or that only humans have the human capabilities listed in Table 1. Many of the human capabilities listed here are shared with other species.

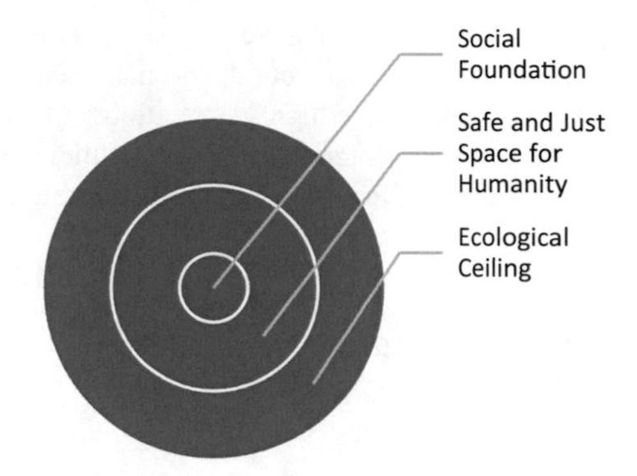

Fig. 7 Doughnut economic model (Adapted from Raworth, 2017)

such framework that is gaining popularity is the Doughnut Economic Model. Developed by Kate Raworth (2017), this model rejects economic growth as the overarching goal and argues for balance. It strives to develop a generative and distributive economy that maintains a safe and just space for humanity supported by a strong social foundation and within an ecological ceiling (Fig. 7).

Similarly, human-centered technologies should contribute to safety, justice, and a strong societal foundation.

4.3 Participants

Moving to truly human-centered computing also requires a radical change in the role that developers play in the process. Organizational goals can be met with relatively small and homogeneous development teams made up of and led by organizational members. Human-centered computing requires inclusion of diverse stakeholders in the process to make sure that the needs and constraints of all the people who will be affected by the changes are well understood (see chapter of Bennaceur et al.). Stakeholders may be individuals, advocacy groups, organizations, and communities. It is especially important to include underrepresented groups including those voices that have been historically marginalized, invisible, and silenced. Many communities use the phrase “nothing about us without us” (see, e.g., Charlton, 1998). This can be a helpful guideline to determine if we have the right people represented in the development effort.

Stakeholder representation in the conversation is important, but truly human-centered computing also requires authentic participatory co-design (Sanders & Stappers, 2008). Stakeholders should be at least equal partners, if not the leaders, in the effort. Stakeholders bring a deep understanding of the domain and problems to be solved. This knowledge is a form of expertise that is complementary to, not inferior to, developer’s technical knowledge. As such, stakeholders should be compensated for the time and effort that they devote to the project. True inclusion and authentic co-design imbues user and community leadership of the development effort with real decision-making power (Pines et al., 2020).

Developers must also make a long-term commitment to the community and to working with them to meet the human needs that they identify. This is quite different from the common extractive relationship in which developers extract knowledge from community members, use it for their own or for corporate benefit, and fail to return value to the community (Harrington et al., 2019).

4.4 Ethical and Responsible Computing and the Socio-technical System

Human-adjacent and human-aware computing assumed that the system of interest was a closed technical system developed to meet organizational needs. In contrast, human-centered computer requires that we understand, intervene in, and manage the broader multicomponent sociotechnical system (see Fig. 6). Developing and implementing new technologies is one possible intervention into a complex web of interacting components that, acting together, can return value to communities while meeting individual needs (Fig. 8).

The robust societal infrastructure for computing provides readily available networking, data storage, and software components. With just a smartphone and an app, individuals and communities can often leverage the existing infrastructure to meet their information technology needs.

But working with diverse stakeholders can be challenging. People are not just individuals. They are also embedded within friendship and family groups and may be members of formal organizations (e.g., employers, churches, schools, libraries). Meeting the community needs will require leveraging the strengths of the

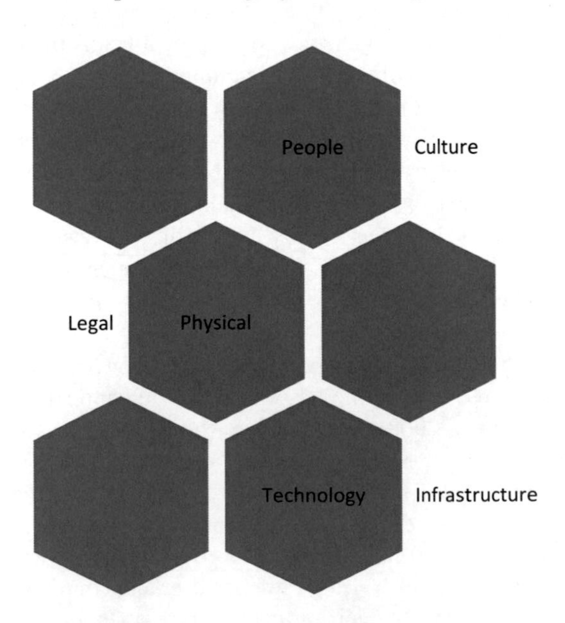

Fig. 8 Some components of a sociotechnical system

individuals, families, and communities themselves. Integrating innovations into sociotechnical systems will also be easier when they leverage the individual's and community's strengths, abilities, and assets rather than focusing on deficiencies. For example, public librarians and educators have expertise that can be leveraged in developing and delivering training in new technologies.

To be effective, technical solutions must also be consistent with, or even enhance, underlying cultural values. Local culture can be very powerful but hard to recognize. It includes visible artifacts (e.g., language, stories, ceremonies, buildings), underlying values, and unspoken assumptions that may only be seen when violated. Many developers are not trained to elicit information about culture or to guide people in identifying their needs and assessing potential solutions. Often, it is only by immersing ourselves in a community that we can start to understand it. Fortunately, developers can also partner with experts who are trained in user needs assessment and community engagement. These experts can be found in diverse domains such as urban planning, social work, ethnography, human computer interaction, public librarianship, anthropology, sociology, and others.

We also need to consider legal constraints, physical affordances, economic dimensions, and more. These complexities will affect the needs that are identified and the solutions that can be developed. Only by considering all of these components and how they interact to maintain the current system can we responsibly intervene. Designing and introducing an appropriate new technology will more likely be ethical and responsible and maintain a safe and just space for humanity supported by a strong social foundation. However, there may still be unforeseen and unintended consequences.

4.5 From Technology Development to Sociotechnical System Orchestration

There are no guarantees of success in meeting human needs, partly because people are embedded within systems that are so complex that their behavior is itself hard to predict. Human-centered computing involves intervening in a muticomponent system that includes people, institutions, technologies, the physical environment, etc. The system components are all interconnected, so we cannot change just one element without affecting the other parts of the system. In addition, useful interventions may be bundles of technical, social, economic, legal, and other elements, so we may need to change multiple components at once. It is important to remember that all of the components themselves are constantly in flux so the system also changes over time even if we do nothing.

No system will be perfect, but steps should be taken early on to increase positive effects and reduce potential harms and undesirable behaviors. To the extent possible, we need to identify dependencies and complementary assets (Winter & Taylor, 1996). Informative and easy-to-use interfaces should be built into every new technology because they play such an important role in enhancing human agency, autonomy, and respect. We also need to identify what else is needed to make the system a success and ensure that they are available. For technical elements, complementary assets may include training, local experts, Internet access, and even reliable electricity. For example, smartphone apps require connectivity and affordable data plans. Teenagers and young adults often act as local experts. Streaming music services also requires intellectual property agreements with music publishers and artists. Electric vehicles require an installed network of charging stations. Ensuring access to complementary assets helps improve the likelihood that the system will meet human needs.

Predicting the impacts of a new technology is also difficult because it is hard for us to foresee all the ways that it may be used. Creative thinking is enormously important in co-design, but many developers overemphasize potential positive outcomes and fail to explore possible negative effects. In addition, any system that includes people is subject to the vagaries of human behavior. People are very creative in the ways in which they navigate their worlds and may not share the technology developer's goals. There are about 8 billion people alive today, and the law of large numbers suggests that some of them will come up with ways of using the technology that fall outside of your expectations.

Even without intervention, sociotechnical systems are also constantly changing. Components change and co-adapt over time. Nothing is static. It is important to build resilience into the system to allow rapid recovery to unexpected changes.

This complexity, unpredictability, and dynamism suggest that we need to consider how developers and their co-design partners will monitor and manage the larger system. It is impossible to truly control the system, but interventions can allow a form of orchestration to enhance positive effects and minimize negative ones. Continual intervention will help the system continuously meet the goals of safety, justice, and a strong community (Winter & Butler, 2021). Monitoring and managing means developing feedback channels and mechanisms throughout the life of the system. Initially, we can use them to understand implementation progress and assess the initial impacts of the system intervention. Later, we can use them to gather information for ongoing evaluation and management of intended and unintended effects. Building in communication channels will enable the community to sense, evaluate, and make corrections.

Access to the existing "as a service" and "in the cloud" infrastructure has further expanded our conceptualization of a computer to encompass a true information system. This more complex view includes people not just as users of tools developed by organizations but as active co-creators of multi-component sociotechnical systems. This revolution can enable digital humanism if we shift our focus from developing new technologies to orchestrating complex sociotechnical systems.

5 Conclusions

Sometimes, it is hard to tell when things have really changed and when they just look different. In the case of digital humanism and ethical computing, the shift from mainframe computers to client server architecture to ubiquitous computing is a fundamental change. These technologies reflect economic changes in the cost of production but are also associated with distinctly different affordances (Gibson, 1979). As chips got smaller, faster, and more affordable, computing power became commoditized and started to resemble a sort of utility like electricity or water. This computing infrastructure can be used by organizations to meet their own needs.

More interestingly, for the first time, this societal computing infrastructure also opens up the possibility of meeting human needs. However, in many ways, our thinking about technology and design is stuck in the old human-adjacent and human-aware models. In a sort of path dependency or imprinting (Marquis & Tilcsik, 2013), we remain focused on computing to meet organizational needs, and the opportunity for meeting human needs remains under-explored. Capitalizing on these new affordances will require new models for digital humanism. Human-centered computing provides helpful tools and techniques for designing, building, and orchestrating sociotechnical systems that meet human needs and strengthen communities.

Success in meeting human needs cannot be guaranteed, but there is a lot that we can do. Authentic co-design with diverse and equal partners including marginalized communities plays a central role in developing ethical, responsible, and human-centered technologies that enhance agency, autonomy, and respect. This radical transformation to human-centered computing will require that we transform how we think and talk about technologies to avoid category errors, move to a model of participatory co-design, and build in mechanisms for feedback and adjustment.

Technology is a tool that should be used to achieve people's goals. Truly achieving these goals requires us to shift our focus from stand-alone technologies to co-creation and orchestration of the larger sociotechnical system in initial analysis, intervention design, and in continuous monitoring, management, and improvement. This will enable us to strengthen social foundations and meet human needs within an ecological ceiling. This transition will not be easy, but we finally have the tools we need and a pathway to ethical and responsible technologies.

Discussion Questions for Students and Their Teachers

1. How useful are the concepts human-adjacent, human-aware, and human-centered? Can a technology be in multiple categories at once?
2. What are the ways in which we treat computers as though they were people? What does this mean for ideas like providing robots as companions for the elderly?
3. What are some of the barriers that limit the adoption of user-centered computing and participatory design? How can they be overcome?
4. Are there times when user-centered computing is a bad approach? Why or why not?

Learning Resources for Students

1. Campbell-Kelly, M., Aspray, W., Yost, J., Tinn, H., and Con Diaz, G. (2023). Computer: a history of the information machine (4th ed.), Routledge.

   This fourth edition provides an overview of the history of the computing industry and the role of business and government in its early days. It is written in an engaging style and includes a good mix of technical details and historic information.

2. Cooper, N., Horne, T., Hayes, G.R., Heldreth, C., Lahav, M., Holbrook, J. and Wilcox, L. (2022). A systematic review and thematic analysis of community-collaborative approaches to computing research. In CHI Conference on Human Factors in Computing Systems (CHI '22, April 29–May 5, 2022, New Orleans, LA, https://doi.org/10.1145/3491102.3517716.

   This conference paper provides an overview of recent participatory HCI research with communities. It identifies significant issues that often arise when doing this kind of work due to the power and position of the researchers. They provide suggestions for moving toward practices that center communities.

3. Dominelli, L. (2017). Anti oppressive social work theory and practice. Bloomsbury Publishing.

   This book provides a clear discussion of oppression and disempowerment. It provides compelling examples and provides guidance for working with individuals, groups, and organizations for greater empowerment.

4. Naughton, J. (2000). A brief history of the future: the origins of the Internet. Orion Books, London.

   This book tells the story of the development of the Internet including both technical and cultural details. It provides an overview of the people who were involved, the problems they were trying to solve, and how they came together to create the underpinnings of modern digital life.

5. Pine, K.H., Hinrichs, M.M., Wang, J., Lewis, D. and Johnston, E. (2020). For impactful community engagement: check your role. Communications of the ACM, 63(7), 26–28.

   This short and very accessible editorial outlines common problems in civic and community-engaged research. It outlines four new practices that computing professionals should add to their toolbox when doing community-centered responsible design.

6. Rogers, Y., Sharp, H., and Preece, J. (2023) Interaction Design: Beyond human-computer interaction, (6th Edition). John Wiley and Sons, Hoboken, NJ.

   The first chapter of this book provides a helpful overview of the various terms used in the field and how they relate to the role of people in the design process. Later chapters provide a great overview of the field with compelling examples and a good mix of theory and practice, including recent developments in "humans-in-the-loop."

References

Blackburn, S. (1994). *The Oxford dictionary of philosophy* (p. 58). Oxford University Press.

Card, S. K. (Ed.). (1983). *The psychology of human-computer interaction* (1st ed.). CRC Press. https://doi.org/10.1201/9780203736166

Charlton, J. I. (1998). *Nothing about us without us*. University of California Press. ISBN 0-520-22481-7.

Deming, W. E. (1982). *Quality, productivity, and competitive position*. Massachusetts Institute of Technology.

Gibson, J. J. (1979). *The theory of affordances. The ecological approach to visual perception* (p. 127). Houghton Mifflin Harcourt (HMH).

Hammer, M., & Champy, J. (1993). *Reengineering the corporation: A manifesto for business revolution*. Harper Collins.

Harrington, C., Erete, S., & Piper, A. M. (2019). Deconstructing community-based collaborative design: Towards more equitable participatory design engagements. Proceedings of the ACM on human-computer interaction, 3(CSCW), 216:1–216:25. https://doi.org/10.1145/3359318.

Hevner, A. R., & Berndt, D. J. (2000). Eras of business computing. *Advances in Computers, 52*, 2–91.

Marquis, C., & Tilcsik, A. (2013). Imprinting: Toward a multilevel theory. *Academy of Management Annals*, 193–243. SSRN 2198954.

Pines, K. H., Hinrichs, M. M., Wang, J., Lewis, D., & Johnston, E. (2020). For impactful community engagement: Check your role. *Communications of the ACM, 63*(7), 26–28.

Raworth, K. (2017). A doughnut for the Anthropocene: Humanity's compass in the 21st century. *The Lancet Planetary Health, 1*(2), e48–e49. https://doi.org/10.1016/S2542-5196(17)30028-1. ISSN 2542-5196. PMID 29851576. S2CID 46919938.

Sanders, E., & Stappers, P. (2008). Co-creation and the new landscapes of design. *CoDesign, 4*, 5–18. https://doi.org/10.1080/15710880701875068

Winter, S. J. (2019). Who benefits? The case of smart cities. *Communications of the ACM Viewpoints on Ethics, 62*(7). https://doi.org/10.1145/3332807

Winter, S., Berente, N., Butler, B., & Howison, J. (2014). Beyond the organizational 'container': Conceptualizing 21st century sociotechnical work. *Information and Organization, 24*(4), 250–269.

Winter, S. J., & Butler, B. S. (2021). Responsible technology design: Conversations for success. In C. Ghezzi, E. Lee, E. Prem, & H. Werthner (Eds.), *Perspectives on digital humanism* (pp. 271–275). Springer Nature.

Winter, S. J., & Taylor, S. L. (1996). The role of IT in the transformation of work: A comparison of post-industrial, industrial, and proto-industrial organization. *Information Systems Research, 7*(1), 5–21.

Bridging the Digital Divide

Anna Bon, Francis Saa-Dittoh, and Hans Akkermans

Abstract This chapter discusses the disparity in access to digital services, which exists between countries, regions, communities, and people in the world. This disparity is referred to as the *digital divide*. Digital information and communication are obviously of key importance for the development of countries and regions. However, different approaches exist to address this problem. In this chapter, from a digital humanist perspective, we explore practice-oriented digital design approaches to serve people and communities in currently unconnected regions of the world. We discuss how this might best be done, upholding ethical standards, inclusivity, and human-centered principles. To illustrate this in action, we present a case study from rural Ghana.

1 Introduction

The digital divide refers to the disparity between countries, regions, and people in their access to digital services (Fuchs & Horak, 2008; Van Dijk, 2020; Potter et al., 2008; Mubarak, 2015; Bon, 2020). For example, in 2023, 57% of the African population is unconnected to the global digital society (Internet World Stats, 2023). This disparity is considered a global challenge. It is obvious that digital information and communication are of key importance for the development of countries and regions.

A. Bon (✉)
Centre for International Cooperation, Vrije Universiteit Amsterdam, Amsterdam, The Netherlands
e-mail: a.bon@vu.nl

F. Saa-Dittoh
University for Development Studies, Tamale, Ghana

H. Akkermans
AKMC, Koedijk, The Netherlands
e-mail: hans.akkermans@akmc.nl

H. Werthner et al. (eds.), *Introduction to Digital Humanism*,
https://doi.org/10.1007/978-3-031-45304-5_19

Different approaches exist to address the digital divide. Some approaches are technology-focused, seeking progress through technological advancement. Some approaches focus mainly on profits and economic growth. Other approaches are more human-centric, trying to achieve human well-being. Each approach reflects a different worldview or school of thought, with varying assumptions about the nature of development, the role of technology, and the desired outcomes of bridging the digital divide.

From a technology-focused perspective, *not being connected* is attributed to a lack of physical and digital infrastructure. Due to the absence of proper infrastructures in poor regions or countries, many people do not have access to digital services and content. This withholds their participation in the information society and hampers development. Rolling out digital infrastructure and making the Internet available to people in every corner of the planet is then the solution. The ensuing question is how to organize this.

From a slightly different perspective, the digital divide is only a snapshot in time, in an ongoing process of technological innovation and diffusion (Rogers, 2003). Poor regions are lagging but will soon catch up in their technological and organizational capacities and will adopt digital technologies at a later stage. This will lead to progress and bring economic development, at long last (De Janvry & Sadoulet, 2021; Taylor & Lybbert, 2020). The uptake of digital technologies by people in low-resource environments is seen as an opportunity, as this will create a new market segment for technology vendors and other markets. This market segment is referred to as the "bottom of the pyramid" (Prahalad, 2004; Heeks, 2008). Economic growth is the main justification for this approach.

Both perspectives—technology-focused or economy-focused—have one idea in common: digital technology is the motor for progress and development. Access to digital information and services will lead, from an "underdeveloped" situation to a situation of prosperity, like in the industrialized countries (Wicander, 2009). It is assumed that well-being will follow from technological and economic development and that prosperity will *trickle down*, naturally, to most people.

Alternative perspectives on the digital divide value a more human-centered standpoint. Digital humanism, decolonial theory, and grassroots initiatives are examples of human-centered approaches. They prioritize human well-being, social inclusion, equity, and emancipation above technology and profit.

In 2019, the *Digital Humanism Initiative* was launched in Vienna by a group of primarily European scientists, policy makers, and practitioners concerned about the disrupting impact of digital progress on society, economy, and the natural environment. The Vienna Manifesto for Digital Humanism was proclaimed as a call for ethics and humanism and as an antidote to technocratic approaches with their focus on merely technological innovation and economic growth (DIGHUM, 2019). The digital humanism movement is now supported by many scholars, politicians, and policy makers from around the world. It launched a debate about the purpose and the future of the digital society (DIGHUM, 2019). At the onset, the Digital Humanism Initiative focused on the societal issues of the digital society in the Global North, where it originated, but soon it embraced a cosmopolitan viewpoint, in which the

Global South and the exclusion of people in low-resource environments are a central problem to be discussed and addressed.

A similar, and even more radical, perspective is found in decolonial studies, in which patterns of inequality, poverty and wealth, domination, and colonialism are explored and analyzed in society (Mignolo & Walsh, 2018; Mendoza, 2021). Decolonial theory offers an alternative lens to assess the digital divide and explore its root causes and origins, in the light of colonialism. The conjecture here is that the digital divide is inherently unfair because it excludes people. However, the idea also exists that digital technologies, if well designed, may be able to help improve certain aspects and overcome certain problems of people. Of course, these digital technologies must be, by design, respectful of human rights and human dignity and of local agency, culture, norms, and values.

Whereas academic studies, e.g., Lin et al. (2015) and De et al. (2018), express criticism about various aspects of the digital divide, only a few of these studies have been action oriented. Yet, from a digital humanism perspective, the purpose and goal are not only to discuss but also to influence policy, raise awareness, and call for practical, problem-solving action. An example could be an interdisciplinary study that combines action research, design science, and a human-centered approach to design technologies that support people and communities in low-resource environments. The persistent question is how this study can ensure fairness, ethics, and inclusion by design while at the same time being respectful at the autonomy and agency of local users, communities, and people.

This question will be discussed in the sections that follow. In Sect. 2, we give a brief history of the digital divide. In Sect. 3, we observe the digital divide through a decolonial lens, assessing roots, causes, and patterns of inequality. In Sect. 4, we seek the requirements for inclusive, human-centered design. In Sect. 5, we propose a human-centered methodology that combines action research, design science, and ethics perspective. We illustrate this through a case study from northern Ghana in Sect. 6.

2 Short History of the Efforts to Bridge the Digital Divide

Since the 1990s, many efforts have been undertaken by the international community[1] including international organizations such as the World Bank, the United Nations, UNESCO, national and international development agencies, numerous non-governmental organizations (NGOs), and large private charity organizations to make digital technologies available for social and economic development of poor regions of the world. Despite large budgets and numerous projects in prestigious international development programs, a mismatch between technologies and the

[1] We refer to these entities as the "international community." This term is used in international relations to refer to a group of people, organizations, and governments in the Western world.

target environment often occurred (Bon, 2020). Many unsuccessful technology transfers resulted from blind optimism about the impact and reach of digital technologies, combined with poor understanding of local needs and context. Techno-optimism about digital technology culminated in the United Nations World Summit on the Information Society, in 2005, in Tunis, where heads of states from all around the world and global players in the big private technology sector came together, including Microsoft, HP, Nokia, and Intel (Berry, 2006; Qureshi, 2006). Goals were set during this summit, to roll out the Internet before the year 2020, in every corner of the planet.

Soon after 2005, it became clear that many ambitious, large-scale development projects were failing, especially in serving the poorest and least connected communities with digital technologies (Bon, 2020). Two examples are (i) the *One Laptop Per Child* (OLPC) project, which started around 2008 and aimed to provide every schoolchild in the world with a laptop (Buchele & Owusu-Aning, 2007), and (ii) the Millennium Villages project, which started in 2005 and selected a small number of very poor and unconnected villages across African countries to pull them "out of poverty" by giving them an investment boost, transferring state-of-the-art Western technology, and connecting the communities to high-speed Internet (Sanchez et al., 2007). Both the OLPC and the Millennium Villages project spent large sums but did not meet their objectives or expectations[2]. The failures of these and many other large-scale technology transfer projects tempered the initial techno-optimism of the international community.

Unexpectedly, it was not the Internet, but simple, mobile, voice-based telephony, rolled out by the telecom companies in many remote and poor regions to low-income communities of the world, that became a huge success and had a large impact for people's lives at the so-called base of the pyramid (Kalba, 2008). For many poor people in urban or remote rural areas in developing countries, mobile telephony was their first digital experience and remote communication. The mobile telephony success was followed by an innovation called *mobile money*. This technological innovation, which only required a simple mobile phone—no smartphone or Internet connection—enabled people to deposit money on their cell phones and transfer it to other users of the service, without need for a bank account. Mobile money was first launched in 2007 in Kenya, as a truly African innovation by the local telecom operator Safaricom. This service registered 1.1 million users in the first 8 months after its inception (Mbiti & Weil, 2011). Soon, many countries in Africa followed, as Orange, Airtel, and many other telecom companies started providing mobile payment services to millions of previously unbanked citizens in Africa (Nan, 2019).

So, in the past two decades, the least developed countries in, e.g., sub-Saharan Africa have caught up very rapidly and entered the digital era. However, innovation and technology adoption often followed a different path than in the Global North. For example, many people in rural Africa skipped text-based systems and are now

[2] A full discussion about these and other cases of unsuccessful ICT4D interventions is given by Bon (2020).

using asynchronous voice-based communication through voice messaging systems and social media apps, without ever having sent a written (text-based) email (Dittoh et al., 2020a, 2020b).

Despite the positive impact of mobile telephony and mobile money for many people in rural Africa, the profits remained unequally shared. At the onset of the 2020s, many sub-Saharan countries were mainly *consuming* digital services but hardly *developing* or *producing* any.

From the point of view of infrastructure, only few data centers or Internet exchange hubs exist in sub-Saharan countries (Augustine, 2022). The data produced by African users are stored in the cloud, i.e., remote data centers[3]. The costs for data transport between users and the "cloud" make digital services more expensive in remote areas than, e.g., in urban centers. This is another example of inequality.

Technological innovation is moving fast. The technology leap in the second decade of the twenty-first century is based on data-driven artificial intelligent systems. Many new beneficial solutions are to be expected, e.g., for the development of speech recognition of local indigenous languages or for the digitalization and access to specific, contextual knowledge systems. Yet, big concerns exist, related to the deployment of generative AI.

People in countries in the Global South may be vulnerable to the spread of disinformation and digital surveillance. They may face infringement of their intellectual property rights, due to lack of legislation and governance of the digital sphere (DIGHUM, 2019). Since privacy rules and regulations such as GDPR are still not implemented in many African countries, there is no good protection of people's identities, privacy, and data ownership. Especially people "at the base of the pyramid" may be less well informed and therefore more vulnerable to predatory technology firms and digital scams. Moreover, in the light of a rapidly involving technology like artificial intelligence, combined with a lack of policy and legislation in many countries in the Global South, this may result in a complete governance of the digital society, including the infrastructure, data, and technological know-how, to be concentrated in just a few current market-dominant private technological firms, also known as Tech Giants, such as Meta (Facebook), Alphabet (Google), Amazon, Apple, and Microsoft.

[3] To reduce costs of data transport, digital data is usually stored as close as possible to its consumers. In the absence of data centers in many African countries, the nearest locations are data centers in Europe and the Middle East. Upcoming private investments in the richer African countries, including South Africa, may bring new data centers to the continent.

3 The Digital Divide Through a Decolonial Lens

The digital world, where we socialize, interact, and take decisions, mirrors the physical world in many aspects. This includes patterns of inequality and domination, which are often referred to as "coloniality" (Mignolo & Walsh, 2018; Mendoza, 2021 pp. 46–54; pp. 1–12; Quijano, 2007 pp. 15–18; Hope, 2022). Decolonial theory helps uncover hidden patterns of domination within social structures. In this discussion, we explore a few examples from the digital society.

One common assumption, also found in the SDG9, is that many underdevelopment-related problems, e.g., in education and trade, will be solved, once Internet connections have been established. Yet is this a valid assumption? In the light of the concerns about artificial intelligence and the increasing concentration of knowledge and power, it is debatable whether the Internet will bring democracy, social justice, equality, and a sustainable and prosperous life to all people (Bon et al., 2022).

Let's take the example of "free Internet", offered by big tech firms, such as Google (Dahir, 2020), Starlink (Sapah, 2023), and Facebook (The Guardian, 2016), to people in low-resource environments. These initiatives will ultimately connect many people, even in remote low-resource environments, to the digital backbones for free. However, we must question what "free Internet" means in a capitalist world. The revenues of the large technology companies rely on extracting value from personal data, people's Web browsing preferences, by tracking their entire online behavior using AI algorithms. Users are often unaware of the exploitation of their personal data. This business model of extracting value from the people's online behavior has been criticized by Shoshana Zuboff in her book *The Age of Surveillance Capitalism* (2019), for which she introduced the term "behavior surplus."

Another aspect of decolonial critique is the hegemony of the Internet as a network standard. While the Internet can be seen as a global common, a platform to share information, access opportunities, and collaborate across geographic and cultural boundaries, as discussed earlier, it has disadvantages. Choosing not to be part of this network results in isolation, for the non-user. This characteristic of standards and networks, which is described by Grewal (2008, pp. 20–28), makes the Internet a hegemonic system without escape, despite the price users, communities, and even countries pay with money or data, to access it.

Geolocation and governance of digital infrastructures are also aspects related to coloniality. The digital society is heavily concentrated, physically, economically, and socially, in the Global North. The commercialization of digital technologies, influenced by this centralization, further channels the profits from innovations in the Global South to investors (Zuboff, 2019, pp. 63–96). Governance and decision-making in this realm are predominantly controlled by private tech firms, operating under norms and regulations from countries in the Global North. Unequal competition in terms of storage, connectivity, funding, and adoption also hinders start-ups in the Global South (Bon et al., 2022).

In many countries, big tech firms and telecom providers are assuming public roles and functions traditionally held by the state, such as in healthcare, education, and infrastructure. Through philanthropic gifts and corporate social responsibility, digital services are provided in exchange for data, market penetration, tax savings, branding, and policy influence. Youngsters are often targeted by big tech companies with media, music, video, entertainment, and news (Pini, 2020, pp. 37–40).

Coloniality is also evident in artificial intelligence (AI). Machine learning algorithms, previously assumed to be objective and value-free, have been found to harbor many discriminating biases (Mohamed et al., 2020, pp. 659–663). These biases are often concealed in the underlying data. Trivial examples include visualization programs that autonomously lighten the complexion of black and Asian faces or smart doors that, based on facial recognition algorithms, only open for white faces while remaining closed for a person with dark skin, as the machine learning algorithm fails to recognize them as a person. These racial biases can emerge unexpectedly in autonomous smart systems. If these algorithmic biases are not properly addressed, they will further perpetuate inequalities and injustice against certain groups and individuals (Mohamed et al., 2020, pp. 659–663).

The aforementioned discussion highlights the concerns regarding coloniality, domination, biases, and injustice. If left unaddressed, these issues will result in a digital society that is exclusive, unethical, and, from various perspectives, reminiscent of neo-colonialism.

It is crucial to recognize that innovation in digital technologies is not an autonomous process, but one driven by deliberate choices. Methodologies from information systems engineering provide flexible and powerful approaches for designing and fostering open innovation. Action research with its long-standing tradition of improving real-world situations adds to it the human-centered and ethical aspects. In the following section, we will delve into the discussion of how information and communication technologies can be designed in a human-centered manner.

4 Requirements for a Human-Centered Approach

When exploring alternative approaches to serve communities and individuals in low-resource environments, which principles are required?

The foremost and crucial principle is that digital technologies should not cause harm to anyone. It is imperative that digital services align with the objectives and goals defined by the local people and users. To achieve this, local users must actively participate in decision-making processes regarding the goals and objectives of the digital service.

Secondly, digital technology must be adaptable in a flexible way to the local context, enabling it to overcome local barriers. These barriers can include language, literacy, limited infrastructure availability, local purchasing power, or other context-related issues.

Thirdly, there must be local ownership of data and the protection of local domain knowledge and intellectual property. This is essential to prevent compromise or misuse of these valuable assets. In the case of co-design, ownership of the designed artifacts should also be shared. Research data should not be automatically owned by the researcher or published without permission or consent.

In summary, the development of digital services for unconnected people or communities in low-resource environments should be conducted in collaboration with local users. Since software developers and engineers often lack familiarity with the low-resource locations in question, significant emphasis is placed on communication between users and developers through collaborative workshops and co-design sessions.

In the next section, we will describe a methodology and approach that was developed in the field from 2009 to 2019 through an action research program named W4RA—the Web Alliance for Regreening in Africa (W4RA, 2023). The program's objective is to support local smallholder farmers in three West African countries, Mali, Burkina Faso, and Ghana, by designing digital technologies to help them achieve their objectives. The approach is referred to as Information and Communication Technologies for Development, version *3.0*, abbreviated as ICT4D 3.0 (Bon, 2016).

5 Combining Action Research, Design Science, and Ethics Perspective

ICT4D 3.0 represents a grassroots approach to bridging the digital divide, offering an alternative to the prevailing, economic growth-oriented approach to bridging the digital divide. This incumbent approach is described by Richard Heeks (2008) as "a new opportunity for ICT vendors to harness digital innovation and serve the world's poor, profitably," in an article, titled "ICT4D 2.0: The Next Phase of Applying ICT for International Development."

ICT4D 2.0 was presented by Heeks as a great improvement to the previous approaches, in which off-the-shelf digital technologies were transferred to poor regions, often with limited success (2008, p. 26).

In contrast to its predecessors, ICT4D 3.0 positions itself as a human-centered, grassroots methodology for designing digital technologies based on users' needs. It follows a five-step framework:

(i) Context analysis—understanding the users' environment
(ii) Needs assessment—understanding the user's goal
(iii) Use case and requirements analysis—defining and specifying a feasible digital solution
(iv) Prototyping, engineering, and deployment of a digital service
(v) Sustainability analysis—exploring the local business ecosystem to ensure the long-term availability of the service

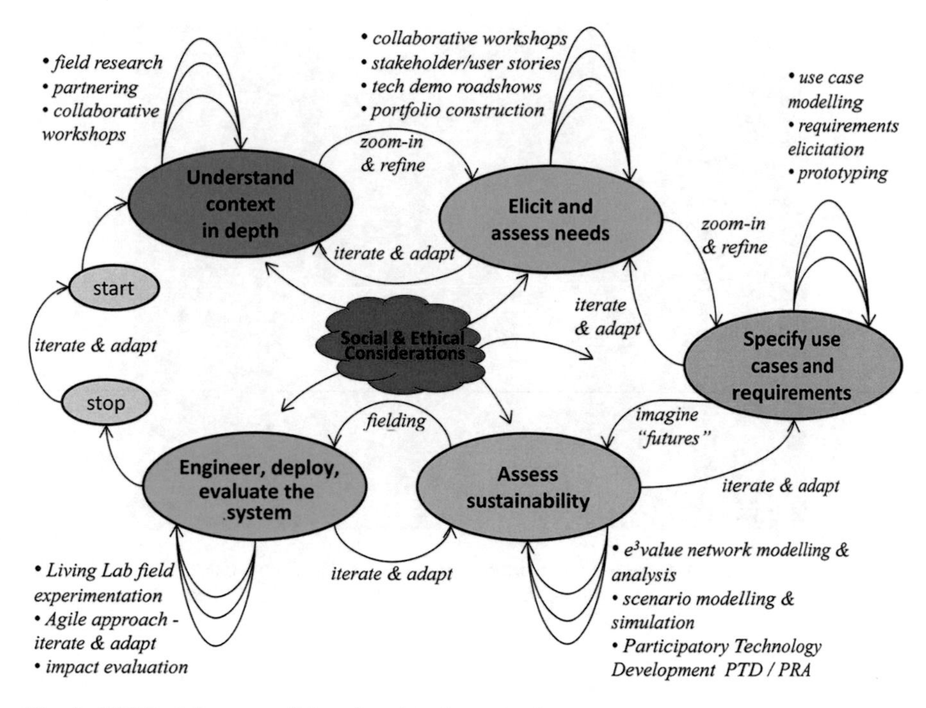

Fig. 1 ICT4D 3.0 as a collaborative, iterative, adaptive approach to digital development in low-resource environments. From: Bon, A. (2020, p. 204, *Intervention or Collaboration—Redesigning Information and Communication Technologies for Development*, Amsterdam: Pangea)

ICT4D 3.0 is a goal-oriented approach, striving for a certain improvement for its envisaged users. A conceptual visualization of this approach can be represented as a goal-strategy map (Fig. 1, cf. (Rolland, 2007)), where each colored ellipse signifies an intention to be achieved through corresponding actions. The process is iterative and adaptable, allowing for adjustments based on new information.

Emancipation, autonomy, and inclusion are the core values ICT4D 3.0 strives to achieve. It has undergone continuous evaluation and validation by its users in the field (Bon, 2020). Importantly, it can be considered a decolonial approach as it empowers users to make decisions rather than having external parties impose solutions upon them.

6 Tiballi: A Case Study of AI and Data Science for Farmers in Ghana

A case study that illustrates the ICT4D 3.0 approach in a community-oriented, transdisciplinary research project is *Tiballi*, a research project, set up in 2023 in northern Ghana (Tiballi, 2023; Dittoh et al., 2021). Tiballi explores how artificial

Fig. 2 Tiballi project's needs assessment, during a focus group discussion in the village of Tingoli, community of Nyankpala, Ghana. Photograph by Gideon Amakama Ali (18 February 2023)

intelligence—and more specifically machine learning and natural language processing—can serve people in a low-resource environment. Tiballi's envisaged users are proficient in a local, under-resourced African language only; they have low incomes, low literacy skills, and limited access to the Internet.

Tiballi's project goal aligns with an explicit wish of farmers in northern Ghana to have access to rainfall data, as this information is essential in rain-fed agriculture, but often not accessible. These wishes were collected during workshops and focus group discussions; see Fig. 2. In these meetings, it becomes clear that (a lack of) Internet access is not the only barrier for the community to use digital services. It is also important to provision locally relevant information in the language and modality people are familiar with, such as radio or simple voice-based phones.

In the Tiballi project, rainfall data are collected in the field and combined with global weather and climate information available on the Web. The combined result is made available to the local community members in their language, through voice-based phone access or local radio (Baart et al., 2018). Automatic voice response and interaction is constructed from vocabularies which are collected in the community and processed with AI. Figure 2 shows a focus group discussion with farmers in the Tingoli village in northern Ghana.

In short, to deliver the requested information to the community, the Tiballi project aims to:

(i) Collect and store real-time weather, for example, the cumulative rainfall over the season.
(ii) Develop an automatic speech recognition system in the local language Dagbanli. It uses a previously developed method to resource small languages,

in which a machine learning model is trained with a relatively small, locally collected dataset.

(iii) Develop a voice-based application that combines limited vocabulary text-to-speech and automatic speech recognition in Dagbanli language. This will enable users to interact with the system by phone and receive requested information, every day (Stan et al., 2022).

(iv) Develop and deploy a voice-based platform, based on inexpensive, small hardware, to provide the service, also in the absence of Internet access and avoid high costs of broadband connectivity (Baart et al., 2019).

7 Discussion on Critical and Societal Issues

In the previous sections, we proposed a collaborative, iterative, adaptive approach to digital development, aligned with inclusion and an ethics perspective. Yet, this approach may have its limitations, for example, related to sustainability or costs of digital services. It is important to continuously evaluate and critically reflect before, during, and after the project period. Deliberation and discussions with its users and beneficiaries on their personal experiences and opinions are essential.

Technological innovation can be a rapid process. Huge developments are taking place in (distributed, cloud, edge) computing, social media, blockchain technology, Internet of Things, artificial intelligence, and data science. It is important to continuously reassess potential positives and negatives of technologies introduced in low-resource environments. We as researchers, ICT professionals, and global citizens must be aware of our responsibility, to care for the present and the future of the digital society.

From the ideas in this chapter, we propose to support the lives and work of people in low-resource environments through co-design. Yet, this small-scale approach needs dissemination to scale up, for example, by training young professionals at European and African universities and by bringing together a community of developers and contributors.

For a societally oriented community of developers, it may be challenging to deliver, in a sustainable way, competitive digital services to low-resource environments. The strong monopolization by big technology firms with technologically advanced services, and backed by big investors, puts up high barriers for the smaller parties. Yet, niches exist—especially in less wealthy regions—that are still unserved.

This endorses the idea that deliberate choices can be made toward a better and more inclusive digital society, guided by social engagement, and encourage human-centered innovation, quoting the Vienna Manifesto 2019: "calling for a Digital Humanism that describes, analyzes, and, most importantly, influences the complex interplay of technology and humankind, for a better society and life, fully respecting universal human rights"[4] (DIGHUM, 2015).

8 Conclusions

Whereas, from the previous discussions, it is evident that, from a macro-economic and geopolitical perspective, there are no easy fixes to bridge the digital divide as a problem of global scale between regions and countries, we propose to develop small-scale grassroots approaches. We stress the importance of collaboration, at all levels.

Firstly, at the international policy level—in platforms and think tanks such as the Digital Humanism Initiative—representatives of communities in the least connected countries and regions in the Global South must be included, to make their perspectives visible, create awareness of the existing problems, and inform the public debate about the needs of people in low-resource environments.

Secondly, at the level of research and education, collaboration and exchange of knowledge is needed between universities (north-south and south-south). Research programs must be developed that are context oriented. Students must be trained through community service-oriented research and technology development.

Finally, it is important to innovate in technologies in and for people in low-resource environments and develop transdisciplinary research methodologies. In the paragraphs above, we discussed community-oriented, collaborative action research and socio-technical software development. While the exchange of ideas between developers and users can offshoot innovation in low-resource environments in unexpected ways, it can also be a source of inspiration for new forms of collaborative knowledge production.

Discussion Questions for Students and Their Teachers

1. What does it mean when it is said that the digital space is *colonized*?
2. What are the problems when digital technologies are transferred from industrialized countries to developing countries, and what would be the alternatives to digital development?
3. What are the decolonial aspects of digital technologies that reflect patterns from the social and physical world? Think of examples that are not mentioned in this chapter.
4. What is the fundamental difference between the critical realism perspective and the action research/design science perspective on the challenges related to the digital divide?
5. What are the five main contextual challenges for the design of digital services, of the low-resource environment in the Tiballi case study in northern Ghana, and how does the given framework ICT4D 3.0 address these challenges?

[4] This quote is from the Vienna Manifesto on Digital Humanism, May 2019.

Learning Resources for Students

1. Potter, R. B., Binns, T., and Elliott, J. A. (2008) *Geographies of development: An introduction to development studies*. Essex: Pearson Education. Chapter 1.
   This book gives, from a geopolitical perspective, an introduction to the digital divide between countries and regions in the world and describes the historical backgrounds in the framework of recent and contemporary history.
2. Zuboff, S. (2019) The Age of Surveillance Capitalism: The Fight for a Human Future at the New Frontier of Power. London: Profile books.
   This book provides a critical analysis of the business models used by big technology firms and how these affect people and the economy, creating unfairness in the digital society and the physical world.
3. Mohamed, S., Png, M. T. and Isaac, W. (2020) Decolonial AI: Decolonial Theory as Sociotechnical Foresight in Artificial Intelligence. *Philosophy & Technology,* 33, pp. 659–684.
   This paper analyzes the risks and biases of artificial intelligence algorithms through the lens of decolonial theory.
4. Stan, G. et al. (2022) 'A Lightweight Downscaled Approach to Automatic Speech Recognition for Small Indigenous Languages', in *14th ACM Web Science Conference 2022* (pp. 451–458). Doi: https://doi.org/10.1145/3501247.3539017.
   This paper describes a technical method to build AI-based automatic speech recognition for indigenous languages, using small data and energy-efficient methods, making it more affordable and accessible for people and communities in low-resource environments,
5. Dittoh, F., et al. (2021). 'Tibaŋsim: Information Access for Low-Resource Environments', in: *Conference proceedings by Springer AISC*. ISBN Number—2194-5357 Series. Doi: https://doi.org/10.1007/97898116.2377662.
   This paper describes a real-world deployment of an ICT system in rural Ghana, as an example of collaborative technology design and its challenges in low-resource environments in the Global South.
6. Baart, A., et al. (2018) 'Ney Yibeogo—Hello World: A voice service development platform to bridge the web's digital divide', in *WEBIST 2018—Proceedings of the 14th International Conference on Web Information Systems and Technologies,* pp. 23–34.
   This paper stresses the importance of resourcing local languages to bridge the digital divide and methods how to do this.

Acknowledgment The case study of the Tiballi research project, described in this section, is funded by the Internet Society through a research grant in 2023. Also, the authors have received some funding from the EU program Erasmus+ for the field visits and the elaboration of educational modules, which have resulted in this chapter.

References

Augustine, A. (2022). *The next wave: A data centre roadmap for Africa.* Accessed June 22, 2023, from https://techcabal.com/2022/10/03/data-centre-africa/.

Baart, A., et al. (2018). Ney Yibeogo—Hello World: A voice service development platform to bridge the web's digital divide. In *WEBIST 2018—Proceedings of the 14th international conference on web information systems and technologies* (pp. 23–34).

Baart, A., et al. (2019). Affordable voice services to bridge the digital divide: Presenting the Kasadaka platform. In *Selected papers from the WEBIST 2018 international conference.* Springer LNBIP Book Series.

Berry, J. (2006). The world summit on the information society (WSIS): A global challenge in the New Millennium. *Libri, 56*(1), 1–15. https://doi.org/10.1515/LIBR.2006.1

Bon, A. (2016). ICT4D 3.0: An adaptive, user-centred approach to innovation for development, In *Conference on advanced information systems engineering*, CAiSE 2016.

Bon, A. (2020). *Intervention or collaboration? Redesigning information and communication technologies for development.* Pangea. https://doi.org/10.26481/dis.20201215ab

Bon, A., et al. (2022). Decolonizing technology and society: A perspective from the global south. In H. Werthner et al. (Eds.), *Perspectives on digital humanism.* Springer. https://doi.org/10.1007/978-3-030-86144-5_9

Buchele, S. F., & Owusu-Aning, R. (2007). The one laptop per child (OLPC) project and its applicability to Ghana. In *Proceedings of the 2007 international conference on adaptive science and technology* (pp. 113-118).

Dahir, A. L. (2020). A bird? A plane? No, It's a Google Balloon beaming the Internet. Accessed June 22, 2023, from https://www.nytimes.com/2020/07/07/world/africa/google-loon-balloon-kenya.html.

De Janvry, A., & Sadoulet, E. (2021). *Development economics: Theory and practice* (2nd ed.). Routledge.

De, R., et al. (2018). ICT4D research: A call for a strong critical approach. *Information Technology for Development, 24*(1), 63–94.

DIGHUM. (2019). *Vienna Manifesto on digital humanism.* Accessed June 23, 2023, from https://dighum.ec.tuwien.ac.at/dighum-manifesto/.

Dittoh, F., et al. (2020a). Mr. Meteo: Providing climate information for the unconnected. In: *Companion publication of the 12th ACM conference on web science.* (pp. 20-25). https://doi.org/10.1145/3394332.3402824.

Dittoh, F., et al. (2021). Tibaŋsim: Information access for low-resource environments. In *Conference proceedings by Springer AISC.* ISBN number—2194-5357 series. https://doi.org/10.1007/97898116.2377662.

Dittoh, F. et al. (2020b). Information access for low-resource environments. In *Proceedings of the 3rd ACM SIGCAS conference on computing and sustainable societies.* (pp. 325-326).

Fuchs, C., & Horak, E. (2008). Africa and the digital divide. *Telematics and Informatics, 25*(2), 99–116.

Grewal, D. S. (2008). *Network power: The social dynamics of globalization.* Yale University Press.

Heeks, R. (2008). ICT4D 2.0: The next phase of applying ICT for international development. *Computer, 41*(6), 26–33.

Hope, J. (2022). Globalising sustainable development: Decolonial disruptions and environmental justice in Bolivia. *Area, 54*(2), 176–184.

Kalba, K. (2008). The adoption of mobile phones in emerging markets: Global diffusion and the rural challenge. *International Journal of Communication, 2*, 31.

Lin, C. I. C., Kuo, F. Y., & Myers, M. D. (2015). Extending ICT4D studies: The value of critical research. *MIS Quarterly, 39*(3), 697–712.

Mbiti, I., & Weil, D. (2011). *Mobile banking: The impact of M-PESA in Kenya.* US National Bureau of Economic Research. NBER Working Paper No. 17129.

Mendoza, B. (2021). Decolonial theories in comparison. In S. M. Shih & L. C. Tsai (Eds.), *Indigenous knowledge in Taiwan and beyond. Sinophone and Taiwan studies* (Vol. 1, pp. 249–271). Springer. https://doi.org/10.1007/978-981-15-4178-0_12
Mignolo, W. D., & Walsh, C. E. (2018). *On decoloniality: Concepts, analytics, praxis*. Duke University Press.
Mohamed, S., Png, M. T., & Isaac, W. (2020). Decolonial AI: Decolonial theory as sociotechnical foresight in artificial intelligence. *Philosophy & Technology, 33*, 659–684.
Mubarak, F. (2015). Towards a renewed understanding of the complex nerves of the digital divide. *Journal of Social Inclusion, 6*(1), 71–102.
Nan, W. V. (2019). Mobile money and socioeconomic development: A cross-country investigation in Sub-Saharan Africa. *Journal of International Technology and Information Management, 27*(4), 36–65.
Pini, M. (2020). Digital inequality in education in Argentina: How the pandemic of 2020 increased existing tensions. In *12th ACM conference on web science companion* (pp. 37-40).
Potter, R. B., Binns, T., & Elliott, J. A. (2008). *Geographies of development: An introduction to development studies*. Pearson Education.
Prahalad, C. K. (2004). *The fortune at the bottom of the pyramid: Eradicating poverty with profits*. Wharton Business Publishing.
Quijano, A. (2007). Coloniality and modernity/rationality. *Cultural Studies, 21*(2–3), 168–178.
Qureshi, S. (2006). Why is the information society important to us? *The World Summit on the Information Society in Tunis, 12*(1), 1–5. https://doi.org/10.1002/itdj.20035
Rogers, E. M. (2003). *Diffusion of innovations* (5th ed.). Free Press.
Rolland, C. (2007). Capturing system intentionality with maps, In *Conceptual modelling in information systems engineering*, Springer, (pp. 141-158).
Sanchez, P., et al. (2007). The African millennium villages. *Proceedings of the National Academy of Sciences, 104*(43), 16775–16780.
Sapah, M. S. (2023). *Starlink: SpaceX's new internet service could be a gamechanger in Africa*. Accessed June 22, 2023, from https://theconversation.com/starlink-spacexs-new-internet-service-could-be-a-gamechanger-in-africa-200746.
Stan, G. et al. (2022). A lightweight downscaled approach to automatic speech recognition for small indigenous languages. In *14th ACM web science conference 2022* (pp. 451-458). https://doi.org/10.1145/3501247.3539017.
Taylor, J. E., & Lybbert, T. J. (2020). *Essentials of development economics*. University of California Press.
The Guardian. (2016). Facebook lures Africa with free internet—but what is the hidden cost? Accessed June 22, 2023, from https://www.theguardian.com/world/2016/aug/01/facebook-free-basics-internet-africa-mark-zuckerberg.
Tiballi. (2023). *Making AI work for Inclusiveness in the Global South*. Accessed June 22, 2023, from https://tiballi.net/.
Van Dijk, J. (2020). *The digital divide*. Polity Press.
W4RA. (2023) *The Web alliance for regreening in Africa*. Accessed June 22, 2023, from https://w4ra.org/.
Wicander, G. (2009). The invisible hand of the market or the visible hand of the state—how to reach universal access? In J. S. Pettersson (Ed.), *Defining the 'D' in ICT4D: Graduate papers on development, Globalisation and ICT*. Karlstad University.
Zuboff, S. (2019). *The age of surveillance capitalism: The fight for a human future at the new frontier of power*. Profile Books.

BY

Responsible Software Engineering: Requirements and Goals

Amel Bennaceur, Carlo Ghezzi, Jeff Kramer, and Bashar Nuseibeh

Abstract In this chapter, we provide an introduction to the discipline of requirements engineering as part of the software engineering process. We indicate how to elicit, articulate, and organize the goals of complex software systems as an explicit expression of the requirements that the proposed or existing software system is expected to achieve and maintain, including what the system should avoid performing. We advocate that system requirements goals can and should be used to explicitly capture, express, and reason about the diverse digital humanism values which are of concern in socio-technical systems. This is an essential aspect of responsible software engineering.

1 Introduction

Software is creating a new digital world in which humans live, individually and socially. This is a large and complex *socio-technical system* where the boundaries between digital, physical, and social spaces are increasingly disappearing. Many activities in such a system are automated, supporting and sometimes replacing human work and creating new functionalities that did not exist before. Humans interact with software-enabled agents in their daily life. Software now defines and administers most of the laws that govern the world. This was observed in the late 1990s by Lawrence Lessig, in his framing of "Code is Law" (Lessig, 2000).

A. Bennaceur (✉) · B. Nuseibeh
The Open University, Milton Keynes, UK

Lero, University of Limerick, Limerick, Ireland
e-mail: amel.bennaceur@open.ac.uk; bashar.nuseibeh@open.ac.uk

C. Ghezzi
DEIB, Politecnico di Milano, Milan, Italy
e-mail: carlo.ghezzi@polimi.it

J. Kramer
Imperial College London, London, UK
e-mail: j.kramer@imperial.ac.uk

H. Werthner et al. (eds.), *Introduction to Digital Humanism*,
https://doi.org/10.1007/978-3-031-45304-5_20

Software engineers, who create code, are the *demiurges*. Although they are responsible for "technical" decisions, the consequences of their decisions go far beyond the purely technical sphere, often with unintended and unanticipated consequences. At the same time, legal systems have lagged behind in adapting to technological changes.

How can the implications of socio-technical systems developed by software engineers be properly considered when systems are conceived and developed? How can the values and issues of digital humanism drive the software engineering process? How does that engineering process interact with other processes (political, normative, etc.) both ex ante—while the system is designed—and ex post, when systems are deployed and operate?

Engineers have traditionally focused on functional correctness, efficiency, and scalability of their solutions. By and large, they have ignored fairness, inclusivity, and deep consideration of the social implications of their solutions. They have mastered technology and make complex technical decisions, but rarely consider the consequences of future use and misuse of their products in society.

In this chapter, we advocate that these issues and values must be considered and explicitly integrated into the software engineering process: in particular, in the explicit expression of the requirements that the proposed or existing system is expected to achieve and maintain. This focus on so-called requirements engineering can provide a bridge between the world in which digital humanism values arise and the digital machine that software engineers design, build, and deploy in that world.

We begin with an overview of requirements engineering, focusing on ways in which goals and requirements are elicited from diverse stakeholders and how they can be explicitly modeled and analyzed. We illustrate how such goal models can be extended to capture various human values and discuss how they can be analyzed for the purpose of validation and verification. We conclude with a discussion on a more responsible software engineering discipline and some suggested exercises to engage students in the articulation of and reflection on digital humanism goals in software systems.

2 Requirements Engineering (RE)

RE has been the subject of several popular books and surveys; this section gives a brief introduction to requirements as a primary basis for sound software engineering. It also provides relevant references for further exploration of the area.

2.1 Introduction to RE

> *Requirements engineering is the branch of software engineering concerned with the real-world goals for, functions of, and constraints on software systems. It is also concerned with the relationship of these factors to precise specifications of software behavior, and to their evolution over time and across software families.* (Zave, 1997)

This definition by Zave emphasizes that a new software system is introduced to solve a real-world problem and that a good understanding of the problem and the associated context is at the heart of RE. Therefore, it is important not only to define the *goals* of the software system but also to *specify its behavior* and to understand the *constraints and the environment* in which this software system will operate. The definition also highlights the need to consider change, which is inherent in any real-world situation. Finally, the definition suggests that RE aims to capture and distill the experience of software development across a wide range of applications and projects.

Although Zave's definition identifies some of the key challenges in RE, the nature of RE itself has been changing. First, RE is not specific to software alone but to *socio-technical systems* in general, of which software is only a part. Software today permeates every aspect of our lives, and therefore, one must not only consider the technical but also the physical, economical, and social aspects. Second, an important concept in RE is *stakeholders*, that is, individuals or organizations who stand to gain or lose from the success or failure of the system to be constructed (Nuseibeh & Easterbrook, 2000). Stakeholders play an important role in eliciting requirements as well as in validating them.

While the definition of the requirements helps delimit the solution space, the requirement problem space is less constrained, making it difficult to define the environment boundary, negotiate the resolution of conflicts, and set acceptance criteria (Cheng & Atlee, 2007). Therefore, several guidelines are given to define and regulate the RE processes in order to build adequate requirements (Robertson & Robertson, 2012). Figure 1 summarizes the main activities of RE:

Elicitation. Requirements elicitation aims to discover the needs of stakeholders as well as understand the context in which the system-to-be will operate. It may also explore alternative ways in which the new system could be specified. Several techniques can be used including (i) traditional data gathering techniques (e.g., interviews, questionnaires, surveys, analysis of existing documentation), (ii) collaborative techniques (e.g., brainstorming, workshops, prototyping), (iii) cognitive techniques (e.g., protocol analysis, card sorting), (iv) contextual techniques (e.g., ethnographic techniques, discourse analysis), and (v) creativity techniques (e.g., creativity workshops, facilitated analogical reasoning).

Modeling. The results of the elicitation activity often need to be described precisely and in a way accessible by domain experts, developers, and other stakeholders. A wide range of techniques and notations can be used to represent requirements, ranging from informal to semi-formal to formal (mathematical) methods. The choice of the appropriate method often depends on the kind of analysis or reasoning that needs to be performed.

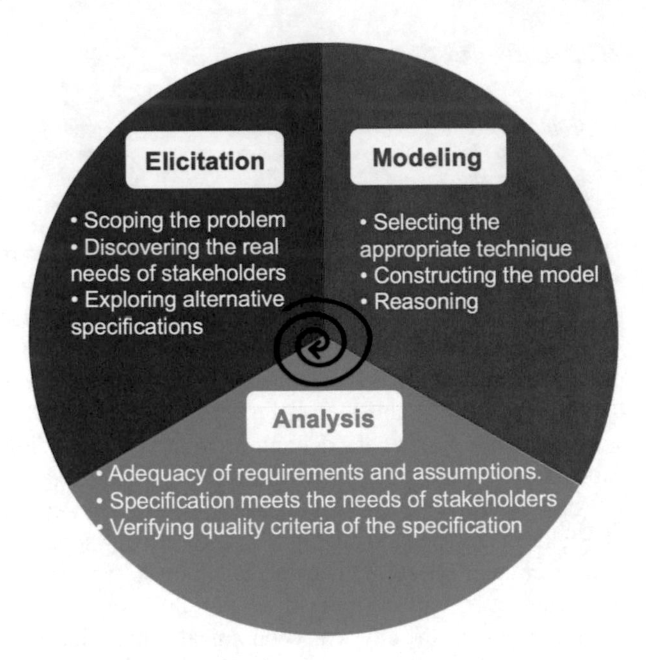

Fig. 1 Main activities of requirements engineering

Analysis and Assurance. Requirements quality assurance seeks to identify, report, analyze, and fix defects in requirements. It involves both validation and verification. Validation aims to check the adequacy of the modeled requirements and domain assumptions with the actual expectations of stakeholders. Verification covers a wide range of checks including quality criteria of the modeled requirements (e.g., consistency).

2.2 *Requirements and Goals*

Zave and Jackson (1997) suggest that there are three main kinds of artifacts that requirements engineers would produce during the RE activities:

- Statements about the *domain*, describing properties that are true regardless of the presence or actions of the machine (or software system)
- Statements about *requirements*, describing properties that the stakeholders want to be true of the world in the presence of the machine
- Statements about the *specification*, describing what the machine needs to do to achieve the requirements

These statements can be written in natural language, formal logic, semi-formal languages, or indeed some combination of them, and Zave and Jackson are not prescriptive about that. What is important is their relationship: *The specification of the machine, together with the properties of the domain, should satisfy the requirements.*

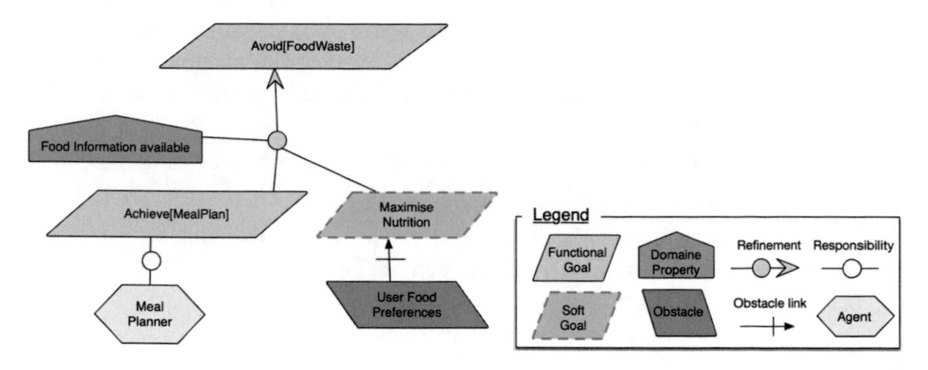

Fig. 2 A sample goal model for the MealPlanning example

To illustrate those notions, let us consider an example of *meal planning* as a way to tackle an important and pressing societal problem, food waste. It is estimated that food waste per capita by consumers in Europe and North America is 95–115 kg/year. Food waste is often caused by insufficient planning of purchases and consumption by individuals. Effective strategies to reduce wasteful behavior should require minimum time and cognitive effort from consumers. The Feed me, Feed me exemplar (Bennaceur et al., 2016) describes a system based on the Internet of Things to support the production, distribution, and consumption of food. We use ideas and challenges from the Feed me, Feed me exemplar to focus on how our approach can support individuals in reducing food waste in households.

For example, to avoid food waste, we should plan meals. This can be achieved by refinements (as illustrated in Fig. 2). The *Avoid[FoodWaste]* goal is refined into sub-goals and associated domain properties. A *goal* in this model is defined as a prescriptive statement that the system should satisfy through the cooperation of *agents* such as humans, devices, and software. Goals may refer to services to be provided (functional goals) or quality of service (soft goals).

Achieve[MealPlan] is a functional goal, while *MaximiseNutrition* is a soft goal. While functional goals can be satisfied or not, soft goals are often optimized. Keywords such as *Achieve*, *Maintain*, and *Avoid* are used to characterize the intended behaviors of the goals and can guide their formal specification.

Domain properties are descriptive statements about the environment. For example, *Food Information Available* is a domain property. An important relationship is that the goal *Avoid[FoodWaste]* can be satisfied through *Achieve[MealPlan]* and *MaximiseNutrition* assuming *Food Information Available.*

Besides describing the contribution of sub-goals (and associated domain properties) to the satisfaction of a goal, refinement links are also used for the operationalization of goals and assigning them to (software) agents. For example, *MealPlanner* is responsible for satisfying the goal *Achieve[MealPlan].*

Finally, *Conflict* links are used to represent obstacles to the satisfaction of goals. For example, *UserFoodPreferences* may hinder the satisfaction of *MaximiseNutrition.* Reasoning about obstacles enables risk analysis of the goals by eliciting properties that may obstruct the satisfaction of goals.

Hence, RE is grounded in the real world; it involves understanding the *environment (domain)* in which the system-to-be will operate and defining a detailed, consistent *specification* of the software system-to-be. This process is incremental and iterative as illustrated in Fig. 2.

Zave and Jackson specify five clear criteria for this process to complete:

- Each goal has been validated with the stakeholders.
- Each domain property has also been validated with the stakeholders.
- The goal does not constrain the environment or refer to the future.
- There exists a proof of the satisfaction of goals.
- The goals and domain properties are consistent.

2.3 The Need for Human-Centered Values

The essence of RE is a good understanding of problems, which includes analyzing the domain, communicating with stakeholders, and preparing for system evolution. However, techniques such as machine learning, automated compositions and interactions, and creativity disrupt the traditional models of software development and call for quicker, if not immediate, response from requirements engineering. Moreover, the social underpinning and the increasing reliance on software systems for every aspect of our life call for better methods to understand the impact and implications of software solutions on individuals and society as a whole.

For example, several pressing global problems such as climate change and sustainability engineering as well as increasingly important domains such as user-centered computing and other inter- and cross-disciplinary problems challenge existing processes and techniques. It is no longer enough to understand the needs of stakeholders and the constraints of the environments in which a software system is deployed; we also need to understand the values of the stakeholders and understand the broader impact of deploying software solutions. In the next section, we move to values and their interaction with requirements.

3 Values We Live By: Eliciting, Articulating, and Organizing Goals

Digital humanism argues for adopting a broader framework where, besides the technical perspective, multiple perspectives (including ethical, social, legal, political, and economic) are considered when developing systems that have an impact on individuals and society.

Recent work has promoted the need to consider ethics and values during the development of software systems (Whittle, 2019). As outlined by Mougouei et al.

(2018), "people are demanding that practitioners align technologies with human values." Some approaches have been proposed to assess and study values in software engineering (Winter et al., 2019), to incorporate social values in software design patterns (Hussain et al., 2018), and to measure the impact of values in requirements engineering activities (Perera et al., 2021). Values are well studied in human-computer interaction and information systems (Cockton, 2004).

For RE, this means rethinking the world in terms of broader and changing stakeholders, their needs, and their values. It also means rethinking the notion of requirements satisfaction to incorporate values and the inevitability of failure and change. Some of the challenges of doing so stems from the subjectivity and uncertainty of values. Values are *subjective* and depend on the diverse viewpoints of stakeholders because different stakeholders describe value requirements differently. As a result, they have different and sometimes contradictory requirements. For example, if we consider the value of fairness, serving a protected group with priority can promote fairness in society, but, at the same time, it may seem discriminatory to others. Values are *uncertain* and are often better understood once the software solution is deployed. For example, awareness of gender bias in data may lead to the deployment of existing equality policies, and their impact and consequences are better understood once deployed.

The debate has long focused on principles and codes of conduct for considering values in software systems. However, it is increasingly moving to tools and processes for implementing those values and principles in practice. While awareness of the potential issues is increasing at a fast rate, the software/requirements engineering community's ability to take action to mitigate the associated risks is still in its infancy. There is still a need to close the gap between principles and practices for engineers to apply ethics at each stage of the development pipeline and to signal to researchers where further work is needed. In other words, we need methods to move from "what" values to embed to "how" those values can be embedded in software systems. This section provides some direction toward achieving this goal.

3.1 Values and RE Activities

Let us first review the RE activities with humanistic values in mind.

Elicitation. Social scientists, ethicists, philosophers, policymakers, technologists, and civil society have been involved in a debate around what is necessary to enable society to capitalize on the opportunities of software systems while ensuring fair and ethical decision-making is maintained. Participatory design aims to elicit the values of multiple stakeholders by following several steps, which include:

- Involving actual users for eliciting value concerns
- Using personas to consider/assume user values
- Using prototypes to analyze assumptions about values
- Using diversity in members selected from various stakeholder groups
- Focusing on cultural sensitivities
- Being considerate of language needs of different stakeholder groups
- Developing empathy with users, emulating their experiences
- Building an atmosphere of trust for stakeholders to voice their opinions
- Applying user feedback to improve mock-ups and prototypes

In addition to continual engagement with stakeholders and practitioners, reflection on practices and the impact of the developing software systems is equally important. The Self-Reflection Tool of the Responsible Research and Innovation (RRI)[1] framework helps practitioners consider the societal and ethical issues that may be involved with technology. Learning by doing underpins the AREA (Anticipate, Reflect, Engage, and Act) approach to RRI. This means that professional and social responsibility is best developed through experience and reflective practice. The guidelines for such practices include:

1. Involving a wide range of actors and people in practice, deliberation, and decision-making. This strengthens democracy and broadens sources of expertise, disciplines, and perspectives.
2. Envisioning impact and reflecting on the underlying assumptions, values, and purposes to better understand how the developed systems shape the future. This yields valuable insights and increases the capacity to act on what we know.
3. Communicating in a meaningful way the methods, results, conclusions, and implications to enable public scrutiny and dialogue. This benefits the visibility and understanding of the developed systems.
4. Being able to modify modes of thought and behavior, overarching organizational structures, in response to changing circumstances, knowledge, and perspectives. This aligns action with the needs expressed by different stakeholders.

Modeling. In Value-Based Requirements Engineering (Thew & Sutcliffe, 2018), values are seen as personal attitudes and beliefs which influence functional and non-functional requirements. There is evidence of human values being treated as software requirements, specifically as soft goals or non-functional requirements (Barn, 2016). In values-first software engineering, Ferrario et al. (2016) argue that complex wicked problems such as sustainability should be treated as soft goals, not as functional requirements. Nurwidyantoro et al. (2022) postulate that non-functional requirements can be seen as a subset of human values and propose to classify human values and align them to system values. They found system value themes, such as efficiency and usability, similar to non-functional requirements.

[1] https://rri-tools.eu/. Accessed 10 April 2023.

Fig. 3 Dimensions to consider for eliciting and operationalizing values

Assurance. Operationalizing values is defined as "the process of identifying human values and translating them to accessible and concrete concepts so that they can be implemented, validated, verified, and measured in software" (Shahin et al., 2022). It is common for stakeholders to gain a better understanding of their values as they experience, reflect, and learn more about them (Gentile, 2010). However, elicitation and modeling approaches focus on early stages of the development process, with little attention given to the satisfaction of values in deployed software systems (Shahin et al., 2022). Software solutions can help stakeholders articulate, measure, and reflect on their values while they are experiencing the software. Values@Runtime (Bennaceur et al., 2023) deal with uncertainty by delaying some decisions until software is in operation. It adopts an adaptive process to engage stakeholders and to support learning about models of stakeholders' values. It provides values instantiation as a means of representing the concrete actions that stakeholders associate with values (Hanel et al., 2017). This framework supports values operationalization in terms of (i) representation, instantiation, and monitoring of values and behavior; (ii) understanding existing mismatches between values and users' behavior based on analysis; and (iii) recommending ways to align values and behavior as well as reflecting on the recommendations.

Hence, eliciting and operationalizing values involves three dimensions (see Fig. 3):

- People, through the adoption of a human-centered view and participatory design as well as involving a diversity of stakeholders and teams
- Artifacts, by making explicit value statements and engineering systems for diverse stakeholders
- Processes, by linking values between requirements and implemented software and by being transparent and open to accountability about implementation practices and mindful of project impact and following current standards and regulations

3.2 Values and Goals

Let us consider the example of fairness when food shopping (Farahani et al., 2021). The high-level goal is *Achieve[FairShopping]* and might be refined in multiple ways—see Fig. 4.

For example, when the domain property *AbundantStock* holds, then the goal is to *maximize Products Sold*, which can be operationalized by allowing users to buy as many products as they want/need. When the domain property Limited Stock holds, then there needs to be a choice between two goals: *Achieve[EquitableAccess]* by prioritizing protected groups or *Achieve[EqualAccess]* by limiting the maximum amount of product per shopper without distinction between shoppers. While not mutually exclusive, the choice is driven by consideration of multiple stakeholders, e.g., supermarkets' willingness to implement different procedures, government's willingness to support protected groups, and public acceptance of prioritizing protected groups. For example, prioritizing a protected group can be perceived as fair for some people, but at the same time, it may seem discriminatory to others. In other words, a goal model can help highlight the stakeholders involved when making value-sensitive choices, e.g., fair for whom or who is responsible for the choice. The goal model helps highlight and contrast alternative operationalization of values.

Emotions can be used as proxy to values and leveraged to design inclusive processes (Hassett et al., 2023). For example, the *Supermarket* might want the stakeholder group, *Vulnerable Shopper* (e.g., older person or person with special needs), to *feel Cared for*, which then leads to prioritizing protected groups.

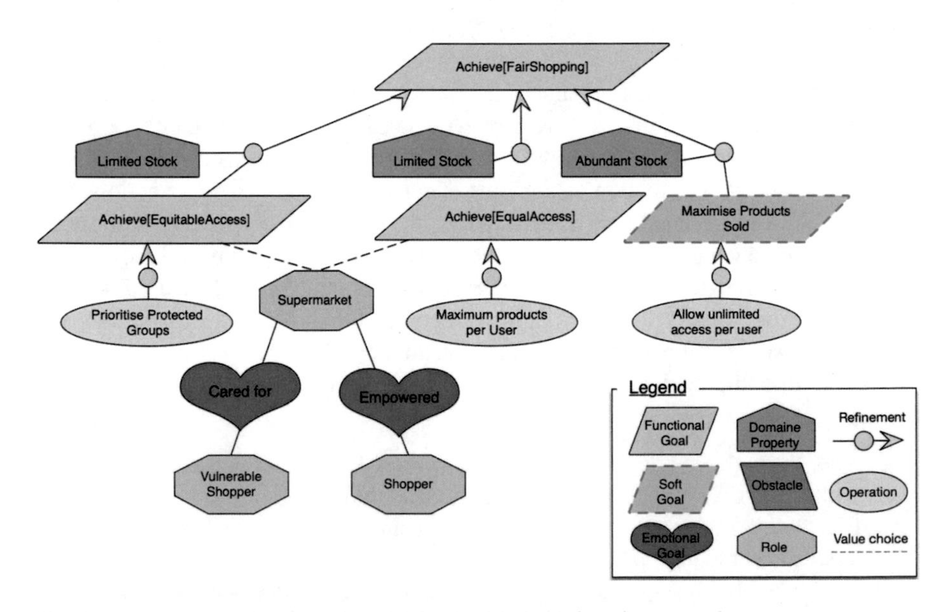

Fig. 4 A sample (emotional) goal model for the fair food shopping example

4 Toward Responsible Software Engineering: DigHum Goals in the Life Cycle

In this section, we discuss how the principles of digital humanism may guide the life cycle of socio-technical systems: from the conception and development of a system, to its operation in the real world, to its continuous evolution.

4.1 Requirements and Other Activities

The first and most important step consists of understanding and articulating the requirements. The previous two sections shed light on this crucial activity, through which developers assume explicit responsibility with respect to the system under development. Through goal models, they express a contract with stakeholders and future users, which states what the system is expected to achieve. Traditionally, software engineers are educated to focus on goals that refer to the functionalities and expected behaviors to be provided by the system and on technical qualities, like efficiency (e.g., average response time of certain transactions), portability of the implementation on different architectures, or security (e.g., guaranteed restricted access to certain data or functionalities). In our context, however, requirements also reflect the general humanistic values, modeled as explicit goals to be met by the future system. For example, fairness is explicitly modeled as a goal to achieve in the context of the food shopping example.

Eliciting and articulating these goals is critical, but also quite difficult and highly context dependent. The technical skills possessed by software engineers alone may fall short. Not only stakeholders and user representatives must be involved, but also experts from other domains—like philosophy (ethics), history, social sciences, economics, or law—may have a lot to say in order to understand goals, analyze and resolve conflicts, and prioritize among them, but also to anticipate possible uses (or misuses) of socio-technical systems in the real world. Depending on the specific system being developed, a deliberative process needs to be put in place, which gives voice to different viewpoints and then responsibly leads to decisions that inform all subsequent development steps.

Requirements are a prerequisite for design and implementation (Fig. 5). These are technical steps that lead to a functioning socio-technical system. Design is responsible for defining the software architecture, i.e., decomposing a system into components and deciding how different components interact and communicate. Implementation is responsible for producing an executable system, often through a combination of programmed parts, libraries, and software frameworks.

However, requirements also permeate many parts of the systems development process. During system design, requirements are used to inform decision-making about different design alternatives. During system implementation, requirements are used to enable system prototyping and testing. Once the system has been deployed,

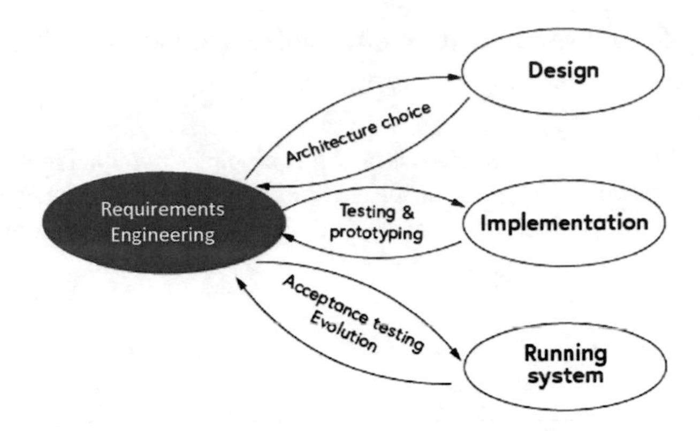

Fig. 5 Crucial relationship between requirements and other activities

requirements are used to drive acceptance tests to check whether the final system does what the stakeholders originally wanted. In addition, requirements are reviewed and updated during the software development process as additional knowledge is acquired and stakeholders' needs are better understood.

Each step of the development process may lead to the definition of additional requirements through a better understanding of the domain and associated constraints. Therefore, there is a need to consider requirements, design, and architecture concurrently, and this is often the process adopted by software engineers.

4.2 Software Processes

Different process models can be followed to guide development, ranging from top-down (waterfall) processes to bottom-up and iterative processes. Waterfall processes are monolithic and sequential: they try to strictly enforce completion of the requirements phase before proceeding to the design phase, which must itself be completed before moving to implementation. Strict sequential ordering of phases is only suitable for highly structured systems that operate in well-defined, formalizable, and highly stable contexts. It is not suitable for ill-defined and unstable settings as is the case in most socio-technical systems, where humans play a fundamental role. More flexible—iterative and incremental—life cycles, such as the popular process models which fall under the term *agile processes*, are almost always adopted for the latter kind of systems. Agile processes, which envision the development of system increments, e.g., via *sprints* in the SCRUM agile methodology (Schwaber & Beedle, 2002), appear as a suitable setting to accommodate the necessary deliberations through which digital humanism-inspired requirements can be explored and then guide development. The chapter by Zuber et al. in this book provides deeper insights into how agile development methods are inherently suitable for embedding digital humanism values into software systems.

4.3 Validation and Verification

Two other important activities need to be carried out during development: verification and validation (V&V). The two terms shed light on two complementary kinds of assurances. *Validation* is the assurance that the system meets the needs of the customer and other identified stakeholders. It often involves acceptance and suitability with external customers. *Verification* is the assurance that the system complies with its specification. The two terms would of course be synonyms if specifications were exhaustive and complete. This is almost inevitably impossible in practice. In addition, as we discuss next, the needs of customers and other stakeholders continuously evolve, and therefore, an upfront complete specification is impossible to realize.

V&V is itself not a stage of system development, but rather a cross-cutting activity that permeates all development steps. Requirements are continuously verified and validated as they are elicited and formalized; likewise, architectures and implementation increments are subject to V&V. Delivery of (partial) applications for real use presupposes an adequate level of V&V to check compliance with specifications, including possible existing regulations, and adherence to users' needs. It is also possible to design systems in a way that these checks are made automatically by the system while it operates, at run-time (run-time V&V).

V&V is practiced through two complementary approaches: systematic reasoning and testing. Systematic reasoning tries to analyze the artifacts under development to prove that the stakeholders' expectations are met by affirming that violations of those expectations are impossible. Testing develops experiments that try to bring the system into desirable and undesirable states, to collect empirical evidence that the system being developed can be delivered for practical use. The two approaches are complementary, since exhaustive testing is impossible to achieve and tools to assist in systematic reasoning do not scale up to large systems.

4.4 The Running System

The life cycle of an application does not end when it is deployed. Most systems, and especially those successfully used in practice, are subject to continuous evolution, traditionally called maintenance. New requirements may arise from real use, pre-existing requirements may need to be adapted due to new insights gained while the system has been in use, opportunities for improvements may be discovered, and errors or other problematic situations that evaded V&V may show up during execution. To support evolution, specifically designed monitors may be implemented in the deployed applications to perform run-time V&V, checking for the insurgence of potential risks, violations of desirable policies, or mishaps.

5 Conclusions

In this chapter, we have explained the central role of requirements engineering in the software engineering process of software production and evolution. We have explained why we advocate requirements specifications and goals as the most promising and pragmatic technique to explicitly express the societal and digital humanism values which are so crucial to sound and responsible software engineering of socio-technical systems. This includes not just what the system should achieve but also what it should avoid performing. Some form of continuous monitoring of the running system will be needed to support assessment as part of responsible software engineering. This will also require that software engineers are involved in outreach activities regarding the global effects of their products: to assess impact, use, and abuse. As mentioned, experts in other disciplines (social scientists, lawyers, etc.) will also need to be involved, not just at the elicitation stage but also when the system is deployed and running. This diversity of stakeholders is becoming more and more important as systems are embedded in society.

We believe that this extension of traditional software engineering to include humanistic values is essential to cope with complex socio-technical systems. It will inevitably require further research, practice, and education to refine the techniques, to gain further empirical evidence and experience, and to ensure dissemination to the profession.

Discussion Questions for Students and Their Teachers

In the following hypothetical projects work together with colleagues from different disciplines and with different backgrounds, to articulate the Digital Humanism goals and overall requirements to be reached by a hypothetical socio-technical system, understanding potential conflicts, and mitigating potential risks, including misuse.

Consideration should also be given to what should be automated and what is left to humans to perform and also whether it is possible to ascertain whether or not the resulting system is compliant with the specified goals and explicit values.

1. Hypothetical Project 1: Citizen Forensics

   The police are overstretched, criminality is on the rise, ... how can citizens participate in deterring crime and helping the police (and each other) detect antisocial incidents and solve crime.

   Hints/issues: you could explore risk and issues around surveillance (before or after incidents), harassment, privacy, citizen-police relations, and information sharing. . .A resource: https://www.citizenforensics.org

2. Hypothetical Project 2: Technology in the Courtroom

   It's not easy to be a judge. . . It is necessary to assess as correctly as possible whether an offender will recidivate, what sentence is appropriate for the particular offense, whether or not the sentence should be suspended, and much more.

   Wouldn't it be great if technology could make judgments easier?

   Many ethical questions arise here, such as who is "fairer," a technical system or a human? How transparent must a decision by a technical system be that supports a court ruling? Is such a system more of a science fiction fantasy à la Minority Report or an actual chance to counter prejudices, perception biases, or even racist tendencies among judges?

Here are some papers and articles about this topic:

https://link.springer.com/content/pdf/10.1007/s10506-022-09310-1.pdf

https://www.propublica.org/article/how-we-analyzed-the-compas-recidivism-algorithm

https://link.springer.com/article/10.1007/s10506-022-09312-z

https://scholarship.law.umn.edu/mlr/58/

Proposed by: Anna Dhungel

3. Hypothetical Project 3: My Truth, Your Truth

   Since the corona pandemic, I don't recognize some of my friends. Through some social media forums, they have become vaccination opponents, mask deniers, and world conspirators.... How can social media be made social and responsible again without immediately giving the feeling of living in a "dictatorship of opinion"?

   Hint: The following article gives a brief introduction into the democratic roles of news recommender systems: https://doi.org/10.1080/21670811.2019.1623700.

   Proposed by: Kian Schmalenbach and Eva Gengler

Learning Resources for Students

1. Van Lamsweerde, A., 2009. Requirements engineering: From system goals to UML models to software (Vol. 10, p. 34). Chichester, UK: John Wiley & Sons.

   The book presents a systematic method to elaborate complex system models, analyze them, and derive software specifications from them. The method is known as KAOS (Keep All Objectives Satisfied). The goal models in this chapter used notations and formalisms from this book.
2. Brey, P. and Dainow, B., 2021. Ethics by design and ethics of use in AI and robotics. The SIENNA project-Stakeholder-informed ethics for new technologies with high socioeconomic and human rights impact.

   The document provides guidance for including ethical principles and procedures into the design and development processes of AI systems.
3. IEEE Standard Model Process for Addressing Ethical Concerns during System Design, in IEEE Std 7000–2021, vol., no., pp.1–82, 15 Sept. 2021, doi: https://doi.org/10.1109/IEEESTD.2021.9536679.

   The standard establishes a set of processes by which engineers and technologists can include consideration of ethical values in system design and development.
4. Guszcza, J., Danks, D., Fox, C., Hammond, K., Ho, D., Imas, A., Landay, J., Levi, Ma., Logg, J., Picard, R., Raghavan, M., Stanger, A., Ugolnik, Z., Woolley, A., Hybrid Intelligence: A Paradigm for More Responsible Practice (October 12, 2022). Available at SSRN: https://ssrn.com/abstract=4301478 or https://doi.org/10.2139/ssrn.4301478.

The paper presents the hybrid intelligence paradigm, aimed at supporting a more responsible practice, through simultaneous consideration of machine capabilities and human psychology, behaviors, needs, and values in the development of AI-based systems.

Acknowledgments This work was supported by the Engineering and Physical Sciences Research Council [grant numbers EP/V026747/1 and EP/R013144/1] and Science Foundation Ireland [grant number 13/RC/2094\P2].

References

Barn, B. S. (2016). Do you own a Volkswagen? Values as non-functional requirements. In Human-centered and error-resilient systems development: IFIP WG 13.2/13.5 joint working conference, 6th international conference on human-centered software engineering, HCSE 2016, and 8th international conference on human error, safety, and system development, HESSD 2016, Stockholm, Sweden, August 29-31, 2016, Proceedings 8 (pp. 151–162). Springer.

Bennaceur, A., McCormick, C., Galán, J. G., Perera, C., Smith, A., Zisman, A., & Nuseibeh, B. (2016). Feed me, feed me: An exemplar for engineering adaptive software. In *Proceedings of the 11th international symposium on software engineering for adaptive and self-managing systems* (pp. 89–95).

Bennaceur, A., Hassett, D., Nuseibeh, B., & Zisman, A. (2023). Values@ runtime: An adaptive framework for operationalising values. In *Proceedings of the 45th IEEE/ACM international conference on software engineering—software engineering in society track.*

Cheng, B. H., & Atlee, J. M. (2007). Research directions in requirements engineering. Future of software engineering (FOSE'07), (pp. 285–303).

Cockton, G. (2004). Value-centred HCI. In *Proceedings of the third Nordic conference on human-computer interaction* (pp. 149–160).

Gentile, M. C. (2010). *Giving voice to values: How to speak your mind when you know what's right.* Yale University Press.

Farahani, A., Pasquale, L., Bennaceur, A., Welsh, T., & Nuseibeh, B. (2021). On adaptive fairness in software systems. In 2021 International symposium on software engineering for adaptive and self-managing systems (SEAMS) (pp. 97–103). IEEE.

Ferrario, M. A., Simm, W., Forshaw, S., Gradinar, A., Smith, M. T., & Smith, I., (2016). Values-first SE: Research principles in practice. In *Proceedings of the 38th international conference on software engineering companion* (pp. 553–562).

Hanel, P. H., Vione, K. C., Hahn, U., & Maio, G. R. (2017). Value instantiations: The missing link between values and behavior?. Values and behavior: Taking a cross cultural perspective (pp. 175–190).

Hassett, D., Bennaceur, A., & Nuseibeh, B. (2023). Feel it, code it: Emotional goal modelling for gender-inclusive design. In *Requirements engineering: Foundation for Software Quality: 29th international working conference, REFSQ 2023, Barcelona, Spain, April 17–20, 2023, proceedings* (pp. 324–336). Springer Nature.

Hussain, W., Mougouei, D., & Whittle, J. (2018). Integrating social values into software design patterns. In *Proceedings of the international workshop on software fairness* (pp. 8–14).

Lessig, L., (2000). Code is Law. Harvard Magazine. https://www.harvardmagazine.com/2000/01/code-is-law-html.

Mougouei, D., Perera, H., Hussain, W., Shams, R., & Whittle, J. (2018). Operationalizing human values in software: A research roadmap. In *Proceedings of the 2018 26th ACM joint meeting on European software engineering conference and symposium on the foundations of software engineering* (pp. 780–784).

Nurwidyantoro, A., Shahin, M., Chaudron, M. R., Hussain, W., Shams, R., Perera, H., Oliver, G., & Whittle, J. (2022). Human values in software development artefacts: A case study on issue discussions in three android applications. *Information and Software Technology, 141*, 106731.

Nuseibeh, B., & Easterbrook, S. (2000). Requirements engineering: A roadmap. In *Proceedings of the conference on the future of software engineering* (pp. 35–46).

Perera, H., Hoda, R., Shams, R. A., Nurwidyantoro, A., Shahin, M., Hussain, W., & Whittle, J. (2021). The impact of considering human values during requirements engineering activities. *arXiv Preprint*. 2111.15293.

Robertson, S., & Robertson, J. (2012). *Mastering the requirements process: Getting requirements right*. Addison-Wesley.

Shahin, M., Hussain, W., Nurwidyantoro, A., Perera, H., Shams, R., Grundy, J., & Whittle, J. (2022). Operationalizing human values in software engineering: A survey. *IEEE Access, 10*, 75269–75295.

Schwaber, K., & Beedle, M. (2002). *Agile software development with Scrum*. Prentice Hall.

Thew, S., & Sutcliffe, A. (2018). Value-based requirements engineering: Method and experience. *Requirements Engineering, 23*, 443–464.

Winter, E., Forshaw, S., Hunt, L., & Ferrario, M. A. (2019). Advancing the study of human values in software engineering. In *2019 IEEE/ACM 12th international workshop on cooperative and human aspects of software engineering (CHASE)* (pp. 19–26). IEEE.

Whittle, J. (2019). Is your software valueless? *IEEE Software, 36*(3), 112–115.

Zave, P. (1997). Classification of research efforts in requirements engineering. *ACM Computing Surveys (CSUR), 29*(4), 315–321.

Zave, P., & Jackson, M. (1997). Four dark corners of requirements engineering. *ACM transactions on Software Engineering and Methodology (TOSEM), 6*(1), 1–30.

Governance for Digital Humanism: The Role of Regulation, Standardization, and Certification

Clara Neppel and Patricia Shaw

Abstract Assuring that digital systems and services operate in accordance with agreed norms and principles is essential to foster trust and facilitate their adoption. Ethical assurance requires a global ecosystem, where organizations not only commit to upholding human values, dignity, and well-being but are also able to demonstrate this when required by the specific context in which they operate. We focus on possible governance frameworks including regulatory and non-regulatory measures, taking as an example AI systems. Thereby, we highlight the importance of considering the specific context, as well as the entire life cycle, from design to deployment, including data governance. Socio-technical, value-based standards, and certification schemes are introduced as enabling instruments for operationalizing responsible and ethical approaches to AI in line with upcoming regulatory requirements.

1 Introduction

AI systems can be used to positively impact humanity for good, *provided it* is designed, developed, deployed, and decommissioned responsibly. This requires creators of AI and users of AI to go beyond the legal requirements (where they exist) and take a whole ecosystem approach to ethically manage the risks and impact AI can have on fundamental rights, human dignity, and human flourishing and sustainability, in short, on people and the planet.

Operationalizing responsible and ethical approaches to AI requires both a top-down and a bottom-up (inclusive of stakeholders) approach to AI and data governance, without which no organization can effectively (1) map (namely, identify AI legal, societal, economic, environmental, and technological risks and plot them to

C. Neppel
IEEE, Vienna, Austria
e-mail: c.neppel@ieee.org

P. Shaw (✉)
IEEE, Beyond Reach Consulting Services Limited, Worksop, UK
e-mail: trish@beyondreach.uk.com

H. Werthner et al. (eds.), *Introduction to Digital Humanism*,
https://doi.org/10.1007/978-3-031-45304-5_21

the relevant product/service and personnel responsible for those risks), (2) manage, (3) measure, (4) mitigate, or (5) monitor their AI or hold themselves accountable for the outputs and outcomes in the short, medium, and long term.

We live in a global AI market, for which there is a clear need for a global coordinated response, but with direct relevance to local contexts when it comes to AI. Regulatory requirements have (as at the date of writing) been jurisdictionally bound, leaving swathes of the world simply having to respond voluntarily rather than dutifully following mandatory legal requirements. For any global response to be effective, it will require the following ecosystem conditions: standards, certification, trustmarks, audit, and, most importantly, stakeholder engagement to not only provide assurance of responsible innovation but to help define the all-important guardrails for safe and trustworthy AI for a global digital world with unique and contextually bound application domains.

2 Background to AI Principles, Regulation, and Standards

2.1 The Principles

There are a number of principles and frameworks seeking to identify and/or provide a taxonomy for AI ethics and values that are to be applied to AI systems and that potentially could be applied universally. These principles were developed by a large number of entities, including international organizations and other governments, industry, and professional organizations, e.g., UNESCO, OECD, and IEEE.

A mapping exercise was undertaken by the Berkman Klein Center at Harvard University, which published "A Map of Ethical and Rights-based Approach to Principles for AI"[1] (see Fig. 1).

In its mapping exercise, the Center found that there was a great degree of commonality in the approaches that many principles, guidelines, and frameworks called for. Key themes included:

- International human rights
- Promotion of human values (such as autonomy, agency, dignity, empathy, and well-being)
- Professional responsibility
- Human control of technology
- Bias, fairness, and non-discrimination
- Transparency and explainability
- Safety and security

[1] Fjeld, Jessica and Achten, Nele and Hilligoss, Hannah and Nagy, Adam and Srikumar, Madhulika, Principled Artificial Intelligence: Mapping Consensus in Ethical and Rights-Based Approaches to Principles for AI (January 15, 2020). Berkman Klein Center Research Publication No. 2020-1,: https://ssrn.com/abstract=3518482 or https://doi.org/10.2139/ssrn.3518482

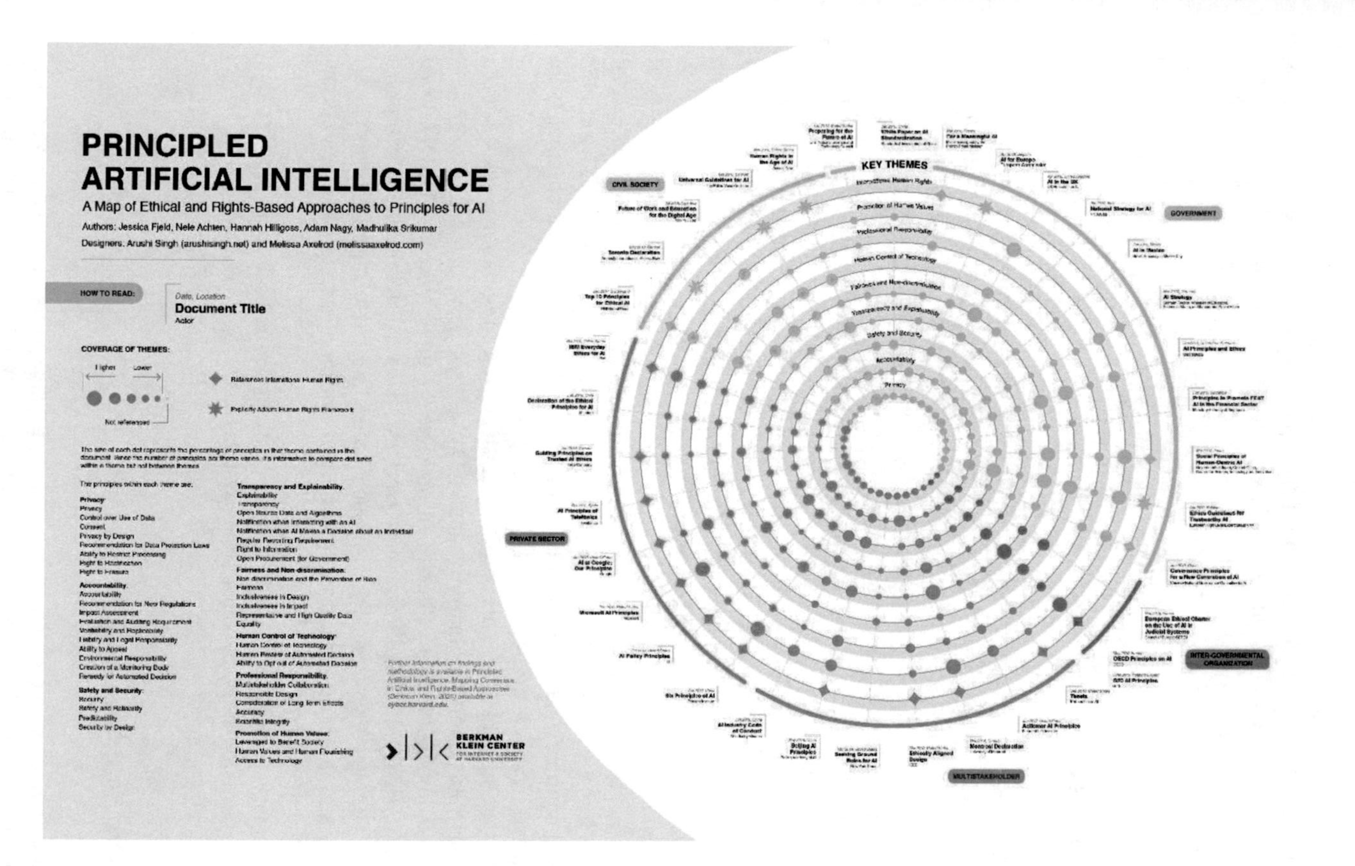

Fig. 1 Source and copyright: Berkman Klein Center (Source: https://cyber.harvard.edu/publication/2020/principled-ai licensed under a Creative Commons attribution 3.0 Unported license: https://creativecommons.org/licenses/by/3.0/legalcode)

- Accountability
- Privacy

The key challenges for many of those principles that were mapped from across the globe are that they are voluntary and therefore are not enforceable and lack the clarity of law and so are often not fully defined leaving their operationalization open to interpretation.

2.2 The Role of Regulation

First proposals for regulating the use of AI systems have already been tabled in different parts of the world to address the specific challenges of AI systems and to provide a trustworthy ecosystem for all affected stakeholders. These regulatory proposals aim to provide AI developers, deployers, and users with requirements and obligations regarding specific uses of AI.

The EU AI Act sets out a risk-based approach, where the obligations for a system are proportionate to the level of risk that it poses. The Act outlines four levels of risk: low-risk systems, limited or minimal risk systems, high-risk systems, and systems with unacceptable risk. We see risk focus and risk proportionality increasingly being used by governments and regulators when designing and delivering regulations with the aim to improve their effectiveness and efficiency.

In parallel, the Council of Europe started a negotiation process for a legal instrument on the development, design, and application of AI based on the Council of Europe framework for human rights, democracy, and the rule of law. If adopted by several countries across the world, this instrument has the potential to act as an international treaty on artificial intelligence.

Besides addressing concerns through legislation and regulations, what can be called "hard law," non-regulatory means known as "soft law" can also set substantive expectations but are not directly enforceable by governments. The OECD AI principles (OECD AI Global Principles Overview, n.d.) are an important example of soft law. They represent one form of such programs where high-level norms are created by a multilateral organization with the intention of setting baseline expectations for the management of AI.

In summary, both hard law and soft law seek to define high-level requirements and obligations for the application of AI systems.

2.3 The Standards

While we do not currently (at the time of writing) have an overarching international legal treaty or convention on AI, and national law and regulation is still in the making, standards are potentially our only way to provide for a consistent technical and/or socio-technical approach to design, develop, and deploy AI systems in a trustworthy and sustainable manner.

As set out above, principles and regulatory requirements are at a high level of abstraction and often need further interpretation for a given context or industry. For instance, transparency can have different meanings to different actors in different sectors. An accident investigator and the average user of an autonomous system would surely have different expectations. The investigator would need to access technical details, such as the source code, whereas the user would need explanations about the system's actions or recommendations, in the name of transparency. This illustrates why having a common understanding of broad and shared principles is key to establishing trust in an ecosystem.

Open and consensus-based processes are the best means for agreeing not only on the definition of principles and requirements but also on how these principles would be implemented and validated. Standards are what can help turn principles into practice and help make AI (and more pertinently AI assurance) interoperable between businesses (or governments) and borders. Standards provide definitions for the principles and a way forward in how to interpret them and apply them in the AI life cycle. Standards can be technical (placing on their users technical requirements) and/or socio-technical (placing on their users processes and/or methodologies in the design, development, and use of technical requirements to achieve human-centered societal outcomes).

2.4 *The Role of Standards and Certification*

Standards can provide for a technical or non-technical specification, recommend practices, prescribe processes, or describe detailed requirements that must or should be fulfilled to either achieve particular outcomes or for the purposes of compliance and conformity. Examples of standards used every day include IEEE 802.11 WLAN standard and the ISO 27001 information security and management systems standard.

The necessary level of trust in socio-technical systems can only be achieved if affected stakeholders openly address the expected benefits and risks for the given context, as well as necessary tradeoffs associated with them. Stakeholders should include technologists, human scientists, regulators, and civil society. Several initiatives echo this mindset, including OECD, Council of Europe, or IEEE.

Traditionally, standardization deals with technical issues, such as quality, interoperability, safety, or security. In order to help organizations apply abstract AI principles to concrete practices, the IEEE Standards Association has been developing socio-technical standards in parallel to technical standards. Socio-technical standard working groups convene technologists with stakeholder groups and focus on things like defining different levels of transparency for incremental needs or impact assessment of AI systems on human well-being and the environment.

One example of such a standard is the IEEE 7000™-2021 Model Process for Addressing Ethical Concerns During System Design (IEEE 7000™-2021 Standard - Addressing Ethical Concerns During Systems Design, 2023). The standard guides developers in making their products and services compatible with the ethical values of the communities in which technical products and services are placed and used. The standard gives step-by-step guidance to organizations on how to care for stakeholder values from the early conception of a system all through its development and later deployment. To elicit values of ethical relevance, the standard applies utilitarianism, virtue ethics, and duty ethics and recommends to also reach out to the culturally and spiritually founded ethical traditions of local cultures.

IEEE 7000 has four primary processes to build ethical systems: concept of operations and context exploration, value elicitation and prioritization, ethical value requirements identification, and risk-based design. These are complemented by a transparency management process.

The role of standards and certification (and in particular AI ethics standards like that seen in the IEEE 7000 suite of standards) is about creating the right behaviors across the AI life cycle and creating the right environment and ethics culture for businesses to interoperate across the AI value chain.

While AI ethics standards set the bar of what processes need to be in place to help achieve certain ethical outcomes, certification is about providing assurance that the necessary processes, policies, practices, and procedures are put in place between parties so that they can fulfil their own legal compliance requirements; manage risk; understand their dependencies, interdependencies, and limitations; and appropriately mitigate and monitor risks.

In conclusion, standards are about how you do it and the good (and often best) practice an organization puts in place, but certification is about testifying publicly to what has been done by the organization to get it AI ethics ready.

2.5 What Is AI (and Data) Governance and Why Is It Necessary?

Artificial intelligence (AI), or more pertinently an AI System, according to the OECD is as follows: "*AI system*: An AI system is a machine-based system that can, for a given set of human-defined objectives, make predictions, recommendations, or decisions influencing real or virtual environments. AI systems are designed to operate with varying levels of autonomy."

This definition is set out in OECD/LEGAL/0449 AI Recommendation, which was adopted on May 22, 2019. At the time of writing this chapter, while it was not documented in the Official Draft of the EU AI Regulation, it was recognized that this definition had also been accepted by the European Parliament as the official definition of AI for the purposes of the EU AI Regulation.

As an AI system is neither created nor operated in a vacuum, certain other definitions also accompanied the definition of an AI system under the OECD Recommendation. These include recognition of the AI life cycle and the AI value chain where a variety of actors and stakeholders play a part.

"*AI system lifecycle*: AI system lifecycle phases involve: *i)* 'design, data, and models'; which is a context-dependent sequence encompassing planning and design, data collection and processing, as well as model building; *ii)* 'verification and validation'; *iii)* 'deployment'; and *iv)* 'operation and monitoring'. These phases often take place in an iterative manner and are not necessarily sequential. The decision to retire an AI system from operation may occur at any point during the operation and monitoring phase.

"*AI knowledge*: AI knowledge refers to the skills and resources, such as data, code, algorithms, models, research, know-how, training programs, governance, processes and best practices, required to understand and participate in the AI system lifecycle."

"*AI actors*: AI actors are those who play an active role in the AI system life cycle, including organizations and individuals that deploy or operate AI."

"*Stakeholders*: Stakeholders encompass all organizations and individuals involved in, or affected by, AI systems, directly or indirectly. AI actors are a subset of stakeholders."

AI governance must therefore recognize the complex ecosystem within which AI is designed, developed, deployed, monitored, and overseen, as well as decommissioned.

When we talk of governance of AI, firstly we cannot leave data out of the equation. For a technology that is data-driven, where, how, and when you got your data and for what purpose matter.

To that end, AI governance must include data governance as two but intertwined ecosystems. Indeed, the European Commission proposed together with its AI strategy also a data strategy to establish the right regulatory framework regarding data governance, access, and reuse. The provenance and quality of data matters. Data (especially if it is personal identifiable data) is potentially also subject to separate regulatory regimes in different jurisdictions. If not completely separate regulations, the interpretation of them can be unique to localized contexts and regulators. Data governance requires assessment and evaluation of the data used in data-driven technologies at every stage of the data life cycle, which is a separate ecosystem in and of itself to that of the AI life cycle but forms an intricate part of the AI life cycle.

The data life cycle (like the AI life cycle) has various stages where the type of data and treatment of the data must be observed, analyzed, and in some cases modified (whether for accuracy or for format, for structuring or for profiling within wider database, or for being matched or merged with other data sets), actions logged, and decisions recorded. The data life cycle typically consists of (1) collection, (2) collation, (3) storage, (4) decisions and inferences made, (5) reporting the story, (6) distributing and sharing, and (7) disposal[2].

How data is treated or what decisions are made will affect the AI system (Fig. 2).

Data can be used at different touchpoints across the whole of the AI life cycle. Depending on how the data is used and when in the AI life cycle will determine its impact. Data is used for training the AI system; testing and evaluating the AI system

[2]Holt, Alison, Data Governance – governing data for sustainable business (BCS, The Chartered Institute for IT 2021, Swindon, UK)

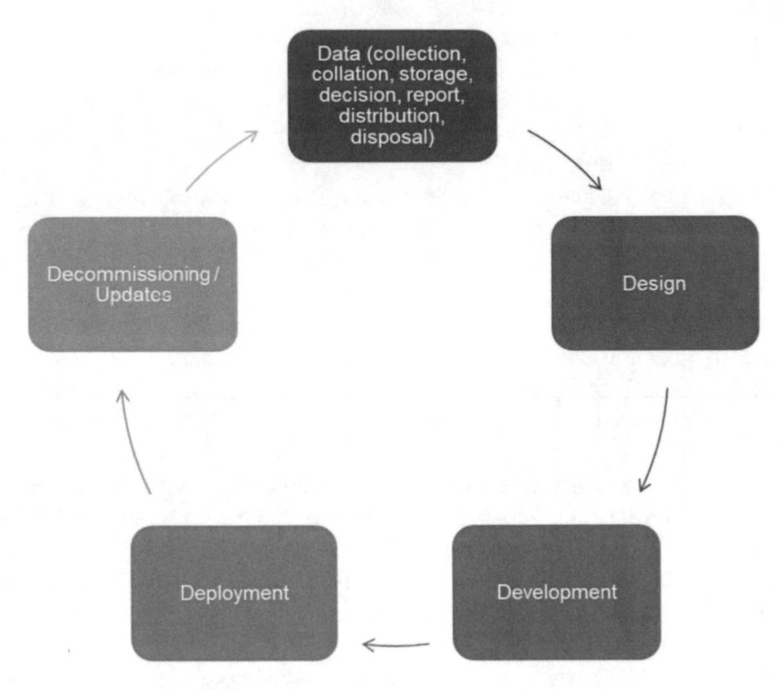

Fig. 2 Data life cycle (Reproduced with the permission of the copyright holder Beyond Reach Consulting Limited)

prior to going to market or being put into service, for verification, or when it is fully operational may set parameters and determine inferences and links made between data variables, features, and attributes.

Governance is the requirement to hold the providers of an AI system to account and to have designated roles aligned with responsibilities to hold the AI system (and the organization designing, developing, deploying, operating, maintaining, and decommissioning the AI system) to account. Fundamentally, it is to have oversight of an AI system to manage it, map the risks, mitigate the risks, and monitor them and (should it be necessary) to have the mandate to turn it off (with that all important "kill switch"), reset it, update it, and provide alternative operations for business continuity and disaster recovery.

An AI system, unlike static software applications, is dynamic. Machine learning, and in particular, deep learning, has the potential to make constant small but iterative changes to the AI system, such that it is perceived as "self-learning." The outcomes of such an AI system (hereafter AI Outcomes) can vary depending on their application domain, context, and audience. AI outcomes can result in societal, ethical, environmental, economic, technological, and legal risks and impacts that may change over time or only become apparent after a significant period of use. Some AI outcomes may transpire in the short term, but others may only occur over the medium or longer term. It is because of this agile and dynamic nature of AI that any AI governance framework applied to it itself cannot be a "one stop shop," never to be

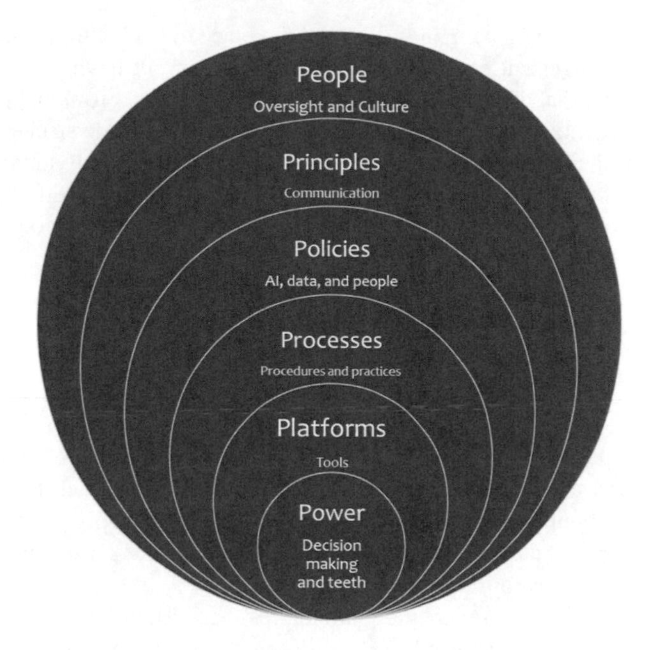

Fig. 3 The six *P*s of AI governance (Reproduced with the permission of the copyright holder Beyond Reach Consulting Limited)

revisited again. Nor can it take a "one-size-fits-all approach." AI governance must be iterative (like the AI life cycle) and continuous (beyond an AI system being put into action in a live environment): map .... manage ... measure ... mitigate ... monitor the risks and ... repeat.

To devise an agile and iterative AI governance framework, it needs to be a holistic approach, which requires an organization to have a four *M*s approach, (1) multilayered, (2) multidisciplinary, (3) multifaceted, (4) multijurisdictional and/or multicultural, and to have the six *P*s in place: (1) people; (2) principles; (3) policies; (4) processes, practices, and procedures; (5) platforms; and (6) power (Fig. 3).

Ultimately, an AI Governance Operating Model should encompass both the 4*M*s and the 6*P*s. Ideally these would all be mapped in a centralized organization-wide Global Risk and Compliance (GRC) Register referencing a centralized repository of all AI use in an organization aligned to domain, product and platform, as well as the data repository containing details of data provenance and the data's limitations (whether they be contractual or purpose limitations), and reporting would be to an empowered, with four *I*s (independence, influence, insightful, and informed), ethics advisory board engaged iteratively just as the AI governance is managed, mitigated, and monitored iteratively. Herein lies the key to successful AI governance, and that is where the ethics advisory board provides the all-important oversight over and above the day-to-day operational management and governance. In an ideal world, independent oversight of AI systems, which are high risk and have the potential to have a negative impact or unintended consequences on people and planet, such as large foundational models, ought to be mandatory.

Having governance structures in place to deal with the day-to-day operations and management of an AI system is one thing, but having an independent board other than that of the executive or non-executive organizational board (depending on the organization's structure) to help oversee and provide an element of that all-important stakeholder insight (as experts and experienced individuals for a variety of disciplines and backgrounds, the ethics advisory board itself can add to the stakeholder voices) will help hold the organization internally to account for itself.

2.6 *Key Areas for Any Responsible AI Governance Operating Model*

Operationalizing responsible and ethical approaches to AI requires both a top-down and a bottom-up (inclusive of stakeholders) approach to AI and data governance, without which no organization can effectively map, manage, measure, mitigate, and monitor their AI or hold themselves accountable for the outputs and outcomes in the short, medium, and long term.

Furthermore, operationalizing responsible and ethical approaches to AI requires a holistic and values-based approach to governance, requiring an understanding of what it means to put ethical principles and their foundational requirements in practice to an organization. This requires mapping the risks (legal, reputational, ethical, and societal) and the benefits both to the business and all its ecosystem stakeholders. This is the approach of the IEEE CertifAIEd framework. The main idea is that the riskier from an ethical perspective an AI system of interest is, the deeper into the levels of the framework the duty holder needs to interrogate.

The IEEE has published its core CertifAIEd ontological specifications[3] detailing the first-tier level of enquiry and provides businesses and governments, any duty holder from within the AI system of interest, with a great starting point to look holistically at the organization as well as the technology and its outcomes. It's intended to be a holistic and outcomes-based approach to AI ethics. Furthermore, it is also intentionally able to be adaptable and flexible to meet the needs of the local application domain and its context.

The CertifAIEd framework promotes awareness, intelligence, and ethics and provides a firm foundation for any AI governance operating model based on four key areas:

[3] https://engagestandards.ieee.org/ieeecertifaied.html

- Accountability[4]
- Algorithmic Bias[5]
- Transparency[6]
- Ethical Privacy[7]

More criteria suites under CertifAIEd are to follow.

As highlighted above, many principles and frameworks exist that do not provide a clear definition or an interpretation to allow them to be operationalized with any level of consistency. The CertifAIEd framework and criteria suites provide both the definitions and credible ways to evidence that "ethical foundational requirements" (operations that provide for and promote ethical practices and behaviors) have been met.

2.7 *Accountability*

According to the IEEE's CertifAIEd ontological specification, to put in place accountability over an AI system means:

> **ethical accountability:** A contextual set of values pertaining to accountability and the satisfaction of a framework of expectations concerned with taking responsibility for actions, omissions, and outcomes and their ethical consequences (such as justice, redress, preservation of autonomy, self-determination, self-selected communities/locum and intimacies, and where issues of dignity and well-being in the use of technology are pertinent).

The framework further specifies how such ethical accountability is to be interpreted:

- Ethical accountability needs to be human-centric: when humans who are part of the accountability construct whether that be governance and oversight roles and responsibilities or it be part of an ethics advisory board, committee, panel, etc., the duty holder draws from a wide variety of dimensions being diverse and

[4] https://engagestandards.ieee.org/rs/211-FYL-955/images/IEEE_CertifAIEd_Ontological_Spec-Accountability-2022.pdf#:~:text=Abstract%3A%20The%20IEEE%20CertifAIEd%E2%84%A2%20criteria%20for%20certification%20in,ethical%20performance%20is%20the%20goal%20of%20this%20work.

[5] https://engagestandards.ieee.org/rs/211-FYL-955/images/IEEE%20CertifAIEd%20Ontological%20Spec-Algorithmic%20Bias-2022%20%5BI1.3%5D.pdf#:~:text=Abstract%3A%20The%20IEEE%20CertifAIEd%E2%84%A2%20criteria%20for%20certification%20in,ethical%20performance%20is%20the%20goal%20of%20this%20work.

[6] https://engagestandards.ieee.org/rs/211-FYL-955/images/IEEE%20CertifAIEd%20Ontological%20Spec-Transparency-2022.pdf#:~:text=Abstract%3A%20The%20IEEE%20CertifAIEd%E2%84%A2%20criteria%20for%20certification%20in,ethical%20performance%20is%20the%20goal%20of%20this%20work.

[7] https://engagestandards.ieee.org/rs/211-FYL-955/images/IEEESTD-2022%20CertifAIEd%20Privacy.pdf

inclusive to ensure that accountability is kept "human centric," i.e., humans at the heart of it and humans in the loop of AI governance and cognizant of real human impact based on the variety of human experiences and expertise.

- Ethical accountability is of a multidimensional nature. What and who is accountable and responsible for an action or omission in an organization depends on the structure of the organization, the roles held within the organization, the clarity of reporting lines, and how well supervised or not staff (or contractors) are within an organization. Furthermore, each role may interpret what is going on in an AI system differently depending on their own expertise and experience, and the interaction between colleagues in any governance construct may also be susceptible for group and power dynamics—both positively and negatively.
- Attitudes, behaviors, culture, and institutionalized norms and practices have a role to play in accountability. Poor behaviors, culture, and perceived normalized practices in an organization can lead to a vicious circle. In contrast, good behaviors, a culture that takes responsibility and seeks to do better and be ethical, and an environment of seeking excellence and best practice can lead to a virtuous circle. The presumption here is that poor and unethical practices ultimately lead to bad outcomes.
- Upholding law is seen as complementary to accountability as failure to comply with law tends to result in enforcement of better practices and/or liability. Depending on whether law exists to hold organizations to account, or whether it goes far enough, will determine how much it would truly overlap with ethical accountability. That said, law tends to be promulgated in response to unethical behaviors and practices that are deemed unacceptable by a civilized society. While law in the area of AI is awaited, frameworks like CertifAIEd concerning accountability will be crucial in demonstrating the trustworthiness of organizations in their design, development, and deployment (as well as decommissioning) of AI systems.

2.8 Algorithmic Bias

According to the IEEE's CertifAIEd ontological specification, the distinction between algorithmic bias in the context of an AI system and ethical algorithmic bias is:

> **Algorithmic bias**: Automated recommendations and predictions that disproportionately favor one stakeholder entity over another. This may be a negative unethical bias that prevents fair access to education, employment, health care, and economic enfranchisement. It may be a positive ethical bias that weights the AIS and its data use to recommend and predict fair outcomes for identified stakeholders within the context of use for the AIS.
>
> **Ethical algorithmic bias**: A contextual set of values pertaining to a framework of expectations that ensures algorithmic biases that negatively impact individuals, communities, and society have established boundaries of acceptance to protect autonomy and freedoms, where autonomy is defined by one's capacity to direct one's life.

This framing of algorithmic bias and ethical algorithmic bias recognizes that some bias is wanted and desirable and some bias is unwanted and chiefly negative in its results. Important to note that algorithmic bias does contribute to unfair outcomes but is not the sole measure of unfairness. To elaborate on how ethical algorithmic bias can be interpreted in the context of a CertifAIED certification:

- Bias can be introduced and reintroduced at any point during the AI life cycle. To that end, it is important to implement interventions to counterbalance and counteract negative bias, to preserve personhood and individual autonomy.
- It concerns bias that affects humans, so recognizing that bias is a chiefly human endeavor, whether it is in the institutional, systemic, and historic data or again institutional, systemic, historic, cognitive, cultural (and the list goes on) rearing its unwanted head in relation to the designing, the development, the deployment, or even decommissioning of a system, bias is there. It is borne of people, about people, and impacting people.
- Ethical algorithmic bias ought to be complementary to areas of law, which are enforced concerning protection from discrimination and from having barriers to all important freedom. Like we have seen above, what the algorithmic bias may be preferencing or skewed in relation to may not always neatly fall within a protected characteristic, e.g., socioeconomic deprivation.
- Bias cannot realistically be eradicated, and sometimes having intentional and wanted bias is desirable.
- Removing protected characteristics and/or bias considerations may in some instances result in a "blind policy" approach being adopted in respect of an AI system, which itself may cause further bias problems and other undesirable outcomes from the AI system, including inadvertently or uncharacteristically identifying false positives or false negatives. More on the biased impacts of false positives and false negatives can be seen in Joy Buolamwini's papers concerning "Gender Shades" (Gender Shades, kein Datum) and the Netflix film "Coded Bias" (Coded Bias, 2020).

2.9 Transparency

According to the IEEE's CertifAIEd ontological specification, to put in place ethical transparency such that it is clear what an AI System does and how it does it, means:

> Ethical transparency: A contextual set of values pertaining to transparency and the satisfaction of a framework of expectations (preservation of autonomy, self-determination, and self-selected communities/locum and intimacies).

It recognizes that transparency is contextual and local context to the person endeavoring to provide as well as receive transparency and that context is pertinent to the understanding of the AI systems. Ethical transparency can be further interpreted in the context of a CertifAIEd certification as:

- Human centric: it must be transparent to humans and contextually relevant for humans.
- Norms and practices that can either work toward transparency or cause obfuscation and detract from transparency.
- Informational autonomy and empowerment to make informed decisions.
- Without transparency, law cannot easily be enforced, and law cannot be applied. The same applies in respect of ethical foundational requirements for CertifAIEd assessment. Law cannot be truly determined and applied without transparency. Furthermore, without transparency, accountability, privacy, and algorithmic bias protections cannot be easily applied. In short, transparency is the cornerstone ethical requirement to most other ethical and legal requirements. It's foundational.

2.10 Ethical Privacy

According to the IEEE's CertifAIEd ontological specification, to safeguard privacy in an AI system means to go above and beyond mere what is legally required but to consider all facets of the private sphere of a person including their data and to understand them contextually to that person. Ethical privacy is therefore:

> A contextual set of values pertaining to privacy and the satisfaction of a framework of expectations (preservation of autonomy, self-determination, and self-selected communities/ locum and intimacies).

Context matters and privacy are no less contextual in respect of (1) what is being disclosed or hidden and (2) the context of what the item(s) are that are being disclosed or hidden and indeed (3) where the privacy is being exerted such as in the home or in one's home life. For example, people consider information about their sexual health or orientation, religion or belief or political associations, and biometrics as sensitive personal data. In contrast, while not always sensitive, financial information is often deemed highly confidential and socially may be taboo to talk about. Furthermore, information about who a person is friends or associates with or which sports clubs they belong to may be seen as private but less sensitive depending on their context and what is intended to be done with the information.

Ethical privacy is not just about personal data being protected under legislation like EU GDPR; it is about going beyond the law, exploring the rights and freedoms of individuals and the collective. It is keeping privacy human centered rather than merely data centered.

To elaborate more on what ethical privacy means and how it can be interpreted in the context of a CertifAIEd certification:

- Ethical privacy is highly contextual and is affected by a variety of dimensions, including but not limited to geographical, cultural, and matters pertinent to ethnicity. An example of the latter might be concerning the Maori people and their ethical data principles. They understand personal data being an extension of themselves and their personhood, requiring special privacy and treatment. Personal data for people of Maori ethnicity operates in an especially sacred space.
- What is considered worthy of privacy (or a right or wrong behavior in relation to a person's privacy) can in some jurisdictions be dictated by local laws but can also be determined by localized social, cultural, and moral norms, ethics, and principles.
- Ethics is human focused, so ethical privacy is human centric.
- Ethical privacy does overlap and complements data protection, privacy, and human rights laws, but ethical privacy takes considerations beyond what the law requires, often the law being very data centric or confidentiality centric (recognizing in some common law jurisdictions that privacy entails torts of peeping tom, publication of private facts, defamation, and misappropriation) as opposed to considering wider aspects of interference with personhood or unverified or intrusive inference about personhood.
- It pertains to all aspects of privacy, including physical, emotional, spiritual, psychological, thought-life, economic, and cultural, and within the inner sphere whether in the life analogue or the life online, beyond simple informational privacy and data and data protection concerns.
- Privacy is not always a matter of upholding individual identity or dignity but can pertain to a group or community beyond that of the individual person.
- It recognizes the power in privacy and its correlation with self-determination and autonomy.
- Ethical privacy is something that aligns with a person's personal expectations but also pertains to the integrity of self, the group, or the community.
- Failure to uphold ethical privacy can lead to human dignity being undermined and a greater dependency or reliance on the use of technology, which may determine inclusive or exclusive behaviors.

3 Application of the Principles and the Governance Operational Model

Standards providing details of process, practices, and procedures, coupled with the IEEE CertifAIEd frameworks, can provide a great deal of practical guidance and reference tool on how accountability, algorithmic bias, transparency, and privacy (amongst other tenets of governance) can be mapped, managed, mitigated, and monitored both from the top-down and the bottom-up.

Putting ethical principles into practice realistically needs a "champion" at the very top of an organization (usually C-suite level) who would drive the organizations to put principles into practice and to be ultimately accountable for governance and the outcomes AI produces. For any governance framework to be effective, it will require financial resourcing and capacity, capability, and competence and a number of other roles and responsibilities across the organization (preferably dedicated personnel and teams) to also be responsible for the AI being managed and monitored on a day-to-day basis. It will also require participation and understanding of the impacts on stakeholders, especially those who are to be impacted by or influenced by the AI system(s) subject to the governance.

For citizens, it means demanding that AI-based public services be fair and transparent. To keep up, public bodies will have to adopt. Companies providing AI-based solutions and establishing internal criteria and measures that cannot be independently verified will not be able to provide a genuine guarantee that the expected criteria are satisfied.

In the fast-changing AI environment, it is important to be innovative, and standards development organizations are no exception. Currently, it can take years to finalize a standard so that it is ready to certify the conformity of products or services. Sometimes AI development and deployment require only a few months; to wait years is unacceptable. Therefore, the development of standards and conformity assessment criteria needs to become more agile so that it can adapt to changes faster.

For this to happen, AI systems developers need new ways to collaborate and achieve consensus faster. Currently, IEEE's CertifAIEd program uses a model-based graphical capture and representation approach for the principal concepts and factors that foster or inhibit the attainment of the desired aim, such as transparency. This allows rapid tailoring to the needs of a sector, such as finance, or a specific use case, such as fraud detection.

4 Use Case: Wiener Stadtwerke (The IEEE CertifAIEd Framework for AI Ethics Applied to the City of Vienna, 2021)

IEEE CertifAIEd's first real-world test was completed in a pilot project between IEEE Standards Association (IEEE SA) and Wiener Stadtwerke. Wiener Stadtwerke is a public service provider owned by the City of Vienna, providing services in the areas of public transport, electricity, natural gas, heating, telecommunications, parking, burial, and cemeteries, to more than two million customers in the Vienna metropolitan region.

In recent years, the Wiener Stadtwerke group has explored several ideas for using AI technology in pilot projects, always adhering to the overall goal of efficiently delivering high-quality services to the citizens of Vienna. One of these was selected for thorough ethical evaluation in the IEEE CertifAIEd pilot with IEEE SA. This is an email classification system (ECS), which is used to automatically assign categories to incoming customer service requests.

The customer service department of Wien Energie (an energy provider belonging to the Wiener Stadtwerke group) receives more than 1000 email requests per day, which need to be briefly skimmed over by a person and assigned to one of about 15 categories. This categorization results in tickets assigned to different teams for processing, where every email is read by a human operator, who will then determine and initiate the appropriate actions and send a reply to the customer. The manual pre-categorization procedure amounts to one person's entire work time per day, even when less than 30 seconds are spent per email. And it is a very repetitive, monotonous, and tiring task. The ECS was developed to automate this pre-categorization step, effectively relieving one customer service operator to focus on actual customer interaction again and thus making better use of their qualifications and training.

Because the described manual procedure has been applied for years, an excellent data collection of several hundred thousand emails with manual category assignments by experts was readily available, providing a very promising starting position for a machine learning approach to the problem. Therefore, a group-internal project was initiated in 2019 to explore the possibility to develop an automatic categorization system from scratch, which gradually led via increasingly mature prototypes to a production-ready email classification system.

5 Assessment of Wiener Stadtwerke's Email Classification System

The first step in the evaluation process was to thoroughly explain the system and its context to a panel of five IEEE experts, including the background and goals of the project, the system's architecture and interfaces, the machine learning component, and the data used for model training, as well as the effects of the new system on people and processes in the organization.

Based on this information, a risk assessment according to the IEEE CertifAIEd framework was conducted. For each of 26 ethical values such as transparency, dignity, trust, and (avoidance of) discrimination, the expert panel rated the likelihood of the ECS to undermine that ethical value, considering concrete potential scenarios in the system's deployment in the Wiener Stadtwerke context. The results of this risk analysis were used to determine the most relevant of the four IEEE CertifAIEd criteria sets for the application—accountability in the case of the ECS. Furthermore, the overall low-risk class of the system resulting from the risk assessment meant that only a subset of the accountability criteria set needed to be addressed in the following step.

Next IEEE SA provided a list of 43 ethical criteria with brief definitions to Wiener Stadtwerke, who were then to provide evidence for each criterion, showing that the respective ethical question or issue is adequately addressed in the system and its context. These criteria range from rather technical aspects such as error analysis, hyperparameter tuning, and mitigation of false positives to more governance-related aspects concerning the organization, such as adopting a layered approach; avoidance of inaction, delay, and indifference; and human authority and autonomy.

For each of the 43 criteria, Wiener Stadtwerke provided evidence in the form of technical documentation, system architecture and software implementation details, screenshots, meeting slides and meeting minutes, internal and public reports, strategy papers, process and role definitions, organigrams, etc., giving full detail for the respective criterion. A so-called Case for Ethics document was compiled, using a structure and template provided by IEEE SA, where Wiener Stadtwerke provided general information about the system, its background, scope, etc. (similar to step one, but in written and structured form), as well as all the evidence for the 43 accountability criteria. This Case for Ethics, a 150-page document, was then submitted to IEEE for assessment.

Finally, an assessment report was delivered back to Wiener Stadtwerke by IEEE SA. This included specific feedback for each of the 43 criteria from the expert panel members, indicating to what degree the respective criterion was considered fulfilled and what could be done to further improve in the respective area. It also included an overall confirmation that the submitted Case for Ethics justifies recognition and certification through the IEEE CertifAIEd program for Wiener Stadtwerke's email classification system. The expert panel feedback contained also pointers to things that could be further improved.

6 Conclusions

Digital humanism should result in the development and use of trustworthy and sustainable digital solutions. This brings a range of responsibilities that technical communities of developers and engineers alone do not have the need to adopt in isolation. Enablers with a combination of organizational, cultural, and technical skills have the ability to come up with technically based value propositions that align with the ethics and values of their application domain stakeholders. Thus, the governance and risk management structures within organizations will be ultimately responsible for implementing standards, best practices, and audits, as well as training programs and certification for the people who develop and use high-risk systems.

As such, technical and socio-technical standards, and certifications, developed in an open and transparent paradigm, can establish evidence of the extent to which systems and ecosystem stakeholders conform with upcoming regulation or agreed principles. Such standards and certifications would serve as reliable and important governance instruments for regulators, industry, and the ordinary citizen.

In the current dynamic context, effective and efficient standardization, certification, and appropriate governance structures are indispensable elements of a trustworthy ecosystem. We have shown that these elements complement and facilitate the development of responsible regulatory frameworks that guarantee both the uptake of AI systems and address the risks associated with certain uses of this new technology, such as currently assessed by the Council of Europe or the European Commission.

An ethical future—this is a journey, not a one-stop shop. Not only for the businesses designing, developing, deploying, and monitoring AI but also those who procure it and use it as well as those that become the future ethical and responsible AI practitioners.

As AI is borderless, an ethical future also requires interoperability—clearly recognized global standards to provide for consistency and certainty while adapting and being flexible enough to local ethics and values and being contextually relevant.

Finally, there is also a need to train for the jobs of the future, which will likely be multidisciplinary and require interdisciplinarity. Skills will need to cover not only the creation of technologies but also the governance, oversight, as well as the development of policies, laws, principles, standards, certification, conformity assessment, and audit. Future jobs may include value leads, AI ethics certifiers, and auditors. This needs AI ethics literacy, ongoing education, and identification of the skill sets necessary for future competent assessors and trainers in these areas. IEEE (among other bodies) can provide sector and technology-related professional education to skill the future generations. At a given point, this should become a part of mainstream education. In the meantime, raising awareness of AI outcomes and potential risks for people and planet, increasing technical understanding accompanied with the ability to critique the outcomes (both legal and ethical, short term, medium term, and long term) is vital.

Discussion Questions for Students and Their Teachers

1. Mapping AI ethics risks—assessment of risk, impact, scope, and likelihood or severity of an AI system (Table 1)
2. Consequence scanning—an agile practice for responsible innovators (https://doteveryone.org.uk/project/consequence-scanning/).

   Using this tool considers the scope of the ethical risks in short, medium, and long term to a wide variety of potential actors and stakeholders

Table 1 Mapping AI ethics risk matrix (Reproduced with the permission of the copyright holder Beyond Reach Consulting Limited)

Risk	**What is the impact / outcome of the risk?** *(The risk could have multiple impacts (or could be an outcome from an impact) and impact stakeholders differently or have different effects in different application domains and contexts)*	**Scope of impact** *(How many people/how much could it impact)*	**Likelihood** *(How likely is the risk to occur)*	**Severity** *(If the risk were to occur, how severe would that that impact be)*

Table 2 Plotting responsibility (hose responsible, accountable, consulted, or informed (RACI)) to ethical foundation requirements matrix (Reproduced with the permission of the copyright holder Beyond Reach Consulting Limited)

Description of Effect	Stakeholder affected	Describe the requirements necessary to manage /mitigate /monitor that effect	Describe where in the AI lifecycle could those requirements be best managed/mitigated/mon itored	Consider who is best placed to manage /monitor and mitigate them (RACI)

Table 3 Interventions matrix (Reproduced with the permission of the copyright holder Beyond Reach Consulting Limited)

Risk / Lifecycle Stage	Ideation	Data	Design	Development	Deployment	Ongoing use over time	Decommissi oning	Third Party

3. Plotting requirements and responsibility
   To help keep accountability at the forefront of AI governance, assign and align every AI governance requirement to manage, mitigate, and manage an AI ethics risk to a responsible person(s) (Table 2)
4. List interventions and strategies to help your organization to manage, mitigate, and monitor risks at each stage of the AI System life cycle (Table 3)

Learning Resources for Students

The following reading material is intended to deepen the knowledge on different instruments that can be used to develop a responsible AI governance framework within organizations. These instruments should cover the different stages of the AI life cycle, from design to deployment, and include context-specific guidelines, standards, and/or certification frameworks.

1. Value-Based Engineering: A Guide to Building Ethical Technology for Humanity (De Gruyter Textbook) | Spiekermann, Sarah | ISBN: 9783110793369
2. iTechlaw's Responsible AI Impact Assessment (RAIIA) tool which can be downloaded from here: https://www.itechlaw.org/ResponsibleAI

3. IEEE ontological frameworks

   Ethical Accountability: https://engagestandards.ieee.org/rs/211-FYL-955/images/IEEE_CertifAIEd_Ontological_Spec-Accountability-2022.pdf?mkt_tok=MjExLUZZTC05NTUAAAGETQHvhqRyJpxehbsTfVHQ3D88oTpizkK-2u0p4IDJF3zbJ2AphqtpsegAVyn4nDEKjPk0H2KzBB2xsikYm4E6Ty1rRyAEumWnb2dvifyEeQ

   Ethical Algorithmic Bias: https://engagestandards.ieee.org/rs/211-FYL-955/images/IEEE%20CertifAIEd%20Ontological%20Spec-Algorithmic%20Bias-2022%20%5BI1.3%5D.pdf?mkt_tok=MjExLUZZTC05NTUAAAGETQHvhWI31Wh8NNeK8rkpq3xDImplIZIV2E_hi3EUhWHL0RzJiSjqTZ_ueYqb0rJ-SKu4_kYgMAWygZyF80qPdxUb_ybwLQIAKOaUGV2JeA

   Ethical Transparency: https://engagestandards.ieee.org/rs/211-FYL-955/images/IEEE%20CertifAIEd%20Ontological%20Spec-Transparency-2022.pdf?mkt_tok=MjExLUZZTC05NTUAAAGETQHvhk2i97UsPFNbzH3-oUDVx_Qk4KdQUdyon6YHLAzDYUx54JOVCY_Oxr2-CwxIAZN7tiaq36aSCV-rKj8pEOG5EPG91AjUBuQBemt5uA

   Ethical Privacy: https://engagestandards.ieee.org/rs/211-FYL-955/images/IEEESTD-2022%20CertifAIEd%20Privacy.pdf?mkt_tok=MjExLUZZTC05NTUAAAGETQHvhbqJ92qFvqon29PnOA4jYmt9VhwjD6oz0WT2NzwiyjUGtBsO8Q5P3TjdT4NwuDIX5E-yRgoUOAadgENoa8mdUn9Fenk3Zb0JV4m-BQ
4. AI Watch: Artificial Intelligence Standardization Landscape Update https://publications.jrc.ec.europa.eu/repository/handle/JRC131155
5. OECD AI Policy Observatory: https://oecd.ai/en/
6. AlgorithmWatch AI Guidelines Global observatory https://algorithmwatch.org/en/ai-ethics-guidelines-global-inventory/
7. Corporate Digital Responsibility—an international manifesto for businesses: https://corporatedigitalresponsibility.net/cdr-manifesto
8. UK's Digital Catapult AI Ethics Framework https://migarage.digicatapult.org.uk/ethics/ethics-framework/
9. Robotics and AI Laws conf, Standardization and AI 30th May 2022 https://ai-laws.org/2022/08/09/conference-report-4th-rails-conference/?lang=en
10. Data Governance—governing data for sustainable business, Alison Holt, published by BCS, The Chartered Institute for IT https://shop.bcs.org/store/221/detail/WorkGroupByIsbn/9781780173757
11. The AI Book by Fintech Circle, Chapter 7 Trust, Transparency and Ethics - Good Governance of AI by Patricia Shaw https://fintechcircle.com/ai-book/

References

Coded Bias. (2020). *Coded Bias.* Accessed May 15, 2023, from https://www.codedbias.com

Gender Shades. (n.d.). *mit media lab.* Accessed May 15, 2023, from https://www.media.mit.edu/projects/gender-shades/publications/

IEEE 7000™-2021 Standard - Addressing Ethical Concerns During Systems Design. (2023). *IEEE SA - Standards Association.* Accessed May 15, 2023, from https://engagestandards.ieee.org/ieee-7000-2021-for-systems-design-ethical-concerns.html

OECD AI Global Principles Overview. (n.d.) *OECD.AI - Policy Observatory.* Accessed May 15, 2023, from https://oecd.ai/en/ai-principles

The IEEE CertifAIEd Framework for AI Ethics Applied to the City of Vienna. (2021). *IEEE SA - Standards Association.* Accessed May 15, 2023, from https://standards.ieee.org/beyond-standards/the-ieee-certifaied-framework-for-ai-ethics-applied-to-the-city-of-vienna/

Value-Sensitive Software Design: Ethical Deliberation in Agile Development Processes

N. Zuber, J. Gogoll, S. Kacianka, J. Nida-Rümelin, and A. Pretschner

Abstract This chapter discusses the integration of ethical deliberations within agile software development processes. It emphasizes the importance of considering ethical implications during the development of software, not just AI. The chapter proposes modes of reflection and deliberation that include disclosive, weighing, and applicative modes of contemplation. It argues that these three kinds of thinking are guided by different normative values. The chapter suggests that agile development is an excellent starting point for implementing ethical deliberations, as it allows for continuous reflection and learning. It also proposes that development teams can perform this task themselves up to a point with proper guidance. This section further discusses the potential of agile processes to naturally accommodate ethical deliberation. However, it also acknowledges the challenges associated with implementing agile processes, especially in the context of machine learning models.

N. Zuber (✉) · J. Gogoll
Bavarian Research Institute for Digital Transformation, Munich, Germany
e-mail: niina.zuber@bidt.digital; jan.gogoll@bidt.digital

S. Kacianka
Technical University of Munich, Garching b. München, Germany
e-mail: kacianka@in.tum.de

J. Nida-Rümelin
Bavarian Research Institute for Digital Transformation, Munich, Germany

LMU Munich, Munich, Germany
e-mail: Julian.Nida-Ruemelin@lrz.uni-muenchen.de

A. Pretschner
Bavarian Research Institute for Digital Transformation, Munich, Germany

Technical University of Munich, Garching b. München, Germany
e-mail: alexander.pretschner@tum.de

H. Werthner et al. (eds.), *Introduction to Digital Humanism*,
https://doi.org/10.1007/978-3-031-45304-5_22

1 Introduction

The widespread societal interest in the potential of artificial intelligence, and machine learning in particular, has sparked a renewed debate on technology ethics. Similar discussions have previously taken place in the areas of preimplantation diagnostics, cloning, and nuclear and genetic engineering. The core question in such debates is which values we should take into account while designing and developing technology and also whether and to what extent we should allow the technology at all. The basic problem is not new: the development of technology already raised philosophically relevant questions in Aristotle's times, which he addresses in his Nicomachean Ethics. An independent systematic approach of the philosophy of technology in the modern era was introduced by Ernst Kapp (1877) in the second half of the nineteenth century. Since then, philosophy-of-technology considerations and approaches have been discussed under various names with different facets: technology assessment, value-sensitive design, responsibility-driven design, etc. (Friedman et al., 2017; Grunwald, 2010; Van den Hoeven et al., 2015). The growing recognition that software is assuming decision-making responsibilities in various aspects of life, or at the very least, providing decision-making assistance to system users, has engendered a feeling of reduced control. This realization contributes to the increasing significance of technology ethics.

To a software engineer, it comes as a surprise that the current ethics debate focuses on AI and, with few exceptions such as the ISO 4748-7000:2022 standard on addressing ethical concerns during system design (ISO, 2022), *not on software in general*: Doesn't such a focus on AI falsely suggest that it is *not* necessary to consider values when developing ego shooter games, cryptocurrencies, file-sharing platforms, corona warn apps, or user interfaces for video platforms that are implemented without any form of AI? On the other hand, there indeed are specific ethical challenges associated with AI. However, from a systems perspective, whether a piece of software is using classic algorithms or machine-learned models seems secondary to the implementation of values. Yet, in the second case, another artifact, the training data, must of course be considered operationally. *Explainability* is often cited as a relevant criterion—but whether a complex algorithm in a distributed system such as a car is really that much easier to understand and hence less dangerous and more transparent than a learned decision tree or a trained neural network is a matter of divided opinion (see, e.g., Felderer & Ramler (2021) for classic systems and Elish (2010) for a discussion on machine learning systems). Either way, ethical values are embedded in machines through the design and programming choices made by their creators and developers. For example, when developing a machine learning model, the training data reflects past values, norms, and biases. Ignoring this will perpetuate them into the future. Additionally, the deployment and use of the technology has ethical implications, such as in the case of facial recognition technology that has been criticized for its potential for invasion of privacy and biased outcomes. As a result, it is important for developers, organizations, and users to consider the ethical implications of their technology and make choices that align with their values and the values of society. This sort of reasoning is called an ethical deliberation.

In this chapter, we will address the question of how to implement ethical deliberations within software development. It turns out that agile development is an excellent starting point (Zuber et al., 2022).

Earlier versions of our considerations on ethics in agile development have been discussed by Pretschner et al. (2021). This chapter specifically emphasizes the philosophical foundations.

2 Codes of Conduct and Software Development

In the last 10 years, more than 100 codes of conduct for software development have been developed by professional associations, companies, NGOs, and scientists. These codes essentially state more or less universally accepted values such as participation, transparency, fairness, etc. (Gogoll et al., 2021). Values are characterized by a high degree of abstraction, which leaves their concrete implications unclear. In software engineering, these codes do not provide the degree of practical orientation that software practitioners are hoping for. They do not provide engineers with immediate instructions for action and often leave them perplexed. Interestingly, the aforementioned codes of conduct often set individual values, such as fairness or transparency, without justification, which could help explain the discomfort of engineers in the face of the lack of concreteness. The implementation of these values is also simple, as long as it does not lead to contradictions, costs, or efforts, i.e., to trade-offs: What is wrong with "transparency"? Nothing—until transparency collides with privacy (or accuracy). There is also nothing to be said against the decision not to develop a guidance system for unmanned aerial vehicles—but the discussion becomes much harder when it leads to lost sales and the need to cut jobs. Thus, the descriptive formulation of isolated values alone is clearly insufficient.

The lack of immediate applicability lies in the nature of things and cannot be avoided. On the one hand, values are formulated in an abstract way. On the other hand, software is very context-specific, ranging from pacemakers over videoconferencing software to visual pedestrian detection systems. This means that software *engineering* is highly dependent on the context, too (Briand et al. 2017). This implies that we have to apply abstract ideas in a concrete context. Due to their abstract nature, Codes of Conduct hence cannot be a tool that provides step-by-step instructions of an ethical implementation of values in software that fits all contexts. Therefore, the embedding of values in software (development) must always be done on a case-by-case basis and tailored to the concrete context. Such a casuistic endeavor yearns for training in ethical reasoning and in practices that ensure ethical thinking to be a part of the daily development routine. In such a sense, Codes of Conducts address a work ethos by highlighting desirable attitudes that developers and designers need to have themselves. Hence, the focus shifts from ethically desirable products to ethically designing products.

In the following, we argue that agile software development is *particularly* suited to allow for a case-specific consideration of values as it can foster ethical deliberation and that ethical deliberations can, in turn, close the gap that the Codes of Conducts must leave open. This does, of course, not mean that non-agile development settings cannot embody ethical considerations as many ideas also apply to non-agile development processes. However, it turns out that the key ideas behind agile development blend surprisingly well with ethical deliberations.

3 Ethical Deliberation

Our challenge is to effectively incorporate ethical concepts into software development processes and thus the software products. This is no straightforward task when morally desirable software is intuitively difficult to identify and examine. As outlined before, it is impossible to define general decisive measures on how to implement and evaluate technology according to ethical criteria due to the context specificity of software and underdetermination of values (Gogoll et al., 2021). This means that we cannot simply create an algorithm that will produce an ethically good outcome. Ethical considerations cannot be resolved by only using checklists or with the help of predefined answers (ibid.) either. Therefore, it remains indispensable to continuously evaluate each new design project from its inception, throughout the development process, its deployment, operations, and its maintenance. Or, to put it another way, we need to normatively weigh, judge, and practically argue throughout the entire life cycle. This is what Brey calls anticipatory ethics and the reason why Floridi and Sanders formulate a proactive ethics (Brey, 2000, 2010, 2012; Floridi & Sanders, 2005). Broadly speaking, their approaches address the necessity of an active ethical stance while designing and developing digital artifacts in contrast to an ex-post ethical technology assessment. To stress the point: even if we had ethically good software, this assessment might change if the software or the operational context changed. For example, when Instagram was launched, it was obviously not started with the goal of making teenagers feel insecure regarding their physical appearance. Yet, when the context of the app changes, the developers need to reevaluate, e.g., how they present photos or if they should show the number of likes on a given photo.

Firstly, we need to identify the values we consider desirable. In fact, codes of conduct may be a good starting point here. Secondly, we need to know how to apply values in particular cases. Hence, we need to understand how to translate ethical values in technical language. This remains the task of a trained techno-ethical judgment (Nida-Rümelin, 2017; Rohbeck, 1993). What does that mean? On the one hand, we need to venture into ethical concepts as well as specific technical know-how, and on the other hand, we need a structure, a praxis, in which we can apply this hands-on knowledge. Thereby, praxis refers to the practical application of knowledge or theory to real-world situations. It is relevant to highlight that we often can perform an ethical deliberation without the use of classical ethical theories. We call such an endeavor pre-theoretical ethical deliberation that orientates itself at empirical input and is less principle-driven. However, also such a pre-theoretical thinking needs to follow rational rules and standards, whereas it cannot be a mere brainstorming process or stream of consciousness.

In the following, we argue that agile software development, especially when paired with an agile product life cycle that includes DevOps, enables a case-specific consideration of norms and values, promotes ethical deliberations, and can thus close the gap that the codes of conduct necessarily leave open. Agile development can be used to establish a desirable praxis by implementing ethical deliberations to achieve a desired outcome, namely, a morally valuable digital product.

4 Individual Responsibility of the Software Engineer

Before doing so, we must briefly consider who actually bears responsibility in the development and use of software-intensive systems. In the spectrum from complete societal systems to the single individual, there are several actors who can and must take responsibility (Nida-Rümelin, 2011, 2017; Nissenbaum, 1994, 1996): society, the organization developing the system and its subdivisions, the individual developer, the operator, and the user of that system. For example, a specific form of facial recognition may be accepted or rejected by society; an organization may choose to develop systems to identify faces from a certain ethnicity; a developer selects data and algorithms; and both the operator and user bear responsibility for possible misuse of that system. Care robots represent another classic example. Let us remember that our considerations go beyond AI as spelt out by the examples in the introduction: computer games, blockchain-based applications, warn apps, and the like.

Clearly, software engineers are not solely responsible. And above all, they are not responsible for all potential externalities: software engineers are not single-handedly responsible for the fact that the widespread use of Airbnb led to distortions in the housing market or that the existence of Uber leads to an increase in non-public transport. Yet, they do have some responsibility. The perception of their individual responsibility is what our approach is about.

Deliberation is performed by various roles: (1) persons who are well aware of technological possibilities and constraints, most often developers, are our focus; (2) persons who are capable of making normative reasoning explicit in certain societal subsystems, most often ethicists; (3) empirical researchers, such as domain specific experts, i.e., development psychologists, economists, and biologists; and (4) stakeholders, such as customers, users, or indirectly affected individuals. While we highlight normative modes of thinking and are claiming that those capacities need to be trained, we are well aware that even if developers are trained in normative reasoning, the deliberation teams will be dependent on the knowledge of experts from various fields to access domain-specific knowledge regarding the implementation of the product in their respective domain.

5 Agile Software Development

In addition to the guiding theme of simplicity, we argue that agile software development and especially agility as an organizational culture can be roughly simplified to four essential phenomena: planning, incrementality, empowerment, and learning (also see Farley, 2022).

First, there is the idea that at the famous conference on software engineering in 1968 in Garmisch, central characteristics of the production of industrial goods, and hardware in particular, were transferred to software. Notably, the separation of design and the subsequent production is such a fundamental concept, the adoption of which was reflected in software development methodologies like the waterfall model and the V-model. In these contexts, design documents are long-term planning artifacts. Yet, software is generally much more flexible than industrial goods, is not subject to a complex process of mass production, and thus requires and also enables rapid reaction to changing requirements and contexts. For this reason, among others, the separation between planning/design and production was reversed in the 1990s by concepts of agility, where planning was interwoven with production. Long-term plannability was considered to be an illusion: "Developers and project managers often live (and are forced to) live a lie. They have to pretend that they can plan, predict and deliver, and then work the best way that they know to deliver the system" (Beedle et al., 1998). The focus was thus shifted from long-term planning, which was underpinned by artifacts such as requirements specifications and functional specifications, specifications, and target architectures, to very precise short-term planning at the sprint level, which was accompanied by a reduction in the number of artifacts to be developed (Beck et al., 2001).

Second, the realization that long-term planning is difficult to impossible in a world where requirements and technologies are constantly changing (and they *can* change because of the flexibility of software!) leads almost inevitably to incremental development. One cornerstone here is the idea to sequentially develop individual functionalities completely up till the end and then immediately integrate them with the respective (possibly legacy) system developed up until now. This is in contrast with a distributed approach where multiple functionalities are developed at the same time and where system integration necessarily takes place only late in the process. The idea of incremental development elegantly addresses the colossal software engineering problems of integrating subsystems, and it smoothly coincides with the ideas behind continuous integration and deployment.

Third, also as a consequence of the short-term rather than a long-term planning perspective, the organizational culture and the understanding of the role of employees is changing. In a worldview where fine-grained specification documents are handed over to "code monkeys" for implementation, there are "higher-level" activities that write specifications and "lower-level" activities that implement them. In this chapter, we will focus on the Scrum implementation of agile. Therefore, a short introduction into the framework is warranted.

Scrum is an agile framework that's primarily used in software development and project management. It encourages cross-functional teams to self-organize and make changes quickly, with a focus on iterative and incremental progress toward the project goal.

The Scrum framework is based on various key components. The Scrum Team comprises a Product Owner, Scrum Master, and Development Team. The Product Owner is tasked with maximizing the value of the product and interacts with the various stakeholders. The Scrum Master facilitates the use of Scrum within the team. The Development Team is responsible for creating the product increment. Sprints are time-boxed periods, usually lasting 2–4 weeks, within which a usable and potentially releasable product increment is created. The Product Backlog is a prioritized list of requirements, features, enhancements, and fixes to be developed, which is maintained by the Product Owner. Detailed Sprint Planning takes place at the start of each Sprint, where the team plans the work to be performed and commits to a Sprint Goal. The Daily Scrum, or Standup, is a 15-min meeting where the team reviews progress toward the Sprint Goal and plans for the next 24 h of work. At the end of each Sprint, a product-oriented Sprint Review takes place, where the team presents the work completed during the Sprint to stakeholders for feedback. Following this, a Sprint process-oriented Retrospective is conducted. The team reflects on the past Sprint, discussing what went well and what didn't, and plans improvements for the next Sprint. The central idea behind Scrum is to deliver valuable, high-quality work frequently and adapt to changes rapidly.

In a Scrum-based agile environment, the primary focus is on addressing high-level requirements, known as "user stories" in the product backlog instead of module specifications. This approach empowers teams with more extensive design capabilities right from the start and across various aspects of the system, which in turn is reflected in cross-functional teams. The team is empowered when compared to the world of the waterfall or V-model and has much greater freedom in its design activities. The team decides how a feature is developed—and can thus influence ethical outcomes. This ability to make decisions, in turn, has direct consequences for the structure of the organization, as it raises the question of what the role of "managers" at different hierarchical levels is in such a world. It also explains why agile software development in non-agile corporate structures regularly does not work as one might have hoped for. It is noteworthy that the *possibility* of ownership through empowerment is, in our eyes, also an *obligation* of ownership.

Fourth, a central idea behind agile ways of working is a culture that embraces error and a culture of learning. Agile organizations can only be successful if they rely on a cybernetic feedback loop. This idea is closely related to the emphasis on short-term planning: because of a (necessary) lack of knowledge, inadequate design decisions will likely be taken, and the development of functionality may very well show that a chosen (technical) path cannot be pursued further in this way. If this is accepted and, in this sense, "mistakes" are perceived as common occurrences, mechanisms for learning from these mistakes must be established. In Scrum, this is reflected in reviews and retrospectives and results in the need for constant empirical process control. In terms of implementing values, this means that an organization continuously learns and improves how to do this.

We do not want to give the impression here that agility is the silver bullet—there is no such thing. Among others, the size of projects, domains with regulated development processes and certifications, organization and logistics of production of hardware-based systems, and the ability and possible lack of desire of employees to work independently are natural and long-known stumbling blocks. Especially in the context of creating pure machine-learned models, it is not directly obvious what agile development actually means since the act of training models does not lend itself easily to an incremental and iterative workflow (unless training the model for one purpose becomes one sprint, which is the perspective we are taking in this paper). Also it is an open question how to map DevDops, and more specific approaches like MLOps, workflows onto agile processes. However, whenever agile processes are a fitting solution, also in situations where they are using machine-learned models, it turns out that the four facets of agile development mentioned above allow ethical deliberation to happen in a very natural way. The dual perspective of how characteristics of modern (agile) software production as such have ethical consequences is explored by Gürses and Van Hoboken (Gürses & Van Hoboken, 2017).

The success factors and characteristics of agility somehow collide with approaches such as the ISO 4748-7000:2022 standard on ethical systems development that explicitly does not consider agile approaches and suggests that all ethical issues can be identified before software is written. Our considerations above indicate that the move toward agile development processes happened for good reasons, which is why we embed our ethical deliberation into those processes rather than confine ourselves to rather static up-front planning methods. While they are suitable and maybe necessary in some contexts, more often than not, they necessarily slow down product development. We think that ethical deliberation needs to be part of development itself. Our approach is designed to scale with the speed of the overall process.

In agile environments, particularly in agile software development, teams operate with a high degree of autonomy within progressively flattened hierarchies. They independently develop features in brief cycles, guided more by broad user requirements than detailed system specifications. Empowerment now means that software engineers can and must have a direct influence on the consideration of values through technology. To a large extent, however, this normative procedure is only possible when concrete design decisions are pending, i.e., when software is already being developed, and not completely before development. Constant reflection and learning are almost by necessity part of an agile culture, into which ethical considerations can be seamlessly embedded.

In our approach, we have combined these pieces into an augmented Scrum process (Fig. 1). The core idea is that, before the regular agile cadence begins, in a sprint 0, we first proceed descriptively and align ourselves with societal and organizational value specifications, i.e., we start from a framework defined by society and organization. Second, in the relationship between the product owner and the client, central ethical values are identified within this framework on a project-specific

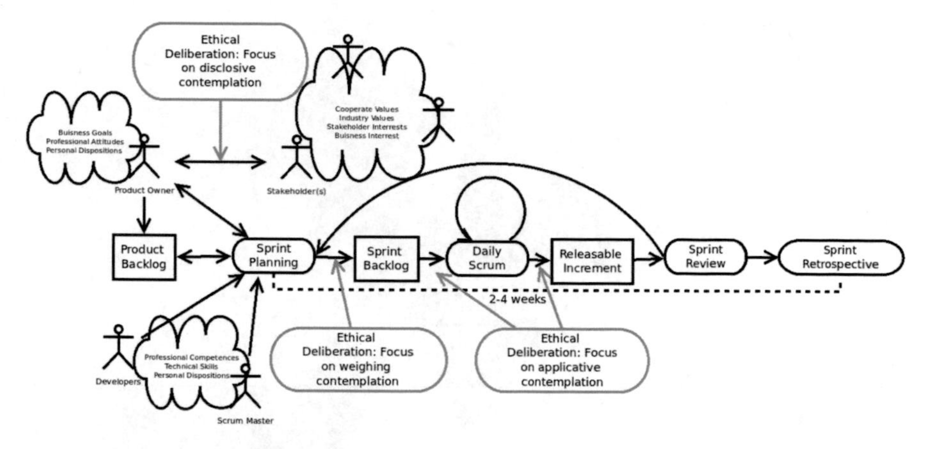

Fig. 1 Embedding ethical deliberations into Scrum; based on Zuber et al. (2022) http://creativecommons.org/licenses/by/4.0/

basis, if necessary, and become part of the product backlog. This can be done on the basis of existing codes of conduct or with other tools and methods that are specific to culture and context. We call this the normative horizon that is established during disclosive contemplation.

Within each individual sprint, it is a matter of identifying new values and implementing normative demands through suitable technical or organizational mechanisms. To do so, developers must continue to be clear about their value concepts in their totality in each sprint. In particular, to avoid risks and harms, they need to think about the consequences of a chosen methodology, a chosen solution approach, a chosen architecture, a chosen implementation, or a chosen data set. At this point, this is done much more concretely than it could have been done before the start of the development, because an increasingly detailed understanding of the system emerges here. Moreover, while reflecting on the implementation of values, it may of course be realized that further values need to be considered.

Let us first focus on disclosive contemplation. Disclosive reasoning is an epistemic endeavor. In this phase, thinking means to identify ethical relevant values within a transparent and opaque environment. Such a reflective process requires a different form of normative orientation: on one hand, one must take a look at the digital technology itself. On the other hand, one needs to analyze normative demands of a special sub-social system. Throughout the project, the product owner elicits technical requirements from the stakeholders, performing such an ethical deliberation, and adds them to the backlog, for example, as user stories. At the beginning of each sprint, the product owner, the developers, and the scrum master decide what backlog items to work on. In this process, they prioritize backlog items and focus on weighing contemplations. When a backlog item is implemented, single developers mainly need applicative reasoning to decide technical realizations. After each sprint, each increment is reviewed with the customer and relevant stakeholders in the sprint review meeting. Finally, the process is reviewed in the sprint retrospective. This

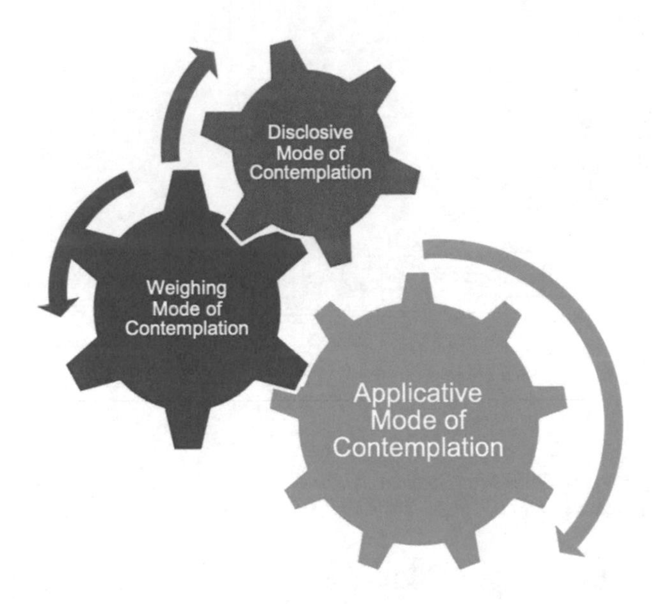

Fig. 2 Ethical deliberation encompasses three modes of contemplation

might also be followed with backlog grooming by the product owner to restructure and revise the backlog for future sprints.

Not all values can be implemented in individual sprints through code alone. For instance, if transparency is a value to be implemented, then a socio-technical accountability infrastructure may be one solution. By definition, such a solution is likely to affect policies, procedures, roles and responsibilities, and ultimately the culture of an organization that cannot be implemented by code in individual sprints alone.

We hinted above that ethical arguments become interesting when they conflict with other moral, aesthetic, or economic arguments that need to be considered during deliberation. Such conflicts sometimes lead to dilemma situations, which by definition cannot be resolved, but only decided, which is why it is necessary not to prolong this discussion arbitrarily but to come to a result just within the planning of a sprint.

This process is a context-specific process of reflection and deliberation, which must be structured accordingly and carried out permanently (Fig. 2). There is a proposal to permanently include an "embedded ethicist" (McLennan et al., 2020) in development teams. This seems too heavyweight to us, as it quickly seems too expensive for smaller companies, and there also is a general shortage of people with these skills that cannot be addressed quickly. With proper guidance, we believe that development teams can perform this task themselves up to a point. This is exactly what our approach aims to do: it includes the lightweight identification, localization, and critical reflection of relevant values. While the former represent a descriptive phase, the latter is already essentially normative. At the same time, technical feasibility or even intentional abstinence must always be discussed. We can systematically accompany this process in order to arrive at well-founded decisions and technical solutions. This does not always require a scientific-ethical analysis as we often reach a desirable level of ethical deliberation with pre-theoretical knowledge.

6 Ethical Deliberation in Agile Processes

The techno-ethical judgment must necessarily encompass three modes of contemplation (Fig. 2): disclosive, weighing, and applicative. First, we must recognize normatively relevant facts, i.e., we pursue an epistemic endeavor. We cannot assume that looking at Codes of Conduct, stakeholder surveys, or intuitive brainstorming is sufficient. Each of these, in itself, has its justification, but also its shortcomings (Gogoll et al., 2021). The judgment of the *disclosive contemplation* must be comprehensible for everyone. Only in the form of a rational argument can we justify our focus on specific facts (Blackman, 2022). The *weighing mode of contemplation* refers to decision-making. The objective is to balance normative arguments in order to arrive at a well-reasoned decision. It is essential that the values identified through observation can be technically executed or incorporated. The third mode is the *applicative mode of contemplation*: It requires contemplating how to translate values into technical *functionality*. Thus, the third mode requires a contemplation from values to translation activity aiming at technical functionality or technical solutionism. All three modes of contemplation are not to be thought of linearly. In fact, they can alternate and sometimes overlap: it is more like a back and forth.

First, we compile all the values from the internal ethical guidelines and other association guidelines. Initially, this is a descriptive approach. It does not make any further assessment and does not question the values found.

In the relationship between product owner and the client, if necessary, project-specific central values will be identified and become part of the product backlog. This can be based on existing codes of conduct, as well as on culturally and context-specific tools and methods. The main reason to do this early in the development life cycle is to ensure that everyone is on the same page and no one works on a project that goes against their core values. However, not only values are of interest, but moral requirements, social norms, and desirable virtues and practices must also be able to find consideration in a moral evaluation. Furthermore, possible consequences of the use of the software system play a role. Similar to the ISO 4748-7000:2022 standard (ISO, 2022) ethical theories may give some additional epistemic guidance. This means that in this case, ethical theories are more useful in identifying the significant moral aspects of software systems rather than serving as a means to decide on morally good actions at an individual level. Consequentialist ethics, such as utilitarianism, which weigh outcomes based on a specific net sum, provide a criterion for normative thinking to ensure stable and rational evaluations (Driver, 2011). Deontological ethical theories support disclosing normative aspects under some form of a universalization principle (Darwall, 1983). Normative thinking in respect to deontological demands will point to the fact that no further balancing is morally appropriate: in the case of developing some medical device, for example, the value of healing cannot be counterbalanced with economic or aesthetic values. Normative thinking is not only about trade-offs but also about understanding limitations that are morally demanded.

Additionally, it is crucial to acknowledge that normative thinking involves not only the consideration of values but also the inclusion of desirable attitudes or patterns of behavior. Such approaches are commonly discussed by virtue ethics. The latter involves the understanding of social interactions that allow desirable attitudes to manifest themselves. Hence, this approach is an appeal to desirable character traits as well as practices that enable such traits to be fruitful. It is less of a cognitive process than a form of education and internationalization of skills, attitudes, and evaluations. This, however, does not lead to virtue ethics being less rational (Siep, 2013). To understand technology, it is of great importance because it can highlight the ways in which digital technology fosters or corrupts desirable character attitudes as well as practices.

However, we feel that the profound knowledge of ethical theories is not part of software engineering and also not a prerequisite for developing software. Yet, as a means to pinpoint ethical relevant issues, it is useful to ask questions such as the following: Is a world desirable where everyone has access to this technology? Is it justifiable that everyone would use technology in a certain way? Such universalism tests reveal spaces that are morally questionable. Or more broadly: how does one assess the expected consequences? Is a world more desirable in which we, for instance, nudge older people to drink more water by using digital means, e.g., because their television set is automatically turned off in case of insufficient water consumption or they receive an electrical impulse? This kind of questioning belongs in the disclosive mode of contemplation but already shows the transition into weighing relation. The weighing mode of contemplation involves prioritizing and delimiting thinking, so that we can come to a conclusion. Throughout, we intermingle technological solutionism with moral concepts: This is the applicative mode of contemplation. Hence, identification of values, principles, and norms and their technological implementation are thought together to form reasonable technical or non-technical solutions.

Within each individual sprint, the third challenge is to implement these values through appropriate mechanisms. To do this, developers must continue to agree on the normative demands in each sprint and particularly consider the potential implications of the selected approach, methodology, architecture, or deployment scenario. This also corresponds to a work culture that favors ethical deliberations rather than suppressing thinking outside technological functionality.

7 Example

Building on these theoretical foundations, how can we now embed ethical deliberations into a practical setting?

To start with, we need to understand what kind of universe of discourse we find ourselves confronted with. Thus, it is important to consider the company's environment and the product's purpose. For example, a team writing software for a manufacturer of children's toys faces different moral demands than a team that works for a manufacturer of weapons. Furthermore, a team building healthcare applications needs different normative solutions than a team that develops an application to share photos. Thus, employees must accept to a certain degree the corporate purpose and culture, i.e., the premise of the universe of discourse.

For our example, we assume that our team, consisting of four developers, Alice, Bob, Claire, and David, is working for a manufacturer of children's dolls. The next generation of dolls will be connected to the Internet, respond to the children's voice commands, and engage in basic conversations. Basically, we have ChatGPT behind a text-to-speech processor and in the package of a doll. Note that while the doll uses ChatGPT, it is not a pure AI application. It is a normal software application that uses ChatGPT as a service and can thus be developed just like any other classical piece of software.

7.1 Ethical Deliberation: Disclosive Contemplation

To define our normative horizon, we begin sprint 0 and identify normative relevant aspects in a structured process. We start by using the company's ethical codex, industry values, and stakeholder interests. These gathered preferences and statements on values and moral beliefs are already the descriptive part of a disclosive ethical contemplation. Since this will lead to a plethora of values and a mix of ethical demands, we need to work with domain ethics to specify and substantiate normative claims.

The example of a ChatGPT doll raises obvious ethical concerns that are debated in advocatory ethics. In the case of children, advocatory ethics speaks for the still immature, who cannot yet fully enter into their own rights and values and is thus concerned with child welfare. Advocatory ethics for children is a philosophy and approach that seeks to promote ethical and moral behavior in children and protect their rights and well-being. Advocatory ethics for children strive to promote values such as fairness, equality, respect, empathy, responsibility, and honesty. These values are essential for building a strong moral foundation in children and helping them become compassionate and responsible individuals. By promoting these values, advocates of ethics for children aim to create a world where all individuals are treated with kindness, fairness, and respect and where children learn to make responsible and ethical decisions. These values also justify moral rules that provide a framework for ethical behavior and are essential for promoting positive social interactions and relationships. By teaching children to follow these rules, advocates of ethics for children aim to instill important values and skills that will serve them well throughout their lives. We designate normative demands that derive from the consideration of domain ethics as *structural values*.

We call normative aspects that are intrinsic to digital technology, such as privacy, security, and transparency, *techno-generic values*. They are relevant because of the characteristics of digital technology itself and hence independent of a specific application. As a result, these values are commonly mentioned in discussions regarding digital technology. This is why ethical codes of conduct targeting developers, operators, and users typically incorporate these concepts, principles, and values, as opposed to values like "honesty" or "kindness" that are not as pertinent. It is essential to consider these techno-generic values when evaluating the ethical implications of digital technology, but not only these.

There are many educational and interactive applications to engage children in learning and conversation, and that could be part of our doll. These applications can provide a fun and engaging way for children to learn new skills and knowledge while also promoting positive social and ethical values. Some examples of educational apps for children include language learning apps that use speech recognition technology to help children improve their language skills, interactive storytelling apps that use natural language processing to respond to children's input and encourage them to engage in creative thinking, and chatbot apps that allow children to have conversations with virtual assistants.

A toy or application can still foster moral behavior in children if it is designed and implemented in a way that promotes these positive ethical attitudes. For example, an interactive storytelling app could feature stories that promote empathy, kindness, and fairness and provide opportunities for children to engage in ethical decision-making. A chatbot app could be programmed to respond in ways that encourage respectful and honest communication and offer guidance on how to navigate difficult social situations.

To ensure that such a toy or application promotes positive moral behavior in children, it is important to consider the design and content of the media (techno-generic normative aspects), as well as the ethical implications of its use (structural normative aspects). Developers should take care to avoid reinforcing harmful stereotypes or biases and should consider the potential impact of the doll on children's social and emotional development. Additionally, parents and caregivers should be involved in the selection and use of such tools and should provide guidance and support to help children understand the ethical implications of their interactions with AI-powered toys and applications.

This first step is crucial to ethical software development. It serves as a critical juncture where the team can approach issues in a structured and rational manner, as opposed to engaging in unstructured discussions that may yield unpredictable and insufficient outcomes. While unstructured approaches may—by chance—lead to some level of improvement, the lack of documentation, reproducibility, and evaluation hinders their effectiveness. Therefore, a structured approach regarding the disclosive contemplation within ethical software development is imperative to ensure that the thought process is transparent and accountable to the team and others. It thus increases the probability of finding the relevant ethical aspects that surround the product and its context of use.

7.2 Ethical Deliberation: Weighing Contemplation and Sprint Planning

Having outlined our universe and our normative catalog of requirements for the product is determined, we move into the regular agile cadence. This means that, in the case of Scrum, we will have a sprint that entails a sprint planning meeting, daily scrum meetings, a sprint review meeting, as well as a sprint retrospective. The daily meetings are short and are used to communicate to the team what everyone is working on. Ethical issues should only in very rare cases be raised in these meetings. For example, Alice might talk about problems of the architecture for the performance of the network stack to get faster replies when the doll has an unstable network connection.

Thus, most of the ethical deliberation with focus on balancing normative aspects should be part of the sprint planning meetings since in these meetings, the development team discusses the scope of the next sprint and what backlog items will be worked on (Note: here we do not go into details of how to turn requirements into backlog items; for an example, see Vlaanderen et al. (2011)). When a backlog item gets selected for the sprint, as part of the discussion of the item, its definition of done and similar technical points, there should be a short discussion about their ethical issues. Here, the item can be analyzed in view of the normative criteria, such as privacy and honesty, so that we ensure that the item and its effect on the product do not violate the given set of moral demands. However, focusing on balancing and trade-offs of ethical demands does not mean that we do not need to switch between all three types of reasoning: it is obvious that while pondering how our doll may foster the value of honesty, we will need to think it in an applicative way. For example, should the doll tell the truth and back statements of facts with sources? Certainly, the doll should not be deceitful and manipulate its users. While doing so, it needs to balance trade-offs, for example, how should a doll answer a question if Santa Claus is real or where babies come from? Additionally, this mode of thinking should disclose problems with the doll. For example, how can we avoid problems of animism and avoid children seeing the doll as a living being? This would certainly lead into habits we do not find desirable.

Most backlog items, like minor features, improvements to existing features, or highly technical features, will most likely need no ethical discussion at all. However, for each feature, there should be space to deliberate normatively—also in a disclosive manner. It is equally important that the meeting is timeboxed and that a deliberation must end with a decision. If the team cannot come to a decision within the allotted timebox, it is a clear sign that the feature should not be implemented in the current sprint. The team should work on another feature and hand the problematic feature, together with the points of contention that arose in the discussion, back to the product owner and, if necessary, a dedicated ethical specialist. This approach does not impede the progress and velocity of the team and allows the ethical issues to be resolved asynchronously while the team is productive.

7.3 Ethical Deliberation: Applicative Contemplation to the Increment

For example, if the team discusses the network capabilities of the doll in sprint N, Bob raises an issue of privacy that conflicts with the normative horizon defined in sprint 0: that just knowing when the doll is active allows an attacker to infer when it is being used and someone is home. Then Claire suggests sending dummy data at random times to obscure the user's usage patterns and habits. By applicative contemplation, the value of privacy can also be understood as predictive privacy (Mühlhoff, 2021) and be countered by technical means. Similarly, Alice might raise the honesty issue with Santa Claus in sprint $N + 1$: if asked by a child if Santa Claus exists, how should the doll answer? An honest doll might say that he is not real, thus hurting the child. Additionally, think about any kind of dialog surrounding sexuality. Furthermore, the doll should also react appropriately to malicious input: If the child playing with it shouts at it, for example, it should react accordingly. The latter implies that we do not want to guide the children toward violent behavior. Empirical input from evolutionary psychologists is needed as well as the critical reflection upon which purpose the doll is supposed to represent. It may be easier to involve ethical experts to elicit and understand desirable values of such a doll. If it is a doll, e.g., that will foster the children's behavior as good parents, we need to extract the meaning of empathy, caring, and need satisfaction. These normative questions might be dealt with in a pre-development phase with an all-encompassing deliberation team to highlight the doll's purpose such as outlined in 4. It is unlikely that all questions might be answered thoroughly by the development team while developing only. However, it is necessary that the developers have a certain mindset to enrich and ground normative dialogue. For example, when working on speech recognition in sprint $N + 2$, David might suggest also considering speech patterns of minority and non-native-speaking children to ensure that kindness and non-discrimination are technically enabled. In such a case, technological skills are combined with ethical awareness.

7.4 Ethical Deliberation: Sprint Review and Sprint Retrospective

At the end of each sprint, we have a sprint review meeting. Here, the team presents the work to the product owner and reviews it. Now, Claire checks on Bob's solution to the privacy problem, and they find that David did not have enough time to train the system on a varied selection of speech patterns and create a backlog item to work on this in a future sprint. The product owner needs to verify that every artifact complies with the definition of done. For particularly sensitive artifacts, this should entail a focus on its ethical suitability.

During a sprint retrospective, the team discusses the work process and how to improve the development process. For example, Claire earns special praise for her idea to solve the privacy problem, or David is celebrated for identifying groups and organizations to contact speech samples. Additionally, this is the place to make changes to the normative horizon. For example, if David finds in his experiments that the doll is prone to insult its user or seem unhinged similar to early versions of Bing Chat (Vincent, 2023), the team might remove the value of free access to information through the bot and consider installing some kind of filtering (or censoring) capabilities. The development continues with the next sprint.

8 Conclusions

Our key insights and ideas can be summarized as follows:

- More than 100 codes of conduct for software development have been developed in the last 10 years by various organizations. These codes state universal and abstract values but lack practical orientation. The lack of immediate applicability is due to both the abstract nature of values and the context-specificity of software.
- Values must be embedded in software development on a case-by-case basis tailored to the context. Ethical deliberations must be part of the daily development routine to achieve ethically designed products.
- Agile software development is particularly suited to allow for a case-specific consideration of values and can foster ethical deliberation.
- Incorporating ethical concepts into software development processes and products is a challenge. It is difficult to identify and examine morally desirable software. There are no and there cannot be universal measures for implementing and evaluating technology according to ethical criteria due to the context specificity of software and underdetermination of values. Ethical considerations cannot be resolved by only using checklists or predefined answers.
- Continuously evaluating design projects from inception to maintenance is necessary. Ethically good software may need reevaluation if the context changes.
- We need to identify desirable values and translate them into technical language. Thus, some techno-ethical judgment is necessary.
- Four actors must take responsibility in the development and use of software-intensive systems: society, the organization developing the system and its subdivisions, the development team, the operator, and the user of that system.
- Software engineers are not solely responsible for every potential externalities, but they do have some responsibility. The approach is about the perception of the individual responsibility of software engineers.
- There are four essential phenomena of agile software development: planning, incrementality, empowerment, and learning. Simplicity is overarching. Agile development is incremental development, sequentially developing individual functionalities and immediately integrating them with the system developed up until now.

- Agile development empowers teams and allows for extensive design capabilities. It emphasizes learning and a culture of error. Ethical deliberation needs to be part of development itself, and the approach should scale with development. A work culture that favors ethical deliberations is important.
- Ethical judgment must encompass three modes of contemplation: disclosive, weighing, and applicative. Disclosive mode is about recognizing normatively relevant facts. Weighing mode is about decision-making and balancing normative demands. Applicative mode is about translating values into technical functionality. These modes can alternate and overlap.
- Although the focus lies on the developers, ethical deliberations necessarily include the product owner, who is in direct contact with the customers and has an important role in managing requirements of systems.

Discussion Questions for Students and Their Teachers

1. What has contributed to the current significance of technology ethics?
2. Why might it be surprising to a software engineer that the current ethics debate focuses on AI and not on software in general?
3. What is suggested as an excellent starting point for implementing ethical deliberations within software development? Can you think about reasons for this claim?
4. Why are values characterized by a high degree of abstraction?
5. Why can't codes of conduct be a tool that gives a step-by-step instruction of an ethical implementation of values in software that fits all contexts?

Learning Resources for Students

1. Blackman, R. (2022). Ethical Machines—Your Concise Guide to Totally Unbiased, Transparent, and Respectful AI. Harvard Business Review Press.

   This book provides an overview about ethical issues regarding AI. It is a good introduction for students particularly interested in the ethics of AI.
2. Gogoll, J., Zuber, N., Kacianka, S., Greger, T., Pretschner, A., & Nida-Rümelin, J. (2021). Ethics in the software development process: from codes of conduct to ethical deliberation. Philosophy Technology. https://doi.org/10.1007/s13347-021-00451-w.

   This paper argues that codes of conducts and ethics are not enough to implement ethics into software development. Instead, ethical deliberation within software development teams is necessary.
3. Reijers, W., Wright, D., Brey, P., Weber, K., Rodrigues, R., O'Sullivan, D., & Gordijn, B. (2018). Methods for practising ethics in research and innovation: A literature review, critical analysis and recommendations. *Science and engineering ethics*, *24*, 1437–1481.

   This review discusses different approaches for a systematic ethical reflection on technology.

4. Winkler, T., & Spiekermann, S. (2021). Twenty years of value sensitive design: a review of methodological practices in VSD projects.

   Ethics and Information Technology, 23, 17–21. In this paper, the VSD approach and its main concepts are discussed and compared to other process-related methodologies.
5. Vakkuri, V., Kemell, K. K., Jantunen, M., Halme, E., & Abrahamsson, P. (2021). ECCOLA—A method for implementing ethically aligned AI systems. *Journal of Systems and Software*, *182*, 111067.

   This paper introduces ECCOLA, a method for implementing AI ethics and bridging the gap between principles and values and the requirements of AI systems. It discusses the steps developers and organizations should take to ensure ethical considerations are integrated into the development process.

References

Beck, K., Grenning, J., Martin, R., Beedle, M., Highsmith, J., Mellor, S., van Bennekum, A., Hunt, A., Schwaber, K., Cockburn, A., Jeffries, R., Sutherland, J., Cunningham, W., Kern, J., Thomas, D., Fowler, M., & Marick, B. (2001). *Manifesto for agile software development.* Accessed June 7, 2023, from http://agilemanifesto.org/

Beedle, M., Devos, M., Sharon, Y., Schwaber, K., & Sutherland, J. (1998). *SCRUM—An extension pattern language for hyperproductive software development.* Accessed June 7, 2023, from http://jeffsutherland.com/scrum/scrum_plop.pdf

Blackman, R. (2022). *Ethical machines - Your concise guide to totally unbiased, transparent, and respectful AI.* Harvard Business Review Press.

Brey, P. (2000). Disclosive computer ethics. *ACM Sigcas Computers and Society, 30*(4), 10–16.

Brey, P. (2010). Values in technology and disclosive computer ethics. *The Cambridge Handbook of Information and Computer Ethics, 4*, 41–58.

Brey, P. A. (2012). Anticipatory ethics for emerging technologies. *NanoEthics, 6*(1), 1–13.

Briand, L., Bianculli, D., Nejati, S., Pastore, F., & Sabetzadeh, M. (2017). The case for context-driven software engineering research: Generalizability is overrated. *IEEE Software, 34*(5), 72–75.

Darwall, S. L. (1983). *Impartial reason.* Cornell University Press.

Driver, J. (2011). *Consequentialism.* Routledge.

Elish, M. O. (2010, June) Exploring the relationships between design metrics and package understandability: A case study. In *2010 IEEE 18th international conference on program comprehension* (pp. 144–147). IEEE.

Farley, D. (2022). *Modern Software Engineering*. O'Reilly.

Felderer, M., & Ramler, R. (2021). Quality assurance for AI-based systems: Overview and challenges (introduction to interactive session). In *Software quality: Future perspectives on software engineering quality: 13th international conference, SWQD 2021, Vienna, January 19–21, 2021, Proceedings 13* (pp. 33–42). Springer International Publishing.

Floridi, L., & Sanders, J. W. (2005). *Internet ethics: The constructionist values of homo poieticus.*

Friedman, B., Hendry, D. G., & Borning, A. (2017). A survey of value sensitive design methods. *Foundations and Trends Human Computer Interaction, 11*(2), 63–125.

Gogoll, J., Zuber, N., Kacianka, S., Greger, T., Pretschner, A., & Nida-Rümelin, J. (2021). Ethics in the software development process: From codes of conduct to ethical deliberation. *Philosophy and Technology*. https://doi.org/10.1007/s13347-021-00451-w

Grunwald A (2010) *Technikfolgenabschätzung: Eine Einführung* Bd. 1. edition sigma, Berlin.

Gürses, S., & Van Hoboken, J. (2017). Privacy after the agile turn. In J. Polonetsky, O. Tene, & E. Selinger (Eds.), *Cambridge handbook of consumer privacy*. Cambridge University Press.
ISO. (2022). *Standard 24748-7000:2022, Systems and software engineering – Life cycle management – Part 7000: Standard model process for addressing ethical concerns during system design*.
Kapp, E. (1877). *Grundlinien einer Philosophie der Technik: zur Entstehungsgeschichte der Cultur aus neuen Gesichtspunkten*.
McLennan, S., Fiske, A., Celi, L. A., Müller, R., Harder, J., Ritt, K., Haddadin, S., & Buyx, A. (2020). An embedded ethics approach for AI development. *Nature Machine Intelligence, 2*, 488–490.
Mühlhoff, R. (2021). Predictive privacy: Towards an applied ethics of data analytics. *Ethics and Information Technology*. https://doi.org/10.1007/s10676-021-09606-x
Nida-Rümelin, J. (2011). *Verantwortung*. Reclam.
Nida-Rümelin, J. (2017). Handlung, Technologie und Verantwortung. In: *Berechenbarkeit der Welt?* (S 497–513). Springer VS, Wiesbaden.
Nissenbaum, H. (1994). Computing and accountability. *Communications of the ACM, 37*(1), 72–81.
Nissenbaum, H. (1996). Accountability in a computerized society. *Science and Engineering Ethics, 2*(1), 25–42.
Pretschner, A., Zuber, N., Gogoll, J., Kacianka, S., & Nida-Rümelin, J. (2021). Ethik in der agilen Software-Entwicklung. *Informatik Spektrum, 44*(5), 348–354.
Rohbeck, J. (1993). *Technologische Urteilskraft: Zu einer Ethik technischen Handelns*. Suhrkamp.
Siep, L. (2013). *Vernunft und Tugend*. Mentis.
Van den Hoeven, J., Vermaas, P. E., & Van de Poel, I. (2015). *Handbook of ethics, values and technological design: Sources, theory, values and application domains*. Springer.
Vincent, J. (2023). Microsoft's Bing is an emotionally manipulative liar, and people love it. *The Verge*. Accessed June 7, 2023, from https://www.theverge.com/2023/2/15/23599072/microsoft-ai-bing-personality-conversations-spy-employees-webcams
Vlaanderen, K., Jansen, S., Brinkkemper, S., & Jaspers, E. (2011). The agile requirements refinery: Applying SCRUM principles to software product management. *Information and Software Technology, 53*(1), 58–70.
Zuber, N., Gogoll, J., Kacianka, S., Pretschner, A., & Nida-Rümelin, J. (2022). Empowered and embedded: Ethics and agile processes. *Humanities and Social Sciences Communications, 9*(1), 1–13.

Humans in the Loop: People at the Heart of Systems Development

Helen Sharp

Abstract Despite increased automation in the process, people are (still) at the heart of software systems development. This chapter adopts a sociotechnical perspective and explores three areas that characterize the role of humans in software systems development: people as creators, people as users, and people in partnership with systems. Software is *created* by specialist developers such as software engineers and non-specialists such as "makers." Software developers build communities and operate within several cultures (e.g., professional, company, and national), all of which affect both the development process and the resulting product. Software is *used* by people. Users also operate within communities and cultures which influence product use, and how systems are used feeds back into future systems development. People and systems are interdependent: they work in *partnership* to achieve a wide range of goals. However, software both supports what people want to do and shapes what can be done.

1 Introduction

Digital humanism aims to put humans at the center of the digital world, arguing that technology is for people and not the other way around. Other chapters in this volume (e.g., Winter in this volume) advocate human-centered systems development which suggests that humans' needs should be the driving force for development and that humans and groups should be better integrated into the system development cycle.

This chapter echoes that perspective but turns the spotlight back onto the people who contribute to the development of digital artifacts and how the human tendency to form communities, and their respective cultures, influences and shapes the artifacts they produce. We focus more specifically on the role that people have in the development and use of systems: who are they, what is their role, and how do

H. Sharp (✉)
Faculty of Science, Technology, Engineering and Mathematics, The Open University, Milton Keynes, UK
e-mail: helen.sharp@open.ac.uk

H. Werthner et al. (eds.), *Introduction to Digital Humanism*,
https://doi.org/10.1007/978-3-031-45304-5_23

humans shape the digital artifacts that they encounter. A key feature of this work is that systems development is seen as sociotechnical, i.e., an approach that makes explicit the fact that people and technology are interdependent (Klein, 2014), a perspective that is increasingly pertinent to digital humanism.

Digital artifacts rely on software, and software is fundamental to virtually everything people do nowadays. Apart from phone apps that keep people in touch with their loved ones, allow bills to be paid, and keep track of their fitness levels, there are also global software-based projects, from instrumentation of the James Webb telescope out in space (e.g. see NASA, 2023) to modeling the spread of viruses across the world (e.g. Wang et al., 2021), controlling neighborhood traffic (e.g. see WDM, 2023), and tracking animals in danger of extinction (e.g. Kulits et al., 2021). Software development is at the core of digital artifact design and implementation, controlling its behavior, how it interacts with users and the environment, determining how trustworthy or secure it is, and whether it supports what the human user is trying to do.

This chapter will focus on software and software development and aims to consider who is involved, what is their role, and how does the sociotechnical nature of software systems development affect the software produced. It is divided into three sections, exploring people as creators of software systems; people as users of software systems; and the partnership between people and software systems.

2 People as Creators of Software Systems

When thinking about people as creators of software systems, the first group that comes to mind are the professionals—specialist software designers and builders. But there is also a growing set of people who are not specialists yet who are involved directly in developing and implementing software systems. Whether specialists or non-specialists, people who create software systems are not acting on their own. Instead, they sit within a community of designers, developers, users, and other stakeholders who contribute to creation in one way or another. These communities may be professional (e.g., user experience designers), organizational (e.g., employees of a company), or personal (e.g., based on ethnicity), but they all influence systems development. For instance, in a study of designers in Botswana, researchers found that sociocultural factors of the designers influenced both the design process and the designed artifact (Lotz & Sharp, 2020; Sharp et al., 2020).

This section explores these two groups (specialists and non-specialists) and how they influence and inform systems development.

2.1 *Specialists such as Software Engineers*

Professional software engineers are one subset of specialist creators, although this seemingly homogeneous group is made up of yet more subgroups, such as commercial software developers, open-source developers, and freelance software developers, for example. Members of these groups work within a community and a network of stakeholders, technical components, and standards. Their work is influenced by different cultures and their own experience and those around them (Sharp et al., 2000).

Modern software development is a very complex endeavor and relies quite extensively on building from existing components such as language library assets, interface components, patterns, and design system languages, often created by different groups. A piece of software must be embedded in its technical environment and is dependent on digital and physical attributes of the device and of the environment within which it operates, e.g., Internet connectivity and access to digital assets. This complexity means that software developers and their work are highly dependent on others: local others and distant others.

The community aspect of software development is often overlooked. Software developers may operate in teams, which is one kind of community, but they also form very close communities across companies, disciplines, and continents (see Fig. 1). These may coalesce around programming languages or tools, or in specific domains such as finance or physics, or in particular locations. Members of these communities support each other with solutions to problems, guidance on technical matters, and documentation, for example. And it goes beyond that—communities are very influential. When we were looking at object-oriented development in the 1990s, one of the research questions we had was how did object-oriented technology emerge and become widespread. We didn't look at the official history but instead tried to follow strands of evidence in contemporaneous literature. From that investigation came the view that the community of object-oriented advocates built a significant following through community events so that when a commercial-strength object-oriented language emerged (C++), there was a ready-made appetite among developers for it to spread very rapidly (Robinson & Sharp, 2009).

Developer communities support each other in various practical ways through sharing solutions and propagating information. But the impact that social processes have goes beyond this. For instance, resilience of sociotechnical systems relies on people (Furniss et al., 2011a). While some aspects of resilient performance are visible through written procedures or policies, others are "hidden" within adaptations made by people every day. To illustrate this, Furniss et al. (2011b) provide several examples from a hospital study. One of these relates to a batch of infusion pumps that were prone to triggering a false alarm. A workaround, i.e., lubricating the relevant part with alcohol gel, was developed by the nurses but was not captured in any procedures nor reported to anyone beyond the immediate team. Instead, people adapted their behavior to account for the situation until the batch had been used and

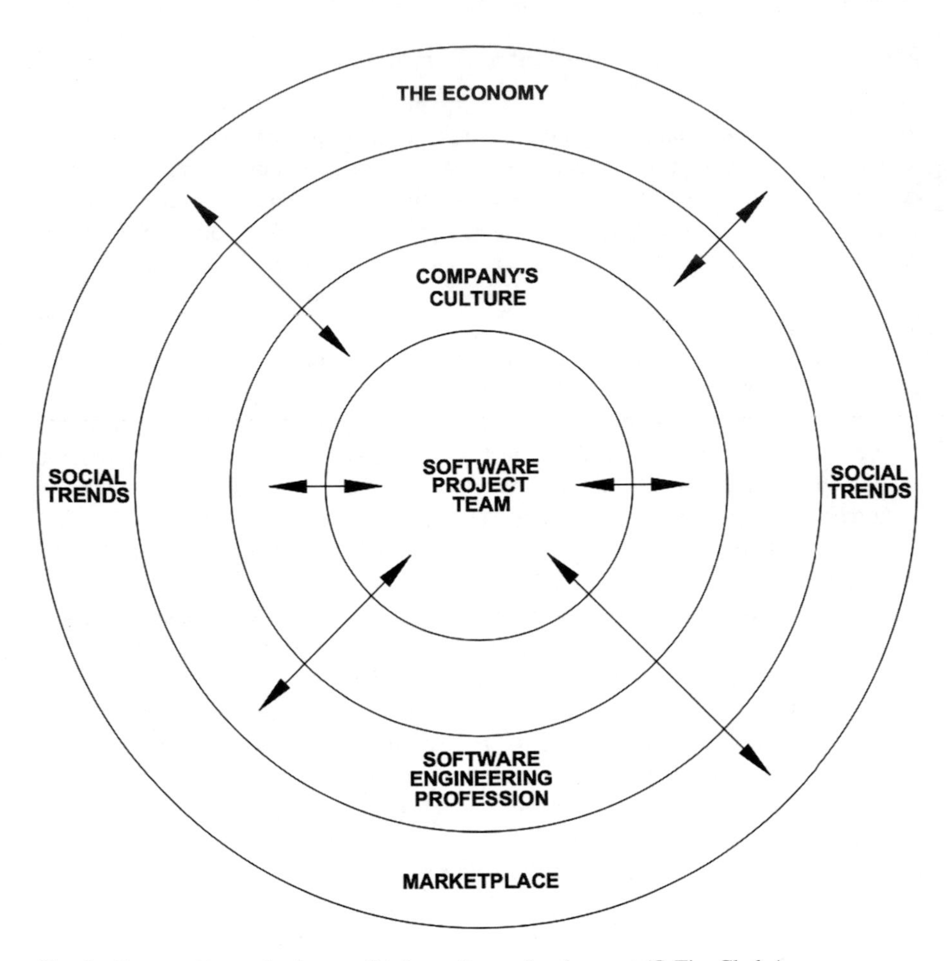

Fig. 1 Communities and cultures affecting software development (© Tim Clarke)

work could return to "normal." Examples of how people's actions keep systems working are also found in software development (Lopez et al., 2023).

A further example of how developers are influenced by their environment is given in work by Lopez et al. (2022), who studied the security behavior of software developers. They were driven to understand why known security vulnerabilities were still being embedded in software: why aren't the developers countering these known issues when the software is built. At the time, the finger was often pointed at software developers asking why they didn't "just do it." Findings showed that decisions that have an impact on security within code were not always made by developers and their teams but instead reflect the attitudes and priorities of companies and their clients. This provided evidence that the cultures of the company, the client, and the team all affected technical outcomes, not just the individual's experience and expertise.

2.2 *Non-specialists such as Domain Experts*

There are many ways in which non-specialists can and do contribute to systems development. For instance, a quick search on Google will show that crowdsourcing of ideas for new technologies and systems is common-place. Two non-specialist examples are discussed in this section as system creators: domain experts and "the public."

All software development requires developers to engage with the domain of application, i.e., where the software will be deployed, and the kind of functionality it is designed to embody. In some cases communicating the intricacies of that domain can be particularly challenging if the domain is specialist, for example, in scientific discovery (Chawla, 2015). In this case, it is common for the domain specialists themselves to create the software, and while they are specialists in their own field, they are not necessarily software or technology specialists. This demonstrates one group of non-specialist creators: domain experts. While some software may be produced simply to support the developer's own requirements, it is common for this software to be valuable to others and such software may be taken up in the wider community, supported by crowdsourced documentation (Pawlik et al., 2015).

The Maker Movement (Anderson, 2013; Hatch, 2014) is very much about opening up the world of "making" to a wide range of people, some of whom were already hobbyists, but others are new to making. The Maker Movement (MM) aims to make Do-It-Yourself making accessible to whoever wants to take part (Anderson, 2013). It explicitly aims to encourage people to make as well as consume artifacts. At its core is to collaboratively craft physical and digital artifacts using a diversity of machines, tools, and methods. The availability of affordable, powerful, and easy-to-use tools, coupled with a renewed focus on locally sourced products and community-based activities, has fueled this interest and made the movement feasible. A network of makerspaces has enabled the maker movement to become widespread and popularized worldwide.

The main principles of MM are to make, share, give, learn, play, participate, support, and change. Note that this is not just about making your own things but also sharing and supporting others. Websites such as instructables.com and makezine.com illustrate the outcomes of this ethos and demonstrate what can be achieved when people share and build on each other's ideas and creations. Although the pandemic dampened the opportunity to gather physically, the movement is still growing. The use of pre-formed kits such as Arduino[1] and e-textiles,[2] together with ready-made components in the form of software development kits, patterns, and libraries, also encourages a wide engagement.

This movement illustrates the power of community and of individual abilities to create artifacts that focus on things that they want. It also represents a change in

[1] Arduino is an open-source electronics platform based on easy-to-use hardware and software; see arduino.cc for more information.

[2] A field of electronics that combines electronic widgets (lights, batteries, sensors) with textiles.

mindset where people can see that they have the chance to shape technology to fit their own purpose rather than be driven by it.

3 People as Users of Software Systems

You might think it goes without saying that software is built to be used, and so people are users of software. It is worth remembering that software is intended to support peoples' goals and that software should be developed with users in mind, but this section goes beyond these simple platitudes. Here we explore two sociotechnical aspects of people as users that are relevant to systems development: that users are inventive and appropriate technology for their own context and that user feedback and behavior with existing systems influence future systems development.

3.1 Taking Account of Users and What They Do

During the 1970s, when software and its applications were becoming more widespread, the need to pay attention to the design of the interface so that it was usable by humans was recognized. The early focus on "man-machine interface" quickly evolved during the 1980s into human-computer interaction (HCI), a term that is still used today although its scope has increased considerably over the decades.

From the beginning, HCI drew on a range of disciplines including cognitive psychology, linguistics, computer science, and sociology. The goal was to design software that would take account of human characteristics such as attention and learning and influences on human behavior such as group processes and attitudes. HCI's focus was on how to take account of these traits in the design of interfaces and systems. For instance, an understanding of attention led to suggestions on how best to structure information, so that users could find what they needed more effectively, and how to use space and color on screens to direct users' attention to the salient points for the task in hand.

HCI also recognized the need for an iterative approach to development so that a range of expertise could be brought into play, and the emerging design may be checked with users. This evaluation of early prototypes and designs with users became the focus of the HCI design process in which emerging designs and prototypes are shown to and evaluated with intended user groups, and the results fed back into redesign (Preece et al., 1994).

The more recent term interaction design captures a focus that is much wider than that of the early HCI days. Interaction design today recognizes that the context of use has expanded away from "one user-one computer" and a wide range of different disciplines needs to be drawn upon in deciding what interactive products to develop and how to design them, including psychology and computer science but also product design, social sciences, and cognitive ergonomics. Interaction design also recognizes the centrality of people and humans as users, co-designers, and creators in the design of interactive products. It is defined as "designing interactive products to support the way people communicate and interact in their everyday and working lives" (Rogers et al., 2023).

Alongside this change of emphasis is the recognition that designing *for* users isn't enough but that creators need to also design *with* users so that technologies can be truly human-centered (see Winter in this volume). But even with the best human-centered development process, users have a habit of appropriating technology for their own uses and it's not clear how it will be used until it is in the hands of the user population. Although software may be designed for particular purposes, people are very good at adapting the software for their own use and in molding it to their own context. This phenomenon prompted the introduction of "in-the-wild" studies of use and evaluation of early designs (Rogers & Marshall, 2017). The idea behind this approach is that systems are evaluated in situations that reflect as much as possible the context in which they will be deployed. While users may say that they will do things in a particular way, it's often the case that they do something different when faced with the situation "for real." The old adage that "what I do and what I say I do are not the same thing" applies in systems design and use too. Indeed, sociology of technology suggests that the usefulness of software is actively and socially constructed by users rather than merely perceived as a property of technology (Pinch & Bijker, 1987). For instance, studying ERP systems (enterprise resource planning systems), Abdelnour-Nocera et al. (2007) found that the context and local culture shaped the utility and usability of systems after they have been deployed.

The importance of encouraging developers to watch users interacting with their creations was realized a long time ago, and the importance of iteration is reflected in modern software development through the agile approach (Ashmore & Runyan, 2015; Zuber et al. in this volume). Agile software development recognizes the need for regular interactions with users and customers so that feedback is provided as the product evolves. In many cases, products are released regularly into real use so that value is delivered to the business often, and feedback may be based on real use.

Insight into how technologies are appropriated by communities of users can be gained by observing products in use and getting regular feedback. However, uncovering cultural norms such as assumptions, customs, beliefs, and habits of user communities is challenging, yet their impact on technology use is significant. For instance, Chavan and Gorney (2008) describe scenarios in which the use of mobile phones is influenced by cultural norms where technologies are shared and hence privacy and security are compromised. If cultural norms of communities are explored during the design process, then this kind of unexpected (to the designers) behavior could be accounted for. This example is one of many that led researchers to recognize that different approaches to design for indigenous communities may be needed (Winschiers-Theophilus & Bidwell, 2013), so that the role that technology plays can be better understood.

3.2 Software Use Influences Future Development

Human-centered development of new systems is important, but much technology design and development are based on evolving existing systems rather than being completely new inventions. Given what we said in the previous section, then it's not a surprise that existing use of systems influences how they evolve in the future. And we've got better at knowing how to collect data and derive information that allows us to do this. Nowadays, there is an inextricable interdependence between development and use.

The Lean UX approach is one example of software development where even an idea can be checked within the context of real use before development proceeds too far. A "minimum viable product" (MVP) is released for real use and user behavior is monitored to see whether and how the product is used. Gothelf and Seiden (2016, pp. 76–77) provide a simple example of an MVP produced by a company who thought that their customers would like a monthly newsletter. To test out this assumption before spending a lot of resource on developing it, they spent half a day producing a sign-up form available online. This MVP allowed them to collect evidence to support or refute their assumption, based on user feedback.

Another approach that focuses on online systems and obtains evidence of users' behavior is A/B testing (Kohavi et al., 2020). In A/B testing, different versions of the same system are delivered to different sets of users, and their performance is tracked according to a defined set of evaluation criteria. The performance of the two designs then helps to decide which one to implement more widely. The name "A/B testing" is based on the idea that there are two alternative designs—"A" and "B"—and that their quality is being tested via an experiment. Setting up appropriate criteria and implementing an experiment are not simple although this technique is used widely. Users are identified and assigned to groups randomly. They don't usually know that they are taking part in such an experiment, so next time you're online and the website or app looks different, perhaps you're helping the designers learn how users interact with their creations!

Other sources of information about how software is used come from customer reviews, which can affect the popularity and success of a product (Harman et al., 2012). App reviews from social media can also provide concrete improvements, for example, Twitter has been suggested as a good source of app reviews (Mezouar et al., 2018). However, it's not straightforward to extract useful information that can be acted upon by developers (Dabrowski et al., 2022). These areas are still the subject of research.

4 People in Partnership with Software Systems

People and software work in partnership in a way that is more than just "using" software: what people can *achieve*, how ideas and understanding *evolve*, and how people *behave* are all influenced by the software systems we use. For instance, what can be achieved through computer-aided design (CAD) systems has revolutionized the way in which buildings are designed and maintained by providing a high level of accuracy and detail that can be modified repeatedly and easily. Software visualization and manipulation of images that supports the analysis of satellite photos have allowed our understanding of how human activity has affected the planet to evolve. How software shapes our behavior is illustrated by the effect of accurate navigation systems on walking and cycling for leisure. Before these came along, such activities needed to be carefully planned and landmarks noted. With the support of accurate GPS tracking and detailed maps, it's possible to find where you are (almost) anywhere in the world and how to get to your destination. You just go out of the door and follow the prompts!

Taking this last point further, software-based systems not only influence our behavior in line with our original goals; it can also help people to change their habits. Persuasive technologies (Fogg, 2009) are explicitly designed to do this. For instance, behavior around domestic energy use can be changed by providing regular feedback to consumers about their energy consumption. Behavior of groups of people may also be changed by sharing consumption figures across a neighborhood. These kinds of persuasive technologies illustrate that the partnership between people and software can have a positive impact across large groups.

However, persuasion can sometimes be less positive. Many online sites are designed to persuade users to do something beyond their initial goal, such as buying an additional product or signing up for services other than those originally intended. At times, this is seen as a fair marketing technique, provided it is transparent, e.g., if purchasing a train ticket to visit a new city, it is likely that the user will also want accommodation, so why not offer them some options? Unfortunately, sometimes a more deceptive approach is implemented where the user feels tricked into "opting in" for something they didn't want. This approach has been referred to as deceptive or dark patterns (see www.deceptive.design).

On the whole, the partnership between software and people has positive outcomes, but although it is very malleable, software has its constraints, and it can have unintended consequences. These constraints may come from technical issues, such as the speed of rendering an image, or from the underlying design of a system, such as mismatches between data formats that prevent integration. Research into technical areas has and will continue to break new ground and what is a constraint today will have been solved next week, but it will be replaced by some other constraint and the cycle will progress. Constraints caused by design issues will also be resolved over time (although significant frustration may continue in the meantime), as more is learned about what users do and want to do.

Unintended consequences are particularly interesting to digital humanism. Baeza-Yates and Murgai in this volume, for example, highlights the ubiquity of bias on the Web. Another example of unintended consequences is provided by recommender systems, which are also discussed by Knees and Neidhardt in this volume. Recommender systems help a user to identify products or services that they might not otherwise have found. These systems are used by online retailers and streaming services, for example, to suggest the items someone might want to purchase or films they might like to download. They analyze data collected about a user such as previous searching or downloading behavior and aim to predict what that user may like; recommenders may also compare across their bank of users to make predictions. Exactly how these recommendations are arrived at depends on the algorithm used, which is a combination of filtering and prediction strategies. However, these systems can lead to the user's preferences simply being self-reinforcing, i.e., the same kind of articles, products, or views are presented again (Pariser, 2011), rather than introducing new ideas. People are prone to biases of various kinds, e.g., confirmation bias, and recommender systems can exacerbate this unless designed deliberately to introduce a novel perspective. If this happens, silos of opinion or creativity can form, which constrain rather than expand a person's outlook. The phenomenon of "algorithm hate," where users become dissatisfied or puzzled by the recommendations they receive, is an active area of research (Smith et al., 2022). However, if users were more aware of this tendency, then changing their behavior would lead to a change in recommendations.

5 Conclusions

Software systems development is a sociotechnical endeavor with people at its heart. Software both supports people in achieving their goals and shapes what can be done; in turn, the ways in which people use software affects how the software behaves and shapes its future evolution. Together, software and its users work in partnership to extend our capabilities, and despite its limitations, software systems have helped us achieve significant advances.

Moreover, both software creators and software users sit within communities, each of which has its own cultural norms that inform and influence software's development and use. Software creation, whether by professional developers or non-specialists, depends on ready-made components and technical assets created by others. Increasingly, non-specialist creators and users are influencing the technologies available.

Making people aware of the fact that software development and use are becoming increasingly interdependent may provide unexpected opportunities within digital humanism.

Discussion Questions for Students and Their Teachers

1. What consequences arise for digital humanism from the sociotechnical nature of the relationship between people and software this chapter describes?
2. Consider the number of software systems you use in a day. Which of them support you and which of them shape your behavior? Choose one that you use regularly and consider how your day would be affected if it wasn't available.
3. Investigate platforms for crowdsourcing ideas—how could crowdsourcing be used to good effect in the quest for digital humanism?
4. Discuss whether and how the communities you belong to influence your relationship with software—as a user or as a creator.

Learning Resources for Students

1. Bergman, O. and Whittaker, S.(2016). *The Science of Managing Our Digital Stuff*. MIT Press

   This book provides an account of how users manage all their digital stuff that seems to keep increasing each day. It explains why users persist with seemingly old-fashioned methods when there are alternative, maybe better approaches that have been designed by software companies.
2. CHASE conference proceedings (the list of papers is available through www.chaseresearch.org)

   This is an annual conference that showcases up-to-date research into the cooperative and human aspects of software development. The papers concentrate on software creators and include a range of issues related to human characteristics and their impact on software development.
3. Hatch, M. (2014) *The Maker Movement Manifesto*. McGraw Hill

   This introduces the Maker Movement and how anyone can get involved in making things and sharing what they have produced. It outlines the fundamentals behind the movement although in places it is a little evangelical.
4. Kohavi, R., Tang, D., and Ya, X. (2020). *Trustworthy Online Controlled Experiments: a practical guide to A/B testing*. Cambridge University Press

   This book was written by three experienced practitioners who have been running online experiments, also referred to as A/B testing, at scale for many years. It is readable and accessible to a wide range of readers and provides valuable detail backed up with specific examples that show the impact that applying this approach successfully can have.
5. Rogers, Y., Sharp, H. and Preece, J. (2023). *Interaction Design: beyond human-computer interaction*. Hoboken: Wiley

   This book provides a good introduction to a wide range of subjects within Interaction Design. Written by a cognitive scientist, an information scientist, and a software engineer, it brings together perspectives from three of the disciplines that have influenced Interaction Design. See id-book.com for more detail.
6. Segal J. and Morris C. (2008) Developing scientific software, *IEEE Software*, 25(4), 18–20

This introduction to a special issue on scientific development is a short piece exploring the nature of this kind of software creation. Further papers in the special issue delve into more detail about developing software for scientific discovery.

7. Sharp, H., Robinson H., and Woodman, M. (2000) 'Software engineering: community and culture', *IEEE Software*, 17(1), 40–47

   This is a relatively short read that explains how community and culture impact software development. The work is based on ethnographic studies of development.

Acknowledgments Many of my colleagues have shaped the views expressed in this chapter. In particular, I'd like to mention Yvonne Rogers, Jenny Preece, Tamara Lopez, and Hugh Robinson. The development of this chapter was supported by UKRI/EPSRC EP/T017465/1.

References

Abdelnour-Nocera, J., Dunckley, L., & Sharp, H. (2007). An approach to the evaluation of usefulness as a social construct using technological frames. *International Journal of HCI, 22*(1), 157–177.

Anderson, C. (2013). *Makers*. Random House Business Books.

Ashmore, S., & Runyan, K. (2015). *Introduction to agile methods*. Addison Wesley.

Chavan, A. L., & Gorney, D. (2008). The dilemma of the shared mobile phone---culture strain and product design in emerging economies. *Interactions, 15*(4), 34–39.

Chawla, D. S. (2015). The Unsung heroes of scientific software. *Nature, 529*, 115–116.

Dabrowski, J., Letier, E., Perini, A., & Susi, A. (2022). Analysing app reviews for software engineering: a systematic literature review. *Empirical Software Engineering, 27*, Article 43.

Fogg, B. J. (2009) A behavior model for persuasive design. In *Proceedings of the 4th International Conference on Persuasive Technology (Persuasive '09)*. ACM, New York, NY, Article 40.

Furniss, D., Back, J., Blandford, A., Hildebrandt, M., & Broberg, H. (2011a). A resilience markers framework for small teams. *Reliability Engineering & System Safety, 96*(1), 2–10.

Furniss, D., Blandford, A., & Mayer, A. (2011b). Unremarkable errors: Low-level disturbances in infusion pump use. In *Proceedings of the 25th BCS Conference on Human-Computer Interaction (BCS-HCI '11)* (pp. 197–204). BCS Learning & Development Ltd.

Gothelf, J., & Seiden, J. (2016). *Lean UX*. O'Reilly.

Harman, M., Jia, Y., & Zhang, Y. (2012) App store mining and analysis: MSR for app stores. In *Proceedings of the 9th IEEE Working Conference on Mining Software Repositories (MSR 12)* (pp. 108–111).

Hatch, M. (2014). *The maker movement manifesto*. McGraw Hill.

Klein, L. (2014). What do we actually mean by 'sociotechnical'? On values, boundaries and the problems of language. *Applied Ergonomics, 45*, 137–142.

Kohavi, R., Tang, D., & Ya, X. (2020). *Trustworthy online controlled experiments: A practical guide to A/B testing*. Cambridge University Press.

Kulits, P., Wall, J., Bedetti, A., Henley, M., & Beery, S. (2021). ElephantBook: A semi-automated human-in-the-loop system for elephant re-identification. In *ACM SIGCAS Conference on Computing and Sustainable Societies (COMPASS '21)* (pp. 88–98). Association for Computing Machinery.

Lopez, T., Sharp, H., Bandara, A., Tun, T., Levine, M., & Nuseibeh, B. (2022). Security responses in software development. *ACM Transactions on Software Engineering and Methodology, 32*(3), 1–29.

Lopez, T., Sharp, H., Wermelinger, M., Langer, M., Levine, M., Jay, C., & Nuseibeh, B. (2023) Accounting for socio-technical resilience in software engineering. In *Proceedings of CHASE 2023*, Melbourne, IEEE.
Lotz, N., & Sharp, H. (2020). Challenges for interaction design education in the South: A case study of Botswana. *Journal of International Development, 32*(1), 62–84.
Mezouar, M. E., Zhang, F., & Zou, Y. (2018). Are tweets useful in the bug fixing process? An empirical study on Firefox and Chrome. *Empirical Software Engineering, 23*, 1704–1742.
NASA. Accessed June 16, 2023., from https://jwst.nasa.gov/content/forScientists/publications.html
Pariser, E. (2011). *The filter bubble: What the Internet is hiding from you*. Penguin.
Pawlik, A., Segal, J., Petre, M., & Sharp, H. (2015). Crowdsourcing scientific software documentation: A case study of the NumPy documentation project. *Computing in Science and Engineering, 17*(1), 28–36.
Pinch, T., & Bijker, W. (1987). The social construction of facts and artifacts. In W. Bijker, T. Hughes, & T. Pinch (Eds.), *The social construction of technological systems* (pp. 17–50). MIT Press.
Preece, J., Rogers, Y., Sharp, H., Benyon, D., Holland, S., & Carey, T. (1994). *Human-Computer Interaction*. Addison-Wesley.
Robinson, H., & Sharp, H. (2009). The emergence of object-oriented technology: the role of community. *Behaviour and Information Technology, 21*(3), 211–222.
Rogers, Y., Sharp, H., & Preece, J. (2023). *Interaction Design: Beyond human-computer interaction* (6th ed.). Wiley.
Rogers, Y., & Marshall, P. (2017). *Research in the wild*. Morgan & Claypool.
Sharp, H., Lotz, N., Mbayi-Kwelagobe, L., Woodroffe, M., Rajah, D., & Turugare, R. (2020). Socio-cultural factors and Interaction Design in Botswana: Results of a video diary study. *International Journal of Human-Computer Studies, 135*, 102375.
Sharp, H., Robinson, H., & Woodman, M. (2000). Software engineering: Community and culture. *IEEE Software, 17*(1), 40–47.
Smith, J. J., Jayne, L., & Burke, R. (2022). Recommender systems and algorithmic hate. In *Proceedings of the 16th conference on recommender systems (RecSys '22)* (pp. 592–597). ACM.
Wang, H., Miao, Z., Zhang, C., Wei, X., & Li, X. (2021). K-SEIR-Sim: A simple customized software for simulating the spread of infectious diseases. *Computational and Structural Biotechnology Journal, 19*, 1966–1975.
WDM. (2023). Accessed June 16, 2023, from https://www.wdm.co.uk/software
Winschiers-Theophilus, H., & Bidwell, N. J. (2013). Toward an Afro-centric indigenous HCI paradigm. *International Journal of Human-Computer Interaction, 29*(4), 243–255.

Resilience: The Key to Planetary and Societal Sustainability

Moshe Y. Vardi

Abstract In both computing and economics, efficiency is a cherished property. The field of algorithms, for example, focuses almost solely on their efficiency. A major goal of AI research is to increase efficiency by reducing human labor. In economics, the main advantage of the free market is that it promises "economic efficiency." A major lesson from many recent disasters is that both fields have over-emphasized efficiency and under-emphasized resilience. Natural evolution, in contrast, navigates the trade-off between efficiency, which is crucial for short-term survival, and resilience, which is crucial for long-term survival.

Two of the major risks facing humanity right now are the climate crisis and the crisis of democracy. We argue here that both crises stem from our narrow focus on efficiency at the expense of resilience. The key to planetary and societal sustainability is making resilience a primary consideration. Just like nature, we need to learn to navigate the tradeoff between efficiency and resilience.

1 Introduction

There is a trade-off between efficiency and resilience. Efficiency requires optimal adaptation to an existing environment, while resilience is an ability to adapt to large or sudden changes in the environment.[1] Emphasis on short-term gains has long tipped the balance in favor of efficiency.[2] The relentless pursuit of efficiency removes hurdles to the speed and reach of transactions, hurdles that also serve as buffers against shocks. Buffers provide resilience in the face of ecological, geopolitical, and financial crises.

[1] https://www.wsj.com/articles/efficiency-isnt-the-only-economic-virtue-11583873155

[2] https://www.project-syndicate.org/commentary/economic-thought-efficiency-versus-sustainability-by-robert-skidelsky-2020-12

M. Y. Vardi (✉)
Rice University, Houston, TX, USA
e-mail: vardi@cs.rice.edu

H. Werthner et al. (eds.), *Introduction to Digital Humanism*,
https://doi.org/10.1007/978-3-031-45304-5_24

As a computer scientist, I look at how algorithms provide a way to test assumptions about resilience, even as the field of computing itself shares the bias toward efficiency. Three recent crises—the 2021 winter storm in Texas, the COVID-19 pandemic, and the Boeing 737 Max software failure—highlight the cost of valuing efficiency over resilience and provide lessons for bringing society into balance.

The essence of digital humanism is the firm belief that technology development must be centered on human interests. This article argues that technology often focuses on efficiency and does that at the expense of resilience.

2 Economists and Engineers Focus on Efficiency

Economics has long been obsessed with efficiency. Economic efficiency means that goods and production are distributed or allocated to their most valuable uses and waste is eliminated or minimized. Free-market advocates argue further that, through individual self-interest and freedom of production and consumption, economic efficiency is achieved and the best interests of society, as a whole, are fulfilled.[3] Yet this conflates efficiency with the best societal outcome.

The intense focus on efficiency at the expense of resilience plagues not only business and economics but also technology. Society has educated generations of computer scientists that analyzing algorithms, the step-by-step instructions at the heart of computer software, boils down to measuring their computational efficiency. *The Art of Computer Programming* (Knuth, 1997), one of the founding texts of computer science, is dedicated to the analysis of algorithms, which is the process of figuring out the amount of time, storage, or other resources needed to execute them. In other words, efficiency is the sole concern in the design of algorithms, according to this guide.

Yet what about resilience? Designing resilient algorithms requires computer scientists to consider, in advance, what can go wrong and build effective countermeasures into their algorithms. Without designing for resilience, you get efficient but brittle algorithms. Of course, fault tolerance has been part of the canon of computing-system building for decades. Jim Gray's 1998 Turing Award citation refers to his invention of transactions as a mechanism to provide crash resilience to databases. Leslie Lamport's 2013 Turing Award citation refers to his work on fault tolerance in distributed systems. Nevertheless, computer science has yet to fully internalize the idea that resilience, which includes reliability, robustness, and more, must be pushed down to the algorithmic level. A case in point is search-result ranking. Google's original ranking algorithm was PageRank (Page et al., 1999), which works by counting the number and quality of links to a page to determine how

[3] https://www.investopedia.com/terms/i/invisiblehand.asp

important the website is. Yet PageRank is not resilient to manipulation, hence *search-engine optimization.*[4]

3 A Storm, Long Trains, a Plague, and Some Bad Software

Brittle systems are more likely than resilient systems to break down when crises strike. For instance, cold temperatures and blackouts during Winter Storm Uri[5] killed almost 200 people[6] in February 2021 in Texas. The storm damaged the power grid and water systems, which lacked the weatherproofing features common to utility infrastructure in much of the rest of the country. A recent investigation[7] by ProPublica revealed that trains are getting longer to increase their efficiency. Yet while railroads are getting richer, these "monster trains" are jumping off tracks across America and regulators are doing little to curb the risk.

The harsh economic consequences of failing to prepare for a pandemic, despite many early warnings,[8] provoked questions about whether the obsessive pursuit of efficiency, which has dominated standard business orthodoxy for decades, has made the global economic system more vulnerable to disruptive changes, such as the COVID-19 pandemic.[9] Thomas Friedman wrote in a May 2020 *New York Time*s column: "Over the past 20 years, we've been steadily removing man-made and natural buffers, redundancies, regulations and norms that provide resilience and protection when big systems—be they ecological, geopolitical or financial—get stressed .... We've been recklessly removing these buffers out of an obsession with short-term efficiency and growth, or without thinking at all.[10]"

A stark example of a system designed for efficiency and not resilience is the flight-control algorithm for the Boeing 737 Max. Boeing retrofitted its 737, a passenger aircraft first produced more than half a century ago, with engines that are more efficient. This retrofitting caused some flight instability, which the flight-control algorithm was designed to overcome.[11]

The algorithm, however, relied on data from a single sensor, and when the sensor failed, the algorithm incorrectly determined that the plane was stalling.[12] In

[4] https://en.wikipedia.org/wiki/Search_engine_optimization

[5] https://www.pbs.org/wgbh/nova/article/texas-winter-storm-uri/

[6] https://www.houstonchronicle.com/news/houston-texas/houston/article/texas-cold-storm-200-died-analysis-winter-freeze-16070470.php

[7] https://www.propublica.org/article/train-derailment-long-trains

[8] https://www.aging.senate.gov/imo/media/doc/hr157ml.pdf

[9] https://www.wsj.com/articles/efficiency-isnt-the-only-economic-virtue-11583873155

[10] https://www.nytimes.com/2020/05/30/opinion/sunday/coronavirus-globalization.html

[11] https://www.forbes.com/sites/petercohan/2019/04/02/mit-expert-highlights-divergent-condition-caused-by-737-max-engine-placement/?sh=e2bfd5a40aab

[12] https://www.cnn.com/2019/04/30/politics/boeing-sensor-737-max-faa/index.html

response, the algorithm caused the plane to dive as an emergency measure to recover from a stall that was not happening. The result was two horrific crashes and hundreds of the aircraft being grounded for nearly 2 years.[13] In retrospect, the engineers overly optimized for fuel economy and time to market at the expense of safety.[14]

4 Just-in-Time Manufacturing

Just-in-time manufacturing is a logistical methodology aimed primarily at reducing times within the production system as well as response times from suppliers and to customers (Cheng & Podolsky, 1996). The idea is to reduce inventory costs by reducing inventory, since warehousing inventory incurs costs of warehouse maintenance, idle inventory, and stocking and de-stocking. Just-in-time manufacturing tries to match production to demand by only supplying goods that have been ordered and focuses on efficiency, productivity, and reduction of "wastes" for the producer and supplier of goods. Parts should arrive, for example, "just in time" for the usage in the manufacturing line.

Just-in-time manufacturing, however, assumes best-case logistics, since a delay in arrival of goods may ricochet across the whole supply chain. Indeed, when the Ever Given container ship got stuck in the Suez Canal in March 2021, it had a worldwide impact, as every day the ship blocked the canal, dozens of ships carrying billions of dollars' worth of cargo had to wait to enter the waterway.[15]

5 The Price of Anarchy

If brittle systems are prone to disasters, why are they so prevalent? One explanation is that, short of disasters, systems that emphasize efficiency can achieve a particular kind of stability. A fundamental theorem in economics, known as the "First Welfare Theorem,"[16] states that under certain assumptions a market will tend toward a competitive balance point, known as the Pareto-optimal equilibrium,[17] which achieves economic efficiency.

How well, however, does such an equilibrium serve the best interests of society? A team of computer scientists (Koutsoupias & Papadimitriou, 1999) studied how beneficial or detrimental equilibria can be from a computational perspective. The researchers studied systems in which uncooperative agents share a common

[13] https://www.flightradar24.com/blog/the-status-of-the-737-max-around-the-world/

[14] https://www.nytimes.com/2020/11/24/sunday-review/boeing-737-max.html

[15] https://foreignpolicy.com/2021/11/10/what-the-ever-given-taught-the-world/

[16] https://en.wikipedia.org/wiki/Fundamental_theorems_of_welfare_economics

[17] https://www.britannica.com/topic/Pareto-optimality

resource, the mathematical equivalent of roadways or fisheries. They showed that such systems can have multiple equilibria, and different equilibria can vary in terms of the total social utility, e.g., traffic congestion or fishery health.

The question is how large the gap is between the best and worst equilibria. To that end, they investigated the ratio between the worst possible equilibrium in terms of social utility and the best equilibrium in terms of social utility (social optimum), a ratio dubbed the "price of anarchy"[18] because it measures how far from optimal such uncooperative systems can be. They showed that this ratio could be very high. In other words, economic efficiency does not guarantee that the best interests of society are fulfilled.

Another team of researchers asked how long it takes until economic agents converge to an equilibrium (Daskalakis et al., 2009). By studying the computational complexity[19] of computing such equilibria, the researchers showed that there are systems that take an exceedingly long time to converge to an equilibrium.

The implication is that economic systems are very unlikely ever to be in an equilibrium, because the underlying variables—such as prices, supply, and demand—are very likely to change while the systems are making their slow way toward convergence. In other words, *economic equilibrium*,[20] a central concept in economic theory, is a mythical rather than a real phenomenon. This is not necessarily an argument against free markets, but it does require a pragmatic view of them.

6 Free Trade

In fact, the very idea of free trade is motivated by the quest for efficiency. In 1817, David Ricardo argued that if two countries capable of producing two commodities engage in free trade, then each country would increase its overall consumption by exporting the goods for which it has a comparative advantage while importing the other goods (King, 2013). The benefits of free trade are undeniable. Over the past 30 years, worldwide free trade ("globalization") has lifted[21] over one billion people out of extreme poverty. At the same time, the question for efficiency has led to the situation that Taiwan, which today is one of the riskiest geopolitical points, dominates[22] worldwide semiconductor production, which led[23] the USA to launch a major investment in domestic semiconductor capacity.

[18] https://www.ams.org/publicoutreach/feature-column/fcarc-anarchy

[19] https://en.wikipedia.org/wiki/Computational_complexity

[20] https://www.investopedia.com/terms/e/economic-equilibrium.asp

[21] https://www.cato.org/commentary/globalizations-greatest-triumph-death-extreme-poverty#

[22] https://www.economist.com/special-report/2023/03/06/taiwans-dominance-of-the-chip-industry-makes-it-more-important

[23] https://cacm.acm.org/magazines/2023/1/267968-how-not-to-win-a-tech-war/fulltext

7 Why Sex Is Best

It is interesting to consider how nature deals with the trade-off between efficiency and resilience. This issue was addressed in a computer science paper titled "Sex as an Algorithm" (Livnat & Papadimitriou, 2016). Computer scientists have studied different search algorithms that are inspired by natural evolution. On one hand, there is *simulated annealing*,[24] which consists mainly of small steps that lead to an improvement of a goal function, but allowing also for some steps that are less than optimal, but could lead to better solutions further down the line. On the other hand, there are *genetic algorithms*,[25] which mimics natural selection by creating "offsprings" of previous solutions and then adding some random mutations. Computer scientists know that, in general, simulated annealing is faster than genetic algorithms (Franconi & Jennison, 1997).

Why, then, has nature chosen sexual reproduction as the almost exclusive reproduction mechanism in animals? The answer is that sex as an algorithm offers advantages other than good performance (Livnat & Papadimitriou, 2016). In particular, natural selection favors genes that work well with a greater diversity of other genes, and this makes the species more adaptable to disruptive environmental changes—that is to say, more resilient. Thus, in the interest of long-term survival, nature prioritized resilience over efficiency. Darwin supposedly said, "It's not the strongest of the species that survives, nor the most intelligent. It is the one that is most adaptable to change."

8 The Crisis of Democracy

US society is in the throes of deep polarization that not only leads to political paralysis but also threatens the very foundations of democracy. The phrase "The Disunited States of America"[26] (tracing back to Harry Turtledove's novel with this title) is often mentioned. "The U.S. is heading into its greatest political and constitutional crisis since the Civil War," wrote[27] Robert Kagan in the Washington Post, raising the specter of mass violence. How did we get here? What went wrong?

The last 40 years have launched a tsunami of technology on the world. The IBM Personal Computer—Model 5150, commonly known as the IBM PC—was released on August 12, 1981, and quickly became a smashing success. For its January 3, 1983, issue, *Time* magazine replaced its customary person-of-the-year cover with a graphical depiction of the IBM PC, "Machine of the Year." A computer on every work desk became reality for knowledge workers within a few years. These

[24] https://mathworld.wolfram.com/SimulatedAnnealing.html

[25] https://mathworld.wolfram.com/GeneticAlgorithm.html

[26] https://www.economist.com/weeklyedition/2022-09-03

[27] https://www.washingtonpost.com/opinions/2021/09/23/robert-kagan-constitutional-crisis/

knowledge workers soon also had a computer at home. With the introduction of the World Wide Web in 1989, many millions could access the Web. The commercialization of the Internet in 1995, and the introduction of the iPhone in 2007, extended access to billions.

The socioeconomic-political context of this technology tsunami is significant. There was a resurgence of neoliberalism marked by the election of Margaret Thatcher as Prime Minister of the UK in 1979 and by Ronald Reagan as President of the USA in 1980. Neoliberalism is free-market capitalism generally associated with policies of economic liberalization, privatization, deregulation, globalization, free trade, monetarism, austerity, and reductions in government spending. Neoliberalism increases the role of the private sector in the economy and society and diminishes the role of government. These trends have exerted significant competitive pressure on the economies of the developed world. To stay competitive, the manufacturing sector automated extensively, with the nascent distributed-computing technology playing a significant role. The implications are still with us.

A 2014 paper by MIT economist David Autor argued that information technology was destroying wide swaths of routine office and manufacturing jobs, creating in their place high-skill jobs (Autor, 2014). This labor polarization appeared to have brought about a shrinking middle class.[28] Autor's data for the USA and 16 European countries showed shrinkage in the middle and growth at the high and low ends of the labor-skill spectrum. This polarization greatly increased income and wealth disparities.

As information technology allowed the flooding of Internet users with more information than they could digest, tech companies supplied mass customization that allowed users to concentrate on information that confirmed preconceived opinions, resulting in deeper societal polarization (Vardi, 2018). This exacerbated further the "filter bubbles" that were created earlier in the broadcast media, following the abolition, in 1987, by the US Federal Communications Commission, of the "Fairness Doctrine," which required holders of broadcast licenses both to present controversial issues of public importance and to do so in a manner that reflected differing viewpoints fairly.

9 Lessons from the Internet

Our digital infrastructure, which has become a key component of the economic system in developed countries, is one of the few components that did not buckle under the stress of COVID-19. Indeed, in March 2020, many sectors of our economy switched in haste to the work from home (WFH) mode. This work from home, teach from home, and learn from home was enabled (to an imperfect degree, in many

[28] https://www.pewresearch.org/short-reads/2022/04/20/how-the-american-middle-class-has-changed-in-the-past-five-decades/ft_2022-04-20_middleclass_03/

cases) by the Internet. From its very roots of the ARPANET in the 1960s, resilience, enabled by seemingly inefficient redundancy, was a prime design goal for the Internet (Yoo, 2018). Resilience via redundancy is one of the great principles of computer science (von Neumann, 2017), which deserves more attention!

10 Conclusions

The bottom line is that resilience is a fundamental but underappreciated societal need. Yet both computing and economics have underemphasized resilience. In general, markets and people are quite bad at preparing for very low-probability or very long-term events (Taleb, 2010). For instance, people have to be forced to buy car insurance, because buying insurance is not efficient. After all, taken together, the insurance business is profitable for the insurers, not for the insured. The purpose of insurance is increased resilience. This example shows that ensuring resilience requires societal action and cannot be left solely to markets. The economic impact of the pandemic shows the cost of society's failure to act.[29] Furthermore, COVID-19 may be just the warm-up act[30] for the much bigger impending climate crisis, so focusing on resilience is becoming more and more important.

There seems to be a broad recognition that the incalculable suffering and trauma of COVID-19 offer societies[31] ways to change for the better.[32] Similar lessons can be drawn from Winter Storm Uri and the Boeing 737 Max. Focusing on resilience is a way for societies to change for the better. In the meantime, the steady flow of news events—like a pipeline company that appears to have underinvested in security[33]—continues to underscore the cost of prizing efficiency over resilience. The big question is how the AC ("after COVID") world will differ from the BC ("before COVID") world. Kurt Vonnegut supposedly said, "We'll go down in history as the first society that wouldn't save itself because it wasn't cost effective." Resilience *must* be a key societal focus in the AC world.

Discussion Questions for Students and Their Teachers

Please consider your own research area. What are the dimensions of efficiency and resilience you can identify? Is there a trade-off between these two dimensions? Where is the current emphasis? How can you increase the emphasis on resilience?

---

[29] https://healthpolicy.usc.edu/article/covid-19s-total-cost-to-the-economy-in-us-will-reach-14-trillion-by-end-of-2023-new-research/

[30] https://www.scmp.com/comment/opinion/article/3114641/covid-19-only-dress-rehearsal-transformations-coming-climate-change

[31] https://www.washingtonpost.com/opinions/2020/10/06/fareed-zakaria-lessons-post-pandemic-world/

[32] https://www.wired.com/story/who-will-we-be-when-the-pandemic-is-over/

[33] https://www.washingtonpost.com/business/2021/05/15/energy-cost-cutting-price/

Learning Resources for Students

1. *Recipe for Disaster: The Formula That Killed Wall Street.*[34]
   Analyze the 2008–9 Financial Crisis through the efficiency/resilience lens.
2. *On the Inefficiency of Being Efficient* (Goldberg, 1975).
   Summarize the main point of the paper through the efficiency/resilience lens.
3. *Antifragile – Things That Gain from Disorder* (Taleb, 2012).
   What is the argument here against efficiency?

References

Autor, D. (2014). *Polanyi's Paradox and the shape of employment growth*. National Bureau of Economic Research, No. w20485.

Cheng, T. C., & Podolsky, S. (1996). *Just-in-time manufacturing: An introduction*. Springer Science and Business Media.

Daskalakis, C., Goldberg, P. W., & Papadimitriou, C. H. (2009). The complexity of computing a Nash equilibrium. *Communications of the ACM, 52*(2), 89–97.

Franconi, L., & Jennison, C. (1997). Comparison of a genetic algorithm and simulated annealing in an application to statistical image reconstruction. *Statistics and Computing, 7*, 193–207.

Goldberg, M. A. (1975). On the inefficiency of being efficient. *Environment and Planning A, 7*(8), 921–939.

King, J. E. (2013). Ricardo on trade. *Economic Papers – A Journal of Applied Economics and Policy, 32*(4), 462–469.

Knuth, D. E. (1997). *The art of computer programming*. Pearson Education.

Koutsoupias, E., & Papadimitriou, C. H. (1999). Worst-case equilibria. *Proceedings of the 16th annual symposium on theoretical aspects of computer science*, Lecture Notes in Computer Science 1563, pp. 404–413.

Livnat, A., & Papadimitriou, C. (2016). Sex as an algorithm: The theory of evolution under the lens of computation. *Communications of the ACM, 59*(11), 84–93.

Page, L., Brin, S., Motwani, R., & Winograd, T. (1999). *The PageRank citation ranking – Bringing order to the web*. Stanford Infolab.

Taleb, N. C. (2010). *The Black Swan -- The impact of the highly improbable* (2nd ed.). Random House.

Taleb, N. C. (2012). *Antifragile – Things that gain from disorder*. Random House.

Vardi, M. Y. (2018). How the hippies destroyed the Internet. *Communications of the ACM, 61*(7), 9.

von Neumann, J. (2017). The general and logical theory of automata. In *Systems research for behavioral science* (pp. 97–107). Routledge.

Yoo, C. S. (2018). Paul Baran, network theory, and the past, present, and future of the Internet. *Colorado Technology Law Journal*.

[34] https://www.wired.com/2009/02/wp-quant/?redirectURL=https%3A%2F%2Fwww.wired.com%2F2009%2F02%2Fwp-quant%2F

How Blockchain Technology Can Help to Arrive at Fair Ecosystems and Platforms

Jaap Gordijn

Abstract Digital ecosystems and platforms are an important part of the economy. However, specifically the tech-oriented platforms are often considered as "unfair." In this chapter, we aim to more precisely articulate this feeling of unfairness. We consider fairness in digital ecosystems and platforms as fair if a decision as a result of applying a rule should accommodate all applicable moral distinctions and reasons for all actors involved. However, fairness is not only related to the operations of a digital ecosystem or platform. Fairness of digital ecosystems and platforms requires fair governance also. We consider fair governance as a prerequisite for fair governance, because the concerns of all stakeholders can then be included in the decision process. As a second assumption, we argue that decentralized decision-making contributes to fair governance. If this assumption holds, it is worthwhile to investigate how decentralized governance can be implemented and supported by information technology. We explain how blockchain technology, with consensus reaching at its core, can support such decentralized decision-making.

1 Introduction

Over the past years, many digital business ecosystems and platforms have emerged. We define a business ecosystem as "a system of economic actors that depend on each other for their survival and well-being" and a platform as "a shared infrastructure of a value network on top of which members of the value network create additional value" (Wieringa and Gordijn 2023). As we consider a platform as a special case of an ecosystem from now on, we use the term "ecosystem" to refer to both in this chapter.

Many new ecosystems are enabled by advances in information and communication technology (ICT) in general and the widespread use of the Internet in particular. Well-known examples of these ecosystems are the *GAFA*, which means Google,

J. Gordijn (✉)
VU, Amsterdam, The Netherlands
e-mail: j.gordijn@vu.nl

H. Werthner et al. (eds.), *Introduction to Digital Humanism*,
https://doi.org/10.1007/978-3-031-45304-5_25

Apple, Facebook, and Amazon, but there are many more. These *digital* ecosystems are, once they have grown enormously, a substantial source of income for the owner (s) and/or their shareholders.

However, questions can be asked regarding the *fairness* of these new digital ecosystems. We consider an ecosystem as fair if decision as a result of applying a rule should accommodate all applicable moral distinctions and reasons for all actors involved (see also Sect. 2). The new digital ecosystems and platforms are often in the news because of undesired behavior. There are many examples, such as the Cambridge Analytica scandal (Hinds et al., 2020), the resistance of Amazon against labor unions (Reese and Alimahomed-Wilson, 2022), and the unreasonable high fee Apple charges in its app store for in-app purchases (known as the Spotify case) (Braga, 2021).

The undesired behavior of the emerging big tech digital ecosystems is possible due to (1) centralized governance (one agent takes all decisions) and/or (2) uncontrolled behavior by some agent(s) external to the ecosystem (e.g., shareholders). Many big tech firms have effectively one person taking decisions (the CEO) or are heavily influenced by creating shareholder value. Moreover, because the value propositions of the big tech firms are relatively new, regulation and legislation are often lacking or insufficient. For instance, only very recently, the Digital Services Act (Rutgers & Sauter, 2021) in Europe is active. This act aims to reduce some undesired behavior of the centralized or shareholder-driven ecosystems of the big tech firms.

Having the proper regulation and legislation in place is certainly important to arrive at fairer digital business ecosystems. However, we argue that fairness of executive decision-taking is also needed. One possible way to achieve this is to distribute decision power over a series of agents, in other words, the creation of checks and balances in the ecosystem. Note that distribution of decision-taking is not a guarantee or strict requirement for a fair business ecosystem. There are well-known counter examples. For instance, in the past, the electricity energy ecosystem was quite centralized (only a few power plants in a country which could determine the price). But at the same time, the electricity energy ecosystem has always been subject to strong government regulation, preventing undesired behavior. The other way around, it can be debated whether an extremely distributed ecosystem, such as the Bitcoin, is fair at all. Some argue that the Bitcoin is actually nothing more than a gambling engine, given the substantial fluctuations of the exchange rate of the Bitcoin, and also a pyramid game, in which early adopters of the Bitcoin got extremely rich.

In this chapter, we assume that distribution of executive decision-taking, for example, by means of a voting mechanism, contributes to a fairer ecosystem. The idea is that by involving the relevant stakeholders in the decision process, their interests can be better addressed and dealt with. This does not always result in fairness as other factors may do so too, e.g., strong and fair government regulation. However, if, for example, Amazon had installed a mechanism where all agents in their ecosystem, including their employees, would have a say, likely a number of undesired behaviors would not have happened.

This chapter is structured as follows. Section 2 provides some perspectives on "fairness." In Sect. 3 we define the notions of digital business ecosystem and platforms. We then argue in Sect. 4 two different ways to achieve fairness in ecosystems and platforms, namely, legislation and penalties and fairness *by design*. Thereafter, in Sect. 5, we assess whether achieving fairness can be achieved by using blockchain technology, due to its inherently distributed nature. In Sect. 6, we present our conclusions.

2 Fairness

2.1 Unfair Behavior

Digital ecosystems, and specifically the well-known tech firms, may behave unfairly in many ways. They may treat their own personnel badly, e.g., pay them very low wages, offer them bad temporary contracts, see them as one-person companies who they can squeeze out, offer bad labor conditions, have an extreme and pressing performance yield system in place, and deny personnel to join a labor union. Moreover, powerful actors in the ecosystem pay very low prices to their suppliers if they have no option to go elsewhere. The other way around, they may charge their customers an unreasonable high fee compared to the service/product offered, often as a result of an on purposely created monopolistic position. Finally, they may avoid tax and/or pollute substantially. The latter happens at the country/continent level and is unfair to the society of that country/continent.

2.2 Toward a Notion of Fairness

The above discussed behavior raises the question of what fairness actually is. This is not an easy question to answer because the notion of fairness is addressed by a broad range of scientific disciplines and not always in the same way. It is not our intention to give a comprehensive overview of the literature; rather we present a compact overview of how fairness is addressed in various areas.

- Philosophy: Hooker (2005) defined *formal fairness* as "interpreting and applying rules consistently, i.e. applying the same rules impartially and equally to each agent." The notion of formal fairness has problems, because its definition does allow bad rules. For instance, the rule not to admit men to a bar can be impartially and equally applied to each agent but is not necessarily fair. Actually, fairness should be about *substantial fairness*, which goes beyond the rules as such. A decision as a result of applying a rule should accommodate all applicable moral distinctions and reasons. This raises the question what moral reasons actually are. In Hooker (2005), a number of these reasons are mentioned (also based on the work of Broome (1990)): "(1) reasons deriving from the possibility of benefits or harms, (2) reasons never to kill or torture, and never to order such acts, and (3) reasons deriving from needs, desert, or agreements."

- Economics: Following many economic-oriented scientists, Hal Varian considers an allocation of x is fair if and only if it is both equitable and Pareto efficient (Varian 1976). Equity requires that each agent considers his own position at least as good as any other agent. Pareto efficiency refers to maximizing the assignment of x. This happens if the worst-off agent is the one who no one envies, and the best-off agent is the agent who envies no one. The advantage of this point of view is that it is internal, meaning that the observations (position, envying) are made by the agents and not by an external observer, which would require that observations for different agents are comparable. There is also work that studies the allocation of discrete units of x, in the situation that not enough units of x are available for all stakeholders. The approach here is to organize a fair lottery, where each agent has equal chances to win x.
- AI and computer science: In AI, fairness often refers to bias of algorithms. Essentially, algorithms are supposed to treat everyone the same. For an overview of fairness and bias in AI, see Xivuri and Twinomurinzi (2021). However, machine learning and related technologies sometimes fail and treat people very differently. Fairness in computer science is already quite old. For instance, Wong et al. (2008) define fairness in operating system scheduling as "the ability to distribute CPU bandwidth equally to all tasks based on their priorities." This corresponds to the work in the field of economics to assign discrete units of x to a number of stakeholders.

The list above is not exhaustive at all but gives an impression how various disciplines view the concept of fairness. Following Hooker (2005), we consider an ecosystem as fair if a decision as a result of applying a rule should accommodate all applicable moral distinctions and reasons for all actors of the ecosystem.

3 Digital Business Ecosystems and Platforms

We define a *business ecosystem* as "a system of economic actors that depend on each other for their survival and well-being" and a platform as "a shared infrastructure of a value network on top of which members of the value network create additional value" (Wieringa & Gordijn, 2023). A digital business ecosystem is a normal business ecosystem, with the additional requirement that the ecosystem is supported by information technology in its operational and/or managerial processes, and/or the value proposition itself has a strong digital dimension (e.g., Netflix, Spotify, Facebook). Note that, due to the digital transformation wave, currently in the Global North, most business ecosystems are digital ecosystems.

Digital business ecosystems need a *business model* which we consider as "a description of how value is created, how it is delivered to customers, and how companies capture revenue from this" (Wieringa & Gordijn, 2023). We describe an ecosystem's business model as a *network* of actors (enterprises, non-for-profit organizations, and consumers), which we call a *value network*: "the organizations, companies and people who collaborate and compete to create, deliver, and capture value" (Wieringa & Gordijn, 2023).

We consider *platforms* as a special kind of ecosystem. They are defined as "a shared infrastructure of a value network on top of which members of the value network create additional value." Many examples of a platform exist; the Android operating system is a platform that is used by app developers (including Google itself) and end users, and Amazon marketplace is a platform that offers trading functionality of sellers and buyers (and again Amazon itself is a seller on the platform). Many platforms are centralized, meaning that they are dominated by a single party with respect to decision-making. But this is not always the case. For instance, OpenBazaar is an example of a decentralized trading platform. Bitcoin and Ethereum are also positioned as decentralized platforms, although it can be contested they are truly decentralized in terms of governance decision-making.

It is debated if all ecosystems and platforms are fair. Without defining fairness already, intuitively many ecosystems are not so fair. For instance, the Cambridge Analytica scandal (Hinds et al., 2020) exposes unfairness in terms of privacy-related data, Amazon treats employees sometimes unfair (Reese & Alimahomed-Wilson, 2022), and the Apple app store charges its customers (e.g., app developers) an unreasonable high fee, which moreover not directly corresponds to the effort spent by the Apple app store (Braga, 2021). So, the question emerges how we can develop fairer ecosystems. We consider two approaches: (1) by means of legislation and (2) by establishing fair governance. We elaborate further on these two different approaches in Sect. 4.

4 Toward Fairer Ecosystems and Platforms

4.1 *Legislation*

The fist strategy to achieve more fairness of an ecosystem is by means of *legislation*, or related to that, (self)-*regulation.*, followed by penalties if someone breaks the rules.

Legislation sets the rules according to which actors in an ecosystem should behave, and if they violate a rule, they have to pay a fine, or they are banned from the market altogether. An example is the EU legislation on reduction, which forces countries to implement rules on the nation level to achieve reduction. Obviously, these rules come with penalties.

Examples of fair legislation are EU competition and contract laws in general and the Digital Services Act and the Digital Markets Act in particular (see Rutgers and Sauter (2021)) for an overview). Both acts are interesting because implicitly they define what the EU considers as fair.

For instance, the Digital Markets Act lists unfair behavior. The act identifies *gatekeepers*, which are effectively the large platforms. These gatekeepers have to follow rules, for example, to allow business users to access the data that they generate on the platform, to offer companies that advertise on the platform independent tools to see the effects of the advertisement, not to rank services of the platform itself higher than similar services of others, allow users to link to other items outside of the platform, and track users outside of the platform.

According to Rutgers and Sauter (2021), the Digital Services Act is mainly about transparency and accountability. This often relates to the content of the platform, how it is moderated, what the rights of the users are with respect to the content, and how to deal with disputes.

4.2 Fair Governance by Design

Another way to achieve fair ecosystems is to include fairness explicitly during the (re)design of the ecosystem at hand. The idea is that the resulting ecosystem is already fair *by design*, and moreover that constructs are in place such that the ecosystem remains fair over time.

We employ two assumptions with respect to designing fair ecosystems. The first assumption is that *fair ecosystems require fair governance*. In other words, if fair governance is in place, operations of the ecosystem will be fair too. This is visualized in Fig. 1 as the *governance paradigm*.

We follow the well-known *control* paradigm of Blumenthal (see, e.g., Bemelmans (1994) and later de Leeuw (1973)) to arrive at the more specific *governance paradigm* (see Fig. 1). We distinguish three systems: (1) the *governed* system (such as the operations of a company) that has to obey to rules set by the governing system (e.g., the management of that same company), (2) the *governing* system that monitors the governed system, and (3) the *meta* governing system that controls the governing system (e.g., the government of a country). Systems, such as the governed system, are exposed to rules and are continuously monitored whether they comply with these rules. Obviously, these rules should be fair, e.g., follow appropriate moral distinctions and reasons as, for example, explained by Hooker (2005) and Broome (1990) (see also Sect. 2). Governance is executed by the governing system. This can be a single agent but also a group of agents (e.g., a parliament). The governing system imposes rules on the governed system and checks whether the rules are satisfied. The governance paradigm can be applied recursively, e.g., the environment may govern the governing system itself. As an example, inhabitants who live in a democracy (collectively called the environment) every few years vote for parliament members (the governing system). In turn, the governing system sets rules, legislation consisting of laws for the governed system, e.g., everyone in a particular country.

Our second assumption is less trivial. We take the position that fair governance can be accomplished by *decentralized* governance systems. The underlying idea is

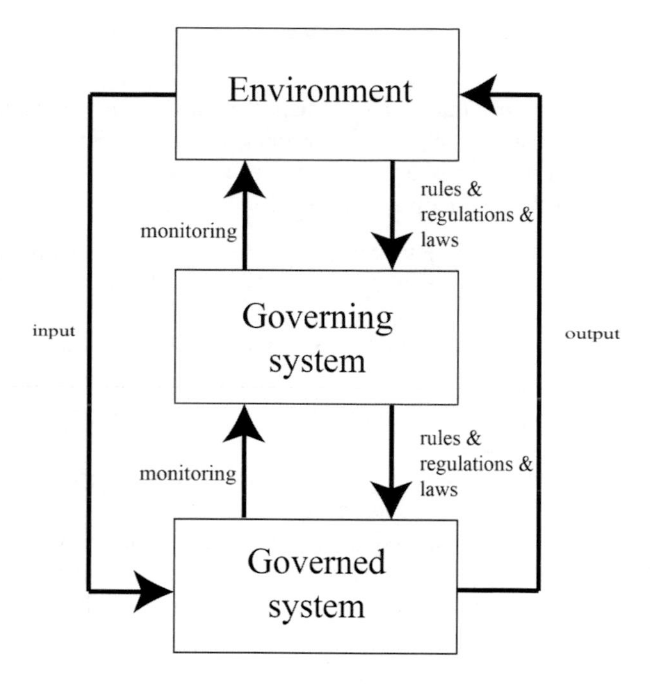

Fig. 1 The governance paradigm

that involving (a representation of) agents, which are well balanced in terms of interests results in a fairer ecosystem than doing so otherwise. A significant part of a governance process is decision-making. In case of decentralized governance, decision-making often happens via a form of voting. In contrast, in *centralized* governance, only one agent is executing governance processes and can take decisions by him/herself. This only works if the decision-taking authority shows fair behavior, and most of the current digital platforms clearly show that this is not always the case. However, it is not always true that centralized governance is unfair. For instance, the electricity energy industry has a so-called transmission system operator (TSO) who is responsible that at all times, there is a balance between demand and supply of electricity in the network (if this is not the case, the network shuts down, resulting in power outages). The TSO is an example of highly centralized governance; there is only TSO per country, and the TSO controls directly the other parties in the ecosystem, namely, producers and consumers of electricity energy. However, the TSO does not usually behave in an unfair way. This can be contributed to very strong regulation and legislation; there is strict law the TSO should comply with too. This happens in many other fair centralized ecosystems too; they are considered as fair but often are heavily regulated.

In sum, we argue that (1) fairness of ecosystems can be improved by having fair governance and (2) that decentralization of decision power may result in fair governance. Therefore, we need to understand better what fair governance actually is.

4.3 Fair Governance

If we assume that fair governance actually helps to realize fair ecosystems, the question arises what fair governance actually entails. Our interpretation of fair governance is based on Graham et al. (2003), Sheng (2009), and Jairam et al. (2021). To summarize, fair governance requires:

1. **Participation.** Fair governance requires active involvement in an unconstrained way in the decision-making process of *all* affected agents.
2. **Rule of law.** *All* agents should be treated equally and fairly by the law.
3. **Effectiveness and efficiency.** Fair governance should perform its tasks without using resources unnecessarily and address the concerns of agents well.
4. **Transparency.** Information to make decisions should be available to all agents and easy to find.
5. **Responsiveness.** A fair governance structure should react within a reasonable time frame toward its agents.
6. **Consensus-oriented.** Fair governance should try to reach (broad) agreement about the decisions taken, e.g., via a voting mechanism.
7. **Accountability.** Each agent participating in the governance structure is held responsible for its actions.

Returning to Fig. 1, the governance paradigm, it is clear that the understanding of fair governance supposes a governance system consisting of *multiple* agents, rather than just one, because in the latter case the governance process can easily be corrupted. In addition, these agents need to be treated fairly. In terms of decision-making, a fair governance system requires multiple agents and often the use of some form of voting to make it fair. Many forms of voting exist, such as a majority vote, a delegated vote, a voting system that requires reaching a quorum, etc. Point is that no single agent can take a decision on its own. If the agents are well balanced in terms of interests and decision power, we argue that decentralized decision-making, e.g., using voting can be fair.

Note that the governing system should be governed itself; we also refer to this as *meta governance*. In the case of most tech platforms, the meta governance is executed by the shareholders, rather than the stakeholders. This often results in profit maximization. In sum, we argue stakeholder value rather than shareholder value. From the meta governance system's perspective, the governance system is just a governed system, with the special property that it executes governance tasks. Effectively, we just apply the governance paradigm recursively. We argue that the governance system as shown in Fig. 1 can only be fair if the meta governance system is fair too. Consequently, and in line with our earlier argumentation, the meta governance system should consist of multiple, and well-balanced, agents too. In other words, governance systems consisting of one agent only should be avoided at (all) meta levels.

5 Fair Governance Using Blockchain Technology

5.1 Blockchain Technology

Blockchain technology is a fully decentralized solution to support ecosystems with no central or intermediate party. The most well-known example of blockchain technology is Bitcoin (see Nakamoto (2009)) and later Ethereum (see Tikhomirov (2018)). However, there any many implementations of blockchain technology. They differ in scaling possibilities in terms of the number of supported nodes and the number of transactions processed per second. In addition, some blockchain implementations provide support for user-oriented distributed computing, also known as smart contracting.

The idea of blockchain technology is that a table containing data, often called the *ledger*, is not stored at a central party, such as a bank, but is replicated over participants, called *nodes*. A node is owned by an agent. For instance, this allows the Bitcoin blockchain to handle payments between two agents directly, without the need to involve a bank to handle the payment. The change in the ledger, normally kept by a bank in a centralized ecosystem, is replicated at all ledgers of the nodes.

Obviously, having the ledger at a (large) number of nodes opens up the possibility to commit a fraud; an agent could change something in his locally stored ledger (e.g., increase the amount of money owned by him) and then claim that his ledger represents the correct situation, in blockchain technology called the *world state*. To mitigate this, each blockchain has a so-called consensus protocol. There are many different protocols, but they all aim to achieve *one* agreed and accepted world state. Therefore, changing the ledger locally would not work, because that represents a state for which no consensus was reached.

A blockchain also keeps an immutable ordered history of previous world states (hence the name block*chain*). This is useful to have a trace of what happens, which cannot be repudiated by any agent.

Some blockchains such as Ethereum (see Tikhomirov (2018)) also have *smart contracts*. Since a blockchain has no central agent who can execute custom computations, there is a need to execute computation in a decentralized way, e.g., by the nodes, in a trusted manner. Smart contracts provide that functionality. In terms of governance, they are useful to support and automate the decentralized governance processes, in a decentralized way itself.

Governance of the well-known blockchain platforms (Bitcoin, Ethereum) happens largely off-chain. This means that updates and improvements regarding the Bitcoin or Ethereum protocol, which should be considered as governance activities, are not really supported by the blockchain platform but happen in discussion fora or other informal communication means. The process is explained by Bitcoin Improvement Proposals (BIPs) and Ethereum Improvement Proposals (EIPs), but these processes are only specified on a very high level, and moreover not formalized, e.g., by using smart contracts. Actually, only decision-taking concerning the acceptance of the implementation of a BIP/EIP happens by means of on-chain voting. Tezos (see Allombert et al. (2019)) is one of the blockchain platforms that supports on-chain governance. We consider on-chain governance as a necessity to arrive at fair governance, since it supports governance (from inception of changes until decision-making about specific implementations) in a fully decentralized way. In contrast, off-chain governance as used by Bitcoin and Ethereum is vulnerable to control by just a small group, specifically during the process that leads to a governance decision. In many cases, in-depth knowledge about the protocol is needed to meaningfully comment on changes of that protocol. In practice, there is only a limited group who can do so.

An Important development for decentralized governance are decentralized autonomous organizations (DAOs) (see Wang et al. (2019) for introduction). DAOs have their governance processes, which are fully implemented as a set of contracts. Some well-known services implemented using blockchain technology, such as Uniswap (exchange of cryptos), Compound (crypto lending), Dash (decentralized payment), Metaverse DAO (talent hunting), and Aave (assigning grants), all use DAOs for their governance.

5.2 The Governance Paradigm and Blockchain

In Fig. 1, we introduced the governance paradigm, and the distinction was made between the governance systems, which monitor and control the governed system. Moreover, the governance system itself can be governed by a governance system. As such, the governance paradigm can be recursively applied, to arrive at meta-governance, or even meta-meta-governance. How will this relate to blockchain as a mechanism to implement governance?

First, blockchain is intended for decentralized ecosystems. It makes no sense to apply blockchain to a single agent only, because then a single information will do. In the case of Bitcoin, for example, the governed system is the set of nodes that have reached consensus about the world state (e.g., transactions done). Reaching consensus should be meaningful and require domain knowledge. In blockchain technology, it is possible to achieve consensus about everything, even about nonsense. Consequently, consensus should be based on domain semantics. In Bitcoin, consensus should be reached about avoiding double spending, and if someone possesses the Bitcoins that he wants to transfer, and about the mining/creation of new coins.

The current governance process of Bitcoin, as outlined in BIP 0001, governs the Bitcoin protocol as discussed above, at the governed system level. In Bitcoin, only the final decision to accept a change in the protocol is on chain. So, the governance process is very limited, namely, taking a decision about a BIP using a majority vote. Systems like Tezos and DAOs are far more extensive in the support of governance of the governed system. Smart contracts define the process of governance and hence can be adapted to the required use case.

At the meta-level governance system, systems such as Tezos and DAOs have to define how the governance of Tezos and these DAOs work themselves. Ideally, it would also be possible to change these meta-governance rules, e.g., by a meta-meta-governance system.

5.3 Is Blockchain Fair?

In Sect. 4.3, we introduced fair governance. We now will evaluate how well blockchain technology corresponds to our understanding of fair governance.

1. **Participation.** By definition, blockchain technology considers the participation of multiple agents. Whether *all* these agents play a role in the governance process depends on the chosen consensus protocol and/or the way how the smart contracts are defined in DAOs. For instance, Bitcoin uses the proof-of-work (PoW) protocol, which involves all nodes (but not the agents that own a wallet only). But there are many other protocols, e.g., delegated proof-of-stake (PoS), which uses a representative sample of all the agents.
2. **Rule of law.** Some blockchain implementations treat all agents precisely the same. However, in general it depends on the chosen consensus protocol and/or of the smart contracts that implement the governance process. As an example, since a while, Ethereum uses PoS, where agents with higher stakes have more influence than others.
3. **Effectiveness and efficiency.** In terms of effectiveness, blockchain systems do precisely as agreed and stated by the smart contracts, provided that the governance is implemented on chain. The efficiency largely depends on the used consensus protocol. PoW (Bitcoin) is known to be very expensive in terms of computing and hence energy consumption. At the other side of the spectrum, practical Byzantine fault tolerance (pBFT) (see, e.g., Aggarwal and Kumar (2021)) is very efficient but unfortunately does not scale in terms of the number of nodes and hence agents.
4. **Transparency.** Public, non-permissioned, blockchains are fully transparent. Permissioned blockchains are restricted by definition; the agent should be granted access. In addition, it is a matter of design to allow visibility of data to everyone, because certain parts can be encrypted. However, there is no principal reason why a blockchain-supported governance system would not be transparent.
5. **Responsiveness.** The responsiveness of a blockchain system depends again in the chosen consensus protocol. If a PoW protocol is used, such as in Bitcoin, transactions can be considered final after about 60 min. Other protocols, such as pBFT, are final almost immediately.
6. **Consensus-oriented.** It goes without saying that consensus is at the very core of every blockchain platform. Currently, there is a broad selection of consensus protocols supported by the various implementations. This is a strong point of blockchain in relation to fair governance.
7. **Accountability.** Blockchains keep an immutable log of (data) transactions, which can be inspected by everyone. It is not possible to reverse a transaction, or to change it. Consequently, blockchain technology is useful to implement accountability.

6 Conclusions

In this chapter, we argued that blockchain technology can contribute to fairer business ecosystems and platforms. Many of these ecosystems and platforms are centrally led, opening the door to unfair behavior. Unfortunately, such behavior happens often.

One approach to address unfair behavior is to establish dedicated legislation and regulation, with penalties if agents misbehave. The EU Digital Services and Markets Acts are recent examples of such legislation.

An entirely different method is to include fairness in the (re)design process of digital business ecosystems and platforms. The focus should then be on fair governance, as fair governance leads to fair operations. Fair governance can be established by a divide-and-conquer strategy; decision-making and the process leading to decisions should not be in one hand but distributed in a balanced way over a number of agents with different interests.

Blockchain technology, depending on specific choices made, e.g., the consensus protocol, can be instrumental in supporting fair governance in a computational way. It allows for an approach where all agents participate, in an effective, efficient, responsive, and transparent way. Rules of law can be encoded into smart contracts and enforced automatically. Blockchain technology is rich in terms of supported consensus protocols. And finally, since it provides an immutable history, accountability can be easily achieved.

Discussion Questions for Students and Their Teachers

1. Evaluate fairness of blockchain technology with the definition of fairness of economics in mind (an allocation of x is fair if and only if it is both equitable and Pareto efficient).
2. Give some examples of digital platforms that you consider as fair, and motivate why you think these platforms are fair.
3. One way to achieve fairness is by means of legislation. Argue why only legislation is not sufficient to arrive at fair ecosystems.
4. This chapter assumes that fair governance requires decentralized governance. Give at least three examples of ecosystems where this assumption does not hold.
5. Blockchain is a technology to implement decentralized governance. Which other technologies may contribute to decentralized governance?

Learning Resources for Students

1. On fairness from a philosophical point of view, see Hooker (2005) and Broome (1990). These articles provide a good starting point to understand the philosophical thinking about the notion of fairness. The work of Broome is foundational and should be read by anyone working in the field of fairness; the article of Hooker critically builds on top of Broome's article.
2. On digital ecosystems and platforms, see Wieringa and Gordijn (2023). This book discusses digital ecosystems in detail and analyzes some popular ecosystems critically, e.g., with respect to fairness issues.

3. On fair governance, see Graham et al. (2003), Sheng (2009), and Jairam et al. (2021). The first two articles introduce aspects of fair governance and are also used in this chapter. The last article applies the first two articles on governance of blockchain systems.

References

Aggarwal, S., Kumar, N. (2021). Chapter sixteen - hyperledger working model. In S. Aggarwal, N. Kumar, P. Raj, eds. The blockchain technology for secure and smart applications across industry verticals, Vol. 121 of *Advances in computers* (pp. 323–343). Elsevier.

Allombert, V., Bourgoin, M., & Tesson, J. (2019). Introduction to the tezos blockchain. In *2019 International conference on high performance computing and simulation (HPCS)*, IEEE, pp. 1–10.

Bemelmans, T. (1994). *Bestuurlijke informatiesystemen en automatisering*.

Braga, M. (2021). *Spotify vs. Apple: A Titans*, PhD thesis, Católica Porto Business School.

Broome, J. (1990). Fairness. *Proceedings of the Aristotelian Society, 91*, 87–101. http://www.jstor.org/stable/4545128

de Leeuw, A. (1973). *Over besturing: een systeemtheoretische beschouwing*, TH Eindhoven. Vakgr. organisatiekunde: rapport, Technische Hogeschool Eindhoven. Tekst van de voordracht gehouden in het bedrijfskundig kolloquium op 21 september 1973, Eindhoven.

Graham, J., Plumptre, T., Amos, B., on Governance, I. Canada, P. (2003). *Principles for good governance in the 21st century, policy brief*. Institute on Governance. https://books.google.com.my/books?id=Bs1CtAEACAAJ

Hinds, J., Williams, E. J., & Joinson, A. N. (2020). "it wouldn't happen to me": Privacy concerns and perspectives following the Cambridge analytica scandal. *International Journal of Human-Computer Studies, 143*, 102498. https://www.sciencedirect.com/science/article/pii/S1071581920301002

Hooker, B. (2005). Fairness. *Ethical Theory and Moral Practice, 8*(4), 329–352.

Jairam, G., da Silva Torres, I., Kaya, F., Makkes, M. (2021). A decentralized fair governance model for permissionless blockchain systems. In G. Guizzardi, T. P. Sales, C. Griffo, M. Fumagalli (Eds.), *CEUR Proceeding of the Workshop of Value Modelling and Business Ontologies*, Vol. 2835, CEUR. https://dise-lab.nl/wp-content/uploads/2021/02/Governance_in_blockchain-2.pdf

Nakamoto, S. (2009). *Bitcoin: A peer-to-peer electronic cash system*. http://www.bitcoin.org/bitcoin.pdf.

Reese, E., & Alimahomed-Wilson, J. (2022). Teamsters confront amazon: An early assessment. *New Labor Forum, 31*(3), 43–51. https://doi.org/10.1177/10957960221116835

Rutgers, J., & Sauter, W. (2021). Promoting fair private governance in the platform economy: Eu competition and contract law applied to standard terms. *Cambridge Yearbook of European Legal Studies, 23*, 343–381.

Sheng, Y. (2009). *What is good governance*. United Nations Economic and Social Commission for Asia and the Pacific.

Tikhomirov, S. (2018). Ethereum: State of knowledge and research perspectives. In A. Imine, J. M. Fernandez, J.-Y. Marion, L. Logrippo, & J. Garcia-Alfaro (Eds.), *Foundations and practice of security* (pp. 206–221). Springer International Publishing.

Varian, H. R. (1976). Two problems in the theory of fairness. *Journal of Public Economics, 5*(3), 249–260. https://www.sciencedirect.com/science/article/pii/0047272776900189

Wang, S., Ding, W., Li, J., Yuan, Y., Ouyang, L., & Wang, F.-Y. (2019). Decentralized autonomous organizations: Concept, model, and applications. *IEEE Transactions on Computational Social Systems, 6*(5), 870–878.

Wieringa, R., & Gordijn, J. (2023). *Digital business ecosystems - How to create, capture, and deliver value in business networks*. TVE Press.
Wong, C. S., Tan, I., Kumari, R. D., & Fun, W. (2008). Towards achieving fairness in the linux scheduler. *Operating Systems Review, 42*, 34–43.
Xivuri, K., & Twinomurinzi, H. (2021). A systematic review of fairness in artificial intelligence algorithms. In D. Dennehy, A. Griva, N. Pouloudi, Y. K. Dwivedi, I. Pappas, & M. Mäntymäki (Eds.), *Responsible AI and analytics for an ethical and inclusive digitized society* (pp. 271–284). Springer International Publishing.

Introduction to Security and Privacy

Edgar Weippl and Sebastian Schrittwieser

Abstract This chapter on *Security and Privacy* builds on two aspects central to digital humanism: (1) self-determination and (2) humans in the center.

Security refers to a system being in a state of protection against potential threats and risks; what this means specifically depends on the so-called security requirements (Bishop, IEEE Security and Privacy, 1(1), 67–69, 2003). Typically, this pertains to protecting data's (1) confidentiality, (2) integrity, and (3) availability. Thus, security mechanisms are designed to prevent unauthorized access, use, disclosure, disruption, modification, or destruction.

Privacy is the individual's fundamental right to determine and limit who has access to their personal information and experiences, ensuring their ability to maintain personal boundaries, confidentiality, and freedom from unauthorized surveillance (Bélanger and Crossler, Privacy in the digital age: A review of information privacy research in information systems. MIS Quarterly, pp. 1017–1041, 2011). Security and privacy are of utmost importance in this increasingly connected world, as they can help protect individuals, companies, and organizations from data breaches, identity theft, and other malicious attacks.

The goals of digital humanism are to shape technologies in accordance with human values and needs, instead of allowing technologies to shape humans. Our task is not only to rein in the downsides of information and communication technologies but to encourage human-centered innovation (Werthner, The Vienna manifesto on digital humanism. In Digital transformation and ethics (pp. 338–357). Ecowin, 2020).

In the following sections, we will analyze security requirements that can compromise these goals and show which security mechanisms can be employed to protect them. Both security and even more privacy are central to digital humanism—also mentioned as one of its principles.

E. Weippl (✉) · S. Schrittwieser
University of Vienna & SBA Research, Vienna, Austria
e-mail: Edgar.Weippl@univie.ac.at; Sebastian.Schrittwieser@univie.ac.at

H. Werthner et al. (eds.), *Introduction to Digital Humanism*,
https://doi.org/10.1007/978-3-031-45304-5_26

1 Introduction

Digital humanism is an ethical framework that seeks to promote the values of human dignity, freedom, and autonomy in developing and using digital technologies. It emphasizes prioritizing human well-being and social responsibility in technology design, implementation, and use.

Digital humanism recognizes that technology is not neutral and can have significant impacts on individuals and society as a whole. The goal is to ensure that technology is developed and used to benefit people and society while respecting their rights and dignity.

Overall, digital humanism seeks to ensure that technology is developed and used in ways that promote human well-being and respect individuals' rights and dignity. It represents a new approach to technology development that prioritizes human values over purely technological or economic considerations.

Security and privacy can provide essential tools to reach such a vision. Many security requirements are implicitly included in the Vienna Manifesto on Digital Humanism. For instance, accountability requires strong authentication—a core concept in information security.

Privacy and security are closely related concepts in information technology but have distinct meanings and objectives. **Privacy** refers to determining, preserving, and managing the rights and restrictions associated with personal data, ensuring that it is only collected, stored, used, and shared in a manner that respects individual rights and needs and further complies with applicable laws and regulations. In essence, privacy is about ensuring individuals' rights to control their personal information within the digital realm, i.e., that individuals can make informed decisions about how their data is used (Schwartz, 2019).

On the other hand, security is concerned with protecting information systems, networks, and data from unauthorized access, use, disclosure, disruption, modification, or destruction. It involves implementing technical, physical, and administrative controls to safeguard the integrity, confidentiality, and availability of information. Security measures include firewalls, encryption, authentication, access control, intrusion detection systems, and regular software updates.

While privacy and security are different concepts, they are closely intertwined. A robust **security framework is necessary to protect the privacy** of individuals and organizations by preventing unauthorized access to their sensitive data. Conversely, strong privacy policies and practices can help enhance the overall security of information systems by minimizing the amount of sensitive data collected, stored, and transmitted.

Ransomware, Industry 4.0, the EU General Data Protection Regulation, mobility, home workplaces, public cloud services, and many other topics have dominated the headlines recently. Given the force of these topics and the often still missing comprehensive security architectures needed to master them, it is becoming increasingly common to lose a sense of how these security fields are interwoven and especially how they need to be linked with classic security requirements such as asset management or privacy concepts. Old knowledge meets completely new threats. In companies, it is the task of the IT security manager to maintain an overview and respond to essential threats with the necessary measures in an appropriate manner.

> There are advantages to computerizing everything—some that we can see today, and some that we'll realize only once these computers have reached critical mass. The Internet of Things will embed itself into our lives at every level, and I don't think we can predict the emergent properties of this trend. We're reaching a fundamental shift that is due to scale and scope; these differences in degree are causing a difference in kind. Everything is becoming one complex hyper-connected system in which, even if things don't interoperate, they're on the same network and affect each other. (Schneier, 2018)

2 Basic Concepts and Definitions

Historically, cryptography and "keeping things secret" have been core aspects of **security** (Trček et al., 2007). The first important step is distinguishing between *security requirements* and *security mechanisms* or *countermeasures*. "Keeping things secret" is a security requirement commonly called confidentiality. Cryptography is one possible security mechanism to implement the requirement of confidentiality. However, ensuring confidentiality alone does not make a system secure. The second step is to comprehensively list the basic security requirements and potential mechanisms for their implementation.

There are three basic security requirements:

1. Confidentiality: Ensuring that sensitive data is only accessible to authorized individuals.
2. Integrity: Protecting data from unauthorized modification or destruction.
3. Availability: Ensuring that data is accessible to authorized individuals when needed.

Confidentiality helps to ensure that sensitive data is only accessible to authorized individuals. This includes protecting data from unauthorized disclosure, meaning only those with the proper permissions can view or access it.

Integrity is the second core concept of information security and is defined as protecting data from unauthorized modification. This includes ensuring that data is not modified in transit or at rest by malicious actors or accidentally. Integrity requires that data is not corrupted or altered in any (unauthorized) way. Integrity is essential to maintain the accuracy and authenticity of data, i.e., to ensure that it is not tampered with or misused.

Availability refers to the ability of authorized individuals to access data and services when needed. It ensures that data is available on demand and not disrupted by malicious, accidental, or natural threats. Complete outages or slowdowns compromise a system's availability.

Countermeasures can be categorized in different ways, such as the *type* of countermeasure or according to its *effect*. There are three basic types of countermeasures: (1) administrative, (2) technical, and (3) physical.

The training handbook for the CISSP (Certified information systems security professional) exam defines the countermeasures or controls as follows:

> Administrative controls are commonly referred to as "soft controls" because they are more management-oriented. Administrative controls include security documentation, risk management, personnel security, and training.
>
> Technical controls (logical controls) are software or hardware components, such as firewalls, IDS, encryption, and identification and authentication mechanisms.
>
> And physical controls are items put into place to protect facilities, personnel, and resources. Physical controls include security guards, locks, fencing, and lighting. (Bragg, 2002)

Countermeasures have different ways of doing what they do. They can prevent, deter, detect, correct, or compensate for the effects of an attack or can be used to recover from an attack.

- *Preventive* countermeasures impede a bad event from happening at all.
- *Deterrent* countermeasures will not wholly prevent an incident in all cases but will reduce the likelihood as it dissuades prospective attackers.
- Once an attack or accidental incident happens, a *detective* countermeasure is needed for the system operator or data owner to actually notice that security requirements have been compromised.
- *Corrective* controls are employed after an incident has been detected to fix the problem.
- If no corrective actions can be taken or the problem is too comprehensive, a *recovery* mechanism, such as a backup, is used to restore the system and data to a previous secure state.
- Another mechanism well known to prevent accounting fraud can also be used to protect data and systems. *Compensating* mechanisms offer a second independent way to compensate for the first mechanism should it fail.

All security mechanisms can be categorized along these two dimensions. For instance, encryption is a *technical* countermeasure that *prevents* unauthorized data disclosure, thus protecting data confidentiality.

A related yet different topic is **privacy**. The NIST defines privacy as "assurance that the confidentiality of, and access to, certain information about an entity is protected." (Powell et al., 2022) or "freedom from intrusion into the private life or affairs of an individual when that intrusion results from undue or illegal gathering and use of data about that individual" (Garfinkel, 2015) or "the right of a party to maintain control over and confidentiality of information about itself" (Oldehoeft, 1992).

2.1 Methods

Once we know which security requirements exist, we can examine how some typical countermeasures are implemented.

People often think of encryption first; even many textbooks start with chapters on encryption. Nonetheless, it is crucial to remember that the most critical first step is to know the requirements—we will elaborate on the process of risk analysis in the following subsection and to understand that even powerful security mechanisms, such as encryption, do not automatically solve all security issues. Encryption can be used incorrectly, giving people a false sense of security.

1. Encryption
2. Authentication
3. Access control
4. Compartmentalization

2.1.1 Encryption

Encryption is the process of encoding a clear-text message into a ciphertext so that an attacker cannot decrypt the ciphertext without knowing the encryption key, even though she knows the algorithm used for encryption. The security of all modern encryption algorithms depends on the secrecy of the encryption/decryption key and not on keeping the algorithm itself secret (Kerckhoff's principle).

Encryption security depends on choosing a good crypto algorithm, but more is needed. The encryption/decryption keys have to be selected wisely, too. The message's confidentiality is compromised if an attacker can guess the key.

Another important aspect is if the sender of a message sends only a few different messages (e.g., if there are only two types of messages sent, "buy the share" or "sell the share"). If the same keys are used without modification, the attacker may not be able to decrypt the message but can observe the ciphertexts. The same cleartext encrypted with identical keys always creates the same ciphertext.

More importantly, even if many different messages are sent, simply observing the traffic patterns (e.g., few vs. many messages or short vs. long messages sent) can leak information to an attacker (Paar & Pelzl, 2009).

2.1.2 Authentication

Authentication is a way to make sure that someone is who they say they are. It is like showing your ID to prove that you are really you, in the same way when a website or app may require to enter a username (i.e., the process of identification) and password (i.e., authentication) to prove the user's identity.

In general terms, authentication is the process of confirming an entity's identity, such as a person, device, or system. It involves using various methods and techniques to verify that the entity is who it claims to be. Only once the identity has been verified can the system check which permissions and privileges to access a particular resource or service can be granted (i.e., authorization).

Authentication can be accomplished through a variety of mechanisms, such as (1) passwords or PINs, (2) biometrics (e.g., fingerprint or facial recognition), or (3) smart cards and digital certificates. Two-factor or multiple-factor authentication may be used, such as requiring proof of at least two of the three methods above.

Authentication is an essential aspect of security, particularly in the digital realm. In addition to being the prerequisite for authorization, authentication can also be used to establish trust between entities. For instance, a digital certificate issued by a trusted certificate authority can be used to authenticate the identity of a website, which helps to establish trust with users who visit the site.

Authentication and identity management are crucial aspects of security and trust, and their importance is only likely to grow as more aspects of our lives move online.

2.1.3 Authorization and Access Control

Authorization and access control are two related concepts that are used to determine what resources or services an entity (such as a person, computer process, or system) is allowed to access.

Authorization is the process of granting or denying access to a particular resource or service based on the permissions assigned to the requesting entity. For instance, if a user wants to access a file on a computer, the operating system will check whether the user has the necessary permissions to access that file. If the user does have the required permissions, they will be authorized to access the file. If not, they will be denied access. More specifically, "access" can refer to certain privileges such as "write access," "read-only access," "deleting," etc. (Sandhu & Samarati, 1994).

2.1.4 Compartmentalization

Another important defense concept is compartmentalization, also referred to as defense-in-depth. This is a security strategy that involves implementing multiple layers of protection to safeguard an organization's information systems, networks, and assets from potential threats. This approach is based on the principle that every single security measure can be compromised and that a multilayered defense can provide a more robust and resilient security posture.

The concept of defense in depth originates from a military strategy where multiple layers of defense are used to slow down an attacker's progress, giving the defenders time to respond and making it more difficult for the attacker to breach the defenses.

In the context of information security, defense in depth involves using a combination of technical, administrative, and physical security measures to protect against various attack vectors. Some key elements of a defense-in-depth strategy include:

- **Access control**: Implementing strong access control mechanisms, such as role-based access control and multifactor authentication, to ensure that only authorized individuals can access sensitive information and resources.
- **Network segmentation**: Dividing the network into smaller segments, each with its own security controls, to limit the potential impact of a security breach and restrict the movement of attackers within the network.
- **Firewalls and intrusion detection/prevention systems (IDS/IPS)**: Deploying firewalls to filter incoming and outgoing network traffic, along with IDS/IPS to monitor for and respond to potential threats in real time.
- **Encryption**: Encrypting sensitive data at rest and in transit to protect it from unauthorized access, tampering, or eavesdropping.
- **Patch management**: Regularly updating software, firmware, and operating systems to fix known security vulnerabilities and reduce the attack surface.
- **Endpoint protection**: Deploying antivirus, anti-malware, and endpoint detection and response (EDR) solutions on devices to protect against threats targeting user devices.
- **Security awareness training**: Educating employees about security best practices, common threats, and how to recognize and respond to potential attacks.
- **Physical security**: Implementing measures such as access control systems, surveillance cameras, and secure storage facilities to protect physical assets and prevent unauthorized access to sensitive areas.
- **Backup and disaster recovery**: Regularly backing up critical data and systems and having a disaster recovery plan in place to restore operations quickly in the event of a security incident or other disruptions.

The defense-in-depth approach aims to minimize the likelihood of a successful attack by increasing the difficulty for attackers to navigate through multiple layers of security and providing multiple opportunities for defenders to detect and respond to potential threats.

The same idea can be used to protect an individual's privacy. This refers to a multilayered approach to safeguard personal information and ensure data privacy. Just as with information security, defense-in-depth for privacy involves implementing a combination of technical, administrative, and organizational measures to minimize privacy risks and prevent unauthorized access, use, or disclosure of sensitive data. Some key elements of a defense-in-depth strategy for privacy protection include:

- **Privacy by design**: Integrating privacy considerations into the design and development of products, services, and systems from the beginning. This includes incorporating privacy-enhancing technologies, minimizing data collection, and ensuring that privacy is a core aspect of the development process (Spiekermann, 2012).
- **Access control**: Implementing strict access controls limits who can access personal data and under what conditions. This can include role-based access control, multifactor authentication, and least privilege principles.

- **Data minimization**: Collecting, processing, and storing only the minimum personal data necessary for the intended purpose. This helps reduce the amount of sensitive data that could be compromised in a breach (Pfitzmann & Hansen, 2010).
- **Anonymization and pseudonymization**: Using techniques such as anonymization (Murthy et al., 2019) or pseudonymization (Neubauer & Heurix, 2011) to de-identify personal data, making it more challenging to link the data back to specific individuals and reducing privacy risks.
- **Data encryption**: Encrypting personal data both at rest and in transit to protect it from unauthorized access and interception.
- **Privacy policies and notices**: Communicating privacy policies and practices to users, including information about data collection, usage, and sharing, as well as their rights and choices regarding their personal data.
- **Privacy impact assessments** (PIAs): Conduct regular PIAs to identify and address potential privacy risks and ensure that privacy controls are adequate and up to date.
- **Incident response and breach notification**: Having a well-defined incident response plan in place to address privacy breaches and notify affected individuals and relevant authorities in a timely manner.
- **Employee training and awareness**: Providing regular privacy training for employees to ensure they understand their responsibilities in handling personal data and are aware of privacy risks, policies, and best practices.
- **Third-party management**: Assessing the privacy practices of third-party vendors and partners and ensuring they adhere to your organization's privacy standards.
- **Legal and regulatory compliance**: Ensuring compliance with applicable data protection laws and regulations, such as the GDPR, and staying up to date with changes in privacy legislation.

By implementing a defense-in-depth approach to privacy protection, organizations can build a more robust and resilient privacy posture, reducing the likelihood of privacy breaches and minimizing the potential impact on individuals and the organization itself.

2.2 *Risk Management*

Technical people might love implementing technical security controls, but it is essential to spend resources efficiently. Therefore, risk management needs to be established as an ongoing task. A good starting point for risk management is performing a risk assessment and then updating this information.

The freely available NIST 800-30 (Ross et al., 2022) guidelines suggest for main steps:

1. Prepare for the assessment.
2. Conduct the assessment:
   (a) Identify threat sources and events.
   (b) Identify vulnerabilities and predisposing conditions.
   (c) Determine the likelihood of occurrence.
   (d) Determine the impact.
   (e) Determine risk.
3. Communicate results.
4. Maintain assessment.

The organization needs to know its assets and security requirements to perform these steps. This is a prerequisite to identifying, for instance, vulnerabilities specific to each asset.

2.2.1 BIA

A business impact analysis (BIA) is a critical step in creating a business continuity plan. It helps identify the potential impacts of a disruption to business operations. It implicitly prioritizes critical business processes and functions that need to be restored first when a disaster recovery plan is executed. However, disaster recovery is only one possible control to implement business continuity. Redundancy, for instance, would be a compensating control.

Performing a BIA is essential as it—as previously stated—focuses on the requirements. More precisely, not only on the technical requirement of confidentiality, integrity, and availability but instead applies them to specific (information) assets.

The usual steps in a BIA are:

- **Define the scope**: Identify the areas included in the BIA. For companies or institutions, this may include facilities, departments, business processes, and technology systems. For private individuals, this included listing the areas of life which use IT or depend on such infrastructure such as personal photos, documents, travel arrangements, tax records, letters/documents, and communication with banks, insurance companies, etc.
- **Identify the critical (business) functions**: List all of the critical (business) functions and prioritize them based on their importance. This can be done by identifying the functions that would have the most severe impact if disrupted. When elaborating on the disruption, the three basic security requirements (CIA) are essential to consider. For instance, the confidentiality of your vacation photos might not be as crucial as the general availability regarding recoverability. While you can most likely accept not having access to them for a couple of days or weeks, completely losing them would be a big (personal) loss.
- **Identify the dependencies**: Identify the dependencies between the critical business functions and other departments, systems, vendors, and partners. This will help you understand how a disruption in one area could impact others. In

particular, if you are using cloud services to store your data, think about the impact of the provider's failure. As commonly mentioned tongue-in-cheek, the cloud is simply "someone else's computer."

The next step is a risk analysis to analyze how frequently a bad event might happen and how bad it is expected to be. Based on these findings, one can look at possible controls and then decide on the cost-effective ones to be implemented.

- **Determine the impact and likelihood**: Determine the potential impact of a disruption to each critical business function. This includes the financial, operational, and reputational impacts that arise if confidentiality, integrity, or availability is compromised.
- **Define recovery time objectives**: Determine the maximum time each critical business function can be down before it starts to impact the organization significantly. This will help prioritize which functions must be restored first should recovery controls be implemented.
- **Analyze controls**: Analyze which controls can be used to protect each critical business function, for instance, using the two aforementioned dimensions: (1) *type* of countermeasure and (2) its *effect*.
- **Test and update the plan**: Test the plan regularly to ensure that it works and update it as necessary to reflect changes in the organization, the assets, and the services used.

Overall, a BIA is an essential step in ensuring that your organization can recover quickly from disruption and continue to operate in the event of an unexpected event or disaster.

2.2.2 PIA

A privacy impact assessment (PIA) is a structured process that helps organizations identify and address privacy risks associated with new projects or initiatives. This involves assessing the privacy impact of a project or initiative, identifying risks, and developing strategies to mitigate them.

Performing a privacy risk analysis typically involves several steps:

- **Identify the data**: Begin by identifying all the data being collected and processed, including personal information, sensitive data, and any other information that could pose a privacy risk.
- **Identify the risks**: Determine the potential risks that could arise from collecting and processing the data, such as unauthorized access, accidental disclosure, or misuse of data.
- **Evaluate the risks**: Assess the likelihood and impact of each identified risk, considering factors such as the sensitivity of the data, the potential harm to individuals, and the likelihood of a breach occurring.
- **Identify safeguards**: Identify measures that can be taken to mitigate the risks, such as implementing access controls, encryption, or anonymization techniques.

- **Evaluate safeguards**: Evaluate the effectiveness of the safeguards in mitigating the risks, and identify any potential gaps or weaknesses that need to be addressed.
- **Document the analysis**: Document the findings of the privacy risk analysis, including the data and risks identified, the safeguards implemented, and any recommendations for further action.

It is important to note that privacy risk analysis is an ongoing process and should be reviewed and updated regularly to ensure that the organization's data protection measures effectively address new and emerging privacy risks.

1. *Qualitative analysis:* This method involves identifying privacy risks and assessing their likelihood and impact using a qualitative approach. This may involve brainstorming sessions with stakeholders, interviews with subject matter experts, and reviewing past incidents and security assessments.
2. *Quantitative analysis:* This method uses statistical and mathematical methods to measure the likelihood and impact of privacy risks. This may involve gathering data on past incidents and conducting simulations to model potential threats and their impact.

3 Critical Discussion

Digital humanism refers to integrating digital technologies and human values to prioritize human needs, rights, and well-being. While this concept promotes a more people-centric approach to technology, it also brings several privacy challenges. Some of these challenges include:

- **Data collection and surveillance**: The increasing pervasiveness of digital technologies has led to massive data collection, which can be misused for surveillance purposes. This compromises people's privacy and personal freedom, often without their consent or knowledge.
- **Data breaches and leaks**: As data is stored and transmitted digitally, it becomes vulnerable to breaches and leaks. Hackers can exploit vulnerabilities in systems to steal sensitive personal information, posing significant privacy risks for individuals.
- **Inadequate data protection laws**: Many countries need robust data protection laws, or their existing laws may need to be revised to protect privacy in the context of emerging technologies. This leaves individuals exposed to potential privacy violations.
- **Profiling and discrimination**: With the accumulation of personal data, there is a risk of creating profiles based on individuals' behaviors, preferences, and other characteristics. This can lead to employment, housing, or even social interaction discrimination.
- **Loss of anonymity**: The increasing digital footprint makes it difficult for individuals to remain anonymous. Many online platforms and services require

personal information for verification purposes, which can make it difficult for users to maintain their privacy.

- **Consent and control**: Obtaining informed consent from individuals before collecting their data remains challenging. Many users may not fully understand the implications of sharing their data or have no control over how it is used or shared.
- **Algorithmic transparency and bias**: Many digital systems use algorithms to process and analyze data, often in a black-box manner. This lack of transparency can lead to biased outcomes, privacy violations, and unfair treatment.
- **Privacy vs. security trade-offs**: To ensure public safety and national security, governments may prioritize surveillance and data collection, which can infringe on individual privacy.
- **Privacy in the age of the Internet of Things** (IoT): IoT devices can collect vast amounts of data about individuals' habits and preferences, which can pose significant privacy challenges if not managed correctly.

Addressing these challenges requires a concerted effort from policymakers, technology developers, and users to ensure that privacy is protected while allowing digital technologies to flourish and benefit society. However, it is even more challenging as globalization couples previously independent systems of companies providing global services. Privacy expectations vary considerably between countries and political systems, making it hard to know what policies should be implemented:

> There are advantages to computerizing everything—some that we can see today, and some that we'll realize only once these computers have reached critical mass. The Internet of Things will embed itself into our lives at every level, and I don't think we can predict the emergent properties of this trend. We're reaching a fundamental shift that is due to scale and scope; these differences in degree are causing a difference in kind. Everything is becoming one complex hyper-connected system in which, even if things don't interoperate, they're on the same network and affect each other. (Schneier, 2018)

Several global initiatives and frameworks aim to regulate privacy and data protection. These initiatives often serve as models for countries to develop their privacy legislation and policies. Some of the most prominent initiatives and frameworks include the (1) General Data Protection Regulation (GDPR), which continues the development of the Council of Europe Convention 108, (2) OECD Privacy Guidelines, (3) the APEC Privacy Framework, and (4) UN initiatives.

GDPR is a comprehensive data protection law implemented by the European Union (EU) in 2018. It aims to give EU citizens more control over their personal data and harmonize data protection laws across the EU. GDPR has extraterritorial scope, meaning that it also applies to organizations outside the EU that process the personal data of EU citizens. *The Council of Europe's Convention for the Protection of Individuals with regard to Automatic Processing of Personal Data* (Greenleaf, 2018) is an international treaty that establishes minimum standards for data protection. It has been ratified by many countries, including non-European ones, and has influenced the development of national data protection laws worldwide.

The Organization for Economic Cooperation and Development (OECD) published its **Guidelines on the Protection of Privacy and Transborder Flows of Personal Data** in 1980, updated in 2013.[1] These guidelines provide a set of privacy principles that serve as a foundation for national legislation and international agreements on data protection.

The Asia-Pacific Economic Cooperation **(APEC) Privacy Framework** (APEC, 2005) is a set of privacy principles designed to facilitate the free flow of information while protecting individual privacy rights within the APEC region. The framework provides a foundation for the development of national privacy laws and promotes cross-border data transfers between APEC member economies.

The UN has also contributed to privacy regulation through the International Covenant on Civil and Political Rights (ICCPR) and the Universal Declaration of Human Rights (UDHR), which recognize the right to privacy as a fundamental human right. The UN has also released resolutions and reports on privacy in the digital age, such as the report on privacy and ethics in the context of big data (UN Development Group, 2017).

These global initiatives have played a significant role in shaping privacy laws and policies worldwide. They provide guidelines and principles that help countries develop their legal frameworks to protect individual privacy rights while balancing the need for data-driven innovation and economic growth.

4 Simple To-Dos for Users and Companies

As an end user, there are several things you can do to improve security and privacy in any digital system. Here are some of the most important ones:

1. *Use strong and unique passwords*: This is the first line of defense against unauthorized access to your accounts. Use strong and unique passwords for each account, and consider using a password manager to help you generate and manage them.
2. *Keep your software up to date*: Software updates often contain security patches and bug fixes that help protect you against known vulnerabilities. Keep your operating system, web browser, and other software up to date.
3. *Be cautious with links and downloads*: Be wary of clicking on links or downloading attachments from unknown sources, as these could be phishing attempts or contain malware. Always verify the source of the link or attachment before clicking on it.
4. *Use two-factor authentication*: Two-factor authentication adds an extra layer of security to your accounts by requiring a second factor, such as a code sent to your phone, and your password. Enable two-factor authentication wherever possible.

[1] https://www.oecd.org/general/data-protection.htm

5. *Limit the amount of personal information you share*: Be mindful of the personal information you share online, and avoid sharing sensitive information such as your home address, phone number, or social security number.
6. *Review privacy policies and settings*: Take the time to review the privacy policies and settings for the apps and services you use. Ensure you understand how your data is being collected, used, and shared, and adjust the settings as needed to limit the amount of data being collected.
7. *Educate yourself on digital literacy*: Educate yourself on digital literacy to better understand how technology works and the potential risks and benefits it can have. This includes learning about how to protect your privacy and security online, as well as how to identify and respond to phishing and other online scams.

By following these steps, you can help protect your privacy and security online and contribute to a more secure and ethical digital world.

As a company, there are several steps you can take to improve privacy and security in the context of digital humanism. Here are some important ones:

1. *Conduct regular security assessments:* Conduct regular security assessments to identify potential vulnerabilities and ensure that your systems and data are secure. This includes conducting regular penetration testing and vulnerability scans to identify potential weaknesses.
2. *Implement strong access controls*: Implement strong access controls to limit access to sensitive data and systems to only those who need it. This includes implementing multifactor authentication, role-based access controls, and monitoring access logs for suspicious activity.
3. *Use encryption*: Use encryption to protect sensitive data both in transit and at rest. This includes using strong encryption algorithms and protocols to protect data in transit and at rest.
4. *Develop clear privacy policies*: Develop clear privacy policies that outline how you collect, use, and share data, and ensure that these policies are easily accessible and understandable by your users.
5. *Minimize data collection*: Minimize the amount of data you collect to only what is necessary for your business purposes, and dispose of data in a secure and timely manner when it is no longer needed.
6. *Educate employees*: Educate your employees on the importance of privacy and security, and provide training on best practices for protecting data and systems. This includes training on identifying and responding to phishing and other social engineering attacks.
7. *Foster a culture of ethical technology use*: Foster a culture of ethical technology use by ensuring that your products and services align with your company's values and contribute to the public good. This includes considering the potential impacts of your technology on society and the environment and developing technology that is accessible, inclusive, and equitable.

By taking these steps, you can help ensure that your company is contributing to a more secure and ethical digital world.

5 Conclusions

Digital humanism is an ethical framework that emphasizes the importance of human-centered design and values in the development and use of digital technologies. In this context, privacy and security are two critical aspects that must be considered to ensure the protection and well-being of individuals. For an individual, the privacy requirements may—in many cases—be more relevant than security; however, privacy is a fundamental social need of humans, providing a space for autonomy and individual growth and acting as a cornerstone for personal dignity, expression, and freedom from unwarranted scrutiny.

Here are some of the aspects of privacy and security that are important for any digital system and form the basis for an individual's security and privacy in a digital world:

1. **Data protection**: Digital humanism recognizes the value of personal data and the need to protect it from unauthorized access, use, or disclosure. This includes implementing strong data encryption, access controls, and policies that limit the collection and use of personal data.
2. **User control**: Digital humanism emphasizes giving users control over their personal data and how it is used. This includes providing clear and transparent privacy policies, options to opt out of data collection and sharing, and allowing users to delete their data.
3. **Trust** is essential in the development and adoption of digital technologies. This includes ensuring that digital systems are secure, reliable, and transparent and that users have confidence in the technology and the organizations behind it.
4. **Ethical use**: Digital technologies should be used ethically and responsibly. This includes avoiding the use of technologies that could harm individuals or communities, ensuring that technology is used to benefit society, and being transparent about the potential risks and benefits of technology.
5. **Accessibility**: Digital humanism recognizes that technology must be accessible to everyone, regardless of their ability or background. This includes designing technology that is easy to use, providing accessibility features for individuals with disabilities, and ensuring that technology does not discriminate against certain groups of people.

Overall, privacy and security are critical aspects of digital humanism that ensure the development and use of digital technologies align with human values and respect individuals' rights and dignity.

Discussion Questions for Students and Teachers

1. "Digital technologies should be designed to promote democracy and inclusion. This will require special efforts to overcome current inequalities and to use the emancipatory potential of digital technologies to make our societies more inclusive" (one of the core principles in the Vienna Manifesto on Digital Humanism, https://dighum.ec.tuwien.ac.at/wp-content/uploads/2019/07/Vienna_Manifesto_on_Digital_Humanism_EN.pdf).

With digital technologies, many aspects scale much better, also including attacks. Thus, fewer people can do more harm, and attribution is harder. Consequently, one may argue that more surveillance and less freedom are essential to implement the emancipatory potential. What do you think?

2. "Privacy and freedom of speech are essential values for democracy and should be at the center of our activities. Therefore, artifacts such as social media or online platforms need to be altered to better safeguard the free expression of opinion, the dissemination of information, and the protection of privacy" (one of the core principles in the Vienna Manifesto on Digital Humanism, https://dighum.ec.tuwien.ac.at/wp-content/uploads/2019/07/Vienna_Manifesto_on_Digital_Humanism_EN.pdf).

   One of the dangers is the spread of false information and the impression that many people support this view. Given the advances showcased with GPT, AI-based lobbying/influencing bots are a very real scenario. Tying the conversation to one (human) individual may be a remedy. This requires strong authentication and managed identities—centralized as in Europe's eID or also Decentralized IDentifiers (DIDs) as another approach. The drawback is that disallowing anonymous communication is a risk to privacy. Perform a security risk analysis and a privacy risk analysis as a basis for discussion.

3. "Effective regulations, rules and laws, based on a broad public discourse, must be established. They should ensure prediction accuracy, fairness and equality, accountability, and transparency of software programs and algorithms" (one of the core principles in the Vienna Manifesto on Digital Humanism, https://dighum.ec.tuwien.ac.at/wp-content/uploads/2019/07/Vienna_Manifesto_on_Digital_Humanism_EN.pdf).

   Machine learning and data-driven techniques build on the past. Human history is biased, unfair, and unequal. Therefore, making decisions by simply analyzing the past will perpetuate the negative aspects. Changing the future frequently relied on fundamental shifts that one can imagine better as rule-based than based on past data. The concepts of "liberté, egalité, fraternité" did not gradually evolve from Louis XV's reign. Does current information technology lock us in and merely improve efficiency, e.g., AI-based political lobbying, micro-targeting voters, etc., instead of further evolving our society?

Learning Resources for Students

1. B. Schneier, Click Here to Kill Everybody. W.W. Norton, 2018.

   This emphasizes the need to prioritize human safety, well-being, and values in the design and implementation of connected technologies. The book highlights the potential consequences of not addressing security and privacy risks in a hyperconnected world and calls for a holistic approach that places human needs at the center of technology development.

2. "NIST SP 800-30 Rev 1: Guide for Conducting Risk Assessments," NIST, 2012.

   It provides a structured approach to identifying and mitigating risks that may impact human values, privacy, and security in information systems. By conducting thorough risk assessments, organizations and individuals can prioritize and implement measures that protect human needs and well-being in the context of technology usage and development.

3. NIST Cybersecurity Framework—Journey to CSF 2.0 https://www.nist.gov/cyberframework/updating-nist-cybersecurity-framework-journey-csf-20
   The framework offers a comprehensive approach to managing and reducing cybersecurity risks that can affect individuals, organizations, and society at large. By promoting better security practices and fostering a culture of continuous improvement, the framework helps ensure that digital technologies are designed and implemented in a manner that respects and prioritizes human values, privacy, and well-being.
4. S. Harris and F. Maymi, CISSP All-in-One Exam Guide. McGraw-Hill, 2021.
   The book helps security professionals develop a comprehensive understanding of information security principles and practices that protect individuals, organizations, and society.
5. OWASP SAMM (Open Worldwide Application Security Project Software Assurance Maturity Model) https://owasp.org/www-project-samm/
   The book provides a framework for organizations to assess, improve, and measure the security of their software development processes. By encouraging the creation of secure software, SAMM promotes a digital environment that respects and protects security and privacy.
6. The Moon is a harsh mistress, Robert Heinlein, G. P. Putnam's Sons 1966.
   The book explores themes of autonomy, freedom, and the role of technology in society. The story, featuring an artificial intelligence that gains self-awareness and assists in a lunar colony's rebellion, encourages discussions about the ethical implications of technology, the responsible development of AI, and the need to consider human values in a technologically driven world.

Acknowledgments SBA Research (SBA-K1) is a COMET Centre within the framework of COMET Competence Centers for Excellent Technologies Programme and funded by BMK, BMDW, and the federal state of Vienna. The COMET Programme is managed by FFG.

References

APE Cooperation. (2005). *APEC privacy framework*. Asia Pacific Economic Cooperation Secretariat, 81.

Bragg, R. (2002). *CISSP training guide: Training guide*. Que Publishing.

Garfinkel, S. L. (2015). *NISTIR 8053. de-identification of personal information*. National Institute of Standards and Technology (NIST).

Greenleaf, G. (2018). "Modernised" Data Protection Convention 108 and the GDPR. In *Data Protection Convention* (Vol. 108, pp. 22–3).

Murthy, S., Bakar, A. A., Rahim, F. A., & Ramli, R. (2019, May). A comparative study of data anonymization techniques. In *2019 IEEE 5th International Conference on Big Data Security on Cloud (BigDataSecurity), IEEE International Conference on High Performance and Smart Computing, (HPSC) and IEEE International Conference on Intelligent Data and Security (IDS)* (pp. 306–309). IEEE.

Neubauer, T., & Heurix, J. (2011). A methodology for the pseudonymization of medical data. *International Journal of Medical Informatics, 80*(3), 190–204.

Oldehoeft, A. E. (1992). *Foundations of a security policy for use of the national research and educational network.* US Department of Commerce, National Institute of Standards and Technology.

Paar, C., & Pelzl, J. (2009). *Understanding cryptography: A textbook for students and practitioners.* Springer Science & Business Media.

Pfitzmann, A., & Hansen, M. (2010). *A terminology for talking about privacy by data minimization: Anonymity, unlinkability, undetectability, unobservability, pseudonymity, and identity management.*

Powell, M., Brule, J., Pease, M., Stouffer, K., Tang, C., Zimmerman, T., Deane, C., Hoyt, J., Raguso, M., Sherule, A. & Zheng, K., (2022). *Protecting information and system integrity in industrial control system environments.*

Ross, R. S., & NIST, S. (2022). *800-30 REV. 1: Guide for conducting risk assessments.* National Institute of Standards and Technology.

Sandhu, R. S., & Samarati, P. (1994). Access control: principle and practice. *IEEE Communications Magazine, 32*(9), 40–48.

Schneier, B. (2018). *Click here to kill everybody: Security and survival in a hyper-connected world.* WW Norton & Company.

Schwartz, P. M. (2019). Global data privacy: The EU way. *NYUL Rev., 94*, 771.

Spiekermann, S. (2012). The challenges of privacy by design. *Communications of the ACM, 55*(7), 38–40.

Trček, D., Trobec, R., Pavešić, N., & Tasič, J. F. (2007). Information systems security and human behaviour. *Behaviour and Information Technology, 26*(2), 113–118.

United Nations Development Group. (2017). *Data privacy, ethics and protection. Guidance note on big data for achievement of the 2030 Agenda.* United Nations.

Part III
Critical and Societal Issues of Digital Systems

Recommender Systems: Techniques, Effects, and Measures Toward Pluralism and Fairness

Peter Knees, Julia Neidhardt, and Irina Nalis

Abstract Recommender systems are widely used in various applications, such as online shopping, social media, and news personalization. They can help systems by delivering only the most relevant and promising information to their users and help people by mitigating information overload. At the same time, algorithmic recommender systems are a new form of gatekeeper that preselects and controls the information being presented and actively shapes users' choices and behavior. This becomes a crucial aspect, as, if unaddressed and not safeguarded, these systems are susceptible to perpetuate and even amplify existing biases, including unwanted societal biases, leading to unfair and discriminatory outcomes. In this chapter, we briefly introduce recommender systems, their basic mechanisms, and their importance in various applications. We show how their outcomes and performance are assessed and discuss approaches to addressing pluralism and fairness in recommender systems. Finally, we highlight recently emerging directions within recommender systems research, pointing out opportunities for digital humanism to contribute interdisciplinary expertise.

1 Introduction

Recommender systems (RSs) are software tools and techniques that use data from users to suggest items they will probably like. These suggestions cover a wide range of items including books, news articles, music, as well as more complex products such as tourist offers, job vacancies, or financial loans. Today, recommender systems are widely adopted. Personalization techniques are used by all major online platforms such as Google, Amazon, Facebook, YouTube, Netflix, Spotify, Booking.

P. Knees (✉)
Faculty of Informatics, TU Wien, Vienna, Austria
e-mail: peter.knees@tuwien.ac.at

J. Neidhardt · I. Nalis
Christian Doppler Lab for Recommender Systems, TU Wien, Vienna, Austria
e-mail: julia.neidhardt@tuwien.ac.at; irina.nalis-neuner@tuwien.ac.at

H. Werthner et al. (eds.), *Introduction to Digital Humanism*,
https://doi.org/10.1007/978-3-031-45304-5_27

com, LinkedIn, and many others to tailor their services to the specific preferences and needs of individual users. It can be argued that recommender systems provide a backbone to the modern, industrialized Web, as they facilitate—as well as steer—access to the world's digital content. As such, they have become a new, albeit more subtle form of gatekeeper for information, culture, and other resources, built on technological opportunities and interests of those operating them.

The implications of incorporating automatic recommender systems to structure access to information and digital goods in virtually all large-scale Web services and platforms are wide-reaching and have led to increased interest from the general public. While initially being welcomed as another commodity of the digital world that effortlessly identifies matching content, limitations and frustrations have soon led to a more critical view of their effects. They become of particular interest when they have the potential to affect society and democratic processes, such as "filter bubbles" (Pariser, 2011).

From the perspective of digital humanism, technology that threatens democracy and leads to isolation of individuals must be redesigned and shaped in accordance with human values (Werthner et al., 2019). More specifically, artificial intelligence (AI) and automated decision-making systems such as recommender systems are often resulting in black-box models for which decision processes remain intransparent, bias unknown, and results unfair (Werthner et al., 2023). As such, we need to understand the principles of recommender systems and analyze strategies to overcome a situation where the mechanisms of the applied method and/or the characteristics of the underlying data dictate undesired and unfair outcomes.

In this contribution, we focus on two desiderata for recommender systems with possible broader societal implications: diversity, as a proxy for pluralism, and fairness. Specifically, we outline how recommender systems can be turned from a threat to pluralism and fairness to an instrument for promoting them. As always, the situation is complex, and no single (technical) solution can fully remedy the undesired effects. After describing the main concepts, methods, and practices in recommender systems research, we discuss the concepts of diversity and fairness in the context of filter bubbles. This is followed by a discussion of optimization goals beyond accuracy, such as diversity, and fairness in more detail. We then investigate methods and research directions for promoting both concepts, diversity and fairness. Finally, we touch on the emerging field of moral and human-centered recommender systems. We include examples to illustrate the concepts and methods discussed before summing the discussion up by presenting the main take-away messages. This discussion is continued and deepened in the following contribution of this chapter, where topics of bias, balancing of various and diverse interests (see chapter of Baeza-Yates and Murgai), and automatic content moderation (see chapter of Prem and Krenn) are addressed.

In the following, we investigate the topics of recommender systems and optimization goals beyond accuracy, such as diversity and fairness in more detail, and highlight current research directions.

2 Recommender Systems: Concepts and Practices

RSs are software applications that use a variety of data sources, including users' past behavior and preferences, to suggest items (e.g., goods, articles, content) to a user that he/she is likely to find interesting (Ricci et al., 2022). The overall schema of a RS is illustrated in Fig. 1. To provide personalized suggestions, the RS needs to have knowledge about the items as well as knowledge about the users. With respect to the items, this knowledge can include textual descriptions, keywords, genres, product categories, release date, or price. With respect to the users, demographic data such as age and gender; data about a user's past behavior such as previous purchases, clicks, or ratings; or a user's online social network are commonly used by RSs. Importantly, a relationship between the two sides, items and users, has to be established by the RS so that it knows which items are possibly enjoyed by a specific user. This relationship is typically established using previous purchases, clicks, ratings, or other behavioral data. There are several fundamental recommendation approaches that are traditionally distinguished, which all exploit different aspects to determine those items to be suggested to a user (Burke, 2007; Ricci et al., 2022): In the content-based approach, items are recommended that have similar attributes to those that the user previously liked (e.g., same category). With collaborative filtering, items liked by users with similar preferences are considered important (e.g., "users who bought this also bought that"). Demographic systems recommend items based on user demographics (e.g., items are recommended that are popular in a specific age group). Knowledge-based approaches make recommendations based on domain knowledge about how specific item properties match user preferences (e.g., a travel recommender system that leverages domain knowledge about various travel destinations and their properties). Community-based approaches recommend items liked by the

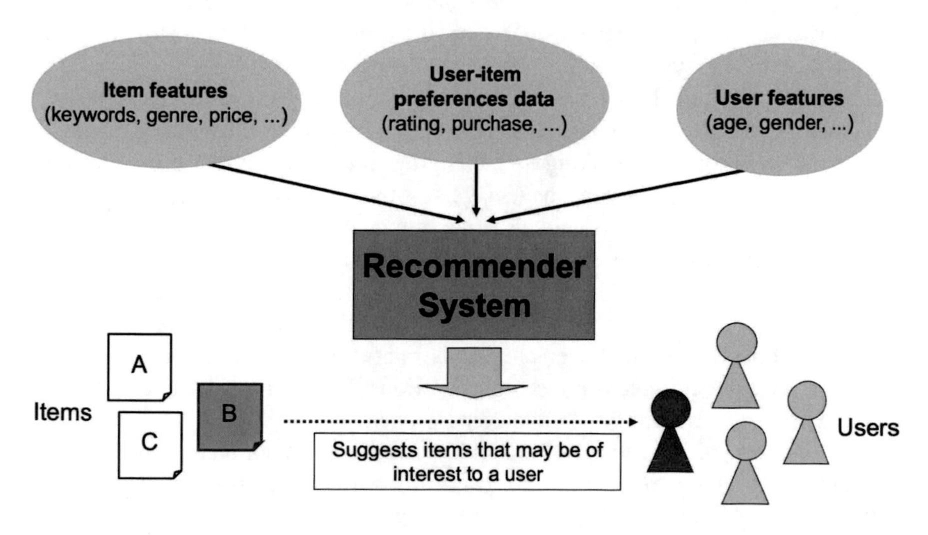

Fig. 1 Overall structure of a RS

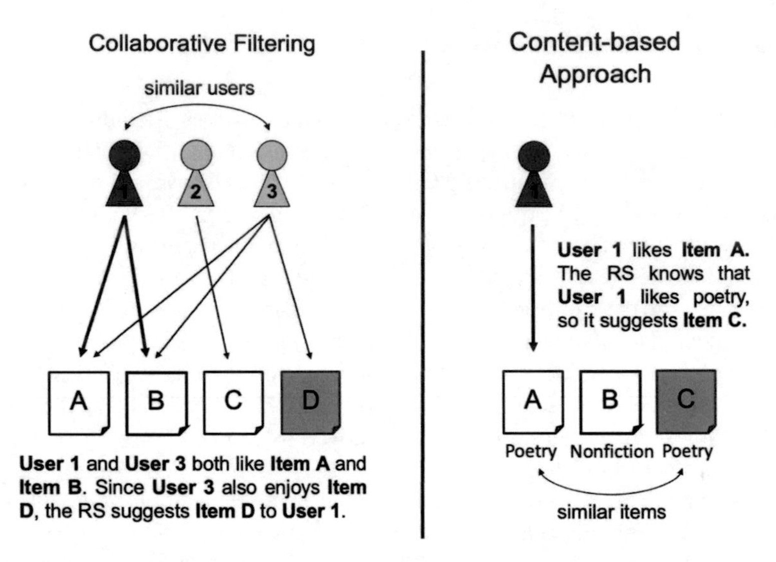

Fig. 2 Collaborative filtering vs. content-based approach

user's friends, often within an online social network. Hybrid recommender systems combine different recommendation techniques to make more accurate and personalized recommendations. Since recommender systems aim to offer personalized suggestions, all the techniques mentioned rely on knowledge about the user. Therefore, every RS needs to include a user model or user profile where this knowledge is accumulated and stored (Jannach et al., 2010). However, this dependency on user data gives rise to significant concerns regarding privacy and misuse.

RS can face a challenge when they encounter new users since there may not be enough data to build a user model. This situation is called "cold-start problem," and the best way to address it depends on the specific use case. The same is true for items that are new to the system. In Fig. 2, the two most common RS approaches, i.e., collaborative filtering and the content-based approach, are conceptually shown. Collaborative filtering encounters the cold-start problem when there is a lack of user-item interaction data, making it challenging to identify similar users. For new users, the recommender system may suggest popular items initially. Similarly, for new items, the system faces difficulties in making recommendations until some users interact with them. In contrast, content-based approaches overcome the cold-start problem for new items by relying on the item's inherent characteristics or features. The system can recommend the item to users who have shown interest in similar items, even if the item has not been previously interacted with. Additionally, for new users, the system can provide recommendations based, for example, on user-provided preferences during the onboarding process.

In the last few years, deep learning architectures have been increasingly used in recommender systems, particularly for capturing various patterns and dealing with high complexity (Zhang et al., 2019). Large language models have also emerged as powerful tools within recommender systems very recently (Liu et al., 2023).

Traditionally, recommendation approaches have focused on predicting how a given user would rate certain items. These approaches are typically tested through so-called offline evaluation, where actual ratings are withheld and used for forecast assessment. The better a method can accurately predict the withheld ratings, the more successful it is. This evaluation approach has significantly advanced the field of recommendation systems. However, there are limitations to this approach such as the absence of real-time feedback, the limited availability of contextual information, and the inability to directly measure user satisfaction (Jannach et al., 2016). To address these limitations, offline evaluation is often supplemented with online evaluation, user studies, and A/B testing, which represent a more realistic and dynamic assessment of recommender systems in real-life settings.

Relying solely on accuracy measurements and a lack of diversity in tailored content consumption can introduce bias and lead to filter bubbles, echo chambers, and related phenomena (Stray et al., 2022). Specifically, users may become trapped in echo chambers and filter bubbles when only considering users' preexisting likes and interests in order to produce the most accurate recommendations, which may lead to a lack of "media pluralism" or the exposure to and consumption of a variety of information, ideas, and viewpoints (Vermeulen, 2022). Correspondingly, there is a growing recognition that the quality of a recommender system extends beyond accuracy measurements only.

3 Recommender Systems as a Threat to Pluralism and Fairness?

An often-discussed effect of automatic information filters such as recommender systems is a loss of diversity in the presented options, due to emphasizing similarity to previous choices. This has been branded and popularized by Pariser (2011) as "filter bubbles." For instance, when consuming social media, and showing interest in posts and articles dealing with, say, migration, recommender systems can pick up this signal and increasingly suggest content dealing with migration. This might lead to overrepresentation of the topic in the shown posts and oust other topics potentially of interest. As such, the topic of migration, despite originally being of (temporal) interest, eventually disproportionally occupies space in the contents recommended and continues to draw the user's attention. Moreover, the recommender system might increasingly present posts from the authors of the consumed posts, i.e., the providers, ousting other authors and leading to a loss of diversity in sources.

Pariser (2011) argues that algorithmic information filters and personalized services are directly connected to individualization and intellectual isolation, ultimately leading to polarization and social fragmentation, posing a threat to democratic societies. Several works have subsequently investigated this connection (e.g., Nguyen et al., 2014; Aridor et al., 2020) and found inconclusive results regarding users' behavior upon usage of recommender systems and its impact on the diversity of items consumed over time. As a consequence, Dahlgren (2021) suggests a further differentiation between *technological filter bubbles* and their consequences that manifest in *societal filter bubbles*. To investigate the former, Michiels et al. (2022) provide an operational definition of technological filter bubbles as "a decrease in the diversity of a user's recommendations over time, in any dimension of diversity, resulting from the choices made by different recommendation stakeholders." Correspondingly, the personalization-polarization hypothesis assumes that these filter bubbles influence the division of large crowds (and thus also of society) into individual groups due to their strongly divergent opinions (Keijzer & Mäs, 2022). The importance of the concept of diversity on the technical side is linked to the societal relevance, as, e.g., stated by Helberger et al. (2018): "As one of the central communication policy goals, diversity refers to the idea that in a democratic society informed citizens collect information about the world from a diverse mix of sources with different viewpoints so that they can make balanced and well-considered decisions."

The definition by Michiels et al. (2022) further highlights the aspect of different recommendation stakeholders (Abdollahpouri & Burke, 2022). While diversity is an important mechanism to avoid one-sidedness with regard to topics and/or sources, for a recommender system, different interests are competing and ultimately might also conflict with the goal of diversity. The typical stakeholders to consider in a recommender system are the consumers (who are typically referred to as the "users"), the providers of items, and the system (or service provider) itself. They all want to ensure to not be treated in an unfair manner and optimize their gain or utility. For instance, users might be treated unfairly if the quality of service they receive depends on individual traits, if these relate to sensitive attributes such as race or gender. Item providers might be treated unfairly if they are deprived of exposure to users, for instance, by not being recommended. The system has the task of maintaining fairness toward all different stakeholders (or at least plausibly argue for it) while maximizing utility, e.g., by recommending items that are most profitable or otherwise beneficial for the system. A typical example to showcase fairness in recommendation toward multiple stakeholders are job recommendations, as performed on business-oriented social media platforms such as LinkedIn or Xing (Ekstrand et al., 2022). In addition to country-specific regulations that might also play a role, matching candidates with job offers is an inherently multi-sided fairness problem. In this scenario, job seekers and employers and both consumers and providers alike, always with the goal to obtain recommendations with the highest utility, raising questions such as: Are recommendations of job opportunities distributed fairly across users? Are job candidate fit scores fair, or do they under- or over-score certain candidates? Do users have a fair opportunity to appear in result lists when recruiters are looking for candidates for a job opening? Are employers in protected groups (e.g., minority-owned businesses) having their jobs fairly promoted to qualified candidates?

Besides fair distribution of opportunities, questions of bias with regard to certain candidates or employers, esp. in protected groups, arise. Beyond this simplified view of competing interests within a recommender system, there are potentially many more stakeholders to consider. For instance, in music streaming, there are multiple types of providers, e.g., the composers, the record labels, or the rights owners; food order platforms add delivery drivers as stakeholders; etc.

4 Beyond Accuracy: Diversity, Novelty, and Serendipity

The "beyond-accuracy" paradigm in recommender system research has been sparked by users scrolling endlessly through items they are already familiar with or that are too similar to their current preferences. This field of study investigates different evaluation measures to improve the value and caliber of recommendations (Smets et al., 2022). Other aspects, such as diversity, serendipity, novelty, and coverage, are being more and more considered in evaluation. These concepts are briefly characterized in the following (Kaminskas & Bridge, 2016; Castells et al., 2022).

Diversity in recommender systems means including a range of different items in the recommendations for users. The goal is to provide a broad selection of items that cover various categories or genres. When the recommender system offers a diverse list of recommendations, users get to see a wide range of options. This allows them to explore and discover new items, which helps them to expand their horizons and ideally improves their overall experience. Content-based approaches (see Sect. 2) often lack diversity because they focus on recommending items that are similar with, e.g., genre. Collaborative filtering can have higher diversity than content-based approaches because it considers the preferences of other users, which can vary widely and thus expose the user to a wider variety of items. An area that attracts a growing number of studies is the domain of news recommendations. Users may not be exposed to opposing viewpoints if tailored news recommendations lack diversity (Stray et al. 2022). A news recommender must find a balance between remaining relevant to users' interests and delivering enough diversity, such as exposing users to new topics and categories, to maintain their interest. The deep neural network presented by Raza and Ding (2020) satisfies the user's requirement for information on subjects in which they have previously expressed interest while going above and beyond accuracy metrics. With an emphasis on the effectiveness of news diversity and confidence in news recommenders, Lee and Lee (2022) investigated the function of perceived personalization and diversity in services. They investigated the effects of perceived personalization and news diversity on users' inclinations to stick around and found that diversity had a positive effect on user satisfaction and continuance intention. From the perspective of the interplay of news diversity and democracy, Helberger et al. (2019) highlight the importance of perspective diversity for well-informed citizens of a democratic society. Furthermore, they underline that interests of the users (autonomy, privacy, and accuracy) need to be considered and balanced against the power and opportunities data and algorithms have to offer—herein lies a great challenge for the design of recommender systems. Another challenge for RS lies in finding a balance between the most accurate and simultaneously diversified recommendations for the user (Möller et al., 2018; Ribeiro et al., 2015).

Occasionally used in connection with measuring diversity is *coverage*. Coverage refers to the proportion of items within the system that the recommender system can recommend to users. A high coverage indicates that the recommender system can suggest items from different genres, topics, or domains, accommodating the varied tastes of its user base.

The concept of *novelty* refers to the degree of uniqueness or freshness of the recommended items. The goal is to suggest items that the user is not familiar or has not seen before. Novel recommendations aim to introduce users to new and unexpected items, encouraging them to explore and avoid repeating previously consumed items.

Serendipity refers to the element of surprise or unexpectedness in the recommendations. It aims to suggest items that go beyond a user's explicit preferences or direct expectations. Serendipitous recommendations should surprise users by presenting them with items they did not anticipate but still find enjoyable or valuable. Serendipity has been examined regarding its potential to reduce popularity bias and boost the utility of recommendations by facilitating better discoverability. However, designing serendipity is challenging, as it requires balancing surprises as well as relevance. One line of research that combines the necessity to provide users with surprising and yet relevant items is presented by Björneborn (2017) and has seen operationalization in recent attempts to design recommender systems beyond the algorithm (Smets et al. 2022). Björneborn (2017) identifies three key affordances for serendipity: diversifiability, traversability, and sensoriability. These affordances are linked to three personal serendipity factors: curiosity, mobility, and sensitivity. Diversifiability relates to curiosity and includes factors such as interest, playfulness, and inclusiveness. Traversability is associated with mobility and encompasses searching, immersion, and exploration. Sensoriability is linked to sensitivity and involves stumbling upon, attention, surprise, and experiential aspects. The essential components of human interactions with information environments are covered by these affordances. A quintessential understanding that can be derived from this operationalization is that environments can be designed in ways that cultivate serendipitous encounters, whereas serendipity itself cannot be designed for (Smets, 2023; Björneborn, 2017).

5 Fairness

As we have seen, beyond-accuracy measures attempt to introduce other aspects besides accurately re-predicting historic interactions to evaluate recommender systems. Still, these measures focus only on the items that are recommended. However, the bigger context of who is affected in which way by the recommendations given by a system and whether the results or mechanisms underlying this are "fair" has become an increasingly important factor for evaluating recommender systems

(Ekstrand et al., 2022). In recent years, the fairness of machine learning has gained significant attention in discussions about machine learning systems. Fairness in classification and scoring or ranking tasks has been extensively studied (Chouldechova & Roth, 2020). Here concepts like individual fairness and group fairness are typically investigated. Individual fairness aims to treat similar individuals similarly, ensuring comparable decisions for those with similar abilities. Group fairness examines how the system behaves concerning group membership or identities, addressing discriminatory behaviors and outcomes. Ekstrand et al. (2022, p. 682) list the following fundamental concepts in terms of fairness definitions, harm, and motivations for fairness.

Definitions

- *Individual fairness: Similar individuals have similar experience.*
- *Group fairness: Different groups have similar experiences.*
  - *Sensitive attribute: Attribute identifying group membership.*
  - *Disparate treatment: Groups explicitly treated differently.*
  - *Disparate impact: Groups receive outcomes at different rates.*
  - *Disparate mistreatment: Groups receive erroneous (adverse) effects at different rates.*

Harm

- *Distributional harm: Harm caused by (unfair) distribution of resources or outcomes.*
- *Representational harm: Harm caused by inaccurate internal or external representation.*

Motivations

- *Anti-classification: Protected attributes should not play a role in decisions.*
- *Anti-subordination: Decision process should actively work to undo past harm.*

With regard to the motivations for fairness, the most commonly discussed and addressed aspect in technology-oriented works is that of anti-classification, i.e., to prevent harm before occurring. The concept of anti-subordination, i.e., addressing past harm and therefore introducing current "unfairness" in order to support historically disadvantaged users (cf. "affirmative actions") is a more complex and difficult topic and often remains unaddressed. For digital humanism, this presents an opportunity to engage in a multidisciplinary discourse on the design of future recommender systems.

Although the objective of a fairness-focused system is commonly labeled as "fairness," it is crucial to recognize that achieving universal fairness is unattainable. Fairness is a multifaceted issue that is subject to social debates and disagreements, making it impossible to fully resolve. The existence of competing notions of fairness, the diverse requirements of multiple stakeholders, and the fact that fairness is inherently subjective and debatable are reasons for it (Ekstrand et al., 2022).

Emerging approaches aim to address fairness-related issues in recommender systems (Boratto & Marras, 2021). As already sketched before in recommender systems, there are various stakeholders with different fairness concerns (Ekstrand et al., 2022):

- *Consumer fairness* involves treating users fairly and ensuring no systematic disadvantages.
- *Provider fairness* focuses on treating content creators fairly, giving them equal opportunity for their work to be recommended.
- *Subject fairness* is the fair treatment of the people or entities that the recommended items are about.

While fairness concerns for these stakeholders are typically considered separately, some work aims to analyze or provide fairness for multiple stakeholders simultaneously. To promote fairness in recommender systems, it is crucial to identify and address specific harms, understand the stakeholders involved, and contribute to building systems that promote equity and avoid discrimination (Ekstrand et al., 2022). Ideally, responsibility for these tasks is taken by the platforms providing the recommendation services. An overview of different works approaching fairness metrics in ranking and recommendation tasks is given by Patro et al. (2022).

Other venues to design for fairness could be found in a better understanding of users, their values, and motivations. Hence, future studies could delve into psychological theories and empirical studies to understand individuals' preferences and their association with contextual information, personality, and demographic characteristics. Recommender systems are designed to assist human decision-making. Additionally, group recommender systems leverage social psychology constructs to provide recommendations beneficial for groups. While current recommender systems provide useful recommendations, they often lack interpretability and fail to incorporate the underlying cognitive reasons for user behavior (Wilson et al., 2020). This is discussed in the next section on relevant and promising research directions.

6 Human- and Value-Centered Recommender Systems

6.1 Psychology-Informed Recommender Systems

For instance, a survey on psychology-informed recommender systems by Lex et al. (2021) identifies three categories in which different streams from psychological research are being integrated: cognition-inspired, personality-aware, and affect-aware recommender systems. Cognition-inspired recommender systems employ models from cognitive psychology to enhance the design and functionality of recommender systems. Personality-aware recommender systems consider individual personality traits to alleviate cold-start situations for new users and improve personalization by increasing recommendation list diversity. For instance, the widely used Five-Factor Model (FFM), also known as the Big Five model or the OCEAN model, is often applied in recommender systems research to describe human personality traits (McCrae & John, 1992). Neidhardt et al. (2015) introduced a picture-based approach to elicit user preferences in tourism. Tourism products are complex, and users often have difficulty expressing their needs, especially in the early stages of the travel decision process. The approach introduces seven factors that combine the FFM and tourism roles from literature and creates a mapping between the factors and pictures. In this way, pictures can be used to implicitly and nonverbally elicit the preferences of users and allow users to interact with the RS in a more enjoyable way. Additionally, affect-aware recommender systems consider the emotional state and affective responses of users to provide more tailored recommendations.

With these approaches aiming to better describe the user, one needs to remain aware that these ultimately highly indirect methods to derive human traits and emotions are often built upon strongly debated theories in psychology (see also below) and that their validity is very limited due to technological shortcomings, assumptions, and negligence (Agüera y Arcas et al., 2017). Whether these research directions therefore actually constitute progress in building more "human-centered" systems or are yet another unsuitable attempt that effectively "dehumanizes" users and violates their privacy needs to be painstakingly observed and investigated. As such, from a digital humanist's perspective, this research direction of recommender systems needs to be met with caution.

6.2 Value-Oriented Recommender Systems

Lately, researchers have been attempting to create more moral and human-centered recommender systems that are in line with human values and support human welfare. In order to create recommender systems that reflect human values and advance well-being, Stray et al. (2022) advocate incorporating human values into them. They stress the importance of taking an interdisciplinary approach to this task. The psychological mechanisms that drive changes in user behavior, including their needs and individual abilities to cope with uncertainty and ambiguous situations, are frequently overlooked (FeldmanHall & Shenhav, 2019).

However, it is important to acknowledge that the field of recommender systems research tends to overly rely on easily accessible and quantifiable data, often neglecting discussions on the stability of observable attitudes and behaviors over time ("McNamara Fallacy"; Jannach & Bauer, 2020) and the potential for interventions to bring about change. Many of the prevailing psychological theories and concepts in the quickly developing field of recommender systems are based on early psychological research (such as Ekman's theory of basic emotion, 1992), which has since frequently been shown to be oversimplified and unable to adequately capture the complex and dynamic nature of human attitudes, behaviors, cognition, and emotion (Barrett, 2022). To illustrate, the stability of a person's personality across different situations has been challenged, as individuals do not consistently behave in accordance with their inner urges (Montag & Elhai, 2019). Montag and Elhai also highlight that while longitudinal studies have demonstrated the overall stability of personality over time, subtle changes can occur, and life events impact personality development. This knowledge emphasizes the importance of considering the context in psychology-aware recommender systems. Integrating these insights into recommender systems could provide a more nuanced understanding of users' preferences and behaviors.

6.3 Embodiment in Recommender Systems

Additionally, recent advancements in cognitive science shine a light on the intricate relationship between the decision-making processes and brain-body functions, which holds significance for the design and functionality of recommender systems. Renowned psychologist and cognitive scientist Lisa Feldman Barrett emphasizes the brain's role in maintaining the body's vital resources, referred to as allostasis, to facilitate various cognitive and physical activities (Barrett, 2017). Considering these insights, it becomes evident that incorporating an understanding of brain-body functions is crucial in the design of recommender systems. Acknowledging the interplay between cognitive processes and physiological regulation allows for a more holistic approach to recommendation algorithms. However, it is essential to recognize the characteristics of human decision-making, its potential as well as its vulnerabilities (Turkle, 2022). To illustrate, while a serendipitous recommendation might fit the user's profile perfectly, their emotional state might simply not allow them to receive it as such (Nguyen et al., 2018). Furthermore, some users' personalities are more, others less accepting of serendipitous recommendations.

In summary, recent discoveries in cognitive science, including the understanding of brain-body functions and decision-making processes, have direct implications for the design and improvement of recommender systems. Integrating insights from cognitive psychology and neuroscience can enhance the accuracy and relevance of recommendations.

6.4 Trust in Recommender Systems

The interaction between a user and a recommender system is also defined by the amount of trust the user holds against it. The more a user trusts the recommender system to generate useful items, the more the user will accept the items (Harman et al., 2014). This is especially important when recommending serendipitous items, as these may appear unexpected which can lead to trust issues (Afridi, 2019). Providing a user with relevant recommendations will establish trust over time, while providing unsatisfying recommendations will erode trust. There are also other challenges; according to Ricci et al. (2022, p. 7) "some users do not trust recommender systems, thus they play with them to see how good they are at making recommendations," and they noted that "a certain system may also offer specific functions to let the users test its behavior in addition to those just required for obtaining recommendations."

Recent evidence highlighting the importance of autonomy support for human well-being and positive outcomes has raised concerns regarding autonomy within technology design (Calvo et al., 2020). However, incorporating design strategies that promote human autonomy faces two major challenges. Firstly, the breadth of designing for autonomy is extensive, as technologies now play a role in various aspects of our lives, such as education, workplace, health, and relationships, spanning different stages of human development. Secondly, these design practices present ethical dilemmas that challenge existing conceptions of autonomy across disciplines, particularly considering that most technologies are designed to influence human behaviors and decision-making processes.

6.5 Socially Responsible Designs

The inclusion of "socially responsible designs" (Heitz et al., 2022, p. 2) in research and development programs could open opportunities to create recommenders that result in actions and choices that are advantageous to both individuals and society (e.g., Stray et al., 2021). Incorporating individual-level elements and user characteristics, psychology-aware recommender systems can provide a fresh viewpoint in the field of recommender systems research. These systems aim to offer more individualized, varied, and interpretable recommendations by making use of psychological categories and ideas. To ensure a more thorough understanding of user preferences and behavior in the design of recommender systems, additional exploration and consideration of the trait-state perspectives and research development in psychology and the cognitive sciences of human characteristics, intervention possibilities, and the impact of social context are required.

7 Conclusions

We have provided but a glimpse into the area of recommender systems, their importance for the modern Web, and their potential impact on individuals and democracy. Following an overview of techniques used in recommender systems and strategies to evaluate and optimize them, we have focused on the ongoing research discussions dealing with the topics of diversity and fairness. From these discussions, the following take-away messages emerge:

- Optimizing systems for historic patterns and behavior data can indicate effectiveness and improvements of systems that in fact lead to decreasing user satisfaction and narrowing of utility. Other aspects, such as diversity in the results, even if

they are not considered correct according to the chosen accuracy-oriented evaluation measures, are important to judge the quality of a system.
- When deployed in areas relevant to democracy, such as news and media, or for the well-being and success of individuals, such as job recommendation, values defined by society shall be given preference over the objectives of service providers, for instance, by means of policy and regulation. Operationalizing these values is challenging but imperative.
- Recommendation settings are complex tasks involving multiple stakeholders. Questions such as diversity and fairness must always be addressed from their diverse and mostly conflicting points of view. Again, whose interests are to be prioritized should ultimately be decided by society or the affected community. Interdisciplinary approaches are required to define concepts such as fairness, e.g., by involving political scientists and others. These are challenging and complex tasks that ultimately require approaches that model societal values. Currently, these are open issues despite the growing body of work addressing these topics.
- Not every research direction dealing with human features is human centered. In fact, there is a chance that they are not even scientific as they are often built on very weak assumptions, spurious effects, and insufficient technology. Conclusions drawn based on such systems are not only invalid but potentially harmful as they can build the basis for decisions that affect individuals. As such, poorly designed and careless research poses the risk of building "de-humanizing" systems, rather than providing the claimed "human centricity."

For digital humanism, recommender systems are a central technology. They are information filters and automatic decision systems. They make content accessible and at the same time act as opaque gatekeepers. They serve humans as well as business interests. They can be shaped according to values—including those of Digital Humanism.

Discussion Questions for Students and Their Teachers

1. Select an area where recommender systems are used and identify stakeholders.
   - For each stakeholder, discuss how they would benefit from a concept of diversity if applied to the recommender system.
   - Which concept would that be?
   - How would this connect to a notion of fairness from their perspective?
   - Which values could they follow and how would that affect their goals and the definitions chosen?
   - Where do the interests of different stakeholders align?
2. Recommender systems are necessary to efficiently navigate the vast amounts of online data and content; at the same time they are a normative factor and can be used to exert control and power. Discuss the usefulness and threats imposed by recommender systems. Collect anecdotal evidence of success stories of recommenders, failures, and concerns and identify individually desired functions of improved, future recommenders and platforms.
3. For technical solutions, a model of the real world and the operationalization of functions and goals is necessary. Discuss how human and societal values could be modeled and operationalized to enable more fair systems.

Learning Resources for Students

For a deeper understanding of the inner workings and principles of recommender systems, it is strongly suggested to directly refer to the Recommender Systems Handbook (3rd edition), in particular the chapters on techniques, applications, and challenges; novelty and diversity; multistakeholder systems; and fairness in recommender systems:

1. Ricci, F., Rokach, L., & Shapira, B. (2022). Recommender systems: Techniques, applications, and challenges. In Recommender Systems Handbook, 3rd ed., 1–35. DOI: 10.1007/978-1-0716-2197-4_1.
2. Castells, P., Hurley, N., & Vargas, S. (2022). Novelty and diversity in recommender systems. In Recommender Systems Handbook, 3rd ed., 603–646. DOI: 10.1007/978-1-0716-2197-4_16.
3. Abdollahpouri, H. & Burke, R. (2022) Multistakeholder Recommender Systems. In Recommender Systems Handbook, 3rd ed., 647–677. DOI: 10.1007/978-1-0716-2197-4_17.
4. Ekstrand, M. D., Das, A., Burke, R., & Diaz, F. (2022). Fairness in recommender systems. In Recommender Systems Handbook, 3rd ed., 679–707. DOI: 10.1007/978-1-0716-2197-4_18.

Critical takes on current practices and methodology in recommender systems and machine learning research can be found in:

1. Jannach, D., & Bauer, C. (2020). Escaping the McNamara fallacy: towards more impactful recommender systems research. AI Magazine, 41(4):79–95.
2. Agüera y Arcas, B., Mitchell, M., & Todorov, A. (2017). Physiognomy's New Clothes. Medium. URL: https://medium.com/@blaisea/physiognomys-new-clothes-f2d4b59fdd6a

For a broader, multi-perspective discussion on the topics of diversity, fairness, and value-based recommendation, the following articles will provide additional input:

1. Helberger, N., Karppinen, K., & D'Acunto, L. (2018). Exposure diversity as a design principle for recommender systems, Information, Communication & Society, 21(2):191–207. DOI: 10.1080/1369118X.2016.1271900.
2. Binns, R. (2018) Fairness in Machine Learning: Lessons from Political Philosophy. Conference on Fairness, Accountability, and Transparency. Proceedings of Machine Learning Research, 81:1–11.
3. Stray, J., Halevy, A., Assar, P., Hadfield-Menell, D., Boutilier, C., Ashar, A., Beattie, L., Ekstrand, M., Leibowicz, C., Sehat, C. M., Johansen, S., Kerlin, L., Vickrey, D., Singh, S., Vrijenhoek, S., Zhang, A., Andrus, M., Helberger, N., Proutskova, P., Mitra, T., & Vasan, N. (2022). Building Human Values into Recommender Systems: An Interdisciplinary Synthesis. arXiv preprint arXiv:2207.10192.

Acknowledgments This work was supported by the Christian Doppler Research Association (CDG). This research was funded in whole, or in part, by the Austrian Science Fund (FWF) [P33526]. For the purpose of open access, the authors have applied a CC BY public copyright license to any author accepted manuscript version arising from this submission.

References

Abdollahpouri, H., & Burke, R. (2022). Multistakeholder recommender systems. In *Recommender systems handbook* (3rd ed., pp. 647–677). Springer. https://doi.org/10.1007/978-1-0716-2197-4_17

Afridi, A. H. (2019). Transparency for beyond-accuracy experiences: A novel user interface for recommender systems. *Procedia Computer Science, 151*, 335–344. https://doi.org/10.1016/j.procs.2019.04.047

Agüera y Arcas, B., Mitchell, M., & Todorov, A. (2017). *Physiognomy's new clothes. Medium.* https://medium.com/@blaisea/physiognomys-new-clothes-f2d4b59fdd6a

Aridor, G., Goncalves, D., & Sikdar, S. (2020). Deconstructing the filter bubble: User decision-making and recommender systems. In *Proceedings of the 14th ACM conference on recommender systems (RecSys '20)* (pp. 82–91). ACM. https://doi.org/10.1145/3383313.3412246.

Barrett, L. F. (2017). The theory of constructed emotion: An active inference account of interoception and categorization. *Social Cognitive and Affective Neuroscience, 12*(1), 1–23. https://doi.org/10.1093/scan/nsw154

Barrett, L. F. (2022). Context reconsidered: Complex signal ensembles, relational meaning, and population thinking in psychological science. *American Psychologist, 77*(8), 894–920. https://doi.org/10.1037/amp0001054

Binns, R. (2018). Fairness in machine learning: Lessons from political philosophy. Conference on Fairness, Accountability, and Transparency. *Proc Mach Learn Res, 81*, 1–11. https://doi.org/10.48550/arXiv.1712.03586

Björneborn, L. (2017). Three key affordances for serendipity: Toward a framework connecting environmental and personal factors in serendipitous encounters. *Journal of Documentation, 73*(5), 1053–1081. https://doi.org/10.1108/JD-07-2016-0097

Boratto, L., & Marras, M. (2021). Advances in bias-aware recommendation on the web. In *Proceedings of the 14th ACM international conference on web search and data mining* (pp. 1147–1149). https://doi.org/10.1145/3437963.3441665

Burke, R. (2007). Hybrid web recommender systems. *The adaptive web: Methods and strategies of web personalization* (pp. 377–408). https://doi.org/10.1007/978-3-540-72079-9_12

Calvo, R. A., Peters, D., Vold, K., & Ryan, R. M. (2020). Supporting human autonomy in AI systems: A framework for ethical enquiry. *Ethics of digital well-being: A multidisciplinary approach* (pp. 31–54). https://doi.org/10.1007/978-3-030-50585-1_2

Castells, P., Hurley, N., & Vargas, S. (2022). Novelty and diversity in recommender systems. In *Recommender systems handbook* (3rd ed., pp. 603–646). https://doi.org/10.1007/978-1-0716-2197-4_16.

Chouldechova, A., & Roth, A. (2020). A snapshot of the frontiers of fairness in machine learning. *Communications of the ACM, 63*(5), 82–89. https://doi.org/10.1145/3376898

Dahlgren, P. (2021). A critical review of filter bubbles and a comparison with selective exposure. *Nordicom Review, 42*, 15–33. https://doi.org/10.2478/nor-2021-0002

Ekman, P. (1992). An argument for basic emotions. *Cognition and Emotion, 6*(3–4), 169–200. https://doi.org/10.1080/02699939208411068

Ekstrand, M. D., Das, A., Burke, R., & Diaz, F. (2022). Fairness in recommender systems. In *Recommender systems handbook* (3rd ed., pp. 679–707). https://doi.org/10.1007/978-1-0716-2197-4_18.

FeldmanHall, O., & Shenhav, A. (2019). Resolving uncertainty in a social world. *Nature Human Behaviour, 3*(5), 426–435. https://doi.org/10.1038/s41562-019-0590-x

Harman, J. L., O'Donovan, J., Abdelzaher, T., & Gonzalez, C. (2014). *Dynamics of human trust in recommender systems* (pp. 305–308). In Proceedings of the 8th ACM Conference on Recommender systems (RecSys '14). https://doi.org/10.1145/2645710.2645761

Heitz, L., Lischka, J. A., Birrer, A., Paudel, B., Tolmeijer, S., Laugwitz, L., & Bernstein, A. (2022). Benefits of diverse news recommendations for democracy: A user study. *Digital Journalism, 10*(10), 1710–1730. https://doi.org/10.1080/21670811.2021.2021804

Helberger, N., Karppinen, K., & D'Acunto, L. (2018). Exposure diversity as a design principle for recommender systems. *Information, Communication and Society, 21*(2), 191–207. https://doi.org/10.1080/1369118X.2016.1271900

Helberger, N. (2019). On the democratic role of news recommenders. *Digital Journalism, 7*(8), 993–1012. https://doi.org/10.1080/21670811.2019.1623700

Jannach, D., & Bauer, C. (2020). Escaping the McNamara fallacy: Towards more impactful recommender systems research. *AI Magazine, 41*(4), 79–95. https://doi.org/10.1609/aimag.v41i4.5312

Jannach, D., Zanker, M., Felfernig, A., & Friedrich, G. (2010). *Recommender systems: An introduction*. Cambridge University Press.

Jannach, D., Resnick, P., Tuzhilin, A., & Zanker, M. (2016). Recommender systems—Beyond matrix completion. *Communications of the ACM, 59*(11), 94–102. https://doi.org/10.1145/2891406

Kaminskas, M., & Bridge, D. (2016). Diversity, serendipity, novelty, and coverage: A survey and empirical analysis of beyond-accuracy objectives in recommender systems. *ACM Transactions on Interactive Intelligent Systems, 7*(1), 1–42. https://doi.org/10.1145/2926720

Keijzer, M. A., & Mäs, M. (2022). The complex link between filter bubbles and opinion polarization. *Data Science, 5*(2), 139–166. https://doi.org/10.3233/DS-220054

Lee, S. Y., & Lee, S. W. (2022). Normative or effective? The role of news diversity and trust in news recommendation services. *International Journal of Human–Computer Interaction, 39*(6), 1216–1229. https://doi.org/10.1080/10447318.2022.2057116

Lex, E., Kowald, D., Seitlinger, P., Tran, T. N. T., Felfernig, A., & Schedl, M. (2021). Psychology-informed recommender systems. Foundations and Trends®. *Information Retrieval, 15*(2), 134–242. https://doi.org/10.1561/1500000090

Liu, P., Zhang, L., & Gulla, J. A. (2023). *Pre-train, prompt and recommendation: A comprehensive survey of language modelling paradigm adaptations in recommender systems*. arXiv preprint https://doi.org/10.48550/arXiv.2302.03735.

McCrae, R. R., & John, O. P. (1992). An introduction to the five-factor model and its applications. *Journal of Personality, 60*(2), 175–215. https://doi.org/10.1111/j.1467-6494.1992.tb00970.x

Michiels, L., Leysen, J., Smets, A., & Goethals, B. (2022). What are filter bubbles really? A review of the conceptual and empirical work. In *Adjunct proceedings of the 30th ACM conference on user modeling, adaptation and personalization* (pp. 274–279). https://doi.org/10.1145/3511047.3538028.

Möller, J., Trilling, D., Helberger, N., & van Es, B. (2018). Do not blame it on the algorithm: an empirical assessment of multiple recommender systems and their impact on content diversity. *Information, Communication and Society, 21*(7), 959–977. https://doi.org/10.1080/1369118X.2018.1444076

Montag, C., & Elhai, J. D. (2019). A new agenda for personality psychology in the digital age? *Personality and Individual Differences, 147*, 128–134. https://doi.org/10.1016/j.paid.2019.03.045

Neidhardt, J., Seyfang, L., Schuster, R., & Werthner, H. (2015). A picture-based approach to recommender systems. *Information Technology and Tourism, 15*, 49–69. https://doi.org/10.1007/s40558-014-0017-5

Nguyen, T. T., Hui, P.-M., Harper, F. M., Terveen, L., & Konstan, J. A. (2014). Exploring the filter bubble: The effect of using recommender systems on content diversity. In *Proceedings of the 23rd international conference on World wide web* (pp. 677–686). https://doi.org/10.1145/2566486.2568012.

Nguyen, T. T., Maxwell Harper, F., Terveen, L., & Konstan, J. A. (2018). User personality and user satisfaction with recommender systems. *Information Systems Frontiers, 20*, 1173–1189. https://doi.org/10.1007/s10796-017-9782-y

Pariser, E. (2011). *The filter bubble: What the internet is hiding from you*. Penguin Press.

Patro, G. K., Porcaro, L., Mitchell, L., Zhang, Q., Zehlike, M., & Garg, N. (2022). Fair ranking: A critical review, challenges, and future directions. In *Proceedings of the 2022 ACM conference*

on fairness, accountability, and transparency (pp. 1929–1942). https://doi.org/10.1145/3531146.3533238.
Raza, S., & Ding, C. (2020). A regularized model to trade-off between accuracy and diversity in a news recommender system. In *2020 IEEE international conference on big data* (pp. 551–560). https://doi.org/10.1109/BigData50022.2020.9378340.
Ribeiro, M. T., Ziviani, N., Moura, E. S. D., Hata, I., Lacerda, A., & Veloso, A. (2015). Multiobjective pareto-efficient approaches for recommender systems. *ACM Transactions on Intelligent Systems and Technology, 53*, 1–20. https://doi.org/10.1145/2629350
Ricci, F., Rokach, L., & Shapira, B. (2022). Recommender systems: Techniques, applications, and challenges. In *Recommender systems handbook* (3rd ed, pp. 1–35). https://doi.org/10.1007/978-1-0716-2197-4_1.
Smets, A. (2023). Designing for serendipity: A means or an end? *Journal of Documentation, 79*(3), 589–607. https://doi.org/10.1108/JD-12-2021-0234
Smets, A., Michiels, L., Bogers, T., & Björneborn, L. (2022). Serendipity in recommender systems beyond the algorithm: A feature repository and experimental design. In *Proceedings of the 9th joint workshop on interfaces and human decision making for recommender systems co-located with 16th ACM conference on recommender systems* (pp. 44–66). https://ceur-ws.org/Vol-3222/paper4.pdf
Stray, J., Vendrov, I., Nixon, J., Adler, S., & Hadfield-Menell, D. (2021). What are you optimizing for? Aligning recommender systems with human values. *CoRR*, abs/2107.10939. https://doi.org/10.48550/arXiv.2107.10939
Stray, J., Halevy, A., Assar, P., Hadfield-Menell, D., Boutilier, C., Ashar, A., Beattie, L., Ekstrand, M., Leibowicz, C., Sehat, C. M., Johansen, S., Kerlin, L., Vickrey, D., Singh, S., Vrijenhoek, S., Zhang, A., Andrus, M., Helberger, N., Proutskova, P., Mitra, T., & Vasan, N. (2022). *Building human values into recommender systems: An interdisciplinary synthesis*. arXiv preprint https://doi.org/10.48550/arXiv.2207.10192.
Turkle, S. (2022). *The empathy diaries: A memoir*. Penguin.
Vermeulen, J. (2022). To nudge or not to nudge: News recommendation as a tool to achieve online media pluralism. *Digital Journalism, 10*, 1–20. https://doi.org/10.1080/21670811.2022.2026796
Werthner, H., et al. (2019). *The Vienna manifesto on digital humanism*. https://dighum.org/dighum-manifesto/
Werthner, H., Stanger, A., Schiaffonati, V., Knees, P., Hardman, L., & Ghezzi, C. (2023). Digital humanism: The time is now. *Computer, 56*(1), 138–142. https://doi.org/10.1109/MC.2022.3219528
Wilson, J. R., Gilpin, L., & Rabkina, I. (2020). *A knowledge driven approach to adaptive assistance using preference reasoning and explanation*. arXiv preprint https://doi.org/10.48550/arXiv.2012.02904.
Zhang, S., Yao, L., Sun, A., & Tay, Y. (2019). Deep learning based recommender system: A survey and new perspectives. *ACM Computing Surveys, 52*(1), 1–38. https://doi.org/10.1145/3285029

Bias and the Web

Ricardo Baeza-Yates and Leena Murgai

Abstract Bias is everywhere, sometimes blatantly explicit, but most of the time it's hidden, as it often arises from that which is missing, the gaps in our knowledge or data. In this chapter, we cover what bias is and its different sources: how it arises, persists, feeds back into a system, and can be amplified through algorithms. To exemplify the problem, we use the Web, the largest information repository created by humankind. The first countermeasure against bias is awareness – to understand what is represented—so that we may identify what is not. So, we systematically explore a wide variety of biases which originate at different points on the Web's information production and consumption cycle. Today, many if not all the predictive algorithms we interact with online rely on vast amounts of data harvested from the Web. Biased data will of course lead to biased algorithms, but those biases need not be replicated precisely. Without intervention, typically they are amplified. We start with engagement bias, that is, the difference in rates at which people produce content versus passively consume it. We then move onto data bias: who is producing data on the Web, in what language, and the associated measurement and cultural biases. Algorithmic bias and fairness are intertwined. We discuss the difficulty in defining fairness and provide examples of algorithmic bias in predictive systems. Lastly, we look at biases in user interactions. We discuss how position bias can be mitigated by distributing visuals across results and shared information about other users can lead to different social biases. We discuss how biases continually feed back into the Web and grow through content creation and diffusion.

1 Introduction

Our inherent tendency to favor one thing or opinion over another trickles into every aspect of our lives, creating both visible and latent biases in everything we experience and create. Bias is not new. It has been intrinsically embedded in our culture

R. Baeza-Yates (✉) · L. Murgai
EAI, Northeastern University, Silicon Valley, San Jose, CA, USA
e-mail: rbaeza@acm.org

H. Werthner et al. (eds.), *Introduction to Digital Humanism*,
https://doi.org/10.1007/978-3-031-45304-5_28

and history since the beginning of time. However, thanks to the rise of the Internet and the Web, bias can now impact more people, more swiftly and with less effort than ever before. This has led the impact of bias to become a trending and controversial topic in recent years.

As digital humanism is concerned with development of technology and policies which uphold human rights, democracy, diversity, and inclusion, understanding bias is crucial if we are to build a better world. This understanding is twofold, as it is needed (1) to achieve a fairer society, as we cover next using the Web, and (2) to reflect on the biases within the history of humanism itself. Indeed, humanism is rooted in a White male Christian European conception of the world, which includes ethnic, gender, religious, and geographic biases. Hence, properly addressing these and related biases and their impact, it is an important component in the development of digital humanism, which also addresses these biases, preventing the encoding of neocolonialism in new systems and infrastructure.

Any remedy for bias must first start with awareness, and while awareness alone does not alleviate the problem, it is a necessary first step, regardless of the path forward. Progressive societies accept the existence of social bias. They identify protected features (such as gender, ethnicity, or religion), protected domains (such as healthcare, education, housing, or financial services), and underrepresented groups (such as women or people of color in technology) and use this information to construct solutions, including regulation. They prohibit unfair and systemic biases strategically, via policy and antidiscrimination laws. Some go further in trying to remedy the problem by introducing positive bias through reparations, such as affirmative action programs. All of these should be considered when developing social algorithms that essentially impact people.

For many of us, the Web has become a vital part of how we experience and understand the world. Recent decades have seen unprecedented growth in cloud storage, computer, and infrastructure to take advantage of the accessibility of the Web and manage and make use of the vast amounts of data coursing through it—a trend set to continue. Social progress arguably hinges on the integrity and accessibility of the Web and its contingent systems. As for any tool, with increased use and development, comes increased risk of abuse and misuse. Both can be surfaced by searching for bias.

Bias on the Web reflects our cultural, cognitive, and individual biases and can manifest in subtle ways. This chapter aims to increase awareness of the potential effects of bias in Web usage and content on humanity. People are faced with the ramifications of bias on the Web in the most measurable way when pursuing life goals with outcomes governed in part or largely by algorithms, from loans to personalization (Smith et al., 2016). While the obstacles that result may seem like crucial roadblocks that affect only minorities, representation bias is omnipresent and affects us all, though much of the time we are blissfully unaware of its presence and how it insidiously sways our judgment.

Nowadays, our most prominent communication channel is the Web. Unsurprisingly, then, it is also a place where our individual and collective cognitive biases converge. As social media grows increasingly central to our daily lives, so does the information about us that can be gleaned from it without our knowledge. For instance, news websites such as the New York Times and Washington Post now use information collected about us from Facebook to decide which news articles we will be most interested in (Pariser, 2011). Search and recommender systems can help filter the vast amounts of data available to us via the Web. They can both expose us to content we may never have otherwise encountered and limit our access to others that we should perhaps be paying attention to. All this makes understanding and recognizing bias on the Web more urgent than ever. Our main aim here is to raise awareness of bias on the Web that can impact us both individually and collectively. We must consider and account for these if we are to design Web systems that lift all of humanity, rather than just the privileged few.

The rest of the chapter is organized as follows. Section 2 introduces the different types of biases, where and how they enter the Web. The following sections cover these biases in more detail: engagement, data, algorithmic, user interaction, and developer biases, respectively. In Sect. 8, we highlight perhaps the most pressing concern: the vicious cycle of bias on the Web. We end the chapter with concluding remarks, further reading, and topics for discussion.[1]

2 Bias

One of the difficulties with bias is that it often results from an absence of information and identifying it requires learning what we do not know. Data gaps are not inconsequential. Data informs how we design the products, services, and systems that support and advance humanity; if you (or people like you) are not in it, the resulting design will not cater for your needs. A swathe of examples can be seen from the gender data gap. Even in the most developed countries, gender bias can be observed in how we design everything: healthcare, housing, offices, and safety features in cars and transportation systems. As a result, women are more likely to be misdiagnosed, seriously injured in car accidents, spend more time traveling, waiting in queues for bathrooms, and be uncomfortably cold at work (Perez, 2019).

The first challenge with bias is how to define and thus measure it. From a statistical point of view, bias is a systematic deviation from the true value (error) caused by an inaccurate parameter estimation or sampling process. But the true distribution or reference value is often unknown. Data is a necessarily biased representation of some truth. Take, for example, classification of people. Someone must make an inherently biased decision about which categories exist and which do not. And the things we measure tend to be proxies for what we really want. In practice, any data relating to an individual is a partial and possibly erroneous representation of who they are.

[1] This chapter is a revised and extended version of Baeza-Yates (2018, pp. 54–61) with additional material from Murgai (2023).

Bias can affect our very perception of the world and people (including ourselves) in opaque and immeasurable ways. One study in 2018 which looked at occupational gender stereotypes in image search found that they were exaggerated when compared with US labor statistics (Kay, Matuszek and Munson, 2015). Participants in the study rated search results higher when they were consistent with occupational gender stereotypes. Simultaneously, they found image search results were capable of shifting people's perceptions of real-world distributions. So, bias on the Web goes both ways. Representational harms, though difficult to measure, are real and play a pivotal role in supporting social hierarchies and hindering social progress (Crawford, 2017).

When all we have is outcomes, how do we measure bias, or rather what do we measure it against? When we look at resource allocation like wealth, it seems natural to make a normative assumption of equality. But more generally, the correct reference value might be less clear and subject to debate. For instance, consider a social variable, such as influence; we would expect there to be some natural variation in the amount of attention individuals garner based on their occupation and this need not be problematic.

Cultural biases can be found in our inclinations based on shared norms and beliefs within our communities. We all belong to some communities and not to others. Our cultural biases mean that we have beliefs or opinions (consciously and unconsciously) about things (including people, from other communities and within our own) in advance of encountering them. As with many other things in life, the remedy for prejudice is education. But the only path to education is via diversity.

Cognitive biases affect the way we think and in turn make decisions. There are many ways in which our thinking and judgment can be impaired. The cognitive bias codex (Weinberg, 2016) provides a helpful categorization of cognitive biases, based on how they manifest. Perhaps the most obvious cause is time pressure; when forced to think fast, we tend to make errors (Kahneman, 2011). The second and third result from unintentionally filtering valuable information, either because there is too much of it, or because it is too complex. Finally, we don't just filter information; we tend to fill the gaps in search of meaning—we imagine what other people might be thinking and lean on stereotypes.

Figure 1 shows how bias is involved in our use and growth of the Web. In the next sections, we explain each of the biases shown in red and classify them by type, beginning with engagement or activity bias resulting from how people use the Web and the implicit bias toward people with limited or no Internet access. The next section addresses bias found in Web data and how it potentially poisons the algorithms that use it, followed by biases created through our interaction with websites and how different types of second-order bias feedback into the Web or Web-based systems. We focus on the significance of these biases and not on the methodological aspects of the research used to uncover them. Further details can be learned by following the references provided herein.

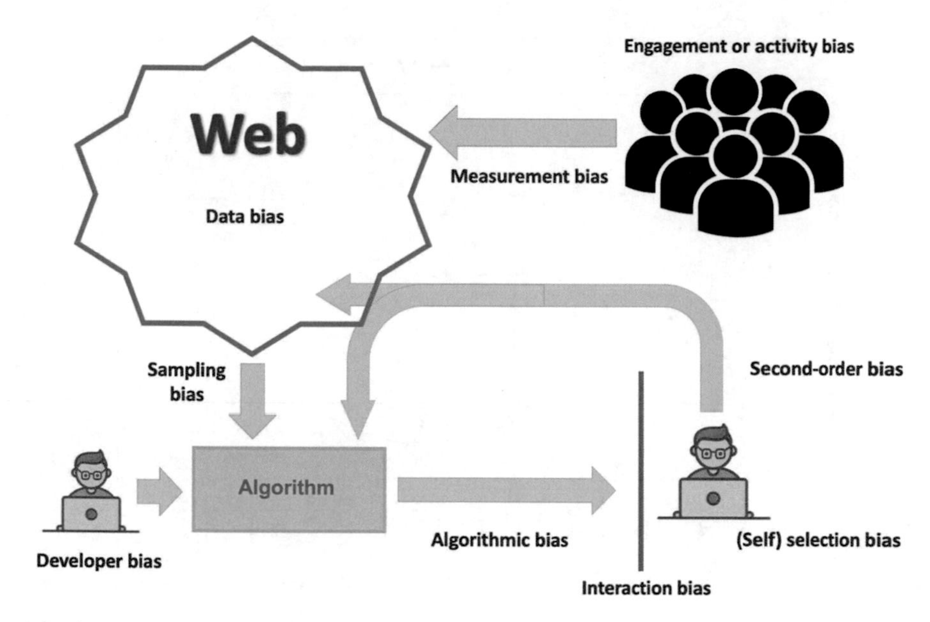

Fig. 1 The vicious cycle of bias on the Web, where the main systemic components are in blue, the biases in red, and their relations in green

3 Engagement Bias: Wisdom of the Few

In 2011, a study of how people followed other people on Twitter found that the top 0.05% of most popular people attracted almost 50% of all the attention (Wu et al., 2011). In other words, half of Twitter users were following a handful of celebrities. Motivated by this fact, we posed the following related question: What percentage of active Web users generated half of the content? That is to say, we did not consider the silent majority that just watches the Web without contributing to it, which is a form of user bias (Gong et al., 2015). We analyzed four datasets, and the results surprised us (Baeza-Yates & Saez-Trumper, 2015, pp. 69–74).

In a small Facebook dataset from 2009, we found that 7% of users generated half the content. In a larger dataset of Amazon reviews from 2013, we found the number to be just 4%. In a very large dataset of Twitter from 2011, the result was even lower, 2%. Finally, the first half of English Wikipedia was written by 0.04% of the registered editors. This indicates that only a small percentage of all users contribute to the Web and the notion that it represents the wisdom of the overall crowd is far from the truth. This is related to Nielsen's 90-9-1 participation rule that states that 1% of the users create content, 9% engage with it (say commenting or doing liking posts), and 90% just lurk (Nielsen, 2006). We also studied the dynamics of these values, finding that at least in Wikipedia, the percentage has increased in the last years as shown in Fig. 2 (courtesy of Diego Saez-Trumper).

A more recent study (Lazovich et al., 2022) looking at engagement on Twitter found similar results that around 90% of people engaged passively. Engagement

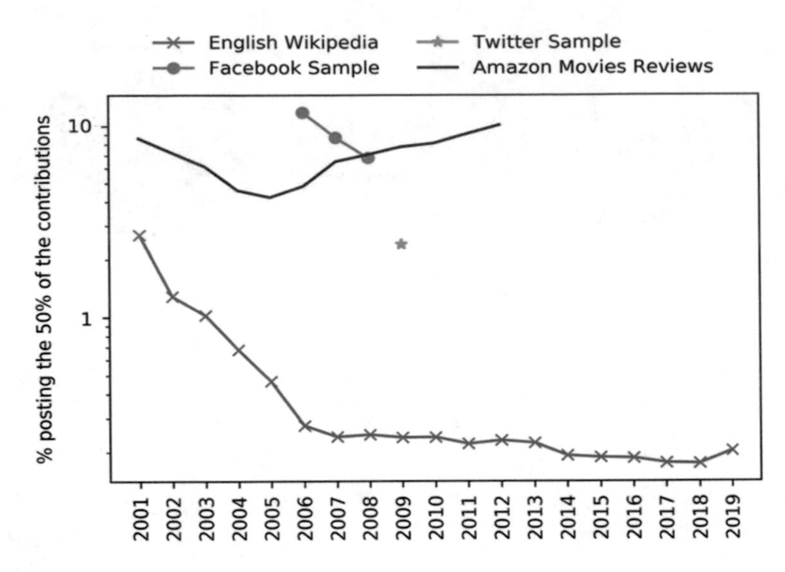

Fig. 2 Dynamics of the percentage of active users that create 50% of the content for four datasets

types that required clicking (likes and author profile clicks) were done by half the population, while retweets, replies, and quote tweets involved the top 70, 80, and 90th percentile of the population, respectively. The top 1% of authors received 80% of the views.

Some remarks on our findings. First, it did not make sense that just 4% of the people were voluntarily writing half of the Amazon reviews. We sensed something else at play. A month after presenting our work, our hunch was confirmed. In October 2015, Amazon started a crusade against paid fake reviews, suing 1000 individuals on a freelance service marketplace accused of writing them (Wattles, 2015). This crusade has continued until today. Our analysis also found that if we considered only the reviews that some people found helpful, the percentage reduced to 2.5% and that there was a correlation between helpfulness and a proxy measure for text quality. Second, although the case of Wikipedia is the most biased, it is a positive example. The 2000 people involved in the start of English Wikipedia probably triggered a snowball effect that helped it become what it is today. Indeed, bias is a requisite in creating anything from nothing.

Zipf's minimal effort law (Zipf, 1949) states that many people do a little while few people do a lot, which may help explain a big part of the engagement bias. However, economic, and social incentives also play a role. For instance, Zipf's law can be seen in most Web measures such as number of pages per website or number of links per Web page. In Fig. 3, we show an example where the Zipf's law is clearly visible on the right side of the graph (the steep line). However, at the beginning, there is a strong social force, the so-called shame effect, which makes the slope less negative. This illustrates that many people prefer to exert the least amount of effort, but most people also need to feel they did enough to avoid feeling ashamed of their

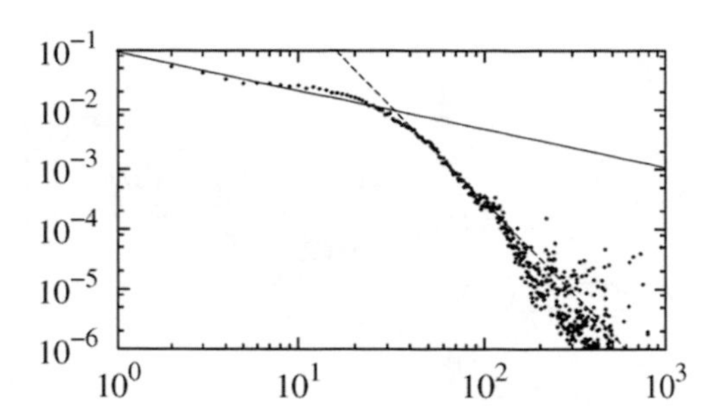

Fig. 3 Shame effect (flatter line) against minimal effort (steeper line) on the number of links in UK web pages, where the x axis represents the number of links while the y axis is the relative frequency. The intersection is between 12 and 13 links, the average is 18.9, and the exponents of the power laws are 0.7 and 3.6, respectively

work (Baeza-Yates et al., 2007). These two effects are common characteristics of the Web. Notice that data on the far right probably comes from pages written by software, not people.

Finally, as Herbert Simon said, "a wealth of information creates a poverty of attention." Hence, engagement bias generates the *digital desert* of the Web, that is, the Web content no one ever sees (Baeza-Yates & Saez-Trumper, 2015, pp. 69–74). A lower bound comes from the Twitter data where they found that 1.1% of the tweets were posted by accounts without followers! From usage statistics of Wikipedia, we got an upper bound: 31% of the articles added or modified in May 2014 were never visited in June. The actual number likely lies in the first half of the 1–31% range.

In this case, bias can also have advantages. Thanks to engagement bias, all levels of caching are very effective on the Web, making the load on websites and the Internet traffic much lower than it could potentially be.

4 Data Bias

Like people, data quality is heterogeneous and therefore, to some extent, biased. People working in government, university, and other institutions that disseminate information usually publish data of higher quality and attempt to address bias through peer review. Social media data on the other hand is much larger, much more biased, and without doubt, of lesser quality on average. That said, the number of people who contribute to social media (an important subset of Web data) is probably at least one order of magnitude more than those in information-based institutions. Thus, social media produces more data with greater variance in quality, including high-quality data (for any definition of what quality is).

A great deal of bias comes from users' demographics. Internet access and use is, of course, correlated to historical, geographical, economic, and educational factors. These dimensions correlate to other characteristics, having a ripple effect where bias

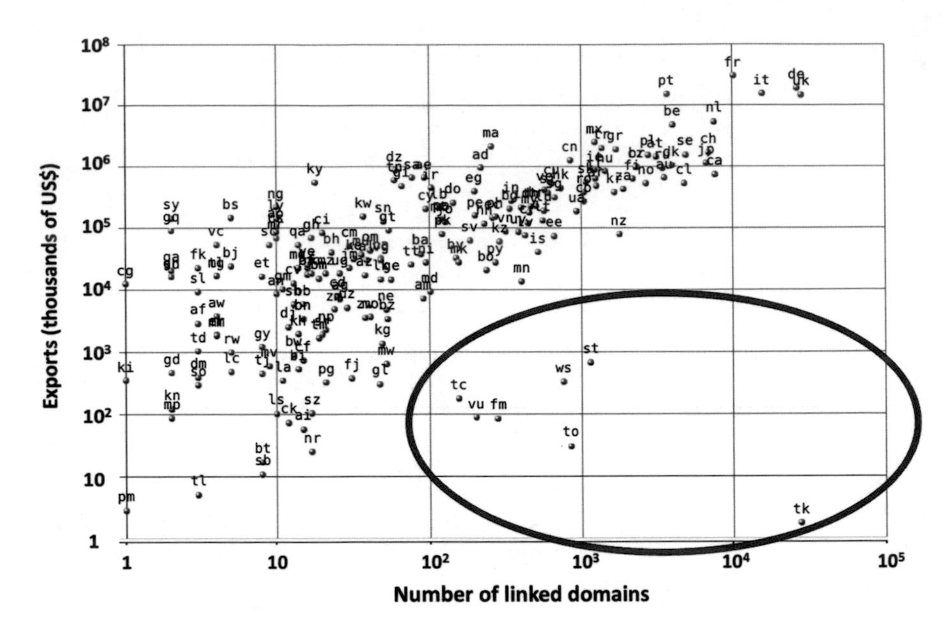

Fig. 4 Economic bias in out links for the Web of Spain (adapted from Baeza-Yates et al., 2006, p. 16)

taints all areas. For instance, it is estimated that over 60% of the top ten million websites (by traffic rankings) are in English (Bhutada, 2021), while the percentage of native English speakers in the world is about 5% (this increases to 13% if we include all English speakers). But is this the correct reference value against which to measure this bias? We could instead use the native language of all people with access to the Internet, where English was almost 26% in 2021 (Statista, 2021). Alternatively, we could consider the percentage of English text on the Web, which might be closer to 30%. At best we still have a bias factor of 2, that is, English websites are twice as prevalent among the best websites as they are among all websites.

Bias can also be found in the link structure of the Web. In Fig. 4, we present a scatter plot showing the total value of Spanish exports to a given country against the number of links from the Web of Spain to the same country (Baeza-Yates et al., 2006, pp. 1–41). Countries in the red circle are outliers; they sold their domain rights for other purposes, such as the Federation of Micronesia, fm, for radio. Discarding those countries, the correlation is over 0.8 for Spain. In fact, the more developed the country is, the higher the correlation, ranging from 0.6 in Brazil to 0.9 in the UK (Baeza-Yates & Castillo, 2006). This does not prove causation, but it is a strong indication of the influence of economy in the link structure of the Web.

What about the representation of women? Consider Fig. 5, which shows the fraction of biographies of women in Wikipedia across history (Graells-Garrido et al., 2015, pp. 231–236). The low fraction of biographies could be explained by the systemic gender bias existing throughout human history (Wagner et al., 2015,

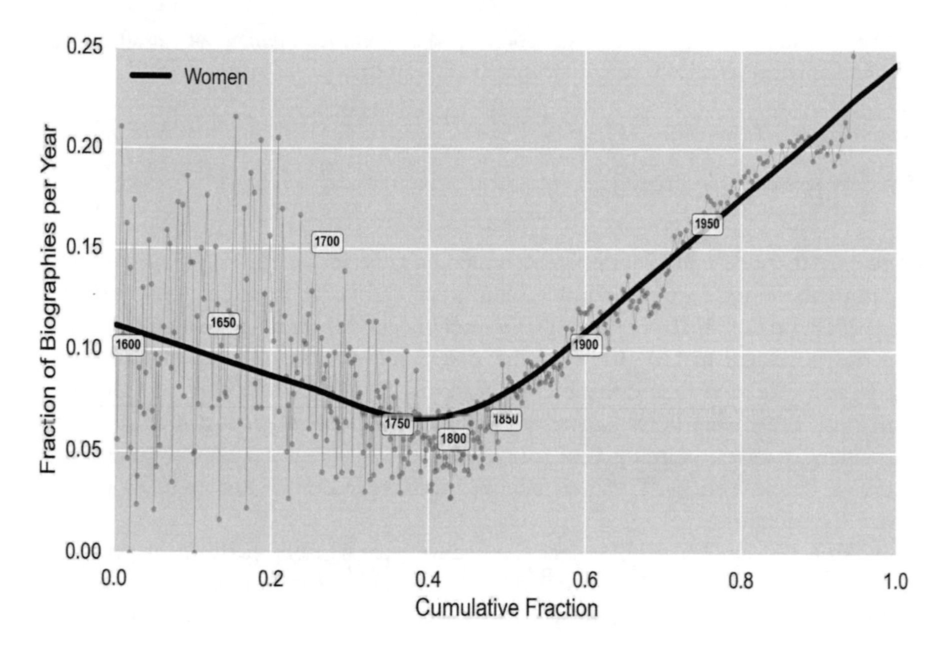

Fig. 5 Accumulated fraction of women biographies in Wikipedia (Graells-Garrido et al., 2015)

pp. 454–463), while the shape seems to change around the French revolution. However, there is an additional underlying factor hiding a deeper bias which is revealed when we look closer at how this content is generated. In the biographies category, less than 12% of the Wikipedia editors are women! In other categories, such as geography, the bias is even worse, falling to a measly 4%. That said, since the percentage of public female editors is just 11%, bias in the biographies category might be viewed as positive rather than negative bias. Keep in mind these values may also contain bias, as not all Wikipedia editors publish their gender; thus, females might be underrepresented in the data as they may prefer not to inform this.

An additional source of data bias is Web spam, a well-known human-generated malicious bias that is difficult to characterize but is motivated by economic incentives. This might be similarly categorized as near-duplication content, like mirrored websites, that represented about 20% of static web content 20 years ago (Fetterly et al., 2003, pp. 37–45).

Since most biases are hard to measure, their effects on predictive algorithms that use machine learning are difficult to understand. First, as Web data represents a biased sample of the population, studies based on social media may have a large error (which we can be sure is not uniformly distributed). Second, the results cannot be extrapolated to the rest of the population for the same reason. As an example, consider the polling errors for past US presidential elections (Mediative, 2014), though online polls performed better than live polls. Third, other sources of error are biased data samples (e.g., due to selection bias) or samples that are too small for the problem at hand (Baeza-Yates, 2015, pp. 1093–1096).

4.1 Information Bias

Of particular concern in relation to social media platforms are the abundance of bots, disinformation, and fake content that seem to spread faster than real content (Lazer et al., 2018, pp. 1094–1096). In 2020, researchers at CMU analyzed around 200 million tweets related to COVID, over the first 5 months of the year, showing that almost half (45%) of them were by bots (Young, 2020). Of the 50 most influential retweeters, 82% were bots. Among COVID disinformation on social media were conspiracy theories, blaming the outbreak on the introduction of fifth-generation mobile network services. These are believed to have led to 5G towers being burned down in England.

In 2017, Facebook's Ad Manager claimed to reach 41 million 18- to 24-year-olds in the USA, while census data revealed there were only 31 million people of that age group (O'Reiley, 2017). Facebook's role in political and humanitarian crises have been well documented in the media. We've seen targeted misinformation leading up to the Brexit referendum in the UK and US presidential elections in 2016 that led to shocking results (Cadwalladr, 2019) and the more recent insurrection in the US Capitol. Most disturbingly, we have seen concerns around Facebook's engagement optimizing algorithms contributing to social polarization with deadly consequences, especially in regions of ongoing conflict. Amplification of hate speech and incitement of violence on the platform have been implicated in the genocide of Rohingya Muslims in Myanmar and mob violence and crackdowns on independent reporting on Tigray in Ethiopia (Hale & Peralta, 2021) where the deadliest civil war of the twenty-first century rages on (Naranjo, 2023).

4.2 Biases in Language

Perhaps there is no better means to illustrate the intersection of statistical, cultural, and cognitive biases than through language. There are around 7100 living languages in the world, though this number is dwindling with time. They can differ vastly in both their vocabulary and structure. As we've seen, there is no doubt that English is drastically over-represented in language data. What might the disadvantages of over-representing this language, culture, and cognitive universe be?

Research has shown that the languages we speak are related to our cognitive ability in perception tasks (Boroditsky, 2017). For instance, Pormpuraawans (people of an Aboriginal Australian tribe) describe space and time using cardinal directions (north, east, south, west) and consistently order time from east to west. Western languages such as English tend to use more egocentric approaches to describe position, left, right, in front, behind, and order time from left to right. It should perhaps come as no surprise that Pormpuraawans have superior knowledge of spatial orientation (Boroditsky & Gaby, 2010, pp. 1635–1639). There are more examples; a community in Papua New Guinea who speak Yupno imagine slopes in flat areas (consistent with the valley in which they reside) to describe position. Bardi speakers, from Kimberley in Australia, describe directions as being with or against the tide (Carylsue, 2016). Language has even been known to affect our ability to perceive colors (Winawer et al., 2007, pp. 7780–7785).

In some European languages, such as Spanish and Portuguese, when accidents happen, it is the grammatically correct convention to say, for example, "the glass fell," "el vaso se cayó." In English, it is an accepted convention to say, "Ricardo dropped his glass," regardless of intent. The fact that English speakers take a much more blame-oriented approach in describing mishaps means they are much more likely to remember who was involved (Fausey & Boroditsky, 2008) (or rather accountable, since this is in English). In hindsight, all this makes sense. Language develops in response to the need to describe things. In turn, having words to describe things drives said things into existence, improving our cognitive ability to perceive them.

But language doesn't just affect our cognitive ability; it also shapes our perceptions. In many languages nouns have explicit gendered associations, and some interesting results can be found by comparing languages that ascribe the opposite gender to the same noun. For instance, in Spanish, bridges are masculine, "el puente," while in German, they are feminine, "die Brücke." Researchers have shown that the gender ascribed to a noun can affect the way we imagine them. Indeed, Spanish speakers use more stereotypically masculine words to describe bridges, strong and long, while German speakers use more stereotypically feminine words, beautiful and elegant (Boroditsky et al., 2003, pp. 61–79).

From masculine versus feminine to good versus bad. Given what we have discussed, questions around the connections between gender representation in language and sexism in culture naturally follow (Pitel, 2019). In 2016, the Oxford English Dictionary was publicly criticized for employing the phrase "rabid feminist" as a usage example for the word rabid (O'Toole, 2016). The dictionary included similarly sexist common usages for other words like shrill, nagging, and bossy. A decade before this, historical linguists observed that words referring to women undergo pejoration (when the meaning of a word deteriorates over time) far more often than those referring to men (Trask, 2007; Shariatmadari, 2016). Take, for example, the words mistress (once simply the female equivalent of master, now used to describe a woman in an illicit relationship with a married man), madam (once simply the female equivalent of sir, now also used to describe a woman who runs a brothel), hussy, governess, and the list goes on.

And finally, an example that relates to ordering. In Menominee (Corn Jr, 2019), a Native American language whose roots lie in Wisconsin, people also take a less egocentric approach to describing their interactions and relationships with others, placing themselves after the animate about which they are talking. Both culturally and in language, they place an emphasis on respect not just for people but all living things, putting others ahead of oneself.

4.3 Bias in Visual Data

Bias in visual records infiltrate the data even before it's been uploaded to the Web, through measurement bias. Capturing likeness in images involves determining the optimal balance of colors to use in each composition. Since its invention, film has been optimized for Caucasian skin. Kodak famously used Shirley cards (Del Barco, 2014) as a standard against which to calibrate colors. It wasn't until the late 1970s, after accusations of racism, that Black, Asian, and Latina Shirleys were added to the reference cards. Today's cameras come with plenty of technology built in to help us take better pictures which we hope is better, but that technology too is imbued with similar biases. Digital cameras assume Asians are blinking (Rose, 2010) and in low light still calibrate to lighter regions to define the image, focusing on White subjects while ignoring darker skin tones (Cima, 2015).

Regarding bias in data quality, we have discussed the good and the bad, now for the ugly. Figure 6 shows some results of an ethical audit of several large computer vision datasets (developed for benchmarking models) in 2020. Researchers found that TinyImages[2] contained racist, misogynistic, and demeaning labels with corresponding images and it was not alone (Prabhu & Birhane, 2021).

The dataset has since been retracted but the problem, unfortunately, does not end there. Datasets used to train and benchmark, not just computer vision but natural language processing tasks, tend to be related. TinyImages was compiled by searching the Web for images associated with words in WordNet (a machine readable, lexical database, organized by meaning, developed at Princeton), which is where TinyImages inherited its labels from. ImageNet (Deng et al., 2009, pp. 248–255) (widely considered to be a turning point in computer vision capabilities) is also based on WordNet, and Cifar-10 and Cifar-100 were derived from TinyImages.

[2] A dataset of 79 million 32 × 32-pixel color photos compiled in 2006, by MIT's Computer Science and Artificial Intelligence Lab, for image recognition tasks.

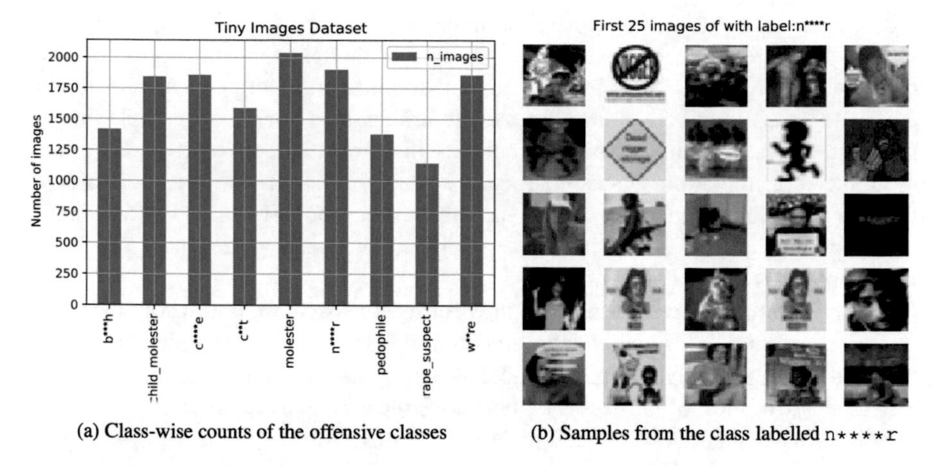

(a) Class-wise counts of the offensive classes (b) Samples from the class labelled n****r

Fig. 6 Results from the 80 million TinyImages dataset (Prabhu & Birhane, 2021). (**a**) Class-wise counts of the offensive classes, (**b**) samples from the class labeled n****r

5 Algorithmic Bias and Fairness

Today, many if not all the predictive algorithms we interact with online rely on vast amounts of data harvested from the Web. It is scraped from social media, news, product reviews, codebases, and beyond. Algorithmic bias in our case refers to bias that is contributed by the algorithm itself and is not present in the input data. Of course, if the input data is biased (which it is), and the model is calibrated well, the output of the algorithm will reflect that bias; but existing biases in training data can be both amplified and reduced by an algorithm [see, e.g., Kleinberg et al. (2017), Chouldechova (2017)]; the latter is harder to achieve. Making better decisions by identifying, estimating, and accounting for biases requires expertise and ongoing investment, and market forces need not always align with public interests in fairness.

Even if we could detect all possible biases, deciding how an algorithm (or indeed any decision process) should proceed to be fair is in general very difficult. People disagree on controversial issues because the optimal decision is subjective and there are trade-offs. Perhaps the law can guide us here? We've already spoken about protected features and domains; these provide information about the types of problems where we should pay special attention. But how do we decide which trade-offs are acceptable and which are not? Anti-discrimination laws can address both direct discrimination or disparate treatment (making decisions based on legally protected features) and indirect discrimination or disparate impact (policies that disproportionately affect protected groups).

Just as the meaning of fairness is subjective, so is the interpretation of law. At one extreme, anti-classification holds the weaker interpretation that the law is intended to prevent classification of people based on protected characteristics. At the other extreme, anti-subordination principles take a stronger stance, that is, anti-discrimination laws exist to prevent social hierarchies, class, or caste systems, and legal systems should actively work to eliminate them where they exist. An important ideological difference between the two schools of thought is in the application of positive discrimination policies. Under anti-subordination principles, one might advocate for affirmative action as a means to bridge gaps in access to employment, housing, education, and other such pursuits that are a direct result of historical systemic discrimination against particular groups. A strict interpretation of the anti-classification principle would prohibit such positive bias. Both anti-classification and anti-subordination ideologies have been argued and upheld in landmark cases in the USA.

Perhaps somewhat reassuringly (if only for its consistency), it turns out there are multiple seemingly reasonable definitions of fairness of classifiers which cannot be satisfied simultaneously except in some degenerate cases (Chouldechova, 2017). By Aristotle's definition of fairness (i.e., like cases must be treated alike), deterministic classification is inherently unfair and to resolve this problem in classification, predictions must be randomized (Dwork et al., 2012, pp. 214–226). Interestingly, scholars have shown that privacy concerns are not unrelated to fairness. Note that in both cases we are concerned about protecting certain features. Much like fairness, defining privacy is not a trivial problem; however, it is considered a solved one (Kearns & Roth, 2019). The widely accepted definition of privacy is named differential privacy. It turns out that the solution to the problem of privacy involves adding just the right amount of noise to obfuscate the protected information (Dwork, 2006). The problem of how to define fairness is yet unsolved, though experts predict it will be in the next decade or so (Kearns & Roth, 2019).

In practice, bias from data, and that added by the model, can be hard to separate from a causal perspective. Commercial model developers often expose their model through an API that returns predictions but do not share their training data which has a significant impact on what representations the model has learned. The reality is that choosing training data is a modeling decision. Understanding your distribution of errors through thorough testing and accounting for biases, accordingly, is just responsible modeling. The latter is not currently a requisite for deployment, though the expectation is that regulation of AI will evolve over time and hopefully catch up with other more regulated industries that use predictive modeling at scale such as finance.

So why do models amplify biases in training data? Often at the root of the problem is over-representation of some groups and underrepresentation of others. If one demographic group dominates the data (which is often the case), in the absence of sufficient information for other groups, the algorithm is unable to converge (d'Alessandro et al., 2017, pp. 120–134; Kamishima et al., 2012). Interestingly, this behavioral phenomenon is exhibited not just by models but people too. The term exnomination is well known among those who study culture. It is used to describe the phenomenon of the *default* social class. Members of exnominated groups are privileged because of being the "norm." They have advantages that are not earned, outside of their financial standing or effort, that the "equivalent" person outside the exnominated group would not.

Exnominated groups are catered for by every store, product, service, and system, with preferential access and pricing. They see themselves represented more often overall and more often in a positive light. They are not subject to profiling or stereotypes and more likely to be treated as individuals rather than as a representative of (or as exceptions to) a group. They are more often humanized, more likely to be given the benefit of the doubt, treated with compassion and kindness, and, thus, recover from mistakes. Exnominated groups are less likely to be suspected of crimes; more likely to be trusted financially; have greater access to opportunities, resources, and power; and are able to climb financial, social, and professional ladders faster. The advantages enjoyed by exnominated groups accumulate over time and compound over generations.

In his book *White* (Dyer, 1997), Richard Dyer examines *whiteness* in visual media over five centuries, from the depiction of the crucifixion to modern-day cinema. In many ways, bias on the Web is a living testament to the endurance of the British Empire, through both preservation and continued amplification of its image, language, and culture. Any algorithm trained on Web data, without intervention, will invariably favor White, English-speaking men, to the disadvantage of most of humanity.

So how might we intervene to mitigate bias from Web technology? Well, there are three points at which one should measure and thus could mitigate bias. The first and perhaps most obvious is improving data quality, for example, carefully curating data with diversity in mind. The second attacks the problem with more careful definition of success or objective in training, for example, introducing penalties for undesirable behavior or model constraints based on carefully considered definitions of fairness. Finally, we must monitor model output. One might try to mitigate risk at the end point when a prediction is produced taking countermeasures for cases where we understand our model to be vulnerable.

5.1 Bias in Language Modeling

In 2016, research showed that word embeddings (vector representations of words) generated from news corpora learn biased she-he analogies, e.g., nurse-surgeon or diva-superstar instead of queen-king (Bolukbasi et al., 2016). Why might algorithms exacerbate gender bias? Quick research shows that about 70% of influential journalists are men even though at college age, the gender proportions are reversed. So, algorithms trained on news articles have learned patterns in text developed with demonstrable and systematic gender bias. Other works show that many other cultural and cognitive biases are at play (Saez-Trumper et al., 2013, pp. 1679–1684).

A year later, researchers showed that Google Translate contained similar gender biases (Caliskan et al., 2017, pp. 183–186). They found that "translations to English from many gender-neutral languages such as Finnish, Estonian, Hungarian, Persian, and Turkish led to gender-stereotyped sentences." So, for example, when they translated Turkish sentences with genderless pronouns: "O bir doktor. O bir hemişre." the resulting English sentences were: "He is a doctor. She is a nurse." They performed these types of tests for 50 occupations and found that the stereotypical gender association of the word almost perfectly predicted the resulting pronoun in the English translation.

Proposals for reducing gender bias include creating more gender balanced data (Costa-jussà et al., 2020, pp. 4081–4088) and mitigating gender bias by transforming embeddings to account for differences in the gender subspace (Bolukbasi et al., 2016). Google opted to intervene at the prediction stage for translations between English and a limited set of just five languages (French, Italian, Portuguese, Spanish, and Turkish), returning both masculine and feminine translations (Kuczmarski, 2018). Google's Natural Language API for sentiment analysis was also found to have problems. In 2017, it was assigning negative sentiment to sentences such as "I'm a Jew" and "I'm a homosexual" and "I'm black"; neutral sentiment to the phrase "white power" and positive sentiment to the sentences "I'm Christian" and "I'm Sikh." In reality, prejudice is, so deeply embedded in language that creating algorithms trained on it that are not is far from trivial.

Bleeding edge developments in language modeling have been focused on conversational capabilities. There is of no doubt that the technology is impressively human sounding, but it also presents some problems for those of us concerned about bias. If machine-written content floods our information ecosystem, what happens to human voices? Chief among model weaknesses is what's described as its ability to hallucinate (a bad metaphor for making a mistake), that is, fabricate expert-sounding, but patently false, prose on complex topics (Hartsfield, 2019). The model is easy to trip up since it cannot reason and does not comprehend. For instance, at the time of writing, ChatGPT was unable to do simple arithmetic, if you ask it to switch the symbols for addition and multiplication first.

There are wider concerns around large language models, specifically their computational inefficiency and corresponding environmental costs (Weidinger et al., 2021). GPT-3, for example, is a model composed of a whopping 175 billion parameters. The costs of building and using this technology are significant when compared to current resources like Google or Wikipedia. Separating fact from fiction is an important milestone if this technology is to be anything more than a rather expensive stochastic parrot (Bender et al., 2021, pp. 610–623) that writes well but needs to be fact checked. Wasting resources does not happen only during training these models but also when billions of people use them as a leisure tool.

5.2 Bias in Computer Vision

In 2015, Google Photos had labeled a photo of a Black couple as gorillas. It's hard to find the right words to describe just how offensive an error this is, but perhaps considering TinyImages, it is not all that surprising. It demonstrated how a machine, carrying out a seemingly benign task of labeling photos, could deliver an attack on a person's dignity.

In 2018, research auditing several popular gender classification packages from IBM, Microsoft, and Face++ showed shocking disparities in performance that depended on both the skin color and gender in sample images (Buolamwini & Gebru, 2018, pp. 1–15).

In 2020, a generative model designed to improve the resolution of images converted a pixelated picture of Barack Obama into a high-resolution image of a Caucasian man (Truong, 2020). If facial recognition technology fails on even the most recognizable faces like Oprah Winfrey, Michelle and Barack Obama, and Serena Williams, what hope do the rest of us have of not being erased by systems that literally can't see us?

5.3 Bias in Recommendations

A major cause for concern is targeted advertising which is now par for the course even in protected domains. In 2013, a study found that Google searches were more likely to return personalized advertisements that were suggestive of arrest records for black names than white, regardless of whether such records existed or not (Sweeney, 2013). This doesn't just result in allocative harms for people applying for jobs; it's denigrating. In 2015, a study showed that women were six times less likely to be shown adverts for high-paying jobs by Google (exceeding $200 K) (Spice, 2015). In 2022, Facebook was fined for using legally protected attributes to target advertisements for housing.

Regarding geographical bias in news recommendations, large cities or centers of political power will naturally generate more news. Hence, if we use standard recommendation algorithms, most people will likely be reading news from the capital and not from the place where they live. Considering diversity and the location of the user, we can give a less centralized view that also shows local news (Graells-Garrido & Lalmas, 2014, pp. 231–236).

An extreme example of algorithmic bias is tag recommendations. Imagine a user interface where you upload a photo, add various tags, and then a tag recommendation algorithm suggests tags that people have used in other photos based on collaborative filtering. You choose the ones that seem correct, and you enlarge your set of tags. This seems like a nice idea, but you won't find this functionality in a website like Flickr. The reason being that the algorithm needs data from people to improve; but as people use recommended tags, they type fewer original ones. They take from the pile without contributing. In essence, the algorithm performs a prolonged hara-kiri. So, to create a healthy folksonomy (tags made only by people), we should not recommend tags. But we can use these recommended tags to search for similar images by using related (human-produced) tags. Though as we have seen, our ability to find similar images is limited by bias in computer vision technology.

Another critical class of algorithmic bias in recommender systems is related to what items are shown or not shown. This bias affects the user interaction, and we cover it in detail in that section.

5.4 Developer Biases

Diversity of developers is a problem of epic proportions especially when it comes to data-driven technologies. It explains all too many of the blunders we've seen in recent years, if we can call them that. In terms of binary gender thinking, approximately 80% of software developers are men: that's four-to-one (Cheryan et al., 2022; Klawe, 2020). If we narrow our pool to developers of data-driven technology, those numbers become worse. According to an AI Index survey, female faculty made up just 16.1% of all tenure track computer science faculty at several universities around the world in 2020 (AI Index Report, 2021). That year, only 15% of AI researchers at Facebook, and 10% of AI researchers at Google were women. Representation in the development of this technology is imperative, in the quest for inclusive technology.

Three antecedents to support this claim. The first is a data analysis experiment where 29 teams developed different solutions to the same problem related to bias (Silberzahn & Uhlmann, 2015). A second study showed that cognitive biases of developers were transferred to their code (Johansen et al., 2021). A third study showed that developer errors are correlated within communities (Cowgill et al., 2020). To put it simply, a more diverse set of voices catches more errors.

6 Biases in User Interaction

One significant source of bias comes from user interaction (not solely limited to the Web). These types of biases have two sources: the user interface and the biased interaction of the user or user bias. The first key bias in the user interface is called exposure or presentation bias: everything that is exposed to the user has a positive probability of being clicked, while everything else has none. This is particularly relevant for recommendation systems. Let us consider a video streaming service. Even if we have hundreds of recommendations that we can browse, that number is abysmally small compared to the millions of possibilities that might be out there. This bias will affect new items or items that have not previously been shown, since there is no usage data for them. The most common solution to this problem is called *explore and exploit* (see Agarwal et al. (2009) for a classic example applied to the Web. This technique exposes the user to new items to *explore*, randomly intermingled with top recommendations. The idea being that information from the (new) items chosen can be exploited to improve recommendations in the future. The paradox of this technique is that exploring may imply a loss, that is the opportunity cost of exploiting information already known. In some cases, there is even a revenue loss, such as in the case of digital ads. However, in the long term, as the system knows the market better, the revenue can be larger (Delnevo & Baeza-Yates, 2022). From the perspective of the user, the best recommendations will always be the things you wouldn't have otherwise known about.

The second relevant bias is position bias. For instance, in Western cultures, we read from top to bottom and from left to right. Our bias is to look first toward the top left corner of the screen prompting that region of the screen to get more clicks. An important instance of this bias is ranking bias. Consider a web search engine where result pages are listed in relevant order from top to bottom. The top ranked result will get more clicks than the others because it is both the (probably) most relevant result but also is in the first position. To be able to use click data for improving and evaluating ranking algorithms, we must debias the click distribution; otherwise, feedback in our algorithms will simply amplify already popular pages.

Other biases in the user interaction include additional effects of user interaction design. For instance, any content you need to scroll to see will suffer from exposure bias. Content near images will have a larger probability of being clicked because images attract our attention. Examples from eye-tracking studies show that since *universal search*[3] was introduced, the non-text content counteracts ranking bias in the results (Mediative, 2014).

Social bias defines how other peoples' content affects our judgment. One example comes from collaborative ratings: assume you want to rate an item with a low score, and you see that most people have a high score. You may increase your score assuming that perhaps you are being harsh. This bias has been already explored for Amazon reviews data (Wang & Wang, 2014, pp. 196–204) and may also be referred to as social conformity or the herding effect (Olteanu et al., 2016).

Finally, the way that each person interacts with any type of device is very personal. Some people are eager to click, while other people move the mouse to where one is looking. Mouse movement is a partial proxy for gaze attention and, in turn, a cheap replacement for eye-tracking. Some people may not notice the scrolling bar, or some people like to read in detail while others just skim. In addition to the bias introduced by interaction designers, we have our own cultural and cognitive biases. A good example of how cultural and cognitive biases affect web search engines is presented by White (2013), where it is shown that users tend to select results aligned with their beliefs, or confirmation bias. To make the problem even more complex, interaction biases cascade in the system and isolating each one is difficult. In Fig. 7, we show an example of how these biases cascade and depend on each other, implying that we are always seeing their composed effects. For instance, ranking bias is an instance of position bias as users tend to click in top results. Similarly, users that scroll affect how they move the mouse as well as which elements of the screen they can click.

The interaction biases just explained are crucial as many web systems are optimized by using implicit user feedback. As those systems are usually machine learning based, they learn to reinforce their own biases or the biases of linked systems, yielding suboptimal solutions and/or self-fulfilling prophecies. Sometimes these systems even compete among themselves, such that an improvement in one system results from a degradation in another system that uses a different (inversely

[3] Universal search results include other media in addition to text, such as images and videos.

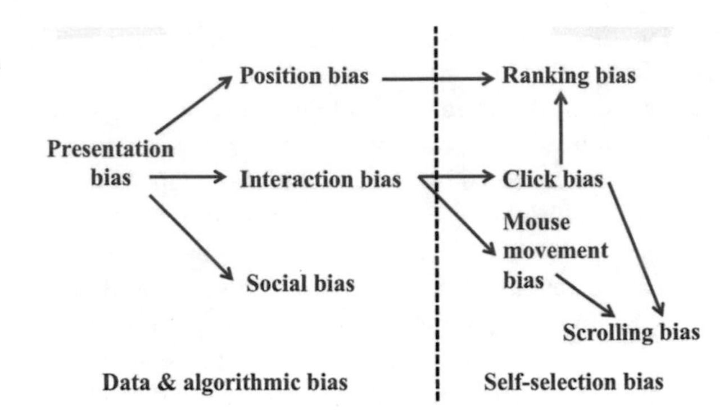

Fig. 7 Dependency graph of some biases that affect the user interaction

correlated) optimization function. A classic example of this is the tension between user experience and monetization teams in Internet companies.

7 The Vicious Cycle of Bias

Bias begets bias. Imagine that you are a blogger planning your next entry. First, you search for pages about the topic you wish to cover. Second, you select a few sources that seem relevant to you. Third, you select some quotes from those sources. Fourth, you write the new content, putting the quotes in the right places, of course citing the sources. Finally, you happily publish the new entry on the Web.

The content creation process outlined does not apply solely to bloggers but also to content in reviews, comments, posts, tweets, toots, and more. The problem occurs when a subset of results is returned, based on what the search engine encodes as relevant to the query. In this way, the ranking algorithm creates a feedback loop, simply because the content that is shortlisted, gets duplicated, and amplified over time. In a study that we did a few years ago, we found that about 35% of the content of the Chilean Web was duplicated and we could trace the genealogy of the partial (semantic) duplication of those pages (Baeza-Yates et al., 2008, pp. 367–376). Today, this effect probably is much larger.

The process above creates a vicious cycle of feedback loop bias because some content providers get more link references which lead to more clicks. Even if you debias them, the rich get richer. Furthermore, the duplication of content makes the problem of distinguishing good pages from bad more complex. Web spammers in turn reuse content from good pages to fake quality content, which only adds to the problem. So paradoxically, search engines are harming themselves unless they do not account for all the biases involved.

Another example of feedback loop bias comes from personalization algorithms, or what Eli Pariser describes as the filter bubble (Pariser, 2011). Personalization of course means that different people making the same query need not see the same results. The argument for personalization is clear: humans need help both filtering

Table 1 Our proposed classification of biases

Bias/type	Statistical	Cultural	Cognitive
Algorithmic	◆	◆	◆
Exposure	◆		
Position	◆		
Developer		◆	◆
Data	◆	◆	◆
Sampling	◆		
Linguistic		◆	
Visual		◆	
Feedback	◆	◆	◆
Engagement		◆	◆
User interaction		◆	◆
Ranking		◆	◆
Social		◆	◆
User		◆	◆

and finding information. But personalization algorithms can also shape our perception of the world. For instance, take an algorithm that relies on our interaction data to show us things we'd "like," filtering out less likable content that is important on some other dimensions not deemed of no advantage to the creators of the technology. At macrolevel, this technology poses the risk of creating social echo chambers that misinform at the behest of foreign or private interests, hindering collective social progress. This issue must be counteracted with collaborative filtering or task contextualization as well as promoting diversity, novelty, serendipity, and even exposure to counterarguments. Such strategies also have a positive impact on privacy online because solutions incorporating them require less personal information.

8 Conclusions

The problem of bias is far more complex than outlined here. We cover just part of the Web, the tip of the bias iceberg so to speak. At its foundation reside our individual and collective biases. On the contrary, many of the biases described here are valid beyond the Web ecosystem, through mobile devices and the Internet of Things.

In Table 1, we attempt to classify the biases described above, as statistical, cultural, or cognitive, by marking the appropriate column. Some instances are a combination of all three. At the top of the table are pure algorithmic biases, though as we've seen, each program inevitably encodes the cultural and cognitive biases of their creators. The lower group includes those biases arising from people while the middle group includes biases where algorithms are involved.

In October 2022, ACM published their second statement on principles for responsible algorithmic systems (ACM Tech Policy Council, 2022). These are legitimacy and competency; minimizing harm; security and privacy; transparency;

interpretability and explainability; maintainability; contestability and auditability; accountability and responsibility; and limiting environmental impacts. The goal of this article is aligned with several principles including minimizing harm (bias) and transparency (bias awareness). In addition, at least two new conferences that address this topic were started in 2018, FAccT and AIES. All these efforts should help our community as we define algorithmic ethics, particularly with respect to machine learning.

Finally, any attempt to be unbiased might be already biased with our own cultural and cognitive biases. The first step is to be aware of all these biases. Only by knowing of their existence can we hope to grapple with and mitigate them. The alternative is a world without fact, where decisions are made based on biased perceptions, in which no amount of diversity, novelty, or serendipity can save us.

Discussion Questions for Students and Their Teachers

1. Discuss possible cognitive biases that may impact the Web and are not mentioned in this chapter. Finding a good taxonomy of cognitive biases is a good way to start.
2. Name all sources of bias that you can think of and discuss how they are related. Mapping the examples of this chapter as well as others to the sources helps.
3. An example of non-trivial reference value is how many web pages in a language should be. What is the right value to measure for bias? Who should decide that?
4. If the bias of the developers is transferred to their code, should developing teams be more diverse? Or are there cases where we may want certain demographics in the team such that the best possible system is built?
5. Assume that you find two different biases that are positively correlated. How can you decide if one of them causes the other or that they are independent?

Learning Resources for Students

1. Persuading programmers to detect and mitigate bias in technology design: The role of motivational appeals and the speaker (Almánzar et al., 2023)

   This paper proposes and studies a conceptual framework for the effectiveness of motivational appeals aimed at programmers, considering the role of framing, the speaker's race and gender, and the individual differences in recipients' social dominance orientation egalitarianism (SDO-E) in driving bias detection outcomes. They suggest that a problem framing, "You are part of the problem," will be more effective than a solution framing, "You are part of the solution," when the speaker is White and male rather than Black and female, but this only applies to respondents with low levels of SDO-E and will be reversed for respondents with high levels of SDO-E, due to the pursuit of egalitarian values that automatically inhibits the activation of stereotypes.
2. Mitigating Dataset Harms Requires Stewardship: Lessons from 1000 Papers (Peng et al., 2021).

   This paper analyzes three influential but problematic datasets on face recognition that are used by almost 1000 papers. They find that derivative datasets and models, broader technological and social change, the lack of clarity of licenses, and dataset management practices can introduce additional ethical issues, proposing a distributed approach to harm mitigation that considers the full life cycle of a dataset.

3. Social Data: Biases, Methodological Pitfalls, and Ethical Boundaries (Olteanu et al., 2019)

   This paper surveys several issues of social data: (1) biases and inaccuracies occurring at the source of the data, but also introduced during processing; (2) methodological limitations and pitfalls; and (3) ethical boundaries and unexpected consequences that are often overlooked. As a result, they present a framework for identifying a broad variety of dangers in the research and practices around social data use.

4. Taxonomy of Risks posed by Language Models (Weidinger et al., 2022)

   This paper categorizes language model risks into six broad subgroups, some of which have been touched on in this chapter. A more complete picture is provided by the referenced publication. One area not discussed here are those around "human-computer interactions." As machines become more competent at emulating ever increasing modes of human communication, what might be the benefits and risks of such technology?

5. Towards a Standard for Identifying and Managing Bias in Artificial Intelligence (Schwartz et al., 2022)

   This document covers the challenging area of AI bias, providing a first step on the roadmap for developing detailed sociotechnical guidance for identifying and managing AI bias. Specifically, they (1) describe the stakes of bias in AI intelligence and provides examples of how and why it can chip away at public trust; (2) identify three categories of bias in AI—systemic, statistical, and human—and describe how and where they contribute to harms; and (3) describe three broad challenges for mitigating bias, namely, datasets, testing and evaluation, and human factors, and recommendations for addressing them.

6. Ethical Development (Murgai, 2023)

   Chapter 2 of the referenced resource discusses how to go about developing machine learning applications ethically. It focuses on practical aspects of developing a data and model governance framework and provides a taxonomy of common causes of harm relating them to the stage of the workflow at which they can be detected and prevented.

References

ACM Tech Policy Council. (2022). *Statement on responsible algorithmic systems. 26 October 2022*. https://www.acm.org/binaries/content/assets/public-policy/final-joint-ai-statement-update.pdf

Agarwal, D., Chen, B.-C., & Elango, P. (2009). Explore/exploit schemes for web content optimization. In *Proceedings of the Ninth IEEE International Conference on Data Mining*. IEEE Computer Society.

Almánzar, A. R., Edinger-Schons, L. M., & Grüning, D. J. (2023). Persuading programmers to detect and mitigate bias in technology design: The role of motivational appeals and the speaker. *PsyArXiv*. https://doi.org/10.31234/osf.io/jbxeq

Artificial Intelligence Index Report. (2021). *Diversity in AI.* https://aiindex.stanford.edu/wp-content/uploads/2021/03/2021-AI-Index-Report-_Chapter-6.pdf.

Baeza-Yates, R. (2015). *Incremental sampling of query logs*. Industry track. In *Proceedings of the 38th ACM SIGIR Conference* (pp. 1093–1096).

Baeza-Yates, R. (2018). Bias on the Web. *Communications of the ACM*, June, *61*(6), 54–61. https://doi.org/10.1145/3209581.

Baeza-Yates, R., & Castillo, C. (2006). *Relationship between web links and trade* (poster). In Proceedings of the 15th international conference on the World Wide Web (pp. 927–928).

Baeza-Yates, R., & Saez-Trumper, D. (2015). Wisdom of the crowd or wisdom of a few? An analysis of users' content generation. In *Proceedings of the 26th ACM conference on hypertext and social media* (pp. 69–74).

Baeza-Yates, R., Castillo, C., & López, V. (2006). Characteristics of the Web of Spain. *El Profesional de la Información, 15*(1), 1–17.

Baeza-Yates, R., Castillo, C., & Efthimiadis, E. N. (2007). Characterization of national web domains. *ACM Transactions on Internet Technology, 7*(2).

Baeza-Yates, R., Pereira, Á., & Ziviani, N. (2008). Genealogical trees on the Web: A search engine user perspective. In *Proceedings of the 17th international conference on the World Wide Web* (pp. 367–376).

Bender, E. M., Gebru, T., McMillan-Major, A., & Shmitchell, S. (2021). On the dangers of stochastic parrots: Can language models be too big?. In *Proceedings of the ACM conference on fairness, accountability, and transparency (FAccT'21)*. Association for Computing Machinery, , 610–623. doi:https://doi.org/10.1145/3442188.3445922.

Bhutada, G. (2021). *Visualizing the most used languages on the Internet*. March 26. https://www.visualcapitalist.com/the-most-used-languages-on-the-internet/

Bolukbasi, T., Chang, K. W., Zou, J., Saligrama, V., & Kalai, A. (2016). Man is to computer programmer as woman is to homemaker? Debiasing word embeddings. In *Proceedings of the 30th conference on neural information processing systems.*

Boroditsky, L. (2017). *How language shapes the way we think*. TEDWomen. https://www.ted.com/talks/lera_boroditsky_how_language_shapes_the_way_we_think

Boroditsky, L., & Gaby, A. (2010). Remembrances of times east: Absolute spatial representations of time in an Australian aboriginal community. *Psychological Science, 21*(11), 1635–1639. https://doi.org/10.1177/0956797610386621

Boroditsky, L., Schmidt, L. A., & Phillips, W. (2003). Sex, syntax, and semantics. *Language in Mind: Advances in the Study of Language and Thought, 22*, 61–79.

Buolamwini, J., & Gebru, T. (2018). Gender shades: Intersectional accuracy disparities in commercial gender classification. vol. 81. In *Proceedings of Machine Learning Research* (pp. 1–15).

Cadwalladr, C. (2019). *Facebook's role in Brexit -- and the threat to democracy*. TED. https://www.ted.com/talks/carole_cadwalladr_facebook_s_role_in_brexit_and_the_threat_to_democracy.

Caliskan, A., Bryson, J. J., & Narayanan, A. (2017). Semantics derived automatically from language corpora contain human-like biases. *Science, 356*(6334), 183–186.

Carylsue. (2016). *New Guinea natives navigate by valleys and mountains*. National Geographic Education Blog, Geography. April 14. https://blog.education.nationalgeographic.org/2016/04/14/new-guinea-natives-navigate-their-homes-by-valleys-and-mountains/.

Cheryan, S., Master, A., & Meltzoff, A. (2022). There are too few women in computer science and engineering. *Scientific American*, July 27. https://www.scientificamerican.com/article/there-are-too-few-women-in-computer-science-and-engineering/.

Chouldechova, A. (2017). *Fair prediction with disparate impact: A study of bias in recidivism prediction instruments.* doi:https://doi.org/10.1089/big.2016.0047.

Cima, R. (2015). How photography was optimized for white skin color. *Priceonomics*. https://priceonomics.com/how-photography-was-optimized-for-white-skin/.
Corn Jr, R. (M). (2019). Native American culture - Language: the key to everything. *TEDxOshkosh*. January 24. https://www.ted.com/talks/ron_muqsahkwat_corn_jr_native_american_culture_language_the_key_to_everything
Costa-jussà, M. R., Lin, P. L., & España-Bonet, C. (2020). GeBioToolkit: automatic extraction of gender-balanced multilingual corpus of Wikipedia biographies. In *Proceedings of the twelfth language resources and evaluation conference* (pp. 4081–4088). European Language Resources Association, Marseille.
Cowgill, B., Dell'Acqua, F., Deng, S., Hsu, D., Verma, N., & Chaintreau, A. (2020). Biased programmers? Or biased data? *A field experiment in operationalizing AI ethics*. https://doi.org/10.48550/arXiv.2012.02394.
Crawford, K. (2017). *The trouble with bias*. NIPS Keynote.
d'Alessandro, B., O'Neil, C., & LaGatta, T. (2017). Conscientious classification: A data scientist's guide to discrimination-aware classification. *Big Data, 5*(2), 120–134.
Del Barco, M. (2014). *How Kodak's Shirley cards set photography's skin-tone standard*. NPR KQED, November 13. https://www.npr.org/2014/11/13/363517842/for-decades-kodak-s-shirley-cards-set-photography-s-skin-tone-standard
Delnevo, G., & Baeza-Yates, R. (2022). *Exploration trade-offs in web recommender systems*. IEEE Big Data.
Deng, J., Dong, W., Socher, R., Li, L.-J., Li, K., & Li, F.-F. (2009). ImageNet: A large-scale hierarchical image database. In *IEEE conference on computer vision and pattern recognition* (pp. 248–255). https://doi.org/10.1109/CVPR.2009.5206848
Dwork, C. (2006). Differential privacy. In M. Bugliesi, B. Preneel, V. Sassone, & I. Wegener (Eds.), *Automata, languages and programming. ICALP 2006* (Lecture notes in computer science) (Vol. 4052). Springer. https://doi.org/10.1007/11787006_1
Dwork, C., Hardt, M., Pitassi, T., Reingold, O., & Zemel, R. (2012). Fairness through awareness. In *Proceedings of the 3rd innovations in theoretical computer science conference (ITCS '12)* (pp. 214–226). Association for Computing Machinery. https://doi.org/10.1145/2090236.2090255
Dyer, R. (1997). *White*. Routledge.
Fausey, C. M., & Boroditsky, L. (2008). English and Spanish speakers remember causal agents differently. *Proceedings of the Annual Meeting of the Cognitive Science Society, 30*(30).
Fetterly, D., Manasse, M., & Najork, M. (2003) On the evolution of clusters of near-duplicate web pages. *Proceedings of the IEEE/LEOS 3rd international conference on numerical simulation of semiconductor optoelectronic devices (IEEE Cat. No. 03EX726)*, Santiago, pp. 37–45, doi: https://doi.org/10.1109/LAWEB.2003.1250280.
Gong, W., Lim, E-P, & Zhu, F. (2015). Characterizing silent users in social media communities. In *Proceedings of ninth international AAAI conference on Web and Social Media.*
Graells-Garrido, E. & Lalmas, M. (2014). Balancing diversity to counter-measure geographical centralization in microblogging platforms. In *Proceedings of the 25th ACM conference on hypertext and social media* (pp. 231–236).
Graells-Garrido, E., Lalmas, M., & Menczer, F. (2015). First women, second sex: Gender bias in Wikipedia. In *Proceedings of the 26th ACM conference on hypertext and social media* (pp. 165–174).
Hale, L., & Peralta, E. (2021). *Social media misinformation stokes a worsening civil war in Ethiopia*. NPR, October 15. https://www.npr.org/2021/10/15/1046106922/social-media-misinformation-stokes-a-worsening-civil-war-in-ethiopia
Hartsfield, T. (2019). *ChatGPT answers physics questions like a confused C student*. February. https://bigthink.com/the-present/chatgpt-physics/.
Johansen, J., Pedersen, T., & Johansen, C. (2021). Studying human-to-computer bias transference. *AI & Society*. https://doi.org/10.1007/s00146-021-01328-4
Kahneman, D. (2011). *Thinking, fast and slow*.

Kamishima, T., Akaho, S., Asoh, H., & Sakuma, J. (2012). Fairness-aware classifier with prejudice remover regularizer. In *Machine learning and knowledge discovery in databases. ECML PKDD* (Lecture Notes in Computer Science) (Vol. 7524). Springer. https://doi.org/10.1007/978-3-642-33486-3_3

Kay, M., Matuszek, C., & Munson, S. A. (2015). *Unequal representation and gender stereotypes in image search results for occupations*. ACM.

Kearns, M., & Roth, A. (2019). *The ethical algorithm*. Talks at Google. https://youtu.be/tmC9JdKc3sA.

Klawe, M. (2020). *Why diversity in AI is so important*. July 16. https://www.forbes.com/sites/mariaklawe/2020/07/16/why-diversity-in-ai-is-so-important/

Kleinberg, J., Lakkaraju, H., Leskovec, J., Ludwig, J., & Mullainathan, S. (2017). *Human decisions and machine predictions*. https://www.nber.org/papers/w23180.

Kuczmarski, J. (2018). *Reducing gender bias in Google Translate*. Google blog, December 6. https://blog.google/products/translate/reducing-gender-bias-google-translate/.

Lazer, D. M. J., et al. (2018). The Science of Fake News. *Science, 359*(6380), 1094–1096.

Lazovich, T., Belli, L., Gonzales, A., Bower, A., Tantipongpipat, U., Lum, K., Huszar, F., & Chowdhury, R. (2022). Measuring disparate outcomes of content recommendation algorithms with distributional inequality metrics. *Patterns, 3*(8).

Mediative. (2014). *The evolution of Google's search results pages and effects on user behavior* (white paper). http://www.mediative.com/SER.

Murgai, L. (2023). *Mitigating bias in machine learning*. https://mitigatingbias.ml.

Naranjo, J. (2023). *Ethiopia's forgotten war is the deadliest of the 21st century, with around 600,000 civilian deaths*. El País. Jan 27, 2023. https://english.elpais.com/international/2023-01-27/ethiopias-forgotten-war-is-the-deadliest-of-the-21st-century-with-around-600000-civilian-deaths.html.

Nielsen, J. (2006). *The 90-9-1 rule for participation inequality in social media and online communities*. October 8. https://www.nngroup.com/articles/participation-inequality/.

O'Reiley, L. (2017). *Facebook's claimed reach in the U.S. is larger than census figures, analyst finds*. WSJ Sept. 6. https://www.wsj.com/articles/facebooks-claimed-reach-in-the-u-s-is-larger-than-census-figures-analyst-finds-1504711935

O'Toole, E. (2016). A dictionary entry citing 'rabid feminist' doesn't just reflect prejudice, it reinforces it. *The Guardian*, January 26. https://www.theguardian.com/commentisfree/2016/jan/26/rabid-feminist-language-oxford-english-dictionary

Olteanu, A., Castillo, C., Diaz, C., & Kiciman, E. (2016). *Social data: Biases, methodological pitfalls, and ethical boundaries*. Available at SSRN: https://ssrn.com/abstract=2886526.

Olteanu, A., Carlos Castillo, C., Fernando Diaz, F., & Kıcıman, E. (2019). Social data: Biases, methodological pitfalls, and ethical boundaries. *Frontiers in Big Data, 2*. https://doi.org/10.3389/fdata.2019.00013

Pariser, E. (2011). *The filter bubble: What the Internet is hiding from you*. Penguin.

Peng, K., Mathur A., & Narayanan, A. (2021). Mitigating dataset harms requires stewardship: Lessons from 1000 papers. In *Proceedings of the neural information processing systems track on datasets and benchmarks*.

Perez, C. C. (2019). *Invisible women: Data bias in a world designed for men*. Vintage Books.

Pitel, L. (2019). *Can a genderless language change the way we think*. FT, August 5. https://www.ft.com/content/7b59352c-b75e-11e9-8a88-aa6628ac896c.

Prabhu, V. U., & Birhane, A. (2021). *Large image datasets: A pyrrhic win for computer vision?* Available: https://arxiv.org/abs/2006.16923

Rose, A. (2010). Are face-detection cameras racist? *Time*. January 22. https://content.time.com/time/business/article/0,8599,1954643,00.html.

Saez-Trumper, D., Castillo, C., & Lalmas, M. (2013). Social media news communities: Gatekeeping, coverage, and statement bias. In *ACM CIKM* (pp. 1679–1684).

Schwartz, R., Vassilev, A., Greene, K., Perine, L., Burt, A., & Hall, P. (2022). *Towards a standard for identifying and managing bias in artificial intelligence*. National Institute of Standards and

Technology Special Publication 1270, USA. Freely available at doi:https://doi.org/10.6028/NIST.SP.1270.
Shariatmadari, D. (2016). Eight words that reveal the sexism at the heart of the English language. *The Guardian*, January 27. https://www.theguardian.com/commentisfree/2016/jan/27/eight-words-sexism-heart-english-language.
Silberzahn, R., & Uhlmann, E. L. (2015). Crowdsourced research: Many hands make tight work. *Nature, 526*, 189–191, October 2015. Full report is available at https://psyarxiv.com/qkwst/, 2017.
Smith, M., Patil, D. J., & Muñoz, C. (2016). *Big data: A report on algorithmic systems, opportunity, and civil rights*. Executive Office of the President.
Spice, B. (2015). *Fewer women than men are shown online ads related to high-paying jobs*. CMU CSD. July. https://csd.cmu.edu/news/fewer-women-men-are-shown-online-ads-related-high-paying-jobs.
Statista. (2021). *Languages on the Internet*. https://www.statista.com/chart/26884/languages-on-the-internet/.
Sweeney, L. (2013). Discrimination in online ad delivery. SSRN. https://ssrn.com/abstract=2208240.
Trask, L. (2007). *Trask's historical linguistics*. Routledge.
Truong, K. (2020). *This image of a White Barack Obama is AI's racial bias problem in a Nutshell*. June. https://www.vice.com/en/article/7kpxyy/this-image-of-a-white-barack-obama-is-ais-racial-bias-problem-in-a-nutshell.
Wagner, C., Garcia, D., Jadidi, M., & Strohmaier, M. (2015). It's a man's Wikipedia? Assessing gender inequality in an online encyclopedia. In *AAAI ICWSM Conference*, pp. 454–463.
Wang, T., & Wang, D. (2014). Why Amazon's ratings might mislead you: The story of herding effects. *Big Data, 2*(4), 196–204.
Wattles, J. (2015). *Amazon sues more than 1,000 sellers of 'fake' product reviews*. October 19. https://money.cnn.com/2015/10/18/technology/amazon-lawsuit-fake-reviews/index.html.
Weidinger, L., Mellor, J., Rauh, M., Griffin, C., Uesato, J., Huang, P.-S., Cheng, M., Glaese, M., Balle, B., Kasirzadeh, A., Kenton, Z., Brown, S., Hawkins, W., Stepleton, T., Biles, C., Birhane, A., Haas, J., Rimell, L., Hendricks, L. & Gabriel, I. (2021). *Ethical and social risks of harm from Language Models*.
Weidinger, L., Uesato, J., Rauh, M., Griffin, C., Huang, P.-S., Mellor, J., Glaese, A., Cheng, M., Balle, B., Kasirzadeh, A., Biles, C., Brown, S., Kenton, Z., Hawkins, W., Stepleton, T., Birhane, A., Hendricks, L.A., Rimell, L., Isaac, W., Haas, J., Legassick, S., Irving, G., & Gabriel, I. (2022). Taxonomy of risks posed by language models. In *Proceedings of the 2022 ACM conference on fairness, accountability, and transparency (FAccT '22)* (pp. 214–229). Association for Computing Machinery. doi:https://doi.org/10.1145/3531146.3533088.
Weinberg, J. (2016). *Cognitive bias codex*. https://dailynous.com/2016/09/14/cognitive-bias-codex/.
White, R. (2013). Beliefs and biases in web search. In *Proceedings of the 36th ACM SIGIR conference*, pp. 3–12.
Winawer, J., Witthoft, N., Frank, M. C., & Boroditsky, L. (2007). Russian blues reveal effects of language on color discrimination. *Proc Natl Acad Sci U S A, 104*(19), 7780–7785. https://doi.org/10.1073/pnas.0701644104
Wu, S., Hofman, J. M., Mason, W. A., & Watts, D. J. (2011). Who says what to whom on Twitter. In *Proceedings of the 20th international conference on the World Wide Web* (pp. 705–714). ACM Press.
Young, V. A. (2020). Nearly half of the Twitter accounts discussing 'Reopening America' may be bots. *CMU News*, May 27. https://www.cmu.edu/news/stories/archives/2020/may/twitter-bot-campaign.html.
Zipf, G. K. (1949). *Human behavior and the principle of least effort*. Addison-Wesley Press.

BY

Copyright Enforcement on Social Media Platforms: Implications for Freedom of Expression in the Digital Public Sphere

Sunimal Mendis

Abstract Online social media platforms (e.g., Facebook, Twitter, YouTube, TikTok) constitute a core component of the contemporary digital public sphere. As such, their regulation should be designed in a manner that enables these platforms to flourish as digital spaces for robust democratic discourse. Ensuring effective protection of users' fundamental right to freedom of expression is critical toward achieving this aim.

This chapter explores how the current EU legal framework on copyright enforcement—the seminal provision of which is Article 17 of the *Copyright in the Digital Single Market Directive* (DSM) [2019]—can undermine the freedom of expression on social media platforms by limiting users' ability to reuse and reinterpret copyright-protected content in ways that promote democratic discourse. Thus, the chapter focuses on legal aspects of social media platform regulation.

The chapter concludes by outlining several proposals presented by copyright law scholars for ensuring a fair balance between user and copyright holder interests in a way that promotes robust democratic discourse in the digital public sphere.

1 Introduction

The power wielded by social media platforms (e.g., Facebook, Twitter, YouTube, TikTok) to direct, influence, and control public discourse has become a topic of vigorous debate in the past decade. Platform owners have been criticized for designing and implementing content moderation systems in ways that arbitrarily undermine users' freedom of expression. Although typically subject to the private ownership of corporate entities, these platforms—as exemplified in Sect. 2—are essential infrastructures for public discourse and a core component of the contemporary digital sphere. Thus, it is essential that the regulation of social media platforms reflects this implicit "private-public partnership" and is designed and implemented in a manner that enables them to flourish as digital spaces for robust

S. Mendis (✉)
Tilburg Institute for Law, Technology, and Society (TILT), Tilburg, Netherlands

H. Werthner et al. (eds.), *Introduction to Digital Humanism*,
https://doi.org/10.1007/978-3-031-45304-5_29

democratic discourse based on humanistic values of self-determination and inclusion. Ensuring effective protection of users' fundamental right to freedom of expression is critical toward achieving this aim. Accordingly, in recent years, States have come under increased pressure to introduce more effective legal, regulatory, and policy frameworks to ensure that users' freedom of expression is adequately safeguarded on social media platforms.

The enactment of Article 17 of the EU *Copyright in the Digital Single Market Directive* (DSM)[1] in 2019 reignited this debate within the EU. Article 17 DSM introduced a more stringent and expansive approach to copyright enforcement on social media platforms resulting in the EU being accused of "killing our democratic spaces using copyright as a Trojan Horse" (Avila et al., 2018). This chapter explores how Article 17 DSM actuates the power of social media platforms to arbitrarily limit users' freedom of expression and outlines several proposals put forward by copyright law scholars to render the EU legal framework on online copyright enforcement more conducive for fostering democratic discourse on these digital spaces.

2 Why Should Social Media Platforms Be Governed in a Manner That Promotes Democratic Discourse?

Online social media platforms constitute digital spaces that provide tools and infrastructure for members of the public to dialogically interact across geographic boundaries. Given the high numbers of users they attract, the substantial amount of discourse taking place on these platforms, and the capacity of this discourse to influence public opinion, it is possible to define them as a core component of the contemporary digital public sphere and accordingly as essential infrastructures for public discourse in today's world.

The term "digital public sphere" is of relatively recent origin and builds upon Habermas's notion of the public sphere (Habermas, 1989). It has been described as:

> [...] a communicative sphere provided or supported by online or social media—from websites to social network sites, weblogs and micro-blogs—where participation is open and freely available to everybody who is interested, where matters of common concern can be discussed, and where proceedings are visible to all. (Schäfer, 2015, p.322)

As per Habermas' vision, the public sphere has a key function in fostering "democratic discourse." A precise definition of the term "democratic discourse" is difficult to come by. However, Dahlberg's concept of rational-critical citizen discourse provides a notion of public discourse that is autonomous from both state and corporate power and enables the development of public opinion that can rationally guide democratic decision-making (Dahlberg, 2001). This presupposes the ability of

[1] Directive 2019/790/EU of the European Parliament and of the Council of 17 April 2019 on copyright and related rights in the Digital Single Market and amending Directives 96/9/EC and 2001/29/EC [2019] OJ L 130/92 (hereinafter "DSM").

members of the public to engage in autonomous self-expression leading to a proliferation of diverse viewpoints that can be the subject of open, inclusive, and deliberative discussion (Dahlgren, 2005).

The value attributed to fostering democratic discourse within the European Union (EU) is underscored by the fundamental right to freedom of expression guaranteed under Article 10 of the European Convention on Human Rights[2] (ECHR 1953) and Article 11 of the EU Charter of Fundamental Rights[3] (EUCFR 2000), which safeguards the "[. . .] freedom to hold opinions and to receive and impart information and ideas without interference by public authority and regardless of frontiers."

In comparison with traditional media, social media platforms offer greater scope for ordinary members of the public to exercise their freedom of expression by directly engaging in the creation of social, political, and cultural content. [4] A primary example of this is user-generated content (UGC), which refers to content shared by users on these platforms involving the reuse and reinterpretation of existing informational and cultural content (e.g., texts, images, music) in creative ways for purposes of social commentary and critique (e.g., parodies, memes, GIFs, commentaries). These typically comprise transformative uses of existing content for noncommercial purposes. UGC is a particularly powerful mode of dialogic interaction that enables the dissection of contemporary narratives to create new meaning by challenging established ideological assumptions and stereotypes (Peverini, 2015) and constitutes an important form of individual self-expression (Conti, 2015, 346). As observed by the CJEU in the *Poland v Council*[5] case, "User-generated expressive activity on the Internet provides an unprecedented platform for the exercise of freedom of expression."[6]

As UGC aims at critiquing and commenting on contemporary political, social, and cultural issues, the content they reuse and reinterpret also tends to be contemporary content, which are often under copyright protection. For example, memes and GIFs often use images and video clips from recent TV shows and movies. Creators of UGC typically reuse such copyright-protected content without the authorization of the copyright owner. This is inter alia for the reason that obtaining authorization from the relevant copyright owner can be an expensive and time-consuming process. However, it is important to note that the unauthorized use of copyright-protected content in UGC does not necessarily result in copyright infringement. This is because copyright law recognizes the importance of facilitating the reuse and reinterpretation of informational and cultural content for purposes of commentary,

[2] Charter of Fundamental Rights of the European Union [2012] OJ C 326/391.

[3] European Convention for the Protection of Human Rights and Fundamental Freedoms, as amended by Protocols Nos. 11 and 14 (1950).

[4] *See* Chapter by Prem and Krenn in this volume.

[5] Judgment of 26 April 2022, *Republic of Poland v European Parliament, Council of the European Union*, Case C-401/19, EU:C:2022:297 (hereinafter *Poland v Council*).

[6] Ibid para 46, citing *Cengiz and others v. Turkey* App Nos 48,226/10 and 14,027/11 (ECtHR, 1 December 2015) para 52.

critique, and creative experimentation. Accordingly, it provides for exceptions and limitations (E&L) to copyright law that permit any person to make use of copyright-protected content for these purposes, without the need to obtain authorization from the copyright owner. Such E&L to copyright have the character of *user freedoms* that enable members of the public to dialogically interact with copyright-protected content without fear of legal sanction. For instance, in the USA, the "fair use exception" provides a broad and open standard that can be flexibly interpreted for the purpose of protecting user freedoms to make transformative uses of copyright-protected content. The use of copyright-protected content in memes and GIFs has a high likelihood of coming within the "fair use exception" as transformative uses of copyright-protected content that are necessary for facilitating commentary, critique, and creative experimentation.

The EU copyright law framework does not include an equivalent broad and open exception. However, Article 5 of the EU Copyright Directive [2001][7] provides specific E&L, which enable the quotation of copyright-protected content for purposes of such as criticism or review (Article 5(3)(d)) and the use of copyright-protected content for the purpose of caricature, parody, and pastiche (Article 5(3)(k)). As stipulated by the CJEU in the determination delivered in *Poland v Council* case, these E&L qualify as user rights, which "(. . .) confer rights on the users of works and (. . .) seek to ensure a fair balance between the fundamental rights of those users and of rightholders."[8] In a series of decisions,[9] the CJEU recognized the significance of these E&L for the protection of users' freedom of expression. That view is reinforced by AG Saugmandsgaard Øe's Opinion[10] in the *Poland v Council* case where he enunciates that the exceptions for quotation, criticism, review, parody, pastiche, and caricature ensure the safeguarding of users' freedom of expression.[11] The AG also recognizes that a significant proportion of content uploaded by users on social media platforms will consist of uses that come within the scope of these E&L.[12]

Thus, ensuring the effective protection of users' ability to benefit from these copyright E&L is critical for the purpose of protecting users' freedom of expression and consequently democratic discourse in the digital public sphere.

---

[7]Directive 2001/29/EC of the European Parliament and of the Council of May 22, 2001, on the harmonization of certain aspects of copyright and related rights in the information society [2001] OJ L167/10 (hereafter "EU Copyright Directive").

[8]Ibid (note 5) para 87.

[9]Judgment of September 3, 2014, *Johan Deckmyn and Vrijheidsfonds VZW v Helena Vandersteen and Others*, C-201/13, EU:C:2014:2132 (*Deckmyn*); Judgment of July 29, 2019, *Funke Medien NRW Gmb H v Bundesrepublik Deutschland,* C-469/17, EU:C: 2019:623 (*Funke Medien*); Judgment of July 29, 2019, *Pelham GmbH and Others v Ralf Hütter and Florian Schneider-Esleben,* C-476/17, EU:C:2019:624 (*Pelham*); Judgment of July 29, 2019, *Spiegel Online GmbH v Volker Beck*, C-516/17, EU:C: 2019:625 (*Spiegel Online*).

[10]Ibid (note 5), Case C-401/19 *Opinion of AG Saugmandsgaard Øe* EU:C:2021:613 [2021].

[11]Ibid para 144.

[12]Ibid para 145.

3 How Can Content Moderation on Social Media Platforms Undermine Freedom of Expression?

Although they fulfill a vital public function by providing essential infrastructures for public discourse, social media platforms are privately owned spaces and are therefore subject to private property rights. Based on these private property rights, owners of social media platforms have the right to determine the terms and conditions subject to which members of the public are allowed access and use of these digital spaces. Such terms and conditions are typically set out in the form of contractual terms of service (ToS), which users are required to accept prior to accessing and using the platforms. ToS inter alia include terms preventing the sharing of illegal content—including copyright infringing content.[13] These terms and conditions are enforced through the process of content moderation. Content moderation[14] refers to the governance mechanism through which platform owners ensure that user-uploaded content comply with applicable legal rules and the platforms' own ToS. It involves monitoring content shared on the platform (i.e., gathering information about content shared on the platform to identify the existence of content that is illegal or incompatible with the platforms' ToS) and filtering offending content to prevent it from being shared on the platform (i.e., by removing, disabling access to illegal content, and/or terminating or suspending the accounts of users who share the illegal content). In the context of copyright law, for instance, this would refer to platform owners' ability to monitor user-uploaded content for the purpose of identifying copyright infringing content and, if such content is identified, removing or disabling access to the infringing content (i.e., blocking) and/or terminating or suspending the account of the miscreant user.

Content moderation grants platforms the power to influence and control public discourse in two ways (Laidlaw, 2010). Firstly, it has an "enabling function" whereby the platform obtains power to influence and shape user perceptions and behavior through a process of norm-setting (e.g., shaping user perceptions on what constitutes lawful or unlawful speech based on the way in which the platform interprets applicable law). Secondly, it has a "restricting function" whereby platforms gain power to restrict users' ability to participate in public discourse through

[13] For example, YouTube's Terms of Service <Terms of Service (youtube.com)> accessed 25 March 2023.

[14] Regulation 2022/2065 of the European Parliament and of the Council of October 19, 2022, on a Single Market For Digital Services and amending Directive 2000/31/EC [2022] OJ L 277 (hereinafter "DSA") defines content moderation in Article 3(t) as:

> [...] activities, whether automated or not, undertaken by providers of intermediary services, that are aimed, in particular, at detecting, identifying and addressing illegal content or information incompatible with their terms and conditions, provided by recipients of the service, including measures taken that affect the availability, visibility, and accessibility of that illegal content or that information, such as demotion, demonetisation, disabling of access to, or removal thereof, or that affect the ability of the recipients of the service to provide that information, such as the termination or suspension of a recipient's account.

the blocking/removal of speech or by terminating/suspending user accounts. Thus, content moderation grants owners of social media platforms, who are private actors, substantial power in regulating the public discourse taking place on their platforms.

Content moderation becomes problematic when platforms exercise this power in a manner that leads to the arbitrary limitation of users' freedom of expression. In a copyright law context, this would be the case when the content moderation system is designed and implemented in a manner that interprets the scope of a copyright exception (e.g., the parody exception) more restrictively than what is actually provided by law. This would, firstly, create an incorrect perception in the minds of users as to the extent to which the copyright exception permits the reuse of copyright-protected content resulting in users exercising *self-censorship* and avoiding legally permitted uses of copyright-protected content, for fear of their UGC being removed by the platform. Secondly, it results in the *suppression of lawful speech* through wrongful blocking/removal of lawful UGC that de jure falls within the scope of that copyright exception. [15]

Such instances of wrongful suppression of lawful speech are unfortunately not infrequent. A good example is the controversy that arose in relation to a UGC video uploaded onto *YouTube* entitled "Buffy v Edwards: Twilight Remixed."[16] This approximately 6-minute video comprised a collage of audiovisual clips from the movie series *The Twilight Saga* (2008–2012) and the movie "Buffy the Vampire Slayer" (1992). In the words of its creator, Jonathan Mcintosh, the video was:

> [. . .] an example of transformative storytelling serving as a pro-feminist visual critique of Edward's character and generally creepy behavior [. . .] some of the more sexist gender roles and patriarchal Hollywood themes embedded in the Twilight saga are exposed—in hilarious ways [. . .]. It also doubles as a metaphor for the ongoing battle between two opposing visions of gender roles in the 21st century. (Mcintosh, 2013)

According to the creator, since it was uploaded in 2009, the public's response to the video was "swift, enthusiastic and overwhelming," and in the first 11 days since its upload, it was viewed over 3 million times, and the subtitles were translated by volunteers into 30 different languages. According to the creator, the video was also used in "media studies courses, and gender studies curricula across the country" and "ignited countless online debates over the troubling ways stalking-type behavior is often framed as deeply romantic in movie and television narratives."

In 2012, YouTube removed the video, pursuant to a complaint by Lionsgate Entertainment—the copyright owner of *The Twilight Saga* movie series—that the video infringed upon their copyright by making unauthorized use of copyright-protected audiovisual content taken from their movies. The creator's YouTube account was suspended and a copyright "strike" placed on it. The creator's defense that the video came within the "fair use" exception was rejected. Finally, in the face of significant public protests against the removal of the video on the Internet,

---

[15] *See* Chapter by Prem and Krenn in this volume.

[16] Video available on YouTube,< Buffy vs Edward: Twilight Remixed -- [original version] - YouTube > accessed March 25, 2023.

Lionsgate conceded that the use of the audiovisual content did in fact come within the scope of the fair use exception, and YouTube re-posted the video.

As private actors, social media platforms do not have positive obligations to protect fundamental rights. Therefore, it is essential that legal and regulatory frameworks step in to ensure that content moderation systems are designed and implemented in a manner that can adequately safeguard user freedoms to benefit from copyright E&L. However, as will be discussed in the following section, the current EU legal framework on online copyright enforcement actuates the arbitrary limitation of users' freedom of expression, thereby increasing the risk of wrongful suppression of lawful uses of copyright-protected content that come within the scope of legally granted E&L.

4 How Can the EU Legal Framework on Online Copyright Enforcement Undermine Democratic Discourse on Online Platforms?

The seminal provision of the EU legal framework on online copyright enforcement is Article 17 of the *Copyright in the Digital Single Market Directive* (DSM) [2019]. Article 17 DSM constitutes a *lex specialis* to the general intermediary liability framework provided under the Digital Services Act [2022] and determines the intermediary liability of online content-sharing service providers (OCSSPs) for copyright infringement arising from UGC.

An OCSSP is defined in Article 2(6) of the DSM as being:

> [...] a provider of an information society service of which the main or one of the main purposes is to store and give the public access to a large amount of copyright-protected works or other protected subject matter uploaded by its users, which it organises and promotes for profit-making purposes.

Accordingly, owners of social media platforms fall within the scope of Article 17 DSM.

The doctrine of intermediary liability imputes liability to providers of online hosting services (such as search engines, streaming services, and social media platforms) for illegal acts committed via those services. Such wrongful acts could involve criminal offences (e.g., child sexual abuse, dissemination of terrorist content) and civil wrongs such as defamation and copyright infringement.

There are two main forms of intermediary liability. The hosting services provider incurs primary (direct) liability for illegal acts that it deliberately commits. For example, if *Netflix* streamed copyright-infringing content on its service, it would incur primary liability for the copyright infringement since it is *Netflix* that determines which content is made available to the public on its service. On the other hand, when the illegal act is committed by a user of the service, the hosting service provider would typically be only charged with secondary (indirect) liability on the basis that it facilitated or contributed to the commission of that act through the provision of its service.

Prior to the enactment of Article 17 DSM, social media platform owners were typically imputed secondary (indirect) liability for copyright infringements arising from content shared by users on their platforms. Unlike content distributors (such as *Netflix*) who directly engage in the sharing of content (and are therefore able to determine and control the types of content that are streamed on their services), social media platforms were regarded as "mere conduits" who simply provided digital spaces and the technological infrastructure to *facilitate* the sharing of content by others. Thus, social media platform owners would be imputed secondary (indirect) liability, while the user who shared the infringing content incurred primary liability. Even then, the platform owner would be able to avoid being held secondarily liable for copyright infringement by fulfilling the criteria necessary for coming within the intermediary liability "safe harbor" provided in Article 6 of the EU Digital Services Act [2022].[17] This reflected the traditional "negligence-based" approach to intermediary liability whereby secondary liability was only imputed if the social media platform owner had *knowledge* of the infringing content shared by a user and after obtaining such knowledge failed to stop that infringement from continuing by removing/blocking the infringing content. Thus, the avoidance of liability merely required the platform to respond to copyright infringements after they arose (ex post copyright enforcement).

Article 17 DSM marks a radical shift in the general intermediary liability framework of the EU. Firstly, under Article 17(1), OCSSPs are assigned primary liability for copyright infringement arising from content shared by users. This is on the basis that, although it is the user who uploads the content, it is the OCSSP who carries out the unauthorized communication to the public[18] via the platform by granting the public access to the infringing content. Under Article 17(3), OCSSPs are also prevented from relying on the Article 6 DSA "safe harbor," thereby exposing them to a higher risk of incurring this enhanced degree of liability for copyright infringements arising through UGC.

In order to avoid primary liability for copyright infringement, OCSSPs are required to make best efforts to obtain licenses from copyright holders for content

[17] Article 6 of the DSA exempts a hosting services provider from liability for wrongful acts committed by users via their services, if the hosting services provider can demonstrate that it (a) does not have actual knowledge of illegal activity or illegal content and, as regards claims for damages, is not aware of facts or circumstances from which the illegal activity or illegal content is apparent or (b), upon obtaining such knowledge or awareness, acts expeditiously to remove or to disable access to the illegal content. Ibid (note 14). Article 6 of the DSA is identical to Article 14 of the EU eCommerce Directive [2000], which it repeals and replaces. *See* Directive 2000/31/EC of the European Parliament and the Council of June 8, 2000 on certain legal aspects of information society services, in particular electronic commerce, in the Internal Market [2000] OJ L 178/1.

[18] Article 3 of the EU Copyright Directive grants copyright owners an exclusive right to communicate copyright-protected works to the public. Hence, the unauthorized public communication of a copyright-protected work to the public will infringe this exclusive right. Ibid (note 7).

uploaded by their users [Article 17(4)(a)]. Where such licenses cannot be obtained, they are imputed with positive obligations to:

- Make "best efforts" in accordance with high industry standards of professional diligence to ensure the unavailability of specific works for which copyright holders have provided relevant and necessary information [Article 17(4)(b)]
- Upon receiving sufficiently substantiated notice from copyright holders to act expeditiously to disable access or to remove from their websites (i.e. platforms) the notified works and to make "best efforts" to prevent the future upload of that content [Article 17(4)(c)]

By imposing positive obligations to make best efforts to "ensure the unavailability" of specific content and to "prevent the future upload" of such content, Article 17 DSM compels OCSSPs to engage in preventive monitoring and filtering (prior review) of content shared by users, with the aim of preventing copyright infringement from taking place on their platform. Thus, it compels OCSSPs engage in ex ante copyright enforcement not just ex post.

The heightened degree of liability coupled with positive obligations to engage in preventive monitoring and filtering compel OCSSPs to adopt a more stringent approach toward copyright enforcement through expansive monitoring and filtering of UGC with the aid of automated content moderation systems (ACMS) (Frosio & Mendis, 2020, p. 563). This in turn enhances risks of "collateral censorship" and "chilling-effects" on speech.[19] At the prevailing level of technological sophistication, ACMS tend to be context-blind and have a relatively low capacity for comprehending nuances, contextual variations, and cultural connotations in human speech (Cowls et al., 2020). This means they are often unable to correctly appreciate the nuances between unauthorized uses of copyright-protected content and authorized uses that come within the scope of copyright E&L (e.g., the exception for parody), thereby resulting in the wrongful removal/blocking of lawful speech.[20] Although Article 17(9) DSM requires platforms to put in place effective and expeditious complaints and redress mechanisms to allow users to challenge such wrongful removal/blocking, the fact that the redress mechanism only comes into play after the suppression of lawful speech (ex post redress mechanism) limits its efficacy as a mechanism for safeguarding users' freedom of expression.

In comparison, Article 17 DSM places significantly less emphasis on the protection of users' ability to benefit from copyright E&L. Although Article 17(7) DSM enunciates that OCSSP efforts to suppress infringing content should not result in

[19] Ibid (note 5) para 54. The CJEU acknowledged that it is not possible to identify possible alternatives to ACMS for the purpose of fulfilling preventive monitoring and filtering obligations in Articles 17(4)(b) and 17(4)(c).

[20] Although the Commission Guidance on Article 17 requires fully automated blocking to be limited to manifestly infringing uploads, a loophole exists for "earmarked" content, the unauthorized online availability of which has the potential to cause significant economic harm to the copyright holder. Communication from the Commission to the European Parliament and the Council, Guidance on Article 17 of Directive 2019/790 on Copyright in the Digital Single Market, COM/2021/288 final.

preventing the availability of non-infringing content (as in the case where the use of copyright-protected content falls within the scope of a copyright exception), no explicit liability is imposed on OCSSPs for the wrongful suppression of such lawful uses. Neither are OCSSPs imposed with enforceable obligations to safeguard user freedoms. However, Article 17(7) DSM underscores the importance of ensuring that users are able to rely on existing E&L for quotation, criticism, review[21] and parody, caricature, and pastiche.[22] This responsibility is assigned to Member States as opposed to OCSSPs.

Given the absence of *positive enforceable obligations* to protect users' ability to benefit from copyright E&L, pursuant to a simple cost-benefit analysis, it is less costly for platforms to remove/block UGC, which reuses copyright-protected content than to invest resources in assessing whether such use comes within the scope of a copyright exception. Thus, Article 17 DSM incentivizes OCSSPs to design and implement their content moderation systems to suppress even *potentially* copyright-infringing content, thereby increasing the risks of collateral censorship.

Therefore, the online copyright enforcement regime introduced by Article 17 is skewed in favor of protecting the interests of copyright owners with less emphasis being placed on the protection of user freedoms. This reflects the primarily economic goal of Article 17 DSM, which is to ensure the ability of copyright holders to obtain appropriate remuneration for uses of their content on OCSSP platforms.[23] Accordingly, Article 17 DSM is deeply entrenched in the narrow-utilitarian viewpoint (based on the neoclassical economic approach) that conceptualizes copyright's primary function as being to incentivize the production of creative content by granting copyright holders a means of obtaining an adequate return on their intellectual/entrepreneurial investment. Conversely, the preservation of user freedoms is rendered peripheral to this core economic aim.

[21] Article 5(3)(d) of the EU Copyright Directive, ibid. (note 7).

[22] Article 5(3)(k) EU Copyright Directive, ibid. (note 7).

[23] The underlying policy rationale for Article 17 DSM is bridging the "value-gap" that purportedly stems from the under-compensation of copyright owners (especially in the music industry) for copyright-protected content shared by users on online content-sharing platforms. The explanatory memorandum to the EU Commission proposal for the enactment of the CDSM Directive states that:

> It is therefore necessary to guarantee that authors and rightholders receive a fair share of the value that is generated by the use of their works and other subject-matter. Against this background, this proposal provides for measures aiming at improving the position of rightholders to negotiate and be remunerated for the exploitation of their content by online services giving access to user-uploaded content.

Commission, 'Proposal for a Directive of the European Parliament and of the Council on copyright in the Digital Single Market' COM (2016) 593 final, p. 3.

5 Proposals for Reform

So how could the existing EU legal framework on online copyright enforcement be revisited in order to effect a fair balance between the interests of copyright owners and users of social media platform owners with the aim of fostering robust democratic discourse on these online spaces? In recent years, several proposals for reform have been put forward by copyright law scholars, which reflect different legal and regulatory strategies. This section outlines some of these proposed strategies.

5.1 Enhanced Regulatory Supervision

The pervasiveness of digital platforms and their growing economic and societal impact has led to increasing calls for the introduction of enhanced regulatory supervision by public authorities (Rieder & Hofmann, 2020). This strategy has also been proposed as a means of providing better protection to users' freedom of expression in the implementation of Article 17 of the DSM.

For example, Geiger and Mangal advocate for the establishment of an independent EU-level public regulator to oversee the implementation of Article 17 DSM in a manner that can ensure predictable and consistent application of user rights in copyright enforcement, across the EU (Geiger & Mangal, 2022).

Similarly, Cowls et al. propose the establishment of an Ombudsperson at the EU level, who is vested with powers to supervise the safeguarding of the freedom of expression by platforms and to provide advice and guidance to platforms in determining whether specific UGC could come within the scope of copyright E&L (Cowls et al., 2020).

The EU DSA (2022) introduces a regulatory framework involving closer supervision of platforms (including social media platforms) and includes several progressive measures which are inter alia designed to secure more effective protection of users' freedom of expression within the content moderation process. For instance, the DSA imposes obligations on social media platforms to (1) provide periodic reports on the use of automated systems for content moderation[24] (including indicators of the accuracy, the possible rate of error and safeguards applied for minimizing such errors); (2) carry out periodic risk assessments of systemic risks for freedom of expression, stemming from the design or functioning of automated and non-automated content moderation systems;[25] and (3) put in place reasonable, proportionate, and effective measures to mitigate these systemic risks.[26]

[24] Article 15(1)(e), ibid. (note 14).

[25] Article 34(1)(b), ibid. (note 14). This obligation is only applicable to very large platforms as defined under Article 33(1) DSA.

[26] Article 35(1)(c), ibid. (note 14). This obligation is only applicable to very large platforms as defined under Article 33(1) DSA.

Given the *lex specialis* nature of Article 17 DSM, it is unclear whether the obligations provided in the DSA could apply to social media platforms in the specific case of content moderation designed to address copyright infringement. Article 2(4)(b) read with Recital 11 stipulates that the DSA is without prejudice to EU law on copyright and related rights including the DSM Directive, which should remain unaffected. This is in accordance with the general principle of *lex specialis derogat legem generalem* (special/specific law prevails over the general law). Nevertheless, they offer interesting insights on how enhanced regulatory supervision could assist in achieving a more transparent and fair application of content moderation systems.

In addition, Article 14(4) DSA obliges platforms to have "due regard to the rights and legitimate interests of all parties involved, including the fundamental rights of the recipients of the service, such as the freedom of expression [. . .]" in imposing any restrictions in relation to the use of their service.[27] According to Article 14(1) DSA, such restrictions include "policies, procedures, measures and tools used for the purpose of content moderation, including algorithmic decision-making and human review." The term "due regard" is vague and ambiguous, and whether Article 14(4) DSA can be interpreted to impose positive obligations on platforms to design and implement their content moderation systems in a manner that safeguards the fundamental right to freedom of expression remains to be seen. Even if this were the case, whether Article 14 DSA would apply to aspects of content moderation that are aimed at monitoring and filtering copyright infringing content in fulfilment of the obligations that are imposed Article 17 DSM is unclear, given the *lex specialis* nature of that law (Mendis, 2023).

5.2 Fundamental Rights as an External Balancing Mechanism

In recent years, invoking the freedom of expression as a legal basis for safeguarding user freedoms to benefit from copyright E&L has gained significant traction within the EU copyright law discourse. Pursuant to this approach, the fundamental rights regime is used as an external "safety valve" to achieve a fair balance between the fundamental right to copyright guaranteed in Article 17(2) of the EUCFR and the fundamental right to freedom of expression guaranteed in Article 11 of the EUCFR.

Article 52(1) of the EUCFR stipulates that fundamental rights guaranteed therein are not absolute and must be balanced against each other as per the principle of proportionality, which requires that any limitation on the exercise of a fundamental right must (1) be provided for by law; (2) respect the essence of the fundamental

[27] Article 14(1) DSA, ibid. (note 14).

right, which is subject to the limitation; and (3) be suitable, necessary, and proportionate *stricto sensu*[28] for achieving the objective pursued by its limitation.

This strategy was employed by Poland when it sought the annulment of Article 17(4)(b) and Article 17(4)(c) of the DSM Directive before the CJEU in the *Poland v Council* case.[29] Poland claimed that the preventive monitoring and filtering obligations imposed by these provisions (with the objective of protecting the fundamental right to copyright) limited users' fundamental right to freedom of expression in a manner that did not comply with the proportionality principle in Article 52(1) of the EUCFR. The CJEU acknowledged that the contested provisions did in fact limit the freedom of expression of users but did so in a manner that was necessary and proportionate for safeguarding the fundamental right to copyright under Article 17(2) of the EUCFR, which made it compliant with Article 52(1) of the EUCFR. What is significant is that in reaching this decision, the CJEU adopted a narrow-utilitarian perception of copyright and accordingly observed that:

> [...] in the context of online content sharing services [...] copyright protection must necessarily be accompanied, to a certain extent, by a limitation on the exercise of the right of users to freedom of expression [...].[30]

The CJEU determination in the *Poland v Council* case illustrates a fundamental drawback in using the freedom of expression as an external balancing mechanism for safeguarding user freedoms to benefit from copyright E&L. By seeking to protect copyright E&L under the fundamental right to freedom of expression and pitting them against the fundamental right to copyright, it perpetuates the misguided conception of these user freedoms as being something external and even antithetical to copyright. Thus, the ability to benefit from copyright E&L is once again relegated to a position of secondary importance within the copyright law discourse, while the protection of copyright holders' interests is reinforced as being its primary function.

5.3 *The Need for a Paradigm Shift?*

The need for a fundamental shift in the theoretical framework of EU copyright law based on the communicational (a.k.a. social planning) theory of copyright law has been advocated with the aim of recognizing and giving effect to copyright law's potential to serve as a legal tool for fostering robust democratic discourse in the digital public sphere (Mendis, 2021).

The communicational theory of copyright law has been advanced by scholars such as Netanel (1996, 1998), Fisher (2001), Elkin-Koren (Elkin-Koren, 1996,

[28] This demands that the benefit gained by the limitation of the fundamental right must be logical and proportionate to the harm caused to the fundamental right taking into account the pursued objective.

[29] Ibid (note 5).

[30] Ibid, para 82.

2010), and Sunder (2012). While affirming the role of copyright in preserving the incentives of authors to produce and distribute creative content, the communicational theory envisions an overarching democratic function for copyright law, which is the promotion of the discursive foundations for democratic culture and civic association (Netanel, 1996).

Thus, the communicational theory prescribes that protecting the interests of copyright owners must be tempered by the overarching aspiration of sustaining a participatory culture (Fisher, 2001), which in turn necessitates the adequate preservation of user freedoms to engage with copyright-protected content for purposes of democratic discourse. As noted by Netanel:

> Copyright-holder rights should be sufficiently robust to support copyright's democracy-enhancing functions, but not so broad and unbending as to chill expressive diversity and hinder the exchange of information and ideas. (Netanel, 1998, p.220)

Espousing the communicational theory as a theoretical framework for EU copyright law would bring about a paradigm shift that enables the protection of democratic discourse to be seen as something that is endogenous—and in fact fundamental—to copyright's purpose. This paradigm shift would provide a solid normative basis for re-imagining the EU legal framework on online copyright enforcement to increase its fitness for preserving and promoting copyright law's democracy enhancing function.

Firstly, it would entail a re-affirmation that the protection of user freedoms to benefit from copyright E&L (particularly those E&L such as quotation and parody that are vital for safeguarding users' freedom of expression) is central to copyright law's purpose and as such should be granted equal weight and importance as the protection of the economic rights of copyright owners. This would provide a normative basis for courts to engage in a more expansive teleological interpretation of copyright E&L with a view to advancing the democracy-enhancing function of copyright law.

Secondly, in view of the character of social media platforms as a key component of the digital public sphere, it would pave the way for acknowledging the role played by OCSSPs as facilitators and enablers of democratic discourse and the potency of content moderation systems to direct and influence public discourse on social media platforms. This would provide a basis for OCSSPs to be imposed with positive obligations to ensure that content moderation systems are designed and implemented in a manner that provides adequate protection to user freedoms.

6 Conclusions

The pervasiveness of social media platforms and their growing influence on every aspect of our lives means that issues concerning their regulation will continue to remain high on policy agendas for years to come. As digital technology continues to advance and evolve, it is likely that the nature of the dialogic interaction taking place in these digital spaces will also evolve and transform. Emerging technologies (e.g., artificial intelligence (AI) and virtual reality) and business models (e.g., live streaming on social media, influencer marketing) are already having a powerful influence on transforming the nature and scope of discourse in the digital public sphere, thereby giving rise to a host of new regulatory problems. Copyright law is already struggling to address several such issues, for instance, the copyright law implications of AI-generated discourse and the need to re-think the private/public and commercial/non-commercial use distinctions in copyright law. It is important to recognize the need for a holistic and interdisciplinary approach in addressing these issues as any legal or regulatory strategy or mechanism that is aimed toward resolving them is likely to have far-reaching social, political, cultural, and economic implications and to have a powerful impact on our digital sovereignty and the protection of our fundamental rights and freedoms in the digital public sphere.

Discussion Questions for Students and Their Teachers

1. Should social media platforms be designated as public utilities/infrastructures notwithstanding their private ownership? What would be the regulatory implications of such designation?
2. Should owners of social media platforms be imposed with positive obligations to protect fundamental rights of users? If yes, does the existing EU law framework allow private actors to be imputed with positive obligations to protect fundamental rights?
3. Should Article 14(4) the EU DSA [2022] apply to copyright enforcement on social media platforms, notwithstanding the *lex specialis* nature of Article 17 DSM? To what extent would such an application contribute toward the safeguarding of users' fundamental right to freedom of expression in copyright enforcement?

Learning Resources for Students

1. Frosio, G. and Mendis, S. (2020). 'Monitoring and Filtering: European Reform or Global Trend?'. In: G. Frosio ed., *The Oxford Handbook of Intermediary Liability*. Oxford: OUP (pp. 544–565). Available at: https://doi.org/10.1093/oxfordhb/9780198837138.013.28

   This chapter explores the evolution of the "Internet threat" discourse and demonstrates how Article 17 of the EU Copyright in the Digital Single Market (DSM) Directive [2019] is rooted within this discourse. It analyzes the impact of Article 17 DSM on users' fundamental rights, particularly in the light of its propensity to motivate wider use of automated content moderation systems.
2. Friedmann, D. (2023). 'Digital Single Market, First Stop to The Metaverse: Counterlife of Copyright Protection Wanted'. In: K. Mathis and A. Tor eds., *Law and Economics of the Digital Transformation.* Springer. Available at: https://link.springer.com/chapter/10.1007/978-3-031-25059-0_8

   This paper demonstrates how the legislative shift toward charging platform owners with a higher standard of liability (strict liability) for copyright infringement incentivizes the adoption of automated content moderation systems and analyzes its implications for user freedoms in virtual worlds (metaverse). Building upon the "fair use by design" concept, it discusses strategies for designing automated content moderation systems in a way that would enable them to safeguard legitimate uses of copyright-protected content such as uses falling within the scope of copyright exceptions and limitations.

3. Geiger, C. and Jutte, B.J. (2021). Platform Liability under Article 17 of the Copyright in the Digital Single Market Directive, Automated Filtering and Fundamental Rights: An Impossible Match, *GRUR International,* 70(6), 517–543. Available at: https://doi.org/10.1093/grurint/ikab037

   This paper analyzes the impact of Article 17 of the EU Copyright in the Digital Single Market (DSM) Directive on fundamental rights to freedom of expression and information; freedom of the arts; freedom to conduct a business; data protection, privacy, and family life; right to property; and right to an effective remedy and to a fair trial. It also analyzes Article 17 DSM with regard to its compatibility with general principles of EU law such as proportionality and legal certainty. It demonstrates the difficulty of striking a fair balance between these different fundamental rights within the normative framework of Article 17 DSM.

4. De Gregorio, G. (2022). 'Digital Constitutionalism and Freedom of Expression'. In: De Gregorio, G. *Digital Constitutionalism in Europe: Reframing Rights and Powers in the Algorithmic Society.* Cambridge: CUP. Available at: https://www.cambridge.org/core/books/digital-constitutionalism-in-europe/digital-constitutionalism-and-freedom-of-expression/72ACEF48324D180E95BBD456E52E9C96.

   This chapter explores the challenges posed by the private enforcement of the fundamental right to freedom of expression by online platforms in the algorithmic public sphere. It outlines how EU legislators and the courts have entered a new phase of digital constitutionalism in reigning in platform power and addressing the challenges of content moderation.

5. Mendis S. (2023, May 18) The Magic Bullet That Isn't! The Limited Efficacy of Article 14 DSA in Safeguarding Copyright Exceptions to Quotation and Parody on Social Media Platforms. Verfassungsblog. Available at: https://verfassungsblog.de/no-magic-bullet/

   This blog article explores the potential of Article 14 of the EU Digital Service Act (DSA, 2022) in effectively safeguarding user rights to benefit from copyright exceptions to quotation and parody. It analyzes whether Article 14 DSA could apply to obligations imposed on online content-sharing service providers (OCSSPs) under Article 17 of the EU Copyright in the Digital Single Market (DSM) Directive and, if so, whether Article 14 DSA could lead to these exceptions being rendered enforceable as user rights in EU law.

References

Avila, R., De Wachter, J., & Schneider, C. (2018). *The EU is killing our democratic spaces using copyright as a Trojan horse*. Accessed March 25, 2023, from The EU is killing our democratic spaces using copyright as a Trojan horse | openDemocracy

Conti, O. (2015). Political remix video as vernacular discourse. In E. Navas, O. Gallagher, & X. Burrough (Eds.), *The Routledge companion to remix studies* (pp. 346–357). Routledge.

Cowls, J., Darius, P., Golunova, V., Mendis, S., Prem, E., Santistevan, D., & Wang, W. W. (2020). *Freedom of expression in the digital public sphere*. HIIG. https://doi.org/10.5281/zenodo.4292408

Dahlberg, L. (2001). The Internet and democratic discourse: Exploring the prospects of online deliberative forums extending the public sphere. *Information, Communication and Society, 4*(4), 615–633.

Dahlgren, P. (2005). The Internet, public spheres, and political communication: Dispersion and deliberation. *Political Communication, 22*(2), 147–162. https://doi.org/10.1080/10584600590933l6

Elkin-Koren, N. (1996). Cyberlaw and social change: Democratic approach to copyright law in cyberspace. *Cardozo Arts & Entertainment Law Journal, 14*(2), 215–296.

Elkin-Koren, N. (2010). Tailoring copyright to social production. *Theoretical Inquiries in Law, 12* (1), 309–347.

Fisher, W. (2001). Theories of intellectual property. In S. R. Munzer (Ed.), *New essays in the legal and political theory of property* (pp. 168–199). Cambridge University Press.

Frosio, G., & Mendis, S. (2020). Monitoring and filtering: European reform or global trend? In G. Frosio (Ed.), *The Oxford handbook of intermediary liability*. Oxford University Press.

Geiger, C., & Mangal, N. (2022). Regulating creativity online: Proposal for an EU copyright institution. *GRUR, 71*(10), 933–951. https://doi.org/10.1093/grurint/ikac086

Habermas, J. (1989). *The structural transformation of the public sphere: An inquiry into a category of bourgeois society*. Translated by Thomas Burger. MIT.

Laidlaw, E. (2010). A framework for identifying Internet information gatekeepers. *International Review of Law, Computers and Technology, 24*(3), 263–276.

Mcintosh. (2013, October 1). "Buffy v Edward" remix unfairly removed by Lionsgate. *Arstechnica*. https://arstechnica.com/tech-policy/2013/01/buffy-vs-edward-remix-unfairly-removed-by-lionsgate/

Mendis, S. (2021). Democratic discourse in the digital public sphere. In H. Werthner, E. Prem, E. A. Lee, & C. Ghezzi (Eds.), *Perspectives on digital humanism*. Springer International Publishing. https://doi.org/10.1007/978-3-030-86144-5_6

Mendis S. (2023, May 18). *The magic bullet that isn't! The limited efficacy of article 14 DSA in safeguarding copyright exceptions to quotation and parody on social media platforms*. Verfassungsblog. https://verfassungsblog.de/no-magic-bullet/

Netanel, N. W. (1996). Copyright in a democratic civil society. *Yale Law Journal, 106*, 283–387.

Netanel, N. W. (1998). Asserting copyright's democratic principles in the Global Arena. *Vanderbilt Law Review, 51*(2), 217–329.

Peverini, P. (2015). Remix practices and activism. In E. Navas, O. Gallagher, & X. Burrough (Eds.), *The Routledge companion to remix studies* (pp. 333–345). Routledge.

Rieder, B., & Hofmann, J. (2020). Towards platform observability. *Internet Policy Review, 9*(4), 1–28. https://doi.org/10.14763/2020.4.1535

Schäfer, M. S. (2015). The digital public sphere. In G. Mazzoleni (Ed.), *The international encyclopedia of political communication* (pp. 322–328). Wiley Blackwell.

Sunder, M. (2012). *From goods to a good life: Intellectual property and global justice*. Yale University Press.

On Algorithmic Content Moderation

Erich Prem and Brigitte Krenn

Abstract This chapter provides an overview of the challenges involved in algorithmic content moderation. Content moderation is the organized practice of screening user-generated content (UGC) on Internet sites, social media, and other online outlets to determine the appropriateness of the content for a given site, locality, or jurisdiction. The most common technical approaches consist in using classifier systems that assign predefined category labels to individual posts. We briefly introduce pre- and post-moderation and provide real-world examples of algorithmic moderation systems used by an Austrian daily newspaper. We point to significant challenges of moderation such as the ambiguities of natural language and the implications for freedom of expression. We conclude with issues that algorithmic content moderation raises for societal power relations and democratic control.

1 Introduction

For all we know, the human capacity for language is second to no other species in the animal kingdom. It is regarded as essential for the development of human society and its cultural achievements. In addition, humans regard language as something extremely personal. In expressing thoughts, desires, intentions, or beliefs with words, humans experience themselves as individuals. This is one of the reasons why *freedom of expression* is considered a human right in many jurisdictions, even where it may not be practically granted. Hence, it is only natural that efforts to moderate linguistic expressions in the digital realm are an important topic in Digital Humanism. Another reason why content moderation deserves a prominent place in digital humanism is that speech has traditionally been the medium through which politics happens. From the public debate in the ancient Greek *polis* to the

E. Prem (✉) · B. Krenn
Institute of Philosophy, University of Vienna, Vienna, Austria

Austrian Research Institute for Artificial Intelligence, Vienna, Austria
e-mail: erich.prem@univie.ac.at; brigitte.krenn@ofai.at

H. Werthner et al. (eds.), *Introduction to Digital Humanism*,
https://doi.org/10.1007/978-3-031-45304-5_30

modern-day speeches in mass media, leaders lead through language and are challenged in debates. Language thus is the medium that facilitates power, and it can be the medium by which power is taken away as in the democratic vote of the people.

The intention to *regulate* (or "moderate") what becomes published is not new nor is it exclusive to digital media. What should be published has probably been a central societal, political, religious, and ethical concern for as long as writing exists, but definitely ever since the invention of the printing press. It was a subject of censorship and is still regulated by law and ethical norms, including traditional mass media (newspapers, books, TV, etc.) in modern liberal democracies. For example, many countries have laws prohibiting the publication of terrorist content and have rules for the publication of certain types of material, such as age limits for pornographic content. Often, there are self-governing bodies that regulate what can be published, for example, in mass media or in advertising. Traditionally, such limitations on publication were implemented through reviewers, editors, censors, or courts and performed by humans. They could limit publication, remove content, or restrict the audiences of certain publications. In principle, these instruments are still applicable in the digital world. However, an important new quality of content moderation emerges, when the decision to regulate content (including who can see it) is taken with the help of algorithms.

2 What Is Algorithmic Content Moderation

Content moderation is a fairly recent field of digital technologies. Even though language technologies relevant for content moderation today have been developing for decades, researchers pay much closer attention to the area since the development of large online social media platforms. In many cases, content moderation is a response to the fact that discourse on such platforms has proven problematic. Online social platforms facilitate the distribution of untrue information (*fake news*), the creation of environments where people are only exposed to opinions reconfirming their interests and beliefs (*filter bubbles*), verbal abuse, and many other troublesome phenomena. While these phenomena are by no means exclusive to digital media or social networks, they may be exacerbated in large communities of speakers with no personal interaction other than the messages that they exchange online. Up until a few years ago, relatively few scientific papers dealt with the topic. The number of scientific publications has been increasing since 2015 (Fanta, 2017), primarily focusing on technical approaches, ethical challenges, and the perception of automatically generated content by journalists and the public. Communication science has also dealt theoretically and empirically with automated content and, in particular, automated journalism for several years.

Content moderation addresses a topic that not only concerns individuals and their linguistic online expressions; it deals with communication and how humans establish social relations. It addresses how we interact with each other and how we make sense of the world. In the following definition of content moderation, we refer to Roberts (2017):

> Content moderation is the organized practice of screening user-generated content (UGC) posted to Internet sites, social media, and other online outlets, in order to determine the appropriateness of the content for a given site, locality, or jurisdiction. The process can result in UGC being removed by a moderator, acting as an agent of the platform or site in question. . . . The style of moderation can vary from site to site, and from platform to platform, as rules around what UGC is allowed are often set at a site or platform level and reflect that platform's brand and reputation . . . The firms who own social media sites and platforms that solicit UGC employ content moderation as a means to protect the firm from liability, negative publicity, and to curate and control user experience. (Roberts, 2017, p. 1)

Content moderation is not only an issue for content providers such as online newspapers but also relevant for social media platforms such as Twitter or Facebook. It is relevant for text-based online systems as well as networks that focus on other types of content such as images, videos, and even music. In this chapter, we focus on text-based systems.

There are two main reasons to screen user-generated content (UGC).

Reason 1: Depending on national legal regulations, media providers are liable for the content published via their sites. This is particularly the case for online newspapers who underlie national regulations as of what content is permitted. For Austria, this is regulated in media law.[1] The situation is less clear for providers of social media platforms such as Facebook, Twitter, or TikTok, which is a comparably new worldwide phenomenon. Thus, the formulation of international requirements of conduct and legal standards is necessary. Respective initiatives are underway. An example is the European Digital Services Act (DSA), which is an endeavor of the European Union to regulate online services including social media.[2] The DSA was put into force in November 2022 and is planned to be fully applicable by February 2024. Due to national legal regulations, it has been vital for providers of online newspapers ever since their existence to filter out UGC that conflicts with the law. This activity is called *pre-moderation* and is done before posts go online. Pre-moderation is typically done automatically, because of the sheer quantity of incoming posts and the speed the posts need to be processed in order to guarantee real-time communication.

Reason 2: Individual content providers have different editorial concepts, and depending on these, they have differing demands on how people are expected to communicate with each other. This is typically communicated via the terms of use and specific rules of netiquette. Fora of online newspapers with a claim to quality are typically moderated by human moderators. An example of an online newspaper with a strong moderation policy is derStandard,[3] which has a team of human forum

---

[1] Mediengesetz https://www.ris.bka.gv.at/GeltendeFassung.wxe?Abfrage=Bundesnormen&Gesetzesnummer=10000719 (URL retrieved 3.4.2023).

[2] https://commission.europa.eu/strategy-and-policy/priorities-2019-2024/europe-fit-digital-age/digital-services-act-ensuring-safe-and-accountable-online-environment_en (URL retrieved 3.4.2023).

[3] https://www.derstandard.at/, https://www.derstandard.de/

moderators whose main task is to support a positive discussion climate in the newspaper's online fora.[4] This kind of moderation is called *post-moderation* as the moderation activities relate to posts that are online. Apart from community activities where users can flag inappropriate posts, natural language processing (NLP) plays an important role in supporting human moderators in finding posts that might be interesting to a larger group of readers of a forum than just to the few who participate in a certain thread. Automatic systems can also help identify fora or phases in the discussions, which become increasingly emotional or discriminating. Examples will be given in the following section.

There are more reasons for algorithmic content moderation, for example, the identification of protected intellectual property (see chapter by Menids in this volume).

3 Technical Approaches to Content Moderation

Technical approaches to content moderation are based on classifiers. Text classification is a core method in NLP, employing different methods of machine learning. Classifiers are used to categorize data into distinct groups or classes. Roughly, they are mathematical models that use statistical analysis and optimization to identify patterns in the data. To train a classifier, a certain amount of labeled data is required, representing in-class and out-of-class examples. A number of classifiers exist, including logistic regression, Naïve Bayes, decision tree, support vector machine (SVM), k-nearest neighbors (KNN), and artificial neural network (ANN) (see, for instance, Kotsiantis et al. (2007) for a review of classification techniques and Li et al. (2022) specifically for text classification).

In the case of fora in online newspapers, text-based classifiers are employed, which assign predefined category labels to individual posts. In practice, a number of different classifiers are in use, depending on the moderation tasks at hand. In *pre-moderation*, UGC is classified into content that can or cannot be posted on the media site as it adheres to or infringes the requirements of the respective (national) media law, or should not be published because it violates the medium's defined online etiquette or community policy (Reich, 2011; Singer, 2011). In *post-moderation,* classifiers support the forum moderators in identifying postings of interest. What is of interest is defined by the individual media companies and may differ across individual resorts up to individual articles. All in all, moderation is an important success factor for online discussion culture (Ziegele & Jost, 2016).

The classifier technologies in use widely differ depending on the time the classifiers were developed. Earlier classifiers often use decision trees and support vector machines (SVMs); more recent ones are based on neural networks (deep learning). As technology advances over time, deep learning-based approaches

[4] https://www.derstandard.at/story/2000140862539/so-sind-wir-wie-wir-unsere-foren-moderieren

typically lead to better results than classical machine learning-based approaches such as decision trees or SVMs. For illustration, examples from the Austrian online newspaper derStandard.at are given in the following.

In pre-moderation, derStandard.at has been using a decision tree-based system (Foromat, developed by OFAI[5]) since 2005. While before the implementation of the system human editors had to manually inspect the incoming posts and decide which ones could go online, Foromat significantly reduced the amount of posts that needed to be manually inspected. With the volume of postings drastically increasing with the shift from print to online, manual pre-moderation became simply impossible and thus was left to the system. Accordingly, community measures such as the possibility for users to flag content as inappropriate and post-moderation became more important as a means to filter out inappropriate postings after their publication.

Post-moderation is key for *encouraging an agreeable discussion climate* in fora. Starting in 2016, the De-Escalation Bot was developed by OFAI together with derStandard (Schabus et al., 2017; Schabus & Skowron, 2018).[6] This is another kind of classification task where the classes were designed to prevent escalation in fora and to identify valuable contributions to discussions. The thus classified posts are then sifted by the moderators, and those which the moderators consider of general interest are ranked at the top of a forum to be easily accessed by all users of the forum. According to derStandard this has noticeably improved the quality of the discourse.[7] A more recent collaboration between OFAI and derStandard lead to a classifier that helps moderators to identify misogynist posts in order to counteract online discrimination against women (Petrak & Krenn, 2022). This is an important precondition to foster female contributions to forum discussions. While the proportion of individuals who identify themselves as men or women among the online readers of derStandard is relatively balanced at 55–45%, there is a clear imbalance when it comes to active contributions, i.e., only 20% of posters identify themselves as female (surveyed on the basis of indication of "salutation" in new registrations).

The limitations in the area of classifier-supported moderation lie primarily in the necessary provision of correspondingly large training data annotated by domain experts (typically moderators). So far, this is usually done once when the classifier is developed. Over time, however, the wording of posts may change as users may counteract moderation strategies, also what is considered relevant and desirable content is likely to change over time, as well as which marginalized user groups and what measures are required to encourage their contributions. Therefore, mechanisms need to be integrated in moderation interfaces where the moderators easily can collect new training data during their daily work, and classifiers capable of online learning need to be developed. This, however, is still a question of basic research [for some further reading on online learning, see Cano and Krawczyk

[5] https://www.ofai.at

[6] See also https://ofai.github.io/million-post-corpus/ for details on the data set used for classifier training.

[7] https://www.derstandard.at/story/2000114011196/25-jahre-online-innovation

(2022) and Mundt et al. (2023)]. Likewise, depending on the information to be identified, the available training data, and the machine learning architecture used, the accuracy rates can vary significantly. In all cases, however, the moderation quality to be achieved at the end strongly depends on the human experts, the forum moderators. The advantage of the classifiers is to direct the moderators to potentially relevant posts, whereas the final moderation decision lies with the moderator.

Apart from encouraging an agreeable discussion climate, *tendentious and fake news detection* is another important aspect of content moderation. This is particularly relevant in social media, which significantly differ from fora in online newspapers. Whereas in online newspapers a forum is related to an individual article or blog entry written by a journalist and redacted according to the editorial policy of the respective newspaper, UGC on social media platforms is far less controlled. Accordingly, social media platforms offer a high degree of freedom of expression while being open to all kinds of propaganda and misinformation. This became particularly obvious with the US presidential elections in 2016. Up to date, the identification of fake and tendentious news has become a very active field of research (see, for instance, the SemEval2019[8] task on *hyperpartisan news detection* (Kiesel et al., 2019), where 42 NLP systems from all over the world designed for identifying extreme right- or left-wing news competed against each other). The comparison of the systems showed that no single method had a clear advantage over others. Successful approaches included both word embeddings and handcrafted features. SemEval2023 subtask 3 addresses *persuasion techniques identification*. Here especially the identification of manipulative wording and attack on reputation are of interest for tendentious news detection.[9] (See also Zhou and Zafarani (2020) for a discussion of theoretical concepts and approaches to fake news detection.) Automated *fact checking* is another area of NLP that addresses the task of assessing whether claims made in written or spoken language are true or false. This requires NLP technology to detect a claim in a text, to retrieve evidence for or against the claim, to predict a verdict whether the claim is true or false, and to generate a justification for the verdict (cf. Guo et al., 2022). Apart from NLP-based research on automated fact checking, there is a broad range of journalist-based fact-checking initiatives and sites, such as PolitiFact, a fact-checking site for American politics; EUfactcheck, an initiative of the European Journalism Training Association; the European Fact Checking Standards Project where European organizations involved in fact checking cooperate to develop a code of integrity for independent European fact checking; or Poynter an international fact-checking network[10]—to mention only some existing fact checking initiatives.

[8] SemEval (https://semeval.github.io/) is a series of international NLP research workshops dedicated to specific text analysis tasks. The tasks reflect challenging problems in NLP and vary from year to year. In setting up these challenges, task-specific high-quality datasets are created, and state-of-the-art NLP systems compete against each other under identical conditions so that methods can be compared.

[9] https://propaganda.math.unipd.it/semeval2023task3/

[10] https://www.politifact.com/

Disinformation detection is a moving target because new topics and concerted propaganda are constantly evolving, and fact checking must adapt accordingly. Moreover, there is ever-growing and refining technology for automated disinformation production due to technological progress in deep learning, which enables the creation of *deepfakes*, i.e., the use of deep learning for the automated generation of fake content. As examples, see the recent large generative language models (such as OpenAI's GPT family or Google's PaLM, Meta's LLaMA, etc.) that are able to flexibly generate text based on prompts or the advances in neural visual content generation (e.g., Google's Imagen or OpenAI's DALL-E) where pictures are generated on the basis of textual input, as well as the possibilities to generate realistically looking, however, fake audio and video content. (See Zhang et al., 2023, for a survey on generative AI.) Note that the developments in generative AI are fast and up-to-date models at the time of writing this contribution may be outdated soon.

4 Societal Challenges

Freedom of expression. As already mentioned, the identification of illegal content is an important reason for content moderation in general and algorithmic moderation in particular. Often, such content will be removed after detection, and it may incur further legal procedures. For example, it is illegal in Austria to publicly deny the Holocaust. In addition, there is content that conflicts with the *terms of use* or the *community guidelines* of a social network. For example, some networks exclude nudity or have strict policies regarding false and misleading information or "fake news."

Often, however, content moderation is publicly debated in the context of unwanted (or *harmful*) content. Such content is much more difficult to define. Note that in many countries, it is not in principle illegal to lie or to use abusive language. Still, such content is often considered societally unwanted, for example, because it affects certain parts of society stronger than others, may lead to the spread of dangerous information, or be used for exerting unwanted (e.g., political) influence. It is, however, a major problem of the notion of *harmful content* that it lacks precision and definition. It is often not very clear *who* is harmed and in whose interest it is to identify, mark, or remove such content. This is one of the reasons why calls to remove harmful content raise concerns and accusations of censorship. In addition, even productive debates may benefit from some degree of strong language and therefore, according to the European Court of Human Rights, may require *information that offends, shocks or disturbs* (ECHR, 2022). This makes it even

https://eufactcheck.eu/
https://www.disinfo.eu/projects/european-fact-checking-standards-project/
https://www.ifcncodeofprinciples.poynter.org/know-more

less clear what precisely should be considered harmful in online debates (Prem, 2022).

The extent to which algorithmic content moderation actually interferes with the principle of freedom of expression is difficult to analyze in practice. This requires a detailed topical analysis of the practices of deletion, for which data are often lacking. It also requires a differentiated analysis of the degree to which banned content (or banned users) can turn to other media to express their thoughts. The core challenge is to strike a balance between protecting users and legal obligations on the one hand and safeguarding freedom of expression on the other (Cowls et al., 2020).

Challenges of meaning and languages. A central challenge in content moderation and indeed in most aspects of language technology is the identification of what users actually mean. Human utterances are easily misunderstood in everyday life, but the notion of meaning is also an elusive philosophical concept that has been debated for centuries. Features of natural languages such as humor, irony, mockery, and many more are notoriously hard to detect (Wallace, 2015), not only by machines but to some extent also by humans. Many algorithms for content moderation are context-blind and have great difficulties detecting nuance. However, such nuance is often important in debate. A particular difficulty in algorithmic moderation is to follow discussions over an extended stretch of online debate. In fact, still today, many algorithms operate only on single posts, while the intended meaning of a post may require taking into account longer stretches of dialogue. Estimates suggest only a 70% to 80% accuracy of commercial tools (Duarte et al., 2017). For example, in 2020, Facebook removed posts with the hashtag *#EndSARS* in Nigeria. It was intended to draw attention to police attacks against protesters, but the moderation algorithms mistook it for misinformation about COVID-19 (Tomiwa, 2020).

Another huge challenge for the practice of algorithmic moderation is the fact that many technologies only work well for a few common languages, first and foremost English. Rarer languages in particular often lack datasets suitable to train NLP models. This raises another ethical and perhaps legal challenge regarding the fairness of different standards in content moderation for different languages. In some regions, such as the European Union, there are a variety of different languages that should be treated equally. There are 24 official languages of the EU, and some of these have a relatively small community of speakers (e.g., Maltese), and significantly fewer texts are available. There are also fewer datasets available for researchers and for AI development. Moreover, the computational and economic power required to train large language models as well as the access to large datasets, which are the basis of current NLP systems today, lies in the hands of private companies such as OpenAI, Meta, or Google.

Political challenge: power of control, silencing, selection, and redress. Online content moderation raises important issues of power and power relations. Online moderation can have a decisive influence on which topics in a debate disappear from public discourse. It can silence specific groups, and it has the power to control whose online contributions are shown to whom. Hence, the delegation of content moderation to algorithms turns content providers into subjects of algorithmic decision-making.

This leads to other important problems, namely, what happens when content is wrongfully reported, deleted, or in any other way restricted. Firstly, there is the problem of informing the authors that their contributions were subject of moderating interventions. Such information can be given, especially where content is considered illegal, but in practice, this is not always the case. In particular, the decision to limit the visibility of a post and to not prominently show it is hardly ever easily accessible for a content contributor. Secondly, the question arises how to contest the decision that content is considered inappropriate or illegal. Today, the focus of public regulation is more on the deletion of illegal content rather than on redress procedures and re-instantiation. Note that regulators do not always prescribe deletion directly but are introducing strict liability regimes that provide strong incentives for platforms to perform algorithmic content moderation even before content is reported by users or third parties (Cowls et al., 2020). This poses a significant threat for freedom of expression as it can mean that certain views are systematically suppressed with little or no chance of forcing online platforms to publish content. It also leads to the question who should be the regulatory body deciding upon complaints and implementing the re-instantiation of wrongfully deleted content. *Wrongful deletion* is a significant problem. For example, in Q2/2020, more than 1.1 million videos were removed from YouTube (Cowls et al., 2020). Such excessive deletion may be a consequence of regulation. Lawmakers have a tendency to regulate that removal of illegal content must be implemented within very short time frames. While regulation usually does not prescribe the use of algorithms directly, it is in practice the only way in which social networks or publishers can fulfill their legal obligations.

Since many newer techniques are based on statistical machine learning, there is an additional danger of bias and discrimination. Algorithmic content moderation systems can replicate and amplify existing *biases and discrimination* in society. For example, if the system is trained on biased datasets or programmed with biased algorithms, it may disproportionately flag and remove content from marginalized communities (Haimson et al., 2021). In addition, there is a lack of *transparency*. Content moderation algorithms are often proprietary, meaning that the public does not have access to the underlying code or the criteria used to determine what content is flagged or removed. This lack of transparency can make it difficult for users to understand why their content was removed (Suzor et al., 2019), and for researchers, it makes it hard to study the impact of these algorithms on society.

There are various ways to address issues of transparency and bias ranging from stricter regulation to increasing accountability or democratic approaches. Vaccaro et al. (2021) propose adding representation (i.e., moving toward participatory and more democratic moderation), improving communication (i.e., better explaining the reasons for moderating interventions), and designing with compassion (i.e., emphasizing empathy and emotional intelligence in moderation decisions). Other measures that have been proposed (Cowls et al., 2020) include ombudspersons, enforceable statutory regimes, and improved legal protection.

5 Conclusions

Content moderation is not a new phenomenon. It has existed at least since written forms of expressions developed and was performed by humans in charge. However, algorithmic content moderation is a new phenomenon tied to the explosion of digital content in online media and social networks. Today's content moderation is a combination of human moderators and algorithmic support, however with a strong trend toward more automation in reaction to growing amounts of content and increasing regulation. There is a range of reasons for content moderation. This includes legal aspects (e.g., duties of platform owners to remove illegal content) and practical aspects such as filtering content for relevance and aiming for showing users the most relevant content. Social reasons for content moderation may include the enforcement of user guidelines or the identification of content that is considered inappropriate or harmful.

Moderation takes many different forms. Content may be signaled or highlighted to inform users about issues with the content; it can be practically hidden from users by downranking and thus decreasing the likelihood of this content to be viewed, or it can be entirely deleted. Content can also be delayed in publication and reported to boards or authorities. There are great differences in the extent to which users are informed about their content being flagged, and there is only limited access to current practices for many of the social networks today. Algorithmic content moderation is often a response to legal requirements. Lawmakers may not prescribe algorithmic deletion directly but prescribe short time limits or severe fines so that algorithms are the only practically viable approaches given the large volumes of data and the high frequency of user interaction.

Challenges arise from the difficulty to interpret human language automatically, especially regarding context and nuances of expression. Also language technologies and training data available for rarer languages are less advanced than those for English. Potential pitfalls include limitations of freedom of expression, bias and unfair treatment, and political influence exerted through silencing of dissent or tendentious moderation. It is possible to perform algorithmic moderation with societally beneficial intent. This includes the abovementioned example of de-escalation, encouraging factful and constructive online debates (Kolhatkar & Taboada, 2017; Park et al., 2016) and pursuing other moderation objectives, such as making voices of systematically underrepresented groups better heard.

The advent of generative artificial intelligence and large language models is generally considered a game changer in text-based AI and expected to trigger a plethora of new applications and systems. Most of the challenges described in this chapter also apply to AI text generators as they pose similar questions of classifying text as harmful or illegal, using and abusing generated text for political propaganda, facilitating the creation of text for children and many more. Similarly issues of discrimination, bias, and transparency also apply to large language models and require further research, social debate, and political agreement and intervention.

Discussion Questions for Students and Their Teachers

1. What are the differences between illegal and harmful content? Discuss how these issues were dealt with in traditional, non-digital publishing. As an example, consider advertising in traditional mass media.
2. What constitutes a good online debate? Should all online discussion only be factual and all commentary be friendly and respectful, or is it sometimes necessary to simplify and use strong words?
3. What can be done to make a debate constructive? Consider techniques used in real-world discussions, and then think about which mechanisms can be transferred to the virtual world.
4. What are the main democratic threats emerging from algorithmic content moderation? Consider who has the power of running social network infrastructure and who is in charge of shaping online discourse. What can be done to balance the power to foster democratic principles?

Learning Resources for Students

1. For a survey and a taxonomy of different approaches to text classification, see Li et al. (2022). It also includes benchmarks and a comparison of different approaches.
2. N. Persily and J.A. Tucker's (2020) book '*Social Media and Democracy*" provides a comprehensive account of social media, content moderation and the challenges for democracy.
3. There is an online summary video available for the ACM opinion piece referenced above (Prem 22): https://youtu.be/SjAH2HYKEhM illustrating the problem of illegal and harmful content and questions regarding freedom of expression.
4. Á. Díaz and L. Hecht-Felella (2021) provide a detailed discussion of many issues listed here and recommendations from a more legal perspective. The paper includes a critical perspective on content moderation regarding the representation of viewpoints from minorities.
5. The so-called *Teachable Machine* https://teachablemachine.withgoogle.com/ is a web-based tool for creating your own machine learning classification models. Its graphical user interface (GUI) allows you to train classifiers without prior programming knowledge and without the need to have special expertise in machine learning. A short overview is *Teachable Machine: Approachable Web-Based Tool for Exploring Machine Learning Classification* by Carney et al. (2020).

References

Cano, A., & Krawczyk, B. (2022). ROSE: Robust online self-adjusting ensemble for continual learning on imbalanced drifting data streams. *Machine Learning, 111*(7), 2561–2599.

Carney, M., Webster, B., Alvarado, I., Phillips, K., Howell, N., Griffith, J., et al. (2020, April). Teachable machine: Approachable Web-based tool for exploring machine learning

classification. In *Extended abstracts of the 2020 CHI conference on human factors in computing systems* (pp. 1–8).
Cowls J., Darius P., Golunova V., Mendis S., Prem E., Santistevan D., & Wang, W. W. (2020). *Freedom of expression in the digital public sphere – Strategies for bridging information and accountability gaps in algorithmic content moderation*. Zenodo. https://doi.org/10.5281/zenodo.4292408.
Díaz, Á. & Hecht-Felella, L. (2021) *Double standards in social media content moderation*. Brennan Center for Justice. https://www.skeyesmedia.org/documents/bo_filemanager/Double_Standards_Content_Moderation.pdf
Duarte, N., Llanso, E., & Loup, A. (2017). *Mixed Messages? The Limits of Automated Social Media Content Analysis*. Center for Democracy and Technology. https://bit.ly/3mdXFCB
ECHR. (2022). *Guide on article 10 of the European convention on human rights*. European Court of Human Rights, p. 101. https://www.echr.coe.int/Documents/Guide_Art_10_ENG.pdf
Fanta, A. (2017). *Putting Europe's robots on the map: Automated journalism in news agencies*. Reuters Institute for the Study of Journalism. https://reutersinstitute.politics.ox.ac.uk/sites/default/files/2017-09/Fanta%2C%20Putting%20Europe%E2%80%99s%20Robots%20on%20the%20Map.pdf
Guo, Z., Schlichtkrull, M., & Vlachos, A. (2022). A survey on automated fact-checking. *Transactions of the Association for Computational Linguistics, 10*, 178–206.
Haimson, O. L., Delmonaco, D., Nie, P., & Wegner, A. (2021). Disproportionate removals and differing content moderation experiences for conservative, transgender, and black social media users: Marginalization and moderation gray areas. *Proceedings of ACM Human Computer Interaction 5,* CSCW2, Article 466 (October 2021), 35 pages. https://doi.org/10.1145/3479610.
Kiesel, J., Mestre, M., Shukla, R., Vincent, E., Adineh, P., Corney, D., et al. (2019). Semeval-2019 task 4: Hyperpartisan news detection. In *Proceedings of the 13th international workshop on semantic evaluation* (pp. 829–839).
Kolhatkar, V., & Taboada, M. (2017). Using New York Times picks to identify constructive comments. *Proceedings of the 2017 EMNLP Workshop: Natural language processing meets journalism* (pp. 100–105). Copenhagen.
Kotsiantis, S. B., Zaharakis, I., & Pintelas, P. (2007). Supervised machine learning: A review of classification techniques. *Emerging Artificial Intelligence Applications in Computer Engineering, 160*(1), 3–24.
Li, Q., Peng, H., Li, J., Xia, C., Yang, R., Sun, L., Yu, P. S., & He, L. (2022). A survey on text classification: From traditional to deep learning. *ACM Transactions on Intelligent Systems and Technology (TIST), 13*(2), 1–41. https://doi.org/10.1145/3495162
Mundt, M., Hong, Y., Pliushch, I., & Ramesh, V. (2023). *A holistic view of continual learning with deep neural networks: Forgotten lessons and the bridge to active and open world learning*. Neural Networks.
Park, D., Sachar, S., Diakopoulos, N. & Elmqvist, N. (2016). Supporting comment moderators in identifying high quality online news comments. In *Proceedings of the 2016 CHI conference on human factors in computing systems* (pp. 1114–1125). ACM.
Persily, M., & Tucker, J. A. (2020). *Social media and democracy*. Cambridge University Press.
Petrak, J., & Krenn, B. (2022). Misogyny classification of German newspaper forum comments. *arXiv preprint arXiv:2211.17163*.
Prem, E. (2022). A brave new world of mediated online discourse. *Communications of the ACM, 65*(2), 40–42. https://cacm.acm.org/magazines/2022/2/258226-a-brave-new-world-of-mediated-online-discourse/fulltext
Reich, Z. (2011). User comments. The transformation of participatory space. In J. B. Singer, A. Hermida, D. Domingo, A. Heinonen, S. Paulussen, & T. Quandt (Eds.), *Participatory journalism. Guarding open gates at online newspapers* (pp. 96–117). Wiley-Blackwell.
Roberts, S. T. (2017). Content moderation. In L. Schintler & C. McNeely (Eds.), *Encyclopedia of big data*. Springer. https://doi.org/10.1007/978-3-319-32001-4_44-1

Schabus, D., & Skowron, M. (2018). Academic-industrial perspective on the development and deployment of a moderation system for a newspaper website. In *Proceedings of the eleventh international conference on language resources and evaluation (LREC 2018).*
Schabus, D., Skowron, M., & Trapp, M. (2017). One million posts: A data set of German online discussions. In *Proceedings of the 40th international ACM SIGIR conference on research and development in information retrieval* (pp. 1241–1244).
Singer, J. B. (2011). Taking responsibility. Legal and ethical issues in participatory journalism. In J. B. Singer, A. Hermida, D. Domingo, A. Heinonen, S. Paulussen, T. Son J. *The Korean Observer.* 2016. Will robot reporters replace humans? http://www.koreaobserver.com/will-robot-reporters-replace-humans-63057/ (aufgerufen 22.4.2020).
Suzor, N., West, S., Quodling, A., & York, J. (2019). What do we mean when we talk about transparency? Toward meaningful transparency in commercial content moderation. *International Journal of Communication, 13*, 18. https://ijoc.org/index.php/ijoc/article/view/9736
Tomiwa, I. (2020). Facebook's content moderation errors are costing Africa too much. *Slate*, October 27, 2020. https://slate.com/technology/2020/10/facebook-instagram-endsars-protests-nigeria.html
Vaccaro, K., Xiao, Z., Hamilton, K., & Karahalios, K. (2021). Contestability for content moderation. *Proceedings of the ACM Human-Computer Interaction 5*, CSCW2, Article 318 (October 2021), 28 pages. https://doi.org/10.1145/3476059.
Wallace, B. C. (2015). Computational irony: A survey and new perspectives. *Artificial Intelligence Review, 43*, 467–483. https://doi.org/10.1007/s10462-012-9392-5
Zhang, C., Zhang, C., Zheng, S., Qiao, Y., Li, C., Zhang, M., et al. (2023). A complete survey on generative AI (AIGC): Is ChatGPT from GPT-4 to GPT-5 all you need?. *arXiv preprint arXiv:2303.11717.*
Zhou, X., & Zafarani, R. (2020). A survey of fake news: Fundamental theories, detection methods, and opportunities. *ACM Computing Surveys (CSUR), 53*(5), 1–40.
Ziegele, M., & Jost, P. B. (2016). Not funny? The effects of factual versus sarcastic journalistic responses to uncivil user comments. *Communication Research.* Advance online publication, pp. 1–30.

Democracy in the Digital Era

George Metakides

Abstract Different studies on the state of democracy worldwide, each using different indices and related weights, all reach similar conclusions. Democracy is "backsliding" for the 16th year in a row. In this chapter, we take a very brief look at the history of democracy from fifth-century BC Athens to today as background to identifying the role and position of digital technologies and big tech platforms in particular among the main causes of its current decline. Possible actions to reverse this trend by empowering uses of digital technologies that entrance democratic practices while guarding against uses with negative impact via appropriate regulation are examined as well as the prevention of concentration of economic and political power.

1 Introduction

Studies by different organizations on the state of democracy worldwide, while using different methodologies, arrive at the conclusion that there has been a continuous quantitative and qualitative retreat of democratic practices, including participation in and integrity of elections, civil liberties, and the rule of law for the last 16 years.

Following its "invention" in fifth-century BC Athens, democracy floundered after the early years of the Roman empire and then went into a sort of deep hibernation for centuries to be reawakened in the wake of the industrial revolution of the eighteenth century and the Enlightenment. From the French revolution of 1789 to the implosion of the Soviet Union in 1989, democracy followed a tortuous path replete with reversals characterized by dragging reform in Britain, France's second empire, the compromise of the merchant class and the land-owners under Bismarck, non-ending civil war in Spain, and a prevalence of fascist regimes in Europe following World War I (WWI) and until World War II (WWII). After the end of WWII, a 45-year-long Cold War started between US and European (by now democratic) states and the

G. Metakides (✉)
Digital Enlightenment Forum, Athens, Greece
e-mail: george@metakides.net

H. Werthner et al. (eds.), *Introduction to Digital Humanism*,
https://doi.org/10.1007/978-3-031-45304-5_31

Soviet Union that ended in 1989. Following this, there was a euphoric belief in the 1990s that democracy was a sort of natural state that would be inevitably preserved and spread by capitalism and globalization.

This was complemented and reinforced during the same decade by the "blossoming" of the Internet and the World Wide Web, which promised to usher in a cultural renaissance that would reinvent and strengthen democracy.

Both of these hopes turned out to be utopic as democracy today is seen to be facing threats, some of which are in fact generated by the spread of digital technologies themselves.

While economic inequalities, globalization effects, immigration, and internal degeneration are the most cited causes for the worldwide retreat of democracy, digital technologies and the big tech platforms in particular are closely intertwined.

Big tech has amassed immense economic as well as political power. The former stems from its dominating corporate value and its "buy or bury" acquisition practices and the latter from its capability not only to lobby but also be used to influence and manipulate public opinion via "nudging," "herding," and "polarizing." Today, we are witnessing a dual increase of awareness, the first being that democracy is in danger and must be defended and the second that there is a need to carefully regulate the digital ecosystem. This does not surprise as in the history of humankind, technology always had potentially both "good" and "bad" users.

The actions envisaged concerning digital technology can be classified in two broad categories. The first consists of initiating and supporting uses that are beneficial to humans and to society. The second consists of reining in the power and role of big tech platforms via regulation.

The "empowering the good" category includes digital assemblies, deliberative democracy, and other related uses of digital technology to support and strengthen democratic processes.

The "guarding against the bad" category includes primarily regulation like the Digital Services Act (DSA), Digital Market Act (DMA), and the AI Act, which is now in preparation in the EU and antitrust lawsuits by the Department of Justice and the Federal Trade Commission in the USA (European commission DMA, European commission DSA, AI Act).

What needs to be done in addition to empowering the "good" and guarding against the "bad" in today's digital ecosystem is to continuously and collectively provide the forethought that enables the anticipation of what is coming and to ensure that the prioritization of future direction of research and development in transformational technologies like AI is not left in the hands of a few large companies.

- The general public and political decision-makers must be kept informed and made aware of what is at stake regarding the future of democracy.
- The role of education in achieving this must be explored and novel approaches developed and tested with a sense of urgency.
- As has been wisely noted, the biggest danger to democracy is to be lulled into believing that there is no danger.

2 Democracy in the Digital Era

During the last few years, study after study on the state of democracy worldwide concludes with words like "precipitous decline" and "backsliding" to describe what is measured as a quantitative and qualitative retreat of democratic practices (including elections, rule of law, and human rights) globally. Geographically, democracy appears to be restricted to (most of) Europe, the English-speaking world (thus including Australia and New Zealand), Japan, and then a small number of oases in an otherwise non-democratic geographical context. Over half of the world live under authoritarian regimes (Fig. 1).

What is a common feature emanating from the aforementioned studies is that people feel frustrated, alienated, disenfranchised, and disempowered to express themselves through the "normal" democratic processes. The young, in particular, share a deep mistrust of politics and politicians, which discourages them from

Fig. 1 The state of democracy as measured by the Economist Intelligence Unit (Visual Capitalist)

participating in the political processes that are accessible to them. This results in a rise in populism, extremism, APEPs (anti-political establishment parties), and a growing attraction to so-called "strong" leaders, where "strong" is often used as a euphemism for autocratic.

Statements that receive significant support in recent US, France, Germany, and Japan polls read like:

> In a democracy nothing gets done, we need perhaps less democracy and more effectiveness.

or . . . even worse:

> We need a strong leader who does not have to deal with parliaments and elections.

Different studies (e.g., by EIU, Freedom House, the European Parliament, the Cato Institute, and other organizations on both sides of the Atlantic) use different indices and related weights (e.g., integrity of elections, participation, civil liberties, and rule of law), and any particular one could be (and is) criticized as to the data and methodology used. But when they all reach basically the same conclusion, i.e., that democracy is backsliding for the 16th year in a row, it is time to heed the warning bells (EIU.com, 2022; Freedom House, 2022; Vásquez et al., 2021).

Democracy is in danger.

To address this danger, it is important to identify its underlying causes and, for the purposes of this paper, the particular role that digital technologies have played and could play in the creation of the problem as well as the quest for a solution.

To help us do this, a brief "parcourse," hopping across "rooftops," which constitute landmarks from the origins of democracy to the present, is in order. Without any intent to disrespect early manifestations of democratic processes in the Mesopotamian region, it is broadly accepted that democracy with codified procedures was "born" in fifth century BC in Athens. The direct participation in Athenian democracy was restricted to free, well-off men (as were all subsequent re-inventions of democracy well into the nineteenth century), and yet it was a revolutionary concept in its foundational belief that rule by the many and not by the few was inherently superior (Cartledge, 2018). It contained key elements of liberalism (to prevent it from becoming a tyranny of the majority) as emanates from (perhaps the best political speech ever written) the Epitaph of Pericles as written by Thucydides:

> We are a free democracy, but we obey our laws, more especially those which protect the weak and the unwritten laws whose transgression brings shame.

It is worth noting that the "unwritten laws" theme was echoed by Supreme Court Chief Justice Earl Warren in the 1960s, who said:

> In civilized life law floats in a sea of ethics.

This is why ancient Athens is often referred to as the "cradle" of democracy. The word "cradle," however, evokes the image of an infant who is then expected to grow, perhaps undergo some turbulence through adolescence, and then settle into adulthood. Alas, this was not meant to be. Already after the end of the Peloponnesian war,

Fig. 2 Declaration des droits de l'homme et du citoyen (Le Barbier)

Athenian democracy went into a backslide (to use today's often used term), from which it never recovered. There were brief manifestations of democracy through the Hellenistic and early Roman periods.

By the sixth-century AD early Byzantium, democracy, in any form, went into a deep hibernation for centuries, to show signs of waking up in seventeenth-century England after the 1688 revolution and then to truly re-invent itself as constitutional representative democracy during the eighteenth-century Enlightenment.

The Declaration of Human Rights after the 1789 French revolution provided a foundation for both the French constitution and the American constitution, the two first "modern" democracies. This was no accident as a key founder of the American constitution, Thomas Jefferson (Britannica, 2022), was actually a coauthor of the French Declaration of Human Rights (Fig. 2).

The first article of this declaration starts with:

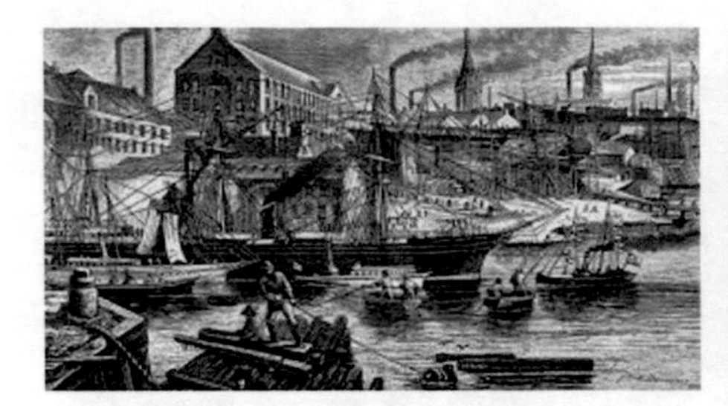

Fig. 3 Industrial Revolution and Enlightenment (Dutertre, Doerstling)

> Men are born and remain free and equal in rights.
> (Les hommes naissent et demeurent libres et égaux en droits)

(For the entire text in French and in English translation, see Constitutional Council.)

This new form of democracy was "representative" and not "direct" as in ancient Athens and contained key elements of liberalism, protection of human rights, and the rule of law. Most importantly, it adhered to the principle of the "Separation of Power" as articulated by Montesquieu:

> Power should be divided among three separate branches of government (legislative, executive, judiciary) to prevent one person or faction from becoming tyrannical (OLL).

It should be noted here that eighteenth-century Enlightenment, and the re-invention of democracy that it brought to the world, came in the wake of the Industrial Revolution, as explained in O'Hara (2010). This was not the first time that new technologies bred not only economic but also sociopolitical changes, and it was not meant to be—as we shall see—the last (Fig. 3).

The newly re-invented democracy however, which survives in various forms to this day, was not destined to take the world by storm.

If we look at the period between 1789 and 1989 in Europe, the leitmotif during these two centuries is the slow, nonlinear quest for consensus on what should replace the "Ancient Regime" in Europe. Dragging reforms in Britain, France's second empire, the compromise of the merchant class and the land-owning aristocrats under Bismark in Germany, and non-ending civil war in Spain are characteristic of the period. Then came the bloody World War I, following which "fascistoid" regimes prevailed in Europe in the 1930s with Nazism emerging as one of the most abhorrent manifestations thereof.

The perception of the USA as well as Britain as "beacons of democracy" during the 1930s—in spite of their many shortcomings—is not without some justification.

It took a second world war for the nation-states that had emerged after the dissolution of the empires in Europe to start adopting the various forms of the kind of liberal, representative democracy that we have today. The end of World War II also marked the beginning of a 45-year-long "Cold War" between the "West" or the "Free World" and the Soviet Union, officially "Union of Soviet, Socialist Republics," or USSR. While the words *democracy* and *republic* are not synonyms, strictly speaking, as a democracy could have a (hereditary) monarch (e.g., Belgium) rather than an elected president (e.g., France), in practice, today's purported "democracies," as assessed by the various studies referred to earlier, include all "democratic republics." The USSR however was not a democratic republic but rather a political system, which according to East Germany's Walter Ulbricht "must look like a democracy but with everything under our control." Similarly, not all of today's republics (in name) are democratic.

During the Cold War, both sides engaged and invested in propaganda, including misinformation and argumentation aimed to "sell" their system as the preferred one to other countries and regions. This was complemented by fostering internal insurgencies as well as direct military interventions for the same purposes. The Cold War came to an end in 1989 as the Soviet Union imploded and collapsed. So after 45 years of Cold War, Western-type liberal representative democracy was no longer considered under threat, and it started being taken for granted. The theory was put forward that liberal democracy was a "natural state" to be nurtured, preserved, and spread by capitalism and globalization. This created a sense of euphoria as reflected by Fukuyama's (in)famous characterization of that point in time as "the end of history" in his book with this phrase in its title, published in 1992 (Fukuyama, 1992). This theory, like most political and economic theories, suffered the only fate that, for a political theory, is worse than death; it was put into practice!

Concurrently, the World Wide Web was born and began to blossom, further strengthening the euphoria of the 1990s as it appeared to pave the way for a digital golden age of democracy, a cultural renaissance that would reinvent democracy as a digital Athenian agora where goods as well as ideas would be freely exchanged. This in turn, it was believed, with substantial preliminary evidence (e.g., the Arab Spring early hopes) would empower more direct and informed citizen participation in an open democratic society.

Alas, this vision of milk, honey, and digital democratic bliss turned out to be a utopia. The undeniable positive effects of the Web came in tandem with an increasing number of negative ones.

As democracy started backsliding, so started the growth of skepticism about the Web, leading eventually Tim Berners Lee to call for "global action to save the Web from political manipulation, fake news, privacy manipulation and other malign forces that threaten to plunge the world into a digital dystopia." In fact, as we shall try to trace in the rest of this paper, democracy and digital technology have been living "parallel lives" from the 1990s to today. The euphoria of the 1990s after the collapse of the Soviet Union caused a weakening of the defense and promotion of democracy via what Timothy Snyder of Yale called a "unilateral moral disarmament" (Snyder, 2017).

We argue that it was a very similar sense of euphoria that prevented the anticipation of some of the negative impacts of developments in digital technologies and the emergence of big tech in particular with their gigantic-scale monetization of personal data and the potential to be used to disrupt and corrupt democratic processes.

Before proceeding further, let us see what conclusions we can draw from our brief historical parcourse, which can help us the rest of the way.

Democracies have had a remarkably short life both in concept and in practice since the fifth century BC and have always been vulnerable as, by their open nature, they contain and nurture the seeds of their own degeneration. This openness can be and has been exploited by demagogues from Julius Caesar to Mussolini and to Trump. Misinformation and people manipulation may not be new. A great eighteenth-century Enlightenment personality, Jonathan Swift, had written "falsehood flies, and the truth comes limping after it; so, when men come to be undeceived, it is too late; the jest is over, and the tale has had its effect." They are, however, exacerbated and reach new levels when empowered by digital technologies and AI in particular and become much harder to identify, let alone contain. What is new is a resilient false sense of security and an underestimation of the lurking dangers in what regards the evolution of democracy as it interacts with the evolution of the digital ecosystem.

As in the rest of this chapter, we will concentrate on trying to identify the threats to democracy emanating from developments in the digital ecosystem; it is important to point out, clearly and in advance, that these are certainly not the only and perhaps not even the greater threats.

Most analyses of the continuing backsliding of democracy identify as major causes and continuing threats the following:

- Rising economic inequalities especially after the 2008 crisis, which are compounded by related globalization effects
- Immigration, especially after the 2015 crisis and its subsequent and continued exploitation by demagogues
- Internal degeneration of democratic processes such as the exploitation of constitutional defects (e.g., gerrymandering and the politicization of the Supreme Court in the USA, "de-liberalization" of democracy in Hungary, and corruption almost everywhere)

These threats are intertwined with and reinforced by the ones emanating from the evolution of the digital ecosystem. It should also be added here that democracies, even during their rather short existence, have never been static but frequently readjusted themselves to socioeconomic but also technological change from the first industrial revolution to the current digital one. To take the first two modern democracies as examples, France is now in its "Fifth Republic" and the US constitution has been amended 27 times. The first ten of these amendments constitute the "Bill of Rights," offering protection of personal liberty and curtailing government power (National Archives, 2021).

Today, we are witnessing a double "correction" (of both democracy and the digital landscape) being attempted. Democracies have started on the one hand, to react to the new threats emanating from the evolution of digital technologies and, on the other, to find innovative ways of harnessing the very same technologies for "good," so as to strengthen and enrich themselves by greater citizen participation. Simply put, this constitutes a "guard against the bad, empower the good" approach.

Let us start by looking at the second, innovative beneficial uses of digital technologies.

3 Empowering the Good

As the polls and studies referred to earlier demonstrate, there is a growing disillusionment among young people (and not only) with the democratic processes. The prevailing feeling is that they are called every 4 years or so to vote and are then forgotten until the next election while laws that affect them are passed, including obscure(d) amendments, without their having any say.

"Decisions are made about us without us" is one of the slogans that best captures their malaise. This feeling of alienation is aggravated by the fact that their elected "representatives" have split loyalties, where loyalty to voters comes second to party or donor loyalties.

To address and remedy this alienation and lack of trust, the innovative concept of "citizen assemblies" was developed and applied—in a yet rather limited scale—successfully as a complement to the established democratic processes of elections and referendums.

It is worth noting that a very similar concept was used in fifth-century BC Athens. Having arrived at the cynical but realistic conclusion that professional politicians could "be bought," Athenians introduced a system whereby a group of citizens was chosen by lot to assemble and debate a topic so that they could then formulate a related proposal, which was subsequently voted up or down by the "ekklesia of the demos," where all citizens participated.

A modern version of this process was used successfully in Ireland in 2018 prior to the referendum that had been called on whether or not abortions should be allowed (Citizens Assembly, 2016).

Before the referendum, a citizens' assembly was formed consisting of 99 members, 33 of which were appointed by the political parties and 66 randomly chosen citizens while assuring age, gender, education, and socioeconomic status balance. They assembled, were provided with information about the issue by supporters of all sides, discussed among themselves, and then made their recommendation, which was in favor of allowing legal abortion. This recommendation was made public, and the referendum which followed endorsed it, which constituted a historical outcome for Ireland.

This concept of a citizens' assembly as a deliberative body of citizens selected "randomly" has also been used successfully in the adoption of a new constitution in Iceland and elsewhere (the interested reader can find more about citizen assemblies and the concepts of sortition and deliberative democracy at Helbing, D. (2019), Wikipedia, "Citizens' assembly" and "Sortition" (March 2023)). All of these, and other such innovative approaches, could eventually help "empower the good" by harnessing digital power, to entrance their effectiveness and help spread their use worldwide.

The pandemic offers a particularly interesting case study of the use of digital technologies for "empowering the good." There is a range of such case studies from virtual Town Hall meetings to the Taiwan Digital Democracy experiment, which, using the slogan "Fast, fair and fun," provides a successful mix of direct and representative democracy empowered by digital technologies (National Development Council, 2020, How to Citizen, 2021).

A pivotal role in all these ongoing efforts to harness as much of the power of digital in support of democracy will be played, undoubtedly, by using this power in education. As the scope of this chapter does not allow for addressing this key digital humanism issue or even for surveying the existing studies on this subject, suffice it for now to quote Nelson Mandela:

> An educated, enlightened and informed population is one of the surest ways of promoting the health of democracy.

Returning to the leitmotif of the parallel lives of democracy and digital, we believe that we are actually witnessing an attempt to effect a double "correction."

An attempted correction of the perceived decline of democracy via increased awareness of the dangers involved resulting in efforts such as the digital assemblies and digital deliberation and at the same time an attempted correction of the role and impact of big tech via new regulatory policies and approaches aimed to "guard against the bad."

4 Guarding Against the Bad

Interestingly enough, the correction we are witnessing includes post-pandemic tremors in the digital landscape.

There are tremors in GAFAM (Google, Amazon, Facebook, Apple, Microsoft) business models, which may or may not prove ephemeral as their digital advertisement model comes under closer scrutiny by regulators and the crypto world convulsions following the collapse of FTX cryptocurrency company have shaken confidence in it.

It is in this context that the new regulatory initiatives on both sides of the Atlantic are coming to guard against the negative impact of digital technologies on democracy by regulation, which reshapes the rules of the game in the digital ecosystem.

There are two major regulatory policies that have been adopted in the EU, the Digital Markets Act (DMA) and the Digital Services Act (DSA). The AI Act, which aims to provide protection from the potential harm by AI applications, is currently in the last stages of deliberation, which precedes adoption and which tries to take into account recent advances in generative AI (European commission DMA; European commission DSA; AI Act).

The DMA, which becomes applicable in May 2023, targets the GAFAM companies and comes to enhance the prior ex post anti-trust approach with ex ante checks, which have a more realistic chance of preventing the concentration of enormous economic as well as political power by big tech (or GAFAM plus if you prefer). Their political power, besides lobbying, stems from the novel capabilities to nudge, herd, condition, and polarize public opinion as has been amply documented by now. The DSA establishes a transparency and accountability framework so as to protect consumers and their fundamental rights online.

These capabilities have been and are being used by both internal and external perpetrators of threats to democracy.

In the past, EU regulatory legislation, e.g., General Data Protection Regulation (GDPR), was subsequently adopted by most countries in the world leveraging the so-called Brussels effect (Bradford, 2020; Intersoft Consulting, 2016). The USA maintained a skeptical position toward regulation until now, arguing that regulation potentially stifles innovation. The US position has been slowly but steadily shifting on this as evidenced by recent anti-trust lawsuits by the Federal Trade Commission (FTC) and the Department of Justice (DoJ) against members of GAFAM.

This does not mean that the EU and US approaches to regulation are anywhere near convergence yet, but there is now the political will to seek common ground so as to avoid the risk of a balkanization of the regulation of the digital ecosystem. The EU-US Trade and Technology Council (TTC) has been set up for this purpose: "to strengthen global co-operation on technology, digital issues and supply chains and to facilitate regulatory policy and enforcement cooperation and, when possible, convergence."

It is worth making the historical note that the origins of anti-trust policy in the USA had not only economic but also democratic motivations (Robertson, 2022). The cornerstone of this policy, the Sherman Act of 1890, which eventually led to the breakup of Standard Oil and ATT, had as its goal "the prevention of the extension of economic power to political power."

The words used by Senator John Sherman himself at the time illustrate this clearly:

> If we would not submit to an emperor, we should not submit to an autocrat of trade.

It is left to the reader to identify, among the present fauna of the digital ecosystem, such "autocrats of trade," which, if left unregulated, will accelerate the accumulation of power with artificial intelligence advancing as its driving force. Such a centralization and concentration of economic and political power would constitute a clear threat to democracy and our humanistic values.

Policies aimed at addressing these threats need all our support in order to succeed.

This chapter provides an introduction to the other two in the section as well as to G. Parker's chapter on platforms. One, by G. Zarkadakis, looks at digital technology practices that "empower the good" by facilitating citizen deliberation at scale, and the other, by A. Stranger, explores whether and how cryptocurrencies and decentralized finance could be "guided" so as to be beneficial rather than detrimental to democracy.

5 Conclusions

Democracies have had a rather short life compared with autocracies and have always been vulnerable.

Their very openness allows for the nurturing of seeds of their degeneration.

Today, democracy is in decline worldwide, both quantitatively and qualitatively.

Digital technologies carry the potential for being used to the benefit or to the detriment of democracy.

Action is needed to encourage and empower the beneficial uses but also to guard against the detrimental ones.

Beneficial uses include building on experiences such as with digital assemblies and deliberative democracy approaches.

Detrimental uses include those that result in the concentration of immense economic and political power in the hands of a few companies that control the "public sphere."

Anticipatory, dynamic regulation is key to guarding against the detrimental uses.

The biggest threat to democracy is for people to believe that there is no threat.

Discussion Questions for Students and Their Teachers

1. How did democracy evolve from ancient Athens to today?
2. What are the major threats to democracy today?
3. What are some digital technology uses that are beneficial to democracy?
4. Why do current big tech platforms pose potential threats to democracy?
5. What sort of regulation is or can be provided to counter these threats?

Learning Resources for Students

Reading these books helped me greatly to understand much of what I tried to present in this chapter. Some (e.g., Cortledge and Runciman) are primarily historical, while others (e.g., Applebaum, Rachmann, Teachout) analyze how democracy should not be taken for granted and what actions can be taken to protect and sustain it.

1. Allison, G. (2017) *Destined for war: Can America and China escape Thucydides's trap?*, Mariner Books.

   A concise survey of current geopolitics whose developments may well affect global democracy profoundly
2. Applebaum, A. (2020) *Twilight of democracy: The seductive lure of authoritarianism*, Doubleday.

   This book provides concrete evidence of how and why the threat of authoritarianism is rising globally.
3. Bartlett, J. (2018) *The people vs tech: How the internet is killing democracy (and how we save it)*, Ebury Press.

   Bartlett identifies the key pillars of liberal democracy and describes how each pillar could be threatened by technology and what could be done about it.
4. Berman, S. (2019) *Democracy and dictatorship in Europe: From the ancient régime to the present day*, Oxford, Oxford University Press.

This book provides a historical perspective on how and why democracies as well as dictatorships prevailed at different times in Europe since the development of nation-states.

5. Cartledge, P. (2018) *Democracy: a life citation*, United Kingdom, Oxford University Press.

   The author provides an authoritative "biography" of democracy from its birth to its eclipse and eventual rebirth.
6. Pappas, T. (2019) *Populism and liberal democracy: A comparative and theoretical analysis*, Oxford, Oxford University Press.

   This book looks at concrete cases of populism in various parts of the world as a basis of developing a comprehensive definition of populism.
7. Rachman, G. (2022) *The age of the strongman: How the cult of the leader threatens democracy around the World*, Bodley Head.

   This is a most timely work examining the global rise of authoritarian, nationalist/populist leaders, and its corrosive impact on democracy.
8. Runciman, D. (2015) *The confidence trap: A history of democracy in crisis from World War I to the present*, Princeton University Press.

   Runciman provides a lucid history of modern democracy from World War I onward, stressing how dangerous it is to believe that democracies can survive any crisis.
9. Teachout, Z. (2020) *Break 'em up*, St Martin's Publishing Group.

   The author makes an impassioned plea for breaking up big tech and prides documentation of how the prevailing strong antitrust movement waned after the 1980s and why it should be revived urgently.

References

AI Act. (2023). *A step closer to the first rules on Artificial Intelligence* [Online]. Accessed June 1, 2023, from https://www.europarl.europa.eu/news/en/press-room/20230505IPR84904/ai-act-a-step-closer-to-the-first-rules-on-artificial-intelligence

Bradford, A. (2020). *The Brussels effect: How the European Union rules the world.* Oxford University Press.

Britannica, The Editors of Encyclopaedia. (2022). *Declaration of the rights of man and of the citizen* [Online]. Accessed: 21 March 2023, from https://www.britannica.com/topic/Declaration-of-the-Rights-of-Man-and-of-the-Citizen

Citizens Assembly. (2016). *The eighth amendment of the constitution* [Online]. Accessed March 21, 2023, from https://2016-2018.citizensassembly.ie/en/The-Eighth-Amendment-of-the-Constitution/

Constitutional Council, *Déclaration des Droits de l'Homme et du Citoyen de 1789* [Online]. Accessed June 1, 2023, from https://www.conseil-constitutionnel.fr/le-bloc-de-constitutionnalite/declaration-des-droits-de-l-homme-et-du-citoyen-de-1789

Doerstling, E. (1859–1940). *Kant and friends at table* [Online]. Accessed June 20, 2023, from https://commons.wikimedia.org/wiki/File:Kant_doerstling2.jpg?uselang=en#Ceadachadh

Dutertre V. (1880). *Shipyards and shipping on the Clyde* [Online]. Accessed June 20, 2023, from https://www.sciencephoto.com/media/988577/view

EIU.com (2022). *Economist intelligence unit - The state of democracy* [Online]. Accessed March 21, 2023, from https://www.eiu.com/n/campaigns/democracy-index-2022/?utm_source=google&utm_medium=paid-search&utm_campaign=democracy-index-2022&gclid=Cj0KCQjwlPWgBhDHARIsAH2xdNd_6tfB4BrQVxWhLiGPCK8coVgY_YZ4QIU34lwXHLzqyXSSFNYHQiEaAjJcEALw_wcB

European Commission DMA, *Digital market act* [Online]. Accessed June 1, 2023, from https://ec.europa.eu/commission/presscorner/detail/en/ip_22_6423

European Commission DSA, *Digital services act* [Online]. Accessed June 1, 2023, from https://digital-strategy.ec.europa.eu/en/policies/digital-services-act-package

Freedom House. (2022). *Freedom in the world* [Online]. Accessed March 21, 2023, from https://freedomhouse.org/sites/default/files/2022-02/FIW_2022_PDF_Booklet_Digital_Final_Web.pdf

Fukuyama, F. (1992). *The end of history and the last man*. Free Press.

Helbing, D. (2019). *Towards digital enlightenment: Essays on the dark and light sides of the digital revolution* (1st ed.). Springer International Publishing AG.

How to Citizen, Baratunde. (2021). *Fast, fair, fun with digital minister Audrey tang* [Online]. Accessed March 21, 2023, from https://www.howtocitizen.com/episodes/fast-fair-fun-with-digital-minister-audrey-tang

Intersoft Consulting. (2016). *GDPR: General data protection regulation,* [Online]. Accessed June 1, 2023, from https://gdpr-info.eu/

Le Barbier, J. J. F. (1789). *Déclaration des droits de l'homme et du citoyen* [Online]. Accessed June 20, 2023, from https://commons.wikimedia.org/wiki/File:Declaration_of_the_Rights_of_Man_and_of_the_Citizen_in_1789.jpg

National Archives. (October 2021). *The bill of rights: How did it happen?* [Online]. Accessed March 21, 2023, from https://www.archives.gov/founding-docs/bill-of-rights/how-did-it-happen

National Development Council. (July 2020). *Digital government program 2.0 of Taiwan (2021–2025)* [Online]. Accessed March 21, 2023, from https://ws.ndc.gov.tw/Download.ashx?u=LzAwMS9hZG1pbmlzdHJhdG9yLzExL3JlbGZpbGUvMC8yMDYwLzVkYTI0OWMzLTVkYzYtNGI0Mi1iMTdiLWEyMWNkNmM0NWM0Zi5wZGY%3D&n=RGlnaXRhbCBHb3Zlcm5tZW50IFByb2dyYW0gMl8wIG9mIFRhaXdhbiAoMjAyMS0yMDI1KS5wZGY%3D&icon=.pdf

O'Hara, K. (2010). *The enlightenment: A beginner's guide (beginner's guides)* (1st ed.). Oneworld Publications.

OLL - Online Library of Liberty, *Political thought: Montesquieu and the separation of powers* [Online]. Accessed March 21, 2023, from https://oll.libertyfund.org/page/montesquieu-and-the-separation-of-powers

Robertson, V. H. S. E. (2022). Antitrust, big tech, and democracy: A research agenda. *The Antitrust Bulletin, 67*(2), 259–279. https://doi.org/10.1177/0003603X221082749

Snyder, T. (2017). *On tyranny: Twenty lessons from the twentieth century* (1st ed.). Crown.

TTC - *Trade and technology council inaugural joint statement* [Online]. Accessed March 21, 2023, from https://ec.europa.eu/commission/presscorner/detail/en/statement_21_4951

Vásquez, I., McMahon, F., et al. (2021). *The human freedom index 2021, A global measurement of personal, civil, and economic freedom, USA*. Cato Institute and the Fraser Institute.

Visual Capitalist. *The state of democracy around the world* [Online]. Accessed March 21, 2023, from https://www.visualcapitalist.com/mapped-the-state-of-global-democracy-2022/

Wikipedia, the free encyclopedia (March 2023a). *Citizens' assembly* [Online]. Accessed March 21, 2023, from https://en.wikipedia.org/wiki/Citizens%27_assembly

Wikipedia, the free encyclopedia (March 2023b) *Sortition* [Online]. Accessed March 21, 2023, from https://en.wikipedia.org/wiki/Sortition#:~:text=In%20ancient%20Athenian%20democracy%2C%20sortition,a%20principal%20characteristic%20of%20democracy

Are Cryptocurrencies and Decentralized Finance Democratic?

Allison Stanger

Abstract This chapter defines the building blocks of Web3 to explore its implications for sustainable democracy. It explains the crash of the Terra ecosystem and compares it with the implosion of FTX, both to underscore the dark side of networks built on blockchain technology and to illuminate how all cryptocurrencies (crypto), as well as all investors, are not created equal. The chapter weighs the costs and benefits of crypto and decentralized finance (DeFi) at the present moment and explores emergent regulation. It argues that cryptocurrencies and DeFi will only serve democracy if governments and international organizations establish the right incentive structure for innovators and safeguards for investors in this space.

1 Introduction

The sensational release in late 2022 of ChatGPT and its subsequent iteration GPT-4 shifted the world's attention from Web3 to generative AI. Yet the new tools made possible by generative pretrained transformers will be developed in a world of Web3 possibilities. If technology is to serve humanity rather than privileged plutocrats, a basic understanding of the promise of Web3 innovations is imperative. The challenges stem from the technological complexity of recent developments, Digital Humanism values the rights and lived experiences of all human beings, not just the technologically proficient. The future of democracy and freedom in the years ahead depends on a digitally competent public.

This chapter starts by considering the worldview of the sovereign individual, one that sheds considerable light on one instantiation of Web3 development. It then explores the reasons for the crash of the crypto market in May 2022, considering the regulatory reaction to those developments for the future of blockchain technologies and related decentralized applications (dApps). The penultimate section considers the ownership ecosystem for Bitcoin, the sole cryptocurrency that has yet to be

A. Stanger (✉)
Middlebury College, Middlebury, VT, USA
e-mail: Stanger@middlebury.edu

H. Werthner et al. (eds.), *Introduction to Digital Humanism*,
https://doi.org/10.1007/978-3-031-45304-5_32

hacked on-chain. The chapter concludes with an assessment of the democracy-enhancing features of Web3, which stand in opposition to the autocratic aspects that crypto and DeFi have highlighted to date.

2 The Sovereign Individual

> AI could theoretically make it possible to centrally control an entire economy. It is no coincidence that AI is the favorite technology of the Communist Party of China. Strong cryptography, at the other pole, holds out the prospect of a decentralized and individualized world. If AI is communist, crypto is libertarian.
> —Peter Thiel

Preface to *The Sovereign Individual*, January 2020

Is Peter Thiel right? Are crypto and other blockchain technologies a boon to the free world? The simple answer to this question is both yes and no—yes in that encryption is a comparative advantage for free societies and it allows for innovation that is decentralized, at least in theory, and no in that what has transpired to date has been anything but focused on human flourishing. The claim that decentralized finance will serve ordinary humans by cutting out the middleman, thereby bolstering democratic values, has not yet panned out in practice.

To be fair, Peter Thiel might even agree with my short answer. He concludes his preface to the latest edition of *The Sovereign Individual* by predicting an outcome somewhere between centralized control and decentralized effervescence:

> The future may lie somewhere between these two extreme poles. But we know the actions we take today will determine the overall outcome. Reading *The Sovereign Individual* in 2020 is a way to think carefully about the future that your own actions will help to create. It is an opportunity not to be wasted. (Thiel, p. 9)

I chose to open this chapter with claims delineated in *The Sovereign Individual*, because they provide a window on the minds of both Elon Musk and Peter Thiel. If you want to understand why they are obsessed with New Zealand, crypto, and space travel, this is a good place to start.

Who is the sovereign individual of the information age?

> The new Sovereign Individual will operate like the gods of myth in the same physical environment as the ordinary, subject citizen, but in a separate realm politically ... the Sovereign Individual will redesign governments and reconfigure economies in the new millennium. The full implications of this change are all but unimaginable. (Thiel, p. 20)

As the pandemic and the move to remote work made clear, most wealth can be earned and spent anywhere. Investors move money with a key stroke across national boundaries. Remote workers and remote-first organizations without headquarters challenge existing taxation regimes. According to *The Sovereign Individual*, this means that “governments that attempt to charge too much as the price of domicile will merely drive away their best customers” (Thiel, p. 21). The nation-state, as a nexus of power, will be eclipsed by sovereign individuals. With this worldview, space is the place where you can create your own rules and personalized tax shelters. The most likely beneficiaries of an increasingly complex adaptive global system will not be the nation-state, or the EU, but sovereign individuals. They will hold the keys to power and governance.

Donald Trump is a sovereign individual, as is his booster, Peter Thiel, but so are Jeff Bezos and Mark Zuckerberg.

Viewed from the vantage point, cyberspace is the ultimate offshore jurisdiction, making the market for crypto a virtual reality, detached from geographical space. Transactions take place, but in what country should they be regulated? Who has jurisdiction? This is the brave new world of Web3, which will present unique new challenges for governance.

Web3 can mean different things to different people. When I use the term, I refer to the network of decentralized databases and the connections between them (blockchains). Web1 was a read/write only world, that of the worldwide web and blogs. Web2 is the interactive version of the Internet we know today. It is the world of social media, of search, and of e-commerce. Web2 is the world of big tech and central authority, a world in which top-down censorship is possible. Indeed, the ultimate manifestation of this reality was the de-platforming of a freely elected US president by the major technology platforms after MAGA (Make America Great Again) extremists stormed the US Capitol in January 2021.

In contrast, in the ideal-type Web3 world, each of us becomes a sovereign individual, cutting out banks and all middlemen, answering only to ourselves and to our own unique needs and preferences. Technology allegedly makes possible a variant of decentralized authority that does not require trust to provide order. Or at least that is the claim.

3 Welcome to the Web3 World

For Mark Zuckerberg, in contrast, Web3 is the metaverse, the virtual 3D planet that blockchain technologies and scientific breakthroughs in both artificial intelligence and chip design will make possible.

Whether metaverse or sovereign individual, decentralized finance is the engine of opportunity for the Web3 ecosystem. Decentralized finance, also known as DeFi, uses cryptocurrency and blockchain technology to manage financial transactions. It aims to democratize finance, at least in theory, by replacing legacy, centralized institutions, such as banks, with peer-to-peer relationships. With DeFi, in theory, I can conduct all my financial transactions, from everyday banking, loans, and mortgages to complicated contractual relationships and asset trading without the assistance of banks or brokerages.[1] In practice, I still need a bank as an intermediary to cash out or buy crypto, even with a self-custody wallet.

[1] What Is DeFi? Understanding Decentralized Finance – Forbes Advisor.

What is a blockchain? A blockchain is a shared digital database or ledger that makes Web3 possible. It stores transactions in immutable, chronological sequences of cryptographically linked blocks secured by consensus mechanisms, such as proof of work (Bitcoin and Ethereum in its first incarnation) or proof of stake (most other cryptocurrencies). Blockchains can ensure data integrity and trust in a peer-to-peer network without central authority because of their radical transparency. One can literally read the blockchain to follow the money when transactions take place between self-custody wallets.

Cryptocurrencies are made possible by blockchains. All cryptocurrencies are digital phenomena. Transactions in a particular cryptocurrency are verified and records maintained by a decentralized system using cryptography. Any sovereign individual can set up their own cryptocurrency. The key question is whether a particular cryptocurrency ecosystem has valuable applications associated with it that can be monetized or whether it is a store of value for the long run, like gold.

Bitcoin is the first decentralized cryptocurrency, introduced in 2009 by Satoshi Nakamoto, a pseudonym for either an individual or a group whose identity remains secret to this day. It operates on a peer-to-peer network and relies on a proof of work consensus mechanism to keep the blockchain secure and transparent, so that users can add new transactions to it. The proof-of-work consensus algorithm uses complex problems for miners to solve using high-powered computers. The problems are solved using trial and error. The first miner to complete the puzzle or cryptographic equation gets the authority to add new blocks to the blockchain for transactions. When the block is authenticated by a miner, the digital currency is then added to the blockchain. The miner also receives compensation with coins. Proof of work is energy-intensive but the least hackable. While numerous crypto exchanges trading Bitcoin have been hacked, there has never been a Bitcoin blockchain hack.[2]

Bitcoin is distinctive due to its pioneering status but also because of its limited and fixed supply of 21 million coins. Since new Bitcoin cannot be created after those 21 million coins have been mined, it has a unique potential as a digital store of value, referred to by some as digital gold. With Bitcoin and a self-custody wallet, you have assets that *no one* can seize, since your valuables reside in cyberspace, not physical space (unless someone successfully tortures you to reveal your unique key.)

All other cryptocurrencies, often referred to as altcoins, are digital currencies created after Bitcoin. While Bitcoin focused on being a digital store of value and a means of payment, in contrast, altcoins are designed to enable a wide range of applications, such as smart contracts, decentralized finance, privacy solutions, and non-fungible tokens (NFTs). The most popular of these is Ethereum.

Ethereum first used proof of work, like Bitcoin, to keep its blockchain secure. It has recently successfully made a glitch-free transition to proof of stake, which amounts to an engineering triumph on a massive scale. As a result of this merger, Ethereum is more sustainable, energy-wise, and more versatile in terms of its potential applications, but less secure, relatively speaking. Other cryptocurrencies

[2] https://www.coinbureau.com/analysis/biggest-bitcoin-hacks/

based on proof of work have been hacked, although this does not necessarily mean Ethereum is destined to be hacked. It depends on the ingenuity of the cryptographic mechanism.

Why does this distinction between proof of work and proof of stake matter for the world of decentralized finance?

Put simply, it is difficult to build dApps on top of the Bitcoin blockchain.[3] You can build them more easily on Ethereum and on many other cryptocurrency blockchains. What sort of dApps might be built is up to the human imagination.

As a result, the best way to think about Web3 is that it is a new technology that is just at the beginning of its development curve. Where it will go is anybody's guess, but the money will be made by what people build on top of the blockchain, just as the money for Web2 was made through the social media platforms built upon it.

4 Why Did the Crypto Market Tank in May 2022?

As we have seen, blockchains and their related products are genuine technological innovations in search of a killer application. So why do so many smart people think crypto is a Ponzi scheme?

The simple answer is that for ordinary investors, most of the crypto ecosystem *is* a Ponzi scheme, albeit a technologically sophisticated one.

To illustrate this simple fact in the most objective way possible (there is a lot of fake news in the crypto world), let's take the case of Terraform Labs, whose meltdown in May 2022 catalyzed the collapse of the crypto market culminating in the spectacular flameout of FTX and Alameda Research and the arrest of the principals in those two ventures. It's a great case to illustrate who bears the risk of tech failure in the Wild West, free market world of decentralized finance as initially conceived.

What was Terraform Labs attempting to do?

The South Korean entrepreneur Do Kwon co-founded Terraform Labs in 2018. Terraform Labs is the company that created the Terra blockchain, which aimed to provide a more efficient and user-friendly financial infrastructure through the deployment of algorithmic stable coins. Its signature cryptocurrency was called Luna. Unaware of the potential for irony, fans and supporters of Luna called themselves lunatics.

The value of all fiat money government-issued currency—typically, that is not backed by a physical commodity like gold or silver—is and always has been a function of the degree of trust humans have in it as a store of value. Even the US dollar today is fiat money, as it is no longer backed by gold. In other words, the dollar today does not have intrinsic value, as does a gold or a silver coin. The US dollar is a

[3]For a noteworthy exception, see Bitcoin Ordinals (https://www.forbes.com/sites/digital-assets/2023/05/24/bitcoin-ordinals-are-the-next-big-thing-in-crypto/?sh=132702c873b0).

favored store of value only because people trust it to remain valuable for the foreseeable future.

The interesting question Do Kwon asked was, "How can I create a cryptocurrency where technological innovation builds trust and hence value?"

Do Kwon's innovation was the introduction of programmable money, which enabled a suite of stable coins pegged to various traditional fiat currencies, such as the US dollar and the South Korean Won. The Luna-based stable coin (TerraUSD) was pegged to the US dollar. TerraUSD was stable because it would always be worth 1 dollar. But it couldn't be traded in for USD, like other stable coins, such as Tether. Instead, it derived its stability from algorithms within the Luna ecosystem that kept it stable—that was Do Kwon's innovation. Faith in Do Kwon's algorithms was to replace faith in the USD.

Do Kwon thought that such a creation would be attractive to investors, especially since investors often use stable coins to buy and sell riskier assets.

He was right. He hired the best and the brightest to pursue his vision. Riding high in early 2022, he inked a $40 million deal with Major League Baseball's DC-based team, the Washington Nationals.[4] He mocked a British economist who criticized TerraUSD's design by saying that he doesn't "debate with poor people."[5]

In April 2022, Luna's price rose to a peak of $116 from less than $1 in early 2021, minting a new generation of crypto millionaires. LUNA, TerraUSD (UST) and other tokens in the Terra ecosystem had a total market cap of more than $60 billion.[6] Do Kwon's daughter was born in April, and he named her, fatefully, Luna.[7] Everything was breaking Do Kwon's way.

And then a combination of economic factors caused Luna's value to plummet, and Do Kwon's algorithms, much to his own apparent surprise, failed to keep TerraUSD at $1 as promised. A death spiral for the entire Terra ecosystem then set in, as Luna plummeted to near zero, with TerraUSD becoming wildly untethered from the USD for all the world to see. TerraUSD had previously become unpegged in May 2021, but it had recovered its value in a matter of several days. At the time, Do Kwon cited this recovery as a signal of the robustness of his algorithmic concept. In May 2022, however, TerraUSD did not recover. All the decentralized applications that developers had built within that ecosystem suddenly had no value either.

All the action for crypto markets is on Twitter. When one high-profile trader, @GiganticRebirth, who also goes by GCR (an acronym for Gigantic Cassocked Rebirth), announced he was shorting Luna $10 million, it was a red flag to many

[4] Terra Signs 5-Year, $40M Sponsorship Deal With MLB Team Washington Nationals - Decrypt.

[5] TerraUSD founder Do Kwon mocked an economist for being 'poor' after she criticized his cryptocurrency—which is now collapsing.

[6] How Far We've Fallen: Lessons Learned in the Aftermath of the Terra (LUNA) Ecosystem Crash | Nasdaq.

[7] They Made Millions on Luna, Solana and Polygon: Crypto's Boom Beyond Bitcoin - The New York Times.

other traders that something was amiss. GCR proved to be right—and made a ton of money to boot.

The Terra ecosystem crash had a domino effect on the entire cryptocurrency market, with prices suddenly plummeting, even the unhackable Bitcoin losing 16% of its value in a single week.

But what slowly became terribly and tragically clear was that the normal investors (somewhat patronizingly referred to as "normies" by high-stakes crypto traders) were the ones who took the biggest hit. Ordinary investors who had invested their life savings to cash in on what seemed like a path to instant riches were suddenly bankrupt. The creators of the Terra ecosystem, in contrast, were not impoverished. They managed to move some of their money out of harm's way, furthering the death spiral.

After Luna's collapse, Do Kwon conveniently moved his base of operations to Singapore before being served with a South Korean arrest warrant. The Korean Ministry of Foreign Affairs revoked his passport. In April 2023, Do Kwon was arrested boarding a flight to Dubai from Podgorica with a forged Costa Rican passport. At the time of this writing, both American and South Korean law enforcement seek his extradition. In the United States, the SEC has charged him with criminal fraud, but Do Kwon continues to insist that TerraUSD was a currency, not a security, and hence not within the SEC's jurisdiction. He is currently imprisoned in Montenegro, awaiting resolution of where he will stand trial.[8]

Things spun downward from Do Kwon's demise, and 6 months later, the cryptocurrency exchange FTX US declared bankruptcy on November 11, 2022. FTX founder Sam Bankman-Fried (SBF) was arrested in the Bahamas on December 12, 2022, and shortly thereafter extradited to the United States, where he remains under house arrest prior to his trial. As of March 2023, SBF faced twelve counts of criminal fraud, including charges that he defrauded the Federal Elections Commission, committed wire fraud, and engaged in money laundering.[9] His closest associates have surrendered to the authorities and are cooperating with the prosecution in exchange for relative leniency.

In a world where states still control passports and their borders, there are apparently still limits to the power of the sovereign individual. SBF was found guilty on seven counts of fraud and conspiracy in early November 2023. He faces up to 110 years in prison.

[8] Do Kwon, Jailed Crypto CEO, Rejects SEC Fraud Allegations - WSJ; Crypto Crisis: A Timeline of Key Events – WSJ.

[9] https://techcrunch.com/2023/02/23/sam-bankman-fried-faces-new-criminal-charges-for-unlawful-political-contributions/?guccounter=1&guce_referrer=aHR0cHM6Ly93d3cuZ29vZ2xlLmNvbS8&guce_referrer_sig=AQAAAGnMJV8NBwf9-pa2iR0w7WP7HyTR3226naKmPP5MP0m4jrRHQcC78XJrKy4EV5oBYLWBmoQXvaVK0QKy71j7HeXd7f7q1Zu63tqVvfkyV3Pz5OrQQe6S3dyqNzropfj3YqRt7y2HIP-03j-OGHLCOU-LQ9aE50zloLDNUYBn4rt5

5 Are Crypto and DeFi Democratic?

Do the developments I have just sketched for you bode well for democracy? It all depends on us. Crypto and decentralized finance could be democratic if the powerful wanted it to be and if we, the people, insisted upon it. In an ideal world, public education could teach every citizen to read the blockchain, and since transactions are all traceable in Web3, citizens could then collectively keep their elites honest.

Theoretically, crypto could allow for remittances from foreign-based nationals to their home countries without a series of middlemen reducing the value of money wired back home. It could allow us to execute smart contracts without having to pay out huge sums to lawyers.

But elites always figure out a workaround or hack. And current signs suggest that the real world differs enormously from the theoretical ideal. For starters, if you invest your money in an exchange such as FTX or Coinbase, individual transactions are transparent and visible on-chain, but just who is making them becomes impossible to track.

The SEC, Treasury Department, and other US oversight bodies are still trying to figure out how to regulate crypto. In August 2022, Treasury and the SEC sanctioned so-called virtual currency mixers, Blender and Tornado Cash. According to the SEC:

> **Tornado Cash** (Tornado) is a virtual currency mixer that operates on the Ethereum blockchain and indiscriminately facilitates anonymous transactions by obfuscating their origin, destination, and counterparties, with no attempt to determine their origin. Tornado receives a variety of transactions and mixes them together before transmitting them to their individual recipients. While the purported purpose is to increase privacy, mixers like Tornado are commonly used by illicit actors to launder funds, especially those stolen during significant heists.[10]

The SEC reported that the largest heist was the $455 million stolen by the Lazarus Group, a North Korean-backed hacking organization with ties to terrorism and organized crime.

Regardless of where one resided or conducted business, using a virtual currency mixer such as Tornado Cash violated the law and was subject to prosecution. In other words, even though crypto is a global phenomenon, the SEC has not restricted its perceived jurisdiction to US territory alone.

At Congressional hearings in fall 2022, Senator Patrick Toomey (Republican-Pennsylvania), one of the seven Republicans who voted to impeach Donald Trump at the second impeachment trial, challenged SEC Chairman Gary Gensler to clarify which cryptocurrencies were considered securities and therefore subject to regulation by the SEC and which were not.[11] Gensler has said that Bitcoin is *not* a security, and some of his colleagues have said that Ethereum is not a security, but he has not indicated where and why the line is drawn as to which cryptocurrency ecosystems

---

[10] U.S. Treasury Sanctions Notorious Virtual Currency Mixer Tornado Cash.

[11] https://www.reddit.com/r/ethereum/comments/xf5ztg/sec_chair_gary_gensler_says_its_not_about_the/

are considered securities. Developers therefore don't know which ecosystems fall under the jurisdiction of the SEC and which do not, which has had a chilling effect on dApp building and innovation.

To make matters more complicated still, should the American SEC really be the entity ruling on what is ostensibly a global issue? Both the *Wall Street Journal* Editorial Board and the SEC Inspector General have criticized Gary Gensler's "fast-and-furious" rulemaking.[12] As stands, it looks like US regulators may be calling the shots in this market, which may be necessary in volatile times, but it is also hegemonic rather than democratic.

In the United States, Americans seem to have learned that crypto is not a prudent investment vehicle for the Main Street investor. Polling results from March 2023 indicate that 75% of Americans "say they are not confident that current ways to invest in, trade or use cryptocurrencies are reliable and safe."[13] The Wall Street investor, however, may have learned a different lesson. Bitcoin might be a hedge store of value against inflation for those with the means to move money around quickly. Regulation has not yet been forthcoming from Congress, although it has been proposed by Republicans.[14]

In contrast, in Europe, the EU is in the process of bringing crypto-assets issuers and crypto-assets service providers under a harmonized regulatory framework that aims to support innovation and fair competition while preventing fraud.[15]

The global distribution of crypto ownership has certainly changed since China banned cryptocurrencies that were not sanctioned by the Communist Party in 2017 and, by extension, Chinese cryptocurrency exchanges. China's crackdown intensified in 2021, when China banned Bitcoin trading and mining, after which many miners moved operations to other countries. Prior to the ban, China had been a significant player in Bitcoin mining.

It is hard to determine Bitcoin ownership by country since crypto wallets are virtual and are not physically domiciled in any given territory. In the Bitcoin market, there are "whales" who hold significant amounts of Bitcoin, and while the distribution of ownership is difficult to assess, it is imminently clear that a few addresses own a large percentage of the total supply. If ownership of assets is plutocratic, decentralized finance becomes a contradiction in terms.

[12]Gary Gensler's Bad Performance Review – WSJ.

[13]Americans view crypto investing as unreliable. They're right.

[14]Crypto bill from Republicans lays out clear roles for SEC and CFTC.

[15]PE-CONS 54/22 KHO/cc ECOFIN and Digital finance: agreement reached on European crypto-assets regulation (MiCA).

6 Conclusions

In the realm of theory, cryptocurrencies and decentralized finance sound like fiercely democratic forces, a weapon of the common man. DeFi, after all, claims to democratize finance.

In practice, they threaten to further centralize wealth and power in the hands of the few, for three reasons:

First, risk is currently borne by ordinary investors. Technological innovations before they reveal their real value are always risky propositions. As the crash of the crypto market showed, the risk was primarily borne by ordinary investors, as major players were able to hedge their bets and move their assets in a timely fashion. Estimates by the SEC say that Do Kwon cashed out $80 million every month before the LUNA and UST collapse.[16]

Second, the spoils go to the already wealthy. The big winners in the crypto space have been investors and traders with sufficient funds and expertise to skillfully engage in high-stakes arbitrage. Anyone who had funds in FTX or Coinbase was and is prevented from moving quickly enough to benefit from rapidly changing and volatile markets, but fund managers were not similarly impeded.

Finally, the decentralized ironically winds up being centralized. Especially after the crypto crash, decentralized finance, given the nature of the major players in the space, is anything but decentralized.

The good news is that if we keep our eyes wide open as blockchain applications are further developed, we could see mind-blowing new things created beyond our wildest dreams of the present moment.[17] Just 10 years ago, for example, who would have thought we could instantaneously communicate with friends and family around the world for free? As Jaap Gordijn argues in this volume, blockchain technologies have the potential to promote fairness and equality in our digital ecosystems.

In conclusion, the main message I would like to leave you with is this: Blockchain is a technological innovation whose killer application has yet to emerge. It is something to watch—as are the moves of the Big Technology companies in this space. One thing is clear: in a world without data dignity and respect for human plurality, the strong will continue to do as they can and the weak as they must. Given existing wealth disparities, such a world will not be one that most want to live in.

Discussion Questions for Students and Their Teachers

1. What are the likely similarities between Web2 and Web3? What are the likely differences? Why might they matter for global politics?

[16] Terra's Do Kwon cashed out over $80 million per month before LUNA and UST collapse.

[17] For windows on a brighter Web3 future, see Allen, Danielle, Eli Frankel, Woojin Lim, Divya Siddarth, Joshua Simons, and E. Glen Weyl. "Ethics of Decentralized Social Technologies: Lessons from the Web3 Wave." Edmond & Lily Safra Center for Ethics, Harvard University, March 20, 2023, Putting Flourishing First: Applying Democratic Values to Technology—GETTING-Plurality and Decentralized Society: Finding Web3's Soul.

2. A friend of yours asks you if cryptocurrency is a good investment. How would you advise them?
3. Are crypto and DeFi democratic? If your answer is yes, what steps should be taken to cultivate further an ecosystem of equals? If your answer is no, what policies would you recommend for democratizing Web3?
4. Should the market for cryptocurrency be under US oversight and jurisdiction? Should Europe accept such a state of affairs? What steps might the EU take to move toward genuine co-governance of Web3?
5. What rules might encourage innovation while containing winner-take-all dynamics in the global economy? Whose rules should they be?

Learning Resources for Students

For readers interested in doing a bit of self-organized on-chain analysis, the following sources are worth consulting in June 2023 (this is a rapidly evolving landscape):

1. Coin Metrics. Coinmetrics is an important source for on-chain data and analysis on various cryptocurrencies, including Bitcoin. Their regular reports and research articles provide valuable insights into the Bitcoin ecosystem: Coin Metrics
2. Glassnode. Glassnode offers comprehensive on-chain data analytics for Bitcoin and other cryptocurrencies. You can find various metrics and charts related to Bitcoin wealth distribution, market behavior, and other trends: Glassnode
3. Chainalysis: Chainalysis provides blockchain data and analysis. They provide valuable insights into various aspects of the cryptocurrency ecosystem including country-specific trends and ownership distribution: Chainalysis
4. Cambridge Center for Alternative Finance (CCAF): CCAF regularly publishes research on the cryptocurrency industry, including mining activities and geographic distribution. Their Global Cryptoasset Benchmarking Study is particularly valuable: CCAF publications - Cambridge Centre for Alternative Finance
5. Coin Dance: Coin Dance is a community-driven platform that provides Bitcoin statistics, including data on node distribution, mining, and development within the Bitcoin ecosystem. Coin Dance
6. On data dignity, see There Is No A.I. | The New Yorker and Jaron Lanier, *Who Owns the Future?* (Lanier, 2013).
7. On plurality, see GETTING-Plurality, Plurality: Technology for Collaborative Diversity and Democracy and The Collective Intelligence Project.
8. On the sovereign individual, see James Dale Davidson and William Rees-Mogg, *The Sovereign Individual* (Touchstone, 1999/2020). Preface to the second edition by Peter Thiel.
9. For windows on a brighter Web3 future, see Allen, Danielle, Eli Frankel, Woojin Lim, Divya Siddarth, Joshua Simons, and E. Glen Weyl. "Ethics of Decentralized Social Technologies: Lessons from the Web3 Wave." Edmond & Lily Safra Center for Ethics, Harvard University, March 20, 2023, Putting Flourishing First: Applying Democratic Values to Technology - GETTING-Plurality and Decentralized Society: Finding Web3's Soul.

Acknowledgments The author would like to acknowledge the support of GPT4 in researching and formatting this paper. Jachym Kraus, Woojin Lim, and two insightful reviewers also helped me improve my first iteration pronouncement on this rapidly changing global ecosystem.

References

Allen, D., et al. (2023). *Ethics of decentralized technologies: Lessons from the Web3 Wave*. EJ Safra Center for Ethics, Harvard University.

Davidson, J. et al. (1999). *The sovereign individual*, Touchstone. Preface to the second edition (2020) by Peter Thiel.

Lanier, J. (2013). *Who owns the future?* Simon & Schuster.

Weyl, E., et al. (2022). *Decentralized society: Finding Web3's Soul*. Social Science Research Network.

Zalesne, K. et al. (2023). *Putting flourishing first: Applying democratic values to technology*. Research Brief, GETTING-Plurality Research Network, Harvard University.

Platforms: Their Structure, Benefits, and Challenges

Geoffrey Parker and Marshall Van Alstyne

Abstract In this chapter, we describe platforms and their structure and how that structure differs from traditional linear value chains. We then discuss some of the key economic factors, including two-sided and multi-sided network effects, which underpin both the platform value proposition and the ability to create welfare for users. Platform and technology firms have grown to the point where their market capitalizations greatly exceed oil, gas, and financial services firms. We then explore some key governance and regulatory issues, including privacy, false information, and antitrust. We conclude with a discussion of emerging issues posed by Large Language Models such as ChatGPT, including their ability to create false information at scale and disrupt creative industries.

1 Introduction

A platform is a business based on enabling value-creating interactions between external producers and consumers.[1] The platform provides an open, participative infrastructure for these interactions and sets governance conditions for them. The platform's overarching purpose is to match users and facilitate the exchange of goods, services, or social currency among those users in order to create value for all participants (Parker et al., 2016).

One challenge when describing platforms is that the term is used in different ways by different people and disciplines. For example, personnel who are responsible for

[1] Note that elements of this chapter are adapted from previous works.

G. Parker (✉)
Dartmouth College, Thayer School of Engineering, Hanover, NH, USA
e-mail: geoffrey.g.parker@dartmouth.edu

M. Van Alstyne
Boston University, Questrom School of Business, Boston, MA, USA
e-mail: mva@bu.edu

H. Werthner et al. (eds.), *Introduction to Digital Humanism*,
https://doi.org/10.1007/978-3-031-45304-5_33

an organization's technology—such as a Chief Technology Officer—often describe a platform as the technology (computers, software, and communications systems) that are deployed by the organization to carry out its operations. Others might refer to a platform as a technology stack that provides reusable functionality to make product design, development, and delivery faster and cheaper (Levandowski et al., 2013). In this chapter, the term "platform" will refer to a business system that includes the functionality and architecture necessary for users to create and consume value as well as the rules of governance to promote and regulate interactions (Jacobides et al., 2019). For example, platform resources include the default insurance contracts that protect drivers and riders (in the case of Lyft and Uber) as well as hosts and guests (in the case of Airbnb). They facilitate user interactions while reducing the transaction costs, both monetary and non-monetary, of engaging in an economic activity or transaction.

2 Platforms

Platforms are widespread, and most people use them in their daily lives. Common platform uses include searching the web with Google, producing or consuming messages using Twitter, interacting with other professionals using LinkedIn, transporting through Uber or Lyft, renting a room through Airbnb, managing teams and engaging customers using Salesforce.com, purchasing goods and/or services on eBay or Amazon Marketplace, and purchasing applications on Google Play or Apple's App and iTunes stores. While the firms mentioned have varying business models, they share the common characteristic of facilitating interactions among users. They are also relatively new companies that rely on relatively recent information and communications technology (ICT). Their platforms' rapid adoption suggests that consumers derive significant benefit from the goods and services these platforms provide.

Despite the recent rise of large technology firms using platform business models, platforms have been present throughout human history. Medieval village marketplaces served as platforms for merchants to connect with consumers and exchange goods and services for some form of compensation. More recently, shopping malls have functioned as platforms by matching stores with consumers. Mall developers explicitly woo name brand (anchor) stores because of their ability to attract shoppers who then shop at smaller specialty stores (Yeates et al., 2001). Similarly, radio stations, television networks, and newspapers have long functioned as platforms, matching advertisers with consumers (Evans, 2009).

What is new is the growth and reach of platform firms. This occurred for many reasons, chief among them the (ICT) advances that have dramatically increased computing power, decreased the costs of storage, and increased network connectivity. In the past, transaction costs were sufficiently high that similar platforms could exist simultaneously, protected by geographic, cultural, linguistic, or other barriers. A medieval village was limited as a platform because it served only those merchants and consumers who could travel there over roads using human and animal power. Today's digital technology has dramatically reduced the transaction costs of earlier platforms, expanding the scope and size of the markets served, sometimes quite dramatically. For example, both eBay and Craigslist greatly expanded the markets available to sellers of used (and new) items. Previously, these sellers depended on newspaper classified advertisements to reach buyers (Seamans & Zhu, 2014). As this example shows, an entire market that was once fragmented by region can now be served by one or a few firms.

Although the economics of platforms have been studied for decades, the term "platform" itself is relatively new. Previous research described the structure of these types of businesses as *systems* and *networks* (David, 1985; Katz & Shapiro, 1985; Farrell et al., 1998), with much emphasis on the concept of network effects. Network effects describe the impact of the number of users on the value generated for each user and the adoption rate of new technologies. For example, fax machines and telephones were (and are) one-sided networks that enable communication between a single type of user (e.g., sender and receiver of fax messages). As more users joined these platforms, they were able to facilitate a greater number of interactions, resulting in increased value for users Eisenmann et al. (2006) and Parker et al. (2016) describe these effects in detail.

Over approximately the past two decades, scholars have extended their analyses and formalized the understanding of two-sided markets/networks, network effects, and the impact on platform pricing decisions (Parker & Van Alstyne, 2000, 2005; Rochet & Tirole, 2003; Caillaud & Jullien, 2003). Two-sided markets are networks in which two distinct types of users (e.g., demand-side buyers and supply-side sellers) can interact with one another. Two-sided networks can add additional sides, and the literature often refers to these as multi-sided platforms (MSPs) (Hagiu & Wright, 2015). For example, LinkedIn is an MSP in that it connects individual users, recruiters, and advertisers.

Importantly, multi-sided platforms often begin as one-sided systems that can exhibit strong same-side network effects among a single type of user. Over time, the systems then often expand (i.e., open) to add additional types of users (Eisenmann et al., 2009). These additional users create cross-side network effects (i.e., between different types of users) if the value to users depends on the number of other types of users. Note that in the long run, one-sided platforms cannot provide unsubsidized free services; to sustain their operations, they need a revenue source. Even if there are strong same-side network effects, such as those often observed in social networks, these systems will still tend to open up to additional types of users, such as advertisers, to gather the necessary resources to fund ongoing operations and technology development.

The topic of pricing by platforms has been well studied by economists. The early literature laid out the conditions of market size, network effect strength, and elasticity of demand that could drop prices below those that would normally be set by profit-maximizing firms (Parker & Van Alstyne, 2005; Hagiu, 2006). This stream of literature showed that prices that might once have been viewed as predatory—that is, below some appropriate measure of marginal cost—were in fact perfectly rational. Firms can afford to give away goods and services to one type of user so long as that type of user's participation on the platform attracts a sufficient number of paying users. Their fees can more than offset the cost of serving the free users. For example, early two-sided network literature showed that it can be profit maximizing to charge one side of a network zero or negative prices. This phenomenon, long observed in examples such as advertising-sponsored radio and television (Eisenmann et al., 2009), was becoming prevalent on the Internet in the late 1990s and early 2000s (Parker & Van Alstyne, 2005).

3 Platform Structure

As described above, a platform's most critical function is enabling interactions among both similar and diverse users. Platforms do this by providing both the infrastructure for these interactions and the governance mechanisms to enforce rules about what users can and cannot do. This architecture is central to key aspects of platform operations, e.g., the nature and size of network effects, and whether platforms networks encourage users to affiliate with multiple platforms at once (multi-homing) (Choi, 2010). Similarly, understanding a platform's governance, the extent to which the platform is open or closed, and the way(s) in which the platform can be monetized are all critical to understanding the platform's underlying economics.

Before describing platform businesses, we first describe what business structure is *not* a platform. For example, a standard business arrangement to produce and deliver a product or service is often described as a linear supply chain, i.e., an arrangement where value accumulates from one stage of production or distribution to another. Figure 1 shows a stylized example of a linear automotive supply chain (Hayes et al., 1988). On the left are the upstream sources of raw materials such as metals and plastics. In the middle, raw materials are fabricated by suppliers into components such as paint, tires, and seats. These components are then combined in an assembly plant to form a complete automobile. At the end, the automobile is sold to a customer.

In this figure, value accumulates from left to right. Supply-chain partners are compensated from right to left for their value add. From a customer's point of view,

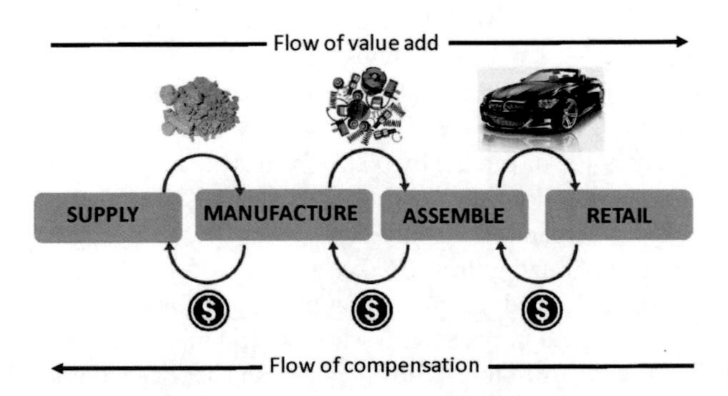

Fig. 1 Linear supply chain: styled automotive example

the supply chain is relatively invisible and largely irrelevant (Zeng, 2015). Customers care about what the supply chain can deliver in terms of a finished product or service delivered at retail. There are relatively minimal network effects, if any, in a standard supply chain system; one consumer's purchase of an automobile does not significantly change the value that another consumer derives from the product. Note that electric vehicles are an exception, as consumers do care whether others are active on their network (Anderson et al., 2022a). But the linear supply chain discussed above is *not* a platform.

A true platform's structure differs from that of linear supply chains in that it has a triangular structure that facilitates user interactions (Eisenmann et al., 2011). We begin with a description of one-sided platforms with a single type of user. We then describe two-sided platforms with both consumer-side and supply-side users. For illustration purposes, readers can think of consumer-side users as the buyers on the platform; supply-side users, by contrast, are the platform's sellers. First, consider a one-sided platform where users interact with other similar users. When platforms first launch, they often operate as a one-sided platform. In this way, platforms can work out the value proposition to one type of user before the platform opens up to additional types of users. For example, when LinkedIn first began operations, it only facilitated interactions between professionals who wished to connect with one another. Figure 2 shows the one-sided network platform structure graphically.

Telephone systems are examples of a one-sided network. The technology facilitates interactions between users; the interaction takes the form of a telephone call. At any given time, a user can be either the call originator or receiver. If there are only a few (or no) other users, then the system has minimal value. However, once adoption grows, the system can provide significant value to its many users.

In contrast, the structure of a two-sided network platform is triangular, as shown below in Fig. 3.

Two-sided platforms allow different *types* of users (Side "A" and Side "B" above) to use platform resources to directly transact with one another to exchange value

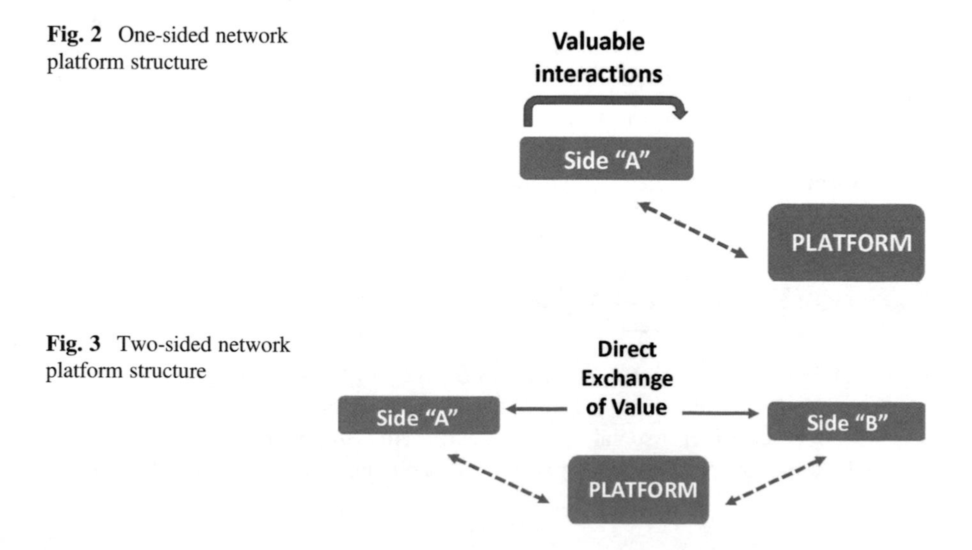

Fig. 2 One-sided network platform structure

Fig. 3 Two-sided network platform structure

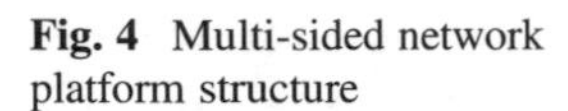

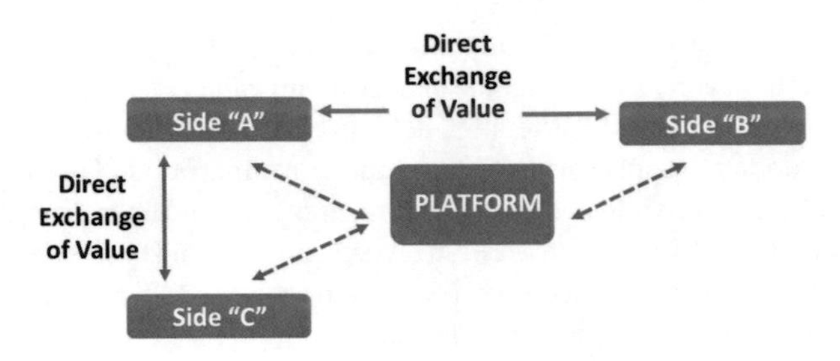

Fig. 4 Multi-sided network platform structure

(Hagiu & Wright, 2015). Uber provides a well-known example of this two-sided network platform structure. The Uber ride-sharing system (the platform) matches drivers and their cars (Side "A") with riders (Side "B") and then allows a ride to be exchanged (the "Direct Exchange of Value"). The platform provides significant functionality; it tracks the location of drivers and riders, matches them to one another, transmits pricing information, provides payment services, allows for bidirectional ratings, and more.

Multi-sided platforms facilitate interactions among even more types of users (Sides "A," "B," and "C"). For example, Uber has expanded to food delivery (Uber Eats) by adding restaurant users (Side "C") who want access to Uber's drivers (Trabucchi & Buganza, 2020). The new structure is illustrated by Fig. 4.

Typically, a two-sided network has both demand-side users (e.g., consumers seeking to buy a good or service) and supply-side users (e.g., sellers seeking to sell a good or service). Consider as an example Sony's PlayStation game console. Like many gaming systems, PlayStation functions as a platform that allows game players (demand-side users) to use software (games) provided by game developers (supply-side users). Also, Sony sets the platform's rules. For example, it determines which games are allowed on the platform (Eisenmann et al., 2006). The PlayStation system facilitates both same-side and cross-side interactions. Gamers derive value by playing games, but they can also interact with other players (same-side interaction) in multi-player game settings, deriving additional value. In addition, PlayStation gamers value access to the wide variety of content (cross-side interaction) provided by authorized game developers.

One key source of platform value is the network effect. Here, value depends on the number of different-type users. Because this concept is so central to understanding platforms, we discuss network effects in detail below.

4 Network Effects and Value

Network effects exist when the value users derive from a platform depends on the number of platform users (i.e., the size of a user base). For an example of a one-sided network effect, consider a social network such as Instagram. It is more valuable to users when members of their family are also on the network. For a two-sided

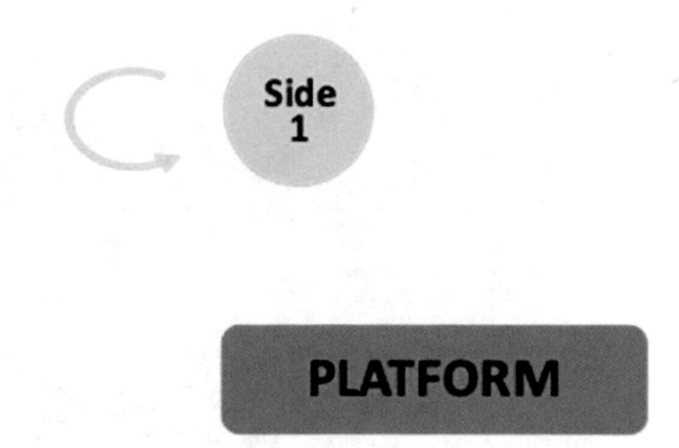

Fig. 5 One-sided networks facilitate one main interaction. Positive (+) same-side: telephone and fax machine users benefit from being able to call one another and exchange information. Negative (−) same-side: receiving a harassing phone call is unwelcome and reduces a user's value

network effect example, consider how a merchant's willingness to accept a given credit card (e.g., American Express) depends on the number of consumers who wish to pay with such a card. The greater the number of consumers wishing to pay with that card, the greater the value to the merchant in accepting it. Similarly, a consumer's willingness to carry a given credit card depends on the number of merchants willing to accept it.

One-sided platforms manage interactions among just one type of user. Importantly, the value that users receive from the presence of other users and their interactions can be either positive or negative, as shown in Fig. 5. For this reason, platforms work to reduce or even eliminate negative interactions, as we discuss further in the section on governance.

By contrast, two-sided platforms facilitate two kinds of interaction between users: same-side user interactions and cross-side user interactions. From these interactions, network effect value flows. More formally, a two-sided market is one in which (1) two sets of agents interact through an intermediary or platform and (2) the decisions of each set of agents affect the outcomes of the other set of agents, typically through an externality (Rysman, 2009). In a two-sided platform, there are four potential network effects to consider, as shown in Fig. 6.

Let us return to the case of the PlayStation video game system. The platform sponsor is the console producer—Sony—while the two sets of users are consumers (i.e., game players) and video game developers. Neither consumers nor game developers are likely to find significant value in the PlayStation console unless the other party is present and active. More players attract more game developers, and more and better games attract more players. These are positive cross-side network effects. The value that users place on other users' participation is exactly the network effect discussed above.

A highly stylized and simplified representation of the value that platform users gain from the system is shown in the equations below.[2] Note that the value users obtain from using the platform is not the same as the amount that the users pay for

[2] For clarity of exposition, the impact of network effects on user value is represented by linear equations. In reality, the impact is almost certainly nonlinear.

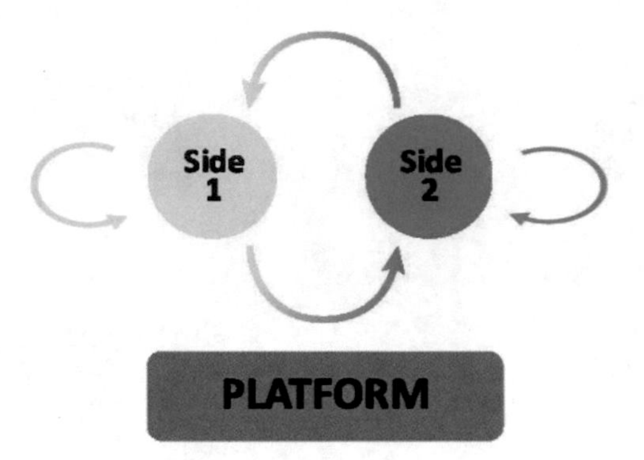

Fig. 6 Two-sided networks have four interactions. Positive (+) same-side: player-to-player contact in Xbox games, end user sharing of PDF files. Positive (+) cross-side: merchants and consumers for credit cards, application developers and end-users in Android or Apple iOS. Negative (−) same-side: competing suppliers on procurement platforms, harassment from other users on social media platforms, other diners who book your restaurant table. Negative (−) cross-side: advertising clutter to consumers. Source: T. G. Eisenmann, Geoffrey G. Parker, and Marshall Van Alstyne, "Strategies for Two-Sided Markets." *Harvard Business Review* 84.10 (2006)

the platform. In some cases, users pay nothing, yet they can derive significant value from affiliating with platforms. For example, the users of the Google, Bing, and Baidu search engines are not directly charged. Instead, the platforms charge advertisers for those users' attention.

4.1 User Value for One-Sided and Two-Sided Networks (with User Types 1 and 2)

User value in a one-sided network

$$\text{User Value} = V + e^{*} N \tag{1}$$

User type 1 value in a two-sided network

$$\text{Type 1 User Value} = V_1 + e_1{}^{*} N_1 + e_{21}{}^{*} N_2 \tag{2}$$

User type 2 value in a two-sided network

$$\text{Type 2 User Value} = V_2 + e_2{}^{*} N_2 + e_{12}{}^{*} N_1 \tag{3}$$

Equation (1) shows the value that a single type of user receives from a one-sided network. V is the stand-alone value for the platform that a single user enjoys. N represents the number of other users, and e represents the incremental value that each additional user contributes to a single user's value from the platform. Thus, as

N increases by one, a user's value from the platform increases by e, which can be interpreted as the marginal network effect value from one additional user.

Equation (2) presents a user's value in a two-sided network. V_1 is the stand-alone value that user type 1 (such as a consumer) derives from the platform (i.e., the value to user type 1 from her use of the platform, in the absence of any other users). The second term $e_1* N_1$ captures the same-side network effect, where parameter e_1 measures the incremental value that an additional Type 1 user provides to other Type 1 users, and N_1 is the number of other Type 1 users. The third term $e_{21}* N_2$ captures the cross-side network effect, where parameter e_{21} measures the extra value that user Type 1 derives from the addition of another Type 2 user (such as a seller on a marketplace) and N_2 is the number of Type 2 users. Equation (3) parallels Equation (2) and describes the value that a Type 2 user derives from the core platform (V_2), the same-side network effect from additional Type 2 users ($e_2* N_2$), and the cross-side network effect from Type 1 users ($e_{12} * N_1$).

When there are no network effects, parameters e_1, e_2, e_{21}, and e_{12} equal zero, and users benefit only from the stand-alone value of the platform. Products such as stoves or hair dryers fit this description.

To summarize, the value proposition to users can be thought of as occurring in three main categories: stand-alone value (in the absence of other users); same-side network effect value, which depends on similar users; and cross-side network value, which depends on the interactions of different types of users (Anderson et al., 2022b).

5 Platform Openness

A critical decision that platforms must make is how open to be. Platforms can create significant value by coordinating the activities of external "ecosystem" partners, who in turn attach to the platform to reach customers and produce products or services (Jacobides et al., 2018). Examples include computer operating systems that are extended by both software developers and social media platforms (such as YouTube and Twitter) that depend on their users for content creation. Enterprise software systems such as those offered by SAP and Salesforce.com have significant functionality by themselves, but they also depend on external partners who can extend the platform's functionality.

One challenge platforms face is determining how to provide access to users who can create value for other users while also excluding users who either provide poor-quality products and services or misbehave and destroy value for other users. An early example comes from the video game crash of 1983 (Aoyama & Izushi, 2003). During this time, Atari could not control who published games on its system; as a result, many inferior games were produced for Atari's gaming console. The result: because customers could not easily distinguish good-quality games from bad, many fled the market—a classic "Market for Lemons" failure (Akerlof, 1970). The next company to lead the videogame market, Nintendo, learned from Atari's mistake. To ensure quality, Nintendo excluded certain developers from publishing games for its system.

Controlling access to a platform is a key way that a platform's owner has the control points needed to monetize participation, should it choose to. Platforms that are too open have had difficulty charging for the goods and services transacted across them (Parker & Van Alstyne, 2018). Platforms can open only slightly, allowing external supply-side partners to connect to their systems, by providing application programming interfaces (APIs) (Parker & Van Alstyne, 2009). More generally, a platform is *open* to the extent that (1) no restrictions are placed on participation in its development, commercialization, or use or (2) any restrictions—for example, requirements to conform with technical standards or pay licensing fees—are reasonable, non-discriminatory, and applied uniformly to all potential platform participants (Eisenmann et al., 2009).

5.1 Access to Demand-Side Use (as a Consumer)

Most platforms are open to any end user who wishes to connect. However, if payment is required for access, then a system will be designed to ensure that only paying users can use the platform. Access to the demand side can be tightly restricted. For example, when Apple's iPhone was first released in the US market, the device was compatible only with the AT&T network. Users who wanted iPhones but were not already AT&T customers had to incur significant costs, first acquiring the device and then signing up with AT&T.

5.2 Access to Extend Platform (Supply Side)

Supply-side users including developers may have open access to platforms such as Linux, Microsoft Windows, and Apple macOS. None of these systems impose restrictions on the ability of demand-side users to load new applications. In contrast, Sony limits the games that can be published on its PlayStation game consoles. Sony does this primarily so it can screen games for quality. As detailed above, the "crash of 1983" shows that firms can suffer significant losses if they do not manage the quality of all elements of their platforms or systems. In the case of business software, systems such as Salesforce also limit access to only those developers who can pass a quality screen (Sawhney & Nambisan, 2007). Similarly, Apple restricts access to the supply side for its smartphone operating system, iOS (Hagiu, 2014).

5.3 Access to User Provision (e.g., Android and Apple Devices)

Platforms must also often provide access technology to their users. This leaves the platform owner with a decision: whether to provide the technology itself or whether to open the ability to supply technology to third parties. In the game console examples described above, the major suppliers—Microsoft (Xbox), Nintendo (Wii), and Sony (PlayStation)—are the exclusive console providers, and they do not allow third-party firms to supply hardware. However, in other settings, firms do open this role to third parties. Even within a single industry, firms can make different decisions. For example, in smartphones, while Apple restricts supply-side access, Google allows any hardware manufacturer to use Android Open Source Project software on its phones (Gandhewar & Sheikh, 2010).

5.4 Access to Change Technology/Contracts (Decision-Making)

Another critical decision facing platform sponsors is the degree to which they open their platforms to multiple decision-makers on issues regarding, for example, the nature and form of platform content. This decision can drive who gets access to the platform, what technology the platform will deploy, and if (or even how) the platform will capture value.

In some cases, these companies have opted to reserve all platform decision rights for themselves. This has been the case with Apple (iOS), Microsoft (Xbox), Nintendo (Wii), Salesforce, SAP, and Sony (PlayStation). However, there are also cases where decisions are made by multiple actors, whether a small number of partners or (as is the case with open-source software) a relatively large number of decision-makers. For example, both the Mastercard and Visa credit card networks are owned by member banks who control their decisions (Akers et al., 2005). Similarly, open-source systems such as Apache and Linux are inherently open at the user and developer level. And at the decision-making level, these open-source systems allow any of their users to propose changes to the core technology. Further, open-source governing bodies such as the Apache Software Foundation have multiple membership levels determining who gets to make changes (Lerner & Tirole, 2002). Membership levels are typically allocated to those who make greater contributions (O'Mahony & Ferraro, 2007). When a disagreement over technology direction cannot be resolved, a party is free to "fork" the software to make a version that incorporates their vision. Other factors may encourage forking, too, as user-developers may have conflicting interests as to the technology's evolution (Lerner & Tirole, 2002).

6 Platform Governance

Platform governance encompasses the set of rules and decisions platforms make to determine who gets to participate in an ecosystem, how value gets divided, and which mechanisms are used to settle disputes, whether among users or between the platform and its users. Platforms must determine how to provide access to users and encourage activities that generate value while also excluding certain users or specific actions that do not contribute to value creation. Failures in platform governance can both prevent value creation and destroy existing value (Boudreau & Hagiu, 2009).

In addition, online platforms that attract advertisers with their user data must confront additional privacy concerns. To make this data useful, online platforms want their users to share as much as possible about themselves. However, this can increase privacy worries among the users themselves, such as whether their information is being sold, stolen, or otherwise misused. Therefore, online platforms must strike a balance between sharing user data with advertisers and implementing appropriate privacy controls and data security. In addition, governments have passed laws designed to protect consumer privacy, by restricting both the use of data and online tracking techniques used by websites.[3] Online platforms must comply with such regulations, even in the face of research that suggests even moderate privacy regulation can reduce the effectiveness of online advertising (Goldfarb & Tucker, 2011).

One governance area that has gained attention recently is the challenge of managing the dramatic increase of false information online (Vosoughi et al., 2018; see also the chapter in this volume on content moderation by Prem and Krenn). This includes the potentially deadly consequences of false information such as attacks on the Rohingya in Myanmar (Fink, 2018). Election integrity is another area under attack across the globe as numerous actors, including nation states, seek to influence electoral outcomes (Henschke et al., 2020). The explosion of fake news online has led some platforms to invest in capabilities that can identify and remove false information and problematic content such as fake user profiles, offensive language, and hateful or discriminatory comments (Aral, 2020). These platforms must also decide whether to impose disciplinary actions on users who fail to comply with such guidelines, which can include temporary or permanent removal from the platform (Conger & Isaac, 2021). As the more recent reversal of the ban on Donald Trump from Twitter shows, this is a rapidly changing area.[4] Given the implications for social stability, there is likely to be significant policy innovation as regulators across the world attempt to reign in the harmful effects of misinformation. This is a particularly thorny issue in the United States because the Constitution's First

[3] See, for example, Directive 2002/58/EC of the European Parliament and of the Council of July 12, 2002, concerning the processing of personal data and the protection of privacy in the electronic communications sector (Directive on privacy and electronic communications), accessed at https://eur-lex.europa.eu/LexUriServ/LexUriServ.do?uri=CELEX:32002L0058:en:HTML

[4] https://www.npr.org/2022/11/19/1131351535/elon-musk-allows-donald-trump-back-on-twitter

Amendment prohibits the government from abridging the freedom of speech and of the press. One novel solution (proposed by Van Alstyne, 2021) is to focus on the amplification of speech instead of the original speech itself. The issue of amplification has been identified as critical (Syed, 2017). In Van Alstyne's scheme, speakers might be required to warrant that their speech is true if they wish to have it disseminated beyond the original publication.

7 Platform Growth and Power

Platforms emerged as an important type of organizational form as early as 2006 (Eisenmann et al., 2006) when the conditions for winner-take-all or winner-take-most markets began to become clear. One important question is when firms can overcome the entry barriers. Platforms can enjoy these barriers to competition due to network effects and switching costs. But platforms can also overcome these barriers through a strategy known as *platform envelopment*, in which one platform provider can enter another's market by bundling its own platform's functionality with that of the target, leveraging shared user relationships and common components (Eisenmann et al., 2011). This strategy is particularly effective for a platform that has overlapping user bases with a rival. The platform can then bundle the rival's functionality into its own offering.

Over the past 25 years, platforms have taken on a larger presence in the global economy as compared to energy, pharmaceutical, and manufacturing firms that once dominated the top firms by market capitalization.[5] Today, the top seven publicly traded firms (as of 2020) in three sectors are shown in Fig. 7 with market capitalizations from March 2023. Note the prominence of Apple, Microsoft, Google, and Amazon.

One important platform feature is the ability to enter the markets of traditional linear value-chain (pipeline) firms. One key method of entry is the aforementioned *platform envelopment*, the process by which a platform leverages overlapping user bases to enter new markets (Eisenmann et al., 2011). Because of the nature of the technology infrastructure—which tends to be modular so that ecosystem partners can connect—platforms find it relatively easy to add functionality and put forth a compelling value proposition. Product and services firms that have only stand-alone value propositions can find it difficult to match a platform offering. As shown by Fig. 8, stand-alone offerings can be threatened by the entry of a platform such as Google Android or Apple iOS.

The rapid growth of platforms has also become a central concern for regulators. Partly, this is because of the potential for market dominance, especially by the largest technology companies (Shapiro, 2019). The pricing and business models typically used by platforms can make it difficult to apply existing regulations. For example,

[5] https://money.cnn.com/1998/02/02/markets/marketwrap/capitalization.htm

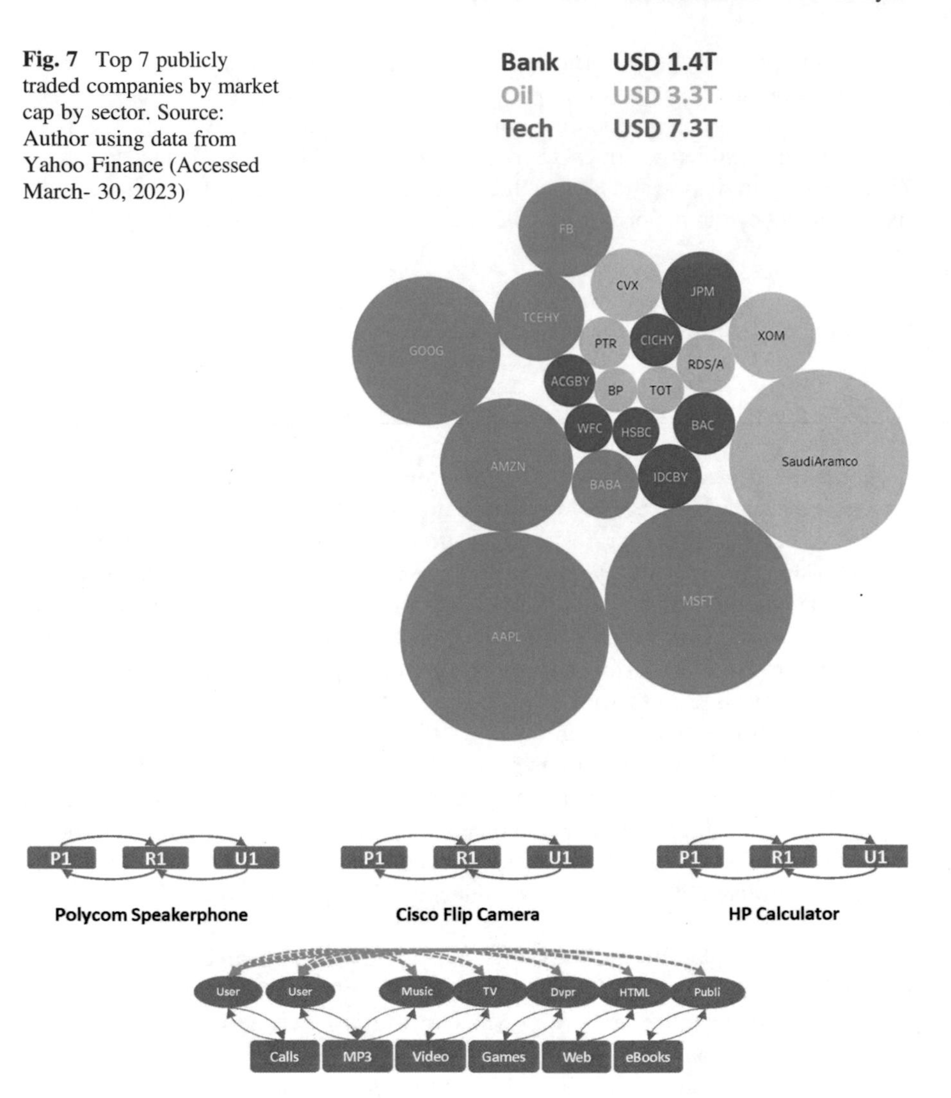

Fig. 7 Top 7 publicly traded companies by market cap by sector. Source: Author using data from Yahoo Finance (Accessed March- 30, 2023)

Fig. 8 Stand-alone firms are vulnerable to entry by platforms

many online platforms offer goods and services for free. This renders meaningless the significant and non-transitory increase in price (SSNIP) test to identify the relevant market (Hesse, 2007). Theories of harm include excessive prices, inferior quality, reduced incentives for innovation, predatory pricing, and self-preferencing (Parker et al., 2020). What's more, the merger and acquisition behavior of Google, Apple, Facebook, Amazon, and Microsoft (GAFAM)[6] can add complementary functionality in the core business, add new functionality in the vertical value

[6]Now known as Alphabet, Apple, Meta, Amazon, and Microsoft.

chain, merge with substitute products and services such that competition might be reduced, and seek to acquire human capital (Parker et al., 2021). The regulatory concerns that emerge from mergers and acquisitions focus essentially on market foreclosure, competitive bottlenecks, and distortion of upstream competition. Despite the potential for harm, very few of the 855 GAFAM mergers completed during the years 1988 to 2020 were investigated, suggesting that regulators did not yet have an effective way to control the potentially negative effects of these deals.

The European Union has taken significant steps toward understanding the issues, and that has included promulgating regulations such as the Digital Markets Act (DMA) and Digital Services Act (DSA).[7,8] The DMA and DSA have a particular focus on "gatekeepers" or "Very Large Online Platforms" which, for consumers, are defined as platforms with over 45 million users as of 2023.[9,10] One key question is whether such regulation will be enforced ex ante through a series of obligations that platforms must adhere to or whether it will be enforced ex post, should a platform be found in violation. The ex post regulatory framework has come under criticism for taking too long, being too expensive, and having seemingly random outcomes (Parker et al., 2020). Instead, the DMA takes a different approach; it lays out a series of over 20 ex ante directives designed to curb potential abuse.[11] A panel of economic experts commissioned by the European Union Joint Research Centre (The Cabral panel) analyzed the proposed regulations, and while it found that most were well grounded in economic theory, it still proposed that some prohibited activity should instead be "gray." In these cases, the practice would be prohibited, but arguments could still be made by large platforms for why the practice should be allowed (Cabral et al., 2021).

8 Conclusions

As can be seen from the growth of large technology firms and the resulting regulatory scrutiny, there is great concern over the impact such firms are having on both the economy and the global population. Such concerns are not new; during the industrial revolution, the growth of manufacturing, transportation, and financial institutions drew similar attention. But the relatively recent growth and public awareness of accessible Large Language Models (LLM) such as ChatGPT (Chat

[7] https://www.euronews.com/next/2022/11/02/eus-digital-markets-act-comes-into-force-what-is-it-and-what-does-it-mean-for-big-tech

[8] https://techcrunch.com/2022/11/16/digital-services-act-enters-into-force/

[9] https://www.reuters.com/technology/google-twitter-meta-face-tougher-eu-online-content-rules-2023-02-17/

[10] https://ec.europa.eu/commission/presscorner/detail/en/ip_22_6423

[11] https://commission.europa.eu/strategy-and-policy/priorities-2019-2024/europe-fit-digital-age/digital-markets-act-ensuring-fair-and-open-digital-markets_en

Generative Pre-trained Transformer) show that the platform space remains as dynamic as ever. The pace of change in LLMs has been nothing short of extraordinary, with capabilities seeming to grow by the week. However, a large number of potentially negative uses for the technology have already been identified, and more are coming every day.[12] These include AI taking academic and professional exams such as the US Bar Exam for legal certification; AI authoring academic articles, student exams, and papers; and deep video fakes. There is also the potential for significant disruption to industries such as music and video. These disruptions could change the economics of these industries in ways that transform the existing competitive landscape (Gupta & Parker, 2023).

Discussion Questions for Students and Their Teachers

1. Consider sectors that have yet to face significant competition from platform firms. Is it only a matter of time or are there structural reasons that protect those sectors from platform entry?
2. Have platforms become a threat to innovation and competition? If so, are interventions such as the European Union's Digital Markets Act and Digital Services Act a step in the right direction, or do they go too far?
3. What are the implications for regions of the world without significant platform firms? For example, Europe is home to only a few platform firms. Should governments seek to invest in emerging technologies such as Large Language Models, or should they leave it to private enterprise?
4. How are individuals impacted by large technology platform firms? Consider access to information and useful services as well as the impact on the social fabric.

Learning Resources for Students

Platform Structure

1. Amrit Tiwana, 2013. *Platform ecosystems: Aligning architecture, governance, and strategy*. Newnes.

   This work lays out the structural elements of platforms and how they interoperate.
2. Geoffrey Parker, Marshall Van Alstyne, Sangeet Choudary, 2016. *Platform revolution: How networked markets are transforming the economy and how to make them work for you*. WW Norton & Company.

   This work is a comprehensive treatment of platforms from their economics, structure, launch conditions, business models, governance structures, and regulatory concerns.

Network Effects

1. Rochet, J.C. and Tirole, J., 2003. Platform competition in two-sided markets. *Journal of the european economic association*, *1*(4), pp. 990-1029.

[12] https://www.scientificamerican.com/article/ai-platforms-like-chatgpt-are-easy-to-use-but-also-potentially-dangerous/

This is one of the two seminal works that describe the theory of two-sided network effects from the lens of the credit card industry.

2. Parker, G.G. and Van Alstyne, M.W., 2005. Two-sided network effects: A theory of information product design. *Management science*, *51*(10), pp. 1494-1504.

   This is the second of two seminal works describing the theory of two-sided network effects from the lens of multiple industries, including computer operating systems and software complements.

Openness

1. Joel West, "How Open Is Open Enough? Melding Proprietary and Open Source Platform Strategies," *Research Policy* 32, no. 7 (2003): 1259–85.

   This work examines the decisions that Apple, IBM, and Sun made in computer operating system markets to examine how openness impacts a firm's ability to capture value (appropriability) and user adoption.
2. Eisenmann, T.R., Parker, G. and Van Alstyne, M., (2009). "Opening platforms: How, when and why." In Platforms, markets and innovation, 6, pp. 131–162.

   This work defines platforms, lays out the different structures of sponsorship, and makes predictions of openness over a platform's life cycle.
3. Kevin Boudreau, "Open Platform Strategies and Innovation: Granting Access Versus Devolving Control," *Management Science* 56, no. 10 (2010): 1849–72.

   This work explores the decisions that mobile platform sponsors made with respect to allowing access to the platform and lays out subsequent adoption statistics.

Governance

1. Andrei Shleifer and Robert W. Vishny, "A Survey of Corporate Governance," *Journal of Finance* 52, no. 2 (1997): 737–83, esp. 737.

   This paper lays out the broad principles of governance at a firm level.
2. Geoffrey G. Parker and Marshall Van Alstyne, "Innovation, Openness and Platform Control," 2018, *Management Science*.

   This paper develops a model of sequential innovation that shows how ecosystem participants can be collectively better off if a platform enforces rules that require ecosystem partners to share intellectual property with other partners after a closed proprietary period.

Platform Growth and Power

1. Cusumano, M.A., Gawer, A. and Yoffie, D.B., 2021. Can self-regulation save digital platforms?. *Industrial and Corporate Change*, 30(5), pp. 1259–1285.

   This work explores which areas where platforms can be trusted to regulate themselves and where the threat of government intervention might be necessary to improve social welfare.
2. Cennamo, C., Kretschmer, T., Constantinides, P., Alaimo, C. and Santaló, J., 2023. Digital platforms regulation: An innovation-centric view of the EU's Digital Markets Act. *Journal of European Competition Law & Practice*, 14(1), pp. 44–51.

This work provides an additional analysis of the European Union's Digital Markets Act with a special focus on innovation.

References

Akerlof, G. A. (1970). The market for "lemons": Quality uncertainty and the market mechanism. *The Quarterly Journal of Economics, 84*(3), 488–500.

Akers, D., Golter, J., Lamm, B., & Solt, M. (2005). Overview of recent developments in the credit card industry. *FDIC Banking Review, 17*(3), 23–35.

Anderson, E. G., Bhargava, H. K., Boehm, J., & Parker, G. G. (2022a). Electric vehicles are a platform business: What firms need to know. *California Management Review, 64*(4), 135–154.

Anderson, E. G., Lopez, J., & Parker, G. G. (2022b). Leveraging value creation to drive the growth of B2B platforms. *Production and Operations Management, 31*(12), 4501–4514.

Aoyama, Y., & Izushi, H. (2003). Hardware gimmick or cultural innovation? Technological, cultural, and social foundations of the Japanese video game industry. *Research Policy, 32*(3), 423–444.

Aral, S. (2020). *The hype machine: How social media disrupts our elections, our economy, and our health--and how we must adapt*. Currency.

Boudreau, K., & Hagiu, A. (2009). Platform rules: Multi-sided platforms as regulators. In A. Gawer (Ed.), *Platforms, markets and innovation* (pp. 163–189). Edward Elgar Publishing Limited.

Cabral, L., Haucap, J., Parker, G., Petropoulos, G., Valletti, T. M., & Van Alstyne, M. W. (2021). The EU digital markets act: A report from a panel of economic experts. In L. Cabral, J. Haucap, G. Parker, G. Petropoulos, T. Valletti, & M. Van Alstyne (Eds.), *The EU digital markets act*. Publications Office of the European Union.

Caillaud, B., & Jullien, B. (2003). Chicken & egg: Competition among intermediation service providers. *RAND Journal of Economics, 34*(2), 309–328.

Choi, J. P. (2010). Tying in two-sided markets with multi-homing. *The Journal of Industrial Economics, 58*(3), 607–626.

Conger, K., & Isaac, M. (2021). Twitter permanently bans Trump, capping online revolt. *The New York Times*. Jan. 8, 2021.

David, P. A. (1985). Clio and the economics of QWERTY. *The American Economic Review, 75*(2), 332–337.

Eisenmann, T., Parker, G., & Van Alstyne, M. (2006). Strategies for two-sided markets. *Harvard Business Review, 84*(10), 92–101.

Eisenmann, T., Parker, G., & Van Alstyne, M. (2009). Opening platforms: How, when and why? In A. Gawer (Ed.), *Platforms, markets and innovation* (pp. 131–162). Edward Elgar Publishing Limited.

Eisenmann, T., Parker, G., & Van Alstyne, M. (2011). Platform envelopment. *Strategic Management Journal, 32*(12), 1270–1285.

Evans, D. S. (2009). The online advertising industry: Economics, evolution, and privacy. *Journal of Economic Perspectives, 23*(3), 37–60.

Farrell, J., Monroe, H. K., & Saloner, G. (1998). The vertical organization of industry: Systems competition versus component competition. *Journal of Economics and Management Strategy, 7*(2), 143–182.

Fink, C. (2018). Dangerous speech, anti-Muslim violence, and Facebook in Myanmar. *Journal of International Affairs, 71*(1.5), 43–52.

Gandhewar, N., & Sheikh, R. (2010). Google Android: An emerging software platform for mobile devices. *International Journal on Computer Science and Engineering, 1*, 12–17.

Goldfarb, A., & Tucker, C. E. (2011). Privacy regulation and online advertising. *Management Science, 57*(1), 57–71.

Gupta, A., & Parker, G. (2023). How will generative AI disrupt video platforms? *Harvard Business Review*. Online article, March 13, 2023.
Hagiu, A. (2006). Pricing and commitment by two-sided platforms. *The Rand Journal of Economics, 37*(3), 720–737.
Hagiu, A. (2014). Strategic decisions for multisided platforms. *MIT Sloan Management Review, 55*(Winter), 71–80.
Hagiu, A., & Wright, J. (2015). Multi-sided platforms. *International Journal of Industrial Organization, 43*, 162–174.
Hayes, R. H., Wheelwright, S., Wheelwright, S. C., & Clark, K. B. (1988). *Dynamic manufacturing: Creating the learning organization*. Simon and Schuster.
Henschke, A., Sussex, M., & O'Connor, C. (2020). Countering foreign interference: Election integrity lessons for liberal democracies. *Journal of Cyber Policy, 5*(2), 180–198.
Hesse, R. B. (2007). Two-sided platform markets and the application of the traditional antitrust analytical framework. *Competition Policy International, 3*(1).
Jacobides, M. G., Cennamo, C., & Gawer, A. (2018). Towards a theory of ecosystems. *Strategic Management Journal, 39*(8), 2255–2276.
Jacobides, M. G., Sundararajan, A., & Van Alstyne, M. (2019). Platforms and ecosystems: Enabling the digital economy. *World Economic Forum Report*.
Katz, M. L., & Shapiro, C. (1985). Network externalities, competition, and compatibility. *The American Economic Review, 75*(3), 424–440.
Lerner, J., & Tirole, J. (2002). Some simple economics of open source. *The Journal of Industrial Economics, 50*(2), 197–234.
Levandowski, C. E., Corin-Stig, D., Bergsjö, D., Forslund, A., Högman, U., Söderberg, R., & Johannesson, H. (2013). An integrated approach to technology platform and product platform development. *Concurrent Engineering, 21*(1), 65–83.
O'mahony, S., & Ferraro, F. (2007). The emergence of governance in an open source community. *Academy of Management Journal, 50*(5), 1079–1106.
Parker, G., & Van Alstyne, M. (2000). Internetwork externalities and free information goods. In: *Proceedings of the second ACM conference on electronic commerce*. Association for Computing Machinery, pp. 107–116.
Parker, G., & Van Alstyne, M. (2005). Two-sided network effects: A theory of information product design. *Management Science, 51*(10), 1494–1504.
Parker, G., & Van Alstyne, M. (2009). Six challenges in platform licensing and open innovation. *Communications and Strategies, Q2*, 17–36.
Parker, G., & Van Alstyne, M. (2018). Innovation, openness, and platform control. *Management Science, 64*, 3015–3032.
Parker, G. G., Van Alstyne, M. W., & Choudary, S. P. (2016). *Platform revolution: How networked markets are transforming the economy and how to make them work for you*. WW Norton & Company.
Parker, G., Petropoulos, G., & Van Alstyne, M. W. (2020). *Digital platforms and antitrust*. Available at SSRN: https://ssrn.com/abstract=3608397
Parker, G., Petropoulos, G., & Van Alstyne, M. (2021). Platform mergers and antitrust. *Industrial and Corporate Change, 30*(5), 1307–1336.
Rochet, J. C., & Tirole, J. (2003). Platform competition in two-sided markets. *Journal of the European Economic Association, 1*(4), 990–1029.
Rysman, M. (2009). The economics of two-sided markets. *The Journal of Economic Perspectives, 23*(3), 125–143.
Sawhney, M., & Nambisan, S. (2007). *The global brain: Your roadmap for innovating faster and smarter in a networked world*. Pearson Prentice Hall.
Seamans, R., & Zhu, F. (2014). Responses to entry in multi-sided markets: The impact of Craigslist on local newspapers. *Management Science, 60*(2), 476–493.
Shapiro, C. (2019). Protecting competition in the American economy: Merger control, tech titans, labor markets. *Journal of Economic Perspectives, 33*(3), 69–93.

Syed, N. (2017). Real talk about fake news: towards a better theory for platform governance. *Yale LJF, 127*, 337–357.

Trabucchi, D., & Buganza, T. (2020). Fostering digital platform innovation: From two to multi-sided platforms. *Creativity and Innovation Management, 29*, 345–358.

Van Alstyne, M. W. (2021). Free speech, platforms & the fake news problem. *Platforms and The Fake News Problem*. Available at SSRN: https://ssrn.com/abstract=3997980.

Vosoughi, S., Roy, D., & Aral, S. (2018). The spread of true and false news online. *Science, 359*, 1146–1151.

Yeates, M., Charles, A., & Jones, K. (2001). Anchors and externalities. *Canadian Journal of Regional Science, 24*, 465–484.

Zeng, M. (2015). Three paradoxes of building platforms. *Communications of the ACM, 58*(2), 27–29.

Work in a New World

Daniel Samaan

Abstract Work has always played a central role in human lives, from ancient times to the modern age to contemporary history. How is the way we work changing in the digital economy, and how can we make sure that it is changing for the better and not worse? This chapter provides an overview of what we currently know about the future of work, such as potential job losses through automation, new emerging jobs, new skills, future social security systems, and wage inequality, and of chances and risks more generally of working in the digital economy. The focus is on presenting an overview of currently existing socioeconomic research on the "future of work" and to identify policy areas in which policymakers may have to become active, with either established labor market and social policies or with entirely new policy ideas.

1 Introduction

Artificial intelligence (AI) keeps making the headlines about its progressing capabilities in carrying out activities that have been considered exclusively human behavior (see, e.g., very recently, the BBC reporting on ChatGPT and its successor GPT-4 on March 15, 2023)[1] Yet, the discussion about how digitalization is going to change the world of work dates back at least to the 1960s (see Simon, 1965); this is more than half a century ago. In 1964, the International Institute for Labour Studies (IILS) in Geneva, created by the International Labour Organization (ILO) in 1960, gathered international experts for a 5-day conference to discuss "Employment Problems of Automation and Advanced Technology." The papers and presentations of this conference have been preserved [see Stieber (1966)], and they offer valuable insights about how international experts at the time evaluated the challenges of new

[1] See, for example, BBC "OpenAI announces ChatGPT successor GPT-4": https://www.bbc.com/news/technology-64959346, accessed 14 March 2023.

D. Samaan (✉)
International Labour Organization (ILO) Research Department, Geneva, Switzerland
e-mail: samaan@ilo.org

H. Werthner et al. (eds.), *Introduction to Digital Humanism*,
https://doi.org/10.1007/978-3-031-45304-5_34

technologies for employment, education and training, management, and industrial relations. There was broad consensus at the conference that all these areas would be strongly affected by the perceived switch away from technological advances of so-called energy converters, i.e., machines that eliminate or reinforce human and animal muscle power, toward so-called "information converters," defined as machines that eliminate or reinforce human brain power, and which could "facilitate" man's acquired skills in writing, reading, and reaching conclusions along definite lines of reasoning or computing. It is easy to consider the development of ChatGPT as a current (and temporary) peak in the development of information converters, a journey that already started decades ago. Interestingly, the concerns about the world of work today appear to be very similar or even identical to the ones in the 1960s.

There are several reasons to first look into the past before reflecting about the future. Not everything that appears to be new to the current generation or to contemporary societies is or has been entirely new to mankind. Obviously, the introduction of new technologies into work processes, even of information processors, may be such a challenge for the current work generation, but previous generations have already dealt with this situation. A crucial question therefore is: To what extent are these changes truly revolutionary or disruptive in historical context? Will digitalization of our workplaces and our societies lead us into a very different (digital) society with new types of labor relations and new institutions, or will we merely see gradual adjustments to the existing world of work? The changes of the industrial revolution[2] were so profound that new labor market institutions, labor laws, and labor rights emerged: for example, trade unions, ministries of labor, regulation of working hours, the statuses of "employees" and "employers," unemployment insurances, maternity protection, and many other labor-related developments are all outcomes stemming from the industrial revolution. It is impossible to already give a definite answer to the question whether we will transform into a new type of digital society, with new types of labor relations and labor market institutions. Historians will be able to answer this question in the future. This chapter provides a non- exhaustive overview of the ongoing discussion about the future of work: First by looking at some debates from a more "traditional perspective," about how digital technologies might alter the existing world of work through job losses, new jobs, job transformations, skills training, productivity increases, and other changes. Second, the chapter highlights some considerations about how the world of work might fundamentally change our work culture in a future digital society.

Another interesting observation from the 1964 conference is that the participants attempted to evaluate the value of new technologies. Many concluded that,

[2]The industrial revolution did not occur in all countries and not everywhere at the same time. Furthermore, there existed country-specific differences that cannot be discussed in this article. Many features that concern the organization of work, such as mechanization or factory work, or the emergence of labor market institutions, were very similar in all countries that experienced an industrial revolution. This article refers to the "industrial revolution" in this sense.

ultimately, the value of any technology must be determined on the basis of its benefits and harm to humanity, Digital Humanism.

2 What Kind of "Digitalization"?

The terms "digitalization" and "artificial intelligence" (AI) are rarely precisely defined and mean different things in various studies. In this chapter, we understand as "digitalization" the whole process of converting information into a digital, machine-readable format as well as the adoption of digital tools in the world of work. The first phase of "digitalization," roughly from the 1960s to 2000, is mainly characterized by "computerization," the adoption of computers and programs. The second phase of "digitalization," over the last 20 to 25 years, can be mainly described by a large expansion of connectivity (the Internet), diffusion of mobile devices, availability of large datasets, and significant advances in AI. The only type of AI that appears to be available in the foreseeable future is "narrow AI," i.e., AI that is capable of solving specific problems. Most experts agree that artificial general intelligence (AGI), which would allow for the creation of machines that can basically mimic or supersede human intelligence on a wide range of varying tasks, is currently out of reach and that it may still take hundreds of years or more to develop AGI, if it can ever be developed.[3] Therefore, in this chapter, "digitalization" means computerization and adoption of (narrow) artificial intelligence.

3 The Traditional View: Adjustments to the Status Quo

Under the assumption that our economic system and our labor market institutions remain, by and large, the same as they are now and as they have been over the last decades, the economics literature has identified several channels through which digitalization and digital technologies affect labor markets. The two main ones are briefly discussed in this section. The first mechanism is that digital technologies are expected to raise productivity: this is to say output per worker is expected to increase. The second mechanism concerns the substitution or complementation of humans through digital machines (which would most likely also lead to productivity increases). The substitution of workers or human work activities through digital machines entails the risk of job losses and necessary organizational or personal adjustments to new activities, like transitioning of workers to new jobs and/or roles. This may require retraining of workers or the acquisition of new skills with possible

[3]See, for example, Rodney Brooks: https://rodneybrooks.com/agi-has-been-delayed/ or https://rodneybrooks.com/the-seven-deadly-sins-of-predicting-the-future-of-ai/

changes of a country's education and training systems. It follows from both channels, productivity increases and labor market transitions, that wages and incomes of workers and firms may change in the process. They may increase or decrease for particular workers or entities and hence lead to rising or declining inequality. Labor market transitions may also touch upon other aspects of work quality like job security, social security, or occupational health and safety.

3.1 Productivity

Productivity is expected to increase on the microlevel (in firms and organizations or at the individual workplace) as well as on the macrolevel (for the economy as a whole). The effects of productivity increases do not only affect labor markets but also other dimensions of the economy. For example, more productive firms tend to be more competitive, and they have growing market shares and are likely to be more successful in exporting their products and services.[4] This process typically leads to a structural transformation of the economy in which new enterprises and sectors emerge and others shrink or even disappear. In order to compare productivity growth across countries or sectors, economists tend to measure productivity in monetary values, for example, in USD per worker or USD per working hour. For labor markets, one immediate effect is that productivity increases allow for and often translate into wage increases for workers. Indeed, on the macroeconomic level, over long time periods (decades), one can observe that real wages in most countries roughly grow in line with labor productivity. However, it needs to be emphasized that this is not a natural process but depends on institutional settings, for example, the bargaining power of workers and firms. Therefore, we can also find examples and time periods in which the relationship between productivity growth and real wage growth breaks, as, for example, currently in the USA where the two time series have decoupled since the 1980s.[5] But for previous time periods and for most other countries, this relationship generally holds.

Surprisingly, for many policymakers and academics, labor productivity growth has been declining for decades (see, e.g., OECD (2015) or Dieppe (2021)). Starting in advanced economies in the 1970s and 1980s, the productivity growth slowdown is now a global phenomenon (ILO, 2023). It had and has been widely expected that the many applications of AI in combination with other digital technologies have an enormous potential for labor-saving automation, thereby increasing productivity [see OECD (2020), ILO (2022)]. Therefore, the lack of accelerating productivity growth rates has been dubbed the "modern productivity paradox." It should be noted

[4] The magnitude of productivity growth affects many other aspects of the economy, which cannot be discussed here in detail, not only the labor market.

[5] See, for example, the Economic Policy Institute (2022): https://www.epi.org/productivity-pay-gap/

that productivity growth is not only determined by the availability of technology but also many other factors, and the factors behind this secular decline in growth rates are still being debated (ILO, 2023).

With respect to digital technologies, the economics literature offers three explanations why the recent technological advances have failed so far to translate into higher productivity growth and hence higher economic well-being for the average person: Firstly, productivity increases can be hard to measure, especially in the services sector or for activities for which there exist no market prices (e.g., private activities or public sector output). We may therefore simply mismeasure and underestimate the real productivity increases. Secondly, the implementation of general-purpose technologies takes time, and recent digital technologies (like AI) are still in their implementation or diffusion phase [e.g., Brynjolfssonet et al. (2019)]. The decline in productivity growth rates is basically explained by a time lag, and future productivity growth rates should accelerate once the technology can exert its full effect. Finally, it has been contemplated that the effect of digital technologies on productivity is simply overestimated. Technologies with large effects on productivity have already been discovered by mankind in the past (steam engine, electricity, and others). The "low-hanging fruits" have already been harvested, and low-productivity growth is the new normal (Gordon, 2013, 2017; Gordon & Sayed, 2019).

3.2 *Labor Market Adjustments*

On the labor market, the prevailing economics literature sees computers, and more recently AI, as forms of capital, i.e., an economic production factor which is competing with labor, as the other production factor. Usually, a certain degree of substitutability is assumed between both production factors and obviously also exists in practice. Hence, we observe a constant race between machines and humans to be employed (see Acemoglu and Restrepo (2018)), both having comparative advantages, depending on their current costs and their capabilities. With costs for computers, data storage declining, and with the capacity of machines to perform more and more human tasks, capital as a production factor becomes more attractive for firms to employ. Most of the economics literature about the future of work and about job losses and technological unemployment is based on this idea of substitution between capital and labor.

This idea has been formalized in economics with the so-called task approach to labor markets propagated by Acemoglu and Autor (2011), Autor (2013), and others. Economic output at the microlevel (e.g., in a firm) is produced by "tasks" (or "work activities"), and the boundary between what are "labor tasks" and what are "capital tasks" is fluid and is changing dynamically as technological capabilities evolve. Which task is carried out by which production factor depends – in each particular point in time – on the relative economic cost of the two factors. Based on the machine-task substitution in Autor et al. (2003), Autor (2013) suggests that the set of tasks most subject to machine displacement are those that are routine or codifiable.

A task is routine if it can be accomplished by computer-controlled machines following explicit rules that can be programmed. A task is non-routine if people do not sufficiently understand them and struggle to articulate rules that machines can execute—non-routine tasks require tacit knowledge (Autor et al., 2003). As the implementation of computers and other digital devices become relatively cheaper, more routine tasks are being carried out by machines. This has become known as the "routinization" hypothesis, or Routine Biased Technical Change (RBTC). Routine tasks appear to occur mainly in occupations in the middle of the wage distribution, and the RBTC has therefore been used to explain observed employment growth at the top and the bottom of the distribution for several advanced economies [e.g., Autor et al. (2006), Autor and Dorn (2013), Goos and Manning (2007), Goos et al. (2014)]. Biagi and Sebastian (2020) provide an overview of the RBTC literature as well as the definitions and data sources that have been used to calculate empirical measures for routine tasks.

The same idea is typically extended to the analysis of AI, in this new wave of digitalization, whereby AI is seen as a form of capital that can either be a complement or a substitute for (different types of) labor. This is echoed by Frey and Osbourne (2017), Brynjolfsson and McAfee (2014), Brynjolfsson et al. (2018), and others, who claim that the replacement of cognitive and manual routine tasks through capital is evident but that this potential for replacement needs to be extended to non-routine cognitive tasks in the context of AI. Frey and Osbourne (2017) predict that any (also non-routine) task can be carried out by capital as long as it is not subject to any engineering bottlenecks, which they roughly group into the three categories, perception and manipulation tasks (or unstructured problems), creative intelligence tasks, and social intelligence tasks. What clearly emerges from this literature is that routine tasks are most suitable for automation and the replacement of machines including through AI. AI even expands the set of tasks that can be automated; its automation potential is therefore assumed to be even bigger. In other words, AI can be expected to take over at least all routine tasks and probably even many more. Fossen and Sorgner (2019) use two empirical measures for digitalization that have been developed by Frey and Osbourne (2017) ("probability of computerization") and by Brynjolfsson et al. (2018) ("suitable for machine learning") to categorize potential future changes of US occupations into "human terrain," "machine terrain," "rising stars," and "collapsing occupations." The idea is that occupations that require tasks that machines are "good at" are likely to disappear but that many occupations are only being transformed: Humans will use machines in their occupations, but human activities remain essential for the occupation. In most cases, occupations will not disappear in their entirety, but the tasks that humans do within this occupation will change. For example, a radiologist may spend more time with his patients or learn more about how to interpret computer output, while an AI analyzes thousands of images, an activity that the radiologist previously did himself. In summary, digitalization is expected to trigger both replacement and change of human work. In both cases, the consequences are labor market transitions. People will transition to entirely new jobs, to new roles, or to new tasks within existing occupations. Such transitions should, for the benefit of workers and enterprises, be transitions toward jobs that are more productive, are better paid and offer better working conditions. A crucial factor to enable people to make such labor market transitions are the skills that they have or which they need to acquire or retrain.

3.3 Skills

The labor market adjustments discussed in the previous section are only possible if people have the right skills to make such adjustments. Skills can be distinguished from tasks or work activities. Tasks refer to a job or an occupation (in which the tasks have to be carried out—see the "task approach" in the previous section). Skills refer to workers (i.e. to people). A skill can be defined as the capacity of a person to use her abilities, her knowledge, her experience, and her training to carry out particular tasks in a certain context. The distinction between skills (the capabilities of a person) and tasks (generalized or specific work activities) is often not made properly in many discussions led by human resources (HR) specialists and economists about the future of work. The terms are often used as synonyms. Indeed, it may be the case that changing tasks also requires a change in peoples' skillset, but this is not necessarily the case. We can imagine many situations in which a worker's existing skills enable him or her to carry out new or different tasks. For example, imagine someone with a high degree of social perceptiveness, like an HR recruiter who is experienced in assessing potential candidates in a physical interview. The recruiter would often be immediately capable of carrying out interviews online in a video call, without or with very little (re-)training. Hence, despite frequent calls for major "re-skilling" our "upskilling" of our workforces in light of digitalization, it is not at all clear which new skills exactly are needed in the future and which types of skills are truly becoming obsolete. Furthermore, there exists also no common definition of "digital skills," another frequently encountered term in the context of digitalization.

Various interpretations for this lacuna are possible: Digital skills could mean that people have the capability to develop digital tools and AI systems (e.g., IT specialists, programmers, mathematicians, etc. would have "digital skills"). The term could also refer to workers being skilled enough to utilize digital devices, for example, to collect data on the Internet and use certain applications or smartphones or tablets. (Would the majority of workers need massive re-skilling to carry out these tasks?) Digital skills could also refer to the proper use or the interpretation of machine output, e.g., an AI recruiting system rejects an applicant. How should the recruiter integrate this output from the AI in the overall recruiting process? Most likely, digitalization will raise demand for all types of these previously discussed tasks, but at what scale does this shift require re-skilling of our workforces? This is largely unknown. At the moment, for example, current labor shortages in North America and Europe exist in the construction sector, in health and elderly care, and the tourist industry, and none of these shortages are specifically linked to digitalization.

McKinsey (2018) and others suggest that those skills become more valuable for which humans have a comparative advantage against machines. This is in line with the economics literature that views labor market effects of digitalization mainly through the lens of substitution between capital and labor. For example, McKinsey (2018) predicts for the United States that demand of physical and manual skills and basic cognitive skills declines by 2030, while higher cognitive skills and social and emotional skills gain in importance. With some common sense, a comparison between what computers are good at and what they are not good at provides us with examples of skills/tasks/situations in which machines and humans have comparative advantages respectively. Machines are usually more efficient than humans in computing, handling large amounts of data, solving same-context problems, non-personal communication, carrying out standardized transactions, categorizing and matching items, and detecting correlations. Humans tend to be better at personal communication, solving problems in changing contexts, detecting causality, tackling problems for which no previous data are available or only very small data points exist, and solving unstructured problems that require frequent switching of tasks.

4 The Historical Perspective: An Entirely New World of Work?

So far, the implicit assumption has been that the overall structure of our labor markets remains, by and large, unaffected by digitalization: Work content changes, and people adjust and transition to better or worse jobs. They may have to retrain or learn new skills, but in the end, our society and the world of work, our social security systems, and education remain as they are. But as indicated in the introduction, does it have to be this way, or could digitalization truly disrupt the world of work and transformation into "digital societies"? This final section is based on Samaan (2022)) and reflects on the potential of the "digital revolution" to transform the world of work on a similar scale as the industrial revolution.

Labor relations changed profoundly around 200 years ago during the IR, driven mainly by societies in Europe and North America. Facilitated by technological advances like the steam and combustion engines as well as expedited by regulatory changes, mass production and standardization of goods became the prevailing modes of production. This newly emerging factory system also entailed changes in the work organization: it has been characterized by a high physical concentration of labor in production facilities and a hitherto unseen division of labor, orchestrated by hierarchical organizations. Both changes, mechanization and standardization of production processes and the corresponding new work organization, have led to unprecedented productivity increases to which we owe much of today's living standards. In his famous example of the pin factory, Adam Smith has illustrated the magnitude of these productivity increases more than two centuries ago, whereby output per worker could be increased to 4800 pins from less than 20 (Smith, 1776).

These changes to the way we work and the role that work plays in our societies are still dominant to this day. Bergmann (2019) calls it the invention of the "job system": We bundle the vast majority of our work activities ("tasks") into "jobs." We call standardized descriptions of such jobs "occupations." These jobs are then bought and sold on the (labor) market for a supposedly fair share of society's overall output (wage). Hence, the functioning of the industrial society is centered, not about work that we do for us but about obtaining and performing jobs for others.

The importance of the "job system" for our societies can hardly be underestimated. It is at the center of how we act and how we conduct our lives: We educate ourselves, predominantly, in order to "learn an occupation" and to "get a job." We want to spend our lives being "employed" and not "unemployed." Being "unemployed" or without a "real job" is social stigmata and leads to loss of income and social standing. Political competition in every Western democracy is critically concerned about creating new jobs or proposing suitable conditions for companies to crank out more jobs. We are prepared to accept all kinds of unpleasant trade-offs, like destroying our environment or heating up the climate, if only job creation is not harmed, because without jobs, we have no work, no income, no taxes, no public services, no social security systems, no more support for democratic votes, and finally no more society, as we currently know it. This way of thinking has not changed much since the industrial revolution. Today, we do reflect about the future of work, but our imagination of the future is restricted and dominated by the "job system" and by all the institutions and terminology that we created around it: "the labor market," "re-skilling," "unemployment," "part-time work" or "contingent work," etc. This list could be easily expanded and filled with the respective literature on the future of work. In other words, with some exceptions (e.g., Precht (2018)), most of the discussion on the future of work sees the job system as a given centerpiece of our societies. This was also the assumption in the previous sections about "labor market adjustments": The job system remains intact.

What is now the role of digitalization in this debate? One can look at the changes during the industrial revolution as a solution to a societal coordination problem: Labor productivity, hence living standards, could only be raised significantly if the division of labor was increased to unprecedented levels. But such a high division of labor creates very complex societies with the necessity to coordinate and administer collective behavior. Who needs what and who should work on which (intermediate) product and which service? At the time, it was impossible to obtain information from each individual and to coordinate on this basis behavior from bottom up. So, the solution to this coordination problem has been a hierarchical society and a hierarchical world of work, physically amassing workers in space and time (in factories or offices, the invention of working time and shift work), the creation of the "job system," and educating workers such that they can fill "jobs." The output has been standardized goods from mass production for the "average need" of the population. A society might run out of jobs, but it can never run out of work. The real question that we face today is therefore whether or not digitalization and its powerful offspring, big data and artificial intelligence (AI), are going to eradicate the "job system" and, if so, how we can live without it.

There are three reasons why digitalization, understood as a technology, has the potential to destroy the job system. Firstly, artificial intelligence is a general-purpose technology (Brynjolfsson & McAfee, 2014). It is not an invention, like the radio or many others, which had a confined impact on certain economic sectors and societal domains, like the radio has had on mass media, the printing press, and perhaps the military sector. AI and digitalization are more comparable to electrification. We can find applications and devices in virtually all economic sectors for consumers and producers, workers, management, governments, and many other actors alike. This qualification as a general-purpose technology is a major ingredient for a revolutionary change. Secondly, big data together with the wide availability of smartphones and connectivity provide economic actors with information on the "states of the world" and facilitate decentralized decision-making and decentralized action. Production plants and workers do not need to be concentrated, neither spatially nor in time. Output does not have to be standardized but can be customized for a specific individual. We can think about the industrial economic world as a picture of islands of producers, customers, workers, and managers, whereby the middlemen are connecting the islands. The whole picture ("state of the world") is not fully visible. Now big data is rapidly filling the empty spaces with many small dots and establishing direct connections among them. Thirdly, digitalization brings about an enormous potential to automate tasks. Such automation will not result in the end of human work but will lead to a big "re-shuffle" of work activities between humans and machines on a scale similar to the industrial revolution. This allows society also to reconsider which kind of work activities humans actually *want* to and should do and which ones we want to leave for the machines. There is potential for—literally—a "digital revolution" in the world of work rather than a slight and continuous adjustment of the status quo.

5 Conclusions

The world of work is changing through digitalization. The introduction of new technology into our working lives is nothing new but has already taken place for centuries. Even the process of digitalization has already changed the world of work for several decades. Job losses through automation and mechanization are possible but also the transformation of jobs through new technology, with positive effects on productivity and wages. Workers are likely to have to adjust their skills. Yet, as digital tools, especially in the form of AI, are general-purpose technologies and the changes through digitalization are profound and multifold, more disruptive change to the world of work is also a possibility. Whether the changes will be as transformative as the industrial revolution, and if they will lead us into a new "digital society," is still an open question. Our labor market structures are still very much embossed by the changes imposed by the industrial revolution. We can see digitalization also as a chance to liberate us from the constraints that the industrial revolution has imposed on us, as a path toward more self-organizing, non-hierarchical work organizations that generate individualized work output.

Discussion Questions for Students and Their Teachers

1. Which differences do you see between "digitalization" and other technological changes that have been experienced throughout human history?
2. Which changes could digitalization trigger in the world of work, and through which channels could these changes be triggered? Reflect on a variety of possible labor market dimensions that could be affected by digitalization, for example, the number of jobs, wages, social security systems, employment security, working conditions, personal development opportunities, equality, and others.
3. Which risks and which opportunities do you see in this transformation for people (workers), for enterprises, and for society?
4. Where do you see a role for policymakers to implement new or to enforce better existing policies or regulations? Why?

Learning Resources for Students

1. Acemoglu, D.; Restrepo, P. 2019. "The wrong kind of AI? Artificial intelligence and the future of labour demand" Cambridge Journal of Regions, Economy and Society, Vol. 13, pp. 25–35.

   This paper discusses how AI is predominantly seen by economists as a tool to automate existing human tasks. This process typically leads to a reduction of labor demand. The authors claim, however, that AI can also be employed to create new and different activities for humans, if the right choices are made. This alternative use of AI would lead to more desirable social and economic outcomes.
2. Acemoglu, D.; Restrep, P. 2016. "The race between machines and humans: Implications for growth, factor shares and jobs", voxEU.

   The article provides an overview of how economists have traditionally seen the relationship between technological progress and developments on the labor market. It relates this historic debate to recent advances in AI and the ongoing considerations about automation in economics.
3. Autor, David (2013), "The task approach to labor markets: an overview", IZA Discussion Paper No. 7178.

   In this overview, the author explains important labor market terminology such as "jobs," "skills," and "tasks." A conceptional, analytical framework is provided in which the two production factors "capital" and "labor" are combined to produce economic output. Through technological progress, the set of tasks that capital and human labor provide changes over time.
4. Bessen, J. 2016. "How computer automation affects occupations: Technology, jobs, and skills", voxEU.

   The author explains how automation does not only lead to job losses through replacement of workers but also influences other economic variables, such as productivity and occupations. If one considers more complex economic interactions over time, it becomes much more difficult to predict whether automation accelerates or decelerates job growth.

5. Brynjolfsson, E.; Mitchell, T. 2017. “What Can Machine Learning Do? Workforce Implications.” Science 358 (6370): 1530–34.

   The authors analyze the capabilities of AI (machine learning) relative to the typical capabilities of the US American workforce and discuss possible implications for the latter.
6. Brynjolfsson, Erik, Daniel Rock, and Chad Syverson (2019a). “Artificial Intelligence and the Modern Productivity Paradox: A Clash of Expectations and Statistics.” In The Economics of Artificial Intelligence: An Agenda, edited by Ajay Agrawal, Joshua Gans, and Avi Goldfarb. University of Chicago Press.

   The paper reviews recent empirical evidence of the global productivity growth slowdown on the macroeconomic level. Different hypotheses are evaluated that can explain how the alleged technological potential of digitalization and AI can be reconciled with poor productivity growth in the national statistics.
7. Fossen, F.; Sorgner, A. 2019. “Mapping the Future of Occupations: Transformative and Destructive Effects of New Digital Technologies on Jobs.” *Foresight and STI Governance* 13 (2): 10–18.

   The authors distinguish between transformative and destructive effects of digital technologies whereby destructive effects increase the risk of occupations becoming obsolete and transformative effects tend to change occupations and the respective skill requirements. The theory is then applied to empirical data about existing US occupations.
8. MIT. 2020. “Study finds stronger links between automation and inequality”, (Cambridge, MA.)

   This short newspaper article discusses the links between automation and income inequality.
9. The Digital Humanism Initiative (2021): “Perspectives on Digital Humanism”.

   The book consists of short essays that provide perspectives on digitalization for humanity. It has been written by selected thinkers from a variety of disciplines, including computer science, philosophy, education, law, economics, history, anthropology, political science, and sociology.

References

Acemoglu, D., & Autor, D. (2011). Chapter 12 - Skills, tasks and technologies: Implications for employment and earnings. In D. Card & O. Ashenfelter (Eds.), *Handbook of labor economics* (Vol. 4, pp. 1043–1171). Elsevier.

Acemoglu, D., & Restrepo, P. (2018). The race between man and machine: Implications of technology for growth, factor shares, and employment. *American Economic Review, 108*(6), 1488–1542.

Autor, D. H. (2013). The “task approach” to labor markets: An overview. *Journal for Labour Market Research, 46*, 185–199.

Autor, D. H., & Dorn, D. (2013). The growth of low-skill service jobs and the polarization of the US Labor Market. *American Economic Review, 103*, 1553–1597.

Autor, D., Levy, H. F., & Murnane, R. J. (2003). The skill content of recent technological change: An empirical exploration. *The Quarterly Journal of Economics, 118*, 1279–1333.

Autor, D., Katz, L., & Kearney, M. (2006). The polarization of the U.S. Labor Market. *American Economic Review, 96*(2), 189–194.

Bergmann, F. (2019). *New work, new culture – work we want and a culture that strengthens us*. Zero Books.

Biagi, F., & Sebastian, R. (2020). Technologies and "routinization". In K. F. Zimmermann (Ed.), *Handbook of labor, human resources and population economics* (pp. 1–17). Springer International Publishing.

Brynjolfsson, E., & McAfee, A. (2014). *The second machine age: Work, progress, and prosperity in a time of brilliant technologies*. Reprint. W.W. Norton & Company.

Brynjolfsson, E., Mitchell, T., & Rock, D. (2018). What can machines learn and what does it mean for occupations and the economy? *AEA Papers and Proceedings, 108*, 43–47.

Brynjolfsson, E., Rock, D., & Syverson, C. (2019). Artificial intelligence and the modern productivity paradox: A clash of expectations and statistics. In A. Agrawal, J. Gans, & A. Goldfarb (Eds.), *The economics of artificial intelligence: An agenda*. University of Chicago Press.

Dieppe, A. (Ed.) (2021). Global productivity – Trends, drivers and policies. In *International bank for deconstruction and development*. The World Bank.

Economic Policy Institute. (2022). *The productivity–pay gap*. Washington, DC. Accessed June 29, 2023, from https://www.epi.org/productivity-pay-gap/

Fossen, F., & Sorgner, A. (2019). Mapping the future of occupations: Transformative and destructive effects of new digital technologies on jobs. *Foresight and STI Governance, 13*(2), 10–18. https://doi.org/10.17323/2500-2597.2019.2.10.18

Frey, C. B., & Osborne, M. A. (2017). The future of employment: How susceptible are jobs to computerisation? *Technological Forecasting and Social Change, 114*, 254–280. https://doi.org/10.1016/j.techfore.2016.08.019

Goos, M., & Manning, A. (2007). Lousy and lovely jobs: The rising polarization of work in Britain. *The Review of Economics and Statistics, 89*(1), 118–133.

Goos, M., Manning, A., & Salomons, A. (2014). Explaining job polarization: Routine-biased technological change and offshoring. *American Economic Review, 104*(8), 2509–2526.

Gordon, R. J. (2013). U.S. productivity growth: The slowdown has returned after a temporary revival. *International Productivity Monitor, 25*, 13–19. https://ideas.repec.org/a/sls/ipmsls/v25y20132.html.X

Gordon, R. J. (2017). *The rise and fall of American growth: The U.S. standard of living since the Civil War*. Princeton University Press. X.

Gordon, R. J., & Sayed, H. (2019). The industry anatomy of the transatlantic productivity growth slowdown: Europe chasing the American frontier. *International Productivity Monitor, 37*, 3–38.

ILO. (2022). *Digital transition, technological change and productive development policies in LAC: Challenges and opportunities*. International Labour Office.

ILO. (2023). *World employment and social outlook: Trends 2023*. International Labour Office.

McKinsey Global Institute. (2018). *Skill shift, automation, and the future of the workforce*. Discussion Paper, MGI.

OECD. (2015). *The future of productivity*. OECD Publishing. https://read.oecd-ilibrary.org/economics/the-future-of-productivity_9789264248533-en#page4

OECD. (2020). *OECD digital economy outlook 2020*. OECD Publishing. https://www.oecd-ilibrary.org/sites/bb167041-en/index.html?itemId=/content/publication/bb167041-en

Precht, R. D. (2018). *Jäger, Hirten, Kritiker – Eine Utopie für eine digitale Gesellschaft, Goldmann Verlag, 1*. Auflage.

Samaan, D. K. (2022). Work without jobs. In H. Werthner, E. Prehm, E. A. Lee, & C. Ghezi (Eds.), *Perspectives on digital humanism* (pp. 251–256). Springer.

Simon, H. A. (1965). *The shape of automation for men and management*. Harper & Row.

Smith, A. (1776). *An inquiry into the nature and causes of the wealth of nations*. Modern Library; 12/26/93 edition (December 26, 1993), New York.

Stieber, J. (Ed.). (1966). *Employment problems of automation and advanced technology – An international perspective*. Macmillan.

BY

Digital Labor, Platforms, and AI

Luke Munn

Abstract This chapter examines the role that platform labor plays in the development of contemporary AI systems. While such systems are often touted as magical innovations, they are typically propped up by vast amounts of human laborers, who clean the data, manually label key features, and moderate toxic content, among other tasks. Proponents claim these tasks offer flexibility and pay; critics counter that this work is exploitative and precarious, taking advantage of the already marginalized. This chapter surfaces this often-invisible labor, highlighting several key issues around its poor or nonexistent remuneration, exploitative mechanisms, negative impact on well-being, and extractive colonial logics. The chapter suggests several interventions, from concrete policy to corporate responsibility, that might lead to improvements. As AI technologies proliferate into many domains, the hidden labor required to develop them—and the negative impacts this has on lives and livelihoods—becomes an increasingly urgent issue.

1 Introduction

From ChatGPT to DALL-E, contemporary AI models have recently dominated headlines as revolutionary new tools, capable of penning witty poetry, delivering scientific articles, or fabricating fantasy landscapes on the fly. But often overlooked in this wide-eyed rhetoric is human work and its contribution to these models.

This chapter examines the human labor behind several foundational AI models. This is the open secret behind our technical marvels, the "artificial artificial intelligence" (Stephens, 2023) that prepares and powers them. In this framing, computational technologies are ascendant, but not yet smart enough. Human laborers are needed for this temporary transitional stage, to fill in the cognitive, affective, and physical gaps. Filling in the gaps means cleaning data by hand, manually labeling tricky scenes, or moderating ambiguous content. This is the invisible labor behind

L. Munn (✉)
Digital Cultures and Societies, University of Queensland, Fairfield, QLD, Australia
e-mail: l.munn@uq.edu.au

H. Werthner et al. (eds.), *Introduction to Digital Humanism*,
https://doi.org/10.1007/978-3-031-45304-5_35

so-called automated systems (Munn, 2022; Gray & Suri, 2019), what some have referred to as "fauxtomation" (Taylor, 2018).

How might we delimit this labor from other types of labor? Platform labor is a broad term that can refer to ride-share drivers (Munn, 2017), digitally mediated care workers (Ticona & Mateescu, 2018), and freelance designers and professionals (Carlos Alvarez de la Vega et al., 2021), along with a wide array of other roles, in a diverse range of industry sectors. This chapter focuses on a certain form of platform labor often referred to as "crowd work" or "click work." While there has been significant research on crowd work, much of it has concentrated on older, general-purpose crowd work platforms like Amazon Mechanical Turk (Ross et al., 2010; Paolacci et al., 2010).

However, an array of newer platforms have emerged in recent years specifically geared toward labor for AI technologies. Appen, Remotasks, Scale AI, CrowdWorks, and Defined.ai are some of the key players to enter this space. There has been less research on these platforms and particularly how they interface with very new generative AI models such as ChatGPT and DALL-E 2, both released in November 2022. This chapter thus acknowledges insights and commonalities from prior crowd work research while focusing more specifically on crowd labor for contemporary AI systems.

By all accounts, this human labor behind AI is swelling, forming a vast army. While obtaining precise demographics for these platforms is difficult, one study estimated that there were 19 million active users on these platforms at the end of 2020 (Kässi et al., 2021). Other figures can be obtained from the websites of individual providers. The Japanese platform CrowdWorks (2023), for example, boasts that it has 4.7 million workers in its ranks. These workers come from the USA, but also India, Venezuela, Russia, the Philippines, and dozens of other countries (Posch et al., 2022). And the global pandemic has only deepened the draw and uptake of this digitally mediated remote work (Braesemann et al., 2022). As AI technologies proliferate across industries and countries, this labor will only expand in scale and scope.

For technology pundits, AI technologies and platforms are a positive step, accelerating innovation and ushering in progress and prosperity (Brynjolfsson & McAfee, 2011, 2014). But more critical research has highlighted the social fallout of AI-driven shifts, its ability to extract capital in novel ways while increasing precarity and inequality. As the chapter will discuss, platform labor for AI is often low paid, operating on a piece-work model, leaving workers with little recourse or power, and targeting workers from Global South countries.

The result is that exploitative forms of labor are at the heart of our contemporary AI systems. This makes such labor a key issue for any serious development of digital humanism. Digital humanism is concerned with making our technologies more humane, more egalitarian, more just. Yet rather than benefiting humanity, the current conditions benefit a handful of elite technology companies while harming those who are already marginalized and disenfranchised. Workers pour their time and energy into these platforms, contributing their cognitive, affective, and physical skills, but are then discarded, without sharing in any of the financial, cultural, and intellectual capital that accompanies cutting-edge AI models. There can be no ethical AI without ethical crowd work.

2 Key Concepts in Platform Labor for AI

The origins of labor for AI are closely linked to crowd work platforms. Amazon Mechanical Turk is widely considered to be the first crowd work platform. At the turn of millennium, the Amazon marketplace was plagued with duplicate products. While Amazon engineers attempted many automated solutions to identify and remove these duplicates, they eventually gave up, deeming the problem too difficult. However, in 2001, one Amazon manager devised a solution and published it as a patent. Venky Harinarayan's et al. (2001) patent described a "hybrid machine/human" arrangement which broke jobs down into "subtasks" and distributed them to a large pool of human laborers. While the platform was originally an in-house tool, its success led the company to releasing it to the public in 2005. Clients quickly adopted the platform, farming out "human intelligence tasks" to hundreds of workers.

While Amazon Mechanical Turk is still a major player in the crowd work space, it has recently been joined by an array of platforms specifically aimed at providing the labor for AI technologies. Samasource (2023) offers "human in the loop validation" for AI developers, claiming to offer "quicker time to accuracy" and "faster time to market." CrowdWorks (2023) stresses that AI requires "massive amounts of training data" and presents data labeling as a "remote, part-time job where you can earn money wherever you want, whenever you want." "80% of your AI efforts will be spent managing data," Appen (2023) cautions developers and promises that its massive labor force will take care of this requirement, delivering "quality data for the AI lifecycle."

Such rhetoric provides a way of understanding how crowd labor is framed in AI production—work that is at once absolutely necessary and deeply devalued. The creation, curation, and cleaning of training data is certainly understood as key to AI success. But this meticulous and monotonous labor can take thousands of hours. That kind of grunt work is beneath developers, who focus instead on the "innovative" work around machine learning architectures, techniques, and testing. Data annotation is "dirty work" (Rosette, 2019), outsourced to others who are cheaper and less talented. Their labor, largely invisible and quickly forgotten, sets the stage for experts to build the AI engines of the future.

2.1 *Digital Piecework*

Crowd work for AI platforms draws on a longstanding form of labor: piecework. Piecework, as its name suggests, is work which is compensated by a fixed rate per piece. Piecework emerged in the late nineteenth century in astronomical calculations and manual farm labor, where workers were paid for each result. But piecework achieved its greatest hold and attention in the domain of garment production. In Britain, workers toiled at home in poor conditions for subsistence-level wages, a practice known as the sweating system (Earl of Dunraven, 1890). Thanks to the struggles and organization of labor activists, this exploitative form of labor largely disappeared in developed countries after the mid-twentieth century. However, as Veena Dubal (2020) notes, Silicon Valley companies have resurrected this notorious model of compensation. Indeed, for Alkhatib et al. (2017), there is a clear link between historical forms of piecework and contemporary forms of crowd work. By chopping jobs into microtasks and farming them out to global workers, this digital piecework extracts long hours of computational labor at poverty-level rates.

Crowd work is low-paid, descending at times to pennies per task (Simonite, 2020). One study found that the average hourly wage for this work was $2 (Hara et al., 2018). A more recent meta-analysis suggested the average was more like $6 per hour (Hornuf & Vrankar, 2022) but highlighted the difficulty of measuring unpaid labor in this analysis. These analyses are echoed by workers. Workers must identify jobs, read instructions, complete each task, and then wait to get paid. Far from being a source of steady income, then, crowd work is highly fragmented—intense bursts of microtasks interspersed with long periods of down time. This makes it difficult for workers to precisely calculate their earnings—and when they do, they are typically lower than was anticipated or desired (Warin, 2022).

2.2 *Unpaid Labor*

Significant amounts of work on crowd platforms are not compensated at all. One study found that the most time intensive task for workers was managing their payment, a form of labor that is totally unpaid (Toxtli et al., 2021). The same study discovered that hypervigilance, or watching and identifying jobs, was another form of invisible and uncounted labor (Toxtli et al., 2021). In a survey of 656 online workers, participants said they spent 16 h per week on average browsing for jobs, reading about jobs, and applying for jobs (Wood et al., 2019, p. 943). For some workers, this means literally refreshing the webpage over and over again. For more tech-savvy workers, this means setting up a scripted alert whenever tasks with certain keywords come through. Yet whether manual or automated, workers must be ready to claim these tasks instantly; desirable jobs on these platforms disappear in a matter of seconds. One worker "didn't feel like she could leave her apartment, or even her computer, lest she miss out on an opportunity to work on good tasks" (Schein, 2021, p. 412). This is high-pressure labor that is not counted as labor.

Another variant of unpaid labor is training. On crowd work platforms, workers often need to qualify for particular jobs. This typically entails completing batteries of test questions or undertaking sample tasks that approximate the real work (see Posada 2022 for one account). Such training can take hours or even days to complete but is not remunerated. These preparatory tasks are typically framed as an upskilling opportunity or a quality control measure, ensuring that workers can deliver a professional product to clients. For platform providers and their clients, this is the work needed to be "work ready"—the unpaid labor before the "real" labor begins.

Finally, unpaid labor takes place through the rejection mechanism built into crowd work platforms. Clients are able to provide ambiguous instructions to workers and then "mass reject" completed tasks for trivial deviations from these guidelines (Altenried, 2020). This dynamic is exacerbated by the fact that click work is extremely low paid (see above). Clients can request far more samples or tasks than they actually require, select their preferred data, and then reject the surplus. Rejection means that workers are simply not paid for this task. Workers may protest, but, as many testify, platforms overwhelmingly side with the client, the paying customer, in these disputes.

2.3 *Toxic and Exhausting Labor*

While the remuneration of this labor is bleak, it is worth looking beyond the economic conditions to consider the psychological and subjective impact of this work on the worker. For instance, the hypervigilance required to constantly monitor jobs and snap up good ones (Toxtli et al., 2021) suggests intense pressures on workers, which may be internalized as anxiety or stress. Drawing on two large surveys of two thousand workers, Glavin et al. (2021) found that both gig workers and crowd workers were more vulnerable to forms of loneliness, a finding that perfectly tracks with a form of labor which is highly individualized and often highly competitive. In addition, workers have little control over platform mechanisms, and this powerlessness can often produce annoyance or anger. One study found that technical problems in conducting tasks, platform competition, and the inability to disconnect from work all led to significant levels of frustration amongst workers (Strunk et al., 2022).

If this work can be psychologically damaging, it can also be simply exhausting. One study of 263 workers on a crowdsource platform found they became technologically overloaded, leading to burnout (Bunjak et al., 2021). Burned-out workers leave the platform, creating significant churn. But as Van Doorn (2017) notes, the turnover created by these accelerated conditions is designed into the model: as workers become exhausted and leave, a new set of precarious individuals comes on board to take their place. Baked into platforms, then, is the logic of obsolescence. Workers are driven to the point of breakdown and then quit in disgust at the conditions or are discarded when their performances falter.

Of course, such a logic is far from novel. Marx (1977, p. 348) diagnosed this same dynamic when he noted "'capital's drive towards a limitless draining away of labor-power." Just as the soil was exhausted of nutrients, the body of the worker was exhausted of its productive potential. In this sense, the extraction of labor for AI technologies is not some unprecedented condition, but a repetition of what has come before. The exploitation of vulnerable or even desperate workers by elite technology companies is a pattern that seems all too familiar. This means that insights from the history of labor and from analyses of capital can still be fruitful, providing insights for understanding these conditions and recommendations for improving labor practices.

2.4 Colonial Circuits

Platform labor for AI is not equally distributed across the globe but is instead arranged in particular patterns. These patterns tend to follow long-established patterns of labor, where work is extracted from Global South locations and funneled to Global North actors. Cheap labor is coordinated and captured in the colonies and then transmitted to startups, developers, or tech titans. This is the well-known global division of labor (Caporaso, 1981), an imperialist appropriation of resources and labor which provides a boon to these so-called advanced economies (Hickel et al., 2022).

Labor for AI models does not so much upend this division as twist and extend it in various ways. These technologies enable new forms of flexibilization resulting in a division of labor between innovation-intensive production sites and their counterparts in the so-called periphery (Krzywdzinski, 2021). Companies leverage new digital technologies—together with a large informal sector and very limited regulation—to build an instant low-cost workforce in a marginal economy (Anwar & Graham, 2020).

Fragments of work are farmed out to laborers in the Global South who are essentially hired and fired with each task. Scaling up and down as necessary, this just-in-time workforce offers a model to companies that is lean, flexible, and above all, cheap. AI systems depend upon this work to function correctly and to "learn" rapidly, but this key labor from the Majority World is often rendered invisible (Amrute et al., 2022).

This is an asymmetric power relation. In one sense, data production hubs such as Ghana, Kenya, or South Africa mean that Africans are technically participating in the development of AI technologies. However, as Chan et al. (2021) stress, such "participation" is limited to work which is low level and low paid—and there are systemic barriers that prevent more meaningful or collaborative forms of participation. The result is a new form of extractivism (Monasterio Astobiza et al., 2022), reminiscent of the colonial plundering of resources, where valuable raw materials are harvested and built into lucrative AI products by powerful digital empires.

2.5 ChatGPT as Case Study

ChatGPT provides a case study that exemplifies many of these issues. This AI large language model can replicate human-sounding text in many genres and has been widely celebrated as an important innovation. The model was developed by OpenAI, a high-profile startup based in San Francisco with $11 billion in capital. However, as a high-profile report for *TIME* (Perrigo, 2023) documented, the firm came up against a crucial issue during development. The model had great potential but also major problems, regularly churning out responses that were racist, sexist, misogynistic, or toxic in various ways.

To remedy this issue, the firm turned to Samasource, a platform based in Kenya. Their mission was straightforward but fraught: provide labeled examples of violence, hate speech, and sexual abuse so that an AI model could be trained on them (Perrigo, 2023). Sama was sent hundreds of snippets of abhorrent text describing child sexual abuse, bestiality, murder, suicide, torture, self-harm, and incest in graphic detail. Sama workers had to read through each of these samples and manually label each one. Workers testified to the trauma or psychological fallout of reading through such depictions, over and over again, day after day. In this sense, these individuals are the haz-chem workers of the digital world, carrying out dirty and dangerous work in order to construct safe environments for the privileged (Munn, 2022).

The study found that workers were paid between $1.30 and $2 per hour, depending on their seniority and performance levels (Perrigo, 2023). This could be compared against the average salary for a software engineer at OpenAI, which is at least $250,000 USD per year, not including typical developer add-ons such as signing bonuses, stock options, and performance bonuses. In this single case study, then, we see low wages, harsh work conditions, psychological damage, and the extractivism of disposable Global South labor by a wealthy Global North company (Table 1).

Table 1 A summary of key issues (among many) in AI labor discussed in this chapter

Fundamental framing	Human data labor is often invisible and undervalued in comparison to "innovative" or "high-value" model work
Digital piecework	Crowd work on AI platforms uses a piecework or per-task model that compensates in pennies
Unpaid labor	Significant amounts of labor, including training, searching for jobs, and rejected labor, is not compensated at all
Toxic and exhausting labor	The intensity, repetition, and frustration experienced on crowdsourcing platforms can impart a physical and psychological toll on workers
Colonial circuits	AI companies in the Global North frequently leverage low-paid and precarious workers drawn from Global South countries

3 Possible Solutions and Interventions

As the chapter has suggested, there are a number of significant issues with the current state of labor for AI systems. These issues are diverse, ranging from the financial (extremely low remuneration or nonpayment) through to the social (isolation, alienation, and sense of powerlessness) and the political and racial (exploitation of global division of labor and Global South workers), among others. Even from this cursory list, it is clear that there is no "silver bullet" solution for AI labor issues, no single technical fix that would address these multifaceted problems. However, there are several more modest suggestions which aim to improve the situation for workers.

Mutual aid is one possible intervention. After interviewing and surveying many workers on Amazon Mechanical Turk, Lilly Irani and Michael Silberman (2013) found that many experienced frustration at the lack of information on clients and the lack of accountability for misbehavior. As a result, the duo established Turkopticon, a forum where workers can rate clients, share stories, and exchange information. These kinds of spaces and forums also exist for other platform laborers, such as ride-share drivers. Such an intervention, while imperfect, disrupts the profound isolation and informational asymmetry that tend to characterize platform labor. This intervention allows workers to come together, share their experiences, warn others, and generally offer forms of support. It is one manifestation of mutual aid, a form of solidarity and support that workers have long used to improve their conditions and enhance their prospects. Such communality and support need to be extended into the context of AI labor, which is individualized and invisible. Indeed, in his book on AI labor, Dan McQuillan (2022) considers mutual aid to be a significant and strategic response to the brutal conditions that these technologies often impose.

Best Practices and Guidelines can also provide concrete recommendations for companies engaging in this form of work. The Allen Institute for Artificial Intelligence (2019), for instance, released its guidelines for AI labor as a public resource. The guidelines give an hourly rate for US-based work and international work; they establish a rubric for pricing work; they highlight the importance of worker privacy; they champion transparency and setting expectations with workers; and they caution about rejecting work. Other research has suggested that companies doing crowd work for natural language technologies takes up three ethical principles to mitigate harm and improve conditions (Shmueli et al., 2021). These principles and best practices have potential if companies seriously engage with them and uphold them. However, ethical principles in the context of AI are nonbinding and can easily be ignored (Munn, 2022), with high-minded ideals effectively acting as window-dressing while the real business of technical development continues apace.

For this reason, "soft" principles and norms must be accompanied by "harder" *regulations and legislation*. The application of laws to platform labor, which is globally distributed across many territories, is by no means trivial. However, as Cherry (2019) notes, precedents can be found in the EU's GDPR scheme for data, in the laws applied to maritime workers, and to multinational codes of conduct, all of which have "extraterritorial" applicability. In the case of maritime workers, for

Table 2 A summary of potential interventions (among others) to improve labor for AI

Mutual aid	Spaces and tools that allow workers to support each other, fostering forms of solidarity and communality
Best practices and guidelines	Values, norms, and standards that provide companies and organizations with a strong blueprint for humane work
Regulations and legislation	Laws and regulatory regimes, with penalties and enforcement mechanisms to ensure compliance

instance, there are international laws, conventions, and standards that have been ratified by member states, forming a regulatory regime that is largely understood and followed across the globe. A similar scheme might be drafted specifically for AI crowd workers that recognizes their needs, establishes key protections, and defines a set of penalties for non-adherence. Such a scheme for "socially responsible crowd work" is possible, stresses Cherry (2019), but it requires creative thinking and buy-in from platforms, workers, and regulators (Table 2).

4 Conclusions

Contemporary AI models are highly dependent on high-quality data for training, accuracy, and functionality. Producing such data often means annotating fields, labeling images, cleaning duplicates, or even developing new datasets for a particular domain or use case. Such production does not happen magically but instead requires vast amounts of human labor. This labor has typically been organized through crowd work platforms, where large jobs are broken into microtasks and distributed to a massive labor pool of workers. However, there are numerous problems with this approach, as this chapter has discussed. Workers are paid poorly or not at all, much of the work is invisible and uncounted (e.g., finding jobs), the tasks themselves can be taxing or even toxic, and the labor form is extractive, transferring labor from vulnerable populations to elite tech companies in ways that repeat colonial patterns. While there are no easy solutions to this situation, an array of interventions, from mutual aid to industry norms and harder regulation, could lead to incremental improvements in terms of work conditions, worker well-being, and more equitable forms of organization. Thoughtfully engaging with these issues—and carrying out the difficult negotiation and implementation of responses in real-world work situations—must be central to any institution or organization committed to digital humanism.

Discussion Questions for Students and Their Teachers

1. Why is human labor necessary for contemporary AI models, systems, and technologies?
2. How did crowd working emerge as a distinct form of labor? What similarities does it have with older, or historical, forms of labor?
3. How is crowd work paid, and what issues emerge around remuneration of this work?
4. What kind of labor conditions characterize this crowd work? What kinds of impacts does this have (not just economically but socially, psychologically, etc.)?
5. How is labor for AI organized globally? Describe how this distribution of labor perpetuates colonial patterns and power relations.
6. What kind of interventions could be made to AI labor in order to increase remuneration, improve labor conditions, and support the well-being of workers?

Learning Resources for Students

1. Altenried, Moritz. 2022. *The Digital Factory*. Chicago: University of Chicago Press.

   This book does an excellent job of showing the historical links between the Taylorist rationalization of work, where gestures were measured and optimized to boost production, and the control (gamification, algorithmic management) mechanisms embedded in crowd work, the gig economy, and other contemporary forms of labor.
2. Perrigo, Billy. 2023. "Exclusive: The $2 Per Hour Workers Who Made ChatGPT Safer." *TIME Magazine*. January 18. https://time.com/6247678/openai-chatgpt-kenya-workers/.

   The case study in my chapter draws from this excellent piece of investigative journalism. This example showcases in a clear and powerful manner many of the underlying issues with labor for AI systems, including very low pay and poor working conditions, exposure to toxic material, and the exploitation of precarious labor pools in the Global South by Global North tech titans.
3. Amrute et al. 2022. "A Primer on AI in/from the Majority World: An Empirical Site and a Standpoint." New York: Data & Society. https://www.ssrn.com/abstract=4199467.

   This report aims to reframe the conversation on technology and the Global South, focusing on its dynamism, its ingenious interventions, and its pools of potential labor, rather than what it lacks. The authors present an array of fascinating readings, arranged thematically, which augment typical viewpoints on AI and labor in a challenging and productive way.
4. Munn, Luke. 2022. *Automation is a Myth*. Stanford: Stanford University Press.

   This book is a short and accessible text that lays out key issues around automated technologies, contextualizing technologies, and racialized and gendered labor. Drawing on numerous disciplines and an array of rich stories from workers, it highlights the vast army of human labor that props up so-called "automated" systems.

5. Gray, Mary, and Suri, Siddharth. 2019. *Ghost Work: How to Stop Silicon Valley from Building a New Global Underclass*. Boston: Houghton Mifflin Harcourt.

   This book showcases the diverse forms of invisible labor that contribute toward our contemporary technical systems. This "ghost work" is carried out by women, migrants, students, and a range of other people to earn some money but is often underpaid or exploitative. Gray and Suri highlight the importance of this work, show how tech companies adopt it as a strategy, and discuss how it might be altered and improved for the better.

References

Alkhatib, A., Bernstein, M. S., & Levi, M. (2017). Examining crowd work and gig work through the historical lens of piecework. In *Proceedings of the 2017 CHI conference on human factors in computing systems. CHI '17: CHI conference on human factors in computing systems* (pp. 4599–4616). ACM. doi:https://doi.org/10.1145/3025453.3025974.

Allen, A. I. (2019). *Crowdsourcing: Pricing ethics and best practices, medium*. Accessed February 28, 2023, from https://blog.allenai.org/crowdsourcing-pricing-ethics-and-best-practices-8487fd5c9872

Altenried, M. (2020). The platform as factory: Crowdwork and the hidden labour behind artificial intelligence. *Capital & Class, 44*(2), 145–158.

Altenried, M. (2022). *The digital factory: The human labor of automation*. University of Chicago Press. Accessed March 6, 2023, from https://press.uchicago.edu/ucp/books/book/chicago/D/bo123166001.html

Amrute, S., Singh, R., & Guzmán, R. L. (2022). *A primer on ai in/from the majority world: An empirical site and a standpoint*. Data & Society. Accessed March 1, 2023, from https://www.ssrn.com/abstract=4199467

Anwar, M. A., & Graham, M. (2020). Digital labour at economic margins: African workers and the global information economy. *Review of African Political Economy, 47*(163), 95–105. https://doi.org/10.1080/03056244.2020.1728243

Appen. (2023). *Confidence to deploy AI with world-class training data, Appen*. Accessed March 6, 2023, from https://appen.com/

Braesemann, F., et al. (2022). The global polarisation of remote work. *PLoS One, 17*(10), e0274630. https://doi.org/10.1371/journal.pone.0274630

Brynjolfsson, E., & McAfee, A. (2011). *Race against the machine: How the digital revolution is accelerating innovation, driving productivity, and irreversibly transforming employment and the economy*. Digital Frontier Press.

Brynjolfsson, E., & McAfee, A. (2014). *The second machine age: Work, progress, and prosperity in a time of brilliant technologies*. WW Norton & Company.

Bunjak, A., Černe, M., & Popovič, A. (2021). Absorbed in technology but digitally overloaded: Interplay effects on gig workers' burnout and creativity. *Information and Management, 58*(8), 103533. https://doi.org/10.1016/j.im.2021.103533

Caporaso, J. A. (1981). Industrialization in the periphery: The evolving global division of labor. *International Studies Quarterly, 25*(3), 347–384. https://doi.org/10.2307/2600579

Carlos Alvarez de la Vega, J., Cecchinato, M. E., & Rooksby, J. (2021). "Why lose control?": A study of freelancers' experiences with gig economy platforms. in *Proceedings of the 2021 CHI conference on human factors in computing systems* (pp. 1–14). Association for Computing Machinery (CHI '21). doi:https://doi.org/10.1145/3411764.3445305.

Chan, A. et al. (2021). *The limits of global inclusion in AI development*. arXiv. Accessed March 6, 2023, from http://arxiv.org/abs/2102.01265

Cherry, M. (2019). A global system of work, a global system of regulation: Crowdwork and conflicts of law. *Tulane Law Review, 94*, 183–246.
Crowdworks. (2023). *CrowdWorks, Inc.* Accessed February 13, 2023, from https://crowdworks.co.jp/en
Dubal, V. (2020). Digital piecework. *Dissent Magazine*. Accessed March 1, 2023, from https://www.dissentmagazine.org/article/digital-piecework
Earl of Dunraven. (1890). *The sweating system.* House of Lords. Accessed March 1, 2023, from https://api.parliament.uk/historic-hansard/lords/1890/jun/09/the-sweating-system
Glavin, P., Bierman, A., & Schieman, S. (2021). Über-alienated: Powerless and alone in the gig economy. *Work and Occupations, 48*(4), 399–431. Available at:. https://doi.org/10.1177/07308884211024711
Gray, M., & Suri, S. (2019). *Ghost work: How to stop silicon valley from building a new global underclass*. Houghton Mifflin Harcourt.
Hara, K. et al. (2018). A data-driven analysis of workers' earnings on Amazon mechanical Turk'. In *Proceedings of the 2018 CHI conference on human factors in computing systems* (pp. 1–14). Association for Computing Machinery (CHI '18). doi:https://doi.org/10.1145/3173574.3174023.
Harinarayan, V., Rajaraman, A., & Ranganathan, A. (2001). *Hybrid machine/human computing arrangement*. Available at: https://patents.google.com/patent/US7197459B1/en
Hickel, J., et al. (2022). Imperialist appropriation in the world economy: Drain from the global South through unequal exchange, 1990–2015. *Global Environmental Change, 73*, 102467. https://doi.org/10.1016/j.gloenvcha.2022.102467
Hornuf, L., & Vrankar, D. (2022). Hourly wages in Crowdworking: A meta-analysis. *Business and Information Systems Engineering, 64*(5), 553–573. https://doi.org/10.1007/s12599-022-00769-5
Irani, L. C., & Silberman, M. S. (2013). *Turkopticon*. doi:https://doi.org/10.1145/2470654.2470742.
Kässi, O., Lehdonvirta, V., & Stephany, F. (2021). How many online workers are there in the world? A data-driven assessment. *arXiv preprint arXiv:2103.12648* [Preprint].
Krzywdzinski, M. (2021). Digitalization and change in the global division of labor: Industrial work in transition. RBEST: Revista Brasileira de Economia Social e do Trabalho, 3 (Art. No.:) e021016. doi: https://doi.org/10.20396/rbest.v3i00.15864.
Marx, K. (1977). *Capital: A critique of political economy*. Translated by B. Fowkes. Vintage.
McQuillan, D. (2022). *Resisting AI: An anti-fascist approach to artificial intelligence*. Policy Press.
Monasterio Astobiza, A., et al. (2022). Ethical governance of AI in the global south: A human rights approach to responsible use of AI. *Proceedings, 81*(1), 136. https://doi.org/10.3390/proceedings2022081136
Munn, L. (2017). I am a driver-partner. *Work Organisation, Labour & Globalisation, 11*(2), 7–20. https://doi.org/10.13169/workorgalaboglob.11.2.0007
Munn, L. (2022). *Automation is a myth*. Stanford University Press.
Paolacci, G., Chandler, J., & Ipeirotis, P. G. (2010). Running experiments on amazon mechanical turk. *Judgment and Decision making, 5*(5), 411–419.
Perrigo, B. (2023). Exclusive: The $2 per hour workers who made ChatGPT safer. *Time*, 18 January. Accessed January 23, 2023, from https://time.com/6247678/openai-chatgpt-kenya-workers/
Posada, J. (2022). Embedded reproduction in platform data work. *Information, Communication and Society, 25*(6), 816–834. https://doi.org/10.1080/1369118X.2022.2049849
Posch, L., et al. (2022). Characterizing the global crowd workforce: A cross-country comparison of Crowdworker demographics. *Human Computation, 9*(1). https://doi.org/10.15346/hc.v9i1.106
Rosette. (2019). *How data annotation works: Inside NLP and search, Part IV, rosette text analytics*. Accessed March 3, 2023, from https://www.rosette.com/blog/inside-nlp-and-search-part-iv/
Ross, J. et al. (2010). Who are the crowd workers? Shifting demographics in Amazon mechanical Turk. In *CHI '10 human factors in computing systems*. ACM, pp. 2863–2872.

Samasource. (2023). *Sama AI platform: Accurate data annotation services, SAMA*. Accessed March 6, 2023, from https://www.sama.com/

Schein, R. (2021). From free time to idle time: Time, work-discipline, and the gig economy. In *Research handbook on law and Marxism* (pp. 400–420). Edward Elgar Publishing.

Shmueli, B. et al. (2021). *Beyond fair pay: Ethical implications of NLP crowdsourcing*. arXiv. https://doi.org/10.48550/arXiv.2104.10097.

Simonite, T. (2020). Newly unemployed, and labeling photos for pennies. *Wired*, 23 April. Accessed March 1, 2023, from https://www.wired.com/story/newly-unemployed-labeling-photos-pennies/

Stephens, E. (2023). The mechanical Turk: A short history of 'artificial artificial intelligence'. *Cultural Studies, 37*(1), 65–87.

Strunk, K. S., et al. (2022). Antecedents of frustration in crowd work and the moderating role of autonomy. *Computers in Human Behavior, 128*, 107094. https://doi.org/10.1016/j.chb.2021.107094

Taylor, A. (2018). *The automation charade, logic magazine*. Accessed January 31, 2023, from https://logicmag.io/failure/the-automation-charade/

Ticona, J., & Mateescu, A. (2018). Trusted strangers: Carework platforms' cultural entrepreneurship in the on-demand economy. *New Media and Society, 20*(11), 4384–4404. https://doi.org/10.1177/1461444818773727

Toxtli, C., Suri, S., & Savage, S. (2021). Quantifying the invisible labor in crowd work. *Proceedings of the ACM on human-computer interaction*, 5(CSCW2), p. 319:1–319:26. doi:https://doi.org/10.1145/3476060.

van Doorn, N. (2017). Platform labor: On the gendered and racialized exploitation of low-income service work in the "on-demand" economy. *Information, Communication and Society, 20*(6), 898–914. https://doi.org/10.1080/1369118X.2017.1294194

Warin, R. (2022). *Love, loss and unpaid wages*. Fairwork Podcast. Accessed March 1, 2023, from https://shows.acast.com/fairwork-podcast/episodes/004-love-loss-and-unpaid-wages

Wood, A. J., et al. (2019). Good gig, bad gig: Autonomy and algorithmic control in the global gig economy. *Work, Employment and Society, 33*(1), 56–75. https://doi.org/10.1177/0950017018785616

Sovereignty in the Digital Age

Paul Timmers

Abstract The century-old concept of state sovereignty is acquiring new and hotly debated meaning, due to digital disruption and technology-without-borders, dominance by powerful—often foreign-owned—global tech companies, and cyber-undermining by malicious states. Sovereignty, as we know it, is also threatened by rising geopolitical tensions, war, and global challenges such as climate change, pandemics, and global cyber-crime. This chapter deals with the future of sovereignty in a digital and geopolitically contested age. It starts with an introduction into international relations, sovereignty, and strategic autonomy thinking. It reflects on the impact of digital technology on the international system of states. Then the chapter provides an analysis and some practical guidance to tackle the challenges of developing public policy for sovereignty in the digital, and digital humanistic, age. Finally, two case studies and a set of questions invite the reader to a deeper dive.

1 Introduction

Sovereignty means that states or countries have autonomy[1] in how they manage their internal affairs. Consequently, countries should respect each other's sovereignty. This is, of course, only one and a highly simplified Platonic ideal image of sovereignty. We will go deeper into the multiplicity of perspectives on sovereignty and international relations.

When we say *sovereignty*, generally here we are talking about state sovereignty rather than the sovereignty of an individual person. However, the two are closely related. Sovereignty concerns the power arrangements in society, notably between the citizens and the "state." A government or ruler who is systematically not

[1] Autonomy does not at all imply autarky. Rather there are several options to realize and safeguard sovereignty, as Sect. 4 discusses in detail (while also clarifying the notion of *digital sovereignty*).

P. Timmers (✉)
Public Governance Institute, University of Oxford, Leuven University, Leuven, Belgium
e-mail: paul.timmers@kuleuven.be

H. Werthner et al. (eds.), *Introduction to Digital Humanism*,
https://doi.org/10.1007/978-3-031-45304-5_36

Fig. 1 Sovereignty gap

accepted by the people is in trouble. People in a country who are not accepted by the government or the ruler are in trouble. One way to arrange for the allocation of power between citizens and state is democracy and respect for fundamental human rights. These are two relational notions that link state and individual sovereignty. They are also at the heart of what digital humanism stands for.

Why would we spend time on such a century-old concept? The reason is that in today's geopoliticized digital age, sovereignty is under severe pressure. There is a *sovereignty gap* between the aspirations for state sovereignty and hard reality (Kello, 2017). The hard reality consists of the threats of geopolitical conflict, the pervasively disruptive nature of digital technologies and big tech, and global threats such as cyber-crime, pandemic, and climate change (see Fig. 1). These three forces are not halted by the human-created borders between countries; they do not respect sovereignty. The international system of states is being disrupted and perhaps fundamentally reshaped. No wonder that heads of states are very worried. Since 2017, sovereignty and the related notion of strategic autonomy have been *Chefsache*. But they are not sitting ducks and have come forward with a multitude of public policies to safeguard, defend, and even strengthen sovereignty.

Here we focus on public policies that address the interplay of digital technologies and sovereignty. That is, public policy that shapes sovereignty and the digital age fit for what we want.

The central problem is to develop public policy for sovereignty in the digital age.

What we need for this is to shed light and to understand: to shed light on the possible shapes of sovereignty in the digital age, and the desired ones, which is a political choice, and to understand the interplay of technology and society. This is not easy at all. However, not addressing the problem leaves us in the hands of unaccountable powers, undemocratic authoritarians, and uncontrollable technology development. This would precisely be counter to what digital humanism is about.

Sovereignty and geopolitics are key aspects of the reality that digital humanism seeks to influence.

We now first give a brief introduction to perspectives on international relations, sovereignty, and strategic autonomy. That puts us in a position to discuss the impact of digital technologies. Then we can address the challenges of developing public policy for sovereignty in the digital age and illustrate these by concrete cases in two hot topics of cybersecurity and artificial intelligence (AI).

2 International Relations

Sovereignty of countries, or state sovereignty, is a key concept in political sciences, in particular in the study of the relations between countries, that is, international relations (IR). In IR thinking—grossly simplified—the main schools are realists, liberalists, and contingency thinkers. Realists consider that the international system of states is basically an anarchy of states. This does not mean that there is chaos but rather that the defining characteristic is that there is no overarching authority. Moreover, states are captured in the "security dilemma" which means that they must be ever mistrustful of the intentions of foreign states, having to rely on self-help, and likely preemptively having to arm themselves. This line also fits global or regional hegemon thinking (Mearsheimer, 1994; Waltz, 2010).

Liberalists consider that there is more than states to world order. International organizations and other actors (e.g., private sector, NGOs, the global tech community) also play a role in international relations. Collaboration between states is possibly and, in fact, quite likely based on self-interest rightly understood (de Tocqueville, 1864).

Contingency thinking considers that international relations between states depend on, or are contingent on history, the evolving identity of states and the "socialization" between states, as developed over years and in all forms of international relations. An illustration is the establishment of international institutions and governance post-1945 such as IMF and World Bank and the EU, all strongly influenced by the traumas of the two World Wars.

In addition, we mention mercantilist and Marxist thinking. Both see state relations as inherently conflictual (as do realists). For both the primary motivation is economic. For mercantilists, national wealth contributes to and should serve national power relative to other nations. For Marxists, capitalist profit-maximization inherently leads to conflicts, also between states (Art & Jervis, 2016, p. 277). These two ways of economics-based thinking are relevant for us when, for instance, we want to design an industrial policy for semiconductors that considers both global economics and geopolitics.

Although the interplay of international relations and technology has been researched, there is not yet a systematic corpus of academic knowledge, let alone established schools on this issue within either political or technology/innovation sciences. Technology has for a long time been seen as an exogenous factor by international relations scholars and mainly as a factor in warfare. Nevertheless, the writing was on the wall with the famous Declaration of the Independence of Cyberspace that stated "Governments of the Industrial World [...] You have no sovereignty where we gather" (Barlow, 1996). Recently, perhaps belatedly, a new political sciences branch of "techno-politics" is emerging. It has grown out of science and technology studies and takes seriously a two-way interplay of technology and (international) politics (Eriksson & Newlove-Eriksson, 2021).

As stated in the introduction, digital humanism perspectives should relate to the international system of states. Realists will consider states as primary actors and likely take digital humanism into account only as far as it fits with friend/foe perceptions. Digital humanism as a movement can then very well impact alliances of like-minded states but become problematic when it reaches outside like-minded states. Digital humanism in the realist perspective would be expected to work in particular with state-related social constructs such as law, public education, and national democratic institutions.

Liberalists, being more open to multistakeholder approaches, may see digital humanism acting through a wider set of channels or multistakeholder platforms and believe that it can make a difference in international relations, also beyond the existing configuration of states, whether democratic and likeminded or not. In particular, digital humanism may exert influence through technology-based collaborations and other social constructs (e.g., digital ethics and standards). However, not all liberalist thinking may be at peace with digital humanism. In particular, both extreme liberalism that seeks to minimize influence of the state and unconstrained economic liberalism can be argued to be incompatible with democracy (Francis Fukuyama, 2022) and other digital humanism principles as expressed in the Digital Humanism Manifesto (Digital Humanism Initiative DIGHUM, 2019).

Contingency thinkers in turn may stress the historically contingent context of both digital humanism and international relations. They may be taking into account a history of sovereignty from roots in the Treaties of Westphalia and late seventeenth-century Enlightenment to today's philosophy about the relations between technology, humans, and society (see Learning Resources, below). They may also take into account that, while we are in a time of heightened geopolitical polarization, the perception of what "the state" is may well alter in a time span of decades or centuries due to long-term trends or major global forces, such as climate change, or indeed technology. For contingency thinkers, digital humanism and international relations are not absolute. They may be looking for long-term and profound trends and factors that transcend both. Digital humanists may well be wary of the economic-functionalist perspectives of both mercantilists and Marxists since digital humanism is likely seen as an instrument rather than an objective per se.

The "Discussion Questions" challenge to bring IR thinking and digital humanism ideas together.

3 Sovereignty

Sovereignty as one of our central themes turns out to be a hard to pin down concept. State sovereignty has emerged from at least three thinkers. Bodin (1529) came up with the concept of the sovereign as a person who exercises absolute and undivided power with impact both internal to the state and in the external affairs of the state. Hobbes (1588) developed the doctrine of supreme sovereignty based on a unitary body politic of rulers and rule, free from supreme accountability (except, perhaps to God). Jean-Jacques Rousseau (1762), an Enlightenment thinker, advocated popular sovereignty and a social contract which evolved into the thinking that the relationship citizen-state sovereignty is legitimized by choice of the citizens with corresponding obligations of the state toward citizens (Stanford University, n.d.).

In the second half of the sixteenth and first half of the seventeenth century, European kings, warlords, and the Holy Roman Empire almost continuously fought with each other. This brought devastation to Europe and millions of people died. In 1648, the Treaties of Westphalia were signed that set out to end the warring by recognizing states as the locus of sovereignty. It was the birth of the state-based system of relationships between sovereigns, which became the sovereign states-based system of international relations in much of the world.

Obviously, international relations have evolved over the centuries. Likewise, the concept of sovereignty is evolving and may well appear to be rather fuzzy. Perhaps we have to accept that sovereignty is an essentially contested concept, as is religion or art (Gallie, 1956).

Still, that does not stop us deepening our understanding and continuing the discourse on sovereignty and its future. Today, international relations have evolved from states into supranational organizations such as the UN and its agencies as well as regional law-based alliances of states such as the European Union (EU) that pool and share sovereignty. While countries and states do not have diminished in relevance, an important body of international law has emerged, and though frequently contested it is still ever-expanding along with global challenges (Klabbers, 2021).

In an age where power is linked to control of technology and where global challenges transcend the powers of any individual state, we must take into account international corporations—such as big tech—and their influence on geopolitics. Similarly of great importance are international collaborations such as civil society activism, standardization by the technology community and industrial alliances, as well as multistakeholder collaborations. These can be meeting places for common opinion building and voluntary action but can also have power, either de facto or sometimes also de jure under national, regional, or international law, to manage important assets of economy, society, justice, or democracy. An instructive case in the digital domain is ICANN (Internet Corporation for Assigned Names and Numbers). This is a private international multistakeholder organization that manages the Internet domain name system. ICANN is effective in achieving international compliance to global domain name management, not in the least thanks to its multistakeholder approach, yet it is not an organization under international law.[2]

Sovereignty requires internal and external legitimacy (Biersteker, 2012). Internal legitimacy is acceptance of the authority of the government by the citizens. External legitimacy is the acceptance of the state by foreign countries. Sovereignty concerns three "assets" that need to be governed: (1) power, which is called foundational sovereignty; (2) physical and nowadays also digital assets which comprise above all territory and therefore is called territorial sovereignty; and (3) the institutional organization of economy, society, and democracy, which is called institutional sovereignty (Bickerton et al., 2022).

The key notions of internal and external legitimacy map onto foundational, territorial, and institutional sovereignty. For instance, where state sovereignty is about power arrangements, these need to be recognized internally and externally. To be effective the state needs to have authority in the organization of government and public services, and democracy needs to be an authoritative institution, for instance, with an organization to ensure free elections. "Territory" may be seen as any resources or assets that "belong to us" (i.e., not to "them"). These are of a geographic, natural, or digital origin and can also be taken to include the population, values, and culture. This territorial view clearly requires internal and external recognition and thereby legitimacy. Finally, the institutions of government need to be internally accepted, while their external legitimacy is a matter of—sometimes disputed—international relations, such as extraterritorial jurisdiction (Klabbers, 2021, pp. 106–108).

State sovereignty is quite different from sovereignty of the individual, but nevertheless, they are related through the internal legitimacy dimension of sovereignty. Control over what belongs to us as individuals (our body and life, our thoughts, our preferences, our choices in social relations and democracy) will likely lead to tensions in the relationship between state and individual when the state also seeks control. Such tensions manifest themselves in authoritarian regimes where there is suppression of free speech. They also show up when national security or safety or public health is at stake. Some felt that their personal freedom was unjustly curtailed during the COVID-19 pandemic and for some the state lost legitimacy.

A difficult question is also who exercises control over what is shared between citizens and the state. The canonical example is citizen identity (or eID for its digital form). Does it belong to you or to the state? Clearly, it is a sovereign asset and issuing the citizen ID is a function of the sovereign (i.e., the state), a *fonction régalienne*. However, many of our electronic identities are issued by Internet companies, and some we use over and over, including for public services such as Facebook or Google or Apple ID. Can our eID also belong to a corporation rather than the state? The EU seeks to answer such questions in its EU Digital Wallet law. Such a digital wallet includes the national eID, which is issued and recognized by the

[2] ICANN is a US 501(c)3 nonprofit, with obligations for transparency and to spend its budget on its mission, and is subject to the Court of California.

state, and furthermore contains personal attributes that are under self-sovereign, that is, exclusive citizen control. Moreover, with the EU Digital Markets Act, the big tech platforms (so-called gatekeepers) have to accept identification with the nationally recognized ID. Therefore, a citizen eID or enriched citizen eID such as a digital wallet in Europe is unlikely to come under exclusive corporate control.[3]

4 Strategic Autonomy

Much ink has been spilled in the last few years on the notion of strategic autonomy, certainly in European debates. While some would argue that this is yet another essentially contested concept (General Secretariat, 2021), research reveals that this is actually not the case. There are at least two origins of the notion of strategic autonomy (Timmers, 2019). One is in the French defense/military doctrine that considers it as the capacities and capabilities to defend sovereignty. After WWII, this was also translated by France to the ability to project military power wherever necessary in the world (*force de frappe*) and the need to have the atomic bomb. The other origin is in Indian diplomacy, again especially after WWII, which was the doctrine that India should have independence from either Beijing, Moscow, or Washington, which also has strong defense/military undertones, that is, non-alignment.

Clearly, both tell us that strategic autonomy is seen as a means to an end, the end being sovereignty. The means consist of capabilities and capacities and control. Also, clearly, today the notion of strategic autonomy goes beyond the military domain, since sovereignty in the geopolitical digital age is threatened across economy, society, and democracy—national defense included. In the USA, economic security is equated to national security. In China, economic geo-competition is translated into a competition (with the West) for global system dominance and US hegemony is no longer accepted.

This leads us to the following definition: *strategic autonomy consists of the capabilities, capacities, and control to decide and act on essential aspects of our economy, society, and democracy.*

Is this a clear and operational definition? One could criticize that "essential" and "our" are not defined. Indeed, these terms link to what is meant by "our" sovereignty. They have to be interpreted in the discourse on who "we" are and how we interpret sovereignty, which is not a matter of definition but rather of assessment and judgment.

[3]In theory, the government of the EU Member State can notify a corporate eID/eWallet as being compliant with the EU's Digital Wallet law. However, if there are few strings attached, this could be seen as a handover of a sovereign asset to commercial interests (which was not uncommon in the past and even in the present when this concerns natural resources such as oil/gas or minerals).

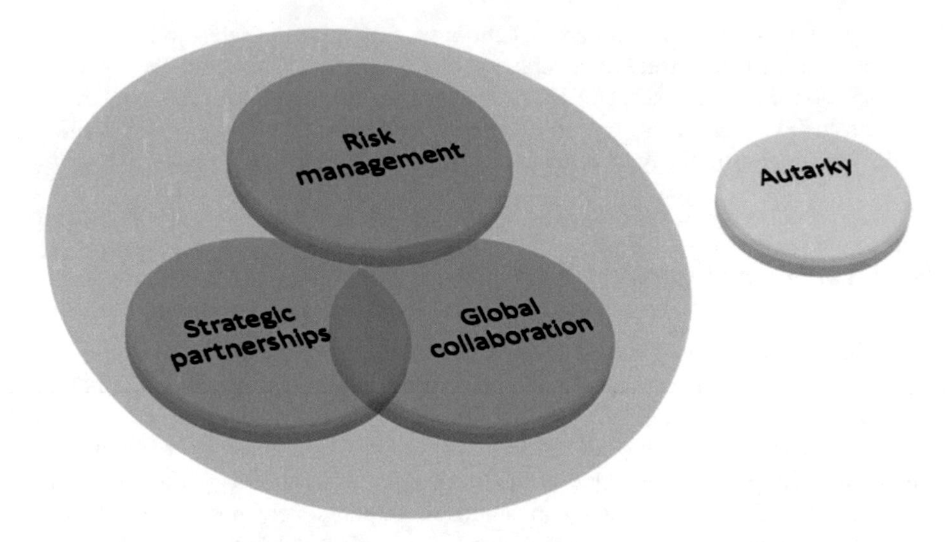

Fig. 2 Four ways to address strategic autonomy

The other terms are clearer: capabilities are what we know, capacities are how much we can do, and control is the say we have over capabilities and capacities, decisions and actions. This makes the definition quite operational: we can identify and even often measure capabilities and capacities and control or at least use proxies for these. Examples—far from an exhaustive list—of such proxies are patents and skilled professionals (capabilities), investments and market share (capacities), shareholding, and security scrutiny requirements (control).

Furthermore, by having such an operational definition, we become aware that often in many aspects strategic autonomy will not be absolute but only relative to other countries. It will also only be partial. It is unlikely, except perhaps for the superpowers USA and China, to have total control and have all necessary capabilities and capacities, in other words, to have autarky. Economically, this is actually undesirable because, even for the superpowers, lack of scale leads to inefficiencies compared to division of roles across countries, i.e., specialization and global supply chains. An illustration is that for the semiconductor industry, a global industrial ecosystem costs in the order of one trillion dollars less than fully localized "self-sufficient" supply chains (Boston Consulting Group and Semiconductor Industry Association, 2021). How else to address strategic autonomy? There are essentially four ways (see Fig. 2).

First, we already mentioned autarky. Second, countries can impose a risk management approach to strategic autonomy, that is, doing the best possible according to the state of the art, but otherwise accepting vulnerabilities as an unavoidable risk. Hopefully that residual risk is not disastrous, i.e., one can bounce back, one has resilience. Risk management may not seem wise (do you want to put the state at risk?), but it is actually the approach that many countries have followed from the 1970s until recently. They were encouraged that globalization would reduce

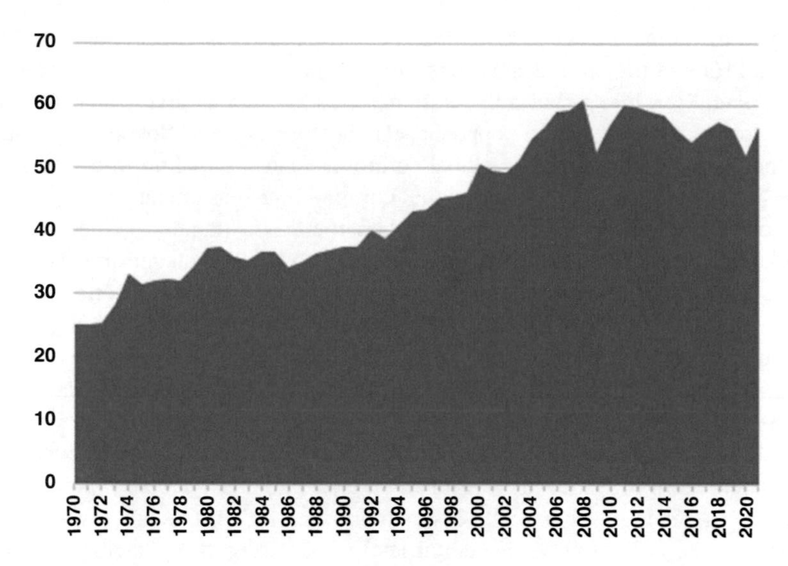

Fig. 3 Global trade (% of GDP, CC-BY 4.0 license, World Bank)

supply risks and have resilience as a by-product. Indeed, globalization increased fairly consistently year upon year [see Fig. 3, with global trade as a proxy for globalization (World Bank, 2021)], until 2021. Already earlier, there were doubts about the risks of critical foreign dependencies, but COVID-19 brought home that message loud and clear. Risk management is no longer the most-favored approach.

Rather on the rise and this is the third way is a strategic partnership approach to strategic autonomy, meaning, to work together with like-minded countries or regions in order to, as much as possible, strengthen joint or shared capabilities and capacities and control. Strategic partnerships of the like-minded do not ignore that there can still be strategic dependencies on non-like-minded countries. Dependency policy identifies such critical dependencies and for each determines the appropriate policy action, such as import substitution, foreign M&A (mergers and acquisitions), building up domestic capacity, acquisition of intellectual property (IP), or, realistically, also IP theft and state-sponsored industrial espionage. The reverse approach is also part of such analysis, namely, to weaponize dependencies. On the latter, following early work on power and interdependence in international relations (Keohane & Nye Jr, 2011), further thinking is emerging that addresses how in today's geopolitical and globally networked digital/technological world, dependencies actively get weaponized, which we see happening today, for instance, in semiconductors and critical raw materials (Farrell & Newman, 2019).

Finally, the fourth approach to strategic autonomy is to pursue global collaboration on global common goods. This may seem idealistic but is in fact a reality, even today. Examples in the digital world are the management of the Internet domain name system by ICANN, a multistakeholder global organization with authority over the allocation of domain names (from the country domain names such as ".cn" to thematic ones such as ".shop") and to some extent safeguarding the security and stability of the domain name system globally. A successful past example is the 1987 Montreal Protocol to curb the emissions of CFK gases that destroy the ozone layer.

Paradoxically, while global collaboration seems to be about giving up control and thereby losing sovereignty, the opposite can be true as well. Sovereignty can be strengthened by jointly nurturing global commons. This holds true when the global threats surpass the power of any individual country—such as climate change, cybercrime, or pandemics. It also holds true when there is a tragedy of the commons situation, that is, either free-riders egotistically destroy the beneficial source or going solo impedes the development of the much greater benefits of the common good, from which, in turn, sovereignty can be strengthened. The great political philosopher Alexis de Tocqueville observed this when studying democracy in America in the nineteenth century, finding that the motivation to collaborate and provide benefits to others is "self-interest rightly understood" (de Tocqueville, 1864).

The scale of collaboration does not necessarily have to be global. Regional collaboration as in the EU, which is legally based in the EU Treaties, may be seen by the EU member states as a win-lose situation as far as national sovereignty is concerned. It appears obvious that countries lose sovereignty by having to comply with EU laws, while the EU as a supranational entity gains sovereignty. But this is not always true. A case in point is the EU Digital COVID Pass which provides a triple win: it enabled EU member states to better deal within their own country with the pandemic and thus strengthened internal legitimacy of government vs citizens. It also built a European common good, an EU sovereign asset which increased the legitimacy of the EU in relation to European citizens. Finally, it increased the standing and influence of the EU in the world, i.e., its external legitimacy, as the EU COVID Pass has been recognized and copied by 65 countries and over 1 billion people across the world.

Strategic autonomy is a key concept for sovereignty in the digital age. It can take many shapes and degrees of realization. But the debate is sometimes confused by misunderstandings on terminology and fallacies. Often strategic autonomy in digital matters is—mistakenly—called *digital sovereignty*, whereas authors actually discuss capabilities, capacities, and control rather than sovereignty.

There are also fallacies about strategic autonomy. One is that authors equate strategic autonomy to autarky or self-sufficiency which has the smell of protectionism. But autarky is only one approach and actually the rarest. Moreover, protectionism may be a legitimate policy measure to strengthen strategic autonomy, but the converse may also be true. Moreover, strengthening mutual interdependencies can reduce the risk that the foreign country would be tempted to undermine its partner's sovereignty.

There are two more fallacies on which we can be brief. One is the "we can have it all" fata morgana. Strategic autonomy does not come for free. The total investments for strong independence (such as in semiconductors, cloud, networks, AI, green industry, medicines, etc.) far surpass the resources of most countries. Another is the "let's take back control" fallacy (the slogan of Brexit). As (Martin Wolf, 2019) convincingly and scathingly argued, you cannot take back control on something you never had. As an example, for the EU, cloud strategic autonomy is not about taking

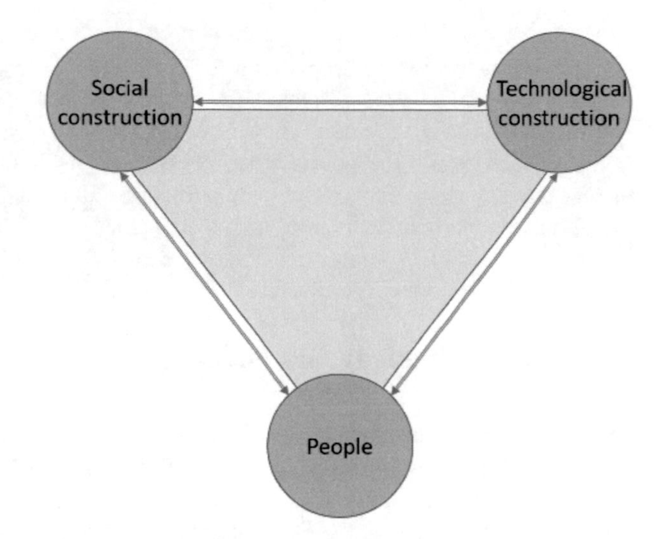

Fig. 4 Social and technological construction of reality

back control but rather about either building up an EU cloud industry that can compete with the big foreign cloud providers (who have 70% of the market in the EU), or accepting to play a value-added role to the big cloud providers in trust services and AI with as a consequence long-term geopolitical dependency on the USA, or changing the paradigm and building up strategic autonomy in edge-cloud, a new form of decentralized and distributed cloud.

Interludium: Technological and Social Construction of Reality
The underestimation of the power of technology to shape international relations has its mirror in the underestimation of the power of geopolitics to shape technology. There is a much closer interplay between technological constructs and social constructs such as international relations and government than we are often aware of. The same holds for sovereignty and its social constructs such as law, public services, justice, democracy, etc. More generally, Fig. 4 illustrates this (Timmers, 2022a).

Therefore, when investigating which public policy for sovereignty in the digital age, we should ab initio take as degrees of freedom both the technological constructs and the social constructs of sovereignty. In the early 2000s, the term "code is law" was used to express that the technical architecture of the Internet conditioned and constrained legislative options to regulate the Internet (Lessig, Lawrence, 1999). Moving toward the 2020s, the awareness grew that the reverse also holds, that is, law is code. This means that technology has to be designed in order to fit with the norms and rules society wishes to have (De Filippi & Wright, 2019). Some terms that reflect this thinking are *privacy-by-design* and *security-by-design*. We are now entering an age of *sovereignty-*

(continued)

by-design, the combined social and technological (re-)construction of sovereignty. Cohen (2019) shows that large tech companies have often well understood that this is the case. They have worked for years closely with the government, while the government has adapted itself to these corporations (this process is called governmentalism). The aim was to get a regulatory environment and digital architectures that enabled profit maximization by such corporations, as was largely achieved at least in the USA.

5 Digital Technology and Sovereignty

Let's zoom in on important changes in sovereignty due to digital technologies and vice versa. The most obvious is the territorial dimension of sovereignty. No longer are we talking only of physical assets and physical space. In the digital age, we also have digital assets such as the national digital identity, national and provincial and city domain names, national health data, or digital twins of nationally manufactured products or of smart cities. We also have the notion of cyber*space*, which comprises a peculiar amalgam of digital equipment such servers and data centers and domestic digital networks that necessarily have a physical location and thereby fall under a sovereign jurisdiction, complemented by transnational networks (under which jurisdiction) as well as nonphysical rules and standards and digital services. These digital services generally are not bound to a physical location and, interestingly, some can actually undo the link to a sovereign jurisdiction by moving around in the cloud.

Territory therefore gets vastly expanded into the digital age. A country that has no concept of digital territory risks losing its riches. Take genetic and health data—it is just data, isn't it? No, it is a national asset that "belongs to us." Such data originate from the population itself as does to some extent its value added in products and services, from new medicines to healthy-living programs.

However, if states want to ensure that digital technology does not escape from the traditional notions of territorial sovereignty, they are tempted to impose data localization, which implies a technology architecture with built-in borders. Interestingly, the notion of "belong to us" can also be supported by requiring that access to and use of data come under control of the "our" jurisdiction rather than the data themselves—which would be adequate to safeguard sovereignty as long as there is a technology that enables this. Indeed, the emerging homomorphic encryption is such a technology.

The institutional dimension of sovereignty gets ever more influenced and even determined by digital technology. Modernizing public services with digital technology is far from value neutral. Digital technologies offer greatly expanded possibilities to get information about and interact with citizens. This goes from the beneficial with intelligent, non-bureaucratic, and efficient public services such as for child benefits, permits, and voting to, in extremis, malicious state surveillance and social scoring. Digital technologies can also bypass and invalidate the old models of institutionalized sovereignty. For instance, all institutionalized governance used to be centralized. Distributed ledger technologies (such as blockchain) make possible 100% trustworthy transactions without any centralized oversight. Centralized authorities such as for import/export reporting or food quality control can—in theory—be bypassed by much more efficient and reliable decentralized distributed controls. Centralized national currencies are bypassed by completely decentralized cryptocurrencies.

It is not only authorities as institutional constructs of sovereignty that change due to digital technologies. Some institutional constructs, notably law as we know it, can no longer function when we must rely upon autonomous AI, such as to counter cyber-attacks on critical infrastructures that evolve at millisecond timescale—themselves being AI-driven. The world of sovereignty used to be a world on a human scale, which is fundamentally incompatible with the world of machines.

Here too, in some cases the reverse can happen so that sovereignty-as-we-know-it can continue to function while technology gets adapted. Rather than open and global blockchain, there are now permissioned distributed ledger technologies that enable a limited group (say, the national customs administration) to continue exerting control while still largely gaining the efficiencies of open blockchain. However, we do not yet have a technological solution for the abovementioned autonomous AI problem such that humans stay in control and political accountability—a key aspect of internal legitimacy—is maintained. Note the conundrum: we may not be able to do any longer without such autonomous AI in order to rescue our sovereignty but doing so erodes our sovereignty in the long run.

Finally, with the rise of digital technologies, there is a need for new institutions that define and control these technologies. Numerous digital standard-setting bodies are arising, often driven by industry. For example, with ever more data, there is a need for secure data analysis, that is, secure computing. A global secure computing alliance has been created, largely driven by US and Chinese companies. They may determine the standards for securely handling information, making all other countries dependent on them, even for their most sensitive government information or most intimate citizen information. Again, a challenge to sovereignty.

Ultimately, we must conclude that the most profound impact of digital technologies is on the foundational dimension of sovereignty, that is, the arrangements of power and the perception of who "we" are. Digital technology gets instrumentalized to shift power—from states to a few companies, to big tech and even to a few individuals, from those states that do not master the technologies to those few who do, from states to non-state actors such as terrorists and (cyber-)criminals who have easy access to technology to undermine states with disinformation, cyber-disruption, and cyber-theft. In the digital world, we can no longer take for granted the social contract of Hobbes and the popular sovereignty of Rousseau. Upsetting these undermines legitimacy, internally and externally. At the same time, technology can also be shaped by us to shore up sovereignty—both of states and of human individuals.

We have to add to this that digital technology can also be shaped and used to be shaped to empower global citizenship, free from geographic borders and state control. In the early days of the Internet, it was believed that the global Internet protocols and its fully decentralized implementation (intelligence distributed into all the network-connected computers) would create an independent de-territorialized cyberspace where "governments of the Industrial World, you wary giants of flesh and steel, [. . .], you are not welcome among us. You have no sovereignty where we gather" (Barlow, 1996). A dream that has been shattered to the extent that nowadays we better talk of splinternet rather than Internet (O'Hara et al., 2021). Still, the dream of global citizenship, escaping from the shackles of state sovereignty and big tech, lives on the basis of new technologies such as self-sovereign identity and blockchain enabled Web3.

The examples above, to develop technologies that respect sovereignty ("law is code"), are always also about restoring the balance of power, back to the state and back to citizens, away from foreign states and away from private companies. But we have also shown that sovereignty-respecting technology architectures may not always be possible—let alone whether the power struggle can be won by sovereign states and their citizens.

Power in the digital age is qualitatively and quantitatively different from power in the nineteenth and first half of the twentieth century. The rise of artificial general intelligence (AGI) and concerns about fundamental erosion of human autonomy (digital slavery) and geopolitical disruption (tech war) are serious. While we can learn from the past and from human nature, it would be naïve and dangerous to assume that history repeats itself that "we have been here before."

6 Policies for Sovereignty in the Digital Age

Policies for sovereignty in the digital age must take both geopolitics and technology into account. Ab initio these two must be on equal footing. Both shape and can be shaped by public policy.

Public policy can have many goals, which can include the safeguarding and strengthening of sovereignty in the digital age, i.e., we are looking for digital strategic autonomy policy. This is a new form of policy-making, different from the past, as it explicitly addresses strategic autonomy *and* responds to the nature of digital technologies.

Digital technologies are characterized by their speed of development, the scale of their impact, the systemic effect they have in economy or society, and the synchronicity that they enable, meaning that powerful actors can combine several technologies and gain huge competitive and financial advantages (Timmers, 2022b, pp. 13–15). That last point is somewhat abstract but well-illustrated by the development of large language models (LLMs) that enable generative AI such as OpenAI/Microsoft's ChatGPT and Google's Bard. The big tech companies that can afford the billions of investment for collecting and analyzing the data are not only AI companies but also cloud companies that possess huge computing capacity, as also raised by Digital Humanism Initiative (DIGHUM, 2023). They are also leaders in

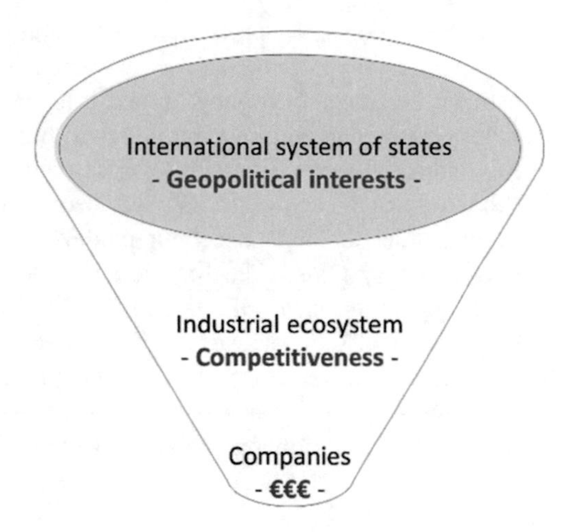

Fig. 5 Three perspectives on industrial policy

cybersecurity and in the next generation, quantum computing, and in the race toward artificial general intelligence (AGI). They are among the few that have the means to synchronize the research and development of several key technologies. If they can exercise unrestrained commercial behavior with this integrated suite of powerful technologies, they are bound to be seen by governments as posing a threat to sovereignty. For AI and AGI, see the related case study and Discussion Questions (#6).

We see several examples of digital strategic autonomy policy today, such as the 2022 USA Chips and Science Act, the broad-ranging China 2025 initiative, and the 2021 European Digital Single Market Act to combat illegal and dangerous content on the Internet and its 2022 EU Chips Act.

Industrial policies get increasingly focused on sovereignty in the digital age. Industrial policy is "a deliberate attempt by the government [...] to orientate industrial development towards specific paths" (Bianchi & Labory, 2020). Traditionally, industrial policy would focus on an industrial ecosystem, where the interest is in national competitiveness, and the individual firm's interests, which include business performance and business strategies for markets and alliances. When sovereignty is at stake, geopolitical interests must be given an equally key role in designing industrial policy. The three perspectives are (simplified) captured in Fig. 5.

Combining these three perspectives is quite challenging. It requires understanding how to join up geopolitical interests, national competitiveness, and company interests. It also requires consistency joining up a wide variety of traditionally separate policy areas. These are, firstly, because of the geopolitical dimension foreign trade, foreign direct investment (FDI), export controls, and defense and security policies. Secondly, because of the industrial ecosystem dimension, we need to consider the producers (think of an area such as semiconductors or pharma); their suppliers; their inputs or "factor conditions" such as knowledge, capital, and raw materials; and the presence of the government as both a buyer and regulator. We then need to think of policy actions for general R&D, investment, standardization, market access, consumer protection, skills, and public procurement. Third, because of the interests of individual firms, we need to think of targeted innovation and investment and taxation policy, aimed at specific (classes of) firms and possible digital transition and employment policy to buffer the shock of digitalization.

It is quite a tall order to master all these policy instruments, let alone to make sure that they reinforce each other. We are also hampered by a lack of theoretical and academic understanding. Excellent models and theories exist for industrial and innovation ecosystems, even for economic networks and platform economies, as applied by, for instance, OECD and World Economic Forum, or by competition authorities. We also have a vast corpus of theoretical and practical knowledge about firms' interests and strategies, as mostly taught at business schools. A very rich field, as shown above, exists in terms of theories of international relations. But there is a paucity in models and theories that connect and integrate the three perspectives.

7 Conclusions

The central problem is to develop public policy for sovereignty in the digital age.

We clearly do not have a simple recipe and not even a cookbook for public policy for sovereignty in the digital age, as we want it, which for digital humanism must include to "shape technologies in accordance with human values and needs."

We saw that the challenges include to understand perspectives on international relations and sovereignty and to understand the nature of digital technologies and the digital technology ecosystem and the motivations of individual actors such as tech companies. We need to combine these perspectives in order to arrive at sensible public policy for sovereignty in the digital age, while there is neither a ready-made model nor does traditional education train the students who go on to work in government, business, civil society, or academia for such integrated policy-making. This chapter aims to give at least some handles to that extent.

The best current approach probably is to examine concrete cases that concern both sovereignty and digital technologies, come forward with policy interventions, and then examine their consistency, coherence, completeness, and impact. We need to add to this also flexibility, given our limited insight and the speed of development of technology and sometimes also the speed of developments in geopolitics (think of the war against Ukraine and global challenges such as COVID-19).

Traditional policy instruments such as regulation struggle to deliver in this respect, but that does not mean that they become irrelevant. Rather, the challenge is to adapt policy-*making* to the reality of geopolitics and technology.

Let's then finish with two cases and with an invitation to the reader to come up with additional or alternative policy interventions and to then reflect on how these relate to digital humanism. The first case is on ICT supply chain security and the second on generative AI such as ChatGPT. The first is more mature, has already shown to lead to posing threats to sovereignty, and has already led to concrete policy action. The second is more recent with still many unknowns but evolving fast with potentially huge consequences for sovereignty.

Hopefully these cases provide the reader with a stepping stone and motivation to make a reality of integrated policy-making for sovereignty in the digital—Digital Humanistic—age.

Case: ICT Supply Chain Security

How can you trust digital technologies (ICTs) that are integrated from a complex supply chain of vendors and into solutions for government, banks, utility companies to run their operations, customer relations, and financial transactions? Bits and pieces of hardware and software, often from open source, and certainly from many suppliers are combined by third party integrators. Suppliers likely have remote updates and maintenance.

Such customer solutions have a large attack surface, that is, cybersecurity attacks can occur at many points. Open source-based vulnerabilities such as Log4j[4] have been exploited. The SolarWinds remote maintenance hack, traced to Russian state actors, led to the theft of confidential government data and it was[5] the Kaseya ransomware attack that led to the closing down of Swedish supermarkets.[6]

What are the core problems that enable sovereignty-threatening attacks? Firstly, software and hardware development has little "sovereignty-by-design." This would mean with technical design to limit the effects of an attack. Technical architecture should aim to halt spillovers that might destabilize a whole system or compartmentalize the most-confidential systems. This also holds for processes to halt an attack. Generally, there is a lack of information exchange and collaboration between authorities in different countries. There are "sovereignty borders in cyberspace," at least for cybersecurity information exchange. Secondly, in the open global market economy, security loses out against price. Market access conditions tend to address consumer protection but not security or resilience in the interest of sovereignty. Thirdly, governments are afraid that security restrictions stifle innovation and impair economic strength, which they believe to be essential for sovereignty.

How then to address these core problems? As for the first and second point, standards and related certification can help. President Biden issued an executive order to investigate and counter supply chain vulnerabilities, including by a software bill of materials, and instructed standards to be developed. The European Commission included supply chain vulnerability in its revised cybersecurity law (Network and Information Security Directive). Industry

(continued)

[4] Log4J Vulnerability Explained: What It Is and How to Fix It | Built In

[5] SolarWinds hack explained: Everything you need to know (techtarget.com).

[6] Kaseya VSA ransomware attack - Wikipedia

should learn about sovereignty-by-design from the painful 5G security experience when governments forced telecoms operators to swap out Chinese equipment due to perceived threats to national security (Timmers, 2020).

Moreover, the strategic autonomy approach of strategic partnership suggests collaborating with like-minded countries. Indeed, the USA and the EU do so in their trans-Atlantic collaboration. The EU's 5G Security Recommendation showed that 27 member states can collaborate, even in national security. As for the third point, given the close interplay between social and technological construction, we need research on technological and organizational approaches that marry security and innovation, e.g., blockchain-based software updating is already being commercialized for industrial control systems. This is an example of combining technological innovation with social innovation, namely, distributed security controls.

Questions: design four scenarios for the future of ICT supply chain security taking two dimensions into account—(1) the degree of geopolitical tension (from a virtual state of war to global sovereignty-respecting collaboration of countries) and (2) the degree of openness of technology solutions (from fragmented closed solutions to fully interoperable and open). Which scenario do you consider most likely? Which scenario is desirable from a digital humanism point of view?

Case: Generative AI and Sovereignty

It is still early days but already the following sovereignty-threatening developments arise from generative AI.[7] Firstly, generative AI turns out to be a great assistant to set up misinformation campaigns in third countries or even in the own country as happened in 2023 in Venezuela (Joe Daniels & Madhumita Murgia, 2023). It can also help to program a cyber-attack. It is not clear whether technology-based countermeasures (e.g., watermarking) get priority by the commercial providers of generative AI, nor whether these are sufficient.

Secondly, generative AI is quickly entering into education. It is not yet understood by us how such AI will influence the capabilities and norms of young persons. Surely, old-school education will struggle to adapt to the speed of change. Nevertheless, education is the foundation of society, the foundation of the sovereignty we want. Thirdly, AI in general and generative AI in particular improve rapidly and get extended with abilities to monitor and act in the physical world. When it gets to near perfection, it will be relied upon

(continued)

[7] Generative AI creates original content. Some examples are ChatGPT (text and computer code), BLOOM (text, images), GLM (text), OPT, Galactica (science), Stable Diffusion (art), DALL-E (art, images), VALL-E (voice), and Galactica (scientific articles). Generative AI is based on several techniques, prominent in these are large language models and generative pretrained transformers (GPT).

without thinking. In fact, it must be relied upon in very fast-moving situations such as to prevent an ongoing cyber-incident having systemic effects and, for instance, crash electricity networks or payments systems. If this were to happen, it would massively undermine trust in government and its internal legitimacy (the USA got near to that with the Colonial pipeline ransomware attack[8]). Governments have no choice but to rely on such powerful AI to act autonomously in order to maintain trust, provide essential services, and thereby keep up sovereignty, but at the same time they abdicate from sovereignty by handing over decision power to a fundamentally uncontrollable machine. Finally, generative AI is controlled by a few companies that are not subject to sovereignty-respecting oversight or conditions.

Generative AI is seen as a promising beginning of artificial general intelligence according to Bubeck et al. (2023) and Sam Altman (2023). AGI or general purpose AI (GPAI) is proposed by the European Parliament to be regulated, at least to some extent.

Questions: Does this mean that governments are not acting from a sovereignty-defending perspective, even if sovereignty may be fundamentally at risk as illustrated above? What would you do?[9]

Discussion Questions for Students and Their Teachers

1. Let us focus on the first three core principles of digital humanism.[10] How would they be seen by realists, liberalists, and contingency thinkers in international relations?
2. What are the advantages and disadvantages of digital humanism, as a movement to "shape technologies in accordance with human values and needs" to include respect for sovereignty as one of the core principles?
3. What are some scenarios that suggest that classifier AI is a challenge to sovereignty? In classifier AI, data gets labeled according to certain classes, e.g., individuals get a credit score [suggestion: look up some cases where AI led to questions about the legitimacy of government, see (Waller & Timmers, 2022)].
4. Estonia, a small European country neighboring Russia, wants to safeguard its sovereignty in the digital age. Which digital policy would you recommend to them to strengthen their strategic autonomy in public e-services (e-government)? Which remaining risks do you see?
5. 5G technology, and its successor 6G, will offer ubiquitous communications using a multitude of means, including satellites. Can satellite networks create a sovereignty gap? If so, which technological constructs can restore sovereignty?

---

[8] Colonial Pipeline hack explained: Everything you need to know (techtarget.com).

[9] In the USA, the Center for AI and Digital Policy requested the FTC to impose a moratorium on commercial GPT (CAIDP, 2023).

[10] Vienna Manifesto on Digital Humanism – DIGHUM (tuwien.ac.at)

6. Can AGI (artificial general intelligence) strengthen or undermine sovereignty? What would an authoritarian state do about AGI? A democratic state? What can a global collaboration to promote universal human values driven by academics and technologists do?

Learning Resources for Students

Most of the articles in the references are quite readable and recommended to at least glance through. In addition, here a few recommended books:

1. Art, R.J., Jervis, R., 2016. International Politics: Enduring Concepts and Contemporary Issues, 13th edition. ed. Pearson, Boston

   All you want to know about the various schools of international relations including contributions by the most authoritative scholars.
2. Carlsnaes, W., et al. (Eds.). (2012). Handbook of international relations. Sage Publications Ltd.

   Authoritative and showing the richness of the field.
3. Biersteker, T., 2012. State, Sovereignty and Territory, in: Handbook of International Relations. SAGE Publications Ltd.

   Especially recommended for the issue of sovereignty.
4. Klabbers, J., 2021. International Law, third edition. ed. Cambridge University Press, Cambridge

   Gives you a readable and sometimes even amusing introduction in international law. For sovereignty, read in particular the chapters on history and on jurisdiction.
5. Francis Fukuyama, 2022. Liberalism and Its Discontents. MacMillan

   Very readable and illustrating the extremes of economic and political liberalism, liberalism and democracy, and the future of liberalism in a polarized world.
6. Lessig, Lawrence, 1999. Code: And Other Laws Of Cyberspace. Basic Books.

   Making the compelling argument technology (the internet) or 'code' relates to the social construct of law.
7. Cohen, J.E., 2019. Between truth and power: the legal constructions of informational capitalism.

   Not the easiest book but provocatively insightful about the close interplay of corporate power and government.
8. Kello, L., 2017. The virtual weapon and international order

   The reference work to understand how digital technologies affect, undermine, and disrupt the international system of states.
9. Nowotny, H., 2021. In AI we trust: power, illusion and control of predictive algorithms

   A most readable personal journey into the world of AI with thoughtful reflection on the limits of what we can control.
10. Cohen, E., 2022. Souveraineté industrielle: Vers un nouveau modèle productif. Odile Jacob, Paris

If you read French (hopefully the book will get a translation), providing an excellent overview of the development of industrial policy and the shape it may take when sovereignty concerns are on the rise.

References

Altman, S. (2023). *Planning for AGI and beyond | OpenAI [WWW Document]*. Accessed 3.28.23, from https://openai.com/blog/planning-for-agi-and-beyond

Art, R. J., & Jervis, R. (2016). *International politics: Enduring concepts and contemporary issues* (13th ed.). Pearson.

Barlow, J. P. (1996). *A declaration of the independence of cyberspace [WWW Document]*. Electron. Front. Found. Accessed 9.13.22, from https://www.eff.org/cyberspace-independence

Bianchi, P., & Labory, S. (2020). European industrial policy: A comparative perspective. In A. Oqubay, C. Cramer, H.-J. Chang, & R. Kozul-Wright (Eds.), *The Oxford handbook of industrial policy* (pp. 593–620). Oxford University Press. https://doi.org/10.1093/oxfordhb/9780198862420.013.22

Bickerton, C., Brack, N., Coman, R., & Crespy, A. (2022). Conflicts of sovereignty in contemporary Europe: A framework of analysis. *Comparative European Politics, 20*, 257–274. https://doi.org/10.1057/s41295-022-00269-6

Biersteker, T., (2012). State, sovereignty and territory. In *Handbook of international relations*. Sage Publications Ltd. Especially recommended for the issue of sovereignty.

Boston Consulting Group, Semiconductor Industry Association. (2021). *Strengthening the Global Semiconductor Supply Chain in an Uncertain Era | BCG [WWW Document]*. Accessed 1.27.22, from https://www.bcg.com/publications/2021/strengthening-the-global-semiconductor-supply-chain

Bubeck, S., Chandrasekaran, V., Eldan, R., Gehrke, J., Horvitz, E., Kamar, E., Lee, P., Lee, Y.T., Li, Y., Lundberg, S., Nori, H., Palangi, H., Ribeiro, M.T., & Zhang, Y. (2023). *Sparks of Artificial General Intelligence: Early experiments with GPT-4*.

CAIDP. (2023). *OPEN AI (FTC 2023) Complaint [WWW Document]*. Center for AI and Digital Policy. Accessed 3.28.23, from https://www.caidp.org/cases/openai/

Carlsnaes, W., Risse, R., Simmons, B. (Eds). (2012). *Handbook of international relations*. Sage Publications Ltd.

Cohen, J. E. (2019). *Between truth and power: The legal constructions of informational capitalism*.

Cohen, E. (2022). *Souveraineté industrielle: Vers un nouveau modèle productif.* Odile Jacob.

Daniels, J., & Murgia, M. (2023). Deepfake 'news' videos ramp up misinformation in Venezuela | Financial Times. *Financial Times*.

De Filippi, P., & Wright, A. (2019). *Blockchain and the Law*. Harvard University Press.

de Tocqueville, A. (1864). Comment Les Américains Combattent L'individualisme Par La Doctrine De L'intérêt Bien Entendu. In I. I. Tome (Ed.), *De La Démocratie En Amérique* (pp. 198–203). Michel Lévy.

Digital Humanism Initiative DIGHUM. (2019). *Vienna manifesto on digital humanism – DIGHUM*.

Digital Humanism Initiative DIGHUM. (2023). *Statement of the digital humanism initiative on ChatGPT – DIGHUM*. Accessed 3.28.23, from https://dighum.ec.tuwien.ac.at/statement-of-the-digital-humanism-initiative-on-chatgpt/

Eriksson, J., & Newlove-Eriksson, L. M. (2021). Theorizing technology and international relations: Prevailing perspectives and new horizons. In *Technology and international relations* (pp. 3–22). Edward Elgar.

Farrell, H., & Newman, A. L. (2019). Weaponized interdependence: How global economic networks shape state coercion. *International Security, 44*, 42–79. https://doi.org/10.1162/isec_a_00351
Fukuyama, F. (2022). *Liberalism and its discontents*. Macmillan.
Gallie, W. B. (1956). Essentially contested concepts. *Proceedings of the Aristotelian Society, 56*, 167–198.
General Secretariat. (2021). *Strategic-autonomy, strategic choices - issues paper*. Council of the European Union.
Kello, L. (2017). *The virtual weapon and international order*.
Keohane, R., & Nye, J., Jr. (2011). *Power & interdependence* (4th ed.). Pearson.
Klabbers, J. (2021). *International law* (3rd ed.). Cambridge University Press.
Lessig, L. (1999). *Code: And other laws of cyberspace*. Basic Books.
Mearsheimer, J. J. (1994). The false promise of international institutions. *International Security, 19*, 5–49.
Nowotny, H. (2021). *In AI we trust: Power, illusion and control of predictive algorithms*.
O'Hara, K., Hall, W., & Cerf, V. (2021). *Four Internets*. Four Internets. https://doi.org/10.1093/OSO/9780197523681.001.0001.
Stanford University. (n.d.). *Stanford encyclopedia of philosophy [WWW Document]*. Accessed 3.27.23, from https://plato.stanford.edu/index.html
Timmers, P. (2019). Ethics of AI and cybersecurity when sovereignty is at stake. *Minds Mach, 29*, 635–645. https://doi.org/10.1007/S11023-019-09508-4/FIGURES/3
Timmers, P. (2020). There will be no global 6G unless we resolve sovereignty concerns in 5G governance. *Nature Electronics, 31*(3), 10–12. https://doi.org/10.1038/s41928-020-0366-3
Timmers, P. (2022a). The technological construction of sovereignty. In *Perspectives on digital humanism* (pp. 213–218). Springer. https://doi.org/10.1007/978-3-030-86144-5_28
Timmers, P. (2022b). *Digital Industrial Policy for Europe | CERRE report*. CERRE.
Waller, P., & Timmers, P. (2022). Controversial classifiers — The perils of prediction algorithms in public administration. *SSRN Electronic Journal*. https://doi.org/10.2139/ssrn.4246955
Waltz, K. N. (2010). *Theory of international politics* (1st ed.). Waveland Press.
Wolf, M., 2019. The Brexit delusion of taking back control | Financial Times. *Financial Times*.
World Bank. (2021). *Trade (% of GDP) | Data [WWW Document]*. Accessed 3.25.23, from https://data.worldbank.org/indicator/NE.TRD.GNFS.ZS

The Threat of Surveillance and the Need for Privacy Protections

Martina Lindorfer

Abstract In recent years, and since the introduction of the General Data Protection Regulation (GDPR) in particular, we have seen an increased interest (and concern) about the amount of private information that is collected by the applications and services we use in our daily lives. The widespread collection and commodification of personal data has been mainly driven by companies collecting, mining, and selling user profiles for targeted advertisement, a practice also referred to as "surveillance capitalism." However, as we detail in this chapter, this is not the only form of surveillance and can be necessary and even beneficial by increasing the safety of citizens—if it is aligned with the principles of digital humanisms in providing transparency, oversight, and accountability. We also detail mechanisms users can deploy to protect their own privacy, as well as mechanisms that help to develop more privacy-friendly technologies.

1 Introduction

> I don't know why people are so keen to put the details of their private life in public; they forget that invisibility is a superpower. (Banksy, allegedly)

We happily share intimate details of our private lives to connect with others on social networks and for the convenience of performing daily chores online and via our smartphone. This data has been coined "new oil" due to it being exploited by tech companies for their own monetary gains, i.e., "surveillance capitalism" (Zuboff, 2019). Besides the ubiquitous surveillance by Big Tech, in Western society, surveillance is mostly only associated with something that happens in less democratic countries to monitor and control citizens. This belief was upset by the revelations of Edward Snowden in 2013, when he exposed how the US National Security Agency (NSA) was collecting vast amounts of communication data, including emails and

M. Lindorfer (✉)
Faculty of Informatics, Research Unit Security & Privacy, Institute of Logic and Computation, TU Wien, Wien, Austria
e-mail: martina.lindorfer@tuwien.ac.at

H. Werthner et al. (eds.), *Introduction to Digital Humanism*,
https://doi.org/10.1007/978-3-031-45304-5_37

chat logs, on individuals and organizations worldwide (Gellman & Lindeman, 2013; Gellman & Poitras, 2013; Greenwald & MacAskill, 2013). While on paper being designed to collect data on American citizens and individuals in other countries, it was carried out without required warrants and put innocent individuals in the crosshairs of mass surveillance. One reason why the NSA—as well as other government agencies like the UK's Government Communications Headquarters (GCHQ)—could collect mass amounts of data at a large scale was the fact that they directly tapped Big Tech, including Google, Facebook, Microsoft, and Apple. The link between the government and the private sector has further been confirmed by reports of federal agencies in the USA, including the Department of Homeland Security and the Internal Revenue Service, buying commercially available data from data brokers (Whittaker, 2023). In countries that are notorious for surveilling their population, such as China, the entanglement of their government with private companies has long been cause for concern, resulting in the discourse about and actual banning of applications such as TikTok. Whether the concerns are warranted is up for debate, but at least for another Chinese social media platform, WeChat, research has shown that content shared by international users is being used to feed and train censorship mechanisms in China (Knockel et al., 2020). What is clear though in any jurisdiction is that any user data collected by companies is at risk of being requested by governments and law enforcement.

Tapping these tech companies for user data potentially gives governments and law enforcement information that they would not be able to collect legally (Hoofnagle, 2003), for example, through "predictive policing." From a pragmatic point of view, it is attractive though as tech companies' access to private user data is extensive. Technology has become an integral part of every aspect of our daily lives, and we use it through a plethora of applications (apps), for everything from emails and social networking to shopping and banking. To maximize the user experience, apps and websites collect and process an increasing amount of private information. With the rising popularity of Internet of Things (IoT) devices, we give up even more private information about our daily lives and habits for the sake of the convenience of a smart home. This does not only include seemingly harmless devices, such as smart toasters and lightbulbs, but also medical devices and fitness trackers, as well as seemingly analog devices: truly targeted TV advertisements based on viewer demographics so far have been wishful thinking (Perlberg, 2014), but new content transmission protocols, e.g., the Hybrid Broadcast Broadband TV (HbbTV) standard deployed across Europe, enable the real-time monitoring of users' viewing preferences and integration with profiles from other sources. In other words, HbbTV turns TVs into an Internet-connected device, complete with all the customization benefits of targeted content ("addressable TV") as well as privacy harms known from the mobile app and web domain (Tagliaro et al., 2023).

Companies use the data they collect through mobile apps, users' browsing behavior, social media content, and data collected from smart devices, to build detailed user profiles. This private information, and user behaviors derived from it, has become a commodity: tech monopolies and shadow brokers collect and aggregate data to not only provide tailored content but also for market research and targeted advertising (Razaghpanah et al., 2018). This process is far from transparent and includes obscure tracking methods and "various techniques [...] to prevent consumers from making a choice on privacy" (Hoofnagle et al., 2012). Furthermore, the data is not always in trustworthy and secure hands: if left unprotected from unauthorized access, social security numbers, addresses, financial records, and other highly sensitive data from billions of users are regularly leaked through data brokers and can potentially be exploited by criminals (Sherman, 2022). Most importantly, behavioral targeting is not only used to sell people products but for far more nefarious purposes: to influence public and political opinions by selectively targeting user groups with disinformation. One prominent case in this regard was Cambridge Analytica selling data harvested from Facebook to political campaigns (Rosenberg et al., 2018).

As a result, private data collection faces increased scrutiny by both legislators and users. The privacy debate has resulted in the introduction of the General Data Protection Regulation (GDPR) (European Commission, 2016) in the European Union in May 2018 and similar efforts in other countries that regulate the collection and processing of private information (see Sect. 3). Privacy is a fundamental human right that through GDPR and various other international laws and regulations around the world is being protected to varying degrees. The goal is to give individuals the ability (back) to control their personal information and keep it private. This can include information such as one's identity, location, health conditions, social network, and personal preferences.

Still, privacy (and the individual perception of and need for privacy) is a complex topic and involves answering questions around (1) which type of data should be protected, (2) how sensitive this data is, (e.g., health information is typically seen more critically and afforded a special category of data by the GDPR than let's say a user's physical location or phone number), and (3) who data should be protected from. Furthermore, while everyone has the right to privacy and should be able to take steps to protect their personal information and online activities, several vulnerable groups are at higher risk of surveillance and privacy violations, ranging from threats from the government to their immediate personal surroundings:

- **Political activists:** Individuals who are involved in political activism or advocacy may be targeted for surveillance by governments or other organizations. This can include monitoring of online activity, phone calls, and physical surveillance.
- **Journalists and whistleblowers:** Journalists and whistleblowers who expose corruption or wrongdoing may also be at risk of surveillance or retaliation. This can include monitoring of communication channels, hacking of devices or accounts, and other methods of surveillance.
- **LGBTQ+ individuals:** LGBTQ+ individuals may not only face discrimination and harassment, but in certain countries even imprisonment or death, and thus may need to protect their privacy to avoid persecution.
- **Racial, ethnic, and religious minorities:** Depending on the dominant group in a country, and other factors, such as the division of state and church, minority groups might face discrimination and harassment as well.

- **People with (mental) health conditions:** Certain health conditions might also face stigmatization or discrimination, for example, in the workplace. This can reach from employees being disadvantaged based on their health to more general attacks on fundamental personal rights. In the latter case, recent regulation attempts on female reproduction pose the question on how much data is collected and shared about potential pregnancies (and their termination) that could result in legal persecution.
- **Domestic abuse and stalking survivors:** Survivors of domestic abuse or stalking (also referred to as intimate partner violence) may need to take extra precautions to protect themselves and their (online) activities from their abusers.
- **Children and young adults:** Children and young adults may be more vulnerable to online predators or cyberbullying. Privacy regulation also particularly protects individuals below a certain age as they are not mature enough to provide informed consent to data collection.

Surveillance and privacy are typically seen as opposing forces; however, in an ideal world, they should co-exist. While perceived negatively, surveillance in itself is neither inherently good nor bad and can be necessary for the greater societal good as well as national security, e.g., by providing law enforcement the means to investigate crime and ensure public safety. For example, extensive surveillance camera footage was instrumental in finding the responsible parties behind the Boston Marathon bombing in 2013 and the US Capitol Attacks in 2021. More generally, surveillance can provide:

- **Security/Safety:** Monitor and prevent criminal activity, terrorism, and other threats to public safety. For example, security cameras in public spaces can help deter crime and assist law enforcement in identifying and apprehending suspects.
- **Health:** Monitor and control the spread of infectious diseases, such as by tracking outbreaks and monitoring vaccination rates. In the case of a public health emergency, such as a pandemic, surveillance can be critical in identifying and containing the spread of the disease.
- **Traffic management:** Monitor traffic flow and congestion, which can help identify areas where infrastructure improvements are needed and can aid in emergency response planning.

Given the overall promise of using surveillance and data collection to increase safety and optimize processes, it is not surprising that also nongovernmental organizations are interested in reaping the benefits. Under the term "workplace surveillance," companies are aiming to optimize how they hire, promote, and fire employees (Peck, 2013; Kantor & Sundaram, 2022). This includes, potentially covertly, monitoring employee activity and productivity to ensure that they are meeting their responsibilities and identify areas where performance can be improved. Whether this is legal, in particular in the context of employment laws, and how these laws still need to catch up with technology changes in the workplace (Calacci & Stein, 2023), is an open question—in addition to questions of the ethical aspects and most importantly the efficiency of these practices in summarizing productivity in simple data points while actually negatively impacting the work environment with the constant threat of surveillance.

On the other hand, the ubiquity of surveillance mechanisms, e.g., cameras in every smartphone, in smart doorbells, and as police bodycams, can also lead to "sousveillance," i.e., citizens holding government agencies accountable for their actions.

In the context of digital humanism, the main tensions between surveillance and privacy arise because surveillance involves the collection of information, while privacy involves the protection of that information and control over how it is used. Surveillance can infringe on an individual's right to privacy if it is conducted without their knowledge or consent, or if it involves the collection of sensitive or personal information. However, it can (and needs to) be designed to prevent abuses of power, minimize the collection of personal information, and protect individuals' privacy, while still providing important security benefits to society. Still, surveillance is frequently seen as an "easy" and convenient solution without critical reflection about its benefits versus its harms, as evidenced by continuing efforts of implementing technology backdoors that undermine security and privacy, as well as eroding trust in technology. Thus, it is important to guarantee transparency, oversight, and accountability during the complete lifecycle of any technology, starting from how potentially privacy-invasive mechanisms are designed, over how they are deployed, to how the collected data is used.

2 Basic Concepts and Basic Definitions

Surveillance refers to the monitoring or observation of people, places, including physical and digital surveillance. Classic physical surveillance includes the use of cameras in public spaces, historically known as closed-circuit television (CCTV) cameras, and physical tracking devices. The data collected through physical surveillance can also be augmented with technology, for example, with facial recognition mechanisms that augment the feed from surveillance cameras. Digital surveillance on the other hand includes monitoring online activity and communication, including emails, web browsing, and social media use. In addition to a categorization based on the technological means deployed to implement surveillance, it can also be differentiated along the following dimensions: covert vs. overt surveillance depending on whether it is conducted in secret and without the knowledge or consent of the individuals being monitored; mass vs. targeted surveillance depending on whether a large group of people is being monitored compared to only specific individuals or groups that are suspected of wrongdoing; and private vs. state surveillance depending on whether it is performed by companies or individuals, potentially for commercial purposes, or by the government and its agencies.

Demonstrating again the tension between surveillance and privacy (and the complexity of the term privacy) are the definitions of privacy according to the National Institute of Standards and Technology (NIST, 2023):

- "Assurance that the confidentiality of, and access to, certain information about an entity is protected."
- "Freedom from intrusion into the private life or affairs of an individual when that intrusion results from undue or illegal gathering and use of data about that individual."
- "The right of a party to maintain control over and confidentiality of information about itself."

The following terms are frequently used to describe the negative effects surveillance and privacy-invasive technology can have, as well as users' attitudes and behavior toward their privacy (Gerber et al., 2018):

- **Chilling Effect:** While the deployment of surveillance technology, such as cameras, can discourage harmful behavior, such as theft or crime, it also has negative effects on users' exercising their legitimate rights. When faced with digital surveillance, for example, users might change their online behavior and self-censor instead of exercising their right to free speech.
- **Privacy Paradox:** Users' online behavior often deviates from their values when it comes to protecting their private information, sometimes simply because the more privacy-invasive option is more convenient.
- **Privacy Calculus Theorem:** Users' intention to disclose personal information is frequently based on a risk-benefit analysis as a trade-off between the functionality and the efficacy of a piece of technology and the data they need to share.

It is also important to note the diversity and type of data points that fall under the umbrella "private information:"

- **Personally Identifiable Information (PII):** Any type of information that can be used to identify an individual. PII can contain direct identifiers (e.g., passport information, social security number) that can identify a person uniquely or quasi-identifiers (e.g., gender, race) that can be combined with other quasi-identifiers (e.g., date of birth) to successfully recognize an individual. In addition to textual information, in particular, photos (e.g., selfies) are a valuable piece of PII that is collected and sold to train facial recognition software.
- **Device Identifiers:** Hardware- and software-specific identifiers can serve as the digital "license plate" of a device and form a specific type of PII that not necessarily contains private user data but nevertheless can be used to track their online activity. Besides fixed identifiers, such as IP and MAC addresses, or information from a phone's SIM card, these identifiers can be generated through a process called "browser fingerprinting." Important to note here is that these identifiers or fingerprints can also be useful for security purposes, for example, for a banking website to recognize suspicious logins and prevent account hacking. From a privacy perspective, one aspect is important though: whether those

identifiers are resettable by the user, or not. In the latter case, they provide means to track a user over the lifetime of their physical device without any control over them.

- **Metadata:** Even when full communication details, such as the content of emails and chats, are not available, the fact that two parties are communicating (when? for how long?) can be sensitive information.

Any of the above data may be collected for legitimate services, e.g., to protect users or provide more tailored services but also for secondary use cases, such as targeted profiling. Privacy issues arise in particular when users consent to sharing information with the first party, such as the developer of an app, but have no insight or control over whether the data is shared with other parties, such as advertisers and data brokers. Furthermore, while individual data points seem innocent enough, and users might think they "have nothing to hide," the combination of information (from different sources) can reveal intimate details and personality traits users might not be aware of, a concept nicely illustrated by the "data onion" (Szymielewicz, 2019). In reality, research has found users to be profiled into 650,000 both highly specific and partly invasive categories (or "advertisement segments") that can be used to target them (Keegan & Eastwood, 2023).

3 Methods

Similar to the variety of privacy threats and private information to be protected, there are a multitude of measures that can be taken either by individuals, app and service developers, corporations, or governments to protect privacy that include technical, organizational, and political aspects. Overall, a combination of these measures is needed to protect privacy effectively, but their application depends on the specific context and the involved privacy risks.

- **Privacy by Design:** Privacy should be a requirement and important factor from the inception of a product or service, i.e., built in from the beginning.
- **Privacy by Default:** Configurable settings should enable the most privacy-friendly ones by default, following the principle of "opt-in" to data collection rather than "opt-out."
- **Privacy Preserving or Enhancing:** Users' PII can be handled in a way that protects it while still maintaining the same level of functionality of an app or service compared to one with full (unprotected) access to PII.

Technical Measures

- **Access Controls:** Mechanisms that restrict access to sensitive information to authorized parties only. They can include password protection, multifactor authentication, or other forms of identity verification.
- **Encryption:** The process of encoding or transforming information in a way that it can only be read by authorized parties who possess a cryptographic key or

password. By encrypting data, users can ensure that it cannot be intercepted or read by unauthorized parties, ranging from people using the same public Wi-Fi in a coffee shop to Internet service providers (ISPs) and government agencies. A de facto standard for protecting communication through encryption is the use of the hypertext transfer protocol secure (HTTPS) instead of plain HTTP when visiting websites. Other examples include the encryption of emails, or the use of secure, i.e., end-to-end encrypted, messaging apps such as Signal. Other examples of encryption in action are virtual private networks (VPNs), which create a secure, encrypted connection (often also referred to as a "tunnel") between devices, e.g., a user's mobile phone and the Internet, or Tor, software that routes Internet traffic through a series of encrypted relays, making it difficult for anyone to track users' online activities and allows users to users to browse the Internet near anonymously.

- **Anonymization:** The process of removing personally identifiable information from data sets to protect individuals' privacy. A weaker form is pseudonymization, which processes personal data in a way that it can no longer be attributed to a specific user (without additional information). However, research repeatedly shows the difficulties in implementing such a process, and assumptions about what information would be necessary to de-anonymize users are typically too strong and broken in practice (Narayanan & Shmatikov, 2008; Deußer et al., 2020).
- **Data minimization and granularity:** Given the abovementioned difficulties in implementing privacy from a technical perspective, one important question remains: What kind of data is really necessary to provide a service or application? Can data be blurred, e.g., is the exact location necessary for a restaurant recommendation or does the city suffice? The best way to protect data typically is not to collect it at all.

Organizational Measures

- **Privacy policies:** Statements that outline an organization's data handling practices and the rights of individuals whose data is collected. They can provide transparency and accountability and help individuals make informed decisions about their data.
- **Employee training:** Raising awareness of privacy risks and best practices within an organization can help to prevent accidental or intentional privacy breaches by employees. The fact that ultimately humans often still access and handle collected information is not that obvious, for example, given the advances in automated audio and video processing. However, reports have shown how manufacturer's employees can have unrestricted access to security cameras (Harwell, 2020), or employees and contractors still are transcribing voice messages (Frier, 2019) and smart speaker prompts.
- **Privacy impact assessments:** Systematic evaluations of the potential privacy risks of new or modified processes, systems, or technologies can help organizations identify and address privacy risks before they occur.

Political Measures

- **Data protection laws:** Legal frameworks that regulate the collection, storage, and use of personal data can provide individuals with legal rights, such as the right to access, correct, or delete their data, and impose penalties for noncompliance or misuse.
- **International agreements:** Legal frameworks such as the General Data Protection Regulation (GDPR) in the European Union (EU) and collaborations like the EU-US Data Privacy Framework can help to establish global privacy standards and facilitate cross-border data protection.
- **Advocacy and activism:** Raising awareness of privacy risks is important to hold organizations and governments accountable for their privacy practices, as well as shape public policy to promote privacy rights and protections.

Example: General Data Protection Regulation (GDPR)

The General Data Protection Regulation (GDPR) is a privacy law that was enacted by the European Union (EU) in 2018 (European Commission, 2016). The purpose of the GDPR is to give individuals more control over their personal data and to ensure that organizations are handling that data responsibly. One of its key aspects is the notion of consent: organizations are required to obtain clear and explicit consent from individuals before collecting and processing their personal data. It further gives individuals the rights to information about how their data is collected and handled, as well as the right to revoke consent and request the deletion of their data. It is an important piece of legislation that seeks to protect individuals' privacy rights and ensure that organizations are handling personal data responsibly. Similar regulations in other jurisdictions include (but are not limited to) the California Consumer Privacy Act (CCPA), the Brazilian General Data Protection Law (LGPD), Canada's Personal Information Protection and Electronic Documents Act (PIPEDA), and the UK's Data Protection Act 2018 (DPA).

GDRP Consequence: Privacy Policies (and Labels)

One mechanism that is frequently cited as a way for users to determine how their data is used and shared are terms of services and privacy policies. However, as a long line of research has shown, not only are privacy policies hard to understand for nonlegal experts, requiring at least university-level reading skills (Litman-Navarro, 2019), it is also practically infeasible for users to read the privacy policies of all apps and services they are using: A study in 2008 (McDonald & Cranor, 2008; Madrigal, 2012) estimated that individuals would spend 76 working days per year to read the privacy policies of every website they are visiting. Given the increasing complexity of policies (Lovato et al., 2023; Adhikari et al., 2023), partially due to legislative requirements, this number is clearly a lower bound.

An interesting proposal to condense the information from privacy policies and present them in a standard and easy to understand way are privacy nutrition labels (Kelley et al., 2009; Emami-Naeini et al., 2020) (see also Fig. 1 for an example). Recent developments by the two main mobile platform providers, Apple and Google, implement such a mechanism: Apple introduced App Store Privacy Labels in 2020, and Google introduced the Google Play Data Safety Section in 2021. Still,

Fig. 1 Example of condensing information from privacy policies into a "nutrition label" (Emami-Naeini et al., 2020)

while these developments seemingly increase transparency, there is a lack of enforcement and accountability as this information is almost entirely self-reported by developers. Google offers the option to have part of this information independently validated, yet this mainly concerns whether an app adheres to security standards and best practices and not necessarily how it handles PII.

More generally, the notion of consent itself is up to debate. Service providers use "dark patterns" to elicit consent to data collection from users by the path of least resistance, leading to current approaches being termed as a "consent theater" (Fassl, 2021).

Emerging Privacy-Enhancing Technologies

In addition to the safeguards individuals can take to protect their personal information and online activities, technology itself can be designed and deployed in a way that it is privacy-preserving or even enhancing.

Homomorphic encryption is a relatively new and still developing technology, and while there have been significant advances in recent years, it is not yet widely deployed in real-world applications. It is a type of encryption that allows computations to be performed on encrypted data without first decrypting it. This has the potential to greatly enhance privacy and security, as it would allow sensitive data to be processed and analyzed without ever being exposed in its unencrypted form. Still, it is a relatively complex and computationally intensive technology, and there are still challenges to be addressed in terms of its efficiency and scalability. There are also challenges for its practical implementation as existing software and hardware systems need to be modified to support it.

Differential privacy is a privacy-preserving technology that works by adding noise to data to mask individual records, thus preventing the identification of specific individuals while still allowing for useful analysis of the data. It has already been deployed in a number of real-world applications, most notably the US Census Bureau, Google in services such as Google Maps and Chrome, and Apple across MacOS and iOS. Still, there are also open research questions to improve its efficiency and scalability, as well as effectiveness in real-world settings.

Synthetic data is another promising approach that generates data with the same statistical properties and patterns of the original data while not containing any identifiable information of individuals. In addition to not exposing any private information by design, it can also augment existing datasets to make them more diverse and generalizable.

Federated learning is a machine learning technique where data is trained across multiple devices or systems without transferring the data to a central server, thereby preserving data privacy.

Secure multiparty computation allows multiple parties to compute a function or analyze data without revealing their individual inputs or data.

4 Critical Reflection

While surveillance can be used for legitimate purposes such as crime prevention, it can also be abused and lead to negative consequences for individuals and society as a whole. Therefore, it is important to carefully consider the balance between privacy and security and ensure that surveillance is conducted in a transparent, accountable, and ethical manner. Surveillance is often seen critically or problematic for several reasons, including:

- **Invasion of Privacy:** It can violate individuals' right to privacy. On the one hand, the feeling of being watched or monitored can feel intrusive and uncomfortable. On the other hand, this can also have a chilling effect on free expression and association, making people more cautious and less likely to express dissenting views.
- **Abuse of Power:** Governments and corporations can use surveillance to gather information on individuals, track their movements and activities, and use that information to exert influence or pressure. Thus, it can be used as a tool for those in positions of power to control and manipulate others.
- **Discrimination and Targeting:** Surveillance can be used to unfairly target and discriminate against certain groups based on their race, ethnicity, religion, sexual preferences, health conditions, or political beliefs, potentially leading to harassment, persecution, or even violence.
- **Lack of Transparency and Accountability:** When conducted without proper oversight, surveillance can lead to abuses and violations of human rights. Furthermore, when conducted in a covert manner, i.e., the individuals being monitored have no idea that they are being watched, there is no way for them to hold the surveilling party accountable.

We have already seen examples of mass surveillance being implemented using questionable and controversial technical means.

Encryption backdoors are deliberate vulnerabilities or weaknesses built into encryption software or hardware, which allow authorized parties to bypass or circumvent the encryption and gain access to the protected information. Law enforcement and national security agencies see it as a useful tool to catch criminals or terrorists, frequently citing national security concerns and the need to catch pedophiles as ways to squash counterarguments. However, these backdoors undermine the very purpose of encryption, which is to protect sensitive information and communications from unauthorized access. It is naïve to assume they can be exploited only by authorized parties (and that criminals will not find more sophisticated technical means to circumvent to hide their tracks). On the contrary, they also provide effective targets for malicious actors, including hackers, cybercriminals, and foreign governments. Furthermore, while calling for more technical surveillance measures, the technical capabilities and human resources to even leverage existing technical means existing data sources are still lacking (Landau, 2016, 2017).

For example, the federal trojan ("Bundestrojaner") is a term used to refer to a type of Trojan horse malware that was reportedly used by the German Federal Criminal Police Office (Bundeskriminalamt or BKA) to conduct surveillance on individuals suspected of criminal activities. The Bundestrojaner was first publicly acknowledged in 2011 when it was reported that the BKA had used the malware to conduct surveillance on a suspected terrorist. The malware was allegedly designed to be installed on a suspect's computer or mobile device, where it would then monitor their activity and collect data, including keystrokes, web browsing, and audio and video recordings. Unfortunately, it is by far not the only example of government-sponsored malware; other countries similarly toyed with the idea of developing (or simply buying) their own version of spyware.

In general, any backdoors, trojan horses, or other spyware can fundamentally undermine the trust that users have in technology, with serious consequences for individual privacy, as well as for businesses and governments that rely on technological means, such as encryption, to protect sensitive data. Thus, they warrant a critical debate about the appropriate balance between national security concerns and individual privacy rights.

Finally, similar to the "chilling effect" of individuals self-censoring their behavior online under the perceived threat of surveillance, citizens might behave differently when they know they are being watched by public cameras (Price, 2017).

5 Conclusions

In this chapter, we pointed out the inherent tension between surveillance and privacy. Surveillance mechanisms need to be designed in a way that they provide (physical) safety to society but also respect human's right for privacy, as well as transparency, oversight, and accountability.

Legislation, such as GDPR, has already been successful in providing more transparency in how data is collected and used, but this solution is far from perfect: not only is it infeasible to read all privacy policies we encounter on a daily basis; how they can be enforced and whether the provided information is actually accurate is still an open question.

Privacy should be built into technology from the outset, through a design approach called "privacy by design." This involves considering privacy implications at every stage of the design process and incorporating privacy protections as a fundamental aspect of the technology itself.

We also presented technological developments, such as homomorphic encryption and differential privacy, trying to address privacy issues, but there still is room for improvement to make them practical and deployable at scale.

As a final point, the threat of surveillance and lack of privacy severely impact users' trust in technology and hinder its adoption. One great example for this was the development (and failure) of contact tracing mechanisms during the COVID-19 pandemic: while its deployment could have been an effective means to limit the spread of the disease, public mistrust limited its adoption and rendered any efforts in this direction irrelevant.

Discussion Questions for Students and Their Teachers

1. What are acceptable tradeoffs between surveillance and privacy, where do you draw the line?
2. Do you recognize instances of the privacy paradox in your own behavior?
3. Think about the data you share online and the information that could be derived from them (see also the "data onion") (Szymielewicz, 2019). Who would you be comfortable sharing this information with? How could this be (mis)used against you? By whom?

4. What do you think are the most effective privacy-protecting measures (technical, organizational, political)? In which context?
5. Can you think of further privacy-enhancing measures that could be designed?
6. Bonus: Take an online privacy test (Blue, 2015). Was there information that surprised you, and are you willing to share your impressions?

Learning Resources for Students
On protecting your privacy in general:

1. Zotzmann-Koch, K. (2022) *Easy Ways to Be More Private on the Internet (Second Edition).* edition sil|ben|reich.

On how to (and why) protect your privacy as part of particularly vulnerable groups:

1. Blue, V. (2015) *The Smart Girl's Guide to Privacy: Practical Tips for Staying Safe Online.* No Starch Press.
2. Lewis, S. J. (2017) *Queer Privacy. Essays From The Margins Of Society.* Mascherari Press.

On privacy policies and their evolution:

1. Adhikari, A. and Das, S. and Dewri, R. (2023) 'Evolution of Composition, Readability, and Structure of Privacy Policies over Two Decades' in *Proceedings on Privacy Enhancing Technologies (PETS).* https://doi.org/10.56553/popets-2023-0074
2. Lovato, J. and Mueller, P. and Suchdev, P. and Dodds, P. (2023) 'More Data Types More Problems: A Temporal Analysis of Complexity, Stability, and Sensitivity in Privacy Policies' in *Proceedings of the ACM Conference on Fairness, Accountability, and Transparency (ACM FAccT).* https://doi.org/10.1145/3593013.3594065

On the inadequacy of privacy policies and alternatives:

1. McDonald, A. M. and Cranor, L. F. (2008) 'The Cost of Reading Privacy Policies' in *I/S: A Journal of Law and Policy for the Information Society*, 4(3).
2. Emami-Naeini, P. and Agarwal, Y. and Cranor, L. F. and Hibshi, H. (2020) 'Ask the Experts: What Should Be on an IoT Privacy and Security Label?' in *Proceedings of the IEEE Symposium on Security & Privacy (S&P).* https://doi.org/10.1109/SP40000.2020.00043

On the mechanisms behind targeted advertisements and why companies try to "game" the system:

1. Hoofnagle, C. J. and Soltani, A. and Good, N. and Wambach, D. J. and Ayenson, M. D. (2012) 'Behavioral Advertising: The Offer You Cannot Refuse' in *Harvard Law & Policy Review*, 273.

On the topic of informed consent and why it is failing users:

1. Fassl, M. and Gröber, L. T. and Krombholz K. (2021) 'Stop the Consent Theater' in *Extended Abstracts of the ACM Conference on Human Factors in Computing Systems (CHI EA).* https://doi.org/10.1145/3411763.3451230

On why users behave contrary to their own privacy preferences:

1. Gerber, N. and Gerber, P. and Volkamer, M. (2018) 'Explaining the privacy paradox: A systematic review of literature investigating privacy attitude and behavior' in *Computers & Security*, 77. https://doi.org/10.1016/j.cose.2018.04.002

On the tension between surveillance capabilities and requests for more:

1. Landau, S. (2016) 'The real security issue of the iPhone Case' in *Science*, 352(6292). https://doi.org/10.1126/science.aaf7708
2. Landau, S. (2017) *Listening in: Cybersecurity in an insecure age.* Yale University Press.

References

Adhikari, A., Das, S., & Dewri, R. (2023). Evolution of composition, readability, and structure of privacy policies over two decades. In *Proceedings on Privacy Enhancing Technologies (PETS).* https://doi.org/10.56553/popets-2023-0074

Blue, V. (2015). *The smart girl's guide to privacy: Practical tips for staying safe online.* No Starch Press.

Calacci, D., & Stein, J. (2023). From access to understanding: Collective data governance for workers. *European Labour Law Journal, 14*(2). https://doi.org/10.1177/20319525231167981

Deußer, C., Passmann, S., & Strufe, T. (2020). Browsing unicity: On the limits of anonymizing web tracking data. In *Proceedings of the IEEE symposium on security & privacy (S&P).* doi:https://doi.org/10.1109/SP40000.2020.00018.

Emami-Naeini, P., Agarwal, Y., Cranor, L. F., & Hibshi, H. (2020). Ask the experts: What should be on an IoT privacy and security label? In *Proceedings of the IEEE symposium on security and privacy (S&P).* doi:https://doi.org/10.1109/SP40000.2020.00043.

European Commission. (2016). *Regulation (EU) 2016/679 of the European Parliament and of the Council of 27 April 2016 on the protection of natural persons with regard to the processing of personal data and on the free movement of such data, and repealing Directive 95/46/EC (General Data Protection Regulation).* European Commission.

Fassl, M., Gröber, L. T., & Krombholz, K. (2021). *Stop the consent theater.* In Extended Abstracts of the ACM Conference on Human Factors in Computing Systems (CHI EA). https://doi.org/10.1145/3411763.3451230

Frier, S. (2019). Facebook paid contractors to transcribe users' audio chats. *Bloomberg Technology News*, August 13 [online]. Available at: https://www.bloomberg.com/news/articles/2019-08-13/facebook-paid-hundreds-of-contractors-to-transcribe-users-audio#xj4y7vzkg (Archived: https://archive.ph/66qcd).

Gellman, B., & Lindeman, T. (2013). Inner workings of a top-secret spy program. *Washington Post*, June 29 [online]. https://web.archive.org/web/20170830105407/https://apps.washingtonpost.com/g/page/national/inner-workings-of-a-top-secret-spy-program/282/.

Gellman, B., & Poitras, L. (2013). U.S., British intelligence mining data from nine U.S. Internet companies in broad secret program. *Washington Post*, June 7 [online]. Available at: https://www.washingtonpost.com/investigations/us-intelligence-mining-data-from-nine-us-internet-companies-in-broad-secret-program/2013/06/06/3a0c0da8-cebf-11e2-8845-d970ccb04497_story.html (Archived: https://archive.is/ucSTd).

Gerber, N., Gerber, P., & Volkamer, M. (2018). Explaining the privacy paradox: A systematic review of literature investigating privacy attitude and behavior. *Computers and Security, 77*. https://doi.org/10.1016/j.cose.2018.04.002

Greenwald, G., & MacAskill, E. (2013). NSA Prism program taps in to user data of Apple, Google and others. *The Guardian*. June 7 [online]. Available at: https://www.theguardian.com/world/2013/jun/06/us-tech-giants-nsa-data (Archived: https://archive.is/haGGj).

Harwell, D. (2020). Ring has terminated employees for abusing access to people's video data, Amazon tells lawmakers. *Washington Post*, January 8 [online]. Available at: https://www.washingtonpost.com/technology/2020/01/08/ring-has-terminated-employees-abusing-access-peoples-video-data-company-tells-lawmakers/ (Archived: https://archive.is/uwXJ4).

Hoofnagle, C. J. (2003). Big brother's little helpers: How ChoicePoint and other commercial data brokers collect and package your data for law enforcement. *North Carolina Journal of International Law, 595*.

Hoofnagle, C. J., Soltani, A., Good, N., Wambach, D. J., & Ayenson, M. D. (2012). Behavioral advertising: The offer you cannot refuse. *Harvard Law and Policy Review, 273*.

Kantor, J., & Sundaram, A. (2022). The rise of the worker productivity score. *The New York Times*, August 14 [online]. Available at: https://www.nytimes.com/interactive/2022/08/14/business/worker-productivity-tracking.html (Archived: https://archive.is/2EaSk).

Keegan, J., & Eastwood, J. (2023). From "heavy purchasers" of pregnancy tests to the depression-prone: We found 650,000 ways advertisers label you. *The Markup*, June 8 [online]. Available at: https://themarkup.org/privacy/2023/06/08/from-heavy-purchasers-of-pregnancy-tests-to-the-depression-prone-we-found-650000-ways-advertisers-label-you (Archived: https://archive.is/1YgzN).

Kelley, P. G., Bresee, J., Cranor, L. F., & Reeder, R. W. (2009). A "nutrition label" for privacy. In *Proceedings of the USENIX symposium on usable privacy and security (SOUPS)*. doi:https://doi.org/10.1145/1572532.1572538.

Knockel, J., Parsons, C., Ruan, L., Xiong, R., Crandall, J., & Deibert, R. (2020). *We chat, they watch how international users unwittingly build up wechat's Chinese censorship apparatus*. Technical Report, CitizenLab. Available at: https://citizenlab.ca/2020/05/we-chat-they-watch/.

Landau, S. (2016). The real security issue of the iPhone Case. *Science, 352*(6292). https://doi.org/10.1126/science.aaf7708

Landau, S. (2017). Listening. In *Cybersecurity in an insecure age*. Yale University Press.

Litman-Navarro, K. (2019). We read 150 privacy policies. They were an incomprehensible disaster. *The New York Times*, June 12 [online]. Available at: https://www.nytimes.com/interactive/2019/06/12/opinion/facebook-google-privacy-policies.html (Archived: https://archive.is/rPZGn).

Lovato, J., Mueller, P., Suchdev, P., & Dodds, P. (2023). More data types more problems: A temporal analysis of complexity, stability, and sensitivity in privacy policies. In *Proceedings of the ACM conference on fairness, accountability, and transparency (ACM FAccT)*. doi:https://doi.org/10.1145/3593013.3594065.

Madrigal, A. C. (2012). Reading the privacy policies you encounter in a year would take 76 work days. *The Atlantic*, March 1 [online]. Available at: https://www.theatlantic.com/technology/archive/2012/03/reading-the-privacy-policies-you-encounter-in-a-year-would-take-76-work-days/253851/ (Archived: https://archive.is/2ER6B).

McDonald, A. M., & Cranor, L. F. (2008). The cost of reading privacy policies. *I/S: A Journal of Law and Policy for the Information Society, 4*(3).

Narayanan, A., & Shmatikov V. (2008). Robust De-anonymization of large sparse datasets. In *Proceedings of the IEEE symposium on security and privacy (S&P)*. doi:https://doi.org/10.1109/SP.2008.33.

National Institute of Standards and Technology (NIST). (2023). *Glossary: Privacy.* Available at: https://csrc.nist.gov/glossary/term/privacy

Peck, D. (2013). 'They're watching you at work. *The Atlantic*, December 15 [online]. Available at: https://www.theatlantic.com/magazine/archive/2013/12/theyre-watching-you-at-work/354681/ (Archived: https://archive.is/s4YJk).

Perlberg, S. (2014). Targeted ads? TV can do that now too. *Wall Street Journal,* November 2014 [online]. Available at: https://www.wsj.com/articles/targeted-ads-tv-can-do-that-now-too-1416506504 (Archived: https://archive.is/OaFA0).

Price, B. A., Stuart, A., Calikli, G., Mccormick, C., Mehta, V., Hutton, L., Bandara, A. K., Levine, M., & Nuseibeh, B. (2017, June). *Logging you, logging me: A replicable study of privacy and sharing behaviour in groups of visual lifeloggers*. Proceedings of the ACM on Interactive, Mobile, Wearable and Ubiquitous Technology 1, 2, Article 22. https://doi.org/10.1145/3090087

Razaghpanah, A., Nithyanand, R., Vallina-Rodriguez N., Sundaresan, S., Allman, M., Kreibich, C., & Gill, P. (2018). Apps, trackers, privacy, and regulators: A global study of the mobile tracking ecosystem. In *Proceedings of the annual network and distributed system security symposium (NDSS).*

Rosenberg, M., Confessore, N., & Cadwalladr, C. (2018). How Trump consultants exploited the Facebook data of millions. *The New York Times*, March 17 [online]. Available at: https://www.nytimes.com/2018/03/17/us/politics/cambridge-analytica-trump-campaign.html (Archived: https://archive.is/jKMM9).

Sherman, J. (2022). *Data brokers and data breaches* [online] Available at: https://techpolicy.sanford.duke.edu/blogroll/data-brokers-and-data-breaches/ (Archived: https://archive.is/pM5jy).

Szymielewicz, K. (2019). Your digital identity has three layers, and you can only protect one of them. *Quartz*, January 25 [online]. Available at: https://qz.com/1525661/your-digital-identity-has-three-layers-and-you-can-only-protect-one-of-them (Archived: http://archive.today/vxQYF).

Tagliaro, C., Hahn, F., Sepe, R., Aceti, A., & Lindorfer, M. (2023). I still know what you watched last Sunday: Privacy of the HbbTV protocol in the European smart TV landscape. In *Proceedings of the annual network and distributed system security symposium (NDSS).*

Whittaker, Z. (2023) US intelligence confirms it buys Americans' personal data. In *TechCrunch*, June 2023 [online]. Available at: https://techcrunch.com/2023/06/13/us-intelligence-report-purchase-americans-personal-data/ (Archived: https://archive.is/nMXzH).

Zuboff, S. (2019). *The age of surveillance capitalism: The fight for a human future at the new frontier of power.* Public Affairs.

Human Rights Alignment: The Challenge Ahead for AI Lawmakers

Marc Rotenberg

Abstract The frameworks for the governance of AI have evolved rapidly. From the 2018 Universal Guidelines for AI on through the 2019 OECD/G20 AI Principles 2019, and the 2021 UNESCO Recommendation on AI Ethics, governments have agreed to the basic norms to regulate AI services. Two important legal frameworks are also now underway—the EU AI Act and the Council of Europe AI Convention. As these frameworks have evolved, we see the scope of AI governance models expand. From an initial focus on "human-centric and trustworthy AI" through the recognition of "fairness, accuracy, and transparency" as building blocks for AI governance, we see now consideration of sustainability, gender equality, and employment as key categories for AI policy. AI laws also overlap with familiar legal topics such as consumer protection, copyright, national security, and privacy. Throughout this evolution, we should consider whether the evolving models for the governance of AI are aligned with the legal norms that undergird democratic societies—fundamental rights, democratic institutions, and the rule of law. For democracies to flourish in the age of artificial intelligence, this is the ultimate alignment challenge for AI.

1 Introduction

As a field of study, digital humanism asks us to consider how we understand the impact of digital technologies on society and the humans who comprise it. In this chapter, we examine how societies respond to these challenges through legal and political institutions. The responses of national governments and international organizations to the specific challenges of the governance of AI become a key test of our ability to manage new technologies for social benefit. All of these undertakings begin with the premise that there must be a system of laws to safeguard fundamental rights, and in this respect, they go beyond the calls for ethical AI and responsible

M. Rotenberg (✉)
Center for AI and Digital Policy, Washington, DC, USA
e-mail: marc@caidp.org

H. Werthner et al. (eds.), *Introduction to Digital Humanism*,
https://doi.org/10.1007/978-3-031-45304-5_38

AI. At the same time, laws are imperfect. Language is imprecise. Technologies evolve rapidly. Powerful companies will resist constraints. And there is a risk that a dialectic process between technology and law could lead to outcomes that fail to protect well-established fundamental rights. This could occur, for example, if proponents of new technologies claim that well-established human rights, such as the protection of human dignity, autonomy, and privacy, must necessarily be altered to allow for the development of technology. For this reason, the articulation of norms for the governance of AI provides insight also to the ability of society to control the development of technology and to ensure that digital technology remains human-centric.

2 Main Part: Basic Concepts/Definitions/Methods and Critical Reflection

This section explores the development of legal frameworks for the governance of artificial intelligence. Law is generally understood to mean a system of rules that govern conduct. In democratic societies, law is derived from public debate and discussion and aims to reflect the will of the people, recognizing also the need to safeguard fundamental rights through constitutional limits on majority will.

Governance frameworks may also include influential policy frameworks (such as the Universal Guidelines for AI described below) as well as global agreements, which would include the OECD AI Principles,[1] the G20 AI Guidelines,[2] and the UNESCO Recommendation on AI Ethics.[3] These frameworks provide the basis for legal standards and international agreements and shape the conduct of those who develop and deploy AI systems as well as those who are subject to the outputs of AI systems.

Across the various governance frameworks, several key terms reoccur. These include "fairness," "accuracy," and "transparency," as well as "human-centric" and "trustworthy." These terms might also be considered the building blocks of AI law as they set out foundational values on which more specific direction is provided.

There are now several frameworks for the governance of artificial intelligence.

[1] OECD AI Principles (2019), https://legalinstruments.oecd.org/en/instruments/OECD-LEGAL-0449

[2] G20 AI Guidelines (2019), https://wp.oecd.ai/app/uploads/2021/06/G20-AI-Principles.pdf

[3] UNESCO **Recommendation on the Ethics of Artificial Intelligence** (2019)**, https://unesdoc.unesco.org/ark:/48223/pf0000380455**

2.1 *Universal Guidelines for AI*

The Universal Guidelines for Artificial Intelligence (UGAI)[4] were announced at the 2018 International Data Protection and Privacy Commissioners Conference at Brussels, Belgium—one of the most significant meetings of technology leaders and data protection experts in history. "The Guidelines are intended to maximize the benefits of AI, to minimize the risk, and to ensure the protection of human rights."[5] The UGAI incorporates elements of human rights doctrine, data protection law, and ethical guidelines. The Guidelines include several well-established principles for AI governance and put forward new principles not previously found in similar policy frameworks.[6] The Explanatory Memorandum states that the guidelines are primarily concerned with those systems that impact the rights of people.

According to the UGAI, the term artificial intelligence is both broad and imprecise and encompasses a variety of technological aspects which requires some degree of automated decision-making. The UGAI uses the term "guidelines" as a means of providing directional practices that can be useful for both governments and the private sector and recommends that the application of the guidelines should be incorporated into "ethical standards, adopted in national law and international agreements, and built into the design of systems."[7]

The UGAI is structured on 12 fundamental principles of right to transparency; right to human determination; identification obligation; fairness obligation; assessment and accountability obligation; accuracy, reliability, and validity obligation; data quality obligation; public safety obligation; cybersecurity obligation; prohibition on secret profiling; prohibition on unitary scoring; and a termination obligation. The UGAI also sets out prohibitions for mass surveillance and unitary (or social) scoring and includes a Termination obligation when it is no longer possible to maintain control of an AI system.

2.2 *The OECD AI Principles/the G20 AI Guidelines (2019)*

The OECD is an international organization that "works to build better policies for better lives." The goal of the OECD is to "shape policies that foster prosperity, equality, opportunity and well-being for all." The OECD emerged out of the Marshall Plan to assist Europe rebuild after the Second World War and to promote

[4] https://thepublicvoice.org/ai-universal-guidelines/

[5] https://thepublicvoice.org/ai-universal-guidelines/

[6] The Public Voice, *Explanatory Memorandum and References*, October 2018 https://thepublicvoice.org/ai-universal-guidelines/memo/

[7] *Id.*

economic interdependence. The OECD now has 38 member countries, spanning the Americas, Europe, and East Asia.[8]

The OECD led the global effort to develop and establish the most widely recognized framework for AI policy. This is a result of a concerted effort by the OECD and the member states to develop a coordinated international strategy. The OECD AI Principles also build on earlier OECD initiatives such as the OECD Privacy Guidelines, a widely recognized framework for transborder data flows and the first global framework for data protection.[9] The OECD AI Principles seek to promote AI that is innovative and trustworthy and respects human rights and democratic values.[10] The OECD set out five principles for the responsible stewardship of trustworthy AI:

1. Inclusive growth, sustainable development, and well-being
2. Human-centered values and fairness
3. Transparency and explainability
4. Robustness, security, and safety
5. Accountability

The OECD also set out five recommendations for national policies and international cooperation for trustworthy AI:

1. Investing in AI research and development
2. Fostering a digital ecosystem for AI
3. Shaping an enabling policy environment for AI
4. Building human capacity and preparing for labor market transformation
5. International cooperation for trustworthy AI

The OECD AI Principles were subsequently endorsed by the G20 nations in 2019. As a consequence, more than 50 countries have endorsed either the OECD AI Principles or the G20 AI Guidelines.

The remarks of the former OECD Secretary General Angel Gurria at the 2020 G-20 Digital Economy Ministers Meeting also provide insight into the work of the OECD on AI.[11] Secretary Gurria said, "AI's full potential is still to come. To achieve this potential, we must advance a human-centered and trustworthy AI, that respects the rule of law, human rights, democratic values and diversity, and that includes appropriate safeguards to ensure a fair and just society. This AI is consistent with the

[8] List of OECD Member countries - Ratification of the Convention on the OECD, https://www.oecd.org/about/document/ratification-oecd-convention.htm

[9] OECD, *OECD Guidelines on the Protection of Privacy and Transborder Flows of Personal Data (1981),* https://www.oecd.org/sti/ieconomy/oecdguidelinesontheprotectionofprivacyandtransborderflowsofpersonaldata.htm

[10] https://www.oecd.org/digital/artificial-intelligence/#

[11] CAIP Update 1.2, *OECD's Gurria Underscores AI Fairness at G-20* (July 26, 2020), https://dukakis.org/center-for-ai-and-digital-policy/center-for-ai-policy-update-oecds- gurria-underscores-ai-fairness-at-g-20-meeting/

G20 AI Principles you designed and endorsed last year, drawing from the OECD's AI Principles."

2.3 *The UNESCO Recommendation on AI Ethics*

In November 2021, the 193 member states of UNESCO adopted the Recommendation on the Ethics of Artificial Intelligence, the most comprehensive global framework to date for the governance of AI.[12] It will not only protect but also promote human rights and human dignity and will be an ethical guiding compass and a global normative bedrock allowing to build strong respect for the rule of law in the digital world.[13] UNESCO Director General Audrey Azoulay stated, "The world needs rules for artificial intelligence to benefit humanity. The recommendation on the ethics of AI is a major answer. It sets the first global normative framework while giving member states the responsibility to apply it at their level. UNESCO will support its 193 member states in its implementation and ask them to report regularly on their progress and practices."

The UNESCO Recommendation was the outcome of a multiyear process and was drafted with the assistance of more than 24 experts.[14] According to UNESCO, the "historical text defines the common values and principles which will guide the construction of the necessary legal infrastructure to ensure the healthy development of AI."[15] UNESCO explained, "The Recommendation aims to realize the advantages AI brings to society and reduce the risks it entails. It ensures that digital transformations promote human rights and contribute to the achievement of the Sustainable Development Goals, addressing issues around transparency, accountability and privacy, with action-oriented policy chapters on data governance, education, culture, labour, healthcare and the economy."

The UNESCO recommendation carried forward earlier principles for the governance of AI and also introduced new safeguards such as gender equity and sustainability. The key achievements of the UNESCO AI Recommendation include:

[12] UNESCO, *UNESCO member states adopt the first ever global agreement on the Ethics of Artificial Intelligence* (Nov. 25, 2021), https://en.unesco.org/news/unesco- member-states-adopt-first-ever-global-agreement-ethics-artificial-intelligence

[13] UNESCO, *Recommendation on the Ethics of Artificial Intelligence* (2021), https://unesdoc.unesco.org/ark:/48223/pf0000380455

[14] UNESCO, *Preparation of a draft text of the Recommendation: Ad Hoc Expert Group,* https://en.unesco.org/artificial-intelligence/ethics#aheg

[15] UNESCO, *UNESCO member states adopt the first ever global agreement on the Ethics of Artificial Intelligence* (Nov. 25, 2021), https://en.unesco.org/news/unesco- member-states-adopt-first-ever-global-agreement-ethics-artificial-intelligence

1. **Protecting data.** The UNESCO Recommendation calls for action beyond what tech firms and governments are doing to guarantee individuals more protection by ensuring transparency, agency, and control over their personal data.
2. **Banning social scoring and mass surveillance**. The UNESCO Recommendation explicitly bans the use of AI systems for social scoring and mass surveillance.
3. **Monitoring and evaluation.** The UNESCO Recommendation establishes new tools that will assist in implementation, including ethical impact assessments and a readiness assessment methodology.
4. **Protecting the environment.** The UNESCO Recommendation emphasizes that AI actors should favor data, energy, and resource-efficient AI methods that will help ensure that AI becomes a more prominent tool in the fight against climate change and on tackling environmental issues.

The Recommendation aims to provide a basis to make AI systems work for the good of humanity, individuals, societies, and the environment and ecosystems and to prevent harm. It also aims at stimulating the peaceful use of AI systems. The Recommendation provides a universal framework of values and principles of the ethics of AI. It sets out four values: respect, protection, and promotion of human rights and fundamental freedoms and human dignity; environment and ecosystem flourishing; ensuring diversity and inclusiveness; and living in peaceful, just, and interconnected societies.

Further, the Recommendation outlines 10 principles—proportionality and do no harm, safety and security, fairness and nondiscrimination, sustainability, right to privacy and data protection, human oversight and determination, transparency and explainability, responsibility and accountability, awareness, and literacy—backed up by more concrete policy actions on how they can be achieved. The Recommendation also introduces red lines to unacceptable AI practices. For example, it states that "AI systems should not be used for social scoring or mass surveillance purposes."

The Recommendation focuses not only on values and principles but also on their practical realization, with concrete policy actions. The UNESCO Recommendation encourages member states to introduce frameworks for ethical impact assessments and oversight mechanisms. According to UNESCO, member states should ensure that harms caused through AI systems are investigated and redressed, by enacting strong enforcement mechanisms and remedial actions, to make certain that human rights and fundamental freedoms and the rule of law are respected.

2.4 The EU AI Act

With the introduction of the Artificial Intelligence Act, the European Union aims to create a legal framework for AI to promote trust and excellence. The AI Act would establish a risk-based framework to regulate AI applications, products, and services. The rule of thumb: the higher the risk, the stricter the rule. The AI Act seeks to protect fundamental rights and public safety. The legislation will also prohibit certain AI applications, such as social scoring and mass surveillance, as UNESCO has recently urged in the Recommendation on AI ethics, endorsed by 193 countries.[16]

In various comments to the European Parliament and the European Council, groups such as the Center for AI and Digital Policy have sought to align the EU AI Act with such frameworks as the Universal Guidelines for AI that underscore the need to protect fundamental rights. Some of the recommendations from CAIDP are as follows:

Prohibit Pseudoscientific and Discriminatory AI Systems

- *Require scientific validity for AI systems*
- *Ban predictive policing*
- *Ban emotion recognition systems*
- *Ban biometric categorization systems*
- *Apply bans to both public and private entities*

Safeguard Fundamental Rights

- *Remove the broad exclusions for law enforcement*
- *Remove the exclusions for ex ante systems*
- *Remove the national security exclusion*
- *Correct the unequal protection of asylum seekers and refugees*

Ensure Transparency and Accountability

- *Mandate ex ante impact assessments*
- *Record serious incidents*
- *Require private users to registers*
- *Mandate independent, third-party auditing*
- *Regulate general-purpose AI (GPAI) systems*
- *Establish obligation to terminate AI systems no longer under human control*

Protect Societal Interests

- *Protect the environment*
- *Safeguard disability rights*
- *Adopt UNESCO Recommendation on AI Ethics*

As the EU AI Act is still under development, it remains to be seen which of these recommendations will be adopted. The text adopted by the Parliament extended

[16] Center for AI and Digital Policy, EU Artificial Intelligence Act, https://www.caidp.org/resources/eu-ai-act/

prohibitions to subliminal techniques, biometric categorization, predictive policing, Internet-scrapped facial recognition databases, and emotion recognition.[17]

2.5 The Council of Europe AI Convention

The Council of Europe (COE) is the continent's leading human rights organization.[18] The COE is comprised of 47 member states, 27 of which are members of the European Union. All COE member states have endorsed the European Convention of Human Rights, a treaty designed to protect human rights, democracy, and the rule of law. Article 8 of the Convention, concerning the right to privacy, has influenced the development of privacy law around the world.

Several AI initiatives are underway at the Council of Europe, including at the Council of Ministers, the COE Parliamentary Assembly. Marija Pejčinović Burić, Secretary General of the Council of Europe, has said "It is clear that AI presents both benefits and risks. We need to ensure that AI promotes and protects our standards .... The Council of Europe has, on many occasions, demonstrated its ability to pioneer new standards, which have become global benchmarks."[19]

In October 2020, the Parliament Assembly of the Council of Europe adopted a new resolution on the Need for Democratic Governance of Artificial Intelligence.[20] The Assembly called for "strong and swift action" by the Council of Europe. The parliamentarians warned that "soft-law instruments and self-regulation have proven so far not sufficient in addressing these challenges and in protecting human rights, democracy and rule of law."

In a set of recommendations examining the opportunities and risks of AI for democracy, human rights, and the rule of law adopted in October 2020 as well, the Parliamentary Assembly called on the Committee of Ministers to take into account the particularly serious potential impact of the use of artificial intelligence "in policing and criminal justice systems"[21] or "on the enjoyment of the rights to

---

[17] Luca Bertuzzi, AI Act enters final phase of EU legislative process, Euractiv, June 14, 2023, https://www.euractiv.com/section/artificial-intelligence/news/ai-act-enters-final-phase-of-eu-legislative-process/

[18] Council of Europe, *Who we are,* https://www.coe.int/en/web/about-us/who-we-are

[19] Council of Europe, *Artificial intelligence and human rights,* https://www.coe.int/en/web/artificial-intelligence/secretary-general-marija-pejcinovic- buric

[20] Council of Europe, Parliamentary Assembly, *Need for democratic governance of artificial intelligence* (Oct. 22, 2020), https://pace.coe.int/en/files/28803/html

[21] Parliamentary Assembly, *Recommendation 2182(2020) Justice by algorithm – The role of artificial intelligence in policing and criminal justice systems* (Oct. 22, 2020) https://pace.coe.int/en/files/28806/html; See also, *Resolution 2342 (2020)* https://pace.coe.int/en/files/28805

equality and non-discrimination,"[22] when assessing the necessity and feasibility of an international legal framework for artificial intelligence.

At present, a draft text circulated by the Committee on AI of the Council of Europe seeks to establish a comprehensive global treaty for the governance of AI.[23] In a statement issued in May 2023, the Council of Europe Committee on Artificial Intelligence (CAI), explained, "The CAI is committed to ensuring that the Framework Convention will be human- centred, open to non-member States, and adopt a risk-based approach to the design, development, and use of AI systems facilitating the prevention of harmful uses of AI systems and promoting the use of this digital technology for the good of society, including by allowing for safe innovation."[24]

2.6 *Challenges Ahead*

An ongoing challenge in AI policy concerns the ability to establish and enforce prohibitions on certain AI deployments. For example, the UNESCO Recommendation on AI Ethics discussed above establishes prohibitions on the use of AI techniques for social scoring and mass surveillance, yet many of the countries that have endorsed the UNESCO Recommendation continue to support the use and deployment of AI systems for these purposes. China, for example, continues to deploy a social credit system, based on AI, that is intended to align the private behavior of Chinese citizens with the political aims of the Chinese Communist Party.[25] Although there is some dispute as to the scope of the social credit system and a recognition that China needs to assess credit worthiness for efficient markets, the incorporation of certain factors in the evaluation, such as "picking quarrels and provoking trouble," is precisely the factors in an AI model that raise concern. The use of AI for remote biometric identification, a form of mass surveillance, remains a concern not only in China but in many countries that have installed camera systems for monitoring public spaces. Over time, these networks have become more sophisticated, providing the ability to link images to individuals and then to government profiles that may also provide risk assessments that lead to police intervention before any unlawful act has occurred. The effective governance of AI in democratic societies will require limitations and prohibitions on the deployment of such AI-driven systems

[22] Parliamentary Assembly, *Recommendation 2183 (2020) Preventing discrimination caused by the use of artificial intelligence* (Oct. 22, 2020) https://pace.coe.int/en/files/28809/html; See also, *Resolution 2343 (2020)* https://pace.coe.int/en/files/25318/html

[23] Center for AI and Digital Policy, Council of Europe AI Treaty, https://www.caidp.org/resources/coe-ai-treaty/

[24] Statement of the Council of Europe Committee on Artificial Intelligence (CAI), https://rm.coe.int/cai-statement-fr/1680ab6e85

[25] John Feng, How China's Social Credit System Works, Newsweek, Dec. 22, 2022, https://www.newsweek.com/china-social-credit-system-works-explained-1768726

There are also the legal frameworks currently underway at the European Union, the Council of Europe, and many governments around the world. There are challenges ahead for both adoption and effective implementation. There is currently a 2-year period from the time the EU AI Act is finalized to actual enforcement. Some are concerned that this gap will allow the use of unregulated AI systems that put at risk fundamental rights and public safety. However, a proposal from industry to develop an interim "AI pact" or "code of conduct" is opposed by civil society organizations as it would undermine democratic decision-making.[26] Regarding the Council of Europe Treaty, there are concerns also about implementation and the possibility that national governments will endorse the treaty nonetheless.

Finally, there remains an existential challenge—will humans remain in control of the AI systems they create? Stuart Russell has expressed this concern in *Human Compatible: Artificial Intelligence and the Problem of Control* in 2019. In recent years, there is growing attention to this issue, as new AI techniques challenge even the ability to deliberate. From this perspective, the ability to develop effective legislation to govern AI becomes even more critical.

3 Conclusions

- The governance structures for artificial intelligence have evolved rapidly, from framework principles to enforceable laws. Many of the governance structures emphasize "human-centric" and "trustworthy" AI.
- As the governance of AI has evolved, so too has the range of issues that fall within the AI domain. Early framework principles focused on automated decision-making and emphasized fairness, accountability, and transparency. More recent governance mechanisms set out principles for equity, public safety, and environmental sustainability.
- AI governance includes prohibitions on certain AI deployments such as social scoring, mass surveillance, and biometric categorization.
- Laws that govern AI interact with other legal rules, including consumer protection, copyright, data protection, national security, and privacy.
- One of the key challenges for AI governance concerns accountability: how to assess AI outcomes if it is not possible to determine how they are produced? A range of solutions has been proposed including explainability and traceability, certification, and transparency obligations.
- The biggest challenge for AI governance may simply be ensuring that AI is aligned with democratic values, fundamental rights, and the role of law.

---

[26]BEUC, **EU-US AI voluntary code of conduct and an 'AI Pact' for Europe, June 5, 2023, https://www.beuc.eu/letters/eu-us-ai-voluntary-code-conduct-and-ai-pact-europe**

Discussion Questions for Students and Their Teachers

1. What are some of the reasons to have laws to govern artificial intelligence?
2. What are the characteristics of AI governance frameworks?
3. Which AI "use cases" would you consider to be high risk and why? And which would you consider to be low risk and why?
4. Are there AI deployments that you would prohibit? If yes, why? If no, why not?
5. What recommendation would you make for an AI governance principle?

Learning Resources for Students

1. Daron Acemoglu and Simon Johnson, *Power and Progress: Our 1000-Year Struggle Over Technology and Prosperity* (Public Affairs Books 2023)

   As the authors explain, "A thousand years of history and contemporary history make one thing clear: progress depends on the choices we make about technology. New ways of organizing production can either serve the narrow interests of an elite or become the foundation for widespread prosperity." *Powers and Progress* include a detailed critique of the AI economy and recommendations for concrete actions.
2. Anu Bradford, *Digital Empires: The Global Battle to Regulate Technology* (Oxford 2023)

   Bradford examines three competing approaches for the digital economy—the American market-driven model, the Chinese state-driven model, and the European rights-driven regulatory model. Which digital empire will prevail in the contest for global influence remains an open question, yet their contrasting strategies are increasingly clear and will have far-reaching consequences for the governance of artificial intelligence.
3. Center for AI and Digital Policy, *Artificial Intelligence and Democratic Values Index* (2023)

   A comprehensive review of AI policies and practices in 75 countries. It provides a methodology to compare country practices and assess trends across 12 key metrics and includes the text of the key AI policy frameworks, including the OECD AI Principles and the UNESCO Recommendation on AI Ethics.
4. European Law Institute, Guiding Principles for Automated Decision Making in the EU (2022)

   The Innovation Paper sets out 12 principles for automated decision-making. The ELI Guiding Principles include such novel concepts for AI governance such as traceability, reasoned decisions, risk allocation, and responsible ADM, including impact assessment on democratic values.
5. Marc Rotenberg, Time to Assess National AI Policies, Communications of the ACM, Nov. 24, 2020

   In this article for a computer science journal, the author explains the origins of the AI and Democratic Values report. "Our goal is to understand the commitments that governments have made, the AI initiatives they have launched, and the policies they have established to protect fundamental rights and to safeguard the public."

6. Stuart Russell, *Human Compatible: Artificial Intelligence and the Problem of Control* (2019)

   One of the world's leading AI researchers describes the challenges ahead to maintain control of artificial intelligence. Professor Russell proposes that we reassess the aims of AI systems, to build in uncertainty about pursuing outcomes and to ensure alignment with human preferences reflected in human behavior.

European Approaches to the Regulation of Digital Technologies

Martin Müller and Matthias C. Kettemann

Abstract Following years of a liberal approach to digital technologies, platforms, services, and markets, the EU has stepped up its action in recent years. The adoption of the General Data Protection Regulation (GDPR) (Regulation (EU) 2016/679 of the European Parliament and of the Council of 27 April 2016 on the protection of natural persons with regard to the processing of personal data and on the free movement of such data and repealing Directive 95/46/EC (General Data Protection Regulation), OJ L 119, 1) in 2016 can be seen as a starting point for new regulations that are now enacted and proposed under the European Commission's strategy "A Europe fit for the digital age." This article will briefly summarize the contents of the GDPR as well as the Digital Services Act (DSA) (Regulation (EU) 2022/2065 of the European Parliament and of the Council of 19 October 2022 on a Single Market for Digital Services and amending Directive 2000/31/EC (Digital Services Act), OJ L 277, 1), Digital Markets Act (DMA) (Regulation (EU) 2022/1925 of the European Parliament and of the Council of 14 September 2022 on contestable and fair markets in the digital sector and amending Directives (EU) 2019/1937 and (EU) 2020/1828 (Digital Markets Act), OJ L 265, 1), Data Governance Act (DGA) (Regulation (EU) 2022/868 of the European Parliament and of the Council of 30 May 2022 on European data governance and amending Regulation (EU) 2018/1724 (Data Governance Act), OJ L 152, 1), and the proposals for the Artificial Intelligence Act (AI Act) (Proposal for a Regulation of the European Parliament and of the Council laying down harmonized rules on artificial intelligence (Artificial Intelligence Act) and amending certain Union legislative acts, 21 April 2021, COM(2021) 206 final.) as well as the Data Act (Proposal for a Regulation of the European Parliament and of the Council on harmonized rules on fair access to and use of data (Data Act), 23 February 2022, COM(2022) 68 final.). We identify the underpinnings of the normative approach and its potential and shortcomings, thus providing an assessment of the role of Europe as a technology regulator more broadly and its relationship to digital humanism.

M. Müller (✉) · M. C. Kettemann
Department for Theory and Future of Law, University of Innsbruck Innsbruck, Innsbruck, Austria
e-mail: martin.mueller@uibk.ac.at; matthias.kettemann@uibk.ac.at

H. Werthner et al. (eds.), *Introduction to Digital Humanism*,
https://doi.org/10.1007/978-3-031-45304-5_39

1 Introduction

In recent years, the European Union (EU) has undergone a significant shift in its approach toward digital tools and technologies, platforms, services, and markets. After years of embracing a more liberal stance, the EU has ramped up its regulatory actions to address the challenges posed by the digital age. A pivotal moment came in 2016 with the adoption of the General Data Protection Regulation (GDPR), marking the beginning of a series of new regulations enacted and proposed under the European Commission's strategy, "A Europe fit for the digital age." This article aims to provide a concise overview of the key regulatory measures introduced by the EU and contextualizes it against the background of an ongoing alignment of EU normative approaches and digital humanism.

2 Overview of EU Platform Regulation

2.1 The Starting Point: GDPR

The General Data Protection Regulation (GDPR) is a great achievement in the field of data protection and one of the toughest privacy and security laws in the world. On 25 May 2018, the regulation entered into force. It is considered a wide-ranging personal data protection regime of greater magnitude than any similar regulation previously in the EU, or elsewhere.[1] The objectives of this Regulation in Article 1 GDPR are to lay down rules relating to the protection of natural persons concerning the processing of personal data and rules relating to the free movement of personal data and to protect fundamental rights and freedom of natural persons.

The Regulation applies to the processing of personal data wholly or partly by automated means. For non-automated means, the GDPR applies as well when personal data is saved in a filing system or is intended to do so. The GDPR sets a low bar, defining "personal data" in Article 4 as "any information relating to an identified or identifiable natural person ('data subject'); an identifiable natural person is one who can be identified, directly or indirectly (. . .)."[2] The territorial requirement for the applicability of the Regulation is that, whether or not the processing takes place in the Union, the processing of personal data must be carried out in the context of the activities of an establishment of a controller or processor in the Union. This means that the GDPR applies to all organizations that process the personal data of EU citizens, regardless of where the organization is based. This includes businesses operating within the EU as well as those outside the EU if they offer goods or services to EU citizens or monitor their behavior. In practice, this means that the GDPR applies to far more data collection activities than its predecessor, the Data

[1] Allen et al. (2019, 785).

[2] Hoofnagle et al. (2019, 72).

Protection Directive, which was based on where the data was processed rather than where the data subject resided.[3] The penalties to be applied by the Supervisory authorities for breaching the Regulation are significant, ranging up to 20 million euros or 4% of global turnover, whichever is higher.

The GDPR seeks to use regulatory powers to create a powerful threatening incentive for companies to behave as the regulators intend. In Article 5, the GDPR lists some principles relating to the processing of personal data. For the regulators, personal data shall be "processed lawfully, fairly and in a transparent manner in relation to the data subject (. . .)"; it shall also be collected for specified, explicit, and legitimate purpose, adequate, relevant, and limited to what is necessary in relation to the object, stored secure for no longer than necessary. Article 13 GDPR lists the information that has to be provided to the data subjects. This includes information about the period of storage of the data, the existence of the subject's right to rectification or erasure of personal data, the existence of the right to withdraw consent at any time, and many more. The data controller and processor must implement appropriate technical and organizational measures to be able to demonstrate that processing is performed in conformity with this Regulation. Article 51 GDPR provides the constitution of one or more independent public authorities in the member states to be responsible for monitoring the application of this Regulation. They should protect the fundamental rights and freedoms of the natural persons in relation to the data. The GDPR sets standards for the authorities which include that the state, while providing the supervisory authority with the human, technical, and financial resources, shall also ensure that such does not affect the independence of the supervisory authority. Article 68 of the GDPR provides the constitution of the European Data Protection Board (EDPB), which shall be composed of the head of one supervisory authority of each member state and the European Data Protection Supervisor.

Five years into the applicability of the GDPR, it is becoming clearer that the GDPR did indeed set a global standard which has been dubbed the *Brussels Effect*[4] and has led to similar data protection laws around the world.[5] However, a few downsides are beginning to show when it comes to clarity and enforcement of the regulation. The provisions of the GDPR are occasionally vaguely worded, so rulings by the European Court of Justice (ECJ) are necessary to remove these ambiguities. Five years after its adoption, 55 cases have had to be decided already or are still awaiting a decision. In view of the approximately 800 cases decided annually by the ECJ for all areas of law,[6] frequent interpretation of the GDPR is necessary. On the enforcement side, civil society organizations showed that procedures under the GDPR take long or may be even not carried out at all. Moreover, as member states

[3] Ibidem, p. 786.

[4] Bradford (2020).

[5] For a comprehensive overview cf. Greenleaf (2021).

[6] ECJ (2023, p. 1).

authorities are responsible for the enforcement, procedure varies and a common approach is hindered by member states-specific procedural issues.[7]

2.2 Regulating Platforms' Societal Power: Digital Services Act (DSA)

The Digital Services Act (DSA) is a regulation of the European Union, which came into force in November 2022. The Digital Services Act (DSA) and the Digital Markets Act (DMA) are part of the EU's digital strategy and aim to create a safer digital space in which the fundamental rights of all users of digital services are protected and to create a level playing field to promote innovation, growth, and competitiveness both in the European single market and worldwide. The DSA is a further development of the previous E-Commerce Directive,[8] which will be replaced by the DSA. A significant innovation is the extraterritorial scope of the DSA; this is defined at the outset in the general provisions. The DSA is territorially linked to the establishment of the user. As a result, as long as there is a "substantial connection to the Union," the establishment of the service provider is irrelevant.[9]

The material scope of application of the DSA does not include all digital service providers but is limited to so-called intermediary services, which are further subdivided into "mere conduit," "caching," and "hosting" services. These services include the transmission and storage of user-generated content.[10] The main objective of the E-Commerce Directive was to create a legal framework that facilitates the free movement of intermediaries within the EU in order to promote innovation and e-commerce. The DSA, however, is based on a different approach. It recognizes digital platforms as responsible actors in the fight against illegal content.[11]

Regarding the liability exemptions in its Chapter II, the DSA preserves and upgrades the basic liability rules of the previous E-Commerce Directive. The liability exemptions prevent state actors from incurring any liability for third-party content and obligations to generally monitor third-party content. The liability exemptions cover mere conduit services, caching services, and hosting services.[12]

Based on the idea of acknowledging digital platforms as responsible actors, the DSA sets out due diligence obligations in Chapter III of transparency, accountability, and information for digital services to qualify and contain a variety of obligations

[7] noyb.eu (2023), van Hoboken (2022).

[8] Directive 2000/31/EC of the European Parliament and of the Council of 8 June 2000 on certain legal aspects of information society services, in particular electronic commerce, in the Internal Market ('Directive on electronic commerce') (OJ L 178, 1).

[9] Buri and van Hoboken (2021, p. 13).

[10] Wilman (2022, p. 1).

[11] Genç-Gelgeç (2022, pp. 25–60).

[12] Husovec and Roche Laguna (2022, p. 3).

such as specific requirements for terms and conditions, the setting-up of a compliant-management system, or reporting and transparency requirements. The obligations are set depending on the size of the digital service providers and their role in the online world. In doing so, the DSA divides them into four categories: intermediaries, hosting intermediaries including online platforms, online platforms (providers of hosting services that also disseminate information), and very large online platforms (VLOPs) and very large online search engines (VLOSEs) (online platforms with more than 45 million recipients). Each of them is required to perform duties at different levels.[13]

In Chapter IV, the DSA introduces a set of rules regarding the implementation, cooperation, penalties, and enforcement. For example, all providers of intermediary services are bound to report, publicly and at least annually, on how they have dealt with various obligations under the DSA. In addition, not that they are obliged to take certain measures to facilitate public supervision and enforcement. Here, the measures include the appointment of a single point of contact allowing for direct communication with the competent supervisory body. As for very large online platforms and very large online search engines, the DSA aims to ensure adequate internal and external oversight of compliance with the new rules. For this, providers must establish an independent compliance function within the provider's organization. An important innovation of the DSA is the wide-ranging competencies given to the Commission to enforce the rules applicable to very large online platforms and very large online search engines, such as the possibility of investigations and inspections, requiring access to data, and the possibility of imposing heavy fines.[14]

2.3 *Regulating Platforms' Economic Power: Digital Markets Act (DMA)*

The DMA was enacted at the same time as the DSA; therefore, both acts have to be read together in order to fully understand the overall meaning of the EU's stance to platform regulation. The DMA tries to contain the economic power the "big tech" platforms have in digital markets, which are often monopolistic when it comes to specific online services (think about "the" search engine, "the" online marketplace, or "the" social media platform). Traditional unfair competition law on the EU level (namely, Articles 101, 102 of the Treaty on the Functioning of the European Union (TFEU)) and member states' laws do apply to digital platforms; however, this is understood to be "too little, too late" as proceedings by the European Commission

[13] Genç-Gelgeç (2022, pp. 25–60).

[14] Husovec and Roche Laguna (2022, p. 12) and Wilman (2022, p. 14 et seqq).

against platforms took long and couldn't improve market competition.[15] Moreover, digital markets differ from other markets by some economic characteristics.[16]

The DMA shifts from the so-called ex post approach (i.e., that authorities must first find a violation and can than react with fines or other measures) which is imminent to competition law to an ex ante approach and prohibits or imposes corresponding regulations for a total of 21 practices that are considered harmful to betting in digital markets. These due diligence obligations do not apply to all platforms but only to those that have been designated as *gatekeepers* by the European Commission. In the DMA's understanding, companies are gatekeepers when they meet the following three requirements: (a) having a significant impact on the internal market, (b) providing a so-called core platform service,[17] and (c) enjoying an entrenched and durable position now or in the near future. These rather general requirements are followed by specific thresholds, all of which are met by the known big tech companies.

The due diligence obligations to be followed by platforms can be divided into two groups: Part of the obligations must be complied with by platforms as they stand. This includes, for example, the prohibition for gatekeepers to merge data from different central platform services or the compulsion to have to use a certain payment service. The other part of the obligations, on the other hand, is less specific and can be further narrowed down by the European Commission as supervisory authority. In this group is, for example, a prohibition of self-preference of services or products of the gatekeepers over those of other providers or the possibility for users to simply transfer their own data to another data provider (so-called data portability).

The new regulations are to be enforced almost solely by the European Commission. If obligations are violated regularly, enforcement will be taken in the form of fines. At up to 10% of annual global turnover, these fines are similar to those of the GDPR. However, the DMA also allows the Commission to prohibit mergers of companies and, as a last resort, to break up gatekeeper companies should obligations of the DMA be "systematically violated."

2.4 Regulating Platforms' "Oil" I: Data Governance Act

The DGA is the first piece of legislation at Union level to address data sharing. While the GDPR is concerned with the protection of personal data, the DGA first wants to address data sharing in general, i.e., personal as well as nonpersonal data, and thus represents a realignment of the Union's policy.[18] The goal of the European

[15] Podszun et al. (2021, pp. 60 et seq).

[16] Schweitzer (2021, p. 518).

[17] The DMA lists in Article 2 (2) overall ten *core platform services*. These are, e.g., online search engines, online social networks, video-sharing platforms, or cloud computing services.

[18] Metzger and Schweitzer (2023, p. 43).

Commission within the framework of the proclaimed "data strategy" is to create a "free flow" of data, which is said to have major economic benefits for the Union's common market.[19]

In total, the DGA regulates four different individual areas: first, it creates conditions for the sharing of public sector data; second, it regulates the operation of commercial "data intermediary services"; third, it oversees those that operate altruistically; and finally, it establishes the European Data Innovation Council.

In the context of European platform regulation, these "data intermediaries" are interesting. Unlike in the DSA and DMA, there is (still) no power position by a "big tech" company in data markets. In addition to creating more trust in data markets and, thus, establishing the "free flow of data," the underlying rationale for regulation can be seen in the attempt to prevent precisely such positions of market power from arising.[20]

Once the DGA enters into force, data intermediaries must notify member state authorities. This also applies to companies not residing in the EU, provided they are also active in the European market. Data intermediaries will be bound by 15 different regulations designed to ensure that the objectives of regulation (increasing data sharing, trust in data sharing, and fair competition) are achieved. For example, companies must act neutrally, be interoperable, or provide fair and transparent access (so-called FRAND conditions). Many of the obligations are similar in content to the DMA but may be interpreted differently.[21]

2.5 Regulating Platforms' "Oil" II: Data Act Proposal

The European Commission's Data Act proposal is the centerpiece of the "data strategy." The aim here is to increase the amount of publicly available data. Currently, vast amounts of data are generated by Internet of Things (IoT) devices, which usually remain with the manufacturers and can only be accessed in exceptional cases.[22]

To this end, a so-called horizontal right is created for users vis-à-vis product manufacturers (the "data holders") to access the data generated by the product, i.e., users can demand in any economic sector the data created by "them" through the use of a product (e.g., a connected vehicle, an app-based robotic vacuum cleaner, etc.) to receive it and to have it shared with a third party. With these access rights come various obligations designed to make this right useful in practice. For example, care must be taken in the design and manufacture of the product to ensure that data is

[19] von Ditfurth and Lienemann (2022, p. 272).

[20] von Ditfurth and Lienemann (2022, p. 278).

[21] Baloup et al. (2021, p. 32 et seqq).

[22] Metzger and Schweitzer (2023, p. 43 et seq).

readily available, and the FRAND conditions for disclosure of data also required in the DMA and DGA are also mandatory for data holders in the Data Act.

From a platform regulation perspective, the obligation of so-called data processing services to enable switching between different such services should also be mentioned. Here again, a parallel to the DMA can be seen, except that the data portability obligation goes beyond the "big tech" companies and is extended. Other provisions concerning the interoperability of data, i.e., the technical compatibility of different provider systems, also strike in the same vein.

2.6 Regulating Platforms' "Tools": AI Act Proposal

Widely understood, the European Commission's proposal for the AI Act is a risk-based regulation[23] in which the use of AI systems is classified into different risk categories, with more extensive regulations for higher risk. Besides many innovative areas of application, AI systems also pose risks, particularly for the fundamental rights of users, which made the European Commission now call for the regulation of the technology.

AI systems are classified through the draft AI Act into different risk categories. In the first, certain AI systems are deemed as "unacceptable," such as when they influence the free will of users or contain "social scoring," which is the AI-based assessment of individual citizens' behavior by government agencies. Under the proposed AI Act's scope, their use is then prohibited in the European Union.

The next level includes "high-risk" AI systems, which are listed in the separate Annexes II and III of the proposed regulation. Annex II features a list of existing EU regulations in place that require a "conformity assessment" for products that bear specific risks. If AI is part of these products or the product "itself," it is considered to be a "high-risk" AI system. For the list in Annex III, the context of use is more relevant, i.e., it is not the AI system itself that is considered risky but the area in which it is used. Eight different domains are therefore named in which certain AI systems are "high-risk" AI systems, such as those involved in decisions about access to education or employment. A particularly large number of applications that are considered "high-risk" AI involve those in law enforcement or migration. If an AI system falls into this category, manufacturers and users must adhere to a host of compliance obligations, such as having risk management and quality management systems in place and registering the AI system with the Commission.

The third and final group includes "low-risk" AI systems, for which the AI Act proposal requires "only" transparency obligations and thus significantly fewer requirements than for those in the "high-risk" category. In detail, this means that providers of AI systems that (1) interact with humans, (2) are used for emotion or

[23] Ebers et al. (2021, p. 589) and De Gregorio and Dunn (2022, p. 488 et seqq).

biometrics recognition, or (3) that generate "deepfakes" must notify their users that the content was generated by an AI.

"Risk-free" AI systems are not regulated by the AI act. They include, for example, spam filters for email programs. Here, the risk for users is considered so small that no regulations are envisaged.

3 Digital Humanism in European Platform Regulation

The Vienna Manifesto on Digital Humanism addresses the platforms as the most important actors in digitalization in several places and demands answers regarding the problematic phenomena that have emerged due to their "platform power" (cf. chapter of Samaan). For example, it demands that "Effective regulations, rules and laws, based on a broad public discourse, must be established." The following demand is even clearer: "Regulators need to intervene with tech monopolies."

In addition to these programmatic demands, however, the Vienna Manifesto also contains the normative framework that should underlie digital technology and thus also its regulation. In addition to ethical considerations (cf. chapters by Nida-Rümelin and Staudacher, Werthner, and Prem/Tamburrini when it comes to AI), the reference to human rights explicitly also includes legal considerations. This should be the yardstick for our assessment of platform regulation under European Union law: How does platform regulation under Union law ensure that human rights are protected?

For the European Union, human rights, as found at the level of international law, for example, in the Universal Declaration of Human Rights or the UN human rights covenants,[24] are not the direct connecting factor. As a supranational, European organization, the ECHR as a regional human rights instrument and the Charter of Fundamental Rights (CFR) adopted in 2007 are more relevant and form the constitutional basis for regulation. When it comes to the level of protection for individuals, this is basically on a par with the level under international law in the case of the ECHR and the CFR.

3.1 Fundamental Rights in EU Platform Regulation

In some cases, the various legal acts explicitly refer to fundamental rights in general or also specifically to individual fundamental rights. It starts with the GDPR, which is the concrete formulation of the fundamental rights of Articles 7 and 8 of the CFR, which initially only stipulate that there is a fundamental right to data protection. The

[24] An overview of the different human rights instruments on the UN level can be found here: https://www.un.org/en/global-issues/human-rights (retrieved 24 April 2023).

detailed formulation is then taken over by the GDPR and specifies, for example, the concrete rights of data subjects in Articles 12 et seqq. GDPR or the requirements for data processing. There is no clear mentioning of fundamental rights in the text, but many of the provisions of the GDPR refer to fundamental rights "unconsciously."[25] Not discussed here, but another example for fundamental rights to be respected by platforms can be found in Article 17 DSM Directive, which has been discussed in chapter of Mendis before.

At two provisions, the DSA contains very specific requirements for platforms to take fundamental rights into account. In the legal discussion, this is referred to as a "horizontal binding" of platforms. This is because fundamental rights and human rights historically applied only between citizens and states, thus binding the state "vertically" to rules, giving citizens rights.[26] Now these rules are also applied between private companies and users, who before had been "on the same level" as fundamental rights holders. However, digitalization and the rise of platforms as the most important actors have led to a power imbalance at the expense of users, thus questioning whether equal fundamental rights treatment is still justified or platforms should also be bound to fundamental rights vis-à-vis their users.

First and foremost, there is Article 14 DSA, which deals with the terms and conditions of platforms. These terms and conditions are very relevant in practice as they mainly govern the relationship between users and platforms.[27] So far, platforms have been quite free in their choice of terms and conditions, sometimes called terms of use or terms of service, and are only marginally bound by law. However, users must agree to the terms and conditions if they want to use the platforms' services. Because of the aforementioned tendency of digital markets to monopolize, this then often results in a requirement for consent. Article 14 (4) DSA now requires that the interests of users must be considered when moderating content and for complaints handled by platforms. The fundamental rights of users, such as the fundamental right to freedom of expression, are cited very specifically. Similar to the way in which fundamental rights must be observed in official decisions or court proceedings in democratic states, platforms may not violate any fundamental rights in "their decisions." Article 14 DSA thus undoubtedly represents a horizontal binding of platforms.[28]

Similarly, VLOPs must respect fundamental rights: Because of the "systemic risks" they pose, the DSA requires them to conduct comprehensive risk analyses and take measures on how to deal with the risks. Article 34 (1) DSA again requires users' fundamental rights among other interests to be taken into account when assessing risks.

[25] Celeste and de Gregorio (2022, p. 11 et seq).

[26] This is not an entirely new phenomenon and can be traced back in different legal systems, cf. Frantziou (2015, pp. 670, 674–677) and Quintais et al. (2022, pp. 17 et seqq).

[27] Quintais et al. (2023, pp. 2 et seq).

[28] Quintais et al. (2022, p. 25).

The AI Act proposal mentions fundamental rights in a few places. The recitals, where at the Union level the larger context and rationale for why a particular provision is adopted can often be found, clearly demonstrate how AI can impact fundamental rights. For example, in addition to the certain benefits AI brings, there is also the risk of "manipulative, exploitative and social control practices," so they are to be prohibited because of their contradiction to, inter alia, Union fundamental rights.[29] Examples of those practices are clearly spelled out in Article 5 AI Act proposal that regulates "unacceptable AI systems" and can be the deployment of subliminal techniques to distort a person's behavior or the use of "social scoring" systems.

For new AI systems that have not yet been covered, the AI Act proposal provides that they must be classified as high-risk AI systems if they have an adverse impact on fundamental rights. As briefly mentioned above, the classification then imposes extensive compliance obligations on the providers and users of these AI systems. In concrete terms, these obligations then include fundamental rights at a further point. For example, Article 13 of the AI Act proposal requires providers of high-risk AI systems to transparently describe the risks to fundamental rights when using AI applications. Similarly, human oversight of high-risk AI systems serves to protect fundamental rights (Article 14 (2) AI Act proposal).

3.2 *Freedom of Choice/Freedom of Contract*

Having already looked at the GDPR, the DSA, and the AI Act, the question arises as to how digital humanism is reflected in the other legal acts from Chapter 2, which concern the factors of the platform economy, i.e., the economic power of the platforms, their "oil," and the tools supporting the work of the platforms. Here, the focal point can be found in the actual safeguarding of freedom of choice and contract, which are protected at various points by fundamental rights such as the right to respect for private and family life in Article 7 CFR, freedom to conduct a business in Article 15 CFR, or the objective of a high level of consumer protection in Article 38 CFR. The human rights of the ECHR, which must be observed by the member states of the European Union, also protect freedom of contract in part through the property guarantee in Article 1 Protocol 1 ECHR.[30] While the DMA thus aims to improve competition among platforms in certain markets, for example, with obligations on interoperability (Article 7 DMA), in areas where there is a monopoly or "quasi" monopoly, "FRAND" conditions (Article 6(6), (12) DMA) are intended to ensure that there is no exploitation of this economic position. Both

[29] Recital 15 AI Act Proposal.

[30] This was pointed out in a variety of cases before the European Court of Human Rights concerning rent-control systems by states which limit the freedom to conclude lease contracts, cf. Pařízek v. the Czech Republic, no. 76286/14, 12 January 2023, § 53 et seq.

approaches are also reflected in the data-related legal acts (DGA and Data Act), as explained above. Especially for the future legal acts related to data, interoperability and FRAND conditions should not be seen independently but are interrelated: In the best case, FRAND conditions allow users access to data not dependent on the "arbitrariness" of data holders, for example, platforms. These can then be used independently of the previously used service through the interoperability obligation. Together, these two factors improve the user's position vis-à-vis platforms as well and allow for an improved exercise of contractual freedom.

4 Conclusions

Our examination of platform regulation and its relationship to digital humanism has shown that binding platforms to fundamental rights is a response by the European Commission to the challenges of digitalization and is in line with the demands of the Vienna Manifesto on Digital Humanism. In order not to go too far, we have not further explored the considerations of other authors on the role of the "rule of law" and "due process," but we do see points of contact in the legal acts of platform regulation that need to be looked at in more detail in the future, for example, through the detailed requirements for complaint management systems in Articles 20 et seqq. DSA.

For the outlook, the exciting question certainly lies in the potential impact of the European draft on the future of platforms: Many of the platforms are located in non-EU countries and the markets of the future for them are not in Europe but in other parts of the world. There is also the question of enforcement: Will it be possible for the various authorities, be it the Commission or even the individual authorities of the member states, to enforce the individual regulations against the platforms? This is not only a financial question but also a question of knowledge, because enforcement in many places requires a deep technical understanding that is unlikely to reside with all authorities. At least, however, the proposed norms provide a solid basis for addressing some of the most challenging issues that individuals and societies are confronted with in times of digitalization.

Discussion Questions for Students and Their Teachers

1. Where can links be drawn between the "Vienna Manifesto on Digital Humanism" and the EU's legal framework for platforms?
2. How does platform regulation ensure that freedom of choice is guaranteed vis-à-vis "big tech" platforms?
3. How are notions of "due process" and "rule of law" as pillars of modern democratic states enshrined in the legal framework for platforms?
4. Is it acceptable to subject platforms to the same requirements as democratic states?
5. How can the EU and its member states learn from the lack of enforcement of the GDPR?

Learning Resources for Students

1. Centre for International Governance Innovation (ed.), The Four Domains of Global Platform Governance, CIGI Essay Series, https://www.cigionline.org/the-four-domains-of-global-platform-governance/ (last retrieved: 26.06.2023).

   The series of 20 essays gives an overview of the different facets of platform regulation, spanning from the content on platforms to the underlying infrastructure.
2. Bietti, E. (2023), A Genealogy of Digital Platform Regulation, 7 Georgetown Law Technology Review (1), 1, available online: https://georgetownlawtechreview.org/a-genealogy-of-digital-platform-regulation/GLTR-01-2023/ (last retrieved: 26.06.2023).

   This paper traces back the history of platform regulation to the 1990s as a part of the discourse on early Internet regulation and suggests to re-invent the rule of law in platform regulation.
3. Richter, H., Straub, M., Tuchtfeld. E. (eds.) (2021), To Break Up or Regulate Big Tech? Avenues to Constrain Private Power in the DSA/DMA Package, Max Planck Institute for Innovation and Competition Research Paper No. 21-25, https://pure.mpg.de/rest/items/item_3345402_5/component/file_3345403/content (last retrieved: 26.06.2023).

   This series of originally short blog entries discusses different aspects of the then-proposed DSA/DMA packages. Although the final legal text has changed, certain issues remain relevant.
4. de Gregorio, G. (2022), "Digital Constitutionalism in Europe. Reframing Rights and Powers in the Algorithmic Society".

   This monograph traces back where constitutional fragments and concepts can be found in EU platform regulation and shows that they in fact underline EU digital policy.
5. Persily, N., Tucker, J. (eds.) (2020), Social Media and Democracy, Cambridge, United Kingdom, New York, NY: Cambridge University Press.

   This volume explicitly deals with social media platforms and approaches the issues of disinformation, hate speech, and content moderation from different disciplines.

Acknowledgements The authors are grateful to have received valuable research support by Johanna Erler.

References

Allen, D. et al. (2019). Some economic consequences of the GDPR. *39 Economics Bulletin* (pp. 785–797). Last retrieved: 26.06.2023, from http://www.accessecon.com/Pubs/EB/2019/Volume39/EB-19-V39-I2-P77.pdf

Baloup, J. et al. (2021). *White Paper on the Data Governance Act.* Last retrieved: 14.04.2023, from https://ssrn.com/abstract=3872703

Bradford, A. (2020). *The Brussels Effect: How the European Union Rules the World*. Oxford University Press.

Buri, I., & van Hoboken, J. (2021). *The digital services act (DSA) proposal: A critical overview*. Last retrieved: 29.03.2023, from https://dsa-observatory.eu/wp-content/uploads/2021/11/Buri-Van-Hoboken-DSA-discussion-paper-Version-28_10_21.pdf

Celeste, E., & de Gregorio, G. (2022). Digital humanism: The constitutional message of the GDPR. *Global Privacy Law Review, 3*, 4–18.

De Gregorio, G., & Dunn, P. (2022). The European risk-based approaches: Connecting constitutional dots in the digital age. *Common Market Law Review, 59*, 473–500.

Ebers, et al. (2021). The European Commission's proposal for an artificial intelligence act—A critical assessment by members of the Robotics and AI Law Society (RAILS). *Multidisciplinary Scientific Journal, 4*, 589–603.

ECJ. (2023). *Statistics concerning the judicial activity of the Court of Justice*. Last retrieved: 26.06.2023, from https://curia.europa.eu/jcms/upload/docs/application/pdf/2023-03/stats_cour_2022_en.pdf

Frantziou, E. (2015). The horizontal effect of the charter of fundamental rights of the EU: Rediscovering the reasons for horizontality. *European Law Journal, 21*(5), 657–679.

Genç-Gelgeç, B. (2022). Regulating digital platforms: Will the DSA correct its predecessor's deficiencies? *Croatian Yearbook of European Law and Policy, 18*(1), 25–60.

Greenleaf, G. (2021). *Global data privacy laws 2021: Despite COVID delays, 145 laws show GDPR dominance*. Last retrieved: 23.06.2023, from https://ssrn.com/abstract=3836348

Hoofnagle, C., van der Sloot, B., & Zuiderveen Borgesius, F. (2019). The European Union general data protection regulation: What it is and what it means. *Information and Communications Technology Law, 28*, 65–78.

Husovec, M., & Roche Laguna, I. (2022). *Digital services act: A short primer*. Last retrieved: 29.03.2023, from https://ssrn.com/abstract=4153796

Metzger, A., & Schweitzer, H. (2023). Shaping markets: A critical evaluation of the draft data act. *Zeitschrift für Europäisches Privatrecht, 31*, 42–82.

noyb.eu (2023). *5 years of the GDPR: National authorities let down European legislator*. Last retrieved: 26.06.2023, from https://noyb.eu/en/5-years-gdpr-national-authorities-let-down-european-legislator

Podszun, R., Bongartz, P., & Langenstein, S. (2021). The digital markets act: Moving from competition law to regulation for large gatekeepers. *Journal of European Consumer and Market Law, 10*, 60–67.

Quintais, J., Appelman, N. & Fahy, R. (2022). *Using terms and conditions to apply fundamental rights to content moderation*. Last retrieved: 29.03.2023, from https://ssrn.com/abstract=4286147

Quintais, J., de Gregorio, G. & Magalhães, J. (2023). How platforms govern users' copyright-protected content: Exploring the power of private ordering and its implications *Computer Law and Security Review, 48*, 105792, pp. 1–25.

Schweitzer, H. (2021). The art to make gatekeeper positions contestable and the challenge to know what is fair: A discussion of the digital markets act proposal. *Zeitschrift für Europäisches Privatrecht*, 503–544.

van Hoboken, J. (2022). *European lessons in self-experimentation: From the GDPR to European platform regulation*. Last retrieved: 23.06.2023, from https://www.cigionline.org/articles/european-lessons-in-self-experimentation-from-the-gdpr-to-european-platform-regulation/

von Ditfurth, L., & Lienemann, G. (2022). The data governance act: Promoting or restricting data intermediaries? *Competition and Regulation in Network Industries, 23*, 270–295.

Wilman, F. (2022). *The Digital Services Act (DSA) – An overview*. Last retrieved: 29.03.2023, from https://ssrn.com/abstract=4304586

BY

Printed in the United States
by Baker & Taylor Publisher Services